REGNUM STUDIES IN MISSION

Pentecostal Mission and Global Christianity

An Edinburgh Centenary Reader

REGNUM STUDIES IN MISSION

Series Preface

Regnum Studies in Mission are born from the lived experience of Christians and Christian communities in mission, especially but not solely in the fast-growing churches among the poor of the world. These churches have more to tell than stories of growth. They are making significant impacts on their cultures in the cause of Christ. They are producing 'cultural products' which express the reality of Christian faith, hope, and love in their societies.

Regnum Studies in Mission are the fruit often of rigorous research to the highest international standards and always of authentic Christian engagement in the transformation of people and societies. And these are for the world. The formation of Christian theology, missiology and practice in the twenty-first century will depend to a great extent on the active participation of growing churches contributing biblical and culturally appropriate expressions of Christian practice to inform World Christianity.

Series Editors

Paul Woods	Oxford Centre for Mission Studies, Oxford, UK
Paul Bendor-Samuel	Oxford Centre for Mission Studies, Oxford, UK
Tony Gray	Words by Design, UK

REGNUM STUDIES IN MISSION

Pentecostal Mission and Global Christianity

An Edinburgh Centenary Reader

Younghoon Lee and Wonsuk Ma, Editors
with Kuewon Lee, Associate Editor

Copyright © Younghoon Lee & Wonsuk Ma 2018

First published 2018 by Regnum Books International
in partnership with
International Theological Institute, Seoul, Korea

Regnum is an imprint of the Oxford Centre for Mission Studies
St. Philip & St. James Church
Woodstock Road, Oxford, OX2 6HR, UK

The right of Younghoon and Wonsuk Ma to be identified
as the Editors of this Work have been asserted by them
in accordance with the Copyright, Designs and Patents Act 1988.

All rights reserved. No part of this publication may be reproduced, stored in a retrieval system, or transmitted, in any form or by any means, electronic, mechanical, photocopying, recording or otherwise, without the prior permission of the publisher or a license permitting restricted copying. In the UK such licenses are issued by the Copyright Licensing Agency, 90 Tottenham Court Road, London W1P 9HE.

British Library Cataloguing in Publication Data
A catalogue record for this book is available from the British Library

ISBN 978-1-506476-44-5
eBook ISBN 978-1-506476-45-2

Typeset by Words by Design

Cover design: Words by Design
Cover photo © Oral Roberts University, 2018

The publication of the book is made possible through the financial support of Yoido Full Gospel Church (Younghoon Lee, Senior Pastor), Seoul, Korea.

Distributed by 1517 Media in the US and Canada

Dedicated to
the fellow Spirit-empowered witnesses,
especially those in the persecuted parts of the world

Contents

Preface xi
Common Call xiii

Pentecostal Mission in the Third Christian Millennium: An Introduction
Younghoon Lee 1

PART ONE

The Missio Spiritus: Towards a Pneumatological Missiology of Creation
Amos Yong 13

The Theological Motivations for Pentecostal Mission
Wonsuk Ma 25

Pentecostal Missions and the Influence of Frontier Mission Missiology
Alan R. Johnson 40

Attitude Is Everything! Defending the Cause of
Latin American Women in Ministry
Mireya Alvarez 55

The Bible in Mission: Evangelical / Pentecostal View In Latin America
Antonia Leonora van der Meer 70

Neo-Pentecostal Paradigms in Latin American Mission:
Microtrends in the Theologies of Mission and Missionary
Practices among Neo-Pentecostals in Peru
Bernardo Campos 83

Straightway Chapel – A Charismatic Theology of Mission
to Muslims in Ghana?
Andreas Heuser 95

A Pentecostal Perspective on the Lausanne Movement
Opoku Onyinah 105

Together towards Life: A Pentecostal Assessment
Timothy T.N. Lim 112

The Challenges of Charismatic Movements to the
Mainline Historical Churches in Africa
Abednego Keshomshahara 126

Bitter and Sweet Tears: Exploring the Spirituality of the Eastern Church Fathers in the Light of Postmodern 'Enthusiastic Christianity' in Russia
Olga Zaprometova 137

Growing Together in Unity and Mission
Veli-Matti Kärkkäinen 149

Cooperation and the Promotion of Unity: A Pentecostal Perspective
Cecil M. Robeck, Jr. 161

The Ecumenism of the Spirit: Emerging Contemporary Contexts of Mission in Latin America
Carmelo Alvarez 174

PART TWO

Deliver Us from Evil: Evangelism, Spiritual Conflict, 'Signs and Wonders'
Tormod Engelsviken 193

Athens 2005: Reconciliation and Healing as an Imperative for Mission
Jacques Matthey 207

Health and Healing: The Maasai Prophet Isaia Orishi Ole Ndokote and his Evangelistic Mission in Kenya and Tanzania
Christel Kiel 222

Power Encounters: Evangelisation and Local Religious Spirits in Latin America
Raimundo C. Barreto, Jr. 233

The Transculturalization and the Transnationalization of the Government of 12: From Seoul to Bogota to Charlotte, North Carolina
Philip Wingeier-Rayo 255

Christian Spirituality and the Diakonic Mission of the Yoido Full Gospel Church
Younghoon Lee 270

Holistic Ministry of the Pentecostal Church
Julie C. Ma 282

The Emerging Church in Africa and Holistic Mission: Challenges and Opportunities
Nicta Lubaale 294

Holistic Mission in Post-Communist Romania: A Case Study on the Growth of the 'Elim' Pentecostal Church of Timişoara (1990-1997)
Marcel V. Măcelaru 305

A Guatemalan Perspective on Pentecostal and Neo-Pentecostal Theology in the Twenty-First Century
Rigoberto M. Gálvez Alvarado 323

Challenges Facing the Ethiopian Evangelical Church Mekane Yesus (EECMY): A Growing Charismatic Churches in the Global South
Dawit Olika Terfassa 339

Mission and Three South African Metropolitan Megachurches: Middle-Class Masses in Search of Mammon?
Genevieve Lerina James 350

Selected Bibliography 365

Contributors 371

Index 375

Preface

In the fall of 2015, world's mission leaders gathered in Oxford to celebrate the completion of the Regnum Edinburgh Centenary Series. Everyone was elated to see the magnitude of the Series: 35 volumes! At the same time, promptly noticing the challenge of valuable studies widely scattered throughout the Series, the leaders of the publisher and the Series editors organized the two Compendium volumes.

The birth of this Pentecostal Reader title is a response to the same challenge. The publication of *Pentecostal Mission and Global Christianity* in the series was highly celebrated with a warm reception by Pentecostals as well as non-Pentecostals. At the same time, it was noticed that about fifty studies on Pentecostal mission were published in the other titles of the Series. The idea of this Reader volume surfaced soon, and the editors caught the vision.

The contributors deserve the editors' warm appreciation for their willingness to participate in the volume project. The process provided an opportunity to correct typos and errors. However, at least two chapters were substantially revised.

The financial assistance of the International Theological Institute (publishing partner) of Yoido Full Gospel Church, Seoul, Korea is gratefully acknowledged. Without this generous help, the book would not have been a possibility. The church was deeply involved, through its Senior Pastor, in the Edinburgh 2010 Conference and the ensuing publication programme. The church sponsored two Edinburgh Centenary titles.

Equally important has been the support of Oral Roberts University for approving a directed study through which the editorial work of the book was completed. The University also provided a superb image of an Empowered21 gathering to be used for the cover. For this permission, the editors are grateful.

To reinforce the 'youthful' nature of Pentecostal Christianity and its mission, besides the cover image, the editors invited two emerging mission leaders from Africa and Asia to offer commendations. They are joined by a well-established mission historian (and practitioner) from North America. Yes, she is very young in heart. We are deeply grateful for their support.

The two editors wish to recognize an important work of Mr. Kuewon Lee, the Associate Editor of the volume. Under the supervision of the editors, he initiated the selection of the studies, communications with the authors, the generation of the Contents, Selected Bibliography, Contributors list, and the keywords for indexing. He has been a special asset to the editorial process.

With all three editorial members coming from Korea, the volume is in part a gift of the Korean church.

The editorial team wishes to express our deep appreciation to the Regnum team in Oxford. Paul Bendor-Samuel, the director of Regnum Books, gladly accepted the volume into the Regnum Studies in Mission series. Tony Gray took the manuscript and magically turned to a beautiful book, including the cover. We are grateful.

However, the ultimate proof of the giftedness of the volume will be realized only at the frontline of mission. It is the Holy Spirit who calls, empowers, and sends God's people to be his witnesses. This book, therefore, brings the dimension of the mission of the Spirit, *missio Spiritus*! This book, to be a tool for the Spirit's empowerment, and to continue the vision of the Edinburgh Centenary Series, the editors envision that shortly this book would be offered as a mission gift through a free download. It is the prayer of the editors and the publisher that this book plays a useful role in the advancement of God's mission.

Editors
Seoul and Tulsa, Oklahoma
Autumn, 2018

Common Call

The Edinburgh 2010 Common Call emerged from the Edinburgh 2010 study process and conference to mark the centenary of the World Missionary Conference, Edinburgh 1910. The Common Call was affirmed in the Church of Scotland Assembly Hall in Edinburgh on 6 June 2010 by representatives of world Christianity, including Catholic, Evangelical, Orthodox, Pentecostal, and Protestant churches.

As we gather for the centenary of the World Missionary Conference of Edinburgh 1910, we believe the church, as a sign and symbol of the reign of God, is called to witness to Christ today by sharing in God's mission of love through the transforming power of the Holy Spirit.

1. Trusting in the Triune God and with a renewed sense of urgency, we are called to incarnate and proclaim the good news of salvation, of forgiveness of sin, of life in abundance, and of liberation for all poor and oppressed. We are challenged to witness and evangelism in such a way that we are a living demonstration of the love, righteousness and justice that God intends for the whole world.

2. Remembering Christ's sacrifice on the Cross and his resurrection for the world's salvation, and empowered by the Holy Spirit, we are called to authentic dialogue, respectful engagement and humble witness among people of other faiths – and no faith – to the uniqueness of Christ. Our approach is marked with bold confidence in the gospel message; it builds friendship, seeks reconciliation and practises hospitality.

3. Knowing the Holy Spirit who blows over the world at will, reconnecting creation and bringing authentic life, we are called to become communities of compassion and healing, where young people are actively participating in mission, and women and men share power and responsibilities fairly, where there is a new zeal for justice, peace and the protection of the environment, and renewed liturgy reflecting the beauties of the Creator and creation.

4. Disturbed by the asymmetries and imbalances of power that divide and trouble us in church and world, we are called to repentance, to critical reflection on systems of power, and to accountable use of power structures. We are called to find practical ways to live as members of One Body in full awareness that God resists the proud, Christ welcomes and empowers the poor and afflicted, and the power of the Holy Spirit is manifested in our vulnerability.

5. Affirming the importance of the biblical foundations of our missional engagement and valuing the witness of the Apostles and martyrs, we are called to rejoice in the expressions of the gospel in many nations all over the world. We celebrate the renewal experienced through movements of migration and mission in all directions, the way all are equipped for mission by the gifts of the Holy Spirit, and God's continual calling of children and young people to further the gospel.

6. Recognising the need to shape a new generation of leaders with authenticity for mission in a world of diversities in the twenty-first century, we are called to work together in new forms of theological education. Because we are all made in the image of God, these will draw on one another's unique charisms, challenge each other to grow in faith and understanding, share resources equitably worldwide, involve the entire human being and the whole family of God, and respect the wisdom of our elders while also fostering the participation of children.

7. Hearing the call of Jesus to make disciples of all people – poor, wealthy, marginalised, ignored, powerful, living with disability, young, and old – we are called as communities of faith to mission from everywhere to everywhere. In joy we hear the call to receive from one another in our witness by word and action, in streets, fields, offices, homes, and schools, offering reconciliation, showing love, demonstrating grace and speaking out truth.

8. Recalling Christ, the host at the banquet, and committed to that unity for which he lived and prayed, we are called to ongoing co-operation, to deal with controversial issues and to work towards a common vision. We are challenged to welcome one another in our diversity, affirm our membership through baptism in the One Body of Christ, and recognise our need for mutuality, partnership, collaboration and networking in mission, so that the world might believe.

9. Remembering Jesus' way of witness and service, we believe we are called by God to follow this way joyfully, inspired, anointed, sent and empowered by the Holy Spirit, and nurtured by Christian disciplines in community. As we look to Christ's coming in glory and judgment, we experience his presence with us in the Holy Spirit, and we invite all to join with us as we participate in God's transforming and reconciling mission of love to the whole creation.

Pentecostal Mission in the Third Christian Millennium: An Introduction

Younghoon Lee

About a decade ago, the historic conference hall of New College of Edinburgh University held the centenary celebration of the Edinburgh Missionary Conference. The monumental Regnum Edinburgh Centenary Series was completed with 35 volumes. Two compendium volumes also appeared. Now that the centenary process has ended, all of the volumes are digitally available to anyone at no cost. The centenary gathering and publishing broke new grounds, which many of the volumes reflect. The most prominent area of reflection was the rise of the churches in the global South. Once called 'new churches,' or 'younger churches' by the western mainstreams, they are no longer the object of western patronization. Those at the conference celebrated this radical development as the success of the modern missionary impulses. At the same time, they constantly asked the heartfelt question, 'What has gone wrong?'

1. The Growth of Modern Pentecostalism

In the midst of this divided sentiments between the north and the south, the conference highly affirmed the rise of Pentecostal Christianity and its contribution to Christian mission. During the period between the 1910 and the 2010 Edinburgh conferences, the Pentecostal and Charismatic block (along with an endless array of independent varieties) has become the second largest Christian block after Catholicism. Since WWI, Christianity has grown rapidly by overcoming strong challenges from rising nationalism, intensifying imperialism, expanding urbanization, and deepening secularization. In 2017 The Center for the Study of Global Christianity published a statistical survey on global Christianity. It showed that the number of Christians has more than doubled by increasing from about 560 million in 1900 to about 1.23 billion in 1970.[1]

In particular, the growth of Pentecostal/Charismatic Christianity is more conspicuous than that of any other Christian group. In 1900 Pentecostals and

[1] Todd M. Johnson, Gina A. Zurlo, Albert W. Hickman and Peter F. Crossing, 'Christianity 2017: Five Hundred Years of Protestant Christianity', *International Bulletin of Mission Research* 41:1 (January 2017), 8.

Charismatics represented 0.18 percent or about 0.98 million of 560 million Christians. By 1970 they constituted 5 percent or approximately 62.7 million of 1.23 billion Christians. By mid-2017 this number was up to approximately 669 million, which meant that 27 percent of the world's 2.48 billion (approx.) Christians were Pentecostal/Charismatics.[2]

Today, there are over 23,000 Pentecostal/Charismatic/Neo-Charismatic denominations globally. Sixteen percent of these denominations are Pentecostals, 39 percent Charismatics, and 45 percent Neo-Charismatics.[3] Pentecostalism grew more than expected during the last quarter of the twentieth century. In 1984, Water Hollenweger, an expert on worldwide Pentecostalism, guessed that Pentecostalism would have about 250 million adherents in 2000.[4] Contrary to Hollenweger's prediction, the number of global Pentecostals reached approximately 460 million in 2000. By 2050 Johnson et al. estimate that about 1.1 billion of the world's 3.33 billion Christian adherents will be Pentecostal, ranking second to Catholicism with 1.61 billion believers.[5]

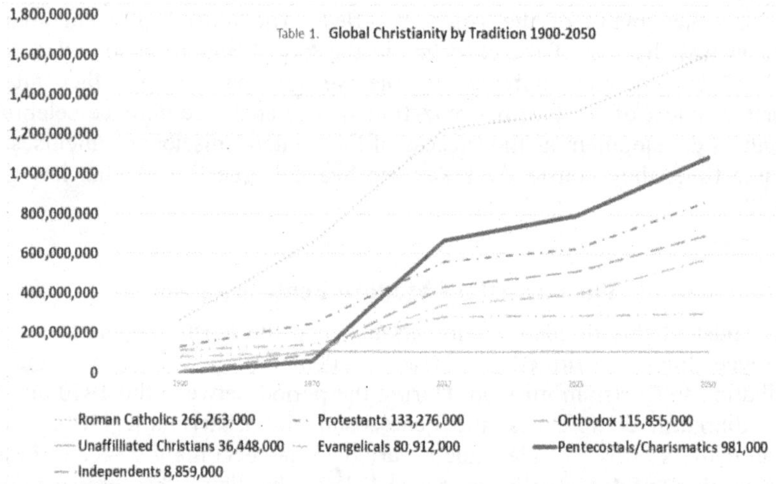

Table 1. Global Christianity by Tradition 1900-2050

---

[2] Johnson et al., 'Christianity 2017', 9.

[3] Association of Religion Data Archives, 'Pentecostal/Charismatic Movement' (http://www.thearda.com/timeline/movements/movement_42.asp), accessed on 10 Sept, 2018.

[4] Walter J. Hollenweger, 'After Twenty Years' Research on Pentecostalism', *Theology* 87 (November 1984), 403.

[5] Johnson et al., 'Christianity 2017', 9.

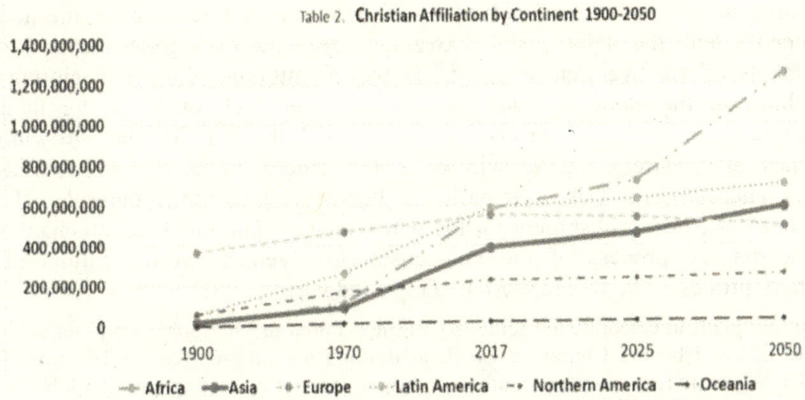

The increase in the Christian population in the Global South is in line with the growth of Pentecostalism there. According to a statistical survey by David Barrett and Todd Johnson on Pentecostalism by continent, Pentecostalism in Africa and Asia recorded the highest annual growth rate of 2.7 percent and 1.9 percent for 2000.[6] In 2014, Johnson estimated that the annual growth rate of Pentecostalism in Africa and Asia was 2.53 percent and 2.95 percent respectively.[7]

As seen above, Pentecostalism has generally led the growth of global Christianity, but particularly in the Global South. The Pentecostal movement has spread to many countries in Asia and grown phenomenally in some places, such as South Korea and the Philippines.[8] In the former, the YFGC not only has led the growth of Korean Pentecostalism, but it has also globally and locally contributed significantly to Christianity by providing insight into church growth.[9]

2. Edinburgh 2010 and Pentecostalism

The reason for the pronounced growth of this family of the world church is because it was not present at the 1910 Conference. The Introduction chapter of the Pentecostal volume of the Regnum Edinburgh Centenary Series explores several interesting insights in this regard. First of all, it argues that the

[6] David B. Barrett and T.M. Johnson, 'Global Statistics', in Stanley M. Burgess and Eduard M. van der Maas (eds), *The New International Dictionary of Pentecostal and Charismatic Movements* (Grand Rapids, MI: Zondervan, 2002), 301.

[7] Todd M. Johnson, 'Counting Pentecostals Worldwide', *Pneuma* 36 (February 2014), 282.

[8] 'Overview: Pentecostalism in Asia', *Pewforum* (http://www.pewforum.org/2006/10/05/overview-pentecostalism-in-asia/), assessed on 10 Sept 2018.

[9] Yeongseung Lee, 'Transnational Networks of Pentecostalism and the Rise of World Christianity in the Twentieth Century', *Journal of Youngsan Theology* (September 2014), 150-51.

Edinburgh movement (which eventually evolved into the ecumenical mission movement) and the Pentecostal movement are the two greatest mission movements of the twentieth century.[10] However, although these two siblings were born in the same decade, they seldom met each other during their development. It was only in the last quarter of the century that growing awareness and desire to interact with each other emerged that the tide began to change. Therefore, the full participation of Pentecostals in the Edinburgh 2010 is a remarkable accomplishment for the world church. The Introduction chapter also details the process of the Pentecostal involvement in the Edinburgh centenary process. The whole section is repeated here.[11]

> The first plans to celebrate the centenary of the Edinburgh Missionary Conference were initiated by the Church of Scotland through the program called Towards 2010. When its first planning conference was organized by calling twenty global mission leaders in May 2005, a Pentecostal delegate was invited from Asia to represent the Asian Pentecostal Society, and this conference proposed nine study themes and transversal themes.[12] The preparatory work of the Towards 2010 was handed to the General Council of the Edinburgh 2010, once it was formed in 2006. Among the twenty General Council members, a Pentecostal delegate represented global Pentecostal Christianity. When the size of the conference was finalised, the Pentecostal delegates were the largest in number among church representatives, reflecting the sheer size of Pentecostal Christianity in the twenty-first century. No one among the 1910 conference leaders would ever have thought that an obscure and ignored Pentecostal Christianity would grow, in a century, to become the second largest Christian group, only after Catholics! Thirty global Pentecostal delegates were invited to the actual conference, representing over 10% of the 250 official conference delegates.[13] On the second day, a Pentecostal leader was among the three plenary speakers.
>
> During the conference, Pentecostal delegates came together for two evenings for fellowship and exchange of views; some Charismatic delegates also joined the meetings. The delegates decided to produce a statement, and this document has become part of the official conference collection.[14] The full text is worth repeating:
>
> We acknowledge the historical significance of Edinburgh 1910 and rejoice that we have been counted among those gathered together in Edinburgh 2-6 June 2010 to mark the centennial. The twentieth century gave clear testimony that although we were not in attendance at Edinburgh 1910, we have taken our rightful place on the landscape of contemporary Christianity. We would like to express our gratitude to those who prepared and participated in the Edinburgh 2010

---

[10] Wonsuk Ma, Veli-Matti Kärkkäinen, and J. Kwabena Asamoah-Gyadu, 'Introduction: Pentecostalism and World Mission', in *Pentecostal Mission and Global Christianity* (Oxford: Regnum Books, 2014), 4.

[11] Ma, et al., 'Introduction', 6-8.

[12] Kirsteen Kim and Andrew Anderson (eds.), *Edinburgh 2010: Mission Today and Tomorrow* (Oxford: Regnum, 2011), 343-34.

[13] The list of the delegates is found in Kim & Anderson, *Mission Today and Tomorrow*, 425-42.

[14] Kim & Anderson, *Mission Today and Tomorrow*, 343-44.

conference and for giving us the opportunity to be able to affirm the significance of the global mission call joining a diverse fellowship of believers in Christ.

As Pentecostal delegates, we participated at Edinburgh 2010 in the nine themes as well as on all levels of the study processes. We have shared issues and concerns. We listened, prayed and learned together, with an attitude of love and respect, building bridges rather than creating chasms, divisions and barriers. We affirm the divine mission mandate to reconcile the whole of God's creation in Christ and do this across denominational and confessional lines. We are to engage in effective witnessing [to] the Good News of Jesus Christ to all parts of the world, in the power of the Holy Spirit and to the glory of God. This vision reflects the heart of God and belongs to the very nature of the Church.

We appreciate that Pentecostals are recognised in a positive way. At the same time we leave with the challenge to find fuller expressions of global Pentecostalism in an ecumenical context. We also noticed a disparity of the language used and concerns expressed between the global North and global South. We must be careful that the academic voices of the North do not wash away the narrative claims of the South. As Pentecostals we are acquainted with both linguistic traditions, we realise that we can play an important role as bridge builders. This would truly benefit the whole Body of Christ.

Furthermore, we are deeply aware that Christians need the help of the Holy Spirit. Through the Spirit's guidance and empowerment we will be able to answer God's mandate to the world. We humbly acknowledge that it is God who has the last word. Issues that relate to mission and unity should not drift into intellectual manoeuvrings. It must be the prayer of all people of God, wherever they are, to hear what the Spirit has to say to the churches so that we can turn to God and our common call can be, 'Come, Lord Jesus!'[15]

The conference statement called 'The Common Call' was viewed as a remarkable achievement of the whole conference process, considering the full breadth and incredible diversity of the participant stakeholders, from the Catholic and mainline churches to the Pentecostal and African Independent Churches. Any Pentecostal believer would detect a strong influence of Pentecostal hands in the formation of the document. The ninth point is a good example:

by the Holy Spirit, and nurtured by Christian disciplines in community. As we look to Christ's coming in glory and judgment, we experience his presence with

[15] Those who signed the statement are: Rev. Dr. Miguel Alvarez (USA), Mr. Kenneth Ben (Cook Islands), Dr. Cheryl Bridges Johns (USA), Dr. David Daniels (USA), Dr. Anne Dyer (UK), Mrs. Dynnice Rosanne Engcoy (Philippines), Dr. Samson Fatokun (Nigeria), Dr. Pamela Holmes (Canada), Rev. Dr. Harold D. Hunter (USA), Rev. Dr. Veli Matti Kärkkäinen (Finland), Dr. Elijah Jong Fil Kim (USA), Rev. Steven K.L. Kum (Malaysia), Dr. Julie Ma (Korea), Dr. Wonsuk Ma (Korea), Rev. Rauno Mikkonen (Finland), Apostle Dr. Opoku Onyinah (Ghana), Rev. Philippe Ouedraogo (Burkina Faso), Rev. Dr. Tavita Pagaialii (Western Samoa), Dr. Jean-Daniel Plüss (Switzerland), Rev. Dr. Daniel Ramirez (USA), Dr. Elisabeth Del Carmen Salazar-Sanzana (Chile), and Rev. Bal Krishna Sharma (Nepal).

us in the Holy Spirit, and we invite all to join with us as we participate in God's transforming and reconciling mission of love to the whole creation.[16]

3. Pentecostal Gifts to Mission

Having surveyed the role of the Pentecostal churches in the Edinburgh 2010 events, in what follows I shall engage with this critical question: 'What gifts can Pentecostals contribute towards engaging and working together with the other churches that experienced and participated in the Edinburgh centenary process?' My experience of serving as Senior Pastor at Yoido Full Gospel Church, Seoul, Korea, will serve as a helpful example.

3.1 Influence on Korean Church

There are three areas that Pentecostalism effected. First, the Korean Pentecostal movement has awakened the Korean church from its spiritual lethargy. It has precluded churches from adopting a legalistic faith, and it has inhibited the ossification of church systems. Also, the Pentecostal movement has led to qualitative and quantitative church growth by renewing the lives of laypeople. In particular, the Holy Spirit movement influenced an intensive prayer movement and cell group system that contributed to Korean church growth regardless of denomination. Precipitated by the Pentecostal movement, Korean churches accomplished astonishingly rapid church growth over the last century, with no parallel in world church history.

Second, from the beginning, the Korean Pentecostal is a movement that gives hope and courage to those in despair and marginalized. As one of the representatives of the Korean Pentecostal movement, since its establishment, YFGC has proclaimed a gospel of hope to the poor, the marginalized, and the diseased. The church has stressed the potential for believers to live successful lives as a result of Jesus' atonement and by also following his model of serving and helping those in need. Recently, YFGC announced that one-third of its budget would go towards helping the socially disadvantaged and missional ministries. This act gained the church a good reputation in both Korean and global Christian circles, and it causes a sensation in Korean society.[17]

Third, since its inauguration, the Korean Pentecostal movement has promoted the ecumenical movement. The 1907 Pyongyang Great Revival was the result of a united ministry between the Presbyterian and Methodist Churches in Pyongyang.

Moreover, all the great revival conventions, such as Billy Graham's Evangelistic Conference, EXPLO 74, and the Korean Evangelical Great Conference, were non-denominational conferences that overcame

---

[16] For the full text, see 'The Common Call' in this volume.

[17] 'A Special Interview with Younghoon Lee, Yoido Full Gospel Church, One of the Largest Churches in the World, "It Is Time for the Church to Contribute and to Help"' [in Korean], *Magazine DongA* 890 (June 2013), 30.

denominational barriers. The AGK to which YFGC belongs has worked ardently for Korean church unification. In 1996, the AGK became a member of the National Council of Churches in Korea (NCCK)[18] and helped successfully manage the 10th World Council of Churches Conference. Pusan, Korea, hosted this event in 2013.

3.2 Influence on the World Church

The following presents another three areas of Pentecostal influence of note. The first area is the role which the YFGC and Cho played in promoting Asian Pentecostalism to the global forum. In 1964, Cho attended the fiftieth anniversary of the American Assemblies of God as a representative of the AGK. AGK later elected Cho as moderator in 1966. He then became one of the most important figures in the global Pentecostal movement. He hosted the third conference for Northern Far East Asian Pentecostals in Korea, which gave momentum to the globalization of Asian Pentecostal denominations.[19] After that, Cho was elected the first chairman of the World Assemblies of God Fellowship at the 16th PWC allowing him to lead the global Pentecostal movement. Through this, the AGK became a leader within the global Pentecostal movement.

The second area is YFGC's contribution to worldwide church growth. While leading the Korean Pentecostal movement, Yonggi Cho also founded Church Growth International (henceforth CGI). CGI explores areas of church growth, and it has contributed towards world church growth. It has established worldwide branches and appointed sixty-three pastors in twenty-five countries as members of boards of directors. The CGI regularly hosts church growth conferences and seminars all around the world. It teaches church growth principles that CGI member churches can easily apply depending upon their contexts. *Church Growth*, the magazine issued by CGI, provides useful information and disseminates church growth principles.[20]

The third area of YFGC's contribution is the expansion of world mission. While experiencing rapid church growth through the Pentecostal movement, YFGC has also conducted missionary works, mostly in North America, Europe, and Oceania. It also broadened its mission fields to people in Third World countries beginning in 1993 with the 20th Full Gospel World Mission Conference. After that, YFGC put its efforts into evangelizing native people and educating pastors by establishing theological schools and colleges. Moreover, the Full Gospel Businessmen's Mission Federation, an organization

---

[18] Younghoon Lee, *The Holy Spirit Movement in Korea: Its Historical and Theological Development* (Oxford: Regnum Books, 2009), 127.

[19] Ig-Jin Kim, *History and Theology of Korean Pentecostalism: Sunbogeum (Pure Gospel) Pentecostalism* (Zoetermeer: Uitgeverij Boekencentrum, 2003), 158-15.

[20] 'About CGI' (https://www.cgikorea.kr/kr/company/about.php), accessed on 10 Sept 2018.

of laymen in YFGC, founded many other small mission organizations to lead world mission.[21]

4. Pentecostals in the Edinburgh Centenary Series

When the editors first envisioned this book they recruited Kuewon Lee as the associate editor. At the time, Lee was a theology graduate student at Oral Roberts University. The editors tasked him to establish a list of Pentecostal chapters published throughout the Edinburgh Centenary Series. He compiled the following data as part of his task. It provides a picture of the role that Pentecostals played in the Edinburgh Centenary Series.[22]

According to Lee's analysis, there are seventy chapters either contributed by Pentecostals or by non-Pentecostals on Pentecostal subjects. Significant as it may appear, this number represents only 8.5% of the entire chapter amount within the Series.[23] According to Lee, this amount does not correlate with the vast number of Pentecostal-charismatic believers at large in the world today. Indeed, with so many Pentecostal-charismatic adherents, including scholars, one expects a more considerable contribution. One reason behind this may be that Pentecostals have traditionally distanced themselves from ecumenical initiatives. On the other hand, perhaps some volume editors were not intentional in reaching out to Pentecostals for their contributions.

In Lee's analysis of the seventy Pentecostal chapters, two sets of data are of interest: regional and gender distribution. The highest number of contributors are from Asia with 23 authors and 32.9% of all the Pentecostal contributions. Europe is second with 17 authors and 24.3% of all the Pentecostal contributions. Africa comes third with 12 authors and 17.1% of all the Pentecostal contributions. Latin America is fifth (10 authors and 14.3% of all the Pentecostal contributions), and North America is sixth (8 authors and 11.4% of all the Pentecostal contributions). The overwhelming presence of the global South is encouraging. However, Africa lagging behind Europe does not reflect the realities. Regarding gender distribution, Lee notices a disappointing imbalance: 52 male authors (or 74.3%) vs. 19 female authors. Considering that the Pentecostal movement has flourished among the marginalized, and its claim that the Holy Spirit empowers every believer, this gender balance does not truly reflect Pentecostalism claims.

5. The Book

This Reader volume is intended to serve as a companion to the Edinburgh Centenary title, *Pentecostal Mission and Global Christianity* (2014). So is the

---

[21] Lee, *The Holy Spirit Movement in Korea*, 125.
[22] Kuewon Lee, 'The Trends in the Theology of Pentecostal Mission: Reflected in the Regnum Edinburgh Centenary Series' (a paper for the class, Trends in Theology of Pentecostal Mission, Oral Roberts University, 2018).
[23] The total number excludes speeches and introductions.

title of this reader volume, *Pentecostal Mission and Global Christianity: An Edinburgh Centenary Reader*. However, the publication of Regnum Edinburgh Centenary Series closed following the publication of the last two compendium volumes, therefore this title is hosted in the Regnum Studies in Mission series.

The first step of selecting contributions was by identifying potential series' chapters. The editors agreed to preclude all the studies in the Pentecostal volume and the compendium volumes. In the end, about 35 studies became available for our consideration. The editors also agreed to limit studies to only one per author. From these decisions, two book sections emerged: theoretical or foundational and practical case studies. When the editors divided the studies between the two sections, they were able to arrange the studies by topics and contexts. At the end of the process, twenty-six studies surfaced for the book. The editorial team was pleased to note a positive geographical distribution. Africa provides six studies, Asia five, Europe six, North America three, and South America six studies. However, the present title fails to keep the gender ratio of the Edinburgh Pentecostal volume: 20 male (or 77%) vs. six female authors.

The first part, Spirit Missiology, includes Pentecostal missiology, engagements with other missiologies, and Christian unity. The second part, Spirit Mission Praxis, includes healing, holistic mission, and challenges which Pentecostal and Charismatic believers face in their mission engagements. The composition of the book reveals that Pentecostal mission thinking is beyond the traditional focus on evangelism and church growth. The editors realized in the early editorial stage that the available studies were heavy on holism and unity. They pointed to the future rather than focusing on the past. We are convinced that this book will serve the Pentecostal, charismatic, and independent churches worldwide, and also the entire global church community.

Part 1

Spirit Missiology

The *Missio Spiritus*: Towards a Pneumatological Missiology of Creation

Amos Yong

Introduction

This chapter triangulates around three theological topics: pentecostal or pneumatological theology, theology of creation, and theology of mission.[1] Although each has an established or emerging literature, they have not, to my knowledge, been brought together in any constructive manner. We thus seek to make contributions along two related lines: that of exploring the possibility of developing an explicitly pentecostal and pneumatological perspective on theology of creation, and that of contributing to thinking about mission theology from within such a framework. The two parts that follow take up these tasks respectively. I conclude with brief recommendations for mission practice from such a pneumatological theology of creation.

Understanding Creation: Pentecostal and Pneumatological Perspectives

We begin by noting that, on the day of Pentecost, the apostle Peter connected the outpouring of the Holy Spirit not only with the charismatic and egalitarian empowering of 'all flesh' (e.g. sons and daughters, young and old, slave and free), but also with 'portents in the heaven above and signs on the earth below' (Acts 2:19).[2] These portents and signs were anticipated long before – by the

---

Originally published in Kapya J Kaoma (ed), *Creation Care in Christian Mission*, Regnum Edinburgh Centenary Series 29 (Oxford: Regnum Books, 2015), 121-133.

[1] For instance, I have written books on each of the three topics: on pentecostal theology in *The Spirit Poured Out on All Flesh: Pentecostalism and the Possibility of Global Theology* (Grand Rapids, MI: Baker Academic, 2005); on the theology of creation in *The Spirit of Creation: Modern Science and Divine Action in the Pentecostal-Charismatic Imagination* (Grand Rapids, MI: Eerdmans, 2011); and on mission theology in *The Missiological Spirit: Christian Mission Theology for the Third Millennium Global Context* (Eugene, OR: Cascade Books, 2014). The following attempts to connect the dots even while forging a synoptic statement.

[2] Unless otherwise noted, all biblical quotations are from the New Revised Standard

prophet Joel (2:28-32): 'blood and fire and columns of smoke, [the] sun shall be turned to darkness, and the moon to blood' – and associated with the salvation expected on the Day of the LORD. While these manifestations are thereby first and foremost signs of God's eschatological salvation, two other observations are pertinent: first, that these heavenly and earthly phenomena are directly connected with the pentecostal outpouring of the Spirit of God, and second, that they serve as capable metaphors for signifying the salvation and eschatological mission of God inaugurated by the gift of the Spirit. Such observations invite further reflection on what might be called a 'pentecostal' or pneumatological theology of creation.

Before proceeding, however, it is important to define our terms. Both Pentecostalism and pneumatological theology are relative newcomers to the religion and science conversation, hence the need to define how they are used in this chapter. *Pentecost* and *Pentecostalism* (both capitalised) refer respectively to the Day of Pentecost described in Acts 2, and to the tradition of Christian churches and denominations linked to the Azusa Street revival in Los Angeles from 1906-1908.[3] *Pentecostals* (also capitalised) are adherents of modern Pentecostalism who often understand the Day of Pentecost not as an unrepeatable historical event, but as paradigmatic and (in some cases) normative for all Christian life and experience. When used adjectivally, *pentecostal* (uncapitalised) is either associated with phenomena on the Day of Pentecost or descriptive of the perspective informed by the experiences of Pentecostals.

The reason for the absence of specifically pentecostal voices in the public domain in general and in the religion and science conversation more specifically is that Pentecostals have only just recently begun to think about what is distinctive about a pentecostal world-view.[4] I suggest that, given the paradigmatic function of the Day of Pentecost for the modern pentecostal experience, and given the centrality of the Holy Spirit to pentecostal spirituality, a pentecostal world-view can and should be developed which is unambiguously pneumatological in orientation. By this, I mean that a distinctive pentecostal perspective should be informed at its core by their experience and understanding of the Holy Spirit, and should be comprehensively extended through the application of this pneumatologically informed frame of reference – what I call the 'pneumatological imagination'[5] – to any and all domains of knowledge.

Version.

[3] This would include denominations like the Assemblies of God, Church of God in Christ, International Church of the Foursquare Gospel, International Pentecostal Holiness Church, Church of God (Cleveland, TN), and Church of God of Prophecy; see Allan Anderson, *An Introduction to Pentecostalism: Global Charismatic Christianity* (Cambridge: Cambridge University Press, 2004), especially chap. 3.

[4] A sketch of a pentecostal world-view can be found in James K.A. Smith, *Thinking in Tongues: Pentecostal Contributions to Christian Philosophy* (Grand Rapids, MI: Eerdmans, 2010).

[5] See part I of my 'Spirit-Word-Community: Theological Hermeneutics in Trinitarian

By 'pneumatological theology', I am referring not to the theological or doctrinal study of the Holy Spirit (pneumatology), but to a comprehensive theological vision starting from and informed explicitly by pneumatology. This work has been in progress across denominational lines – no one Christian tradition corners the market on the Holy Spirit – since the renaissance in pneumatology itself about a generation ago, and has borne impressive results so far, even when limited to the circles of pentecostal theological reflection in mission theology of work, social ethics, and spirituality, among other topics. I suggest that the time has come to ask the specific question: what does a pentecostal perspective and pneumatological theology have to contribute to the Christian understanding of creation and the natural world?

A number of other attempts to develop a theology of nature have drawn upon pneumatological themes and perspectives. In what follows, I highlight the efforts of Sallie McFague, a Protestant feminist theologian, and Denis Edwards, a Roman Catholic theologian. McFague formulates an ecological theology and theology of nature appropriate to the challenges of late twentieth and early twenty-first-century planetary life.[6] Drawing from process theology and feminist/liberationist epistemology, McFague articulates a theology of creation that is both theological and naturalistic. While concerned to avoid any kind of pre-modern supernaturalism, McFague realises that the positivism and scientism of modernity has been destructive for planetary life. As there is a 'more' to the natural world than materialism suggests, McFague exhorts, 'Christians should not only be natural, understanding ourselves as *in* and *of* the earth, but also super, natural, understanding ourselves as excessively, superlatively concerned with nature and its well-being'.[7]

McFague's metaphorical-theological discourse concludes that the incarnation is suggestive not only of the revelation of God in Christ, but also the embodiment of God in Jesus. Jesus Christ reveals (for Christians) the shape of the body of God which is inclusive of all (especially the needy and oppressed), and unveils the scope of the body of God which is inclusive of the cosmos (cosmic Christ). This notion of divine embodiment finds new meaning in the context of our present ecological crisis. Hence the world is reconceived metaphorically as the 'body of God' so as to articulate an interdependence and interrelational model for the God-human-world relationship (rather than a dualistic or hierarchical conception of God and world, or of human beings and creation), encouraging a reverential attitude towards the creation (rather than a

Perspective', in *New Critical Thinking in Religion, Theology and Biblical Studies Series* (Burlington, VT, and Aldershot, UK: Ashgate Publishing Ltd., 2002; reprint, Eugene, OR: Wipf & Stock, 2002).

[6] Sallie McFague's publications are numerous; for our purposes, her more recent trilogy is most pertinent: *The Body of God: An Ecological Theology* (Minneapolis, MN: Fortress, 1993); *Super, Natural Christians: How We Should Love Nature* (Minneapolis, MN: Fortress, 1997); and *Life Abundant: Rethinking Theology and Economy for a Planet in Peril* (Minneapolis, MN: Fortress, 2001).

[7] McFague, *Super, Natural Christians*, 6; italics original.

utilitarian and instrumentalist one), and motivating the development of an ethic of care, reconciliation and liberation (rather than an ethic of domination). Crucial to McFague's proposals is a creation spirituality and praxis aimed at replacing the neo-classical economic structure of middle-class American life with one that attempts to embody the life of Jesus in ways that are more environmentally sustainable and friendly.

It is interesting also to note that McFague develops her panentheistic agential-organic model of the God-world relationship analogously to traditional conceptions of the spirit-body relationship. Even as the human spirit is understood to animate the human body, so also the divine Spirit universally gives life, empowers and energises all things. God as 'spirit-body' is thus neither fully impersonal (hence McFague's anti-modernism) nor fully personal (hence also McFague's anti-premodernism). Instead, Spirit-theology allows for emphasis not only on the divine intellect/Wisdom (Logos theology) transcendent over the world's evolutionary process, but also on the divine enmeshment within creation.

The ecological theology of Australian theologian, Denis Edwards, follows McFague's, but adds an explicitly pneumatological framework.[8] Edwards' thesis is that the story of the Holy Spirit is co-extensive with (what contemporary cosmological science says is) the fourteen-billion-year evolutionary history of the entire universe, not only breathing life into the world but also empowering the creative process. Bringing insights from both the biblical and patristic traditions into dialogue with contemporary science introduces new possibilities into the religion and science conversation. The dynamism of the Spirit or the *ruach* (breath) of God, for example, helps us think about the dynamic and unfinished character of the world. This open-endedness (I would emphasise) is also suggestive of an eschatological (to use theological language) or teleological (a more neutral category) dimension to the universe, and in turn, provides for a connection Edwards sees between pneumatology and the emergence of novelty and complexity in the creation.

Edwards' notion of the Spirit of God immanent to and active within creation's processes contributes towards a more robust theological framework for understanding God as creator. In Edwards' theology of creation, Word and Spirit work mutually and reciprocally as the 'two hands of the Father' (Irenaeus) in the formation and transformation of the universe. Hence the self-organising principles guiding the evolution of complex processes and structures in the universe is inexplicable if a materialistic metaphysics is assumed, but appears to cohere well with the kind of pneumatological theology of creation suggested by Edwards. If the Word (or Logos) provides the divine pattern for creation's forms, then the Spirit is the divine mind (cf. 1 Cor. 2:10-16) that communicates the patterns of the Logos to creatures and the divine breath that empowers creaturely formation. From this, the Spirit is not only the giver of life and the source of novelty and creativity in the world, but

---

[8] Denis Edwards, *Breath of Life: A Theology of the Creator Spirit* (Maryknoll, NY: Orbis Books, 2004), especially chap. 3, 'Breathing Life into a Universe of Creatures'.

also the ontological basis for creation's intricately structured relationships: of each 'creature' with others, its environment, and the divine, and of the whole of creation with the Triune God.

The preceding very succinct exposition leaves much unsaid and only charts two trajectories for considering how to bridge pneumatological theology and theology of creation. Nevertheless, the following gains, at least, can be said to have been achieved: that the spiritual and material dimensions of the world ought not to be bifurcated; that the theological and the natural domains are interrelated; and that the pneumatological and the creational are interconnected. But how might pneumatological theology inform Christian mission? In the following section, I explore how this theology is the foundation of what might be called an environmental or ecological missiology.

Foundations for Christian Mission: Pneumato-Creational Perspectives

The connection between theology of creation and missiology here is pneumatology: the Spirit of creation is also the Spirit that empowers Christian mission. The following discussion unfolds such a pneumatological theology of creational mission in three steps: by following out the salvation historical drama from creation through redemption to eschatological glorification. This will set us up to think about missiological praxis (the final section at the end) in the light of such a pneumatological theology of creation.

Missio Spiritus – The Doctrine of Creation

In thinking about pneumatology, pneumatological theology, and pneumatology of mission, we should begin with the doctrine of creation. This not only helps us to ground pneumatological reflection in the doctrine of God, but it also establishes the cosmic, creational and global scope of the work of the Spirit. Both points are important. Without a link with the doctrine of God as creator, the Spirit may turn out to be less than 'holy', perhaps not even related to the God of Judeo-Christian faith at all, much less to monotheistic or even theistic sensibilities.[9] There are many spirits indeed, so Christian thinking about pneumatology must be defined, at least initially, as the Spirit of the God who created the heavens and the earth. And without relation to the latter, cosmic compass of the Spirit's work, then we may be tempted to merely interiorise or subjectivise the Spirit's presence and activity.

The role of the Spirit in the Christian doctrine of creation has gradually been recognised.[10] In my own work, I have attempted what I have called a

[9] There are also possibilities for thinking about the Spirit of God in relationship to monotheistic traditions more generally and to Islam in particular. I undertake a dialogue with the latter in my *The Spirit Poured Out on All Flesh*, chap. 6.

[10] The major text so far is Jürgen Moltmann, *The Spirit of Life: A Universal Affirmation* (trans. Margaret Kohl; Minneapolis, MN: Fortress, 1992).

pneumatological reading of the Genesis narratives.[11] This begins with the observation that while 'the earth was a formless void and darkness covered the face of the deep', the author of the creation account notes that 'a wind from God [*ruach Elohim*] swept over the face of the waters' (Gen. 1:2). So while traditional creation theologies have highlighted the creation of the world through the word of God, the word of God is uttered through the divine breath and the 'history' of the world is 'blown' or swept along by the presence and activity of the *ruach Elohim*. The partitioning of the waters from land, the emergence of vegetation, the evolution of life itself – each of these can be understood from this pneumatological vantage point as being propelled by the breath of God that transcendentally hovered over the primordial creation.

But the divine breath is not only transcendent over the creation but also immanent within it. This is because all living creatures have been constituted by Elohim's 'breath of life' (Gen. 1:30), and in particular, human beings, who are essentially constituted by the divine breath (Gen. 2:7). As it is said later in the Hebrew Bible, 'If he should take back his spirit to himself, and gather to himself his breath, all flesh would perish together, and all mortals return to dust' (Job 34:14-15). Beyond this, however, the Psalmist indicates that the divine breath not only gives life to creatures, but also that through it, the face of the ground is renewed (Ps. 104:29-30), and the prophet Isaiah proclaims that when 'a spirit from on high is poured out on us, [then] the wilderness becomes a fruitful field, and the fruitful field is deemed a forest' (Is. 32:15). This suggests that the rhythms of creation itself beats to the drumming of the creator Spirit.[12]

It is important to note the missiological implications of a pneumatological theology of creation. If a Logos theology emphasises that the Word became flesh and, as the true light, 'enlightens everyone' in the world (John 1:9), then the doctrine of *creator Spiritus* suggests that such lights are intertwined through the infusion of the divine breath. Thus, as the ancient poets recognised, 'In him we live and move and have our being' (Acts 17:28), and this can be understood both christologically and pneumatologically. On the pneumatological plane, however, when reading in the light of ancient Israelite perspectives (above), humans are pneumatically interrelated not only with one another but also with non-human animals since all of life throbs with and through the breath given by the *ruach* of God. In this sense, Christian mission is thus always and primordially *missio Spiritus*.

---

[11] See Amos Yong, '*Ruach*, the Primordial Waters, and the Breath of Life: Emergence Theory and the Creation Narratives in Pneumatological Perspective', in Michael Welker (ed), *The Work of the Spirit: Pneumatology and Pentecostalism* (Grand Rapids, MI: Eerdmans, 2006), 183-204.

[12] See also Scott A. Ellington, 'The Face of God as His Creating Spirit: The Interplay of Yahweh's *panim* and *ruach* in Psalm 104:29-30', in Amos Yong (ed), *The Spirit Renews the Face of the Earth: Pentecostal Forays in Science and Theology of Creation* (Eugene, OR: Pickwick Publications, 2009), 17-29.

But there is one more layer to pneumatological mission theology of creation that should be lifted up before turning to the doctrine of redemption. Divine redemption is required because although the *ruach Elohim* both hovered over the primordial waters and became the breath of life for all living creatures, nevertheless with the fall of creation, the cosmos and all of its creatures remain alienated from God the Creator. Paradoxically, then, the *ruach Elohim* is both present to all creatures – enlivening and vivifying the creation – and yet also absent from them – in the estrangement creatures feel towards other creatures and to their Creator – simultaneously. In anticipation of this redemptive work, then, the promise is given in the Hebrew Bible that God will redeem the world pneumatologically through the chosen or elect nation of Israel.

There are two moments constitutive of such a pneumatological promise. First, God pledges to Abraham that 'in you all the families of the earth shall be blessed' (Gen. 12:3). Second, however, even the divine promises are insufficient to preserve and ultimately save the people called of God. Rather, God needs to accomplish an internal work, a work of the Spirit: 'A new heart I will give you, and a new spirit I will put within you; and I will remove from your body the heart of stone and give you a heart of flesh. I will put my spirit within you, and make you follow my statutes and be careful to observe my ordinances' (Ezek. 36:26-27). This anticipates the later gift of the Spirit in Christ. But for our purposes at this juncture, it is important to point out that the creational mission of the Spirit not only infuses the dust of the ground with life but also looks ahead to another pneumatic outpouring and infilling. In other words, the creation as a whole, as well as its creatures, is primed to receive the redemptive fullness of the Spirit.

Missio Spiritus – The Doctrine of Redemption

The second moment of the *missio Spiritus* moves us from the universality of the Spirit's presence and activity in the creation to the particularity of the Spirit's historical work in redemption. This redemptive history involves the incarnation of the Son via the power of the Spirit, followed by the Son's gift of the Spirit to the people of God. But why are both essential? For at least two reasons, one historical and the other spiritual: historically, the Son came in order to renew and restore Israel as the people of God, and this renewal and restoration was intended both to serve as a template for the kingdom of God and to inaugurate that kingdom.[13] But God's offer of restoration and renewal in the Son was rejected, and he suffered a violent death; yet his death became salvific for his people because it served as a scapegoat that prevented further outbreaks of violence (at least for one generation). Spiritually, the life and death of the Son represented the obedience that served as the basis of reconciliation of human

[13] Here I am in basic agreement with the central thrust of N.T. Wright's interpretation of the mission of Jesus; my own appropriation of Wright's account is in my *In the Days of Caesar: Pentecostalism and Political Theology* (Grand Rapids, MI: Eerdmans, 2010), chap. 3.

beings in particular and the world as a whole with God; then the resurrection and ascension of the Son confirmed the potentiality of the world's transfiguration in the presence and power of God. Hence, as the ancient church confessed, the Son became human so that human beings might be redeemed as children of God; by extension, the Son was clothed with the dust of the earth so that the creation itself might be renewed as the dwelling place of God.

But the mission of the Son cannot be divorced from the *missio Spiritus*; in fact, they are inextricably intertwined. The Spirit is the power not just of the Son's breath of life but also of the Son's conception and generation in the womb of Mary; just as the *ruach Elohim* hovered over the structural ordering of the primordial chaos, so also did the Spirit both overshadow and come upon Mary (Luke 1:35). Then, the Spirit descends on the Son at his baptism in the Jordan (Luke 3:22) so that he can be filled with the Spirit for his public ministry, itself launched by his spiritual confrontation with the demonic powers of the world (Luke 4:1, 14). Thus does Jesus pronounce that his mission is that of the Spirit's: 'The Spirit of the Lord is upon me, because he has anointed me to bring good news to the poor. He has sent me to proclaim release to the captives and recovery of sight to the blind, to let the oppressed go free, to proclaim the year of the Lord's favour' (Luke 4:18-19). The rest of his public ministry unfolds this agenda according to the power of the Holy Spirit (Acts 10:38).

If Jesus accomplished the saving works of God – proclamation of the gospel to all, in particular to the poor, healing the sick, delivering the oppressed and the captives, and inaugurating the Jubilee year of divine favour and redemption – through the power of the Spirit, then so also did his original disciples. They were initially told to wait in Jerusalem for 'power from on high' (Luke 24:49) and then later promised: 'You will receive power when the Holy Spirit has come upon you; and you will be my witnesses in Jerusalem, in all Judea and Samaria, and to the ends of the earth' (Acts 1:8). Whereas Jesus came first to renew and restore Israel, with forays into Samaria, the Spirit-filled ministry of the earliest followers of Jesus took them to the ends of the earth.

The outpouring of the Spirit at Pentecost brings to historical fulfilment two promises made to ancient Israel. First, if ancient Israel had been disobedient to the covenant with Yahweh due to the hardness of heart, the newly reconstituted people of God were no longer merely bound externally by law but were empowered internally by transformed hearts that had been touched by the Spirit. This is one of the central messages of the New Testament: that the Hebraic law provided for sacrifices for sins, but the gift of the Spirit enables the evangelical obedience that produces sanctified and holy lives (see Heb. 9:13-14 and passim). In other words, the divine breath of life in every person as a result of the creative work of the Spirit is now, potentially, the divine breath of holiness as a result of the redemptive work of the Spirit unleashed on the Day of Pentecost.

Secondly, the Pentecost outpouring of the Spirit inaugurates the promised redemption of the nations derived from the covenant made with Abraham. This occurred in two ways: through the presence at Jerusalem at the Pentecost feast of 'devout Jews [and proselytes] from every nation under heaven living in Jerusalem' (Acts 2:5, 10), and through the apostolic missionary movement that not only went from Jerusalem to Rome (as recounted in Acts) but also commissioned others to take the gospel in other directions (i.e. as did the Ethiopian eunuch in Acts 8). The *missio Spiritus* thus generates ongoing surprises that involve the crossing of borders so that agents of mission continually find a blurring of the lines between 'insiders' and 'outsiders' – at least on this side of the *eschaton* when we all see through a glass dimly – in the divine scheme of things.

The lack of formal closure to the book of Acts invites readers in every place and time since to participate in the work and witness of the Spirit of God in Christ as part of the book's 29th chapter, as it were. The Spirit who empowered the Son and who was poured out upon and filled the apostles is the same Spirit who continues to accomplish the redemptive work of God in Christ and through the church in this post-apostolic period. This ongoing work in history, then, leads us to the third and concluding act of the *missio Spiritus*.

Missio Spiritus – In the Last Days

We began with the work of the Spirit in creation and had in the preceding discussed the Spirit's redemptive work in Christ and the Pentecost outpouring that constituted the church. Now we turn to the eschatological work of the Spirit anticipating the final renewal and restoration of the creation as a whole. This eschatological work was inaugurated in the redemptive work of the Spirit in the life, death, and resurrection of Christ. As the apostle Peter said (quoting the prophet Joel, at least as recorded by Luke the evangelist): '*In the last days* it will be, God declares, that I will pour out my Spirit upon all flesh…' (Acts 2:17, citing Joel 2:28; italics added).[14] Again, there are two dimensions to this eschatological work of the Spirit: the christological and the ecclesiological.

Christologically, the eschatological work of the Spirit is most clearly revealed in Jesus' proclamation regarding the coming kingdom and his accomplishing the signs of the kingdom. These latter include his miraculous deeds, his healings, and his exorcisms of evil spirits. These are signs of the coming kingdom precisely because they can be understood either as enacted by suspensions of the present order of things (i.e., the 'laws of nature' as currently conceived) or as anticipations of the ways in which the coming world will operate. The Spirit enables Christ to accomplish the works that bring about the shape of the coming kingdom, in the process announcing the end of the present cosmic order.

---

[14] Pentecostal mission has by and large been motivated by this eschatological impulse: e.g. James R. Goff, Jr, *Fields White unto Harvest: Charles Fox Parham and the Missionary Origins of Pentecostalism* (Fayetteville, AR: University of Arkansas Press, 1988), and D. William Faupel, *The Everlasting Gospel: The Significance of Eschatology in the Development of Pentecostal Thought* (Sheffield, UK: Sheffield Academic Press, 1996).

Most importantly, however, the Spirit announces the arrival of the kingdom in the resurrection of Jesus. If death is the most ubiquitous sign of the world as we know it, resurrection life provides us with a foretaste of the world to come. Yet even christologically, the fullness of the Spirit is not yet manifest in and through the Christ for that awaits the *parousia*, the return of the anointed Messiah that will finally and fully establish the coming reign of God. As the author of the first Johannine epistle writes: 'When he is revealed, we will be like him, for we will see him as he is' (1 John 3:2).

But again, the work of the Spirit in the life, death, and resurrection of Jesus is now available to the followers of Christ, the church – the body of Christ and the fellowship of the Spirit. We now also have received the Spirit as well as the gifts of the Spirit that are given liberally for the edification of all and for the common good (1 Cor. 12:7-11).[15] The apostolic empowerment by the Spirit thus also enabled them to work miraculous signs and wonders, including healing the sick, exorcising demons, and even raising the dead. These continued the pronouncement regarding the imminence of the coming kingdom even while precipitating its arrival. As people of the eschatological Spirit, the apostolic message was proclaimed 'not with plausible words of wisdom, but with a demonstration of the Spirit and of power' (1 Cor. 2:4). In this sense, then, the church as the people of the Spirit glimpses through the eschatological mirror dimly (1 Cor. 13:12), even now enacting the works of the kingdom in anticipation of the full glory that is to be revealed. There is a fundamental sense, then, in which the Spirit is both present (having already introduced the coming reign of God) and yet also absent (still to fully establish the righteousness of God).

Yet the eschatological work of the Spirit is not merely anthropocentric but has a cosmic scope. The apostle Paul wrote: 'We know that the whole creation has been groaning in labour pains until now; and not only the creation, but we ourselves, who have the first fruits of the Spirit, groan inwardly while we wait for adoption, the redemption of our bodies' (Rom. 8:22-23). On the one hand, the outpouring of the Spirit upon all flesh has already begun the final transfiguration, to the point that the sun, the moon, and the heavenly elements have also begun to anticipate the great and coming Day of the Lord (Acts 2:19-20); on the other hand, the gift of the Spirit here in the second Act has done no more than initiating the eschatological conditions under which the fullness of redemption – the third Act – will be fully accomplished in the coming reign of God. While Easter Sunday has occurred in the resurrection of Christ and in the regenerating work of the Spirit (the 'already' of the Spirit's presence), yet the world nevertheless remains also amidst the Holy Saturday of the present fallen order, betwixt and between the times anticipating the resurrection of all flesh (the 'not yet' of the Spirit's eschatological activity).

But beyond the resurrection of dead bodies, this final eschatological revelation of the Spirit signals the completion of the divine work begun in the

---

[15] For more on my pneumatological theology of the charisms, see *God is Spirit, God is Love: Love as the Gift of the Spirit* (Waco, TX: Baylor University Press, 2012), chap. 7.

creation of the world and brings to fruition what was set in motion in the hovering of the *ruach Elohim* over the primordial waters.[16] All of creation is destined to be reconciled to the Creator: not only human beings but also the entire cosmic order. This is so that all things may be reconciled to God in Christ (Col. 1:15-20) and that 'God may be all in all' (1 Cor. 15:28b): 'For from him and through him and *to him* are all things' (Rom. 11:36, italics added). The dynamic engine driving this eschatological reconciliation, however, is the Spirit. In other words, the Spirit of creation and redemption is also the coming Spirit, the one who enables the renewal and restoration of all things to the image of God in Christ. So if in Act 2 the redemptive work of the Spirit enables her inhabitation of human flesh – first the flesh of Jesus and then that of all flesh – then in Act 3, the eschatological work of the Spirit transforms and transfigures all creation as the dwelling place of the divine Spirit.

Poured Out on All Flesh – To the Ends of the Earth: Towards a Pneumato-Missiological Praxis

I conclude by suggesting three lines of mission praxis. First, if the Spirit of God is also the Spirit of creation as well as the Spirit of mission, then Christian mission ought to be intentional about engaging with the environment. The Spirit is said to groan through human creatures for the redemption and renewal of all creation. If so, then while not all mission work will be environmentally or ecologically directed, such ought not to be wholly ignored. The Spirit poured out at Pentecost on all flesh (Acts 2:17) means that some Christ-followers[17] (not only Pentecostals) will be called towards Creation care even to the ends of the earth (Acts 1:8), and those who are called ought to respond positively to such a vocational undertaking.[18]

Second, it is not only that Spirit-empowered Christian mission is environmentally sensitive and focused, but theological thinking about mission (missiology) ought also to be cognisant of the environmental or ecological horizon within which Christian mission unfolds. This means that every aspect of Christian mission is or ought to be carried out within such an environmental and ecological frame of reference. Missiologies of development, for instance, should be explicated in the light of such constraints, probing not only the challenges but also the opportunities to work missionally in environmentally sustainable ways.[19] The point is that the Spirit of creation is presumed to call

---

[16] See Yong, *In the Days of Caesar*, chap. 8.3.

[17] See also Christopher Wright in this volume.

[18] Such an environmental missiology is further developed in the final chapter of my book, *The Cosmic Breath: Spirit and Nature in the Christianity-Buddhism-Science Trialogue*, Philosophical Studies in Science & Religion 4 (Leiden and Boston, MA: Brill, 2012).

[19] E.g. Bryant L. Myers, *Walking with the Poor: Principles and Practices of Transformational Development* (revised and expanded edition: Maryknoll, NY: Orbis Books, 2011), 183.

and empower Christian mission only through methods and approaches that will not be destructive of their given habitation.

Last but not least, the theological academy ought to be more intentional about developing ministerial and missional curriculum that links pneumatology to theology of creation and missiology. Here I am talking not only about including pneumatological theologies of the environment in missiological courses and seminars, but also about including pneumatological missiologies in theologies of creation courses, and including environmental missiologies in pneumatology and theology courses. In other words, triangulating around these themes ought to generate multi-directional approaches so that each element both informs and receives from the other two, towards an interactive and holistic pneumatology, theology of creation, and missiology. Such a task is necessarily a dynamic one since we see through a glass dimly even as we are committed to working missionally in anticipation of the coming reign of God.[20]

---

[20] Much, although not all, of the material for this chapter has been reworked from two previously published articles of mine: 'The Spirit and Creation: Possibilities and Challenges for a Dialogue between Pentecostal Theology and the Sciences', in *Journal of the European Pentecostal Theological Association* 25 (2005), 82-110; and 'Primed for the Spirit: Creation, Redemption, and the *Missio Spiritus*', in *International Review of Mission* 100:2 (November 2011), 355-66; thanks to John Kaoma for revising and editing into a coherent whole, and for inviting my contribution to this volume, and to Ryan Seow, my graduate assistant, for proofreading the penultimate draft – all obscurities and incoherence remain my responsibility. Notice that my argument for creation care is theological rather than scientific. It is not that I wish to neglect arguments about global warming, for instance, but that there is currently no consensus about the science of this matter. I would invite Christians who are sceptical about the scientific data, however, to consider a Pascalian wager: if we heed the yea-sayers but they turn out to be wrong, one could argue there is no harm done; but if we listen to the nay-sayers and they turn out to be wrong, we have jeopardised our children's future. Conservative Christians are quick to adopt this Pascalian approach for the existence of God and vis-à-vis the stakes related to eternal life, but I am not sure they have considered contested issues in environmental science in these terms.

The Theological Motivations for Pentecostal Mission

Wonsuk Ma

The Growth of Global Pentecostalism

The growth of the modern Pentecostal movement is a remarkable story. During the century of its existence, it has grown from a 'fringe' group congregating every day in a run-down warehouse in downtown Los Angeles whose members were branded as religious fanatics to spread throughout the world, and influence other church traditions. Although numbers vary,[1] there is a consensus that it now numbers around half a billion throughout the world in various forms and traditions, including 'Charismatics' well integrated into various existing church families.[2] This chapter charts the growth of the movement and its developing missiology, demonstrating the complex interplay of Bible, experience, and theology as it does so.

The significance of Pentecostal expansion was evident as the world church celebrated the centenary of the Edinburgh Missionary Conference. In its original 1910 conference, Pentecostals were in their infancy. The disappearance of the Azusa Street Mission in 1909, perhaps the most visible expression of Pentecostal Christianity, after a three-year controversial existence, may have been a relief to some Christian leaders who felt embarrassed by this 'tongue-babbling cultish group'.[3] So, the Edinburgh conference did not need to worry about them. They were already struggling with issues surrounding the Catholic Church. However, Pentecostals did not 'die out'. In fact, the dramatic expansion of Christianity owes much to the exponential growth of Pentecostal

---

Originally published in Emma Wild-Wood and Peniel Rajkumar (eds), *Foundations for Mission*, Regnum Edinburgh Centenary Series 13 (Oxford: Regnum Books, 2013), 220-235.

[1] Todd M Johnson and Kenneth R Ross (eds), *Atlas of Global Christianity 1910-2010* (Edinburgh: Edinburgh University Press, 2010). Henceforth *AGC*.
[2] Johnson and Ross, *AGC*, 103.
[3] Cecil M Robeck, Jr, *The Azusa Street Mission and Revival: The Birth of the Global Pentecostal Movement* (Nashville, TN: Thomas Nelson, 2006), 134.

churches and their variants.[4] The African Independent Churches, most Chinese house church networks, and the majority of Latin American evangelicals are defined as Pentecostal in a broader sense.

By the time the world church came to celebrate the centenary of the Edinburgh conference in June 2010, the radical shift of the landscape of global Christianity was crystal clear. A hundred years ago, about 82% of all Christians lived in the global North, or the 'West,' including Oceania. But today, over 60% of Christians live in the global South, the three major southern continents.[5] A steady decline of western Christianity and a corresponding growth of Christianity in the global South occurred between the two conferences. As much of the new Christianity in the South is Pentecostal or its variation, it is also noteworthy that in the West, growing segments of the church are Pentecostal-Charismatic. For example, in the midst of a rapid decline of Christians in Great Britain, the annual New Wine conferences among Charismatic churches are refreshing. In the 2010 Somerset conference, I witnessed about 15,000 participants of all ages savouring expositions of the Word, praises and various seminars.

The expectation is that the growth of Christianity in the South will continue, and Pentecostal worship and spirituality will also expand. If the twentieth century was marked by the exponential growth of African Christianity, all eyes are now on Asia, where Christianity has reached only 8.5% of its vast population of 3.5 billion (more than half of the world's population). The main growth engine is going to be Chinese Christianity as it is moving toward a 10% goal of the national population.[6] When and if Asia achieves a 15 percent mark it will add 8.5 million to the current number, making Christians exactly one-third level of the world population.[7] The share of Pentecostals will be significant in this growth.

While evangelism and church expansion have been the focus of Pentecostal mission, it is also important to note that so-called 'mercy ministry' has been an integral part of Pentecostal mission practice if not, until recently, its official statements.[8] Countless orphanages, various levels of educational institutions, relief work, and others have been deeply ingrained in 'soul-saving' activities. Often without any intentional or serious theological reflection, Pentecostals, perhaps as they are from lower social strata, have instinctive solidarity with the poor and suffering. Two recent publications may serve as useful illustrations. The first, *Not by Might, Nor by Power*,[9] looks into the Latin American Child

---

[4] Philip Jenkins, *The Next Christendom: The Coming of Global Christianity* (Oxford: Oxford University Press, 2002), 63.

[5] Based on the figures found in 'Distribution of Christians, 1910-2010', *AGC*, 59.

[6] 'Christianity in Eastern Asia, 1910-2010', *AGC*, 140-41.

[7] 'Christianity's Centre of Gravity, AD 33-2100', *AGC*, 53.

[8] Article III, 'Constitution of the Assemblies of God', revised, Aug 8-11, 2007, Indianapolis, in http://agchurches.org/Sitefiles/Default/RSS/AG.org%20TOP/2007_Constitution_and_Bylaws.pdf (accessed 21/07/2011).

[9] Doug Petersen, *Not by Might, Nor by Power: A Pentecostal Theology of Social Concern in Latin America* (Oxford: Regnum, 1996).

Care programme of the US Assemblies of God World Mission. It records the growth of the educational programme for poor families throughout Latin America and its impact on societies. From this success, the author constructs a Pentecostal mission theology of social engagement. The second, *Global Pentecostalism* by Miller and Yamamori,[10] is a summary of a four-year field study of growing congregations in the global South, who were intentionally engaging with issues that societies and communities are facing. It found that most of the congregations meeting these requirements were Pentecostal. This sociological study reveals that Pentecostal mission thinking and practice include care for the suffering. The book, however, challenges Pentecostals on two fronts: to move beyond the evangelism-church planting dimension; and to construct an appropriate theology to provide Pentecostals with a valid conceptual ground for social engagement.

Inquiry at Hand

This study probes the theological motivation for such exponential growth. Considering that such expansion requires the agency of Pentecostal believers, the study looks at hermeneutical roots and missional theology of Pentecostalism. This two-stage inquiry is appropriate for the 'grassroots' nature of Pentecostal theologization a process which is often participatory and context-based: it is undertaken by people in the pews and responds to immediate human needs The crux of this process, therefore, is not trained academic theologians, but preacher-pastors.[11] Consequently, Pentecostal theology is deeply imbedded in prayers, sermons, songs and non-verbal expressions of its spirituality. This makes a theologian's first work a description, articulation, and analysis of embedded theological assumptions and arguments.

Hermeneutical values are a set of orientations inherent in Pentecostal spirituality and theology. These characteristics have critically contributed to the identity of Pentecostal believers and to their theological framework, although implicitly expressed. These values also guide Pentecostals in interpreting the scriptures and their religious experiences. Although evolved throughout its history and expressed in various forms in different contexts, they still remain as constants among Pentecostal believers. They may provide clues to defining Pentecostalism.

---

[10] Donald E. Miller and Tetsunao Yamamori, *Global Pentecostalism: The New Face of Christian Social Engagement* (Berkley: University of California Press, 2007).

[11] Julie C. Ma and Wonsuk Ma, *Mission in the Spirit: Towards a Pentecostal/ Charismatic Missiology* (Oxford: Regnum, 2010), 227-41 under the title 'Local Church, Worship, and Theological Formation'.

Which Pentecostalism?

While Pentecostalism can be defined and characterized in various ways, for this reflection it seems to be convenient to limit to the first wave, denominational (or 'Classical') Pentecostals. They are more identifiable than Charismatics whose mission theology and action is shaped by their denominations. They are less 'messy' than the third category sometimes called indigenous Pentecostals or Neo-Charismatics. Strictly speaking, it is not a category, but a catch-all holding bay for a great diversity of expressions which share Pentecostal core values including Chinese house church networks, African Independent Churches, and the Third Wave movement. Tentatively, therefore, we may be able to claim that the 'values' are more broadly owned by various Pentecostal families, whereas the 'theological threads' are more of the classical Pentecostal families. The longer history of first wave Pentecostals makes them more doctrinally coherent and more articulate in their theology and spirituality than the others. However, even within this group, the matter is not that simple. There is great theological diversity among classical Pentecostals, particularly outside the western hemisphere. For example, the Yoido Full Gospel Church in Korea, the largest single congregation in the world, is part of the global Assemblies of God family. However, some of its theological components and spiritual expressions are vastly different from its western cousins. In the global scene, it is also important to remember that the first category is the smallest among world Pentecostal families.

Pentecostal Hermeneutical Values

Any theological investigation needs to seriously consider hermeneutical strategies of a particular group. Pentecostal's hermeneutical strategy influences how to read the scriptures and interpret one's life towards their theological construct. Obviously, much of Pentecostal's unique hermeneutical ethos was emerging in the nineteenth century. The following discussion is intended to be a brief presentation of key hermeneutical sources for Pentecostal mission theology.

'People of the Book': Scripture and Life

Pentecostals have been called the 'people of the book' for their unquestioned acceptance of the authority, and their literalistic reading of the Bible.

The first characteristic is the non-critical reading of the Bible, or perhaps more accurately the post-critical reading by Pentecostal academics and the pre-critical reading by Pentecostals in the pew. Like their conservative evangelical cousins, early Pentecostals had a firm belief in the (almost mechanical) inspiration of the scripture. This was part of the general trend against the intellectual inquiries and the critical reading of the Bible, originating in nineteenth-century German scholarship and gradually spreading to Europe and North America. Hence, any attempt to critically study the scriptures used to be viewed as a theologically 'liberal' practice. This attitude has been further reinforced among the majority of non-western Pentecostals who live in places where sacred scriptures are never questioned They are objects of reverence and obedience, and this 'evangelical' attitude toward the Bible is believed to be the basis for the Christian dynamic of the global South.[12]

Pentecostals have maintained a notion that the more literally one takes the scripture, the more faithful he or she becomes to the word of God, thus the will of God. Triggered from their reading of narratives in the Gospels and Acts, the historicity of events contained in the narratives is never questioned. Furthermore, the inclusion of certain narratives in the scriptures was also taken as proof for a normative pattern. Speaking in tongues as 'the initial physical evidence' of baptism in the Holy Spirit is based on the recurrence of spirit-filled tongue-speaking in Acts. Naturally, Pentecostals fully subscribe, therefore, to the historicity and authenticity of supernatural events recorded in the Scripture. Their unique view of Scripture and the Holy Spirit allows Pentecostals to collapse the time gap between biblical times and the present establishing a link between the early church and the Azusa Street Mission. They simply assume that miracles included in the biblical narratives are repeatable today. This comes with advantages as well as disadvantages. The Bible to the Pentecostals is not an ancient book at all.

The temporal truncation also collapses the distance between God and humans, or the sacred and the secular. The transcendental God is now immanent. They expect to 'hear the voice of God' from the book. Narratives have a particular appeal as the process of reading will soon become the process of participation: the readers find themselves in the midst of the story, be it of healing or of miracles. This ability to 'time travel' provides lively religious experiences. The God of Exodus, for example, is expected to appear here and now allowing the believers to have a similar experience of God's intervention. Thus the interplay of such a Bible reading and experience-oriented religious life creates a spiral effect to enhance a highly engaged Christian life with God's reality. A Pentecostal's 'pre-critical' reading of the Bible naturally results in a literal reading, leaving little room for spiritualizing or demythologizing any 'irrational' record of the Bible.

Restorational Impulse: Apostolic Vision

As the twentieth century approached, there was a heightened interest in eschatology. One stream was the expectation of the early church restored with the manifestation of the spiritual gifts of prophecy, healing and an outpouring of the Holy Spirit as recorded in Acts and 1 Corinthians. Camp meetings were a common annual feature for devout believers and their families to experience personal revival. One of the most popular words among the late nineteenth century Holiness and early twentieth-century Pentecostal believers was

[12] Philip Jenkins, *The New Faces of Christianity: Believing the Bible in the Global South* (Oxford: Oxford University Press, 2006).

'apostolic', reflecting the expectation and yearning for the restoration of church life as is recorded in the book of Acts. The dawning of the new century reinforced their eager expectation of the 'latter rain' to mark the end of the end time.

The modern Pentecostal movement has developed its unique mission-oriented theology of the Holy Spirit and Christian life. With their unique experiences such as baptism in the Holy Spirit and tongues as its accompanying sign, early Pentecostals understood themselves as being people called for a specific task. Considering that the advent of the Spirit gave birth to the church, the very foundation of its existence is missional. Accordingly, spiritual baptism has been closely linked to witnessing (Acts 1:8), and some early Pentecostal leaders advocated tongues as a practical missionary tool.[13] This unique theological understanding shaped a peculiar self-identity as people empowered for God's mission. Pentecostals were countercultural both in the church and in society, and courageously endured ridicule and marginalization. Yet throughout its history, Pentecostalism has flourished where Christian presence had been in existence, instead of 'virgin' Christian frontiers. In this sense, Pentecostalism is a revival and renewal movement, challenging and energizing the church to recover its 'apostolic' authority and call to witness for Christ to the ends of the earth. Evangelism and church planting have been at the core of Pentecostal mission, partly due to its eschatological orientation, and also as part of the early twentieth century evangelical Christianity.

Participatory Process: Place of Community

The role of community is the focal point of religious life and of the hermeneutical process. The work of the Holy Spirit in community formation is experienced at least on two fronts: bringing people around common spiritual experience, and breaking barriers that divide God's people. In the Azusa Street Mission, the common experience of the Spirit baptism brought together people of different races, social strata, and ecclesiastical affiliations. At the turn of the twentieth century, white and Afro-Americans worshipping together was a radical counter-cultural departure from the norm. The division of the movement along racial lines has become a stark reminder of human sinfulness and failure against the Spirit's intention and work. However, this amazing potential continued to appear throughout its history. In the Philippines in the 1980s, a sociologist discovered close relationships between Pentecostals and Charismatic Catholics despite the hostility between Protestants and Catholics in the Philippines.[14]

---

[13] James R Goff, Jr, 'Initial Tongues in the Theology of Charles Fox Parham', in Gary B McGee (ed), *Initial Evidence: Historical and Biblical Perspectives on the Pentecostal Doctrine of Spirit Baptism* (Peabody, MA: Hendrickson, 1991), 57-71.

[14] Koichi Kitano, 'Socio-Religious Distance between Charismatics and Other Religious Group Members: A Case Study of the Philippines in the 1980s', *Journal of Asian Mission* 5:2 (2003), 231-42.

At the centre of Pentecostal community, formation is worship. It provides a space and time for religious experiences, theological formation and the shared process of theology-making. Worship is incredibly participatory in nature, often blurring the demarcation between the pulpit and the pews. One excellent example is the 'testimony' time, where anyone can be the 'main speaker'. By publicly sharing one's religious experience 'to praise the Lord' or 'to plea to the Lord', any member of the community contributes to the corporate deposit of theology and also for the community to exercise the 'gift' of discernment, evaluation and shared ownership of the presented experience and its interpretation. This 'democratic' nature of Pentecostal spirituality significantly enhances the community formation process. The exercise of spiritual gifts also takes place in a community setting, often a prophecy or a message in tongues ideally accompanied by an interpretation.

Even seemingly individualistic matters are experienced in the community context among Pentecostals. I recall that my own yearning for the baptism in the Spirit, as individualistic as it may seem, became the subject of a community prayer. I walked through this process together with many fellow Pentecostal believers. When I finally 'got it', we together celebrated in praise and worship. In Korea, it is common that a family's prayer becomes the prayer of the entire cell group and sometimes the cell leader will bring the family members to a prayer mountain for prayer and fasting for several days, while the entire cell member families are in prayer. The community-forming potential of the Holy Spirit is experienced in various dimensions.

Experience: Lived-Out Spirituality

Another important aspect of restorational thinking is the recovery of religious experience. Flowing from the Pentecostal view of Scripture, Bible stories are read to experience an encounter with God and to show the miracles that contemporary readers can experience.[15] Pentecostals never 'demythologize' the miracle stories of the Bible. The Pentecostal appropriation of the biblical narratives occurs in two ways: they transport the ancient stories to contemporary life (existentialisation), they also 'slip' themselves into the ancient story of action (identification). The logic is simple: if the God of the Bible acted then, he could do the same today. For this reason, Pentecostals love to affirm that God is 'the same yesterday, today, and forever' (Heb 13:8).

This mindset promotes an expectation of having a tangible encounter with God through worship, prayer, sermons, Bible reading and the like. The nature of such encounters varies, but Pentecostals expect to 'hear from the Lord'. Hearing from God is a common feature of Christianity. The distinctiveness of the Pentecostal experience of hearing is rather concrete and tangible, even if one can argue that tangibility is a subjective notion. Pentecostals are quite open to various channels of such revelation, including dreams, visions, and audible

---

[15] Keith Warrington, *Pentecostal Theology: A Theology of Encounter* (London: T & T Clark, 2008).

or 'inner' voices, mental impressions, or a passage 'being lifted from the page'. Such 'voices' are not limited to matters of spirituality, but apply almost to any issue in life. The other area of encounter is the 'touch of the Lord'. This expression often refers to various experiences of God's reality, be it divine healing, an overwhelming sense of God's presence, relief from physical, emotional or circumstantial difficulties, a deep conviction of God's truth, and the like.

Unlike the Reformers' notion of the Holy Spirit as a shy member of the Trinity, Pentecostals, based on their reading in Luke-Acts, have re-profiled the Holy Spirit as the active player in the birth of the church, initiator of mission, and overseer of the spread of the gospel through empowerment.[16] Many experiences, whether supernatural or circumstantial, are all carefully initiated by the Holy Spirit. This has led Pentecostals into two important theological conclusions: (1) The Holy Spirit interacts with God's people through a wide range of religious experiences, including prophecy (11:22-23; 19:6; 21:9), dreams and visions (9:10; 10:3), hearing voices (10:19; 16:9; 18:9), healings (3:1-8; 4:30), and the like; and (2) such experiences embolden believers in their faith and lead them into opportunities to witness to the risen Lord. However, the role of experience in biblical interpretation is a controversial issue. Ideally, the word should guide, inform and set a parameter to religious experience, while experience affirms the word. Pentecostals are called to guard themselves against the danger of placing experience over the word. Nonetheless, with their literalistic reading of the Bible, religious experiences have a definite role in strengthening their sense of call and commitment to sacred vocation, as baptism in the Spirit as stated below will illustrate so well.

People of the Spirit(s)

Pentecostals assume a worldview distinct from many contemporary western Christians, but closer to a non-western understanding of life and the world. For example, Pentecostals are conscious of spiritual beings, benevolent as well as malevolent, angels, spirits and demons, at work in human lives. For this reason, Pentecostals are the people of the S/spirit(s). With their liberal reading of the Bible, their emphasis on the experiential dimension of religious life, Pentecostals gravitate to the unseen and yet active world of the supernatural.

Two particular areas may be noteworthy. The first is, as noted briefly above, the development of a dynamic theology of the Holy Spirit. Pneumatology that is born out of one's radical experience of the Holy Spirit – be it baptism in the Spirit, healing, exorcism, 'hearing' him or 'seeing' his work – will be explosive. The Holy Spirit has become a miracle-working member of the Trinity. He empowers the church to be victorious in the middle of a hostile world providing signs and wonders as part of Christian witness. This

[16] Roger Stronstad, *The Charismatic Theology of St Luke* (Peabody, MA: Hendrickson, 1984) and Robert P Menzies, *Empowered for Witness: The Spirit in Luke-Acts* (London: T & T Clark, 2004).

orientation gives a shape of empowerment theology that is unique to Pentecostalism. The second area is the similarity between the Pentecostal worldview and that of many non-western cultures where diverse spirits are perceived to operate on a daily basis generating a clash of (supernatural). Only the most powerful spirit (or God) earns a right to be worshipped, and the contest of such spiritual forces has become the basis for mass conversions.[17] The explosion of Pentecostal-type Christianity in Africa, Asia, and Latin America is partly attributed to these worldview similarities[18] and to common interests in life such as healings, blessings, and curses.[19] Pentecostalism can supply functional substitutes to the felt and perceived religious needs because the worldviews have corresponding categories. This helps the missionary recognize the needs of the recipient.

Theological Resources for Pentecostal Mission

The mission implications of four theological beliefs unique to Pentecostalism will be discussed with reference to their historical development. The modern Pentecostal movement as an organized theological and spiritual tradition traces its origin to a conservative form of Protestantism found in the nineteenth century Holiness movement of North America.[20] Charles Parham and William J. Seymour, the two most renowned Pentecostal 'fathers', are Holiness preachers. To illustrate beliefs and practices of early Pentecostals, reports will be used that were published in *The Apostolic Faith* (*TAF*) of the Azusa Street Mission of Los Angeles (1906-1909), the most representative Pentecostal periodical of the formative years of Pentecostal theological construction. A number of key players, already mentioned, are involved in Pentecostal theological construction: Scripture, the Holy Spirit interacting with Scripture, the community of believers,[21] the Pentecostal experience and the wider social context. Context has been recognized as significant as Pentecostals in the global South become more prominent in the movement.

Baptism in the Spirit

This cardinal doctrine makes (classical) Pentecostals distinct from the rest of Christianity. Understood as an experience distinct from and subsequent to

---

[17] Alan P. Tippett, *People Movements in Southern Polynesia: A Study in Church Growth* (Chicago: Moody, 1971).

[18] Walter J Hollenweger, *Pentecostalism: Origins and Developments Worldwide* (Peabody, MA: Hendrickson, 1997), 18-80.

[19] Julie C Ma, *When the Spirit Meets the Spirits: Pentecostal Mission to an Animistic Tribe of the Northern Philippines* (Frankfurt: Peter Lang, 2000).

[20] I am aware of arguments on multiple 'springheads' of the movement. For this reason, I used the qualifier, 'organized' theological and spiritual tradition.

[21] Kenneth J. Archer, *A Pentecostal Hermeneutics for the Twenty-First Century: Spirit, Scripture and Community* (London: T & T Clark, 2004), 156-91.

regeneration, belief in baptism in the Holy Spirit has caused a continuing debate between Pentecostals and Evangelicals. Based on the post-resurrection promise of the Lord that his followers would be baptized in the Holy Spirit, Pentecostals took it as a sign of the restoration of early church spirituality, especially the experience on the day of Pentecost (Acts 2).[22] For the present discussion, three aspects of this belief will be explored with mission as proclamation in mind: experience, its interpretation, and consequences.

As discussed above, Pentecostalism has brought back the significant role of religious experiences. Testimonies abound to the powerful impact of experiences loosely termed 'the baptism in the Holy Spirit'. Various life-changing stories are shared, although most North American classical Pentecostal churches insist on speaking in tongues as 'the physical and initial evidence'. The sense of God's overwhelming presence is a common element of these experiences, as recorded in the first issue of *TAF*:

> Proud, well-dressed preachers come in to 'investigate'. Soon their high looks are replaced with wonder, then conviction comes, and very often you will find them in a short time wallowing on the dirty floor, asking God to forgive them and make them as little children. It would be impossible to state how many have been converted, sanctified and filled with the Holy Ghost. They have been and are daily going out to all points of the compass to spread this wonderful gospel.[23]

Speaking in tongues also brought tangible impact not only to the recipients of the Spirit baptism but also on those who witnessed them. It is no wonder that Pentecostalism spread like wildfire. It is not only understood as a sign of the restoration of early church spirituality, it also shapes the self-identity of people who are called and commissioned to bring the news of salvation to the ends of the earth. It is also interpreted as the reception of power from above for witnessing in the context of Acts 1:8. The early Pentecostal literature made it clear that 'The baptism with the Holy Spirit is not a work of grace but a gift of power.... The baptism with the Holy Ghost makes you a witness unto the uttermost parts of the earth. It gives you power to speak in the languages of the nations.'[24] Its biblical illustrations are often taken from Peter's bold preaching in Acts 2:14-40, and Stephen's courageous sermon in Acts 7:2-53. Last, especially at a popular level, baptism in the Spirit is understood to be the 'floodgate' of spiritual gifts including healing and miracles.

The consequences of this doctrine are evident in an unbending commitment to mission. With a strong sense of calling to be witnesses 'to the end of the earth', this revival movement quickly turned into a missionary movement. A catalogue of heroic missionary achievements, despite little or no training or support, is attributed to this sense of call. A zeal for preaching the 'full gospel' in which tongue-speaking often functions as a reinforcement is another

---

[22] Frank D. Macchia, *Baptized in the Spirit: A Global Pentecostal Theology* (Grand Rapids: Zondervan, 2006).

[23] 'Pentecostal Has Come: Los Angeles Being Visited by a Revival of Bible Salvation and Pentecost as Recorded in the Book of Acts', *TAF* 1 (Sept 1906), 1, col 1.

[24] 'The Enduement of Power', *TAF* 4 (Dec 1906), 2, col 2.

consequence. Some early Pentecostals expected tongues to enable them to bypass laborious language-learning.[25] Third, after the pattern of Acts, signs, and wonders are expected in the context of mission. This power-orientation makes Pentecostals bold witnesses with claims of healings and miracles, albeit with many controversies surrounding them. The net result is the fast spread of the Pentecostal message and the expansion of the Pentecostal movement globally. This pneumatologically-shaped missiology is well attested in a *TAF* report of an Azusa missionary in its early days:

> A Pentecostal missionary has left for foreign lands, Bro Thos P Mahler, a young man of German nationality. He has the gift of tongues besides the knowledge of several. He left here for San Bernardino. He may go by way of Alaska, Russia, Norway, Germany and to his destination in Africa. As our brother was leaving, Bro Post spoke of his call and gave a message in tongues in regard to Bro Mahler which he interpreted as follows: 'I have anointed this dear one with my Spirit, and he is a chosen vessel to me to preach the gospel to many, and to suffer martyrdom in Africa'.[26]

Prophethood of All Believers

This is closely related to the previous discussion on baptism in the Spirit. However, because of its significance in Pentecostal mission, a separate discussion is deemed necessary. This is almost a natural and logical outgrowth of the belief in baptism in the Holy Spirit. Peter's interpretation of the advent of the Holy Spirit on the day of Pentecost is important. In the Old Testament period, only a handful of leaders experienced the coming of the Spirit of God, such as the seventy elders (Num 11), selected judges, the first two kings of United Israel, and selected prophets. However, an eschatological expectation of the Old Testament is to break this exclusivity of the Spirit: everyone in God's community will experience the coming of the Spirit. This is the prophecy by Joel (2:28-29), which has its root in Moses' desire for the whole of Israel (Num 11:29). This democratization of the Spirit is the gist of Peter's sermon in presenting the coming of the Holy Spirit on the day of Pentecost (Acts 2:16-21).

If anyone in God's community is baptized in the Holy Spirit, regardless of age, gender and social status, the calling, empowerment, and commission for God's work is for every believer, thus, 'prophethood of all believers'. This theological paradigm should be understood within the context of Christianity in the West at the turn of the twentieth century. In spite of various expressions of 'every believer's prophetic call', the dominant ministry paradigm among the established churches was clergy-oriented professionalism. Pentecostal theology was a powerful challenge to the established norm.

Of particular note is the significant contribution of women in Pentecostal mission. Later this is expressed in Korea through the mobilization of lay

---

[25] 'Russians Hear in Their Own Tongue', *TAF* 1 (Sept 1906), 4, col 3.

[26] 'The Lord Sends Him', *TAF* 1 (Sept 1906), 4, col 1.

women leaders in David Yonggi Cho's well-known cell group system. Young people are also mobilized for mission in networks, such as Youth With A Mission. This liberates ministry from the exclusive hands of elite clergy. Often advocating short-term missionary service, YWAM and others have 'democratized' ministry and mission for every believer. Thirdly, an extension of this radical mission-thinking is the establishment and empowerment of, and transfer to, national and local leadership at the earliest opportunity,[27] a practice which has made Pentecostalism the fastest growing religious movement in our day.

Eschatology

Early Pentecostals shared their eschatology with the late nineteenth century conservative pre-millennial orientation. The turn of the century provided a naïve expectation of the end of human history. Here is an example found in *TAF*:

> All these 6,000 years, we have been fighting against sin and Satan. Soon we shall have a rest of 1,000 years.... We must go on to perfection and holiness, and get the baptism with the Holy Ghost, and not stop there, but go on to perfection and maturity.[28]

The outpouring of the Holy Spirit was taken as a sure sign of the end of the end time, the last opportunity for the greatest harvest of souls before the return of the Lord. This created an incongruent theological system for Pentecostals, adopting the dispensational scheme of human history. With the fast closure of the church age, or the age of grace, the church is to be taken to heaven, before the return of the age where Jews are dealt with through tribulation. This formed the awareness of living at the 'five-to midnight' moment, giving an extremely small window of opportunity to save as many souls as possible. 'One-way ticket missionaries' were strongly motivated by the eschatological urgency. It was not unusual that engaged young women broke their engagements and left for their mission field.[29] This eschatological consciousness made them other-world oriented Coupled with the religious consciousness of call and empowerment for witness, they are the best ingredients for the significant mission movement we have seen in the last one hundred years.

In spite of the powerful and positive contribution of this form of pre-millennialism with the expectation of the imminent return of the Lord, such clock-setting eschatology must expire sooner or later. As the movement enters the third generation, eschatological messages from Pentecostal pulpits have gradually disappeared to be replaced by this-worldly concerns, such as church

[27] Melvin L Hodges, *The Indigenous Church* (Springfield, MO: Gospel Publishing House, 1963).

[28] 'The Millenium [*sic!*]', *TAF* 1 (Sept 1906), 3, col 3.

[29] For one example see S Shemeth, 'Trasher, Lillian Hunt', in Stanley M Burgess and Eduard M. van der Maas (eds), *New International Dictionary of Pentecostal and Charismatic Movements* (Grand Rapids, MI: Zondervan, 2002), 1153.

growth, the message of blessings and health.[30] Fortunately, the dynamic motive of Pentecostal mission lies in the pneumatological interpretation rather than its temporal eschatological expectation, as the global Pentecostal movement has continued its growth even after the waning of an imminent eschatology.

The Primacy of 'Soul' Matter

Pentecostalism has all the crucial ingredients to become an unprecedented 'religion to travel', as well-evidenced in the exponential growth and spread all over the world in its wild diversity and creativity. Its evangelical heritage and the temporally oriented eschatology has focused Pentecostal missiology on evangelism and church planting. The rise of a social gospel in the middle of the twentieth century may have further encouraged the already narrowly focused attention. Mission impetus was also taken from the mission roadmap found in their favourite passage: '…from Jerusalem, all Judea, Samaria, and (finally) to the ends of the earth' (Acts 1:8). Crossing geographical boundaries, therefore, has been part of Pentecostal mission paradigm. Many brilliant social programmes have soul winning as their ultimate goal.[31]

This, however, may reveal the Pentecostal understanding of humans, sin, and salvation. Every evil, be it personal or corporate, is traced to sin, and to Genesis 3 where separation from God resulted in spiritual damnation, physical suffering, broken society, and cursed environment. The Pentecostal view of restoration, therefore, reverses the order, beginning with the spiritual regeneration, and then personal (including the physical level, such as healing), communal (social) and even environmental, if the notion is conceived in Pentecostal mission framework.[32] The upward social mobility of Pentecostals has been attributed to this paradigm.[33]

Naturally 'revival' or 'renewal' is an important concept in Pentecostal thinking. The Pentecostal movement itself is often classified as a revival movement. The January 1907 issue of *TAF* reveals a glimpse of the Azusa Street revival:

> The meeting went on till morning and all the next day…. Pentecost first fell in Los Angeles on April 9th [of 1906]. Since then the good tidings has spread in two hemispheres…. Wherever the work goes, souls are saved, and not only saved from hell but through and through, and prepared to meet the Lord at his coming. Hundreds have been baptized with the Holy Ghost. Many of them are now out in

[30] For example, Wonsuk Ma, 'Pentecostal Eschatology: What Happened When the Wave Hit the West End of the Ocean', in Harold Hunter and Cecil M Robeck, Jr (eds), *The Azusa Street Revival and Its Legacy* (Cleveland, TN: Pathway), 227-42.

[31] See for example, Calcutta Mercy Ministries, 'History' http://www.buntain.org/about.html (accessed on 15/03/2010).

[32] *Teen Challenge*, the successful drug rehabilitation programme emphasises regeneration and baptism in the Spirit. David Batty and Ethan Campbell, 'Teen Challenge: 50 Years of Miracles', *Assemblies of God Heritage* 28 (2008), 14-21.

[33] David Martin, *Tongues of Fire: The Explosion of Protestantism in Latin America* (Oxford: Blackwell, 1990).

> the field, and some in foreign lands, and God is working with them, granting signs and wonders to follow the preaching of the full Gospel.[34]

As Pentecostal missiology matures, an argument seems to gain ground that spiritual dynamism, evangelism, church growth, and social service are not mutually exclusive.[35]

Conclusion

If this short study in any way leaves an impression that Pentecostals have finally unlocked the secret of Christian mission, the reality is exactly its opposite. In the name of God's kingdom and renewal, church divisions were caused by this movement and unfortunately they have been part of its growth 'strategy'. Some of its serious blind spots, such as its eschatological expectation, are already presented. While they are praised for their creativity in contextualization, Pentecostals are also criticized for the ugly 'prosperity gospel'[36] and their extremely 'western' outlook and ethos. All in all, there is much for further reflection and study.[37]

In the next decades, the progress of Pentecostal mission will depend on how Pentecostals preserve and strengthen their unique spiritual values and understand their changing contexts so that their theological constructs will respond to their missional call and contextual needs The Bible will continue to play an important role, especially as the movement spreads increasingly in the global South. The expectation of the supernatural dimension of Christianity, the role of community and experience, as well as a more holistic worldview, will continue to play critical roles in Pentecostal religious life. Serious challenges and new opportunities will rise on the theological front, and any good theology will need to be locally grounded and relevant. This requires the conscious engagement of Pentecostal values and context. If frontline workers such as pastors, evangelists, and missionaries are to continue their critical role of popular theological construction, the theological formation will be essential. Aided by Pentecostal theologians frontline leaders can protect Pentecostal communities from consumerism-driven, self-serving popular religion, and become relevant to their context. Pentecostal eschatology, as seen in the past, may not serve its earlier pivotal role, and so may be the way of the baptism in the Spirit. However, the latter's empowerment theology, incorporated in the prophethood of all believers, will remain high in Pentecostal theological

---

[34] 'Beginning of World Wide Revival', *TAF* 5 (January 2907), 1, col 1.

[35] Young-hoon Lee, *The Holy Spirit Movement in Korea* (Oxford: Regnum, 2009), 126-27.

[36] See Hwa Yung, 'The Missiological Challenge of David Yonggi Cho's Theology', in Wonsuk Ma, et al (eds), *David Yonggi Cho: A Close Look at His Theology and Ministry* (Baguio, Philippines: APTS Press, 2004), 85-90; Wonsuk Ma, 'David Yonggi Cho's Theology of Blessing: Basis, Legitimacy and Limitations', *Evangelical Review of Theology* 35:2 (April 2011), 140-159.

[37] Ma and Ma, *Mission in the Spirit*.

agendas, if the theology is to remain 'Pentecostal'. The primary purpose of soul-winning is expected to continue, although the Pentecostal horizon in mission thinking and practice has become more holistic and inclusive. At the same time, more locally motivated theological agendas should surface, such as reconciliation in places where religious and racial conflicts raise tensions.

Classical Pentecostals have the most theological and institutional resources. In non-western lands, they look radically different from their North American or European 'mothers', who are not necessarily growing. This is a serious challenge to their century-old theology and constantly institutionalizing ethos. Yet they may also empower the rest of the Pentecostal-charismatic churches. Together they should continue their engagement in new frontiers of mission because to remain faithful to the scriptures, to Pentecostal spiritual heritage, and yet be relevant to the immediate context will pose a significant challenge to emerging Pentecostal mission communities throughout the world.

Pentecostal Missions and the Influence of Frontier Mission Missiology

Alan R. Johnson

At the celebration of the centennial of Edinburgh 1910, we find that the composition and character of global Christianity changed greatly over the past 100 years. The Southern shift in the locus of the Christian faith is now a well-documented phenomenon and the subject of scholarly interest.[1] The past century has also seen the rise of a new stream of Christianity represented in Pentecostal and Charismatic forms of the faith. These two phenomena are related since the shift of the center of gravity of the Christian faith to the south has been statistically a Pentecostal/Charismatic one.[2] The essays in this volume document another megashift that has happened in the past 100 years in the arena of missiology. Corwin observes that the shift was not so much a new vision as it was a new way to look at the old vision: 'that for the first time in the modern period the [mission] task was now couched primarily in terms of *ethne* or peoples and religious blocks, rather than in geographic or geopolitical terms.'[3] Known as frontier mission missiology, the special plea of this stream of mission thinking is to take the gospel to people groups that lack Christians, churches, and church movements adequate to evangelize their people on their own.

My interest here is to explore the relationship between these two megashifts. One is a missiology that has generated an evangelistic focus on people groups that do not have existing church movements, while the other began as an evangelistic church movement that has generated a phenomenal amount of cross-cultural mission with great success in raising up younger churches all over the globe. On the face of things, it would seem that these two shifts were

---

Originally published in Beth Snodderly and A. Scott Moreau (eds.), *Evangelical and Frontier Mission Perspectives on the Global Progress of the Gospel*, Regnum Edinburgh Centenary Series 9 (Oxford: Regnum Books, 2011), 101-116.

[1] Philip Jenkins, *The Next Christendom: The Coming of Global Christianity* (Oxford: Oxford University Press, 2002), 2, 3.
[2] Allan Anderson, 'Towards a Pentecostal Missiology for the Majority World', in Grant McClung (ed.), *Azusa Street & Beyond* (Gainesville FL: Bridge-Logos, 2006), 169-70.
[3] Gary Corwin, 'Sociology and Missiology: Reflection on Mission Research', in Edward Rommen and Gary Corwin (eds), *Missiology and the Social Sciences: Contributions, Cautions and Conclusions* (Pasadena: William Carey Library, 1996), 20-21.

made for each other, with the one calling for an evangelistic activity where the gospel has not been preached or believed, and the other born in the fires of revival with the compulsion of the Spirit to evangelize the world. However, as it played out in the last quarter of the twentieth century, classical Pentecostal mission agencies, in general, did not bend their efforts or structure themselves to mobilize their vast resources for the challenges articulated by frontier mission missiology. What caused the mission arms that developed out of classical Pentecostal denominations to have a relatively slow response to the notion of unreached people groups? I endeavour to build an account to answer this question and then move to a discussion of ways that Pentecostals can draw from their own theological and historical roots to turn their massive numbers and spiritual vitality towards the remaining unreached peoples.

Classical Pentecostals and Their Presence among Unreached Ethnolinguistic Groups

Trying to define Pentecostal/Charismatic Christianity is notoriously difficult. Wonsuk Ma reminds us that these movements are not homogeneous and the terminology used to describe them is not standardized.[4] He offers a classification system with three major streams: Classical Pentecostals (roots in the Azusa revival in 1906, believe in a unique experience of baptism in the Holy Spirit as evidenced by speaking in other tongues); Charismatic (or Neo) Pentecostals (who may not subscribe to the doctrinal position of a separate baptism in the Holy Spirit, but are open to the supernatural work of the Spirit); and Indigenous (or Neo-Charismatic) Pentecostals (highly diverse and often with doctrinal emphases orthodox Christians reject or are uncomfortable).[5] Coming chronologically in the first wave of renewal at the turn of the last century, classical Pentecostal denominational mission structures are older, more established, and have large networks of national churches outside their home borders. Thus it is possible to track their response to the rise of frontier mission missiology from the mid-1970s to the present.

In critically examining the interface between classical Pentecostal mission agencies and the challenge of frontier missions to plant the church among the unreached, some qualifications are necessary. First, to make the assertion that these agencies were slow to respond does not mean that there was no response. Pentecostals place great value on personal calling and the leading of the Spirit. There have always been people called and led to work among groups of people that have had little or no Christian presence. Second, the achievements of the classical Pentecostal denominational mission agencies have been stunning. As an example, the Christians associated with churches planted or associated with

[4] Wonsuk Ma, '"When the Poor Are Fired Up": The Role of Pneumatology in Pentecostal-Charismatic Mission', *Transformation* 24:1 (2007), 28.
[5] Ma, 'When the Poor', 28.

the mission arms of only six of these denominations number nearly 82 million.[6] Third, although full documentation on this does not yet exist, we know that some of the cross-cultural workers generated from these newer church movements are ending up among the unreached. Finally, in the last decade, there is evidence of increasing numbers of workers, structures, and initiatives within many of these agencies and their national churches that are devoted to aspects of frontier mission, often focusing on a particular religious block or the unreached in a geographic region.

It is in point of fact the phenomenal success of classical Pentecostal missions that brings into deeper contrast the realities of their massive growth in some places, and little fruit in others. This is matched by the fact of large numbers of personnel in highly successful places and a corresponding dearth of workers among places and peoples with arguably the least Christian witness. What is at issue here is not the sending of discrete individuals with a call to an unreached people group, but rather the agency level choices that did not utilize their structures and energies to encourage and facilitate new ministry thrusts from their cross-cultural workers and national churches to the ethnolinguistic groups with the least witness of the gospel.

A full documentation of my assertion of a slow response to the challenge of unreached people groups is beyond the scope of this paper. Additionally, there are inherent limitations in trying to gather data related to work that engages unreached groups. Classical Pentecostal missions keep statistics at the level of the nation-state and not by people group, thus it is impossible to know precisely how many actual members of their teams are working directly with such groups. The various missions define their regions in different ways as well, and the countries that make up regions change, making it hard to compare data. The work done by Majority World churches connected to classical Pentecostal movements is still in its early stages and has not been documented for the most part.

However, it is possible to delimit a geographical area that is unreached people group dense, and compare over time the number of personnel located in this area. Taking 1970 as a baseline, before the dissemination of frontier mission missiology post-Lausanne in 1974, we can then see how missionary placement changed or did not change over the decades up to the present. A significant increase in field staff would be a solid indicator that something happened in response to the challenge of unreached peoples. Similarly, if percentages stay relatively the same, and percentages in other areas where the church exists stay the same or grow, it is an indicator that response was limited.

[6] The information here is taken from the denominational websites or from articles in Wikipedia that reference denominational documents and refers to their worldwide constituents/adherents. Assemblies of God 2009 estimated constituents, 63,089,711; Church of God of Prophecy, one million; Church of God (Cleveland), six million; International Foursquare, eight million; International Pentecostal Holiness Church 2000, 3,410,890 including members and affiliates; Pentecostal Church of God (Joplin), 500,000.

The number generated by this exercise is not the actual total of people working among the unreached (due to the fact that many workers are connected to the national church and its needs in these countries) but only the potential maximum number of workers.

The area that I have chosen for comparison among five classical Pentecostal agencies is the region that includes North Africa, the Middle East, Turkey, and the Central Asia republics, and the South Asian countries including India and those surrounding it. For convenience, I am using the Assemblies of God World Missions designation for this area, Eurasia. By Joshua Project database figures this area contains arguably the highest density of discrete unreached ethnolinguistic groups in the world.

	1970	1990	2000	2009
Assemblies of God World Missions				
Total Career Staff	889	1663	2401	2719
Total In Eurasia	78	86	261	308
Percent of Total Staff in Eurasia	8.8	5.2	10.9	14.6
International Pentecostal Holiness Church				
Total Career Staff				97
Total In Eurasia				7
Percent of Total Staff in Eurasia				7.2
Foursquare				
Total Career Staff	71	40	65	88
Total In Eurasia	1	2	4	8
Percent of Total Staff in Eurasia	1.4	5	6.1	9.09

Table 1 Percent of Workers in an Unreached People Group Dense, Part of the World (Eurasia)

What this information shows is that even with the ability to enter the newly accessible countries of Central Asia after the 1989 dissolving of the Soviet Union, the relative percentage of these missions' total field staff in this area has not changed drastically. Two missions have statistical information on their websites measuring their personnel placement in terms of well-known measures relating to the unreached and least-reached. The Assemblies of God 2010 current facts and highlights sheet shows 34.2 percent of their staff working in places that are less than 2 percent evangelical, which are the Joshua Project categories 1 and 2. The Pentecostal Assemblies of Canada website says of their 254 workers that 'Nineteen percent... serve in Restricted Access nations or in places closed to the open preaching of the gospel. Another 18 percent work in the 10/40 window.' While these numbers are very commendable, the fact that 60 plus percent of their mission teams are working where the global church is largest and growing fastest, indicates a less than an aggressive response to the challenge of unreached ethnolinguistic groups.

Missiological Factors Shaping Response

I now want to examine some missiological factors that may have shaped the response of one classical Pentecostal mission agency towards peoples and places in the world with the least Christians. The context for my observations is my own agency, Assemblies of God World Missions, USA. While there are numerous external factors involved in missionary placement, my focus here will be explicitly on internal missiological issues. Although other organizations will have different issues, I believe that much of the discussion that follows will be relevant not only to classical Pentecostal agencies, but to any agency that finds the bulk of their teams working outside of unreached groups.

Conceptions of National Church and the Unintended Loss of the Pioneering Dimension

Founded in 1914, with one of its stated priority purposes being the evangelization of the world, the Assemblies of God noted in their 1915 General Council that missionaries were to evangelize using New Testament methods. At their 1921 Council in St. Louis they formally adopted the goal of establishing three-self 'native churches', [7] and delineated to the Foreign Missions Department the nature of the New Testament practices they were to follow in six key principles.[8] The second stated, 'The Pauline example will be followed so far as possible, by seeking out neglected regions where the gospel has not yet been preached, lest we build upon another's foundation (Rom. 15:20).'[9]

It was not until the 1930s that indigenous self-governing church organizations at the nation-state level began to appear with El Salvador being one of the first.[10] Some twenty years later, veteran missionary Melvin Hodges who worked in Central America, was asked to put the practical steps of indigenous church development into book form. This short and clearly written book became a seminal piece in Assemblies of God missiology, and as testimony to its enduring value, it is still in print nearly 60 years later and remains a popular missions text in the evangelical world.

The power of the indigenous national church concept cannot be underestimated in the exponential growth of the Assemblies of God worldwide fellowship of churches. While recognizing its fruitfulness as a mission concept, I want to look at some of the unexpressed assumptions that grew out of the

---

[7] Gary B. McGee, *This Gospel Shall Be Preached: A History and Theology of Assemblies of God Foreign Missions to 1959* (Springfield MO: Gospel Publishing House, 1986), 95-96.

[8] McGee, *This Gospel*, 95.

[9] McGee, *This Gospel*, 96.

[10] McGee, *This Gospel*, 148.

specific historical context of its development that may have impacted our response to unreached people groups. In current usage national church almost always is equated to mean the church movement within the boundaries of a nation-state. In rereading Hodges, I am not necessarily sure that such jump was in his mind as he wrote.

The book, following its title, is primarily about planting an indigenous three-self church or churches. Only six pages of the text are dedicated to the formation of a national church organization.[11] Indigeneity was much more the focus than the development of a national organization. Although the unifying factor of the Spanish language among the various peoples in his experience in Central America meant that the fledgling national church would encompass the boundaries of the nation-state, his words leave open the possibility for other scenarios. He allows for the needs of geographical features, political boundaries, differences of language, and transportation facilities to be accommodated. 'When distance, language or political barriers make it impractical to unite the churches into one district, it is advisable to divide the district into smaller units with a sectional conference or council in each area.'[12] Hodges used terms like a conference, district, and section, taken from AG organizational structure in the USA, to illustrate the form of organization he is suggesting.[13] Only later does he introduce the term, 'national church'.[14] My sense is that in Hodges' mind the notion of national church and its structure along the lines of AG USA polity was quite clear to his audience thus he felt no need to define or defend it. But his own comments do not demand, and leave the door open for organizing around language or other factors that would separate groups, and not simply geography. Thus it appears that the notion of one national church along nation-state lines came to be assumed, and was not required by the missiological concept.

Another assumption entered the mix as a result of the rapid growth of these national church organizations. There was a natural movement from the idea of the missionary planting the first individual churches and facilitating the development of an indigenous national church movement to partnering with that movement.[15] There is a logical shift in role from the pioneering work that established the church to working with the young organization to strengthen it and pursue its agendas. It is interesting to note that when Hodges did talk about the need for redistribution of missionaries because there were too many in one

[11] Melvin L. Hodges, *The Indigenous Church* (Springfield MO: Gospel Publishing House, 1976), 92-97.

[12] Hodges, *Indigenous Church*, 94.

[13] Hodges, *Indigenous Church*, 93-94.

[14] Hodges, *Indigenous Church*, 95.

[15] Melvin L. Hodges, *The Indigenous Church and the Missionary* (South Pasadena: William Carey Library, 1978), 5. Also see Morris Williams, *Partnership in Mission* (Springfield, MO: Empire Printing Company, 1979).

locale, it was not for the purposes of pioneer church planting among the unreached, but for the good of the indigenous church.[16]

The principle of partnership is also an extremely powerful concept because it forms the basis for an ongoing relationship to help emerging indigenous national church movements grow and prosper. Without such a notion, it is too easy to get something started and then back away, thus truncating the movement and not allowing it to truly become capable of evangelizing its own people without outside resources. For us in the Assemblies of God, the definition of a national church, like Winter's notion of Pauline missiological breakthrough, is a very robust concept.[17] What is problematic however is the unwarranted jump that makes a partnership with the national church such a dominant theme that it suppresses the ability of the mission to act as an apostolic band to take the gospel where it has not been preached. While that conclusion is never formally stated, in practice, partnership becomes a primary value that shapes placement and ministry trajectory. This is true not only on the side of the mission agency, but can come from national churches as well. Majority World church movements, jealous to husband resources for their needs, are capable of citing chapter and missiological verse back to missionaries when they propose working outside of their boundaries to reach out to an unreached people group.

When we stand back for a moment and look at these two concepts, linking the ideas of 'indigenous national church', and 'partnership' enabled a level of fruitfulness that could only have been dreamed for in the early years. However, surfacing some of the assumptions that are currently connected with each reveals ideas that hinder rather than facilitate a move towards unreached people groups. I see the shift in primary emphasis from proclamational pioneer church planting to partnership with existing church movements as something that was never planned. It was a natural change of attention to what was happening as new movements blossomed. However, the unintended consequence of the partnership concept was the erosion of the pioneering dimension of Pentecostal mission that was so salient in their early days. My guess is that this development may have been aided by an assumption that the Pentecostal experience would always lend towards urgency in proclamation and thus it was not something that needed to be worried about. What the passage of time has now revealed is that it is quite possible to remain doctrinally and stylistically Pentecostal, yet lose one's evangelistic fervour.

At the same time, the gradual cementing of the meaning of 'national church' along nation-state lines unwittingly marginalized unreached ethnolinguistic groups outside of the primary ethnicity of the existing national church. Missionaries find that national churches want them to work in their orbit and not with those who they may have a history of problems or animosity. Another problem set has to do with how the new converts in an unreached group will

[16] Hodges, *Indigenous Church*, 96.

[17] See Alan R. Johnson, *Apostolic Function in 21st Century Missions*, J. Philip Hogan World Missions Series (Pasadena: William Carey Library, 2009), 113-14.

relate to the existing church. Do they start their own 'national church'? Do they come under the existing one? Rather than legitimating and validating pioneer work among the unreached, the hardening of these concepts and their associated assumptions slowed the process down by raising concerns were not taken from our reading of Scripture, but rather grew from limitations in our use of these concepts.

The Impact of Missions Success on the Ability to Engage Least-Reached, Resistant, and Unresponsive Peoples

In hindsight, it appears that the incredible success of our mission endeavors actually caught us all by surprise. The doctrine of indigeneity valued and predicted strong, robust, Pentecostal, zealous, evangelistic national church movements. But when it happened so suddenly, it was natural that some missiological points were neglected or lost in the scramble to stay at the front of the wave. The impact of mission success was a key factor in creating a particular ethos and self-understanding in mission; contributed to a lack of reflection on and missions praxis for the unreached, resistant, and unresponsive; and its suddenness hindered the development of missions policy for responding to it. All of these factors combined to work against a systemic response to the challenge of unreached peoples.

THE SELF UNDERSTANDING AND ETHOS OF CLASSICAL PENTECOSTAL MISSIONS

The advent of frontier mission missiology in the mid-1970s came at a time when the national churches founded by classical Pentecostal agencies were beginning to explode exponentially.[18] To put it simply, to be a Pentecostal missionary, meant that it works. The era of painstaking sowing, rejection, and persecution in many fields became memories as big crusades, big churches, big institutions, and big buildings sprung up all over the globe. New missionary candidates raised on stories of powerful Pentecostal mission success came to the agency interested in going to such places and reduplicating such methods. The opposite side of the coin is that this success ethos creates an environment where people working in circumstances with slower response feel a great deal of pressure to 'produce' the results that are expected from Pentecostal mission. Both at the denominational level in the local churches and at the agency level successes were cheered and given a high profile, and it was natural that numerically unfruitful fields among the unreached world received correspondingly less attention. The overall effect of such a self-understanding is to constrain those who will respond to the challenges represented by the unreached.

---

[18] Randy Hurst, 'The Secret of Accelerating and Lasting Growth', *Today's Pentecostal Evangel*, January 26, 2006, 24-25.

Success and the Dulling of Context-sensitivity

Another impact of the success ethos is that the way Pentecostals 'did church' became a part of their style, or mode of faith expression. Pentecostal/ Charismatic worship forms jumped beyond the boundaries of their own churches and became the trademark of cutting edge churches in a globalized world. The difficulty in terms of mission is the fact that while this style fits well in a globalized segment of the world, it does not touch the heart of millions of people in the unreached world who are either turned off, offended, or confused by globalized music, worship styles, and the equation of Christianity with western culture. This stylistic identity that starts at the grassroots level of the constituent churches of classical Pentecostal organizations combined with the success ethos at the agency level means that the cross-cultural workers sent out in the time frame examined here were not well prepared to deal with the context issues that they faced among unreached populations. Their ministry toolkits were limited to reproducing globalized style Pentecostal/Charismatic forms.

A Lack of Theological Reflection on How to Handle the Resistant and Unresponsive

One of the strengths of Pentecostal mission is the emphasis on the leading of the Holy Spirit, and getting involved in what the Spirit is manifestly doing in the world. Wilson, in his biography of J. Philip Hogan, who served for 30 years as the executive director of the Assemblies of God missionary program, provides a number of illustrations from Hogan's thinking that show the sense of dependence on the guidance of the Spirit.[19] It is the Spirit who leads laborers to strategic harvest opportunities [20] and prepares peoples, communities, cities, and nations for sudden harvest.[21] Being strategic in this sense is going where God is pouring out his Spirit.[22] Success in part flowed also from an intentional focus on where the Spirit was working.

Again, it seems natural that in an era of explosive growth all over the globe, there was little time to think about the resistant, unresponsive, and those separated from the gospel by barriers of language, religion, and social standing. The result was that there has not been a serious Pentecostal missiological reflection on working among those who do not respond quickly. There is no theology of sowing and preparation and creating a value system that honours such work. The practical on-field result of this theological gap is that cross-cultural workers find it hard to persevere in the face of no results and

---

[19] Everett A. Wilson, *Strategy of the Spirit: J. Philip Hogan and the Growth of the Assemblies of God Worldwide 1960–1990* (Carlisle, Cumbria: Regnum Books International), 1997.

[20] Wilson, *Strategy*, 64, 136.

[21] Wilson, *Strategy*, 67, 136.

[22] Wilson, *Strategy*, 72.

gravitate towards work with existing churches that is more capable of quantification and amenable to being reported to constituents.

Lack of Reflection on Missiological Principles for Exit from Fully Indigenous National Churches

If there is a lack of theological reflection on how to deal with the unresponsive, the other side of the coin is that we never developed a missiology of success that gave us an explicit exit strategy. By this, I mean how we respond as a mission to the successful formation of strong indigenous national churches which is our stated goal. Indigenous national churches are inherently needy; it never feels as if there are enough workers. Without a theology of success, we have no decision-making tools to help us decide what needs to be done and how to respond to the demands of national churches long after they are fully indigenous or as they are in last stages of the transition time moving towards it. The result is that over time the New Testament dimension of crossing cultural boundaries to present that gospel and the Pauline theme of going where the gospel is not yet present becomes obscured.

Classical Pentecostals and Frontier Missions: Towards a Greater Engagement

If in the past classical Pentecostal agencies have been slow to respond to the challenges of the final unreached peoples, the good news is that the present is showing signs of significant shifts towards a greater engagement. These signs are hopeful that the future will see the turning of the energy of these movements towards the frontier task that remains. I now want to look at some missiological issues that may help facilitate a greater engagement with unreached ethnolinguistic groups by classical Pentecostals all over the world. Each of these points could be expanded upon; my purpose here is not to be exhaustive or comprehensive, but rather is to set forth a tentative outline of a potential agenda that both established and emerging missions can begin to discuss and seek to implement in their work.

I envision this as a reflective process, taking the powerful concepts that have already been developed and proven to bear fruit, and not discard them or move past them, but rather revisit them in light of the challenges of the unreached and bring to them fresh insights that will sharpen our focus and practice. I see the goal of this exercise as synthesizing a conception of mission that:

- Integrates the guidance of the Spirit, the power of the indigenous national church/partnership notions, and a lens to see 'peoples' without the gospel.
- Legitimates the role of the apostolic band that goes where Christ is not known.
- Brings a unified identity to all cross-cultural workers and affirms the value of the multiplicity of gifts in the missionary team.

The series of reflections here provide an outline and some examples of the issues that are potential content for this process.

Reflecting on Pentecostal History: Restoring Evangelistic Zeal

The early Pentecostals saw the coming of the Holy Spirit as a restoration of the church and harbinger of the return of the Lord. The mission impulse was grounded in the sense of urgency that Christ be proclaimed to reap a final harvest. In Assemblies of God history, they pledged themselves to the greatest evangelization the world had ever seen. Now, 100 years distant from the Azusa revival the Lord has not returned, the fires of evangelism have waned among the western based denominations, and the perception of missions on the part of many constituent churches is that missionaries train local people to do ministry. While doctrinally affirming that the coming of the Spirit is empowerment for mission, practically we have developed systems that concentrate on supportive activities among emerging churches. There needs to be an intentional linkage on the part of denominational and missions leaders that the coming of the Spirit is still a relationship that pushes people to go to those who have not heard the gospel. The fact of the documented existence of unreached ethnolinguistic groups needs to be held up to our movements as a primary place of labor for Spirit-empowered workers.

To argue that western originating cross-cultural workers are relegated to only a training role so that Majority World people can finish the task is faulty at two points. First, it assumes that people who themselves are not burning with a zeal to proclaim the good news among the unreached are able to communicate that burden to others. Second, it introduces a limitation that is not warranted by Scripture, restricting the apostolic task to others while ignoring it ourselves, to our spiritual peril. The reality is that the best way to revive evangelistic zeal among the western churches is to trumpet the need of all the tribes and tongues to hear the gospel. For every worker envisioned by the Spirit who moves out of their own cultural setting, there will be dozens that take up the task among their own.

Reflecting on Key Missions Concepts:
Revisiting the Indigenous National Church and Partnership

The problems with some of the unwritten assumptions connected to the concepts of the indigenous national church and partnership I discussed above invite revisiting these notions in order to clarify and strengthen them. Expanding the concepts to make room to enable mission structures to relate to an existing national church while at the same time pioneering in another people group is the first step. This means loosening the connection between national church and the nation-state and opening the doors to creatively structuring varying forms of relationship between church movements with two or more distinct ethnic groups within the boundaries of a single nation-state. Similarly, the notion of partnership needs to be updated so that it allows for an incoming mission team to have the blessing and freedom to work apostolically in planting the church among an unreached group. The bottom line is that we cannot allow the concepts of national church and partnership to harden in such a fashion that they prohibit or inhibit the ability of the mission team to work outside the boundaries of the existing national church and its people group among an unreached group.

Reflecting on the Work of the Holy Spirit

For Pentecostals, the role of the Spirit in calling the workers is central to placement. However, research shows that there are a number of elements that coalesce in the calling to mission. Information via a variety of sources such missionary narratives, missions conventions, missionary experience, and counsel play an important role in this. This means that it is an act of missionary statesmanship to make the needs of the unreached world known. Constituent churches of the home base as well as missionary candidates coming to the agency need to know that there is a world that has not yet heard, understood, or responded to the gospel.

If a candidate comes to a mission organization evincing a call to missions but has never heard of the unreached world, it is incumbent upon the mission leadership to make those facts known and ask that such a candidate spend time in prayer over this information asking God for guidance. I am not suggesting in any way that we squelch the work of the Spirit, nor is this an exercise in suppressing individual guidance in favour of corporate guidance. My point is very simple and is grounded in a big assumption: that it is impossible for the Holy Spirit not to be calling workers to the unreached, given what we know from Scripture about God's concern for all the peoples. The databases of the world's unreached peoples are public documents. At the very least prayer for these groups needs to be engaged at the highest levels of our mission leadership, in our local churches, in our mission teams, and among the emerging national churches, we relate to. To pray seriously about such groups will be to place ourselves in the line of fire to hear the voice of the Spirit who calls workers into the harvest fields.

Reflecting on Our Current Placement: The Need for Spiritual Genetic Modification

If we generate prayer for new workers to the least reached, what do we do with the 60-70 percent working among the existing church? Some have mistakenly taken the call to the unreached as also being a call to redeploy existing cross-cultural workers to work among them, and as an implicit negative judgment upon those working with the church. This is not the case. It was a great misfortune that Ralph Winter's views on this were underplayed and ignored as people group thinking gained more prominence in mission circles.[23] He consistently maintained that to take language and culture competent workers out of their setting and put them into new learning curves among the unreached is not a policy of wisdom. There is much strategic work that can be done for the frontiers of mission from their current place of service.

I like to compare the awakening of having a 'lens' to see 'peoples' as a spiritual genetic modification. This DNA level change in the worker produces changes at the level of why they do things, reorients the ultimate goals of their work, and may even change their whole focus. If our mission staff living among the existing church movements in the Majority World began to turn the energies of those churches towards prayer for the unreached, and to help develop mission sending structures and train workers to go to the unreached, what would the impact be? To infect all of the ministerial training apparatuses among these churches with the biblical theology of mission and a burden for the unreached would be an incredibly strategic work. In my own corner of the world, as I have had opportunities to train Asian leaders, I have discovered that our Majority World churches often do not share our missiology. In addition to this, their views of mission are shaped by the experience of receiving the gospel in a flow of transmission from the West. Too often mission is defined by their perceptions of what western cross-cultural workers have done and are doing. When they have never seen anyone go to the unreached, they do not see it as part of the mission agenda. If our existing mission staff can get the vision for the unreached, they can become key players in passing that burden on to the church movements to which they relate.

Reflecting on the Biblical Text: A Theology of the Hard Work

The Holy Spirit's work in bringing a response to the message and guiding the worker, combined with the ethos of Pentecostal mission success has created a blank spot for what to do with the places that are *not* currently receptive/ responsive. In addition to this, the western passion for tangibility and quantification has shaped a view of mission that makes results the primary evaluative tool for determining success. This results in avoiding work that does not produce immediate and measurable results; thus many important activities that are preparatory to harvest are neglected. This value system is often transmitted from the West into the newer emerging missions, making the criterion of successful mission numerical results alone and discouraging any activity that does not meet that standard. All of this highlights the need for what I call a theology of the hard work. Such a theology is grounded in reflection on the biblical text that will strengthen workers for the foundational tasks of clearing the fields, preparing the ground, and planting the seed needed for harvest.

---

[23] Ralph D. Winter, 'Are 90% of Our Missionaries Serving in the Wrong Places?' *Mission Frontiers* November–December (1991), 34-35.

In John 4:35-38 as Jesus is talking to his disciples about the present harvest, he makes the statement that others have done the hard work (John 4:38), and they are now reaping the fruits of those labours. When I went back and worked through commentaries on this passage, I discovered that scholars are not really sure of the antecedents that Jesus is using here. Who are the 'others'? What harvest Jesus is talking about? Where did he send them to reap? Who are the reapers drawing their wages? and so on. What is quite clear, however, is that Jesus is acknowledging here the well-known agricultural fact that in order to get a harvest you must do hard preparatory work first. It encouraged me greatly that Jesus recognises and honours the hard work. He notes that both the sower and the reaper rejoice together (John 4:36).

A theology of the hard work is founded on Jesus' acknowledgment of the role of hard work in preparing for a harvest. He lets his disciples know that they are standing on the shoulders of others; that those who have gone before have done the really difficult labour and now they will reap. Today, in the excitement of the worldwide expansion of the church there is a diminished tolerance for the often backbreaking labour of preparation for a harvest. I look forward to seeing classical Pentecostal missions new and old fill out their theologies of victory and success with perspectives on hard work in preparation for the harvest that includes the role of suffering, and living among the nations to declare the glory of God. This kind of theological reflection will provide future workers among the hardest places to serve joyfully for God's glory even when they are not seeing tangible results yet.

Reflecting on the Future: Mobilizing Classical Pentecostal Movements to Go to the Unreached

I have saved what is the most important issue and what I consider to be the most exciting possibility for this final point. One thing that makes the Pentecostal/Charismatic stream of faith so dynamic is the continual, unplanned, often unexpected wind of the Holy Spirit that blows and raises up new vision and visits and transforms bodies of believers and their communities. As classical Pentecostals, we need to believe God for a mighty visitation that will bring the vision and spiritual power to turn the movements that are associated with us all over the world towards the unreached ethnolinguistic groups.

Imagine what could happen if tens of millions of believers suddenly could 'see' peoples and begin to order their lives, churches, and movements around making Christ known among such neglected groups. Beyond the obvious benefits of large numbers of people being aware and praying for the unreached, there are two particular ways in which mobilization of classical Pentecostals would have a huge impact for frontier mission. The first is the vast pool of workers that could be released into unreached harvest fields. Majority World missions among classical Pentecostal movements are taking off, and it needs to be steered in the direction of places that do not have existing church movements. It would be a great tragedy for the Majority World churches to develop cross-cultural sending structures only to have people sent to work with the existing church somewhere else. It is entirely understandable how emerging Majority World missions structures want to emulate the work of the missionaries who were sent to them. This highlights the critical need for missions education and information so that these younger agencies can be aware of the needs of the unreached. It is ironic that many younger missions structures have come into existence with a vision to send people not to cross cultural boundaries, but geographic ones, often in pursuit of reaching the diasporas of their own people, while neglecting cross-cultural opportunities right within the borders of their own nation state to work among an unreached people.

The second impact of an awakening to see unreached peoples has to do with the informal ministry of millions of lay people in classical Pentecostal movements around the world that literally rub elbows with unreached peoples every day. If we could bring training down to our local churches and pastors to enable them to bear witness to the Muslims, Hindus, and Buddhists that live around them, these believers would have access to the lives of millions of people that are much more culturally near to them than any expatriate worker.

Conclusion

At the time of Edinburgh 1910, no one could have predicted the megashifts brought to the mission world by the concepts of frontier missions and the vitality and success of Pentecostal churches. Although organizations and missions growing out of classical Pentecostal roots have been slow to respond to the challenges of the unreached world in the past, there are reasons to be very hopeful about the coming together of these streams. The first signs of hope are the explicit structures that are emerging within classical Pentecostal missions in the West that focus on the unreached, and the mobilization for mission happening in the younger churches. The second is that the reasons for slow response are amenable to being addressed, and there is every reason to believe that revisiting key concepts and Pentecostal experiences can lead to a massive turning of the weight and spiritual energy of these movements towards the needs of the unreached.

Attitude Is Everything! Defending the Cause of Latin American Women in Ministry

Mireya Alvarez

This presentation aims at showing how Latina ministers stand out as exemplary leaders in the church despite the challenges, barriers, and limitations encountered in some denominational structures and policies. In recent years, more female pastors are leading growing churches across Latin America. However, some denominations, like the Church of God, are yet to recognize the full ministry of female leaders and have not totally ordained them into denominational leadership or ministry. In spite of the achievements of women in the social, educational and political fields of contemporary society, the church still lags behind in promoting the value and dignity of women in ministry. This paper calls for a renewed reading of the Scripture and church policies. It invites denominational leaders to recognize clergywomen and to formally empower them into church leadership.

While some churches do not set women free to exercise the full privileges of leadership, society has allowed opportunity and space for capable women in administrative and executive positions in many companies and government agencies. 'Several nations have elected women into the presidential office. However, the church does not yet favour a full leadership of women, restricting their development and depriving the church of their great contributions'.[1]

Women obtained the privileges of redemption, which allows them to partake of an unrestricted ministry within the church. How, then, can we speak of redemption if the church continues to deny complete redemption to women? The salvation obtained on the Cross does not exclude people because of race, nationality or gender. It is no longer possible for the Christian church to perpetuate injustice against women. 'There is neither Jew nor Gentile, neither slave nor free, nor is there male or female, for you are all one in Christ Jesus' (Gal. 3:28, NIV). Baptism marked a new dimension of equality and freedom for every believer into the Body of Christ. Racial differences (Jew and Gentile), social status (free and slave), and gender (man and woman), introduced by sin,

---

Originally published in Miguel Alvarez (ed), *The Reshaping of Mission in Latin America*, Regnum Edinburgh Centenary Series 30 (Oxford: Regnum Books, 2015), 87-102.

[1] Yattenciy Bonilla, '¿Hablamos de Redención sin Redimir a la Mujer?' *Boletín Latinoamericano de Estudios Pentecostales* 1:1 (2012), 91-101.

are superseded by the coming of the Kingdom of God, which is 'righteousness, peace… in the Holy Spirit' (Rom. 14:17, NIV).

The Pentecostal tradition celebrates the fulfilled promise of the outpouring of the Spirit upon all flesh, so that 'your sons and daughters… both men and women… will prophesy' (Acts 2:17, 18, NIV). Although the Pentecostal movement continues to expand around the world, some Pentecostal churches have lost the initiative of including women in leadership. Women are excluded in relation to decision-making in the administrative leadership and government of the church. Church policy justifies restrictions by one single phrase about silence (1 Tim. 2:12) rather than expanding upon the promise of empowerment by the Spirit (Acts 2:17).

The Initial Inclusiveness Pentecostal Movement

We will use the Azusa Street revival as the point of reference for the expansion of Pentecostalism in the American continent, although there are evidences of revivals in Mukti, India, led by Pandita Ramabai in 1894 to 1906, and in Valparaiso, Chile, led by Willis C. Hoover in 1902.[2] On the other hand, the revival of Azusa Street 1906-1913, initiated by the African American William Seymour, contributed to the overall global impact of the Pentecostal message. Many people travelled to the city of Los Angeles, California, to attend services and then carried the Pentecostal message to many other cities. Women played an influential role in the expansion of the movement, which took place in an atmosphere of social and racial diversity.[3] Women exercised their ministry gifts, prayed and ministered at the altar. The Azusa revival emphasized the power to perform the work in churches and missionary service.[4] Pentecostals believed that it was the Holy Spirit who enabled them to minister. Women prayed for world evangelization and for the conversion of lost souls.[5] The growth of Pentecostalism is attributed in large part to the mobilization and participation of women in ministry.

Pentecostals broke with the traditional schemes by giving women freedom to preach and prophesy. Unfortunately, the Church of God closed the doors to higher levels of authority to women gifted in the Spirit. In the first meeting of 1907, it was noted that the number of women surpassed the number of men in attendance. Women were granted credentials as evangelists but were restricted from performing ministerial functions. Women were forbidden to officiate at

---

[2] Juan Sepúlveda, 'Pentecostal-Charismatic Movements in Latin America and Among Latinas/os' (presented at the Renewal across the Americas Conference, Regent University, February-March 2014).

[3] See Estrelda Alexander and Amos Yong, *Phillip's Daughters: Women in Pentecostal-Charismatic Leadership* (Eugene, OR: Wipf & Stock, 2009).

[4] David Roebuck, 'Women in God's Army', *History and Heritage* (Fall 1997), 1-2.

[5] See Grant McClung, *Azusa Street and Beyond* (Gainsville, FL: Bridge-Logos, 2006).

baptisms, and in the General Assembly of 1916 women were banned from exercising their right to vote in the General Assembly.[6]

Despite the active participation of women in ministry, Pentecostals missed the opportunity to set the stage for granting them ministerial credentials with all the rights and privileges of ministry. Instead, denominational policies restrained women from positions of authority which led to the exclusion of women in leadership. Moreover, they issued credentials that allowed women to preach but restricted their field of operation to other ministerial roles. Only male ministers were granted ministerial credentials with privileges to officiate marriages, baptism and the reception of new members.

The Church of God created a department for the organization of women to engage in prayer groups, Bible studies, and charitable projects. These groups were designated as Voluntary Workers, Ladies Auxiliary, and Women's Ministry. Such departmentalization constrained the circle of influence of women in the whole mission of the church. It was a way to domesticate the energy and potential of a lot of women. Boundaries were set for women not to overstep the limits of the positions reserved for men. An entire bureaucracy alienated woman from pulpit ministry and administrative leadership positions. Gender segregation was clearly observed in the general council meetings. While male bishops deliberated over church matters, women were marginalized spectators.

During the 1940s the Church of God in the United States joined the interdenominational evangelical movement in its campaign to rescue sacred family values.[7] This new movement, in which Billy Graham was a leading figure, promoted the role of women as the centrepiece of the family.

In traditional evangelical churches, male leadership was emphasized. A woman was assigned a submissive role in the order of creation: home, family and church. It was assumed that the tradition of respect and submission of women in marriage should apply as normative for the church. Clearly, what the Bible teaches is the voluntary submission of women to one man, to her husband, who in turn must exercise dedicated, loyal and consistent leadership. Essentially, marriage partners operate within a relationship of servanthood and mutual submission.

Several writers of the Church of God in recent years suggest a return to our Pentecostal roots, which implies the greater inclusion of all members and a greater dependence on the Holy Spirit for the training of believers. As a result, an increase in the participation of each church member would naturally occur, regardless of gender. In addition, such participation would be consistent with one of the tenets of the Reformation, that is, the priesthood of all believers.

---

[6] Abraham Ruelas, 'A Sociological Perspective on Women, Ordination, and Church Polity: Empowerment or Gender Apartheid?' *Crucible Theology and Ministry* 1:2 (October 2008), 14.

[7] David Roebuck, 'Limiting Liberty: The Church of God and Women Ministers, 1986-1996' (PhD dissertation, Vanderbilt University, 1997).

Unfortunately, the arguments against the full participation of women in ministry have prevailed and are based on biblical texts interpreted in a dogmatic and traditional way. The very formulation of arguments against the ministry of women is indicative of a sinful, unjust and destructive attitude towards woman since she is created in the image and likeness of God.

It is no longer possible for the church to continue closing the door to the ministerial participation of women. There are many women who exercise ministry as pastors, teachers, and evangelists despite the restrictions imposed on their gender. The mission of the church is incomplete if women are deprived of ministerial credentials or if ministerial duties are reserved for males only.

The following section highlights the role of women in the first-century church as observed in the gospels and the New Testament letters. It is essential to review these passages because they emphasize the ministry of women in the early church. This review reveals the manipulation of biblical passages that makes men the protagonists of ministry to the detriment of the names and deeds of extraordinary women in early church history.

The Ministry of Women in the New Testament

The ministry of Jesus reinforced the equality and participation of women in the Kingdom of God. Several women are mentioned in the genealogy of Jesus such as Rahab, Ruth and the wife of Uriah, indicating that Christ came to save all kinds of people. The gospels show that Christ supported women. He conducted his teachings not only to men but also to women who longed to learn (Luke 10:38-42), afflicted and tormented women (Luke 13:10-17; Matt. 15: 21-28), and women who were despised (Mark 5:23; John 4). The Son of God received assistance from female followers 'who supported him with their own means' (Luke 8:2-3).

Jesus defended the rights of women by revealing his thoughts on marriage and divorce (Matt. 5:27-32; 19:3-9). It was the women who remained close to Jesus during his crucifixion and burial while his disciples deserted him (Matt. 27:55-61). Women were the first to see the risen Christ and were sent to tell the good news to the disciples (Matt. 28:8-10; John 20: 14-16). The fact that women were commissioned as evangelists is very significant because in the first-century Jewish context, women could not be considered as witnesses in courts of law.[8]

Mary and Martha exemplify Christian discipleship (Luke 8:1-3; Matt. 12:49-50). Jesus kept a close friendship with them and their brother Lazarus (John 11:8). Mary poured out expensive perfume on Jesus, and he recognized her action (John 12:7). Martha proclaims one of the greatest Christological confessions, 'Yes, Lord... I believe that you are the Messiah, the Son of God, who is to come into the world' (John 11:27). However, it is Peter's confession that has received the attention of preachers.

---

[8] Stanley Grenz, *Women in the Church: A Biblical Theology of Women in Ministry* (Downers Grove, IL: IVP, 1995), 93.

After Jesus' ascension, the apostles remained in prayer 'with the women and Mary the mother of Jesus' (Acts 1:14). It was these women who made up the core of the church and, on the day of Pentecost, the prophecies were fulfilled when the Spirit of God was given equally to men and women (Joel 2:28, Acts 2:4). The Apostle Peter declared the inclusion of women as heirs of the promise: 'Your sons and your daughters shall prophesy' (Acts 2:17c).

Women were part of the fellowship of early believers and were fully integrated into the Christian communities (Acts 5:14; 8:12; 17:4, 12). In Samaria, both men and women believed and were baptized (Acts 8:12). The church of Thyatira began with a women's group that met at Lydia's house (Acts 16:13-15). Among the first converts, there were many widows who depended on the church for their provision (Acts 6:1-6). Women were also persecuted for keeping the faith and were arrested and put into prison by Saul (Acts 8:3; 9:2; 22:4). Obviously, women were considered a threat to the Jewish faith as they shared the gospel with other women in public places like the market-place and laundry.[9]

In Joppa, many believed when Peter prayed for Tabitha who was brought back to life (Acts 9:36-41). In Jerusalem, the disciples prayed together in the house of Mary, the mother of John Mark (Acts 12:12). In Philippi, the women gathered outside the city where they prayed by the river (Acts 16:13). Paul and Silas met with other believers in the house of Lydia, a new convert (Acts 16:40). In Thessalonica and Berea, Paul preached in the synagogue where he persuaded Jews and Greek women of nobility (Acts 17:4, 12). In Athens, a woman named Damaris believed in the gospel message (Acts 17:34). In Corinth, Aquila and Priscilla laboured and travelled with Paul. The narrative discloses that Priscilla and Aquila taught Apollos 'the way of God more adequately' (Acts 18:3, 18.26; Rom. 16:3). The mention of Priscilla's name before Aquila may indicate that she was the more influential of the two.

Several women in the New Testament fulfilled a prophetic mission. Luke referred to the four daughters of Philip who prophesied (Acts 21:9). Mary (Luke 1:46-55), Elizabeth (Luke 1: 41-45) and Anna (Luke 2:36-38) prophesied during the events of Jesus' birth. Paul recognized that women prophesied in the church and instructed them to do so in an orderly manner (1 Cor. 11:5).

In his letter to Rome, Paul greets several women who worked in the church there, and describes their particular function in the church. Paul refers to a servant (*diakonos*), a patron (*prostatis*), a co-worker (*synergos*), a labourer (*kopian*), and an apostle (*apostolos*). Phoebe is mentioned as a deacon (*diakonos*) of the church in Cenchrea (16:1) and a helper (*prostatis*) to many people (16:2). Priscilla is recognized for being a 'co-worker (*synergos*) in Christ Jesus' (16:3). Paul greeted Mary, 'who worked (*ekiopasen*) very hard among you' (16:6). Junia is mentioned as being outstanding among the apostles (*apostoloi*) (16:7). Paul referred to Tryphena, Tryphosa, and Persis for their

---

[9] Michael Green, *Evangelism in the Early Church* (Grand Rapids, MI: Eerdmans, 1970), 178.

'hard work in the Lord' (16:12). He also mentioned the mother of Rufus (16:13), Julia, Nereus and his sister (16:15).

One of the positions of greater authority in the first century was the office of apostle. The term is used to refer to the twelve disciples chosen by Jesus, and Matthias who replaced Judas (Acts 1:26). The apostles were witnesses of the resurrection and commissioned by the church to preach the gospel (Acts 13:2-3; Acts 14:4, 7, 14). In the case of Paul, he was chosen as an apostle to reach the Gentiles (Acts 9:15; 1 Cor. 15:1-7; 2 Cor. 12:11; Gal. 1:17, 19).

The diversified ministry of the apostles included: (a) planting churches (1 Cor. 3:10-11); (b) preaching the gospel in new regions (Rom. 15:20); (c) the appointment and training of leaders (Acts 14:21-23); (d) promoting unity among the churches (Eph. 4:1-16; Rom. 15:25-27); and (e) working miracles (2 Cor. 12:12).

Paul commended Andronicus and Junia as outstanding among the apostles (Rom. 16:7). They were his relatives and fellow prisoners and were Christian converts before Paul (Rom. 16:7). Commentators debate two issues: whether Junia was a female name and if so, was she an apostle? For Tucker and Liefeld, no evidence has been found against Junia being a woman.[10] Both John Chrysostom and Jerome referred to Junia as a woman, and it was not until the fourteenth century that any reference was made to Junia being a man. Most commentators agree that Junia is the feminine form of the longer masculine name Junianus or Junilius, just as Julia is the feminine version of Julius.[11]

Greek and Latin writers before the twelfth century referred to Junia as a woman. The Bible translators of the twelfth century changed the original name Junia for *Junias* since a woman apostle was unacceptable. This practice of setting restrictions was common during the medieval church. Currently, the contribution of women is still restricted through arguments and justifications based on the interpretation of isolated texts inevitably leading to the sidelining of women. It is unfortunate that the very thought of restricting the right of a woman and her ministry in the church endures to this day.

Paul's other letters also recognize the contribution of women among the believers. In Corinth, a church met in the house of Chloe (1 Cor. 1:11). Paul defended the right of the apostles and believers to be accompanied by their wives in the work of the Lord (1 Cor. 9:5). Within the marriage relationship, Paul taught that husband and wife should respect each other, quite an egalitarian position in the context of first-century society (1 Cor. 7:3-5). In a similar passage, Paul tells husbands to love their wives as Christ loved the church and gave Himself for her (Eph. 5:21-33).

Paul refers to Euodia and Syntyche who 'laboured side by side with me in the Gospel together with Clement and the rest of my fellow workers (*synergoi*)' (Phil. 4:2-3). Paul greets Nympha and the church in her house (Col. 4:15), and mentions Apphia who attended church in Philemon's house (Phmn 2). During

[10] Ruth Tucker and Walter Liefeld, *Daughters of the Church: Women and Ministry from the New Testament to the Present* (Grand Rapids, MI: Zondervan, 1987), 13

[11] Grenz, *Women in the Church*, 94. Tucker and Liefeld, *Daughters of the Church*, 73.

the time of the New Testament church, believers had designated groups of women to serve actively in the church. Among these women were deaconesses (Rom 16:1-2; 1 Tim. 3:11), widows and virgins, to all of whom Paul gave specific instructions (1 Cor. 7:25-40).

The first Christian communities appointed women for ministries of service associated with the diaconate.[12] The pastoral epistles were the basis for defending the role of women as deaconesses.[13] Paul wrote in relation to deacons: 'The wives must be of good character' (1 Tim. 3:11). Some commentators conclude that this is evidence of a specific service of women deacons.[14] Others suggest that Paul is referring only to the wives of deacons, since the Greek word *guné* may refer to wife or woman.[15] Although there is no specific Greek word for deacons, the term deaconess appeared in the second and third century for women who exercised that role. Clearly, the reference is to duties that required moral qualities for wives of deacons or for deaconesses.

Widows were recognized as a group of women who ministered at the church and were known as 'the altar of God',[16] Paul instructed the church to provide assistance to widows of sixty years of age or older, who had no family assistance (1 Tim. 5:3). Such women were known for their good deeds such as 'raising their children, showing hospitality, washing the feet of the Lord's people, helping those in trouble' (1 Tim. 5:10).

Paul clarified the state of marriage and singleness as gifts given by God and referred to the blessings and benefits of each (1 Cor. 7:7). The apostle exalted virgins who engaged in the work of God rather than surrender to the obligations of marriage (1 Cor. 7:34). Though Paul advised that the unmarried state allowed greater commitment to ministry, he never forbade marriage (1 Cor. 7:25, 32, 34). Concerning such women as widows and virgins, it was anticipated they would be single.

There are references to women of faith such as Eunice and Lois, the mother and grandmother of Timothy who was his mentors in the way of the Lord (2 Tim. 1:5). Titus advised older women to mentor younger women in their Christian life (Tit. 2:3-5). The book of Hebrews mentions two women of the Old Testament, Sarah, and Rahab, as examples of faith (Heb. 11:11, 31). Women of faith received their dead ones back after they were raised to life (Heb. 11:35). The apostle Peter counselled husbands to treat their wives with respect as heirs of salvation (1 Pet. 3:7). Paul used the feminine figurative language to refer to the church as the bride of Christ (2 Cor. 11:2; Eph. 5:25-27). The book of Revelation refers to the church as a bride and a wife (3:12; 21:9).

---

[12] Grenz, *Women in the Church*, 87.

[13] James B. Hurley, *Man and Woman in Biblical Perspective* (Grand Rapids, MI: Zondervan, 1981), 229-230. See also Tucker and Liefeld, *Daughters of the Church*, 86.

[14] Grenz, *Women in the Church*, 87.

[15] See Philip Graham Ryken, *I Timothy* (Phillipsburg, NJ: P & R Publishing, 2007).

[16] Tucker and Liefeld, *Daughters of the Church*, 91.

In the early Christian communities, women received baptism and worked in the churches because they too were born of the Spirit (John 3:3). As churches spread throughout the Roman Empire, women participated and emerged as leaders.[17] We can conclude that, unlike many churches today, first-century believers honoured women as they fulfilled their ministry.

The Contribution of Women in the Expansion of Pentecostalism

The Pentecostal movement began in the context of holiness revivals of the late seventeenth and early nineteenth centuries. It then became stronger as the contemporary Pentecostal movement grew early in the twentieth century. Pentecostals have been characterized by their passion for the Word of God, their emphasis on a sanctified life, Christ-centred preaching, powerful worship, and their evangelistic devotion.[18] The growth of Pentecostalism is attributed particularly to the mobilization of women in ministry.

In 1901, Agnes Ozman, affiliated with the Assemblies of God, was the first to receive the baptism of the Holy Spirit with the manifestation of speaking in tongues during a prayer vigil in Topeka, Kansas. This event helped establish the doctrine that the initial evidence of the fullness of the Spirit was speaking in tongues. It is undeniable that women were instrumental in the growth and strengthening of the Pentecostal movement. Women preached, prophesied and ministered at the altar.

The Azusa Street revival stressed the importance of the empowerment of the Spirit to do the work of the church and mission. The participation of women in evangelism, prophecy, ministry, and prayer at the altar was the acceptable standard, for the promise embraced, 'Your sons and your daughters will prophesy' (Joel 2:28). During the nascent stage of Pentecostalism, the backing of the power of the Spirit was the acceptable credential for service.

Holiness churches interpreted Scriptures in favour of women in ministry. Luther Lee and B.T. Roberts taught that women could hold office in the church as they had the authority to do so. For both, the subordination of women was a result of the fall; however, women had received their redemption in Jesus Christ according to Galatians 3:28.[19] Within the Holiness movement of the nineteenth century, two women, Phoebe Palmer and Catherine Booth (a founder of the Salvation Army), were defenders of the ministry of women in the nineteenth century.

Women were also founders of Pentecostal denominations. Florence Crawford established the Apostolic Faith Mission in Oregon, and Aimee Semple McPherson founded the International Church of the Foursquare Gospel (ICFG). Two African-American women, Magdalena Tate, and Ida Robinson,

---

[17] Mary Malone, *Women & Christianity: The First Thousand Years* (Maryknoll, NY: Orbis Books, 2000), 80.

[18] Barbara Cavaness, 'God Calling: Women in Pentecostal Mission', in Grant McClung (ed.), *Azusa Street and Beyond* (Gainesville, FL: Bridge-Logos, 2006), 53-66.

[19] David Roebuck. 'Limiting Liberty', 5.

founded churches and were ordained bishops in their Pentecostal denominations.

Fundamentalist Patterns within the Church of God

Several Pentecostal denominations, including the Church of God, joined the North American evangelical movement embracing traditional values that led Pentecostals to slowly eradicate the initial Pentecostal practice of supporting women preachers. A woman's place was in the home, while secular values promoted the emancipation of women. Pentecostal women were excluded from governing positions within the church. Women, however, continued to plant churches, lead prayer groups or Bible studies, in spite of lacking the ministerial privileges granted to men.

In the United States, female ministers continued to lose their freedom after World War II when Pentecostals followed the traditional evangelical movement which argued for the exclusivity of male leadership. Evangelicals warned about the erosion of family values creating concern in Christian circles. Therefore it was generally accepted that women had to carry out domestic duties rather than public participation. The voice of women was silenced, and the image of a woman preacher soon became a forgotten figure. In many churches today, the voice of women is not heard in public, and their participation is unnoticeable in religious services. What message are we sending as a church by publicly silencing the voice of women?

On the other hand, the origins of the Church of God in the rural South, often referred to as the region of the Bible (or the Bible Belt), exerted a powerful influence in policy towards women in ministry. The fundamentalist framework in the history of our denomination, based on the North American evangelical movement, contributed to slowing down the process of the full integration of women in the mission of the church. It was in the early twentieth century that the conservative Protestant churches in the United States reacted to the teachings of theological liberalism and modernism. The so-called fundamentalists defended conservative Christianity, fearing that the church would accommodate to the demands of the modern, secular world. They adopted and promoted doctrinal standards and guidelines, fearing that Darwinism and evolutionary theory postulated a threat to the Christian faith.

Fundamentalism promoted a literal interpretation of Scripture which coincided to a certain degree with a Pentecostal approach to the Word of God. Foundational beliefs and values were adopted at face value, and any association with formal or scientific studies was rejected Fundamentalists taught that the gifts of the Spirit, including the gift of tongues and divine healing, had ceased in the first century, but Pentecostals embraced the fundamentalist doctrine of the premillennial rapture and the second coming of Christ. It was common in Pentecostal circles to reject any formal education, for fear that those who studied could lose their faith. The famous 'Monkey Trial' (1925) in the city of Dayton, a few miles from Cleveland, Tennessee, contributed to the discrediting of fundamentalism. Evangelical followers were perceived as anti-intellectuals who prevented the advancement of society.

In the 1940s, fundamentalist leaders tried to establish a council of Christian churches, since most conservative evangelical leaders chose to move away from the image of the warlike fundamentalist past. In 1942, the new evangelical leaders established the National Association of Evangelicals (NAE), and included the participation of Pentecostals. Consequently, the Church of God joined the new evangelical movement in 1946.

Through the National Association of Evangelicals (NAE), traditional evangelical values have prevailed American Pentecostalism, adopting the conventional perspectives of evangelical churches, perhaps unconsciously assuming discriminatory attitudes against women's ministry. Among the attitudes, beliefs, and values of the North American evangelical church, the exclusive male privilege was emphasized. Proponents of male leadership argued that the government of the church was a matter for men, because Christ chose twelve male disciples. A few restrictive verses defined the role of women, not only at home but also in the church: women were to be subject, and learn in silence. What a contrast with the freedom that the Spirit grants women to minister!

Fundamentalism promoted patriarchy or male privileges because of restrictive hermeneutics or a literal interpretation of Scripture. The fundamentalist theological interpretation influenced the social and political perspective of its followers, often characterized by conservative positions and reflected in racial segregation, the subordination of women and, in the United States, being a member of the Republican Party.

Currently, female ministers of the Church of God do not have a voice in the Executive Council meetings of the General Assembly. During the 2010 General Assembly, more than 62% of the male bishops voted against adopting a new church policy that would make way for the ordination of women.[20] In the book, *What Women Want*, Kimberly Alexander and James Bowers stress that the voice of Pentecostal women could no longer be ignored. From their interviews among female ministers, they gathered insights on the experiences that these women undergo. For example, one woman said, 'I do not attend ministers' meetings, etc., because they are aimed at the men ministers and their wives. My husband… considers the COG "a white, good ol' boys' club" and has pretty much had it with the denomination'.[21] Women are highly involved in church planting, evangelism, and educational opportunities, and it is time for the church to 'support, bless and commission women for greater ministry

---

[20] Adrienne Gaines, 'Church of God Debates Role of Women', *Charisma Magazine*, 2010: www.charismamag.com/site-archives/570-news/featured-news/11656-church-of-god-debates-role-of-women (accessed 2nd May 2015).

[21] Kimberly Alexander and James Bowers, *What Women Want: Pentecostal Women Ministers Speak for Themselves* (Langham, MD: Seymour Press, 2013), 111.

leadership'.[22] It is time for the church to recognize women as strategic leadership partners for the challenges of the twenty-first century.

To conclude this section, the cultural patterns of American evangelicalism and fundamentalism were imposed on Pentecostal churches to exclude women from public office. It is time to distinguish between the authority of Scripture and the traditions inherited in the last hundred years. The following section will review the reality of Pentecostal Latinas in ministry.

Pentecostal Latinas

In the case of Latin American nations, issues of gender equality have impacted society, and more women are participating in politics. In several Latin American countries, about 50% of women occupy political positions of the legislature, mayor and council offices.

In the religious sphere, at least half of classic Pentecostals in the world are in Latin America with an estimated population of 141 million adherents in the year 2000.[23] Pentecostal Latinas have been known for exerting influential leadership as preachers, teachers, and missionaries. The political context of gender inclusiveness and the stimulus generated in thriving Pentecostal congregations could possibly exert influence on women pastors to engage in leadership.[24] As church leaders in the global South, women can most likely become agents of change, as seen in women in the corporate world and women in impoverished settings.[25]

Even though Latina Pentecostals have contributed with solid and spiritual leadership in their churches, there are still obstacles to overcome in order for them to gain equality in leadership with males in the church. Women have learned to navigate a system which does not give them full opportunities, yet they advance in leadership and contribute to the edification of their churches and consequently the Kingdom of God. Several regions have appointed COG women as district overseers or educational directors, positions generally reserved for male bishops.

Latinas are making history and continue to make history within their denominational circles. Seasoned female leaders are setting examples to the younger Latina women who will walk closely in their footsteps. Latinas are indeed hard-working, courageous, and engaged in raising the consciousness of gender equality in the church.

---

[22] Alexander and Bowers, *What Women Want*, 128.

[23] Allan Anderson, *An Introduction to Pentecostalism: Global Charismatic Christianity* (Cambridge: Cambridge University Press, 2004), 63.

[24] Erik Tryggestad, 'As Churches Mature in the Global South, U.S. Christians Find Supporting Roles', in *The Christian Chronicle* (2009): www.christianchronicle.org/article/as-churches-mature-in-the-global-south-u-s-christians-find-supporting-roles (accessed 1st June 2015).

[25] Cynthia Lee Andruske, 'Self-Directed Learning Projects of Women on Welfare as Political Acts', in *Adult Learning*, 14:1 (2003), 13-16.

For Espinosa, Latinas in Pentecostal churches have practised paradoxical roles, that is, as prophetesses in the public sphere, and devoted wives and mothers in the private sphere.[26] Women in the Assemblies of God were ordained, but they were kept out of administrative positions until the 1980s. Within the Church of God in Latina America, women ministers engage in liturgical practices, including some in administrative positions. However, women are still denied the ultimate level of ordination, a status reserved for male bishops.

Pentecostal churches have opened a way for women to participate publicly in ministry. Women in Latin America have been given opportunities to preach, pray and evangelize in home groups.[27] Pentecostalism's teaching and preaching opportunities allow a greater status for women. Pentecostal *cultos a domicilio* [services held in the home] or *células* [cell groups] are largely led by women. Through such activities, women are trained in practical skills, including public speaking, and they may also gain an important measure of confidence.[28]

Women like Maria Atkinson (1879-1963) who was the first woman to take Pentecostalism to Mexico, set a role model for early Latino Pentecostals.[29] Many of the pioneering Pentecostal women dedicated their time and effort to sustain the church in several ways: praying, fasting, offering, cleaning, cooking, and carrying out evangelism and visitation. Pentecostal women gladly adopt roles as servant leaders in the way they approach ministry.

Early studies on Pentecostalism concluded that churches grew because they were closely-knit communities that helped people cope with industrialization and urbanization.[30] Pentecostal groups seem to offer people unique resources that enable them to cope with personal and family problems like alcoholism, poverty, and illness. The charismata of the Holy Spirit are also meaningful and relevant resources. People make changes in their ethical behaviour, and they show an increase in personal discipline.

Gender relations in Latino Pentecostal churches have undergone a transformation in comparison with the traditional culture of *machismo.* The average Pentecostal church attendant is usually under thirty, more often female than male, and of a low to lower middle-class background. Women seem to become more independent in the home and in the public domain. Males shift away from drinking, gambling and adulterous relationships. Pentecostalism is

---

[26] Gaston Espinosa, 'Third-class Soldiers: A History of Hispanic Pentecostal Clergywomen', in Estrelda Alexander and Amos Yong (eds), *Phillip's Daughters: Women in Pentecostal-Charismatic Leadership* (Eugene, OR: Wipf & Stock, 2009), 98, 106, 110, 111.

[27] Verónica Pérez, 'Educación y Liderazgo de la Mujer Pentecostal, Signo de Esperanza para la Iglesia: Una Reflexión', in Daniel Chiquete and Luis Orellana (eds), *Voces del Pentecostalismo Latinoamericano* (Haulpen, Chile: RELEP, 2011), 475-92.

[28] Elizabeth Brusco, *Reformation of Machismo: Evangelical conversion and gender in Colombia* (Austin, TX: University of Texas Press, 1995).

[29] Verónica Pérez, Educación y Liderazgo de la Mujer, 478.

[30] Henry Gooren, 'The Pentecostalization of Religion and Society in Latin America', *Exchange* 39:1 (2010), 355-76.

considered a main social force against *machismo*.[31] A hierarchical male clergy and a high degree of institutionalism characterize North American Pentecostalism. On the other hand, Latino Pentecostalism exerts greater flexibility in gender relations and has the potential to bring about societal transformation.[32]

While the Church of God and many other denominations in North America still debate over the role of women in ministry, a number of Church of God regions in Latin America continue to open opportunities for women to exercise authority, as members in church councils, district overseers and educational directors. Several female pastors have been leading growing churches in Mexico, Honduras, Colombia, and Brazil. Both Latino churches and individual female pastors have challenged denominational standards by allowing greater freedom and inclusion of women in governing boards. In the capital city of Honduras, Tegucigalpa, there are ten female pastors, and one of them is a district overseer, a position reserved for male bishops. A woman minister presides over the Education Department in the Central Region.[33]

From a Pentecostal perspective, leadership is viewed as a gift to one who responds to be a follower of Jesus and a vessel for the power of his Spirit. Leadership is not just a characteristic that can be obtained or learned, since God chooses human leaders in a sovereign way. The greatness of human leadership is measured by how well the leader is a follower of God. Based on Acts 2, Pentecostal and Charismatic churches believe God pours out the ministry and operational gifts equally on all who earnestly seek the Spirit. Within the Pentecostal movement, every member is a potential leader. All genuine leadership is based on spiritual power coming from the Spirit of God, and it is realized in the context of a unified community. Every member is encouraged to learn and publicly recite Scripture and express their gifts of the Spirit in service. Guidance and nurture are offered along with mentoring.

In Pentecostalism, everybody in the congregation is a potential contributor to the liturgy because the movement empowers marginalized people.[34] The participation of women with charismatic gifts was widespread in Pentecostalism. Early Pentecostals affirmed that the same Spirit who was poured out on men also empowered women. Cox affirmed that women, more than men, were the principal carrier of the Pentecostal gospel to many parts of the world.[35]

> Barred from the pulpit, they preached in the streets. Refused ordination, they became missionaries and went to places where men were afraid to go. They

---

[31] Elizabeth Brusco, *Reformation of Machismo: Evangelical Conversion and Gender in Colombia* (Austin, TX: University of Texas Press, 1995), 141.
[32] Cheryl Bridges Johns, *Pentecostal Formation: A Pedagogy among the Oppressed* (Sheffield: Sheffield Academic Press, 1993), 19.
[33] Pedro Guardado, email message to author, October 2012.
[34] Anderson, *An Introduction to Pentecostalism*, 272.
[35] Harvey Cox, *Fire from Heaven* (Cambridge, MA: Da Cappo Press, 1995), 124-25.

became healers and teachers, writers and editors. Without them, Pentecostalism would have died out long ago.[36]

From my ministerial experience in Latin America, I have observed the motivation and persistence in Latina clergywomen of the Church of God in Honduras. Although women still face leadership barriers in the church, it is important to stress that they have overcome barriers and have gained respectable ministerial achievements. Feminine characteristics such as caring, collaboration, sensitivity, helping, have all contributed to the success and ability of women leaders to fit in with a less hierarchical structure in an organization. These feminine principles had little chance of influencing in times when such organizations were 'strictly male cloning production'.[37]

In spite of the barriers and the socio-economic hardships that women face in a Third World country, female clergy seem to have positive outcomes, such as growing congregations, leadership formation, empowered staff, lifelong-learning opportunities, spiritual formation, and others.[38] Some of the obstacles these women encounter include monetary constraints, lack of encouragement from church officials, consuming role demands and an absence of mentoring.[39] The Honduran national bishop stated that several women pastors are currently leading congregations of more than 200 members. One female pastor in a church called *Oasis de Amor* (Oasis of Love) reports more than 3,000 members.[40] The church's website describes their pastor as a woman who has broken church paradigms in a church society generally led by men.[41]

Because male leadership roles, also in the church, have been the norm for so many years, leadership tends to be perceived as a masculine domain exemplified by masculine characteristics such as confidence and dominance.[42] However, female leaders interact in alternative ways in leadership: encouraging participation, sharing information and power, and enhancing others' self-worth.[43] Generally, as organizations shift away from a traditional view of leadership and towards a more democratic and participatory view, women should experience reduced prejudice and gain increased acceptance in leadership roles.[44]

---

[36] Cox, *Fire from Heaven*, 138.

[37] Sally Hegelsen, *The Female Advantage: Women's Ways of Leadership* (New York: Doubleday, 1995), 39.

[38] Aparna Ohlott, Patricia Bhandary, and Joan Tavares Avent, 'What Women Want: Comparing Leadership Challenges in Europe and the US', in *Leadership in Action*, 23:1 (2003), 3.

[39] Celia Rivera Lobo, email message to author, March 2014.

[40] Pedro Guardado, email message to author, September 2013.

[41] Oasis de Amor, Honduras: www.oasisamor.org/Ana.html (accessed 2nd June 2015).

[42] Shawna Lafraniere and Karen Longman, 'Gendered Realities and Women's Leadership Development: Participant Voices from Faith-based Higher Education', *Christian Higher Education* 7:1 (2008), 388-404.

[43] See Judy B. Rosener, *America's Competitive Secret: Utilizing Women as a Management Strategy* (Oxford: Oxford University Press, 1995).

[44] Alice H. Eagley and Steven Karau, 'Role Congruity Theory of Prejudice toward

Women employ democratic relationships, participatory decision-making, delegation, and team-based leadership. In addition, females tend to empower others in making decisions, improving the quality of their work, and removing sources of fear and intimidation from the workplace.[45] Generally speaking, Honduran female pastors have exhibited leadership attitudes, bringing their female qualities to enrich and deepen church ministry.

Female Leaders', *Psychological Review* 109:3 (2002), 573-98.

[45] See Edwards Deming, *Out of the crisis* (Cambridge, MA: Massachusetts Institute of Technology, Center for Advanced Engineering Study, 1986).

The Bible in Mission: Evangelical / Pentecostal View In Latin America

Antonia Leonora van der Meer

I grew up in Brazil in an Evangelical church. As a young adult, I got involved with the Pentecostal movement as well. Later I served for ten years as a missionary in Angola and Mozambique, serving the Evangelical Alliance and a number of Evangelical and Pentecostal churches. One of the very strong influences on my spiritual development was my involvement in IFES (International Fellowship of Evangelical Students), in Brazil, Africa and elsewhere. In that context, I had the privilege of being influenced by models and teachers like John Stott, René Padilla, Samuel Escobar and others, for which I am very grateful.

Traditionally in Brazil, Latin America, Angola and Mozambique mission was understood as the task of preaching to save souls. The goal was for people to make a decision for Christ. To reduce Christian preaching and teaching to the one message caused people to be churchgoers for many years, in order to be ready for heaven, but they never grew up in their faith and did not know how to apply it to their context. In practice, there was compassionate care for suffering members of the church, of the families, and neighbours. But that was not seen as mission.

I remember walking, as a young person, with a Pentecostal friend in São Paulo, and crossing a bridge over the Tietê River. I said to him: 'God must be so sad that we have spoiled his beautiful creation in such a terrible way!' (The river smelled very bad.) His answer was: 'Oh sister, do you really think that God cares for rivers? God wants us to save sinners!'

In Angola, churches stood firm during persecution and restrictions from a Marxist government (from 1975 till 1991, later there was a growing openness) and continued to grow, even though they were not allowed to build new church buildings. Some unregistered churches built simple structures in very poor neighbourhoods; others organized up to 5 services on a Sunday to serve their growing number of members. One pastor would be in charge of several churches. Most did not have any theological or biblical training, due to a lack of training offered by missions that had served in Angola for decades. It is amazing that churches led by such people continued to grow, amidst great poverty and insecurity because of the long war (from 1961 to 2002).

I taught at Bible schools and worked with university students and was always impressed by their desire to learn about the Bible, their faith; they would never become tired from listening and asking questions. Because of these circumstances, there was little room for theological or missiological thinking. But since I came back to Brazil to work at the Evangelical Missions Center, we have had Angolan leaders come to study with us, and usually, their concerns are about how to get their churches involved and committed to mission.

Because of my roots in Latin America, I present mostly, but still in a limited way, the vision of some Latin American theologians, though there are some citations of missiologists from other continents. It is impossible in this paper to write about the whole history of mission, so I deal mostly with the more recent missionary commitment of the Global South, as well as the influence of the Lausanne movement.

The Vision of Some Latin American Theologians[1]

René Padilla

Padilla (from Ecuador) is a leading theologian and wrote that a growing number of Latin American churches are actively involved in cross-cultural mission, sending missionaries to many places, and several institutions are offering missionary courses. But there has not been enough missiological reflection; most books have been translated from English. The Theological Fraternity of Latin America is producing more contextual theological and missiological papers.[2]

Padilla is critical about the way the gospel has been brought to Latin America, Africa, and Asia. Western missionaries were convinced that they had the right vision of translating and preaching the Bible, often with little understanding on contextualization, a message which offered eternal salvation, but many had no concern for people's human struggles. So the gospel came as an alien religion and did not present answers to their needs and questions. Mission should be done following the model of Jesus Christ, who lived as a normal human being in his own context and brought the good news in a way that made sense to the people and answered their needs.

Padilla writes that the gospel comes to human beings in relation to the world of creation, a world made through Jesus Christ that will be recreated through him. The purpose of evangelism is not just to prepare people for the salvation of their soul, but to create a radical re-orientation in their lives, integrating them

---

This is a revised version of the originally published chapter in P. Hoggarth, F. Macdonald, B. Mitchell, and K. Jørgensen (eds), *Bible in Mission*, Regnum Edinburgh Centenary Series 18 (Oxford: Regnum Books, 2013), 93-105.

[1] C. René Padilla, *Bases Bíblicas de La Misión: Perspectivas latinoamericanas* (Buenos Aires: Fundación Kairós, 1998).
[2] R. Padilla, 'Preface', in *Bases Bíblicas de La Misión*, ix.

in the purpose of God to submit all things to the governance of Christ.[3] The church needs to be freed from aspects of its culture that hinder her faithfulness to Christ and her mission. A church has no authority to proclaim reconciliation of man with God, when she denies reconciliation with her fellow men. There is a relation between the life of the church, her prophetical ministry, and evangelism.[4]

He believes that we need to take the unity of Christ's body seriously, denying ethnocentrism and promoting a theological cross-fertilization between different cultures. Each culture has something precious to contribute to the understanding of the gospel.[5] The gospel needs to answer human needs, but we must be careful not to change its nature, only a genuine gospel will produce a genuine conversion, in repentance and faith. In Jesus Christ, the Kingdom of God is manifested, as proclaimed by John the Baptist and by Jesus himself. The content of the gospel is not a new theology but an event: the coming of God's Kingdom, as proclaimed in Isaiah 52.7. People are invited to receive this new life responding through repentance and faith (Is 61:1, 2; Lk 4:20, 21). Jesus teaching about God's Kingdom is that, in anticipation to the end times, the age of the Kingdom is already present through his person and ministry (Mt 4:23, Mk 1:14, 15; Lk 4:43, 8:1). According to Jesus, the Kingdom would be preached until the end of this age (Mt 24:14, Mk 13:10).[6]

The kingdom of God is a present reality as well as a promise which will be accomplished in the future. The end times have come through Jesus, manifesting themselves through his acts of power and mercy (Lk 4:18-19, Mt 11:5). This kingdom will result in the creation of a new community (Lk 9:57-62, 12:32, 14:25-33; Mt 10:34-38, 26:31). The church is not the equivalent of his Kingdom; the Kingdom is God's reign, the church lives under his reign. The church is called to do good works, which manifest the present reality of the Kingdom.[7]

Padilla sees the Kingdom of God as the hermeneutical key to understand the mission of the church. It is a key concept in the Old and New Testament, proclaimed by Jesus and the apostles, and it brings a new age, a life of reconciliation with God, with fellow human beings and with creation, a life in which righteousness and love abound.

Samuel Escobar

Escobar, from Peru, is another leading Latin American theologian. He writes that during the nineteenth and early twentieth century the Bible played a decisive role in the rise of evangelical churches in Latin America. Missionaries

---

[3] René Padilla, *Misión Integral: Ensayos sobre El Reino de Dios y La Iglesia* (Buenos Aires: Ediciones Kairos, 2012), 89.
[4] Padilla, *Misión Integral*, 93-95.
[5] Padilla, *Misión Integral*, 100, 101.
[6] Padilla, *Misión Integral*, 135-41.
[7] Padilla, *Misión Integral*, 283-91.

travelled from place to place, leaving Bibles and New Testaments, and evangelical congregations sprang up, gathering around the Word of God. With the existence of new, thriving churches in many countries, they needed to respond to the pastoral questions that arose in their context and penetrate their cultures with the gospel. Sadly this raised much controversy, and was not accepted by many Protestant missionaries. Missionaries gave the Bible to many tribes and nations, but the way of reading the Bible was conditioned by their culture. This retarded the possibility of people gaining new insights, reading the Bible with their own eyes, and developing a proclamation of the gospel and pastoral practices geared to their own cultures and communities.[8]

Evangelicals of the Third World understand that they are to take seriously the characteristics of their own cultural and historical contexts.[9] 'The new freedom in the Spirit, which enabled these churches to question theological patterns developed in other cultures, also stimulated an effort to take seriously the missionary challenge posed by their own culture'.[10]

According to 2 Corinthians 5, believers have been made new creatures; the old things have passed, which means that there is 'a totally new way to see the earth and human beings (2 Cor. 5:16). A total revolution, a new way to see Jesus, and to see all humanity…'.[11] A new attitude to the Gentiles was developed, in contrast to the hostility that previously characterized the relationships between Jews and gentiles.

The epistle to the Romans Paul writes that:

> God wanted to bring salvation to every human being… and that he had chosen Paul as his instrument. It was not just a mental certainty but a joyful obedience… the proclamation of the gospel among the gentiles and in places where it was not known, was his ambition and specific task…[12]

Paul's goal was to plant churches that would be 'reconciled, integrated, mature, joyful, and healing communities… light amidst darkness (Phil. 2:14-16) and signs of the new creation (Rom. 8:18-23).'

Sadly in Latin America, the tendency has been to reduce the gospel to its minimum in order to keep more church members, and as a result, the church, instead of transforming society, has become an instrument of society to accommodate its members to its materialistic values.[13]

---

[8] Samuel Escobar, *A Time for Mission: The Challenge for Global Christianity* (Leicester: IVP & Langham Partnerships, 2003), 130-34.

[9] David Gitari, 'The Claims of Jesus Christ in the African Context', in *A Time for Mission*, 139, 140.

[10] Escobar, *A Time for Mission*, 141.

[11] Samuel Escobar, 'Pablo y La Misión', in René Padilla (ed), *Bases Bíblicas de la Misión: Perspectivas latinoamericanas* (Buenos Aires: Ediciones Kairós, 2015), 328.

[12] Escobar, 'Pablo y La Misión', 333.

[13] Escobar, 'Pablo y La Misión', 336-37.

Tim Carriker

Carriker, from the USA, has become Brazilian, identifying himself with his adopted country. [14] According to Carriker, the existence of the Bible is clearly missionary: God communicating through Scriptures is proof of his love and concern for humanity. When they receive the Bible, people know God's concern, his love and saving purpose. The Scriptures are a missionary instrument of God.[15]

God gave his people a missionary task and responsibility. When we do not witness, we are separating ourselves from his grace and election. Our role is not to seek power and comfort in our mission, but to follow the footsteps of the Suffering Servant.[16]

Jesus' redemption brings about sincere worship to God and relationships of justice with other human beings and with creation. To be God's people implies reflecting his character and justice. In Brazil, evangelicals became suspicious of a social gospel, and were against the doctrine of good works of Spiritists[17] and Roman Catholics, and against a Marxist understanding of social structures. They followed teachings of foreign missionaries whose sole concern was the conversion of many 'souls'. The church needs to recover a broad Biblical perspective, worshipping the Lord and seeking patterns of justice in the church and society.[18]

Our mission is to reach people from every tongue, tribe, and nation with the gospel of the Kingdom (Mt 24:14). But mission includes stewardship for the whole creation. God's Kingdom is manifested in the proclamation of the gospel for repentance and conversion, but also in the struggle for justice.[19]

The Lausanne Movement

The Lausanne conference of 1974 was influenced by the passionate appeals of Latin American theologians René Padilla and Samuel Escobar for integral mission, which includes care for whole human beings in their context, not only for their salvation. They received support and understanding from John Stott and their message influenced the worldwide evangelical movement, through the Lausanne Covenant. The Lausanne movement resulted in a renewed understanding of the use of the Bible in mission, that it was biblical not only to preach the right message, but to have the right attitudes and actions, following Jesus example and God's compassionate care for the needy, responding to human suffering, poverty, abuse and violence, and caring for God's creation.

---

[14] Tim Carriker, *O Caminho Missionário de Deus*, 2nd ed. (São Paulo: Sepal, 2000).

[15] Carriker, *Caminho Missionário*, 8-9.

[16] Carriker, *Caminho Missionário*, 168.

[17] There are many such different spiritist groups in Brazil from followers of Alan Kardec to several syncretistic cults like Macumba and Candomblé. They have a growing number of followers.

[18] Carriker, *Caminho Missionário*, 174.

[19] Carriker, *Caminho Missionário*, 175-179.

'The Lausanne Covenant' expresses this conviction about the use of Scriptures in Mission:

> To evangelize is to spread the good news that Jesus Christ died for our sins and was raised from the dead according to the Scriptures, and that as the reigning Lord he offers the forgiveness of sins and the liberating gifts of the Spirit to all who repent and believe. Our Christian presence in the world is indispensable to evangelism, and so is that kind of dialogue whose purpose is to listen sensitively in order to understand...
>
> We affirm that God is both the Creator and the Judge of all people. We, therefore, should share his concern for justice and reconciliation throughout human society and for the liberation of men and women from every kind of oppression...[20]

This covenant presented evangelical churches worldwide with a new understanding and commitment to mission, which included concern for whole human beings in context, and the need to respect all cultures.

The Lausanne Movement organized a Third International Conference in 2010, with the participation of representatives of a wide range of churches and movements from almost every nation, where a longer document on the challenge for mission was produced, 'The Cape Town Commitment'.[21]

> We love the word of God.
>
> The Bible tells the universal story of creation, fall, redemption in history, and new creation... At the center of this story are the climactic saving events of the cross and resurrection of Christ which constitute the heart of the gospel. This story of God's mission defines our identity, drives *our* mission... We must make the Bible known...
>
> We confess that we easily claim to love the Bible without loving the life it teaches – the life of costly practical obedience to God through Christ. Yet nothing commends the gospel more eloquently than a transformed life, and nothing brings it into disrepute so much as personal inconsistency.[22]

The Lausanne movement brings together Evangelical and Pentecostal churches worldwide, seeking to involve people from all cultures in all levels of leadership. Lausanne is committed to mission and to the use of the Scriptures in mission.

> We love the Gospel of God
>
> As disciples of Jesus, we are gospel people. The core of our identity is our passion for the biblical good news of the saving work of God through Jesus Christ. We are united by our experience of the grace of God in the gospel and by our motivation to make that gospel of grace known to the ends of the earth....[23]
>
> We love the Mission of God

---

[20] 'Lausanne Covenant' (www.lausanne.org/en/documents), visited on Feb 2, 2013.

[21] 'Lausanne Covenant'.

[22] 'Lausanne Covenant'.

[23] 'Lausanne Covenant'.

> We have been redeemed through the cross and resurrection of Jesus Christ, and empowered by the Holy Spirit to bear witness to what God has done in Christ. The Church exists to worship and glorify God... and to participate in the... mission of God.... All our mission must therefore reflect the integration of evangelism and committed engagement in the world, both being ordered and driven by the whole biblical revelation of the gospel of God.[24]

This is a statement of commitment to mission, which is both bringing good news and a commitment to serve, based upon the gospel. The second part of the Cape Town Commitment is a call to action, which seeks to present what it means to serve in mission in response to the needs of the world, global needs as well as more local suffering. We are called to live the truth of the gospel, to proclaim it clearly, to work for reconciliation between peoples, to care for justice, compassion and empowerment of the poor and needy, as well as caring for the suffering creation as part of our missionary responsibility.

John Stott

Stott was a respected evangelical leader who had a balanced view, committed to Biblical truth and to the need for contextualization.[25] He was committed to the use of the Bible in mission:

> The gospel is thus seen to be one, yet diverse. It is 'given', yet culturally adapted to its audience... This understanding will help us not to make two opposing mistakes: The first is 'total fluidity'... and the opposite mistake is 'total rigidity'... there is a third and better way. It combines commitment to the fact of revelation with commitment to the task of contextualization...[26]

> The Bible gives us the *model* for world evangelization. Through the Bible God is... communicating the good news to the world... the same principle is illustrated in both the inspiration of the Scriptures and the incarnation of the Son.... The divine was communicated through the human. He identified with us, without surrendering his own identity... Some of us refuse to identify with the people we claim to be serving... we do not become like them... others are so determined to identify with the people... that they surrender their Christian standards and values...[27]

> Some people reject the gospel not because they perceive it to be false, but because they perceive it to be alien... All of us need to subject our gospel to more critical scrutiny, and in a cross-cultural situation... need to seek the help of local Christians in order to discern the cultural distortions of our message.[28]

---

[24] 'Lausanne Covenant'.

[25] John Stott, 'The Bible in World Evangelization', in Ralph Winter (ed), *Perspectives on the World Christian Movement: A Reader*, 3rd ed. (Pasadena: William Carey Library, 1999).

[26] Stott, 'The Bible in World Evangelization', 23.

[27] Stott, 'The Bible in World Evangelization', 23-24.

[28] Stott, 'The Bible in World Evangelization', 24.

So it is possible to be faithful and committed to the biblical truth and at the same time open to listen to people from different cultures and ways of understanding. We need to learn to adapt, to incarnate ourselves and our message as followers of Jesus Christ. Missionaries have created barriers to the gospel by their lack of understanding and adaptability. But as evangelicals, we do not want to fall into the trap of creating a different gospel which is more easily acceptable.

Chris Wright

Wright is a theologian, who has followed in John Stott's footsteps as Director of Langham Partnership, an organization with the goal of developing Biblical knowledge especially among leaders in less affluent contexts. He chairs the Lausanne Theology Working Group.

Wright shows that the early church understood their mission and the need to reach out to all peoples because they knew their Scriptures' story and so they found answers at critical moments.

> Jesus, after his resurrection, walking with the two disciples on the road to Emmaus…went through the whole canon of the Old Testament to explain how it all led up to him, the Messiah, and how his death and resurrection were, in fact, the way God had kept his promise to Israel (Lk. 24:13-27)… in order to make sense of the story so far.[29]

> Later the same evening Jesus met the disciples who were gathered in Jerusalem, and…he opened their minds so they could understand the Scriptures…: 'The Messiah will suffer and rise from the dead… and repentance for the forgiveness of sins will be preached in his name to all nations…' (Lk. 24:45-48). Jesus presents the cross and resurrection as the 'central point… of redemption in history… God's answer to every dimension of sin and evil… and all their destructive effects… The cross must be central to every dimension of mission… from personal evangelism… to ecological care for creation.[30]

In his conclusion, Wright writes that he hopes his readers will see the glorious riches of the gospel of God.

> The Bible brings us the most amazing good news that… can transform every area of human life that is touched by sin. What God has joined together, we have put asunder. Then we struggle to articulate how they are 'related' when we should never have separated them….[31]

> The 'bad' news of breaking this whole is that Christians who are evangelized by truncated versions of the biblical gospel have little interest in… God's plan for society and the nations, and even less understanding of God's intention for

---

[29] Christopher J.H. Wright. *The Mission of God's People: A Biblical Theology of the Church's Mission* (Grand Rapids: Zondervan, 2010), 38.
[30] Wright. *Mission of God's People*, 43.
[31] Wright. *Mission of God's People*, 273.

> creation itself... The scale of our mission efforts, therefore, is ... a lot smaller than the scope of the mission of God.[32]

Wright has a firm belief in the Biblical truth that needs to be proclaimed, lived out, and applied to every area of life on our planet and in our society.

Evangelical Writers Committed to a Contextual Use of the Bible in Mission

David Hesselgrave[33]

Hesselgrave has served in Japan and taught mission cross-cultural ministry in the States. He believes that the Holy Scriptures must occupy a central place in the strategy of churches and their mission. Progress in mission is linked with complete confidence in and careful examination and utilization of the Word of God, and not reinforcing a simplistic use of the Bible.[34]

Churches and missions have the tendency to choose one method as the overall strategy for world evangelization. The New Testament uses many words like proclaim, testify, evangelize, dialogue, persuade, tell, warn, prove, beseech. There is a tendency today to promote inter-religious dialogue, but many evangelicals are against it. The emphasis of evangelicals has been proclamation and evangelism. This can imply a limitation of the biblical task.[35] We need to contextualize the proclamation of the Biblical message, not compromising its truth but applying it in an appropriate way, being sensitive to the hearers and their cultural context.

The problem with a one-sided emphasis on proclamation is that it overlooks the need to be effective hearers, who will respond to people's understanding and objections. Jesus used a two-way communication, addressing questions to his hearers' minds and consciences. A biblical dialogue will not compromise the revealed truth, nor refrain from presenting unappealing truths.[36]

N.T. Wright

Wright is an evangelical theologian, a prolific writer. He is one of the present date's most respected biblical scholars. His hermeneutical key also is the Kingdom of God, for understanding how to live our lives, developing a Christian character and learning to become what God has always intended us to be.

---

[32] Wright. *Mission of God's People*, 274.

[33] David J. Hesselgrave, *Scripture and Strategy: The Use of the Bible in the Postmodern Church and Mission*, Evangelical Missiological Society Series 1 (Pasadena, CA: William Carey Library, 1994).

[34] Hesselgrave, *Scripture and Strategy*, 9-11.

[35] Hesselgrave, *Scripture and Strategy*, 89.

[36] Hesselgrave, *Scripture and Strategy*, 92-93.

The kingdom is not a new idea in the Bible; it is present in the creation account of Genesis 1 and 2. What kind of kingdom did God have in mind? Certainly not a human tyranny over nature. Genesis speaks about a garden with a rich variety of life which man has to care for. As God is a God of love, generous and creative, his way of governing is sharing power, acting through those who carry his image, inviting them to cooperate in his project with joy and freedom.[37]

The early Christians rejoiced in the hope of the New Jerusalem, descending from heaven to earth (Rev 21.2), a world flooded with the joy and righteousness of God. To worship and reign are the double calling of the people of the new city (Rev 3:21, 5:9-10, 20:4, 6). It presents a vision of human beings, able to gather the worship of creation and offer it to the Creator, to exercise sovereignty and wise stewardship over the world as God always had planned for them. They will be priests and kings in the New Jerusalem.[38]

Paul presents the anticipation of our future hope that all who are in Christ, in whom the Spirit lives, will reign in glory over the whole creation. Looking at texts like Matthew 19:28-30, it becomes clear that Jesus' teaching about the kingdom is related to the future government of God over the world. His followers need to live in the present, anticipating here and now the role they will receive in the future.[39]

Some Remarks on the Pentecostal View

In Latin America, Pentecostal churches have been very active, both in reaching out to communities, especially among the poor, as well as sending missionaries to other countries. But very little has been written by Pentecostal theologians. A number of articles were published under the title 'In the Strength of the Spirit: The Pentecostals in Latin America, a challenge to the historical churches'.[40]

What has caused the poor classes to be attracted to the Pentecostal churches in Brazil? These churches offer community life and values that help the poor to face their daily struggles, help them in their survival, and to develop a sense of their value as human beings, loved and enabled by God. Pentecostals develop an ascetic lifestyle and dedicate themselves to their family. They help the poor to face and overcome conflicts in their homes.[41]

---

[37] N.T. Wright, *Eu Creio, e Agora? Por que o Caráter Cristão é importante [After you Believe]* (Viçosa: Ultimato: 2012), 81-84.

[38] Wright, *Eu Creio, e Agora?* 85-90.

[39] Wright, *Eu Creio, e Agora?* 100-106.

[40] Benjamim F. Gutiérrez and Leonildo Silveira Campos (eds), *Na Força do Espírito: Os Pentecostais na América-Latina: um desafio às igrejas históricas* (São Paulo: Associação Evangélica Literária Pendão Real, 1996).

[41] Cecília Loreto Mariz, 'Pentecostalismo e a Luta contra Pobreza no Brasil' [Pentecostalism and the Struggle against Poverty in Brazil], in *Na Força do Espírito*, 170-86.

Pentecostal Churches in Cuba arrived in the 1960s but have grown very rapidly, especially in the 90s. Pentecostal as well as historical churches understand mission in two main ways: (a) They consider mission and evangelism as being identical. They will share their experience of faith with others and speak to them about God, encouraging people to be saved. (b) They understand evangelism as speaking the Word of God, as well as witnessing through their lifestyle and commitment in society. They attract people through their lives more than through their words. They see their goal as raising awareness and sowing seeds, so that people start seeking God. They understand their mission as including service and solidarity, acting to promote love and mutual understanding.[42]

Marcelo Vargas

Vargas is a Bolivian theologian, the Executive Secretary of the Latin American Theological Fraternity. He wrote his doctoral thesis on 'The Aimara identity of Neopentecostals in urban La Paz, Bolivia, with specific reference to the Power of God (PoG) Church.' Presented in 2010, for his Ph.D., at the University of Wales-Oxford Centre for Mission Studies.[43]

PoG members repeat the forms of speech used by their leader by heart, and attempt to imitate his lifestyle and practice of Neopentecostal spirituality. The traditional spiritual disciplines of evangelical Protestants have changed in form and content. Prayer, miracles, and evangelism based on their personal experience have replaced the priority given to Bible study in other evangelical churches.

Prayer is by far their most common practice of piety… They speak to God to ask for the power of the Holy Spirit or to find a job. Evangelism means sharing their faith with relatives and friends, talking more about their experience than the content of the Gospel. Their evangelism is motivated by a sense of urgency transmitted by the church, because the task has to be completed and each believer must play his or her part.

The PoG believers not only read their Bibles less frequently, but their capacity to study and understand the biblical text is weaker. Communication based on orality is an Aimara value. They are committed to fasting, visiting the sick, speaking in tongues and the use of the PoG mass media.

Julie C. MA and Wonsuk Ma

The Mas are from Korea and have served in the Philippines. They now direct and teach at the Oxford Center for Mission Studies.

---

[42] Rafael Cepeda, Elizabeth Carillo, Rhode González, and Carlos E. Ham, 'Causas e Desafios do Crescimento das Igrejas Protestantes em Cuba: A Influência do Movimento Pentecostal' [Causes and Challenges Protestant Church Growth in Cuba: The Influence of the Pentecostal Movement], in *Na Força do Espírito*, 121-37.

[43] Vargas paper is so far unpublished.

They write about the development of Pentecostal Mission and Missiology.[44] A good proportion of Southern Christianity is 'Pentecostal', although the term is not used in many churches. The Bible is read to believe it, and to expect to experience the same healings and miracles, and God is expected to 'speak' to his people through visions and dreams. The evangelistic and missionary zeal of these emerging churches is a natural consequence of this type of Christianity, often coupled with a voluntary and involuntary displacement of massive numbers of people.[45]

With a conservative theology, they continue their campaign for the other world, while ignoring the church's missionary call to 'this life' matters. More alarming is a strong leaning towards a theology of (this worldly) blessing, often indistinguishable from the self-centred prosperity gospel.[46]

The outward expression includes vibrant and participatory worship, commitment to prayer for God's direct intervention to human needs, zealousness for evangelism. This form of Christianity tends to attract the poor in society and has brought an empowering effect to masses.[47]

However, there have been signs of a more holistic understanding of mission. The social context of the 'developing' societies requires Christians to take social issues into their mission thinking, such as poverty, health issues (HIV/ AIDS, etc.), education, etc. The biblical base for this broader understanding may be found in John 17:18: 'As you sent me into the world, I have sent them into the world'.[48] A new breed of Pentecostal churches, particularly in the Global South, has taken social service seriously. Miller and Yamamori call them 'progressive Pentecostals'.[49]

Mission in Reverse

Non-Western Christians are attempting to re-evangelize the West. A primary factor making this possible is the movement of migration which is bringing unprecedented numbers of people from the non-Western world to Western countries. Some are worshipping in their mother tongue. Others are worshipping in English but sustaining a cultural identity from their place of origin.

Lucas Njenga in 2003 founded 'Heart for the City', a project in Glasgow which combines biblical witness with concern for social renewal. After six months dedicated to understanding the culture and the people, Lucas and his wife Helen began their work among vulnerable communities. The project

---

[44] Julie C. Ma and Wonsuk Ma, *Mission in the Spirit: Towards a Pentecostal/charismatic Missiology* (Oxford: Regnum Books, 2010).

[45] Ma and Ma, *Mission in the Spirit*, 2.

[46] Ma and Ma, *Mission in the Spirit*, 3.

[47] Ma and Ma, *Mission in the Spirit*, 4.

[48] Ma and Ma, *Mission in the Spirit*, 6.

[49] Ma and Ma, *Mission in the Spirit*, 10.

brings together people from different ethnic and socio-economic groups for Christian teaching and worship.

There can be little doubt that immigration has dramatically changed the character of Christianity in Europe. In Cologne, the largest worshipping congregation is a Korean one. The largest congregation in London is a Nigerian-founded one. The largest congregation in Europe is in Kiev, and again it is Nigerian-founded.

There is no mistaking the fact that the gospel is spreading through migratory movements. It is a spontaneous movement of people making their own connections and developing their own perspectives and networks.[50]

Samuel Escobar observes that: 'Perhaps the biggest challenge is the prophetic task of being a mouthpiece for the poor and downtrodden and pronouncing an unpopular prophetic word for a society that seems to be taken over by panic from seeing these waves of foreigners who have come to stay'.[51]

Conclusion

Evangelical and Pentecostal churches have developed a growing commitment to serve the poor in Brazil, in Latin American, in Africa and Asia. There is a growing number of Christian NGO's and churches serving in many ways. They have learned that in both the Old and the New Testaments God is manifested as a God who cares for the little ones, a God who offers forgiveness and reconciliation with himself, as well as being concerned for justice and service to those who suffer, a God who becomes a humble servant to reach even the most despised human beings.

Many understand that we are called to follow Jesus' model in humble and loving service. Some serve in arts, others in sports, many offer training courses to the young, as well as to women, others serve in literacy and in community development. Sadly a growing number of churches are influenced by the self-seeking theology of prosperity and have lost compassion for the needy. And many still follow the traditional view that our real task is to present the gospel and seek to convert people to Christ. But there is hope, even though the dimension of social needs and suffering continues to be much greater than our possibility to respond adequately and seek the empowerment and restoration of the dignity of people living at the margin of society.

---

[50] Kenneth R. Ross, *Non-Western Christians in Scotland: Mission in Reverse* (www.ctbi.org.uk/pdf_view.p´hp?id=210), accessed on Dec 6, 2013

[51] Samuel Escobar, 'Migration: Avenue and Challenge to Mission', *Missiology: An International Review* 31:1 (January 2003), 19.

Neo-Pentecostal Paradigms in Latin American Mission: Microtrends in the Theologies of Mission and Missionary Practices among Neo-Pentecostals in Peru

Bernardo Campos

This article describes four micro trends in the theologies of mission and missionary practices of Neo-Pentecostalism in Latin America: (1) Restoration and specialization of ministry, especially of apostles and prophets for the establishment of the Kingdom as a global mission; (2) Recovery of the earthly city as the goal of humanizing mission; (3) Inner healing, spiritual warfare and deliverance as a means to recruit disciples who populate the earthly city in the perspective of the Kingdom; and (4) Economic prosperity, a sign and foretaste of the Kingdom of God here and now. Together they could be considered in future as paradigms of mission in Neo-Pentecostalism.

Introduction: Paradigms and Trends

The original meaning of 'paradigm'[1] is 'pattern' or 'model'. For Plato, paradigms are the 'divine models' from which earthly things are made.[2] In modern developmental psychology, a paradigm refers to the acceptance of ideas, thoughts, and beliefs generally built during early life and accepted as true or false without testing them in a new analysis.[3] In the broader sense,

---

Originally published in Miguel Alvarez (eds), *The Reshaping of Mission in Latin America*, Regnum Edinburgh Centenary Series 30 (Oxford: Regnum Books, 2015), 193-205.

[1] The term 'paradigm', as we know, that originates from the Greek word παράδειγμα [paradigm], is a compound word: παρά (para) [together with] and δεῖγμα (deĩgma) [example or pattern]. See Henry George Liddell and Robert Scott, *A Greek-English Lexicon*, revised and augmented throughout by Henry Stuart Jones with the assistance Roderick McKenzie (Oxford: Clarendon Press, 1940).

[2] María Angeles Durán and Francisco Lisi, *Plato's Dialogues* (Barcelona, España: Editorial Gredos, 1996), 132-36.

[3] A paradigm is a set of beliefs and preconceptions, both philosophical and otherwise, that at a certain time shares a scientific community. In a broad sense, it is a new view or

παράδειγμα [*paradeigma* or paradigm] refers to the set of practices or theories that define a scientific discipline that has been or are still being tested and analyzed extensively over time, and therefore are still standing. According to Karl Popper[4] and T.S. Kuhn,[5] who introduced this concept in the theoretical discussion of science in his book *The Structure of Scientific Revolutions*, the paradigm includes 'an entire cluster of beliefs, values, modes of behavior, shared by the members of a given community'.[6]

Applying it to theology, Hans Küng defines paradigm as a model of interpretation, model of knowledge or as a fundamental model (macro model).[7] In my opinion, a set of realities and practices can be considered as 'megatrends' and at the same time be material elements for the configuration and reconfiguration of paradigms. Megatrends are significant social, political, economic and technological changes affecting longer periods of time (ten years or more). One example of megatrend occurred when the industrial society moved on to the information age, which changed the global economy, revived the arts, ignited religious revival and developed a high quality of technology. In our case, a number of theories and practices of the Neo-Pentecostal church that are maintained throughout time could set a mission model or paradigm beyond religious boundaries, whether or not they were shared with other groups.

Kuhn illustrated his thesis with classic examples of the history of science of nature, and analyzed the mechanisms in detail by which the Ptolemaic, Copernican, Newtonian and Einsteinian paradigms were formed and developed. Along the same lines, Hans Küng,[8] in the light of a long history of the church and society, also discussed macro epochal constellations from basic models, i.e., large paradigms that have structured the Christian vision of reality and have been transformed over the history of theology and the church. From this overview of Christianity, Küng distinguishes six major paradigms: (1) the proto-Judæo-Christian apocalyptic paradigm of theology of the church, (2) the ancient ecumenical Hellenistic and Byzantine, (3) the Roman Catholic medieval, (4) the Reformation (evangelical Protestant), (5) the modern enlightenment, and finally (6) the post-modern post-Enlightenment or ecumenical paradigm of trans-modernity.[9]

According to this interpretation, a paradigm is a cluster of ideas and practices that cover a number of years and that mark or point to a specific time

---

new approach. See 'paradigm' at: http://dictionary.reference. com/browse/paradigm (accessed 29th March 2015).

[4] Karl Popper, *La lógica de la investigación científica* (Mexico: Rei, 1991), 78-101.

[5] Thomas S. Kuhn, *La estructura de las revoluciones científicas* (Mexico: Fondo de Cultura Económica, 1962), 18-27.

[6] Thomas S. Kuhn, *¿Qué son la Revoluciones Científicas? y otros Ensayos* (Barcelona, Spain: Paidós, 1989), 21-32.

[7] Hans Küng, *Theology for the Third Millennium: An Ecumenical View* (New York: Doubleday, 1987), 12-18.

[8] Küng, *Theology for the Third Millennium*, 36.

[9] Hans Küng, 'Cambios de Modelo de Iglesia en la Marcha del Pueblo de Dios', in Juan Carlos Núñez Bustillos (ed), *Éxodo* (Madrid: Editorial Trotta, 1997), 77-93.

in one or more aspects of a culture. Now, with this approach in mind, we ask if we can talk about Neo-Pentecostal paradigms in the mission of the church in Latin America. I think not; it's too early for that. Perhaps it is better to speak of 'micro trends' in Neo-Pentecostal theologies of mission and missionary practices in Latin America, which in the future could be the basis for discarding new paradigms in mission. I consider them at a 'micro' and not at a 'macro' level because we are referring to a section of Protestant Christianity (Neo-Pentecostalism), and Neo-Pentecostals are only part of the global range of mission theories. Before continuing, let me first recall four major trends in the classic Pentecostal understanding of mission that, in my opinion, precede Neo-Pentecostalism and from which many reinterpretations have been made that indicate a clear contrast.

Traditional Paradigms in Classic Pentecostal Missiology

The Church (Universal Priesthood) as the Principal Agent in the Mission of God

From very early in the history of Christianity, the church understood that she was a depository of revelation and therefore the custodian of salvation. Outside the church, salvation was not possible (*Extra ecclesia, nullam salus*). According to this tradition, the church is the main agent of God's mission in the world, which is expressed primarily as evangelizing mission. Fortunately, this reductionist perspective of 'mission as evangelism'[10] has been overcome and is now understood as an 'integral'[11] or 'holistic' mission. Integral mission includes worship (liturgy), the proclamation of the gospel (*kerygma*), education in the faith (*didache*), Christian communion or fellowship (*koinonia*) and social action (*diakonia*), along with other Christian services. It is also 'full or total'[12]

---

[10] Cf The Lausanne Covenant Document, available online at: www.lausanne.org/content/covenant/lausanne-covenant – the emphasis is on mission as evangelization.

[11] The term 'integral mission' was widespread in Latin America by René Padilla and La Fraternidad Teológica Latinoamericana [Latin American Theological Fraternity]. Cf René Padilla, *¿Qué es misión integral?* (Buenos Aires: Ediciones Kairos, 2006), 11-48. A review of the impact of the theology of integral mission in Latin America, posted by the Kairos Foundation, can also be found at: www.kairos.org.ar/index.php?option=com_content&view=article&id=48&Itemid=146 (accessed 29th March 2015).

[12] For example, in the summer of 2009, the Iglesia Unida de Cristo [United Church of Christ] at its General Synod, and La Iglesia Cristiana Discípulos de Cristo [The Christian Church Disciples of Christ] at their Assembly, adopted resolutions affirming the pact between the two denominations to be a global or total Mission Church. Incidentally, Amos Yong has stressed the possibility of a 'Global Theology' in his book, *The Spirit Poured Out on all Flesh: Pentecostalism and the Possibility of Global Theology* (Grand Rapids, MI: Baker Academic, 2005), 17-30.

mission that encompasses the entire planet and is not limited to religion, but incorporates the entire culture, society, economics, and politics. In the classic Pentecostal view, the universal priesthood of all believers is emphasized, and that is why 'every believer' was called not only to be a 'disciple' but also to be a 'missionary'.

Heaven, Glory and Christians' Final Destiny

Historically, Christians have pointed to the sky as the final destination for the followers of Christ. Opposed to hell as a place of eternal punishment for sin, heaven is the prize that believers would receive after suffering in the world. It is the crowning for their efforts and loyalty to the gospel and Jesus Christ. The search for the glory of God in the church was already a foretaste of the coming glories with the second coming of Christ. Heaven is the final destination of the faithful.

Empowered for Global Mission

For traditional Pentecostals, the power of the Holy Spirit of God is the engine that moves the missionary task. Without that power, evangelizing, teaching or social work remains sterile or fruitless. Without the Spirit's action, missionary work is reduced to mere social or philanthropic activity. Only the power of God can produce a true transformation of lives and societies. That power is contrasted with the powers of this world. Christians can use earthly powers as part of their work, but they are not confined to them. They are considered as a means to a greater or sublime end. They must distinguish the difference, for political power belongs to the natural order, but the power of the Spirit is supernatural. Christians are citizens of two worlds.[13] Although they move in the earthly city, they seek to reach the city of God as Augustine[14] proposed against the pagans.

Martyrdom as a Prize for Winning the World for Christ

Among classic Pentecostals, it is natural to assume that the prize for following Christ and doing his will is martyrdom, death. Suffering for the cause of faith and the preaching of the Word in hostile environments is almost an expected consequence. Following Jesus implies suffering. Suffering completes the believer and fashions his or her character. The Kingdom of God will be established with the second coming of Christ, but in the meantime, believers should live according to the standards worthy of that salvation wrought by

[13] See Hilario Wynarczyk, *Ciudadanos de dos mundos. El Movimiento Evangélico en la Vida Pública Argentina 1980-2001* (San Martín, Argentina: UMSAM EDITA, 2009), 391. The author shows that double perspective observed in Neo-Pentecostal believers.

[14] Cf. Peter Robert Lamont Brown, *Augustine of Hippo: A Biography* (New York: New York City Press, 1990).

Christ. Poverty and destitution are conditions often used by God to perfect his children.

Missional Paradigms and Megatrends among Neo-Pentecostals

For the purposes of this work, we define Neo-Pentecostals as groups of believers marked by the spiritual experience of Pentecost. These differ from classic Pentecostals by their economic and social status, their theologies of faith and prosperity, pragmatic religiosity which includes belief systems, rituals, forms of organization and ethics. Neo-Pentecostals are spiritually open to the influence of post-modernism and globalization.[15] From a socio-religious perspective, Neo-Pentecostals would fall under Hans Küng's sixth paradigm of enlightened post-modernity.[16]

According to José Mardones,[17] post-modernity shows the following characteristics: (1) A de-modernization and de-historisation that puts people at a post-history that harbours a memory loss attitude. (2) Loss of the unique perspective of mass media by the manipulation of information technology. Neo-Pentecostals enter into a world of images that pushes them to step out of the reality of the world and society. They are taught to access a virtual world that forces a de-realization and relocation of reality. (3) Due to over-dependency on imagery, Neo-Pentecostals are forced to use limited knowledge to overcome weaknesses and limited academic training. This condition generates de-realization of knowledge that moves them to over-emphasize charismatic experiences and spiritual exposure. (4) Socio-politically Neo-Pentecostals replace the political and ideological polarization through widespread spiritual instability cause by evil forces. Politically, they tend to favour nationalistic and conservative movements and, to avoid extremes, they prefer to be known as 'centrists'. (5) To avoid conflict, Neo-Pentecostals prefer to de-politicize and de-bureaucratize the masses that long for close relationships. They prefer to manage people by gathering them in small groups. That way people help each other and lessen the pressure on the leaders. (6) Neo-Pentecostals commercialize the art and spiritualize social evils along with other behavioural conditions of people.

In summary, with its nuances, we see that Neo-Pentecostals manage situations where the heart prevails over reason and feelings over thought. They are led by post-modernism which is characterized by an implicit rejection of the tenets of scientific reason. There is a new logical disclaiming of modernity that

---

[15] An interesting religious socio-Neo-Pentecostal approach is that of sociologist William Mauricio Beltrán, *Del Monopolio Católico a la Explosión Pentecostal: Pluralización Religiosa, Secularización y Cambio Social en Colombia* (Bogotá: Centro de Estudios Sociales de la Universidad Nacional de Colombia, 2013), 223-92.

[16] Küng, 'Cambios de modelo de Iglesia en la Marcha del Pueblo de Dios', 80.

[17] José Mardones, *¿A dónde va la Religión?* (Santander, Spain: Sal Terrae, 1996), 184-85.

is seen as 'autonomy of reason' (Kant) or 'autonomy of the whole man' (Marx) against the tutelage of the church or theology.[18]

Today, we are witnessing a new order in the ideological, cultural, economic and social fields in which globalization, the market economy, modernity, and technology are its main components. Around them, a series of socio-ideological and economic phenomena are produced such as affluence, marginalization, technological dehumanization, addiction to energy sects, and deterioration and dysfunction of the family. Somehow the 'micro' missiological trends of Neo-Pentecostalism are a religious response anchored to post-modern life and the challenges of globalization.

The globalization of knowledge and western culture in developed countries is the most revolutionary and disturbing fact of our times, and the most challenging for the mission of the church in this century. Globalization, according to Guillermo Cook,[19] is technological, economic and religious, and its main instruments are the mass media and the rapid expansion of the neo-liberal economic model. However, the globalization of technology brings a hopeful contradiction. While spreading the 'gospel of the free market' and the values of post-modernism – which some confuse it with the theology of prosperity – it also serves as a means of the search and diffusion of technological, economic, cultural and religious alternative models (or paradigms).

With the neo-liberal economic model, Latin American states have been forced to abandon their responsibilities for the welfare of all its citizens, particularly those living outside the formal economy. Millions of Latin Americans live in extreme poverty. Today, the people are led to accommodate their lives to the demands of the market and are dominated by the philosophy of consumerism that creates artificial needs and deep frustration for those who cannot keep up with it. The vast majority of the world's population tends to be sacrificed to the god of the market. Free market globalization is based on a tragic contradiction: natural and economic resources are not globalized but are under the monopoly of mainstream economics that extracts them from our countries and then sells them at high prices.

The phenomenon of globalization with its universal approach impacts cultures of all peoples in two ways. While the West goes post-modern, secular culture goes global and also causes worldwide changes. The more the dominant cultures grow, the more traditional and alternative cultures extend worldwide.

---

[18] According to Hegel, the movement of the Enlightenment as autonomy of reason of any imposition from outside begins with Kant and ends with the crisis of Christianity's logical positivism. The Enlightenment and autonomy of the whole man, for alienating structures, began with Marx and led to the theory of the Frankfurt School in Germany. See Amady Aly Dieng, *G.F. Hegel, Leçons sur Philosophie de la historie* (Paris: Série de Monographies, 1967), 336-37.

[19] Guillermo Cook, 'La misión de la iglesia en el siglo 21', *BuenasTareas* (February 2011): www.buenastareas.com/ensayos/La-Mision-De-La-Iglesia-En/1498191.html (accessed 2nd March 2011).

In addition, new religious movements grow, using electronic media to network and propagate beliefs. This complex reality presents a unique challenge for the church in Latin America. New technology facilitates communication, which is strategically used by Neo-Pentecostals. In this context, the mission practices of Neo-Pentecostals are perhaps the clearest reflection of this global reaction as a religious response to the new global and post-modern culture.[20] In that context, I consider the following four 'micro trends' to be fundamental in the Neo-Pentecostal mission, which also shows the new paradigms observed at Neo-Pentecostal congregations in the region.

Restoration of the Fivefold Ministries, Especially of Apostles and Prophets

It is a fact that not all Neo-Pentecostals embrace the apostolic and prophetic movement. Recently, some Neo-Pentecostal circles have embraced this doctrine and a new order of ministry. It has been assumed that these ministries are highly specialized in the fields of spirituality and contemporary ministry. The leaders who excel as apostles and prophets are typically seen or revered as 'God's generals'.[21] These generals have become powerful agents specialized in spiritual warfare in a newly engaged holy war. They teach that the world and the church are in permanent spiritual warfare against the forces of evil. They also see this war as an opportunity to further God's mission in the world. The spiritual victory won by the churches is understood as a precondition for mission to be accomplished. In other words, without spiritual warfare, there is no battle to win or to lose.

Neo-Pentecostals understand the mission of the church strictly in 'apostolic' terms. The apostolicity of the church is the very essence of the Kingdom of God. Being an apostle is to be a messenger, an apostle to the nations to extend the Kingdom of God. This naturally implies missionary work, planting cell churches and, with it, the establishment of governments over cities or nations.

Neo-Pentecostals associate the establishment or implementation of the Kingdom of God with global mission. Considering itself as the last Christian reform, the Neo-Pentecostal movement assumes its function basically as the extension of the Kingdom of God on earth. The church is only an agent of the kingdom and, if necessary, it must build enterprises to support its transformational mission. The Kingdom of God is manifested 'here and now'; it has arrived and has been established by Jesus Christ who has commissioned his apostles to govern it.

---

[20] Cook, 'La misión de la iglesia en el siglo 21', 2. See also José Luis Rocha, 'Sincretismo en la Centroamérica Neoliberal: Los Neo-Pentecostales absorben y difunden la cultura gerencial y el pensamiento positivo', in Luis R. Huezo Mixco (ed), *De las Misiones de Fe al Neopentecostalismo. Génesis y evolución del Protestantismo salvadoreño desde el siglo XIX hasta el presente* (San Salvador, El Salvador: Universidad Evangélica de El Salvador, 2013), 271-338.

[21] Cf. Liardon Roberts, *Los Generales de Dios, vols I-II* (Buenos Aires: Editorial Peniel, 2005).

For Apostle Denis Arana Cárdenas, a former Baptist pastor, now a renovated Baptist, apostolic restoration is 'the final act of God'.[22] This means that Neo-Pentecostals relate eschatologically with the fulfilment of mission. According to Arana Cárdenas, God has restored the ministries of apostles and prophets. He has restored the theme of the Kingdom; God has restored the 'Tabernacle of David', which is a metaphorical way of referring to the restoration of the worship of God as a way of life. He has also restored the number of government – the vision of 'The Twelve' as the ideal number for church government and for the implementation of the fivefold ministry. Restoration has also affected the role and interpretation of the written Word, for example, the Holy Spirit could deliver a revelation that is completely new, for it is not found in the Bible. That 'new word' affects theological language and the attitude towards finances, liturgy, evangelism, and doctrine itself.[23]

The centrality of the Kingdom of God is clearly the determining factor in the theology of Neo-Pentecostalism.[24] I believe the theological stance will determine the creed and define the architecture of theology. In Neo-Pentecostal sermons, God is referred to as a sovereign or king. The Kingdom of God is regarded as the exercise of divine power and providence over men and as the historical realization of his plan of salvation. This idea of the Kingdom of God as salvation-liberation must always be taken into account because it belongs to the essential lines of the mission concept. Some Neo-Pentecostal pastors run their congregations as kings. They take their members as subjects of their kingdom.

If the Christological ecclesiology of the 'body of Christ' (*corpus Christi*) was pivotal to the articulation of recent contemporary pentecostal theology, as well as in Roman Catholicism, judging by the thematic relevance of Neo-Pentecostals, who define the apostolic theology of the future as '*regia* ecclesiology' (ecclesiology in the light of the Kingdom of God), the centre is no longer the body of Christ but the apostles who rule over it.

Neo-pentecostal ecclesiology understands the church as 'God's people' that is also an agent of the Kingdom. That does not place conversion as the final requirement to become a member of God's people, because foreigners are also accepted into the extended family of believers converted to Christ and all those that love his Name, even if they are not believers. In other words, the church is no longer the centre in the Body of Christ. The church is an instrument of the Kingdom as a means for spiritual and social transformation. Neo-Pentecostalism includes all humanity in God's Kingdom; that is because the movement wants to include itself as God's agent that seeks to influence society. In fact, many Neo-Pentecostal leaders have taken the initiative to

---

[22] See Denis Heidel Arana Cárdenas, *Restauración Apostólica: La Jugada Final* (Lima: Ministerios Comunidad Apostólica Templo Sion-CATSION, 2005), 137-46.

[23] Arana, *Restauración Apostólica*, 137-196

[24] I have described this concept extensively in my book, Bernardo Campos, *Visión de Reino: El Movimiento Apostólico-Profético en el Perú – Apreciación Fenomenológica de un Movimiento de Restauración y Reforma* (Lima: Editorial Basilea, 2009), 64-83.

'conquer cities for Christ', some in a classic fundamentalist sense, and others as true managers competing for social reforms, 'face to face' with other social movements in the political, social, cultural, economic and religious fields.

Theocracy is referred to as a system or alternative government to democracy.[25] Not because the ideal of democracy is bad in itself, but because it actually has never worked due to man's sinfulness. In Neo-Pentecostalism, there is a reinvention of the pre-monarchic Israelite theocracy. A theocracy lived in a democracy – or in spite of democracy. It is understood that the apostolic office should lead this theocracy. This is clearly a 'reconstructionist' vision, through which theocracy must be restored through the priesthood. This reconstructionist theocratic model promotes the hegemony of religion over political power but at a conservative and neo-liberal ideological level. Thus it is not surprising that apostles such as Harold Caballeros made the radical decision to leave his pastorate to devote the rest of his life to the cause of politics. Through his VIDA (Life) movement, Caballeros seeks to bring a social impact to Guatemala that will transform the country. Caballeros narrowed his 'mission' to bringing improvement to the economic, social, political and cultural situation of Guatemala. He thinks this is the proper way to lead the country to true development.[26]

Recovering the Earthly City as the Goal of Humanizing Mission

Neo-pentecostal ministers understand that they have been called to govern, 'to be the head and not the tail'. For Neo-Pentecostals, politics is not a 'mission field' among others but the very centre or core of the mission. Modern apostles and Neo-Pentecostal leaders believe they have the ministry of government. They have been called to rule the planet, and soon the world powers will be transferred to them.

They understand that the earth, not heaven, is the final destiny of man, so what they should do is to conquer the earthly city, starting with the spiritual conquest of the town. This requires financial prosperity and gradual and strategic integration into public office at the state level.

In this vision, mission is 'humanization', the completion of men and women as men and women here on earth – that is, personal and social development as the way to a complete state of salvation.

According to an apostolic vision of the body of Christ, the church becomes an 'apostolic home'. Cell growth and apostolic presbyteries are simultaneously the mechanism's organization and government. One of the forms of organization that has been effective is that of 'house churches' or homogeneous units, which over time become 'apostolic houses' under the direction of the

[25] Jaime Yupanqui, 'Reforma Apostólica', in *Manual Apostólico II. El Ministerio del Apóstol, Iglesia Ríos de Agua Viva* (Lima: VII Conferencia Internacional del Ministerio Quíntuple en Acción, 2005), 34

[26] Harold Caballeros, *El Poder Transformador del Evangelio de Jesucristo* (Guatemala: Ministerios El Shaddai, 2002), 59; also, Yupanqui, 'Reforma Apostólica', 54-63.

main apostle. The models implemented by Neo-Pentecostals vary widely. They vary from the model known as G12 (a group of twelve) to Christian Family Groups or cells of Christian growth. The use of all these models as 'communities of discipleship'. This model has succeeded in various cases. These apostles have been able to have built 'mega-churches' with such numerical growth that they have acquired political influence. Some have been used to negotiate with political leaders, thus making a significant public impact in their cities.[27]

Inner Healing, Spiritual Warfare, and Deliverance as a Means to Recruit Disciples Who Will Populate the Earthly City in Kingdom Perspective

In the Neo-Pentecostal vision, inner healing is a prerequisite for discipleship. Believers can be possessed by demons, and in fact, when they come to faith in Christ, they need to be healed first. For Neo-Pentecostals, the souls of believers should be healed. So spiritual warfare is necessary for all wickedness and any source of influence from spiritual powers, rulers and principalities be expelled from the life of believers.

Mission can be a 'conquest' of cities and nations. Spiritual warfare is the means by which the minister is able to penetrate areas of reality; otherwise, the natural way would be impossible. The mission of the church is understood as the 'conquest' of cities for God or the 'establishment' of the Kingdom of God here on earth. Spiritual warfare has two distinct levels: a war at 'ground level' that believers wage daily in their fight against spiritual bondage. At this level, people possessed by demons are delivered, and inner healing is imparted.

The 'high-level' of warfare is known in the Neo-Pentecostal jargon as 'war of altars' (i.e., the image of war between Elijah and the prophets of Baal). At this level, ministers are waged by their level of experience in the spiritual realm. 'Strategic spiritual warfare' is the application of a number of techniques designed to 'bind' satanic powers according to their hierarchy. Here four principalities are clearly distinguished: principalities (*archai*), powers (*exousiai*), governors (*dunamis*) and spiritual hosts of wickedness (*kosmokratoras*), so the success of evangelization is connected with the spiritual realm. People today hunger for the supernatural and these apostles know it, so they adorn their methods of deliverance by adding creative forms that captivate their audience.[28] A minister who does not wage war leaves much to be desired, and the veracity of his spiritual 'anointing' comes under suspicion.

It is not surprising that a doctrine of the centrality and presence of the Kingdom of God produces a different understanding of the return of the Messiah. In the said doctrine, God's great plan is that we build his kingdom

---

[27] Bernardo Campos, *¿Mega-Iglesia o Iglesia Minoritaria? Disyuntiva entre Modelos y Principios* (Lima: IPER, 2001), 2.

[28] Bernardo Campos, 'La Guerra Espiritual: Un Desafío a la Misiología', *Signos de Vida* 13 (1999), 2-5.

here and now. Humanity's final destination is not heaven but earth. Therefore, if the promised paradise is here on earth, what sense does it make to expect a fulfilment beyond this world? Christ came to establish his Kingdom, and he commissioned his apostles to make it manifest. Manifesting the Kingdom involves the experience of citizenship, ethics in the vision of the Kingdom, and political behaviour aimed at recovering this earth for the people of God. If that includes making strategic political alliances, then it's right on cue. But where possible, believers are the ones who must take the initiative and must occupy key positions in society. From the perspective of God's Kingdom, entrepreneurs and other professionals should be called and sent to lead social change.[29] It is all about a civilizing mission whose ultimate object is to restore creation to itself but with human effort.

Economic Prosperity, a Sign, and Foretaste of the Kingdom of God

In Neo-Pentecostalism, financial management occupies an important place. On the one hand, large sums of money are used almost beyond measure to send apostles to the nations and even support them during the time of transition. The practice of tithing, offering and firstfruits is a sacred act with much spiritual significance. [30] There is even the custom of tithing personally and hand-delivering offerings to the main apostle, who is responsible for administering and using it for the unique, exclusive and zealous use of sustaining his ministry and his leaders. Covenantal offerings (covenants) for special reasons are also practised according to the intelligent teaching of 'sowing and reaping'.

Poverty, disease, and death are generational curses that must be uprooted from the lives of believers.[31] The children of God are sons of a King who 'owns gold and silver'. Giving a generous offering is actually 'investing' in the Kingdom. God's will is that their children prosper economically. Only then can they work on the extension of his Kingdom without spiritual bondage and claim the nations of the earth for themselves, according to Psalms 2:8.

Economic prosperity is a sign and foretaste of the Kingdom of God and becomes an important element in the mission of God. Mission and finance go hand-in-hand with Neo-Pentecostalism, and they are the priority. Unlike classic Pentecostals, Neo-Pentecostals require from their faithful members large or extravagant sums of money as an act of faith and obedience. The contributors are encouraged to give with the promise of reaping thirty, sixty and one

---

[29] C. Peter Wagner, *Apóstoles en la Iglesia de Hoy* (Miami, FL: Editorial Peniel, 2004), 95-112.

[30] See Samuel Arboleda, *La iglesia: Gobierno y Finanzas* (Lima: IMPACT-PERU, 2006), 26.

[31] See Kenneth E. Hagin, *Redimido de la Pobreza, Enfermedad, y Muerte Espiritual* (Tulsa, OK: Kenneth Hagin Ministries, 1989), Paulo Arieu (ed): http://es.slideshare.net/pauloarieu1/manual-explicativo-que-es-la-teologia-de-la-prosperidad (accessed 31st March 2015).

hundredfold.[32] This is the best economic investment in the kingdom, which brings financial prosperity in return – a financial partnership with God himself.[33]

Conclusion

1. From the perspective of Neo-Pentecostal mission, the mission mandate is linked with the establishment of the Kingdom of God here on earth. This kingdom includes all earthly powers and spheres of government, human and spiritual. To soar in power and establish a theocracy (priestly government), the church must dethrone evil 'principalities' that rule over cities and nations. Christians must pray for the transference of riches from the wicked to the people of God.
2. Mission work is made possible through spiritual warfare and strong discipleship programmes usually organized in cell churches. Mission is also carried by entrepreneurs who willing to finance or invest in building the Kingdom of God.
3. Healthy Christian life is expressed through financial prosperity. The conquest of cities and nations is a sign and foretaste of the Kingdom of God, and at the same time is a public testimony to the power of God. Ultimately, the purpose of mission is to guide people into wholeness as human beings who were created to inherit the land and administer it.
4. The subject of the mission is the new people of God, raised by God as a special lineage amidst a wicked world that is inexorably lost but can be restored by the work of God's children who have been selected to govern the nations.

[32] See John Avanzini, *30, 60 Ciento por Uno* (Fort Worth, TX: His Publishing Company, 1989).

[33] Martín Ocaña, *Los Banqueros de Dios. Una aproximación evangélica a la Teología de la prosperidad* (Lima: Ediciones Puma, 2002), 43-98.

Straightway Chapel – A Charismatic Theology of Mission to Muslims in Ghana?

Andreas Heuser

Introduction

In the euphoria about the upsurge of Pentecostal-type churches in many parts of Africa, Charismatic and neo-Pentecostal alike, one feature remained rather unnoticed. In the mid-1980s the phenomenon of churches founded by former Muslims surfaced. With their fundamental criterion to convert Muslims to Christianity, these churches differ immensely in their theological design from the rest of the movement. One of the pioneering churches of converted Muslims in West Africa is Straightway Chapel, based in Ghana. Its most innovative aspects are the style, method, and strategy of evangelism that is rooted in a still experiential or implicit theology of mission.

Straightway Chapel's founder, Ahmad Aygei, was brought up in a prominent Sunni Muslim family. As a consequence of his conversion to Christianity in 1983, he was banned from his family.[1]

In a post-conversion process, he realised that churches of whatever kind completely lacked a support structure for Muslim converts. His experiences of both rejection and indifference convinced Aygei to initiate an organisational set-up to assist other converts. He experimented with several church structures before he founded Straightway Chapel, in Kumasi, in 1988.[2] It attracts converts by a system of mutual assistance to strengthen the converted Muslims' faith, and by political demands of religious freedom. The name resonates the

Originally published in Claudia Währisch-Oblau and Fidon Mwombeki (eds), *Mission Continues Global Impulses for the 21st Century*, Regnum Edinburgh Centenary Series 30 (Oxford: Regnum Books, 2010), 235-244.

[1] Cf. Ahmad Aygei, *Sharing the Love of Christ with Your Muslim Neighbour* (Kumasi: UGC Publishing House Breman, 2002), 24. His father acted as a spokesperson of the Ghana Muslim Mission that aims at an autonomous expression of Islam in Ghana independent from immigrant Hausa Muslims. On Islam in Ghana, see Nathan I. Samwini, *The Muslim Resurgence in Ghana since 1950: Its Effects upon Muslims and Muslim-Christian Relations* (Berlin: LIT Verlag, 2006).

[2] Elom Dovlo and Alfred Ofosu Asante, 'Reinterpreting the Straight Path: Ghanaian Muslim Converts in Mission to Muslims', *Exchange* 32:3 (2003), 214-38.

Surat-al-Fatiha, the first Sura (1:6-7) that is recited in the five Muslim daily prayers:

> Guide us in the straight path, the path of those whom you have blessed, not those against whom there is displeasure, not those who go astray.

Aygei reinterprets the Qur'anic meaning to identify Jesus Christ as the straight path. In other words, he presents a reading of the Qur'an that points to Christianity as the revealed true religion; he offers a Qur'anic hermeneutics of conversion to Christianity.

Conversion Experience

Aygei's vintage point is his conversion experience. He describes it as an individual process of rational choice and theological reasoning.[3] According to Aygei, his conversion resulted from a critical reading of the Qur'an. Quoting two passages in the Qur'an (Sura 3:55 and Sura 57:27), he concludes that the authority of Jesus Christ and his followers had not ended and were not superseded by a Muslim era. A comparative reading of the holy scriptures, both the Qur'an and the Bible, substantiated his findings. He discovered an inner Qur'anic logic to point to Christianity as the chosen path to God.[4] Aygei leaves the impression of relying on the Word alone as the cornerstone of his conversion.

However, a next stage in the distancing process from Islam is characterised by non-scriptural bodily experiences. His textual analysis was repeatedly backed by visions and auditions of prophets that urged him to convert. In a state of confusion, he resorted to a period of fasting and prayer. When visions reoccurred, he suffered from severe physical trouble. Finally, he accepted Christianity and had to leave his father's house with a curse.[5]

Aygei's conversion narrative contains two sets of arguments. One points to discursive elements, i.e. scriptural analysis, systematic comparison, and rational reasoning. The other circumscribes a complex of non-discursive arguments such as visions, auditions and physical emotions. Embodied experiences are seen in African worldview in general as revelations from the spiritual world. They reveal a manifest reality of invisible powers that cannot be manipulated. As in Aygei's case, visions and dreams can be an avenue for religious conversion.[6] In Aygei's theology of mission, however, the rational set of

---

[3] Contrarily Hollenweger found that in Africa 'people usually become converted either because of a healing (...), because of a dream or vision, or because they have a friend who is Christian. We have found not one single instance where somebody was saved on the basis of arguments (...)'. Walter J. Hollenweger, *Pentecostalism: Origins and Developments Worldwide* (Peabody: Hendrickson Publishers 1997), 255.

[4] Cf. Aygei, *Sharing the Love of Christ*, 21-25, and Ahmad Aygei, *Ishmael Shall Be Blessed* (Kumasi: UGC Publishing House Breman, 2002), 109-110.

[5] Cf. Aygei, *Sharing the Love of Christ*, 21-26.

[6] Following Humphrey Fisher, dreams are a point of contact between African world-views and Islam: 'the very dream ... may be an avenue for the acceptance of new

arguments is over-represented. This contradicts sharply with the ordinary range of Charismatic and neo-Pentecostal theologies in Ghana. Here, essentially non-discursive arguments are used to articulate theology, so that visions or dream images, or bodily reactions describe identity as born-again Christians. Furthermore, churches cope with such bodily experiences by initiating ritual innovations. And finally, the ritual frame serves to effect a 'complete break with the past'.[7] Compared with the surrounding Charismatic and Pentecostal discourse, Aygei marginalises the status of bodily phenomena. Although his conversion process entails elements of vision, dream, and of curse, they do not play a major role to unfold neither his theology nor his ministry. He basically presents a hermeneutics of inter-religious encounter, and he does not urge for a radical break with the past.

Inter-Religious Hermeneutics

An important fragment in Aygei's conversion narrative relates to the question, who interprets the Holy Scripture(s) correctly? Thus, he favours an explicit hermeneutical approach in the context of Christian-Muslim relations. This is, once more, strikingly different compared to other African Pentecostal-type churches. Here you find ritual strategies of the denial of Islam, often seen as a power-encounter situation, in which the 'powers of darkness' are expelled in the name of Jesus.[8] Aygei's interpretation of Islam is more dialectical in nature.

As mentioned, Aygei's conversion process was supported by scriptural evidence and comparative analysis, for an intense reading of the Qur'an accompanied his Bible studies. By insisting on an in-depth study of the Qur'an, he respects Islamic claims to possess the final revelation, believed to be preserved in the Qur'an. Consequently, a thorough understanding of the Qur'an and Islamic theology became a presupposition in Aygei's theological quest. Instead of ritual practices, Aygei initiated several theological training programmes as identity markers of his church. The curricula introduce the logic of theological arguments as well as inter-religious comparison.[9]

The comparative approach advocates a careful study of the Qur'an and sensitizes believers for the interrelatedness of both religions. However, it leaves space for dissonance. Aygei inverses the Islamic exegesis, according to which Christianity is an incomplete earlier phase in the chronicle of salvation history

---

ideas or objects, or even of religious beliefs, being thus in itself a channel of conversion'. Quoted in Peter B. Clarke, *West Africa and Islam: A Study of Religious Developments from the 8th to the 20th Century* (London: Edward Arnold, 1984), 260.

[7] See Birgit Meyer, '"Make a Complete Break with the Past": Memory and Postcolonial Modernity in Ghanaian Pentecostal Discourse', in Richard Werbner (ed), *Memory and the Postcolony: African Anthropology and the Critique of Power* (London: Zed Books, 1998), 182-208.

[8] Cf. Emmanuel Kingsley Larbi, *Pentecostalism: The Eddies of Ghanaian Christianity* (Accra: Blessed Publications, 2001), 388-98.

[9] Theological training is provided in weekly workshops that treat foundations and doctrines of Christianity, and comment the Qur'an from a biblical viewpoint.

that ends with Islam. While examining the revelatory content of the Qur'an, he insists that the scriptural evidence unmistakably points to the Messiahship of Jesus. Considering the Sonship of Jesus Christ, and reflecting the status of prophets, he refutes Islamic assertions that the Qur'an contains the genuine and correct meaning of the Bible. For him, the Qur'an 'aims at abrogating the Bible'.[10] From a discussion of the Qur'anic titles of Jesus, Aygei draws heavy-weight conclusions. Instead of Muhammad who bears the title of a 'Messenger of Allah', it is Jesus, the 'Spirit of Allah' who needs to be considered as the greatest of all prophets. In Aygei's mind, this title of Jesus is even proof of his divine nature:

> As 'His Spirit', he is brought very close to the very being of Allah. Do we not recognise that by identifying Jesus so closely with Himself, Allah is revealing the deity of Jesus Christ, which Muslims vehemently object to?[11]

Aygei's inter-religious hermeneutics uses the methods of exegesis and scriptural comparison. His debate of diverse modes of theological interpretation is controversial as it challenges the Islamic language of faith in its most sensitive layers.

Moralistic Anti-Memory

Aygei stretches this method of comparison to a re-reading of Islamic history. He raises questions of doubt about the life of the prophet Muhammad and his era. In his re-reading of Islamic history, Aygei applies a moral discourse as a tool to discern 'true' prophets from questionable claimants of truth. The recurrent argument in his repertoire to judge the beginnings of the Islamic era is Muhammad's marriage policy. 'He surrendered himself to the cares and discord of polygamy, and the unity of his family was broken, never again to be restored'.[12] The description of the beginnings of Islamic history follows a path of moral failure. The prophet could only settle a series of family disputes caused by his polygamous way of life, according to Aygei, by his imagination of revelatory conflict solving. Thus, Aygei withdraws the prophetic claim from Muhammad to having received divine revelations. Commenting on the marriage intentions of the Prophet, Aygei states, that 'nothing short of a divine revelation could settle the matter'. The Qur'anic verses 'produced' by 'the Prophet (in the name of Allah and His Apostle)' served 'to sanction his heart's desire'.[13] Quite obviously, Aygei aims at the dethroning of the founding prophet by interpreting his personality in terms that derive from present-day Pentecostal-type catalogues of moral behaviour. The moralising re-reading of

---

[10] Aygei, *Ishmael Shall Be Blessed*, 29.
[11] Aygei, *Ishmael Shall Be Blessed*, 111.
[12] Aygei, *Sharing the Love of Christ*, 64.
[13] Aygei, *Sharing the Love of Christ*, 67.

Muhammad's era is biassed in its strong emphasis on sexual ethics and the nuclear family as a God-given institution.[14]

The moralising politics of memory does not only serve to de-construct early Islamic history. The act of reading aims at establishing the difference. Yet, African Pentecostal-type Christianity usually conceptualises difference by means of ritual cleansing and protection. Bodily reactions are seen as part of the permanent spiritual fight between God and Satan. Because the forces of 'evil', emanating from the spiritual world of African religions, are believed to intrude in the life of the saved ones, African Pentecostal-type discourse applies the key category of a 'rupture with the past' in order to distance the new belief from the former other. The notion of rupture enables converts to draw a line between 'them' and 'us', between 'then' and 'now'. This discourse of 'othering' does not rely on rational arguments but on a ritual praxis, oriented towards the individual. One popular ritual to break bonds with the Satanic is 'deliverance', in which the powers of darkness manifest themselves to be exorcised by specially gifted members of a congregation.[15]

Such ritual means to control the influence of demonic bondage are significantly missing in the congregational life of Straightway Chapel. In the liturgical and theological context of Straightway Chapel, the progress in Christian lifestyle also demands a critique of one's past. But the type and the practice of memorialising differ from the mainline African Pentecostal ways. Rather than defining a dualism, Aygei favours a dialectical approach of appropriation and rejection of his Muslim past. And instead of a ritually manifest break with the past, he opts for practice of remembrance by reading the revealed scriptures.

In conclusion, African Pentecostal-type churches perform ritual acts of individual deliverance from demonic bonds primarily identified with the African religious heritage. Straightway Chapel, with a membership of converted Muslims, chooses a different memory praxis. It arranges a collective anti-memory against the mainstream interpretation of the Qur'an and the life of the Prophet Muhammad, canonised in Islamic scriptural memory. The divine revelation in a holy book finds an adequate response in a new community of the 'text'. In other words, in a setting of Muslim converts, textual coherence, infused with moral standards of Pentecostal identity, replaces ritual coherence.[16]

---

[14] Neo-Pentecostal literature sees the family as a daily warzone against demonic powers. Cf. Leonhard Soku, *The Spiritual Warfare in the Warzone* (Accra: Tonia Press, 2003), 37-38.

[15] Allan Anderson, 'Exorcism and Conversion to African Pentecostalism', *Exchange* 35:1 (2006), 116-33.

[16] The shift from ritual to textual coherence has been interpreted as a paradigmatic step in the history of religions, cf. Jan Assmann, *Religion und kulturelles Gedächtnis* (Beck: München, 2000), 148-52.

Theology of Suffering

A similar change in the use of key notions in Pentecostal-type churches takes place in connection with the meaning of curses. In the spiritual mindset of many Pentecostal believers, afflictions caused by curses play a prominent part. Curses are directly addressed towards an individual, but they have a basic social significance. In many instances, individual problems are attributed to influences from existing social relations. Especially family circles are considered potentially dangerous for keeping a born-again lifestyle.[17] Pentecostal-type churches promise solutions to the difficulties caused by curses, and again offer deliverance services. Here, social networks are scrutinised and individuals are asked to separate from them. Thus, born-again consciousness presents an image to be in control of such destinies, propagating an independent individual who deliberately chooses to loosen ties with the past. In contrast, in Aygei's case, being cursed meant the expulsion from his family, and his break with the past was a forced one. His conversion narrative does not mention any ritual support to disengage from social relationships. Instead, he copes with the curse resting on him by a theology of suffering.

For Aygei, being rejected by his family points at an essential dimension in his belief. Circumscribing the consequences of his conversion, he generalises that 'Christian faith is about suffering'.[18] Aygei unfolds his theology of suffering by distinguishing between trials and temptations. He defines temptations as 'strategies and plans designed and purported by Satan to cause us to sin and thus separate us from God'. Trials, on the other hand, 'help us to know God better' and 'to become stronger in our faith'.[19] Aygei equates the curse of his father with the destiny of the Christian martyrs, and all Muslim converts may face such trials. On an existential level, his theology of suffering implies self-control and discipline to endure in the new faith. In his view, his biography as a Muslim turned into a successful church leader, encouraged other Muslims to convert 'because they were no longer afraid of the power of curses in their lives'. Aygei comments:

> I was being maltreated, but now I can testify that the training I had has made me a better person. God was disciplining me as the son He loves.... A positive attitude towards trials and suffering is the key to the triumphant Christian life.[20]

By insisting on the reality of suffering, Aygei complains about converts who downplay the seriousness of trials to look for easy solutions. He advises churches to:

> ...stop pampering new converts. The most common mistake in the Christian circles is that we shower gifts, money, etc. on this new convert. Before long, they

---

[17] African theology classifies curses in detail, cf. Kwaku Dua-Agyeman, *Deliverance from Ungodly Soul-Ties* (Accra: UGC Publishing House, 2001).
[18] Personal communication, 30 January 2006.
[19] Aygei, *Sharing the Love of Christ*, 27.
[20] Aygei, *Sharing the Love of Christ*, 26, 34.

become greedy. That is why many of them go from church to church sharing their testimonies with the intention of being paid for.[21]

With this intervention, Aygei contrasts the politics of conversion in other churches.[22] He disengages from a distinctive form of the Pentecostal-type theology of prosperity that focusses on the material side of celebrating a born-again identity. The prosperity gospel combines material expectations to improve one's personal situation here and now with a spiritual emphasis on individual salvation in the hereafter.[23] Whereas many people are motivated to join Pentecostal-type churches by such promises, Aygei disqualifies those conversion motives. His theology of suffering is far from an enthusiastic approach in mission to Muslims. He rather advocates a self-reflective approach.

Self-Reflexion

According to Emmanuel Larbi, African Pentecostal-type Christianity considers people of the Muslim faith as mere objects of evangelisation:

> The Pentecostals do not see any common ground between themselves and non-Christian religious groups such as Muslims or the priests of the primal religion. The only expectation of the Pentecostals of such groups is that of outright conversion to Christianity.[24]

The imagery invoked is of a complex spiritual battleground. In this picture, Islam is painted as a pillar in the realm of Satan. Remarkably enough, Aygei's writings on Islam dispense with such antagonistic rhetoric. Despite his moralist interpretation of early Islamic history, he portrays Islamic theology in an almost neutral or descriptive style. He clearly aims at facilitating Christian-Muslim encounters in the proximity of daily life. Aygei wants 'to encourage Christians to share the love of God with their Muslim neighbour'.[25]

Aygei's theology of suffering prohibits a triumphant style of the encounter between Christians and Muslims. Outlining the contemporary global religious landscape in terms of a 'Muslim-Christian polarisation', he advocates a self-reflexive attitude. Aygei laments the stance of repulsion toward Islam. The vocabulary chosen to describe the current state of affairs is drastic. It ranges from religious 'prejudice' to a common 'stereotype mentality', all rooted in 'ignorance' of the Muslim world. Aygei criticises the polemics to expose Islam as 'fallacious and an orchestrated lie by the Evil One'. He ends his ideological criticism of Christian misinterpretations of Islam:

---

[21] Aygei, *Sharing the Love of Christ*, 33.

[22] Incorrectly addressing Aygei, John Azumah accuses him of 'parading' Muslim converts to give 'testimonies' about their conversion, 'most of it involve exaggerations and blatant distortions'. John Azumah, 'Interfaith Relations in Ghana: Faith and Citizenship' (http://nifcon.anglicancommunion.org), accessed 10 January 2008.

[23] Cf. Paul Gifford, *Ghana's New Christianity. Pentecostalism in a Globalizing African Economy* (Bloomington/Indianapolis: Indiana University Press, 2004), 90-101.

[24] Larbi, *Pentecostalism*, 435.

[25] Aygei, *Sharing the Love of Christ*, 1.

> What is even more disturbing is the fact that many Christians have fallen victim of this lie and have become partakers in deepening the gulf between the Christian and the Muslim worlds.[26]

Aygei is well aware of one's own bias in the perception of the religious other. The self-reflexive starting point of his approach uncovers projections on the other that are vital specifically within his own Christian tradition. What is important here, is the change of perspective in comparison with current opinions on Islam in African Pentecostal-type Christianity. He does not locate Islam as an entity in the realm of Satan, but identifies the prevailing Christian ignorance on Islam as an element in the Satanic strategy in contemporary society. The missionary answer he opts for is based on interpersonal relationships. Starting from the level of neighbourhood networks, Aygei seeks to bridge those two worlds.

Discourse of Difference

Aygei's request for inter-religious dialogue is incomplete without a defined agenda of his own. The people of the Muslim faith are his target group. Though, even with this zeal in mind, Aygei abstains from objectifying Muslim believers. His esteem for Islam, as claiming divine revelation, is too high. Since his early life, he was convinced that both Islam and Christianity were just similar paths leading to God: 'When I was in Islam, I thought that both Christians and Muslims served the same God, but with differences in approach'.[27] This statement resonates with the basic convictions of a pluralist theology of religion, essential in order to accept the sovereignty of God. But with his conversion, Aygei accentuates differences between the religions. He now dismisses the pluralist categories in inter-religious dialogue, for they declare any evangelising practice obsolete. He states that some Christians:

> …are afraid to cause offence because our modern world teaches that everyone has the right to his own belief and that there are different ways to worship the same God. All these are further lies from Satan to keep Muslims from hearing the truth of the gospel.[28]

Aygei insists on the difference in the understanding of God in Christianity and Islam. The 'straight path' is reserved for the biblical revelation, from where the evangelising motive follows. However, Aygei does not remain with dogmatic orthodoxy. He seeks to engage individual Christians and churches in public debates on religious difference. Claiming difference must be proven in transparent theological discourses. An imperative debate about God belongs to Aygei's concept of mission. The discourse about God is a systematic part in his interpretation of the Great Commission 'to reach all people with the gospel'. This command is sacrosanct for Aygei. It is an incontestable element in

---

[26] Aygei, *Sharing the Love of Christ*, 2-3.
[27] Aygei, *Sharing the Love of Christ*, 21.
[28] Aygei, *Sharing the Love of Christ*, 19.

Christian identity and an axiomatic principle in any Christian initiative of an inter-religious nature. As a consequence, it affects the Christian-Muslim dialogue directly. 'Muslims should, therefore, welcome Christians for peaceful religious discussion'. But also from a Muslim viewpoint, Aygei reckons, there is an incentive for a dialogue with Christians, who are identified by Aygei as the people of the Book. Quoting Sura 10:94, he asserts that Muslims should 'seek clarification from the people of the Book when any doubt arises in the course of reading the Qur'an'.[29]

To sum up, Aygei argues in two directions. Based on the Qur'anic advice, Aygei diagnoses an inner need on the Muslim side to enter into a dialogue with Christians. Moreover, Aygei struggles to harmonise mission and dialogue. He tries to show that the Christian missionary impulse and the insistence on an inter-religious dialogue based on difference can converge.

Concluding Remarks

Aygei's theology of mission in the context of a Christian-Muslim neighbourhood is exceptional for African Pentecostal-type churches. He unfolds a hermeneutic circle according to which the reading of the Qur'an points at the biblical revelation of God. His method of comparison and scriptural interpretation has, in the worst case, a potential to create inter-religious tension.[30] Too drastic appear his inversions of Islamic traditions of knowledge, i.e., his perception of the Qur'an that disarms salient features of Islamic exegesis, or his pleading for a re-orientation of Muslim spiritual life. Nonetheless, Aygei insists on the right to articulate theological difference which is his precondition for any responsible Christian-Muslim dialogue.

His position ranges between two poles of conceptualising Christian-Muslim encounters in Africa.[31] One pole instrumentalises inter-religious dialogue for evangelism. In this respect, a key strategy is to postulate religious difference and to define Muslims as a mere target group of evangelism. Any inter-religious contact is legitimised by the ultimate end of converting Muslims as fast as possible. The method applied is confrontational and the time frame makes neighbourhood relations unnecessary. This objectifying understanding of inter-religious dialogue is well articulated within Pentecostal-type African Christianity. Aygei, however, withdraws from this church heritage. For him, inter-religious dialogue contains a self-critique of stereotypes on the religious other. He seeks to explore the self-understanding of the partner in dialogue and to dismantle prejudices about their counterparts by way of self-reflection. The other pole of Christian-Muslim dialogue in Africa makes use of a romanticising stereotype of Islam. This is an effort to clear the atmosphere of a long-standing

---

[29] Aygei, *Ishmael Shall Be Blessed*, 105-106.

[30] Clashes occurred in the mid-1990s in Kumasi, when Straightway Chapel operated 'crusades' in sections with a dominant Muslim population.

[31] Lamin Sanneh, *Piety and Power: Muslims and Christians in West Africa* (Maryknoll, NY: Orbis, 1996), 80.

antagonism between the cross and the crescent. The vision is to shift the agenda towards a policy of mutual understanding. Aygei is far from any romanticising promotion of Islam. He imagines a scenario of inter-religious communication that balances competing claims of truth. It is at the same time dialogical and self-critical in nature. In a pose of unveiling deficiencies in his own religious tradition, Aygei urges for a direct and sometimes confrontational exchange of primarily theological arguments.

A Pentecostal Perspective on the Lausanne Movement

Opoku Onyinah

Introduction

The Lausanne Movement operates under a memorable mission statement: 'The Whole Church Taking the Whole Gospel to the Whole World'. Since its initial meeting in 1974, the movement has convened large and small gatherings on a wide range of issues – all related to its mission statement regarding world evangelization.[1]

The first Congress convened by Billy Graham was held in Lausanne, and approximately 2,700 Christian leaders from over 150 countries gathered for the ten-day programme. It produced the *Lausanne Covenant*, one of the most profound and influential writings in recent church history. The *Lausanne Covenant* affirmed the necessity of reaching the world with the Gospel, the uniqueness of Christ, the authority of the Bible, the importance of social action, the value of cultural sensitivity, the richness of co-operation, and sorrow for having failed to complete the task of world evangelization. That Congress also produced an immediate impact. Ralph Winter transformed mission strategy by emphasising the need to reach every people group within all the nations of the world. He helped us understand that having a church in a nation did not mean we had reached that nation. What about all the other ethnic groups within that country that spoke other languages and lived quite a distance from that church? To reach them would require intentional cross-cultural efforts that targeted those who had never heard the Gospel. This emphasis on 'unreached people groups' became the new frontier in missions.

Faithful to this clarion call, the Lausanne Movement has organised numerous regional and global conferences since 1974 to constantly urge the church to hasten the task of world evangelization. Prominent among them were the Second Lausanne Congress, convened in Manila, in 1989, and the third Lausanne Congress in Cape Town, South Africa, in 2010. The Manila Congress

---

Originally published in L. Dahle, M.S. Dahle, and K. Jørgensen (eds), *The Lausanne Movement: A Range of Perspectives*, Regnum Edinburgh Centenary Series 22 (Oxford: Regnum Books, 2014), 419-425.

[1] 'Lausanne Gatherings' (www.lausanne.org/en/gatherings), accessed 25th Aug 2012.

focused on the progress, resources, and methods of evangelising the world. It produced the *Manila Manifesto*, which is an elaboration of the *Lausanne Covenant*.[2] Significant in the Manila Congress and its manifesto was the work of the Christian mission strategist Luis Bush, who first highlighted the need for a major focus of evangelism in the 'Resistant Belt', covering the middle of the eastern hemisphere: the 10/40 window.[3]

The third Congress produced the *Cape Town Commitment* (*CTC*), which sought to build upon the previous documents. The *CTC* strongly advocates that 'we must respond in Christian mission to the realities of our own generation'.[4]

In all three Congresses – Lausanne, Manila, and Cape Town – some attention was given to one of the most notable movements within the worldwide church in the last century: the rise of Pentecostalism.[5] The empowering of the Holy Spirit was reflected in all three global Lausanne Congresses and in each of the publications, although less in 1974, a bit more in 1989, and fully in 2010. The Pentecostal perspective is critical in any major global discourse on Christianity. It is from this viewpoint that I examine the third Lausanne Congress on World Evangelization (Cape Town 2010).

Representation and Participation

The third Lausanne Congress on World Evangelization brought together 4,200 evangelical leaders from 198 countries, and thousands more participated online. Cape Town 2010 is considered one of the most diverse gatherings of Christians in history.[6] Participants reflected the worldwide church in its global, ethnic, denominational,[7] age and gender diversity. This broad representation signalled an 'all-hands-on-deck' approach to reaching a lost world. It was also a way of de-emphasising denominational individualism and strengthening co-operation,

---

[2] R.A. Hunt, 'The History of the Lausanne Movement, 1974-2010', *International Bulletin of Missionary Research* 35:2 (April 2011), 81-85.

[3] 'Second International Congress on World Evangelization' (http://en.wikipedia.org/wiki/Second_International_Congress_on_World_Evangelization). This article states, 'Further research in the mid-1990s led to the "10/40 Window" concept, which contrasts the major needs and few resources devoted to this part of the world'.

[4] The Third Lausanne Congress, *Cape Town Commitment* (www.lausanne.org/en/documents/ctcommitment.html, 2011), 8.

[5] W. Hollenweger, *Pentecostalism: Origins and Developments Worldwide* (Peabody, MA: Hendrickson, 1997), 6-17; E.K. Larbi, *Pentecostalism: The Eddies of Ghanaian Christianity* (Accra: SAPC, 2001), 1-11; A. Paul, *Signs and Wonders: Why Pentecostalism Is the World's Fastest Growing Faith* (San Francisco, CA: Jossey-Bass, 2009), 4-17.

[6] John W. Kennedy, 'The Most Diverse Gathering Ever', *Christianity Today* (Sept 29th 2010). Available at: www.christianitytoday.com/ct/2010/september/ 34.66.html

[7] However, the Catholics, who are about 1.2 billion, and the Orthodox were not there. It was possible that other churches affiliated with the World Council of Churches were also not there.

as the Lausanne Movement has always sought to do. The diversity also re-echoed the need to focus on what binds Christians together as we renew all efforts to complete the Great Commission.

Pentecostals were broadly represented among the participants, but unlike the Lausanne II Congress in Manila where Pentecostals fully contributed in the Congress, in Cape Town the Pentecostal voice was lacking on the podium. Commenting about the Manila Congress, Peter Wagner wrote:

> In dramatic contrast to Lausanne I, held in Switzerland in 1974, Lausanne II embraced leaders of the Pentecostal/charismatic movements at all levels from the Lausanne Committee itself through the plenary sessions and workshops to the thousands of participants who regularly worshiped with raised hands. Remarkably, the three most attended workshop tracks (of 48 offered) were on the Holy Spirit, spiritual warfare and prayer. Speakers such as Paul Yonggi Cho, Jack Hayford, Omar Cabrera, Dick Eastman, William Kumuyi and many others like them reflected the lowering of the barriers between evangelicals and Charismatics over the 15 years between the two congresses.[8]

It was thought the trend in Manila would continue, but that was not so in Cape Town. The issue of Spiritual Warfare, for example, which was prominent in the late twentieth century, could have been discussed to find out the progress so far.[9] Pentecostals strongly believe in the imminent coming of Christ and thus embark on aggressive evangelism. Since Pentecostals and Charismatics are perhaps the driving force in mission today, they should have been featured in a plenary session. It is hoped that in future Congress this 'Christian traditional' balance will be considered. The worldwide church needs to learn from each tradition's experiences. In addition, a strong challenge from a Pentecostal for the infilling of the Holy Spirit would have been appropriate at such a strategic gathering.

Cape Town 2010 was on African soil, and Africa is home to some of the emerging largest churches in the world, such as the Church of Pentecost with its headquarters in Ghana, and the Redeemed Christian Church of God headed by Bishop E.A. Adeboye, which has become a city of its own in Nigeria. Though Africa was featured geographically, it was not featured theologically, and some participants were disappointed that none of the African 'mega-voices' had the opportunity to speak. It was felt that the Congress organisers distanced themselves from these ministries, most of which are Pentecostal/Charismatic and are major agents of worldwide Christian transformation.

---

[8] Cited at www.seekgod.ca/darkangels.htm. Accessed Oct 11th 2012.

[9] See for examples, Opoku Onyinah, *Pentecostal Exorcism: Witchcraft and Exorcism in Ghana* (Blandford: Deo Publishers, 2012); and Opoku Onyinah, *Spiritual Warfare* (Cleveland, TN: CPT, 2012).

Opening Celebration

The opening celebration at Cape Town 2010 was colourful, historical and educative. A two-part video presentation entitled 'Turning Points in Church History: From Pentecost to Edinburgh' traced the growth of the church in the face of many obstacles. In addition to the video, dramatic presentations highlighted the expansion of Christianity in China, Latin America, and Africa.

As a result of the impact of the Pentecostal renewal on Christianity since the beginning of the twentieth century, Pentecostals expected the Azusa Street revival that led to the worldwide Pentecostal movement to have been highlighted in such presentations. Instead, it was conspicuously absent. Neither was there any mention of the charismatic renewal in the last century. The video documentary of the history of the Christian church and its development over time stopped at the year 1900. As a result, nothing at all was said about the impact of Pentecostalism in the last 100 years. The impression was that Pentecostalism was being marginalised, and that we had been invited as observers and not participants. Although that was disappointing, everyone could appreciate the central message of the opening ceremony: that from its small beginnings, the church has grown to encompass the world.

The Role of the Holy Spirit in Christian Living and Global Missions

Pentecostalism places much emphasis on the work of the third person of the Godhead, the Holy Spirit, and we believe strongly in a direct personal experience of God through the baptism of the Holy Spirit. One of our central messages is that the Holy Spirit enables believers to live the Christian life and to effectively perform the tasks assigned to each believer. The Spirit gives the supernatural ability to Christians to witness, preach, cast out evil spirits, heal the sick, and defend themselves against unseen evil forces. Likewise, the Spirit is seen as the motivating force behind all Christian mission activities.[10]

The Cape Town 2010 Congress was celebrated as a gathering to re-energise worldwide Christian leaders to complete the evangelization of the entire world. Pentecostals wish there had been a greater emphasis on the necessity of the empowerment of the Holy Spirit in accomplishing this great task.

The Gospel is about Jesus Christ

Pentecostals believe in the preaching of the Lord Jesus as the Saviour, the Baptizer of the Spirit, the Healer, and the soon-coming King. Though we extend emergency humanitarian assistance and social welfare to needy people, we do not believe these should be the central focus of ministry. Pentecostals maintain that the preaching of the Gospel must undergird all social action, such

---

[10] A. Pomerville, *Introduction to Missions: An Independent-Study Textbook* (Irving: ICI University Press, 1987), 100. Cf. W. Hollenweger, *The Pentecostals: The Charismatic Movement in the Churches* (Minneapolis, MN: Augsburg, 1972), 7-21.

as establishing schools, healthcare, recreation, involvement in politics and commerce.[11] In other words, Pentecostals hold that confronting the needs of society demonstrates the reality of the Gospel but does not replace the necessity for its preaching.

Cape Town 2010 prioritised the preaching of the Gospel in the same manner, though there was a certain level of tension about this. Some participants felt the emphasis on social problems was too great. Dr John Piper tried to address this in his exposition of Ephesians 3 when he said that 'for Christ's sake, we Christians care about all suffering, especially eternal suffering'. He said very poignantly that if we are not concerned about the world's suffering, we have a defective heart; if we are not concerned about people's eternal suffering, we have a defective view of hell.

No doubt, presentation after presentation brought us face-to-face with many of the world's problems, such as relativism and pluralism, yet the Gospel which is the power of God was consistently presented as the answer. The Congress affirmed belief in absolute truth, and particularly in Jesus Christ as the Truth. Christians, therefore, were called to live and proclaim the truth in the workplace, in the media, in government, and in academia. Cape Town 2010 encouraged Christians to respond to *post-modern* relativism and pluralism with sound and healthy apologetics. In this regard, Cape Town 2010 was in focus, pointing the church to the commission of its Master, Jesus Christ.

Unreached and Unengaged Groups

The concept of 'unreached people groups' is one of Lausanne's greatest legacies. However, it was a surprise that it was not given enough attention in the plenary sessions. Only Paul Eshleman spoke directly on this topic and provided participants with lists of the unreached people groups in their respective countries. This subject had deserved more attention.

Nevertheless, academic work, literature and video clips on unreached areas were helpful. Thus the Congress helped set participants on course. This focus is vital, because co-ordination, co-operation, and progress of mission activities remain slow in unreached areas. Much work remains to be done in Central and North Africa, Central America, Asia, the Middle East, and the Arabian Peninsula.

Ironically, the label 'unreached' may soon include portions of the west, which is another evangelistic concern that deserved more attention. This area needs renewed ecumenical attention because the west still has a powerful voice in the directing of world Christianity.

From a Pentecostal perspective, the decline of Christianity in the west and the challenge of the unreached areas are important issues that should constantly inform our prayers. We praise God for every strategy that is being marshalled

---

[11] Grant McClung, 'Beyond Basic Evangelism: Pentecostals and a Broadened Lausanne Evangelistic Agenda', Part Two, June/July 2010, Available at: www.lausanneworldpulse.com/perspectives.php.../06-2010?p. Accessed Oct 18th, 2012.

to stem the tide of secularism in the west and to shine God's light among the unreached. However, prayer is one of our most powerful weapons, and little attention or teaching was heard on this great subject and its importance in carrying out the Great Commission. A concerted time to pray for the unreached would have been welcome.

Worship

Generally, the worship before the main services was warming, but the Pentecostal bones cried out for some prayers within the plenary sessions to address the challenges that were brought to our attention day by day (even hour by hour). We heard much talk about living the Christian life. Perhaps what was lacking was a fervent prayer to energise our ability to live the talk.

The *Cape Town Commitment*

The central aim of Lausanne III was to 'bring a fresh challenge to the global Church to bear witness to Jesus Christ and all his teachings in every nation, in every sphere of society, and in the realm of ideas'.[12] The *Cape Town Commitment* is an enduring expression of those goals.

The *Commitment* is in two parts. Part I establishes the boundaries of the evangelical faith, passed down to us in the Scriptures. Here, writers tried to distinguish primary truths (upon which the church must be united), from secondary issues (upon which Christians can thoughtfully disagree). Part II is a call to action with regard to world evangelization. It is hoped that the *Commitment* will serve as the roadmap for the Lausanne Movement in the coming decade.[13]

The *Cape Town Commitment* is a remarkable document, and I was pleased to chair a recent nationwide congress in Ghana that revolved around its teachings. As a Pentecostal, I was immediately drawn to the section in Part I, 'We Love God the Holy Spirit'. It spoke urgently of the need for the Spirit's empowering presence and said our engagement in mission is 'pointless and fruitless without the presence, guidance, and power of the Holy Spirit'. I think all Pentecostals will say a hearty 'Amen!' to that. The caution in that section about charlatans who distort the ministry of the Holy Spirit is in order.

Implementation

In Cape Town 2010, a good attempt was made to translate ideas and strategies into implementable realities. This was evident in the regional meetings. However, in some places, for instance in Africa, such strategies work better when sub-regional groups have a voice in regional planning and

[12] *Cape Town Commitment*, 4.
[13] *Cape Town Commitment*, 5.

implementation. Perhaps this could have been accomplished with specific tasks-and-expectation modules, as well as specific input-output frameworks. In self-supporting Christian ventures, it appears that in Africa the Pentecostal and the Charismatic movements are in better shape to achieve more than the other traditions, which often remain tied to outside funding.

Conclusion

The task of completing world evangelization requires the joint effort of all Christian traditions. The Lausanne Movement has sought to address this. Islamic militancy and renewed fundamentalism in the Middle East and North Africa, as well as recent Buddhist uprisings in South East Asia and Central Asia, should inform the Christian world that theoretical affirmations at well-advertised conferences are not enough.[14] Recent expressions of Nigerian Christianity have shown a certain level of militant resistance in the face of Islam's aggression. Although the posture of the Nigerian church is one of self-defence, the ecumenical reality to push for more civil and political space to evangelise the world has become necessary.

This study has attempted to show that although the Lausanne Movement has achieved a lot, there is still the need to adopt the strengths of all Christian faith traditions to reach the unreached areas. These include the Pentecostal distinctive of emphasising the work of the Holy Spirit in missions and fervent prayers in the life of Christians.

---

[14] J. MacArthur, *Hard to Believe: The High Cost and Infinite Value of Following Jesus* (Nashville, TN: Thomas Nelson, 2003).

Together towards Life: A Pentecostal Assessment

Timothy T.N. Lim

This chapter appraises *Together towards Life* (*TTL*) after a concise account of global Pentecostalism, its ecumenical dialogues, and missional expressions.[1] The appraisal examines aspects of *TTL* that Pentecostals would affirm, are likely to affirm, and not amenable to agree, with reasons and sources for further investigation.

Global Pentecostalism

Contemporary global Pentecostalism traces its origins to William Seymour and an outpouring of the Holy Spirit at Azusa Street in 1901.[2] Reports uncover other indigenous Pentecostal outpourings before, during and after 1901, both at Azusa Street and elsewhere (e.g., Pyongyang).[3] In our milieu, global Pentecostalism contributes to societal transformation and the renewal of Christianity.[4] Pentecostalism transmutes into various streams (classical, neo-Pentecostal, charismatic, neo-charismatic and 'third wave'). Occasionally,

---

Originally published in K.R. Ross, J. Keum, K. Avtzi and R.R. Hewitt (eds), *Ecumenical Missiology: Changing Landscapes and New Conceptions of Mission*, Regnum Edinburgh Centenary Series 35 (Oxford: Regnum Books, 2016), 438-451.

[1] Readers may also be interested in my review essay, 'Comparative Pneumatology in Together towards Life, Evangelii Gaudium, and the Cape Town Commitment', *International Review of Mission* 104:2 (2015), 203-16.

[2] Mel Cecil Robeck, Jr., *Azusa Street Revival* (Nashville, TN: Thomas Nelson, 2006).

[3] A.H. Anderson, 'Pentecostalism in East Asia: Indigenous Oriental Christianity?', *Pneuma* 22:1 (Spring 2000), 115-32; Young-Hoon Lee, 'Korean Pentecost: The Great Revival of 1907', *Asian Journal of Pentecostal Studies* 4:1 (2001), 73-83; Hwa Yung, 'Endued with Power: The Pentecostal-Charismatic Renewal and the Asian Church in the Twenty-First Century', *Asian Journal of Pentecostal Studies* 6:1 (2003), 63-82, esp. 68-69; Sung Won Yang, 'The Influence of the Revival Movement of 1901-1910 on the Development of Korean Christianity' (Ph.D. dissertation, Southern Baptist Theological Seminary, 2002).

[4] Allan Heaton Anderson, *To the Ends of the Earth* (Oxford: Oxford University Press, 2013); Allan Heaton Anderson, 'To All Points of the Compass', *Enrichment Journal* (Springfield, MO, 2006); Donald E. Miller, Kimon H. Sargeant and Richard Flory (eds), *Spirit and Power* (Oxford: Oxford University Press, 2013).

some streams maintain exclusivity from other streams. Nearly all share similar phenomenological experiences of the Spirit – Spirit baptism, *glossolalia*, manifold operations of charismata, power encounters, healing, exorcism, and deliverance ministries.[5] Phenomenological explanations do not fully account for the multi-complex religious, socio-economic-political, divine-temporal engagements or the religious community despite the similar, confluential and convergent narratives about the experiences of the Holy Spirit.[6] The movement's diversity is shaped by global, cultural, theological-ecumenical, linguistic and indigenous expressions in various social locations.[7] And because of the plurality of localised expression, it is almost impossible to gather a team to speak representatively for the varieties within this movement.[8] Statistics report nearly 18,810 independent, indigenous, post-denominational groups of global neo-charismatics, 1,500 intra-denominations in North America, and another fifteen hundred Pentecostal denominations in Chile.[9] The challenges for this global movement abound, as does its potential.[10]

Pentecostals in Ecumenical Dialogue

Ecumenical dialogues have been continuing across various communions.[11] Pentecostals have moved from being a marginalised community to becoming an invited dialogue partner at world, national and regional levels. Pentecostal dialogue with other churches is no longer a novelty.[12] The Joint Consultative Group between the World Council of Churches and Pentecostals formed in 2000 has paved the way for Pentecostal participation in bilateral and multilateral meetings.[13] The *Focolare* movement's course on ecumenism at

---

[5] W. Paul Williamson and Ralph W. Hood, 'Spirit Baptism: A Phenomenological Experience', *Mental Health, Religion and Culture* 14:6 (2011), 543-59; Peter D. Neumann, *Pentecostal Experience*, Princeton Theological Monograph 187 (Eugene, OR: Wipf & Stock, 2012).

[6] Stephen C. Torr, *A Dramatic Pentecostal/Charismatic Anti-Theodicy* (Eugene, OR: Pickwick, 2013), 107. See also Vinson Synan and Amos Yong (eds), *Global Renewal Christianity* (Lake Mary, FL: Charisma House, 2015), 4 vols.

[7] Wonsuk Ma, Veli-Matti Kärkkäinen and J. Kwabena Asamoah-Gyadu, 'Introduction', in W. Ma, V-M Kärkkäinen and J.K. Asamoah-Gyadu (eds), *Pentecostal Mission and Global Christianity* (Oxford: Regnum Books, 2014), 3.

[8] Wolfgang Vondey, *Pentecostalism and Christian Unity*, vol. 2 (Eugene, OR: Cascade, 2012), 4, 9, 10, cf. 1-31.

[9] Ed van der Maas and Stanley M. Burgess (eds), *The New International Dictionary of Pentecostal and Charismatic Movements* (Grand Rapids, MI: Zondervan, 2002), xx.

[10] Nigel Paul Willis, *The Pentecostal Movement: Its Challenges and Potential* (Frankfurt: Peter Lang, 2013).

[11] Example of reports: https://ecumenism.net/docu/dialogue.htm (2015) (accessed 25th April 2015).

[12] Wolfgang Vondey, 'Presuppositions for Pentecostal Engagement in Ecumenical Dialogue', *Exchange* 30:1 (2001), 344-58.

[13] Pentecostals participate in the WCC's Commissions on Faith and Order, World Mission and Evangelism, and in more than forty national councils of churches and other

Castelgandolfo, Italy, in April 2014, emphasised Pentecostal and Charismatic expressions in Protestant and Catholic Christianity.[14] The Vatican claims 120 million Charismatic-renewed faithful worldwide, and with the blessing of various Popes, though not without resistance from some Catholic bishops.[15]

The longest-standing dialogue with Pentecostals, the International Catholic-Pentecostal Dialogue, has continued since 1972 and recently entered its sixth phase. Though Pentecostals showed distrust for theology at the first Quinquennium of the dialogue, Pentecostals engaged in topics of vital importance for Pentecostal-Catholic relations in subsequent phases of dialogue.[16] Hollenweger's lament of the difficulties (in 1999) has since been replaced with Cecil Robeck's appraisal of being warmly welcomed by Catholics although, internally, many Pentecostals are still suspicious about ecumenism.[17]

Reformed-Pentecostal dialogue has entered the third cycle. The first two official dialogues occurred in 1996-2000 and 2002-2011, between the World Alliance of Reformed Churches and the Pentecostal World Conference.[18] In

---

ecumenical agencies. Pentecostals have ongoing dialogues with Roman Catholics (since 1972), World Communion of Reformed Churches, formerly World Alliance of Reformed Churches (since 1996), Lutheran World Federation (since 2005), and World Alliance (since 2011), and have entered informal conversations as steps towards dialogue with the Anglican Communion, Mennonite World Conference, and the Synodal Committee for Inter-Orthodox and Inter-Christian Affairs of the Ecumenical Patriarchate of Constantinople.

[14] www.focolare.org/en/news/2014/04/29/dialogo-con-i-pentecostali (29th April 2014) (accessed 5th February 2015).

[15] Kilian McDonnell (ed/), *Open the Windows* (South Bend, IN: Greenlawn Press, 1989), cited from Cecil M. Robeck, Jr,, 'Creative Imagination and Ecumenism in Light of Global Demographic Changes' (lecture delivered 4th February 2013 at Catholic University of America for Washington Theological Consortium), 19, 18-19, n. 23.

[16] Juan Usma Gomez, 'Dialogue with Pentecostals', Eternal World Television Network (2001): https://www.ewtn.com/library/curia/pccupent.htm (accessed 9th June 2015).

[17] Walter J. Hollenweger, 'Roman Catholics and Pentecostals in Dialogue', *The Ecumenical Review* 51:2 (April 1999),.147-59; Cecil M. Robeck, Jr., 'Cooperation and the Promotion of Unity: A Pentecostal Perspective', in David A. Kerr and Kenneth R. Ross (ed), *Edinburgh 2010: Mission Then and Now* (Oxford: Regnum Books, 2009), 290-303; I analysed the suspicion, not just of Pentecostals, but also of Anabaptists, Baptists, Evangelicals and Presbyterians, towards ecumenism in 'Recognition and Reception: Towards a Joint Commemoration of the Reformation in 2017', in *Ecclesiology*, Part III.

[18] Cecil M. Robeck, 'First International Reformed-Pentecostal Dialogue', *Journal of Ecumenical Studies* 33:3 (June 1996), 442; 'Word and Spirit, Church and World: Pentecostal-Reformed Dialogue 1996-2000' (https://ecumenism.net/archive/docu/2000_pent_warc_word_spirit_church_world.pdf, 2000) and http://pctii.org/cyberj/cyberj8/WARC.html (20th December 2001); Cecil M. Robeck, 'The Challenge of the Pentecostal Movement and the First Dialogue Results on the World Level' (Strasbourg Institute Lecture 2011: http://strasbourginstitute.org/wp-content/uploads/2012/10/Seminar2011-Strasbourg-LW

November 2014, the World Communion of Reformed Churches, the Reformed Church of Hungary and the classical Hungarian Pentecostals held an international dialogue focusing on 'mission' in Berkfürdö, Hungary. Both communions appreciate the principles of mission theologically, and recognise differences in the way mission is practically expressed.[19]

Lutherans, under the umbrella of the Lutheran World Federation, have been dialoguing with other church families since the 1960s. International conversation with Trinitarian Pentecostals, which formally began in 2004, continued for another six years in Strasbourg, Pasadena, Zurich, and Tampere. The exchange focuses on how each tradition encounters Christ in their various charismas, sacraments, and rites, and on each communion's mutual response to the other historically.[20]

Baptists and Pentecostals have agreed to seek common ground, a significant step because of their history of mutual repudiations.[21] Historically, Baptists and Pentecostals disagree about the implications of receiving the Scriptures as the final authoritative revelation for churches of all ages, the continuing work of the Holy Spirit in the life of believers and the church after the apostolic age (known as cessationism and non-cessationism respectively), and the understanding of sanctification and perfectionism (depending on their roots in Calvinistic theology or Arminian theology respectively). While Baptists increasingly adopt Pentecostal modes of worship, Duke University's Baptist theologian Curtis Freeman insists that Baptists are not 'Bapticostals'.[22] Or is a shift to accept Pentecostals possible after the International Missions Board of the Southern Baptist Convention revision of its policy to admit missionary candidates who speak in tongues, a Pentecostal/Charismatic phenomenon of the Spirit?[23] Still, the prospects for better relations are hopeful.

F-Dialogue-Cecil-ROBECK.pdf, 2012); and http://reformatus.hu/mutat/10397/ (7th January 2015), accessed 5th February and 25th April 2015.

[19] http://wcrc.ch/news/wcrc-opens-new-round-of-dialogue-with-pentecostals/ (5th December 2014), accessed 25th April 2015.

[20] www.strasbourginstitute.org/dialog/lutherisch-pfingstlerischer-dialog (Institut für Ökumenische Forschung, 2015), accessed 5th February 2015; Lutherans and Pentecostals in Dialogue (Institut für Ökumenische Forschung in Strasbourg, and David du Plessis Center for Christian Spirituality, in Pasadena, and the European Pentecostal Charismatic Research Association in Zurich, 2015).

[21] http://baptistnews.com/archives/item/7022-baptists-pentecostals-seek-common-ground (20th December 2011), and http://ecclesialtheology.blogspot.com/2012/08/update-on-baptist-pentecostal-dialogue.html (9th Aug 2012), accessed 5th February 2015.

[22] Curtis Freeman, 'Pentecostal Power', *Baptist News Global* (25th May 2012): https://baptistnews.com/opinion/commentaries/item/7452-pentecostal-power (assessed 10th June 2015).

[23] www.religionnews.com/2015/05/14/southern-baptists-open-ranks-missionaries-speak-tongues/ (14th May 2015) and Southern Baptist Convention's perspectives: www.sbc.net/faqs.asp (both accessed 9th June 2015).

Pentecostals have historically adopted a pacifist position as far back as 1917 until the Assemblies of God embraced nationalism and militarism.[24] The historic, mutual contempt between Pentecostals and Mennonites[25] has been ameliorated with dialogues between the Mennonite Church USA and the Church of God Cleveland taking place in 2005 and 2006.[26]

Despite some internal puristic tendencies, the movement has maintained its harbinger role for plurality. Though it may be too early to claim that Pentecostalism is making waves in ecumenism, the hopeful developments in these dialogues show that it has reversed an older negative assessment regarding its potential for participation in collaborative, ecumenical mission.[27]

Pentecostal Missional Expressions

Pentecostal mission expressions are as diverse as the movement's plurality.[28] Several biblical promises provide the foundational premise and approach for Pentecostals' obedience to the Great Commission mandate (Matthew 28): 'You shall receive power when the Holy Spirit comes upon you' (Acts 1:8), the continuing fulfilment of Joel's prophecy on dreams, visions and manifestations of the Spirit (Acts 2:17; Joel 2:28), with healing and restoration as a regular manifestation that continues in Peter's reply: 'Silver and gold I have none' (Acts 3:6-16). Nimi Wariboko claims that the Pentecostal Spirit, who gives the many tongues of the Spirit in the church, is the Pentecostal principle that allowed these many missional manifestations.[29] Among some Charismatics, the gospel mission emphasises the message of prosperity, health and wealth, which proponents read to be implicit in Paul's wishes for the soul's prosperity (3 John 1:2).[30] Global Pentecostalism and Charismaticism have become agents and

[24] Paul Alexander, *Peace to War* (Telford, PA: Cascadia, 2009); Paul Alexander, *Pentecostals and Nonviolence: Reclaiming a Heritage* (Eugene, OR: Wipf & Stock, 2012), 350.

[25] Alan Kreider, *Social Holiness; A Way for Living for God's Nation* (Eugene, OR: Wipf & Stock, 2008), previously published as *Journey Toward Holiness* (Scottdale, PA: Herald Press, 1987), 15-16.

[26] Cheryl Bridges Johns, 'Overcoming the Holy Spirit Shyness in the Life of the Church', *Vision* 13:1 (Spring 2012), 6-15.

[27] www.pctii.org/cyberj/cyberj5/bundy.html (accessed 9th June 2015); cf. the dated article by David Bundy, 'The Ecumenical Quest for Pentecostalism', *Cyberjournal for Pentecostal-Charismatic Research*, n.d.

[28] Ma, Kärkkäinen and Asamoah-Gyadu, *Pentecostal Mission and Global Christianity.*

[29] Nimi Wariboko, *The Pentecostal Principle: Ethical Methodology in New Spirit* (Grand Rapids, MI: Eerdmans, 2011).

[30] This Charismatic prosperity teaching has received several criticisms. For instance, Timothy Lim, 'Blessings in the Prophets and the Wisdom: A Response to Charismatic Christian Hermeneutics and a General Application for Christian Living', *Evangelical Review of Society and Politics* 6:1/2 (2012/2013), 77-103. This is a special edition on 'Money, Prosperity and Economics'.

witnesses of the Spirit's renewal despite the historic churches' contestation of the movement's claims.[31]

Not all missional expressions are affiliated with historic classical Pentecostals. Newer indigenous movements, such as African Initiated Churches, and the Pentecostal-like China house church movements, have been observed.[32] The social and political expressions of Pentecostal mission and witness in North America, Latin America, Africa, and Asia, continue to expand, and these theologians, social and political scientists have analysed these movements.[33] Recent trajectories include a systematic Pentecostal missiology.[34] Do these ecumenical, missional developments within renewal movements (Pentecostals and Charismatic Christianity) signal a positive reception of *TTL*?

Renewed Mission and Evangelism Affirmation

CWME's desire to include older, historic, and newer Christian churches is evident when *TTL* begins with Nicea's Trinitarian position. Though Pentecostals were not major conversational partners in the World Council of Churches' dialogue towards convergence on *Confessing One Faith* in the 1990s, Pentecostals have gradually participated in discussions on *The Nature and Mission of the Church,* and *The Nature and Purpose of the Church*, both of which eventually became foregrounds to the convergence text, *The Church: Towards a Common Vision.*[35] With the exception of Oneness Pentecostals,[36] Pentecostals and Charismatics would strongly welcome *TTL*'s Trinitarian basis of Christian mission as rooted in God who creates, redeems and sustains life

---

[31] Ma, Kärkkäinen and Asamoah-Gyadu, *Pentecostal Mission and Global Christianity*, 1.

[32] Here I register that most Chinese house church movements would not affiliate themselves with historic Pentecostals or Charismatics, despite sharing similar spiritual passion and Pentecostal-like phenomena.

[33] E.g. Timothy J. Steigenga, *The Politics of the Spirit: The Political Implications of Costa Rica and Guatemala* (Lanham, MD: Lexington Books, 2002); Donald E. Miller and Tetsunao Yamamori, *Global Pentecostalism: The New Face of Social Engagement* (Berkeley, CA: University of California Press, 2007); Ruth Marshall, *Political Spiritualities: The Pentecostal Revolution in Nigeria* (Chicago, IL: University of Chicago Press, 2009); Michael Wilkinson and Steven M. Studebaker (eds), *A Liberating Spirit: Pentecostals and Social Action in North America* (Eugene, OR: Wipf & Stock, 2010); Miller, Sargeant, Flory (eds), *Spirit and Power*.

[34] Amos Yong, *The Missiological Spirit: Christian Mission Theology in the Third Millennium Global Context* (Eugene, OR: Cascade, 2014).

[35] See Wolfgang Vondey, 'Pentecostal Perspectives on The Nature and Mission of the Church: Challenges and Opportunities for Ecumenical Transformation', in Paul M. Collins and Michael A. Fahey (eds), *Receiving 'The Nature and Mission of the Church'* (New York: T. & T. Clark, 2008), 55-68.

[36] Gregory A. Boyd, *Oneness Pentecostals and the Trinity* (Grand Rapids, MI: Baker, 1992); Bruce Tucker, *Oneness Pentecostal Churches* (New York: Xlibis, 2011); Matthew J. Cawthorn, *American Oneness Pentecostalism* (CreateSpace, 2012).

with his incarnational love for the world, and his empowerment of the church for renewing the whole creation.

Pentecostalism has always emphasised the ministry of the Holy Spirit in empowering believers for sanctification and in the work of the gospel, although perspectives vary on whether the 'finished work of Christ' on the cross translates into Christians attaining sinless perfection instantly or gradually in this temporal life; the variations depend on whether they are Wesleyan, Keswick or Classical Holiness in conceiving the triumphant Christian life.[37] Still, as Jesus has instructed, the disciples of Christ are to wait for the Spirit to anoint them for ministry. Despite the empowerment on the Day of Pentecost (Acts 1–2), churches disagree as to whether Christ's disciples in each subsequent era have to receive the Spirit's manifold charismas for manifold service.[38]

The Introduction to *TTL* provides the strongest rationales for multi-faceted missional expression.[39] As Pentecostal-Evangelical systematician and missional theologian Amos Yong argues, 'The plurality of tongues of the Spirit' will give witness to the manifold works of the Spirit of the one God so that the church may fulfil her missionary thrust![40] Hence, Christian mission is rightly understood 'in a cosmic sense, and to affirm all life, the whole *oikoumene*, as being interconnected in God's web of life'.[41] 'Life in the Holy Spirit' is conceived as 'the essence of mission', identity, being and doing of Christians.[42] At least two Pentecostal theologians have recently affirmed life in the Spirit as missional, albeit without documenting any awareness of *TTL*.[43] Thus, all Christians and churches are God's messengers and gifts to, and for loving and transforming, the world.[44] *TTL* underscores the need for healing and reconciliation among the churches towards communal inclusivity and unity for her mission.[45]

TTL would appeal to many Pentecostals and Charismatics for various reasons. *TTL*'s explicit recognition of the Trinity in Christian mission – when CWME significantly adumbrates the Spirit of Christian mission and the Spirit's

---

[37] Charles W. Burtner, and Robert E. Chiles (eds), *John Wesley's Theology* (Nashville, TN: Abingdon, 1982), 141.

[38] Some argue that Pentecost is a once-and-for-all event and not repeatable. Others suggest that believers in each era need their initial and continual filling with the Spirit.

[39] *TTL*, §1-11, especially §1-4, 8, 10.

[40] E.g. Amos Yong, *The Spirit Poured Out on All Flesh* (Grand Rapids, MI: Baker Academic, 2005), 26, 124, 173.

[41] *TTL*, §4.

[42] *TTL*, §3.

[43] Andrea D. Snavel and Joel P. Okamoto, *Life in the Spirit* (Eugene, OR: Pickwick, 2015).

[44] *TTL*, §8, 10.

[45] *TTL*, §8, 10. Unlike *TTL*'s introduction, EA begins with the scandal of the churches' divisions before explicating the biblical, theological and ecumenical grounds and convictions for mission and witnessing. Thus, *TTL* would be ecumenically more inviting for churches.

operation in Christian mission – is a favourable change from the Spirit's less prominent role in WCC's earlier mission text, *Mission and Evangelism: An Ecumenical Affirmation* (1982)! *TTL*'s recognition of the renewal movements' global expansion and expressions could correct the historic and mainline churches' negative reception of these global renewal movements in the middle of the twentieth century.[46] While it may be a far cry to say that Pentecostals are now accepted in all churches and traditions, communions outside the Pentecostal movement are more willing to befriend believers outside their fold, even if these communions are still not in theological agreement with Pentecostals, as evidenced in the many dialogue reports. Still, many non-Pentecostal and non-Charismatic churches have renewed their worship services to become more contemporary, or at least participatory, thanks to the 'Spirit-led' worship renewal movements within this diverse tradition that have unfortunately also created 'music wars' when they deviated from the liturgies and practices of classical Christian worship.[47] *TTL*'s multi-faceted recognition of the local praxes to faith, and acknowledgement of the plurality of Pentecostal self-understandings, are important because Pentecostals are experiential in their faith and thus do not receive well a singular, universal concept and practice of the church.[48]

Pentecostals in the Majority World are likely to welcome *TTL*'s dual-direction of pursuing mission. To the older paradigm of 'mission to the margins', *TTL* now adds 'mission from the margins' of the 'powerless', 'the poor', and 'marginalised'. *TTL* affirms that missions could move in both directions simultaneously. *TTL* recognises that the margins possess God-given gifts for serving both in their own contexts and in transnational contexts. They could use their gifts 'to counteract injustices in life, church, and mission' because they experienced the 'misuse of power and use of the wrong kind of power in mission and in the church' from the rich, the powerful, and western centres of power. According to *TTL*, because the western missionary enterprise

---

[46] *TTL*, §5. *TTL* is right in how Christians identify who, where and what the 'centre' of Christianity is, while the outreach missions have been changing as a result of a) the global expansion of Christianity, which is by no means only a consequence of the successes of Pentecostalism (which §5 seems to imply), b) the phenomenon of migration, and c) the increasing trajectory of the margins recognizing themselves as agents of mission (rather than as the targets or recipients of mission). After the introduction, *TTL* did admit to the churches' historic faults in mission when churches denigrated local wisdom and local cultures in their missional history to indigenous peoples (cf. *TTL*, §27).

[47] For a global Pentecostal expression of worship, see Monique M. Ingalls and Amos Yong (eds), *The Spirit of Praise* (University Park, PA: Penn State University Press, 2015). For a different perspective, see Ruth C. Duck, *Worship for the Whole People of God* (Louisville, KY: Westminster John Knox, 2013). For a historic perspective, see James F. White, *Introduction to Christian Worship*, 3rd ed. (Nashville, TN: Abingdon, 2001).

[48] Simon Chan, 'Mother Church: Toward a Pentecostal Ecclesiology', *Pneuma* 22:2 (Fall 2000), 177-208.

had unfortunately perpetuated injustices rather than furthering 'the causes of justice, dignity, and life',[49] the shift in missional paradigm towards 'mission from the margins' is now desirable. The change will find favour with Pentecostals, not merely because *TTL* is now embracing a liberation ethos, articulated decades ago.[50] Rather, *TTL*'s explicit encouragement of 'mission from the margins' affirms that those at the margins have something to teach the rest of the mainstream churches that have marginalised them.[51] Churches at the margins are also God's missional instruments not just to their own local contexts but also to the dominant and powerful in western Christianity. As Kenneth Ross' interpretation of *TTL* in the context of 'liquid modernity' has suggested (and with insights from Lamin Sanneh), re-evangelisation of the western world may occur from the Spirit who actually brings about the transmigration of people in a global world![52]

However, certain formulations in *TTL* may or may not excite some Pentecostals and Charismatics. The reception on these formulations may range from ambivalence to rejection. The first ambivalence concerns *TTL*'s framing of mission inclusively.[53] The current approach towards inclusivity may inhibit a positive reception, especially by churches that see Christian mission either as a counter-cultural force or as focusing primarily on eternal salvation. Though *TTL* has duly acknowledged these perspectives, the inclusive framing will be difficult for some in the Renewal tradition to embrace, for the following reasons.

TTL suggests that evangelism could be understood, not just as the proclamation of the gospel leading the unbeliever to conversion, but also as the witnessing of Christian mission in social justice and solidarity with the poor, oppressed and marginalised.[54] The crux for a proper reception on *TTL*'s views on evangelism boils down to: what constitutes evangelism and gospel proclamation? To be sure, *TTL* affirms that the fundamental basis of their faith and the thrust of the gospel rest on the eternal salvific revelation of Jesus Christ: this explicit affirmation of Christ as the thrust of the gospel might help Evangelicals and Pentecostals overcome their prior assessment of WCC's Justice, Peace and Integrity of Creation projects (JPIC) as liberal deviations

---

[49] *TTL,* §33, 38, 39-42, 45, 46-49.

[50] Liberation theology is much older, although the ethos entered Pentecostal expression only in recent decades, as seen in R. Andrew Chesnut, *Born Again in Brazil* (New York: Rutgers University Press, 1997); Samuel Solivan, *Spirit, Pathos, and Liberation*, Journal of Pentecostal Theology Supplement 14 (New York: Bloomsbury: T. & T. Clark, 1998).

[51] E.g., Chad M. Bauman, *Pentecostals, Proselytization, and Anti-Christian Violence in Contemporary India* (Oxford: Oxford University Press, 2015), ch. 3, 70-93.

[52] Kenneth R. Ross, 'Together towards Life in the Context of Liquid Modernity', *International Review of Mission* 103.2 (November 2014), 249-50; cf. 240-55; Lamin Sanneh, *Summoned from the Margin* (Grand Rapids, MI: Eerdmans, 2012).

[53] *TTL,* §8-10.

[54] *TTL,* §85.

from the gospel.[55] As we now know, some Pentecostals in the Majority World have expressed their faith counter-culturally when they explicitly seek to be conduits of societal transformation through concrete projects in social justice advocacy, but even these social witnesses are conducted without relegating the direct proclamation of the salvific message of Jesus Christ.[56] *TTL*'s inclusivity and reframing of what counts as evangelism would remain a challenge: Pentecostals and Charismatics, together with Evangelicals, would be likely to disagree with *TTL*'s acceptance of solidarity as a form of evangelism, and *TTL*'s relegation of the direct proclamation of Jesus Christ's salvation message as only 'an essential part of the way we convey God's love to the world'. In Renewal and Evangelical understanding, evangelism is not merely an aspect of Christian proclamation; evangelism is primarily about the saving of souls eternally: salvation is the gospel itself![57]

Nonetheless, *TTL* and Renewal churches can affirm that social witnessing does not exclude evangelism. As *TTL* states, because 'the mission of God's Spirit encompasses us all in an ever-giving act of grace ... we are therefore called to move beyond a narrowly human-centred approach and to embrace forms of mission which express our reconciled relationship with all created life'.[58] *TTL* rightly points out that to presume that believers can seek eternal salvation without caring for JPIC is 'to falsely believe [that] we can belong to God without belonging to our neighbour', and in so doing, 'fall into a spirituality that simply makes us feel good while other parts of creation hurt

---

[55] *TTL,* §9; Jonas Jonson and Norman A. Hjelm, *Wounded Visions* (Grand Rapids, MI: Eerdmans, 2013). That said, apart from a few dissenting voices, Pentecostals would readily affirm the need to co-operate with 'other religions and cultures in building societies of love, peace and justice' in our 'multi-religious and multi-cultural' world. Daniel Castello, *Revisioning Pentecostal Ethics* (Cleveland, TN: CPT Press, 2012) proposes an eschatological reframing of Pentecostal moral theology to allow the possibility of Pentecostal mission in the world. Though Castello did not directly address issues of social advocacy, justice, and ecological care, the appropriation is well within an application of Castello's work (cf. Castello, *Revisioning Pentecostal Ethics*, 51). Monte Lee Rice, 'Renewing the Pentecostal Vision and Witness of the Justified People of God', *Asian Journal of Pentecostal Studies* 16:2 (August 2013), 85-98 offers an example of a Pentecostal social witness.

[56] David H. Lumsdaine (ed), *Evangelical Christianity and Democracy in Asia* (Oxford: Oxford University Press, 2009); Allan Anderson and Edmond Tang (eds), *Asian and Pentecostal*, 2nd ed. (Oxford: Regnum Books, 2011).

[57] *TTL,* §8. Here, *TTL*'s use of direct proclamation as 'an essential' in the larger backdrop of the churches' wider witness implies, albeit unintentionally, that direct witness is one among other messages of the gospel witness; the relegation of evangelism as only an essential remains a problem for renewal readers. Nonetheless, the clarification of a more moderate perspective in *TTL,* §19-23 that Christian mission would seek the flourishing of creation eco-justice, and respect of the earth and advocacy for the oppressed and marginalised, against the backdrop of §83 that conceives evangelism as the sharing of faith and conviction with other people as the ultimate gift to another fellow human being, would be more acceptable to renewal readers.

[58] *TTL,* §19.

and yearn'.[59] Also, *TTL* explains that Christian proclamation and witness as 'good news for all' should not succumb to forces of individualism, secularism and materialism 'that end up 'promoting falsehood, injustice and oppression': the caveat would be a lesson for Pentecostal mission, given Pentecostals' varying approaches to secularity and materiality, as we shall shortly examine.[60]

On another aspect of *TTL*'s inclusive missional framing, the inter-faith position articulated in *TTL* may also find an ambivalent reception. *TTL*'s inter-faith position is also rather mild in its presentation. One could easily read *TTL*'s position as arguing for an open, inclusive and collaborative listening and dialogue with other religions towards their shared responsibilities as part of humanity in the protection of religious liberty and solidarity.[61] Here, Pentecostals are unlikely to fully stand with *TTL*, though promoting religious liberty and solidarity are certainly part of Christian witness![62] On the whole, since Pentecostal reflection on its mission is still emerging, one could speculate that Pentecostals are likely to concur with aspects in *TTL* that conceive salvation through evangelism and witnessing through advocacy as necessary to the gospel and the mission of the church, although they would not affirm *TTL*'s relegation of direct proclamation or a subdued role in interreligious engagement.[63]

It would also be interesting to see how Pentecostals and especially Charismatics would respond to both *TTL*'s rejection of the saving power of the market economy and mammon, and *TTL*'s acknowledgement of communicating the gospel in the global market economy.[64] On the one hand, Pentecostals and Charismatics, including factions that embrace a prosperity gospel, seem to use this-worldly materiality as a means or a platform for proclaiming the gospel.[65] Thus, *TTL*'s introduction in §7 and commentary in §31 may offer a pushback for Pentecostals. *TTL*'s point would definitely not

---

[59] *TTL,* §21.

[60] *TTL,* §91.

[61] *TTL,* §93-96.

[62] Tony Richie, *Speaking by the Spirit* (Lexington, KY: Emeth Press, 2011); Tony Ritchie, *Towards a Pentecostal Theology of Religions* (Cleveland, TN: CPT Press, 2013); for a more inclusive and pluralistic voice, see Steven M. Studebaker, 'Christian Mission and the Religions as Participation in the Spirit of Pentecost', in Amos Yong and Clifton Clarke (eds), *Global Renewal, Religious Pluralism, and the Great Commission* (Lexington, KY: Emeth Press, 2011), 71-95.

[63] Ma, Kärkkäinen and Asamoah-Gyadu, *Pentecostal Mission and Global Christianity.* Norbert Hintersteiner, 'From Cultural Translation to Interfaith Witness: The Intercultural Transformation of Missiology', in Linda Hogan, Solange Lefebvre, Norbert Hintersteiner and Felix Wilfred (eds), 'From World Mission to Inter-religious Witness'. *Concilium* 2011/1 (London: SCM, 2011), 85-94.

[64] *TTL,* §7.

[65] Amos Yong and Katherine Attanasi (eds), *Pentecostalism and Prosperity* (New York: Palgrave Macmillan, 2012); Calvin L. Smith, 'The Politics and Economics of Pentecostalism: A Global Survey', in *The Cambridge Companion to Pentecostalism* (Cambridge: Cambridge University Press, 2014), 175-94.

affect groups that see 'the creation of wealth and prosperity' as an end in itself.[66] On the other hand, Pentecostal and Charismatic spirituality would agree with *TTL* that transformational mission would 'confront idolatrous assumptions, unjust systems, politics of domination and exploitation in our current world economic order' so that the church would be motivated 'to serve God's economy of life, not mammon, to share life at God's table rather than satisfy individual greed, to pursue change for a better world'.[67] On either spectrum, there will be respondents who will embrace or critique *TTL*'s rejection of the market economy and mammon: the litmus test will be whether economy and mammon are regarded as a means and instruments of the gospel or ends in themselves. Amid the political economy of exchange, Amos Yong argues that an informal economy is at work when believers share and exchange goods and services in the spirit of Christian love, and hence one cannot totally reject the capabilities of economy and mammon, despite the real dangers of misusing or abusing them.[68]

Ecclesiology underlies the missional expression of the church, and thus one would expect *TTL* to give substantial treatment to the church. *TTL* speaks accurately about the gift of the church to the world: the church transforms society by bringing new life and announcing God's love and presence. *TTL* also affirms the fundamental ecclesiological unity of the church on the basis of the Trinitarian vision, and hopes to facilitate the churches' unitive witness as disciples of Christ and as agents of healing and reconciliation to the world.[69] Pentecostals would concur here. As Peter Althouse suggests, Pentecostal ecclesiology is anchored in the missional life of the Triune God: the church becomes the sent and sending community to live out its mission.[70] Nonetheless, *TTL* frames its ecclesiology to inclusivity without offering substantial qualifiers: the lack of nuance about what sort of inclusivity would characterise the gospel-centric community of disciples is unlikely to find acceptance with puristic churches in Evangelical and Pentecostal communities, although, to a certain extent, the gospel would prize inclusivity. Pentecostal churches, as with Evangelical communities, would wish to remind the drafters of *TTL* that the gospel is also exclusivist – whoever believes in Jesus Christ as Lord and Saviour shall be saved and those who deny Christ will be denied by the Father (Matthew 10:33; 1 John 2:22-23)![71]

TTL drafters may have wanted a wide reception of the text, and hence *TTL* is not formulated only with exclusivist churches, like Pentecostals and

[66] *TTL,* §31.
[67] *TTL,* §30.
[68] Amos Yong, *In the Days of Caesar* (Grand Rapids, MI: Eerdmans, 2010), 304-10.
[69] *TTL,* §10.
[70] Peter Althouse, 'Towards a Pentecostal Ecclesiology: Participation in the Missional Life of the Triune God', *Journal of Pentecostal Theology* 18:2 (2009), 230-45. For a wider study of Pentecostal ecclesiology, both theological and empirical, see Mark Cartledge, 'Renewal Ecclesiology in Empirical Perspectives', *Pneuma* 36 (2014), 5-24.
[71] Clifton Shane, 'Pentecostal Ecclesiology: A Methodological Proposal for a Diverse Movement', *Journal of Pentecostal Theology* 15:2 (2007), 213-32.

Evangelicals, in mind. Still, I wish that *TTL* had presented their alternative model without needing readers to choose between their preferred inclusivity or the implicit contrasting exclusivist approach to gospel mission. *TTL* remains attractive because it clarifies that Christian mission, as a step towards welcoming others, entails not just the practice of hospitality to aid inclusivity, but also implies the crossing of boundaries. The notions of hospitality and crossing boundaries are certainly not foreign to Pentecostal spiritual ethos; from the beginnings of Pentecostalism, it was called a harbinger for plurality. Nonetheless, the movement still has much to do to expand its inclusivity.[72] Thus, *TTL* has unwittingly offered some correctives for Pentecostals and Evangelicals.

> §25: The churches are called to discern the work of the life-giving Spirit sent into the world and to join with the Holy Spirit in bringing about God's reign of justice (Acts 1:6-8). When we have discerned the Holy Spirit's presence, we are called to respond, recognizing that God's Spirit is often subversive, leading us beyond boundaries and surprising us.[73]

> §26: We are led by the Spirit into various situations and moments, into meeting points with others, into spaces of encounter and into critical locations of human struggle.[74]

> §33: Mission provokes in us a renewed awareness that the Holy Spirit meets us and challenges us at all levels of life, and brings newness and change to the places and times of our personal and collective journeys.[75]

> §44: The church's hope is rooted in the promised fulfilment of the reign of God. It entails the restoration of right relationships between God and humanity and all of creation. Even though this vision speaks to the eschatological reality, it deeply energises and informs our current participation in God's salvific work in this penultimate period.[76]

Whether Pentecostals will receive the Spirit's invitation and *TTL*'s pneumatological mission proposal remains to be seen. Many of *TTL*'s encouragements, which could offer correctives for renewal churches, have been raised in one way or another by the late Baptist-Evangelical Renewal theologian Clark Pinnock's programmatic essay, 'Church in the Power of the Holy Spirit'.[77] The question then becomes: Will renewal churches advance the

---

[72] Amos Yong, *Hospitality and the Other* (Maryknoll, NY: Orbis Books, 2008) engages hospitality in the interreligious arena. Still, the principle of hospitality and its applied implication towards crossing boundaries would not be inconceivable for ecclesiology or ecclesiological mission.

[73] *TTL*, §25.

[74] *TTL*, §26.

[75] *TTL*, §34.

[76] *TTL*, §44.

[77] Clark H. Pinnock, 'Church in the Power of the Holy Spirit: The Promise of Pentecostal Ecclesiology', *Journal of Pentecostal Theology* 14:2 (2006), 147-65.

themes in their respective contexts in global, collaborative missions, outside their own communions in the coming era?

The Challenges of Charismatic Movements to the Mainline Historical Churches in Africa

Abednego Keshomshahara

The Fast Growth of the Church in Africa

The church is growing very fast in Africa. This shows how mission work in Africa has been successful in one way or another. But we have to go beyond this achievement and ask ourselves whether this growth is without problems. Although the mainline historical churches (Anglican, Lutheran and Roman Catholic) are growing, the Pentecostal and Charismatic churches are growing faster.[1] Many Christians from the mainline historical churches join the Charismatic churches in order to quench their spiritual needs.[2] This challenges the mainline churches to know what has gone wrong in their approach to doing mission in Africa and elsewhere in the world.

The Charismatic churches emerged mainly in the African cities and towns in the early 1980s. Most of these churches have had financial support from the USA, Canada, and Scandinavian countries.[3] These movements attracted many people with modern media and communication systems while addressing people's needs and expectations. As far as Tanzania is concerned, this movement came when the country was experiencing economic hardships which resulted from the oil crisis and the failure of African socialism. These Charismatic churches promised people a good life if they believed in Jesus

---

Originally published in Claudia Währisch-Oblau and Fidon Mwombeki (eds), *Mission Continues Global Impulses for the 21st Century*, Regnum Edinburgh Centenary Series 4 (Oxford: Regnum Books, 2010), 95-106.

[1] Klaus Koschorke, 'Introduction', in Klaus Koschorke (ed), *African Identities and World Christianity in the Twentieth Century* (Hamburg: Missionshilfe Verlag, 2002), 233-34.

[2] Edward D.O. O'Connor, *The Pentecostal Movement: In the Catholic Church* (Notre Dame: Ave Maria Press, 1971), 239-62.

[3] Jesse Mugambi, *From Liberation to Reconstruction: African Christian Theology after the Cold War* (Nairobi: East African Educational Publishers, 1995), 68-70. Also, Wilson Niwagila, 'Charismatische Bewegung in Tansania' (a paper presented to UEM member churches, 2005), 1-9. Also, Friedrich Durst, *Das andere Afrika: Impressionen, Reflexionen und auch Visionen aus dreißig Jahren kirchlicher Arbeit in Afrika* (Neuendettelsau: Erlanger Verlag für Mission und Ökumene, 2004), 168-71.

Christ, fasted and prayed for healing miracles. They went on to say that even students could pass their examinations if they prayed. Since people were needy, they joined these movements with expectations that their needs would be met. In fact, when you tell people who have no food to fast, such people will accept your appeal not only because of religious factors but also because of economic hardships as they will take fasting as a way of economising their consumption of food.

Again, when you tell people who have no possibility of accessing health services to pray only for healing miracles, your message will be accepted since people have no access to medical facilities anyhow. They are even not ready to go to the traditional healers who charge them money for their healing practices. This was already a challenge to the mainline historical churches which had established centres for health services that serve those who can pay for medical treatments.

The mainline churches stress medical services with less emphasis on prayers for healing, a weakness that makes their Christians leave their denominations and join the Charismatic movements. Moreover, the challenge that faces the mainline historical churches is to empower people to be in a position of improving their economies so that they may be able to pay for health services. At least nowadays the mainline historical churches empower the Christians and the entire community through savings and credit cooperative societies (SACCOS) through which members can access credit and produce to meet their daily needs including health services.

Religion and society are inseparable. The question is how this relationship can be well utilised to bring about social, mental, economic and spiritual development without jeopardizing the integrity of people. This leads us to the challenge of doing mission in a holistic way, addressing both the spiritual and material dimensions of the people. Both the Charismatic churches and mainline historical churches are challenged to address the needs of people without concentrating on one aspect of life, since people have spiritual and material dimensions of life. A good example can be taken from Jesus Christ who preached to people the good news of salvation for the forgiveness of sins while at the same time feeding and healing them.

Theological Differences between the Mainline Historical Churches and the Charismatic Movements

The Role of the Holy Spirit

The difference between the mainline historical churches and the Charismatic movements is mainly found in their understanding of the Holy Spirit and his functions in the church. The mainline historical churches have mainly emphasised the person and work of Jesus Christ with less emphasis on the person and work of the Holy Spirit.[4]

Marie-Henri Keane poses a similar challenge:

> Christ was never forgotten, the God who sent him was never overlooked, but what is surprising is that we who believe in a triune God should have grossly neglected the life-giving Spirit, especially since we know that we cannot say 'Jesus is the Lord' or call God 'God' unless this grace is given to us through the Spirit.[5]

In showing how pneumatology has been neglected or marginalised by some churches, Elizabeth Johnson quotes leading theologians who comment that the Holy Spirit has become 'half known God' (Yves Congar); 'watered down from its Biblical fullness' (Wolfhart Pannenberg); 'homeless in the West' (Joseph Ratzinger); 'faceless' (Walter Kasper) and 'shadowy' (John Mackuarrie).[6] At least Reformation theology puts it very clearly that people by their own reasoning ability and strength cannot believe in Jesus Christ except through the Holy Spirit. The Holy Spirit is responsible for calling, enlightening, sanctifying and preserving the believers in the true Christian faith. Moreover, the Holy Spirit forgives sin and is expected to resurrect and provide the believers with eternal life.[7] The Danish scholar Regin Prenter argues that Lutheran theology gives much attention to the Holy Spirit since it maintains that both justification and sanctification are the work of the Holy Spirit.[8]

However, other functions of the Holy Spirit such as healing through prayers, speaking in tongues, and prophesy (charismatic gifts) have been marginalised or even neglected by Lutheran theology because charismatic gifts are not central to the salvation of people and are not upholding the theology of the cross, instead, they are confined within the theology of glory.[9] But the theology of the cross is not only meant for those who suffer but also those who prosper since both sides are challenged to go beyond their situations and reflect on God's grace of saving humans through Jesus Christ. In addition, the cross does not only imply spiritual aspects of life but also socio-economic and political arenas of life since Jesus' death on the cross was caused by his challenging

---

[4] Lesslie Newbigin, *The Relevance of Trinitarian Doctrine for Today's Mission* (London: Edinburgh House Press, 1963), 77-78.

[5] Marie-Henri Keane, 'The Spirit of Life', in John W. de Gruchy and Charles Villa-Vicencio (eds), *Doing Theology in Context: South African Perspectives* (New York: Orbis Books, 1994), 69.

[6] Keane, 'The Spirit of Life', 72.

[7] Martin Luther, 'The Small Cathechism', in Theodore G. Tappert (ed), *The Book of Concord: The Confessions of the Evangelical Lutheran Church* (Philadelphia: Muhlberg Press, 1959), 45.

[8] Benard Holm, 'The Work of the Spirit: The Reformation to the Present', in Paul D. Opsahl (ed), *The Holy Spirit in the Life of the Church* (Minneapolis: Augusburg Publishing, 1978), 100-103.

[9] Karlfried Froehlich, 'Charismatic Manifestations and the Lutheran Incarnational Stance', in *The Holy Spirit and the Life of the Church*, 136-45.

actions and constant sermons about God's kingdom that challenged exploitation, oppression of people and religious legalism.[10]

But as people, we encounter diseases, pain, and death. Jesus himself prayed in Gethsemane to avoid torture and death, but he prayed while letting the will of God to be done.[11] That is what he taught his followers to pray by saying 'Thy will be done'. In spite of his prayer, he was confronted by torture and death that was meant for the salvation of humans. On the cross, he complained to God as to why he had forsaken him (Mark 15:34-36). But afterwards he placed his soul in the hands of God (Luke 23:46) and died. In this context, we ought to accept the reality of being humans who ought to carry the cross with the hope of resurrection. Otto Markmann says that the Charismatic movements tend to overlook the cross and live as if Christian perfection was possible here on earth, while in reality Christian perfection is expected after the resurrection of the body and life everlasting as we read from Philippians 3:12 and 1 John 3:2.[12]

Some Christians in the Charismatic movements have been tempted to perceive healing as a necessary phenomenon to those who pray and believe. They forget that even those who believe cannot avoid the reality of death. The teachings about charismatic gifts need special theological attention and clarification in doing mission in the light of the Biblical teachings and evangelical theology, lest people are misled by wrong teachings.

Other Theological Differences

Another problem is related to the understanding of God from the perspective of the Trinity, whereby every denomination tends to emphasise only one aspect of the Triune God with less emphasis on the other aspects of the Trinity. For example, while Lutherans put much emphasis on the person and works of Jesus Christ (*solus Christus*), the Roman Catholic Church emphasises the aspect of God as Father. The Charismatic churches stress the works of the Holy Spirit who is associated with the events of healing, prophecy, speaking in tongues, visions, and dreams without attention to the other persons of the Trinity. As such, Lesslie Newbigin challenges all denominations to have a Trinitarian approach in doing mission, an approach that will help the Christians to have confidence in God as creator, redeemer, and sanctifier. The balanced Trinitarian aspects in the task of doing mission will also help the church to overcome the challenge of secularism[13] as long as God is involved in all dimensions of life as creator, redeemer, and sanctifier.

---

[10] Jürgen Moltmann, *The Crucified God: The Cross of Christ as the Foundation and Criticism of Christian Theology*, trans. R.A. Wilson and John Bowden (London: SCM Press, 2001), 46-50, 128-47.

[11] Mark 14:36-15:47.

[12] Otto Markmann, *Charismatische Bewegung: Eine Materialsamlung mit Beurteilung für eine Gutachten über die Charismatische Bewegung* (Berlin: Lutherischer Gemeinschaftsdienst, 1982), 31.

[13] Newbigin, *The Relevance of Trinitarian Doctrine*, 77-78.

Hans-Peter Grosshans observes that the Charismatic churches emphasise living out the faith without a focus on the theological reflections about faith. For them, theology is unnecessary and seems to be a disturbing activity. He admits that there are ways of doing theology which are far away from living out faith, but he maintains that there is also a good theology that does not oppose faith. This kind of theology, he adds, is part of faith or its instrument. Grosshans points out that we need some distance from living out the faith and experiences of the Holy Spirit in order to see and understand what is going on in the church and society. Theology is necessary if at all we want to know and reflect the foundations of our faith. Charismatic churches are interested only in the immediate, direct experiences of the Holy Spirit without theological reflections on the foundations of what they are believing in.[14] Since the Charismatic movements have a negative attitude towards theology and theologians, there has been tension between Charismatic Christians and mainline clergy or theologians. In this context, there is a need for dialogue in which the clergy ought to listen carefully to the challenges of the Charismatic Christians who want to freely express their faith and experiences of their lives in the Spirit. At the same time, Christians in the Charismatic movements should be able to see the relevance of theology in clarifying the foundations of the Christian faith. Church history tells us that there are times when faith without theological reflections leads to danger and death of people. A good example of faith without reflection is when some Charismatic preachers tell people to only pray for healing without going to the hospital. As a result, some people have lost their lives because of faith that lacks theological reflections. Thus, Christian faith must be based not only on the immediate experience of the Holy Spirit but also on the theological reflection for the sake of clarity, certainty, the pursuit of truth, salvation and liberation of humans from obstacles of life by relating faith to socio-economic and political aspects of life.

The Context of African Traditional Spirit Beliefs

The challenge which faces the church in Africa today is caused by what John S. Mbiti observes, namely that Christianity has failed to relate and interpret the Gospel in the context of African spirituality.[15] Since the Gospel was not interpreted in the African cultural and religious context, African Christians became Christians during the day, but in the night they became adherents of their African Traditional Religion (ATR).[16] In African Traditional Religion

[14] Hans-Peter Grosshans, 'The Work of the Holy Spirit in Christian Life and in the Church: Lutheran Theological Reflections', in Karen L. Bloomquist (ed), *Lutherans Respond to Pentecostalism* (Mineapolis: Lutheran University Press, 2008), 119.
[15] John S. Mbiti, *African Religions and Philosophy* (London: SPCK, 1969), 237-38.
[16] Israel Katoke, 'The Coming of the Gospel and African Reaction', in C.K. Omari (ed), *Essays on Church and Society in Tanzania* (Arusha: Evangelical Lutheran Church in Tanzania, 1976), 112-13.

every aspect of life has a connection with the spiritual world hence there is an interrelationship between the material and spiritual dimensions of life.

The emphasis of the Charismatic churches on the functions of the Holy Spirit appeals to many Africans whose traditional spirit beliefs are associated with the miraculous aspects in life.[17] This leads us to the need of interpreting the doctrine of the Holy Spirit in the socio-religious settings of Africans without jeopardizing the essence of the Gospel. Gwinyai H. Muzorewa argues that the role of the Holy Spirit correlates with that of the ancestral spirits in the African Traditional Religion.[18] This implies that Africans whose traditional religion maintains that the ancestral spirits can heal people will likely feel at home when the Charismatic movements emphasise that the Holy Spirit is responsible for healing sick people. The same applies to the functions of the Holy Spirit in prophecy, speaking in tongues, counselling, etc. African ancestral spirits are also involved in prophesying in the sense that they enable those who are possessed by them to predict what will happen in the future. In addition, there are beliefs among Africans that the ancestral spirits can make people speak in a language that is foreign to the hearers.[19] The traditional healers use the ancestral spirits to acquire knowledge for counselling people regarding their needs in society.

When the Bible talks of the Holy Spirit as the one who has the power to counteract the evil spirits, African traditionalists talk of good spirits as protectors of people against them. When the Charismatic preachers emphasise the role and functions of the Holy Spirit against the evil spirits and other calamities in life, their message is well perceived

The question is why are Africans interested in the Holy Spirit if they already have ancestral spirits which play a great role in their lives? The Christian message attracts Africans when the Holy Spirit is presented as God, a message that shows that the ancestral spirits are inferior to God. While the Holy Spirit is the Spirit of God, the ancestral spirits are spirits of humans. This is accepted in African Traditional Religion in which the spirits are graded below God. Thus, the traditional ancestral spirit beliefs should not be an end in themselves; rather, they should be perceived as a background through which the doctrine of the Holy Spirit as God can be interpreted in our endeavour of doing mission in Africa and elsewhere in the world where people still have ancestral spirit beliefs. While there are special traditional spirits for specific purposes like hunting, fishing, farming and having children, the church failed to address the needs of people by asking the Holy Spirit to guide and help them in such daily needs.

---

[17] Abednego Keshomshahara, 'The Lutheran Doctrine of the Holy Spirit and the Challenge of the Traditional Spirit beliefs among the Haya People' (M.Th. Thesis, Makumira University College, 2000), 1-6.

[18] Gwinyai H. Muzorewa, *The Origins and Development of African Theology* (Maryknoll, NY: Orbis Books, 1985), 43.

[19] Keshomshahara, 'The Lutheran Doctrine', 50ff.

African theology has tried to express Jesus as a 'proto-ancestor' bearing in mind that the ancestors play an important role in the lives of the Africans. But the task which ought to be given attention as far as the Charismatic movements are concerned is the correlation between the Holy Spirit and the ancestral spirits. When we do mission in Africa, we should always be careful regarding the aspect of salvation and miracles in view of the role of the Holy Spirit. Although the Bible talks about the aspects of miracles, its essential message is about the liberation and salvation of humans in and beyond history; it encompasses history and eschatology. It is here that we should differentiate between the temporal and eternal needs of humans.

We have to understand that the Holy Spirit provides for temporal and eternal needs in life. Ibrahim Bitrus challenges the historic churches to review their curricula in theological seminaries and universities in order to encounter the challenges of Charismatic and neo-Pentecostal movements by adding courses concerning *charisma*, Spirit baptism, speaking in tongues, healing and deliverances, dynamics of worship, job and wealth creation and capacity building.[20] Galana Babusa Yako depicts how the historic churches in Kenya have started to adjust themselves to the challenges of Charismatic movements by praying for people who have special problems during worship services. He adds that once per month during Sunday sermon, the preacher leads a discussion with members of the congregation on topics such as the Holy Spirit whereby they are given a chance of sharing their views and understanding with one another. Other strategies include allowing lay Christians to preach and the opportunity for afternoon fellowships in which pastors are present to learn from people and help them in their spiritual growth.[21] It is very interesting to note that historic churches which respond to the spiritual needs of their Christians have succeeded in retaining their Christians. Even some of the Christians who leave historic churches and join the Charismatic movements come back when the spiritual needs are met.[22]

The Attractiveness of Charismatic Movements

Other reasons that make African Christians leave mainline churches and join the Charismatic movements include that of seeking a place where they can freely participate in the worship services without depending on pre-determined liturgies. Ibrahim Bitrus observes that liturgies in the mainline churches are associated with cold formalism rather than vibrant worship that is found in the Charismatic and Pentecostal churches. He adds that many worship services in the mainline churches are still centered on the pastor rather than the whole

---

[20] Ibrahim Bitrus, 'The Influence of Neo-Pentecostalism in Nigeria', in *Lutherans Respond to Pentecostalism*, 88.

[21] Galana Babusa Yako, 'One Church's Response to Pentecostalism', in *Lutherans Respond to Pentecostalism*, 89.

[22] Yako, 'One Church's Response to Pentecostalism', in *Lutherans Respond to Pentecostalism*, 89.

congregation. As a result, the congregation becomes passive rather than being active participants in the whole process of worshipping God.[23]

Worship services in the Charismatic movements have room for simple songs that can be sung without hymn books. Such songs can be sung while dancing, twisting, moving and clapping hands, creating an atmosphere of joy and participation. Such worship services attract many youths who like dancing and singing. This, again, is a challenge to the historic churches. It is in this context that creativity and innovation of things that are attractive to Christians in worship should be encouraged to avoid worship services that are boring. Such innovations include liturgies that are flexible and appealing to people. This should go hand in hand with encouraging active participation of all Christians in the worship services. The priesthood of all believers as upheld by the Lutheran doctrines seems to have been marginalised since the participation of all Christians in the Lutheran churches, and other historic churches is not encouraged.[24]

Christians in the Charismatic and Pentecostal churches encourage relationships in the sense that they care for one another, unlike some large established historic churches which may not even know their church members. In addition, Charismatic churches are concerned with solving individual socio-economic and spiritual problems.[25] The fact that Christians in the Charismatic movements participate in the ministry and feel responsible to visit the sick people and pray for them makes Christians in the historic churches leave their churches and join a Charismatic movement. This is a challenge to the mainline historic churches, which ought to involve the Christians in the ministry by encouraging them to visit, counsel and care for one another without waiting for their pastors to do such duties.

Critiquing the Charismatic Movements in Africa

We have seen how the Charismatic churches respond to the social, material and spiritual needs of the people. However, the Charismatic churches which have tried to emphasise the role of the Holy Spirit and his gifts to meet the challenge of African traditional spirit beliefs have created some theological problems which ought to be criticised For example, while they stress the miracles of healing through prayers, they marginalise Western and African traditional medicines[26] as if the Holy Spirit is limited to one form of healing. Moreover, in those churches, prayers to God have predictable results which depend on one's

---

[23] Bitrus, 'The Influence of Neo-Pentecostalism', 86-87. Cf. Musawenkosi Biyela, 'In Spirit and Truth: Liturgy in Dialogue with Pentecostalism', in *Lutherans Respond to Pentecostalism*, 95.

[24] Bitrus, 'The Influence of Neo-Pentecostalism', 87.

[25] Bitrus, 'The Influence of Neo-Pentecostalism', 87.

[26] John S. Mbiti, *Bible and Theology in African Christianity* (Nairobi: Oxford University Press, 1986), 74-78; cf. Keshomshahara, 'The Lutheran Doctrine', 3.

observance of laws and taboos. Failure to follow the rules leads to unsuccessful prayers according to the teachings of these churches.[27]

Another problem is associated with lack of order in the church, especially when every Christian claims to be guided by the Holy Spirit which has led to split of the churches in various small groups and movements of people from one denomination to another. The same applies to the Pentecostal and Charismatic movements' views concerning social miseries, which are attributed to individual sins only without consideration of socio-political and economic structures of evil.[28] All these problems ought to be addressed and solved so that African Christianity may not disassociate people from political engagement.[29]

Charismatic and Pentecostal movements are criticised for reading the Bible literally.[30] It is in this context that we see the relevance of exegetical work in which we are enabled to understand the social, religious, cultural and historical context of the text before we apply it to our life experiences.[31] However, exegesis should be done in a way that does not take over the place of faith, especially when exegesis makes some ordinary Christians doubt if what they read and hear is really God's word or people's words.[32] The Bible is not a book of science but a book which requires us to believe beyond what we can verify scientifically. Paul Tillich warns believers against the problem of literalism and science with regard to faith. He says that reading the Bible literally is superstition, and replacing religious language with science is also superstition. Rather, religion should continue to have its own language and symbols which should not be replaced by science, bearing in mind that religion and science address different fields of human life.[33]

The Challenge of Modernity

Another problem which faces the doctrine of the Holy Spirit is modernity that has made some theologians like Rudolf Bultmann to understand the Holy Spirit as a myth which is unintelligible and useless to modern humans without

---

[27] E. Ikenga-Metuh, 'The Revival of African Spirituality: A Leaf from African Instituted Churches', in *Encounter of Religions in African Cultures* (Geneva: LWF, 1991), 37.
[28] Abednego Keshomshaha, 'A Theology of Poverty Reduction in Tanzania: A Quest for Christian Socio-Economic and Political Vision' (Ph.D. Dissertation, Kirchliche Hochschule Wuppertal/Bethel, 2008), 151.
[29] Keshomshaha, 'A Theology of Poverty Reduction', 151. See Mugambi, *From Liberation to Reconstruction*, 72-85, 149-60.
[30] Bitrus, 'The Influence of Neo-Pentecostalism', 83.
[31] Bitrus, 'The Influence of Neo-Pentecostalism', 83.
[32] Cf. Naaman Laiser, 'Lutheranism in Africa', in Reijo Arkkila and R.O. Olak (eds), *The Theology of the Cross: Second International Lutheran Confessional Conference, 14-18 March 1994* (Helsinki: Sley-Kirjat Oy, 1994), 146. Cf. Keshomshahara, 'A Theology of Poverty Reduction', 90-91.
[33] Paul Tillich, *Systematische Theologie Band II*, 7 (Stuttgart: Evangelisches Verlagswerk Stuttgart, 1981), 121-28, 151, 164ff.

demythologisation.[34] The same applies to the spirits or ancestral spirits which are viewed as myths which ought to be demythologised.[35] From the time of enlightenment rationalism, the reality of spirits has been denied in the light of natural science.[36] Some Western missionaries in Africa were greatly influenced by the enlightenment worldview, and therefore they rejected the existence of spirits[37] although the Bible accepts the existence and miraculous powers of these spirits while warning people not to depend on them except God alone.[38] Michael Green warns that if we reject the existence of the evil spirits on the basis of science and rationalism, there is a danger of not accepting the existence of the Holy Spirit on the basis of science and rationalism since we cannot prove the Holy Spirit's existence by human reason.[39]

However, it should be noted that evil spirits and Satan are not objects or articles of the Christian faith. Sometimes, Christians in the Charismatic movements focus more on Satan and evil spirits to the extent of marginalizing the almighty God. The Nicaean and Apostles' Creeds are very clear on this, especially when they are concerned with God the Father, Son, and Holy Spirit. Nothing is said about Satan except the reality and forgiveness of sin.[40]

The influence of modernity on contemporary African theologians affects communication between them and ordinary African Christians who take seriously the reality of the spiritual world in the light of their African religious heritage and the Bible.[41] Thus, African pastors and theologians find themselves in a conflict between Western and African theology.[42] But all theologies are bound up with the cultural contexts in which they are made although learning

---

[34] Holm, 'The Work of the Spirit', 121-25; Keshomshahara, 'A Theology of Poverty Reduction', 89-90.

[35] Michael Green, *I Believe in Satan's Downfall* (London: Hodder and Stoughton, 1981), 15-20, 84-99. See Keshomshahara, 'A Theology of Poverty Reduction', 90.

[36] Richard Gehman, *African Traditional Religion in Biblical Perspective* (Kijabe: Kesho Publication, 1987), 106-119, 171; Green, *I Believe in Satan's Downfall*, 15-20, 84-99.

[37] John S. Mbiti, 'Eschatology', in Kwesi A. Dickson and Paul Elingworth (eds), *Biblical Revelation and African Beliefs* (Maryknoll, NY: Orbis, 1969), 183. Cf. Gehman, *African Traditional Religion*, 171.

[38] Gehman, *African Traditional Religion*, 176-83. Cf. Kurt E. Koch, *Demonology Past and Present: Inaugural Lecture at the Swaziland Christian University of Theology* (Neuhausen: Hanbler, no date), 4. Cf. I Samuel 28:3-22; Leviticus 19:31; Deuteronomy 18: 10-18; Isaiah 8: 18-20. Keshomshahara, 'A Theology of Poverty Reduction', 52-53.

[39] Green, *I Believe in Satan's Downfall*, 20.

[40] Keshomshahara, 'A Theology of Poverty Reduction', 95.

[41] Muzorewa, *The Origins and Development of African Theology*, 12. Also T.G. Kihogora, 'Angels, Demons and Spirits in African Christianity', in A. Nasimiyu-Wasike and D. Waruta (eds), *Mission in African Christianity: Critical Essays in Missiology* (Nairobi: Uzima Press, 1993), 53. Gehman, *African Traditional Religion*, 107. Mbiti, *Bible and Theology*, 76. Also, Keshomshahara 'A Theology of Poverty Reduction', 5, 90, and Laiser, 'Lutheranism in Africa', 146.

[42] Mika Vähäkangas, 'Genuinely Catholic, Authentically African? The Encounter between Neo-Thomism and African Thinking in Charles Nyamiti's Methodology' (Ph.D. Dissertation, University of Helsinki, 1997), 9.

from different cultures is of cardinal importance. Even when modern science regards the impact of charismatic gifts as sociological and psychological phenomena, some theologians argue that God operates also in the context of sociological, psychological, and natural means to fulfil his purpose of addressing the needs of humans.[43] This echoes what was said by the Lutheran Church in the USA regarding the functions of the Holy Spirit and psychological interpretations. This Lutheran Church states that:

> A combination of personal magnetism of healers and the suggestive atmosphere of the gathered congregation can be explained psychologically, but they can also be seen as God's gift. That a phenomenon has psychological explanation does not prevent it from being a gift of the Spirit.[44]

When the church explains faith and addresses human needs in terms of science and reason only, there is a danger of failing to address needs that are beyond what we can see and verify. As a result, people who have failed to get peace through science and reason tend to find solutions to their problem outside the church. That is why some have resorted to occultism and horoscopes in spite of scientific and technological developments in the world.[45] Although science and technology have improved people's lives, they have also created some problems that need solutions outside of the field of science and technology.[46] These are the challenges which our churches ought to tackle in the sense that our mission is holistic in covering the spiritual, psychological, sociological and material needs of humans, without deviating from the biblical and theological foundations of the Christian faith.

---

[43] Stanley Benson, 'The Conquering Sacrament: Baptism and Demon Possession among the Maasai of Tanzania', *African Theological Journal* 9:2 (July 1980), 58-60.

[44] Paul D. Opsahl (ed), *The Holy Spirit in the Life of the Church* (Minneapolis: Augsburg Publishing, 1978), 262.

[45] *Spirits, Ancestors and Healing: A Global Challenge to the Church, A Resource for Discussion* (Geneva: LWF, 2006), 14-17.

[46] A. Keshomshahara, *A Theology of Poverty Reduction in Tanzania: A Quest for Christian Socio-Economic and Political Vision* (Dodoma: Central Tanganyika Press, 2008), 12, n. 84.

Bitter and Sweet Tears: Exploring the Spirituality of the Eastern Church Fathers in the Light of Postmodern 'Enthusiastic Christianity' in Russia

Olga Zaprometova

The challenges of postmodern pluralism have produced insecurity and made room for doubts and hesitations that go beyond the issue of faithfulness to Scripture. We have more knowledge about God but less knowledge of God, less experiences of His presence and personal encounters with His love. Postmodernity does not trust abstract ideas. Everything is tested through a personal relationship. The crisis of self-identity in contemporary society is often considered to be a result of secularisation, and many Christians are trying to find a solution in the 'fellowship of the Holy Spirit.' In Russia, there is a growing interest in 'enthusiastic Christianity',[1] which some scholars characterise as an extra dimension of emotionalism that sometimes reaches exaltation. Is it possible however to see this phenomenon as a new manifestation of the open emotional expression which was both recognised by Eastern Christianity and formed an integral part of its tradition many centuries ago? Or is it a response to the advent of postmodern symptoms in Russian society?

We have to accept the fact that, as elsewhere in the world, many Russian Christians nowadays feel themselves 'homeless', moving from one church to another as religious institutions become marketing agencies and religious traditions become consumer commodities. Feeling and being 'at home' in this sense is a gift and a call from God. We are immersed in a postmodern[2] identity

---

Originally published in R. Olsen, K. Ahlstrand, J.A. Kirk, T. Petrova, T.F. Rossi, and J.J. Sebastian (eds), *Mission and Postmodernities*, Regnum Edinburgh Centenary Series 10 (Oxford: Regnum Books, 2010), 191-203.

[1] The author is using this term to include Pentecostals, Charismatics and Neocharismatics. See Stanley M. Burgess and Eduard M. van der Maas (eds), *The New International Pentecostal and Charismatic Movements* (Grand Rapids, Michigan: Zondervan, 2003), xix-xxii.

[2] In this study, the author is referring to post-modernity and post-modernism as the terms generally used to describe the aspects of contemporary culture that are the result of the unique features of late 20th century and early 21st century life.

crisis. The postmodern self is de-centered, disoriented, fragmented and tossed by the wind of every impinging image and context. Will this new movement of 'enthusiastic Christianity' be able and ready to envisage its mission calling in such a context? This study is an attempt to do three things:

1) To find answers to many questions posed by those who are taking Christian living as an ongoing drama. Who in Russia today is truly postmodern? To what extent is this so, and in what ways?

2) To show the role of emotions in the development of the practice, as well as the doctrine, of spiritual life by analyzing the teachings of representatives of the Eastern Church (Gregory the Theologian, Isaac of Nineveh and Simeon the New Theologian).

3) To make a link with today's preferences by pointing to the success of 'enthusiastic Christianity' in contemporary Russia. Can this be regarded as a direct response to the advent of postmodern symptoms in Russian society? How does 'rejoicing Christianity' envisage its mission calling in this context?

The First World War witnessed the end of the modern era including its hope to achieve all kinds of progress in society. According to Boris Pasternak, 1913 was the last year during which it was easier to love than to hate. Anna Akhmatova defined 1914 as the beginning of the 20th century. Although the early years of the 20th century seemed promising both for the Orthodox and for Evangelical Protestants in Russia, the declaration that followed the revolution (1918) regarding the separation of the churches from the state and of the schools from the churches, removed the legal basis of all religious institutions, which was not restored till 1989.[3] After the two World Wars, the European countries were disillusioned with the idea of the ongoing progress of civilisation towards a better future. Eurasia was swept by waves of different enthusiastic movements much more than the rest of the world. The utopian ideas required more and more sacrifices, as a kind of 'game', for the sake of 'happiness' promised by all kinds of leaders. As a result, the youth became apathetic toward the enthusiasm of previous generations and did not want to make sacrifices for the sake of a better life. 'Better to take life as it is, to enjoy it for your own good, there is no absolute truth to dedicate your life to totally and so… there is no meaning to this life'.

In the late 1970s and early 80s of the last century, Russian scholars noticed the historical shift that had been taking place in the former Soviet Union, defined by them as a crisis of civilisation. It was considered to be the response to the social and cultural changes that the society had undergone, and the formation of new stereotypes. It was already noticed that postmodernity allowed for plural interpretations. Nowadays, the inner man is fragile and facing problems as never before. The Russian Christian analysts report on the decline of the first wave of religious enthusiasm, which appeared on

---

[3] Walter Sawatsky, 'Orthodox-Evangelical Protestant Dialogue on Mission-Challenges and Shifting Options', *Acta Missiologiae* 1 (2008), 11-31.

post-Soviet territory and of the aspiration for the second one to come.[4] Religion, however, does not disappear from the social stage. Religious experience reflects the multiplicity of transformations and a human being's way of life. The godless way of life, implanted by mass media does not leave us without a perspective on what concerns secularism and religion. Quite the opposite! The deconstruction of traditional dispositions and beliefs, which is now taking place, gives a chance for a new social search for religious truth.[5]

Russian secular philosophers of today envisage the future of humankind to be the acquisition of religious meaning. They are expecting the renaissance of a set of religious beliefs. G. Kiselev, in his paper 'Postmodernity and Christianity', reminds us that the traditional self-identity in Eastern Christianity is fellowship between a human being and God. This mystical encounter is a process. According to this modern Russian scholar, the very first Ecumenical task of contemporary Christianity is to understand its true position and place in world history. Kiselev stresses that Russian religious philosophy has been waiting for the new birth of Christianity since the end of the 19th century. This religious philosophy claimed as well that a true spiritual renaissance of the world might be expected only through the intervention of the Holy Spirit.[6] It definitely seems that the pendulum never stops swinging back and forth, and the ongoing search for truth, for meaning and for experiencing the Absolute (God) is essential for postmodernity as never before. The paradigm of love in contemporary Trinitarian thought might be taken as an example of a synthesis of Western and Eastern Christian thought, that is turning out to be of special interest for the growing 'enthusiastic' Christians.[7]

It is assumed that most Western readers have little experience with the Orthodox tradition, its richness, and variety that so greatly influenced the formation of the 'Russian soul'. The priority given to emotional values over material ones by the Russian character is a well-known fact.[8] Emotions are one of the mightiest powers in history and culture. The academic world is going through a process of analyzing the 'emotional revolution' in the humanities and sees it as a new paradigm shift. In 2007, an international conference on 'Emotions in Russian History and Culture' was held in Moscow. Among the problems raised at this forum were inter alia: emotional responses to the texts

---

[4] Pavel Levushkan, 'The Church proved to be unprepared for the coming of the Google world', *Mirt* 1 (2009), 12-13 (in Russian).

[5] Alexander S. Vatoropin and Konstantin M. Olkhovikov, 'The Perspectives of Secularism and Religion in the Post-modern Era', *Social Sciences and Modernity* 3 (2003), 136-45 (in Russian).

[6] Grigory S. Kiselev, 'Post-modernity and Christianity', *Questions of Philosophy* 12 (2001), 3-15 (in Russian).

[7] See Mikhail Aksenov-Meerson, 'The Love Paradigm and the Retrieval of Western Medieval Love Mysticism in Modern Russian Trinitarian Thought' (Doctoral dissertation, Fordham's University, 1996).

[8] Alla Sergeyeva, *The Russians: Behavior Stereotypes, Traditions, Mentality* (Moscow: Science, 2005), 136 (in Russian).

that represent culture, emotions as a discipline, and the role of emotions and historical memory.

The growing Pentecostal and Charismatic congregations that are often referred to in some circles as 'enthusiastic Christianity', differ from evangelical fundamentalists in their search for truth. This truth can be found, according to them, not only in the sphere of the mind (teaching, doctrine) but also in spiritual experiences. These experiences are followed by a change of attitude and conduct, which is the essential part of the true conversion. The Pentecostal worldview is characterised primarily by the emphasis put on the importance of communion with God, and by the claim that love is an emotional experience.[9]

First, let me remind the reader what is the difference between a Western and an Eastern understanding of 'doing' theology. The very term 'theology' is often misunderstood. It is commonly agreed that theology deals with the knowledge of God which man strives to acquire. It is also often accepted that theology seeks to explain the relations between God and man (God and the created world) and aims at explaining current social problems in the light of the Gospel and the Scriptures. Theology is seen as a contemplative discipline, which helps human beings to have a better understanding of God and the world He created. For the East, theology starts with the *ortho-doxy*, understood as proper worship. According to James Stamoolis, theology is something in which believers must participate: 'For the Orthodox, all theology is worship; all worship is theology'.[10] For the West, *ortho-doxy* is related more to the correct understanding of doctrinal statements (taking a different meaning of the Greek word *doxa* which underlies the second element of the word 'orthodoxy'). It is a rational way of thinking. In other words, the difference is in the emphasis put on the experiential versus the rational way of doing theology. The experiential way is related to the prayer life of a believer and is inseparable from the spirituality of a Christian. However, it does not mean that Western theology excludes the spiritual life of the believer, nor that Eastern theology excludes a correct understanding of doctrine.

Let us turn now to the writings of the Eastern Church Fathers in order to see whether there is any place for emotions that may be relevant to our postmodern era. One of the most famous Jewish exegetes of pre-Christian times, Philo of Alexandria, wrote about *drunkenness, sober ecstasy* and *intellectual rage/fury* when trying to describe his own spiritual/intellectual experience.[11] His approach to biblical exegesis is in accord both with the earlier Jewish tradition (1 Sam 1:13-16) and with that later developed in the New Testament (Acts 2:12-15; Eph 5:18). In the Bible, such an emotional state of praying is compared to drunkenness (1 Sam1:13-16; Acts 2:12-15; Eph 5:18). Tertullian, the

[9] Jackie D. Johns, 'Pentecostalism and the Postmodern Worldview', *Journal of Pentecostal Theology* 7 (1995), 73-96.

[10] James Stamoolis, *Eastern Orthodox Mission Theology Today* (Maryknoll, NY: Orbis Books, 1986), 10.

[11] For Philo it is still more the intellectual experience. See Kenneth Schenk, *A Brief Guide to Philo* (Moscow: St. Andrew's Biblical-Theological Institute, 2007), 23.

3rd-century North African theologian, talked about the marriage of a believer's soul to the Holy Spirit, followed by the physical body. This is his way of explaining how a soul is able to feel God, and to witness His mighty deeds through prophecies and feelings/emotions.[12] Gregory the Theologian (4th century) is considered to be one of the creators of the Theology of Light in the Christian tradition, which later was further developed by the Hesychast movement. His teaching on the vision of God is inseparable from his teaching on the knowledge of God. Gregory the Theologian points out that a person can see God only by feeling His mystical presence. The pinnacle of the whole Christian life, according to him, is *deification* or *theosis* (unification of a human being with God).[13] The term *deification* appears to be a Latinate calque of *theosis* rather than an accurate translation of its meaning, and this serves to obscure rather than illuminate the dialogue between the Eastern and the Western Christianity. *Theosis* includes two complementary stages of deification: the process towards deification and the state of deification. Gregory the Theologian affirms that the first 'stage of theosis' takes place in our current life, and the second one will be accomplished in the age to come; now we only foretaste theosis, but there is the eschatological theosis that is waiting for us at the 'fulfilment of times', the one we will be able to enjoy fully.[14] The way leading to deification is a human being's love for God, as expressed in prayer and mystical experience as well as in the fulfilment of the New Testament commandments. Although God still remains unknowable, inexpressible, unreachable, and invisible, prayer is primarily a meeting with the living God. A human being is seeking God and is in need of fellowship with Him, and God is seeking those who are *thirsty after Him, continually and abundantly outpouring* (Himself) *upon them.*[15] Praying to Christ was an integral part of Gregory's spiritual life. His prayers were filled with a deep personal love for Christ.[16]

---

[12] Quintus Tertullianus, *On the Soul* (St. Petersburg: Oleg Abushko's Publishing House, 2004), 139 (in Russian); www.krotov.info/ (in Russian)

[13] 'Deification' is the ancient theological word used to describe the process by which a Christian becomes more like God through His grace (2 Pet 1:3-4). Because of the incarnation of the Son of God, because the fullness of God has inhabited human flesh, being joined to Christ means that it is again possible to experience *deification,* the fulfillment of our human destiny. According to the Orthodox tradition, nourished by the Body and Blood of Christ, we are partaking in the grace of God, in His strength, in His righteousness, in His love, and are therefore enabled to serve Him and glorify Him. Thus, while remaining human, we are being *deified.*

[14] Alfeyev, *The Life and Teaching of St. Gregory the Theologian* (Moscow: Lovers of Church History Society's Press, 1998), 391, citing Gregory's *Oration* 38, 11, 22-24 (in Russian).

[15] Alfeyev, *The Life and Teaching of St. Gregory the Theologian*, 360 (in Russian).

[16] According to Origen, one has to pray only to God the Father through Christ, because Christ Himself did this and taught it to His disciples (Matt 6:9; 26:39; Lk 11:2; John 12:27; 17:11 et al). All the known Early Church liturgies are addressed to God the Father. Liturgies addressed to God the Son appeared not earlier than in the fifth century, in the era of the Christological controversies.

According to Archimandrite George, 'Theosis is the acquisition of the Holy Spirit, whereby through God's grace Christians become participants in the Kingdom of God.... Theosis begins here in time and space, but it is not static or complete, it is an open-ended progression uninterrupted through all eternity'.[17] This process of deification is a fairly close description of the process that Protestant theology describes as *sanctification* and might be considered as one of the possible themes for the future dialogue between Pentecostal and Orthodox communities.

Bitter and Sweet Tears

The experiences of a person on his journey towards God appear also in the Syrian Christian literature. One of the outstanding representatives of the Syrian tradition in the Eastern Church is Isaac the Syrian (7th century), for whom spiritual life starts with the turning of the soul to God and the rejection of the ways of this world. According to him, the world is the sum of a human's passions. Like Gregory the Theologian, for whom prayer was an encounter with the living God, Isaac the Syrian claimed that *life in God was a sensation or feeling of His presence.* When for some reason this presence is lost, the believer is unable to find peace until he/she feels His presence again.[18]

Here one has to take into consideration that in our postmodern world the word 'passion(s)' has three different meanings: (1) etymologically, the word does mean suffering, but in modern language, this meaning is pretty well restricted to a theological context, speaking about the passion for Christ; (2a) in common usage, the word is often a synonym for emotion, but is rather stronger, meaning an overwhelming enthusiasm for something;[19] (2b) in tabloid style usage, it has strongly sexual overtones, and, for a lot of people, this may even have become the primary meaning. There are several interpretations of the concept of passions in Patristic literature, including two major ones: passion as a sinful inclination and passion as an inherited ability of a soul which might be turned to (for) good as to evil.[20]

According to Isaac the Syrian, there are three stages along the way to a human's unification with God: repentance, purification, and perfection or in other words: change of will, freedom from passions, and the acquisition of perfect love and the fullness of God's grace. Repentance[21] starts when one feels

---

[17] George Archimandrite, *Theosis: The True Purpose of Human Life* (Mount Athos: Holy monastery of St. Gregorios, 2006), 86.

[18] Alfeyev, *The World of Isaac the Syrian* (Moscow: Lovers of Church History Society's Press, 1998), 109 (in Russian).

[19] See Steven J. Land, *Pentecostal Spirituality: A Passion for the Kingdom* (Sheffield, Sheffield Academic Press, 1997). Here is the example that a passion can be a fixed attitude, not just a temporary enthusiasm.

[20] K.T. Ware, *The Meaning of 'Pathos' in Abba Isaias and Theodoret of Cyrus* (Louvain: Studia Patristica XX, 1989), 315-22.

[21] Greek word, *μετανοια*, means 'change of thoughts, change of mind'.

sinful, due to the intervention of God's grace.[22] Teaching on repentance and the encounter of a human soul with God is closely related to Isaac's teaching on tears. When referring to the Saviour's words: *Blessed are they that mourn* (Matt 5:4), Isaac adds that *the one who is in the love of God will never lack the grace of tears because he/she is never lacking the source that is feeding him/her: the remembrance of God. That is why even when he/she is sleeping he/she is talking to God.*[23] Isaac distinguishes between bitter and sweet tears, tears of repentance and tears of affection (*slezy umilenia* – Slavic) given to a person when he or she reaches the purity of heart. The last type of tears means 'tenderness' ('tender-hearted'), 'mildness' or 'meekness'. Tears in prayer testify that prayer is accepted by God. According to Isaac, endless crying may start for any of the following three reasons:

> … from awe and wonder occasioned by the mystery of revelation that is revealed to the mind only rarely – tears begin to pour unbidden and without the will of a person and without forcing… ; …from the love to God that inflames the soul to such an extent that a person cannot bear this love without continuous crying from pleasure because of its sweetness… ; … from great humbleness of heart.[24]

Unification with God is impossible without prayer because prayer is a personal encounter with God. Isaac underlines how one has to pray: attentively, with deep feeling and with tears (because the grace of tears is the fullness of prayer),[25] with fervour and faith. This amazement, wonder, and rapture of the mind under the influence of the Holy Spirit, and seeing the Divine Light in a state of *silence* and *peace* is sometimes called ecstasy. When realizing that one does not belong to oneself but rather to God, one is going out of oneself and can no longer tell whether one exists in present time or in eternity.[26] When the control and supervision of the Spirit rules over the mind… then freedom is taken from nature, and the mind is led instead of leading.[27] An intense personal fellowship between a human being and God is taking place. What a soul is praying for is no longer represented by the words of the prayer itself, but rather by feeling and experiencing the spiritual realities of the world yet to come. These realities are beyond human understanding, except by the power of the Holy Spirit…. From this experience of prayer, the Holy Spirit lifts the soul up to meditation that is called spiritual vision.[28]

---

[22] Augustine, Wesley and many others wrote about the same, while Pentecostals preach about this as well.

[23] Quoted according to Alfeyev, *The World of Isaac the Syrian*, 145.

[24] Quoted according to Alfeyev, *The World of Isaac the Syrian*, 147. At the same time, according to Alfeyev, Isaac does not always define the line between the two types of tears: they are more likely two aspects of the same experience, 148.

[25] Alfeyev, *The World of Isaac the Syrian*, 153.

[26] Vladimir Lossky, *Essays on the Mystical Theology of the Eastern Church* (Moscow: SEI Center's Press, 1991), 156-257 (in Russian).

[27] Quoted according to Alfeyev, *The World of Isaac the Syrian*, 230.

[28] Quoted according to Alfeyev, *The World of Isaac the Syrian*, 23-33.

The image of drunkenness caused by wine helps Isaac describe the experience of a mystical encounter, which is in itself the introduction to the heavenly joy and pleasure of the Kingdom of Heaven.

> … Quite often it happens that a person bows his knees in prayer, his hands are lifted up to heaven, his face is turned to the Cross of Christ, and all his thoughts are brought together in prayer to God, and at the same time, as a human being is praying to God with tears and affections, suddenly a spring starts to spurt in his heart, pouring out pleasure; then parts of his body are weakened, his eyes close, the face bent over to the earth, his thoughts are changing in such a way that he cannot bow down from the joy that is exciting his whole body.[29]

> From time to time, however, the mind is taken from the prayer and carried to heaven as a captive and involuntary tears like springs of water pour over the face and water it. At the same time the person himself feels at peace, is speechless and filled with amazing vision and truly this is a ceasing of prayer; it is a state that is above prayer – a state of constant amazement in the face of every one of God's creatures, like those who have lost their senses because of wine.[30]

> When the soul is drunk with the joy of hope and the joyfulness of God, the body does not feel sorrows…. This happens when the soul enters into the joy of the Spirit.[31]

Such experience is frequently associated by Isaac with the Eucharist, in which the true love of God is revealed to a human being.

Simeon the New Theologian (10th-11th centuries) is regarded in the West as the most outstanding of the medieval mystics for his charismatic approach to Christian life. Like Gregory the Theologian, Simeon speaks about his experiences of the Divine Light and mentions it in all his writings. Besides these experiences, Gregory mentions as well prayer *in other tongues* and how much his *soul suffers* and *cries.*[32] Tears, as a theme in Simeon's writings, are associated with the themes of love for God and vision, as in Isaac's writings. Simeon gives testimony regarding the process of a person's transformation, which takes place in turning to God in prayer, and in shedding bitter tears of repentance and grief. Once the state of a clean heart and the vision of the Divine are reached, there is a consolation, and the person experiencing it sheds sweet tears (Matt. 5:8). When envisaging God and listening to His revelations, the person becomes a light. All of Simeon's personal experiences, which form the basis of his theology, are not just an individual search for God, but rather the very revelation of God Himself to a human being. He perceives this

---

[29] Quoted according to Alfeyev, *St. Simeon the New Theologian and the Orthodox Tradition* (Moscow: Lovers of Church History Society's Press, 1998), 396-97 (in Russian).

[30] Quoted according to Alfeyev, *The World of Isaac the Syrian*, 259.

[31] Quoted according to Alfeyev, *The World of Isaac the Syrian*, 262.

[32] Alfeyev, *St. Simeon the New Theologian and the Orthodox Tradition* (Moscow: Lovers of Church History Society's Press, 1998), 601.

experience as a feeling of light and a flood of tears – a reaction to God's presence unseen by his earthly sight.[33]

It is often argued that deep Christian affections are at the core of Pentecostal spirituality and they are considered by many as essential for understanding theology. For one of the most widely recognised Pentecostal authors of today, Steve Land, deep Christian affections are different from mere feelings or moods. Pentecostal prayer shapes and expresses the affections that Land is interpreting as 'a passion for the Kingdom'.[34] This passion is different from temporary feelings or shallow emotions. Love as such, including the love of God, is a passion. We do not love principles; we love the Person. As defined by Jürgen Moltmann, these differences can be 'noticed when praying to the Father, to Christ and the Spirit, and are reflected in the different forms of intercession, invocation, and adoration'.[35]

One can compare the three components of the Eastern church fathers' mystical encounter with the Holy Spirit which have been discussed in this paper with the three major characteristics of Pentecostal theology: orthodoxy, orthopathy, and orthopraxy. The first concerns prayer, in which an encounter with a living God is taking place. Its goal is a vision of God, knowing His will and accepting it freely. The second corresponds to experiencing the presence of God, as expressed in various ways (tears, ecstasy, etc.). The third is the transformation of a believer's way of life (*deification*) as described by the Eastern Fathers'.[36]

Literally, spirituality means life in God's Spirit, and a living relationship with Him. As we can see, experiencing the Holy Spirit is inseparable from the Spirituality of the Eastern Church tradition. Bitter and sweet tears, as well as joy and love, were a vital part of the transformation process going on in a Christian, which was embraced by the teaching on *deification.* The writings of the Eastern Fathers give us valuable evidence of the variety and richness of the ancient Church's spiritual life, and its ability to incorporate reflections of spiritual experience into its doctrine.

In sum, one may see the important place of emotional experience, not just in the practice of praying, but also in the development of doctrine. This experience was always an integral part of Eastern Christian spirituality.

Theology begins when one first prays, since praying is a deeper mode of understanding than knowing by means of reason alone.[37] Although the term 'deification' is unknown to Pentecostals, most of them speak about the importance of the fellowship of a Christian with the living God. The

[33] Alfeyev, *St. Simeon the New Theologian and the Orthodox Tradition*, 340-50

[34] Land, *Pentecostal Spirituality*.

[35] Jürgen Moltmann, *The Spirit of Life: A Universal Affirmation* (Minneapolis: Fortress Press, 1994), 12.

[36] Olga M. Zaprometova, 'Experience of the Holy Spirit in the Context of Patristic Tradition: The Pentecostal's Reading', *Pages* 13:1 (2008/2009), 63-90 (in Russian).

[37] Don E. Saliers, *The Soul in Paraphrase: Prayer and the Religious Affections* (Akron: OSL Publications, 2003), 70.

Pentecostal movement stresses the value of religious experience, which may transform the postmodern fragmentation. Experiencing the Holy Spirit is inseparable from a Pentecostal spirituality, and it is on these grounds that Pentecostals are often accused of being emotional at the expense of being rational.[38]

Pentecostalism is fundamentally experiential and culturally constructed (formed by the culture). However, it is this experiential and inter-cultural approach which allows for greater possibilities. M. Cartledge defines Pentecostalism as a worshipful experience and a crisis experience (that must be understood in a Christian context). It is also a social context which theologically may be accounted for in a broad sacramental sense.[39] Prayer is the centre of Pentecostal spirituality. Since prayer is communion and a dialogue, which involves a relationship in passion between those who pray and God, it is the place where the encounter between a human being and the living God occurs. The Pentecostal worldview is characterised primarily by the emphasis it puts on the importance of communion with God, and by claiming constantly that love is an emotional experience. Salvation, when conceived of as a communion, involves a response of freely given love, and a sincere turning of the human will towards God and His ways. This makes communion with God deeper and deeper.

As R. Roberts has observed, all the peculiarly Christian emotions are founded on a passionate interest in the Kingdom of God.[40] Some contemporary Pentecostals define their own personal experiences as charismatic manifestations or deeds of the Holy Spirit, which result in the decision to follow Him. Love for God and neighbour is the basis for the mission calling of the new 'enthusiasts': to spread the Kingdom of God through witnessing, preaching and ministering as well as through different forms of social work. T. Richie underlines the importance of the Pentecostal heritage of ecumenicalism and inclusivism, as an answer to the religious diversity and the pluralistic opinions in our contemporary world.[41] 'Rejoicing Christianity' must envisage its mission calling and consider carefully the distinctiveness of its own worldview in the context of the postmodern era.[42] Nowadays Pentecostals (including the Charismatic movement which some Russian authors call Neo-Pentecostalism) are growing in number in Russia, and have become a visible phenomenon in both the religious and the social spheres, attracting the

---

[38] Land, *Pentecostal Spirituality*, 132.

[39] Mark J. Cartledge, 'Pentecostal Experience: An Example of Practical-Theological Rescripting', *JEPTA* 28:1 (2008), 21-33.

[40] Robert C. Roberts, *Spiritual Emotion: A Psychology of Christian Virtues* (Grand Rapids: Eerdmans, 2007), 196.

[41] Tony Richie, '"The Unity of the Spirit": Are Pentecostals Inherently Ecumenists and Inclusivists?', *JEPTA* 26:1 (2006), 21-35.

[42] Jackie D. Johns, 'Pentecostalism and the Postmodern Worldview', *Journal of Pentecostal Theology* 7 (1995), 73-96.

attention of the media and provoking considerable controversy.[43] Still, due to the secularisation of society and to the new phenomenon of postmodernity, unlike in their early years, Pentecostals are no longer regarded as a sect. In general, the crisis of postmodernity in Russia results in longing for a restoration of the supernatural, a strengthening intercultural relation, an attraction to the mystery and an affirmation of the more figurative and symbolic forms of communication. 'Enthusiastic Christianity' has a lot to offer to the unhappy ones in society, who are thirsty and in search of a new spirituality. However, one should not disregard the importance and richness of the spiritual heritage of Eastern spirituality, now embedded in a way in the 'Russian soul'.

This paper has attempted to show that in a sense the new movement of 'rejoicing Christianity' is a direct response to the advent of postmodern symptoms in Russian society. In view of our culture's orientation to success, to production and prestige and to all the requirements that follow such an orientation, our inner being is longing for deeper spirituality, quiet and peace. It is reflected in the search for religious experience, for deeper affections and for meaning in a committed Christian life. The encounter with God's Spirit, i.e., the experiencing of the *Ruakh* of God is first and foremost a stirring one.[44] The intention of this paper has been to create a link to the past, this includes both to find the roots of postmodern Pentecostalism's experiential theology and of its rich emotional outpouring in experiences presented in the Patristic tradition as part of a process of seeking self-identity, and at the same time to strengthen awareness of the inter-cultural relationship between the two eras.

The search for a more solid and constructive dialogue between followers of Eastern and Western Christian traditions is one of humankind's most urgent tasks, especially in the light of globalisation. Let us keep the 'windows of theology open', since this may be the proper answer to both the scepticism and the fundamentalism of our times. Without overlooking the experiential component of conversion, which plays a role in the process of reaching salvation and full communion with God, 'enthusiastic Christianity' has begun to seek its roots in Holy Scriptures and in Church tradition. Will the 'enthusiasts', together with some contemporary Orthodox theologians, choose to follow the way of Neo-Patristic synthesis, or will they claim that this represents only an escape from the problems imposed by postmodernity, an escape which can be no more than a slavish imitation of tradition, one which rejects any theological development? Will also the Orthodox Church, the most prominent religious power in contemporary Russia, be ready to recognise the reality of the encounter with Christ, which 'enthusiastic Christianity' advocates

---

[43] It is a surprise that the denomination, whose history in Russia can be traced to the beginning of the 20th century and which experienced all the difficulties of religious persecution, equally with the representatives of the Orthodox Church and other confessions, though recognised all over the world, in Russia is still sometimes considered to be a cult.

[44] Anton Houptepen, *God, the Open Question: Theological Perspectives of the Modern Culture* (Moscow: St. Andrew's Biblical-Theological Institute, 2008), 330 (in Russian).

and testifies to? Let us remember that, so far, these are open questions, and that the secular analysts are waiting for a response from the Church, not just in the form of official ecclesiological-political acts or documents, but rather in reflections, conjectures or insights from its individual members.

Exploring the spirituality of the early Church Fathers can serve as a helpful way for Pentecostal and Charismatic believers in Russia to overcome the postmodern crisis of self-identity. It may help find in Church history answers relevant to the contemporary Russian context. This will enrich mission activity in Europe both East and West, and even in Asia, due to the spread of Russian Orthodoxy by emigration, and in view of globalisation and the postmodern identity crisis. The emphasis put on 'enthusiastic Christianity' is not a doctrinal question. Instead of logical/rational theological *Regula fidei* formulations/ concepts, it suggests rather an experiential side as the basis of Christian faith. This is a much more promising approach to mission in postmodern Russia. In the postmodern world, one has not just to see with one's own eyes but also to feel with one's own heart, to experience in one's whole being the presence of God and His love. Mission must follow worship/doxology. Thus, we may see in what sense an understanding of the role of emotions in the Eastern Christian tradition might become a bridge to understanding the growth of 'enthusiastic' Christianity in contemporary Russia. The experience of the closeness of God and His intimate presence is greater than theological proofs of God's existence for secularised society. Love is more than an attribute of God! It is His essence. The Christian East with its rich religious experiences, described by the Early Church Fathers, seems to be more attractive to disappointed postmodernists, especially the younger generation. Will its theological treasure be embraced by contemporary 'enthusiasts'?

Growing Together in Unity and Mission

Veli-Matti Kärkkäinen

Introduction: The Urgency and Dilemma of Unity

What the missionary document *Ad Gentes* of the Roman Catholic Church's Second Vatican Council says of the missionary nature of the church is widely embraced by all Christian traditions: 'The pilgrim Church is missionary by her very nature, since it is from the mission of the Son and the mission of the Holy Spirit that she draws her origin, in accordance with the decree of God the Father' (#2). Similarly, the important current ecumenical document, *The Nature and Mission of the Church*, speaks of the mission of the church deriving from the 'reflection of the communion in the Triune God' (#34), meaning that 'mission belongs to the very being of the Church' (#35).[1] These statements anchor the essentially missionary nature of the church in the sending nature of the trinitarian God, the one God.

Consequently, mission and unity are deeply and integrally related. This call for seeking unity in mission and mission in unity in the beginning of the new millennium is succinctly described in the following two statements, the first one from the evangelical Lausanne Movement's Cape Town Commitment and the second from the ecumenical American *The Princeton Proposal for Christian Unity* document:

> We lament the dividedness and divisiveness of our churches and organisations. We deeply and urgently long for Christians to cultivate a spirit of grace and to be obedient to Paul's command to 'make every effort to maintain the unity of the Spirit in the bond of peace'.[2]

Originally published in John Gibaut and Knud Jørgensen (eds), *Called to Unity for the Sake of Mission*, Regnum Edinburgh Centenary Series 25 (Oxford: Regnum Books, 2010), 59-70.

[1] *The Nature and Mission of the Church,* Faith & Order Paper 198 (Geneva: WCC, 2007), #62. For the most recent important ecumenical statement on ecclesiology, see the 2013 'The Church: Towards a Common Vision'.

[2] 'The Cape Town Commitment' of the Lausanne Movement (2011), II.F.1. a; available at www.lausanne.org/en/documents/ctcommitment.html#p2-6 (accessed 16 January 2014).

> In late modernity we fear unity, often with good reason. We cherish our particularity – our family and ethnic heritage, our established patterns of life and thought. We look with suspicion on the political and economic forces that impose homogeneity. We celebrate diversity and pluralism, sometimes as a good in its own right, because we fear the constraints of single sets of ideals.[3]

Rightly, the German Lutheran dogmatician Wolfhart Pannenberg has reminded us that only '[if] Christians succeed in solving the problems of their own pluralism, may they be able to produce a model combining pluralism and the widest moral unity which will also be valid for political life'.[4]

Hence, the Biblical mandate for seeking the unity of the church for the sake of Christ's mission and reflecting the unity between the Son and the Father (John 17:26) is an urgent task given for all the church. 'Visible Christian unity is ... not a modern dream, but a permanent and central aspect of Christian life'. It calls us 'to a deeper unity of common prayer, common witness, shared conviction, and mutual acceptance'.[5] Yet, unlike in modernity, in our age, the concern for diversity and otherness compels us to mind differences as well. 'In our post-modern age, the desire to celebrate the different and suspect the same, to prefer ... the alien over the identical' is the starting-point.[6] How do we balance these two somewhat conflicting tasks – to work for unity and allow for diversity? Negotiating such a balance is the unique challenge of ecumenism for the third millennium. While attending to that task, ecumenists should also consider the implications for the work for unity stemming from both modern missions history and the current global spread of Christianity.

Particularly from the time of the Protestant Reformation, the unity of the church has been threatened and frustrated with ever-intensifying plurality and schisms. While socio-political changes such as industrialisation and colonialisation played a significant role from the beginning of the nineteenth century, nothing probably compares with the role of the modern missionary movement in spreading and diversifying the one church of Jesus Christ. As a result, Christianity became a global religion extending to all corners of the world. Although until the mid-twentieth century the universal church was unevenly spread throughout the continents of Africa, Asia, and Latin America – more often than not following the coastlines of the colonists – by the end of the second millennium a decisive shift had appeared.[7] Most Christians are now found in the global South and, by 2020, Africa will be the largest Christian

---

[3] *In One Body through the Cross: The Princeton Proposal for Christian Unity*, Carl E. Braaten and Robert W. Jenson (eds) (Grand Rapids, MI: Eerdmans, 2003), #2, 12

[4] Wolfhart Pannenberg, 'Christian Morality and Political Issues', in *Faith and Reality* (Philadelphia, PA: Westminster, 1977), 38.

[5] *In One Body through the Cross*, #3, 4 respectively, 12-13.

[6] F. LeRon Shults, 'Theological Responses to Postmodernities or Tending to the Other in Late Modern Missions and Ecumenism' – unpublished presentation for the Nordic Institute for Missiological and Ecumenical Research Annual Meeting at the University of Abo, Turku, Finland, 19-22 August 2007, 1.

[7] See further my 'Ecclesiology', in *Mapping Modern Theology*, Kelly Kapic and Bruce McCormack (eds) (Grand Rapids, MI: Baker Academic, 2012), 345-46 (345-76).

continent. The rise of the Pentecostal and Charismatic movements, which currently comprise more than a quarter of the worldwide membership of the church, along with the steady growth of the closely related Evangelical movement, have further diversified – and helped split! – the one church.

Add to this complex picture the well-known observation that the way of doing mission by the Catholics and Protestants has been vastly different; the difference has a definite bearing on the search for unity. Whereas in the spread of the Protestant church, mission societies and entrepreneurial individuals played a key role, in Catholic missions, monastic and other religious orders were in the forefront. Furthermore, while the Catholic Church virtually withstood the influence of the Enlightenment until Vatican II (1962-65), Protestant churches were from the beginning influenced by the Enlightenment.[8] We should not ignore the missionary enterprise of the Eastern Orthodox Church, notwithstanding its smaller scale: Orthodox priests and monks travelled to Russia, Siberia, Alaska, and other places to establish significant Orthodox constituencies.[9]

All this is to say that, by the opening of the twentieth century, the question of the churches' self-understanding and clarification of their identities in relation to the one church of Christ and other churches had become a major theological task.[10] With this task in mind, let us first examine the differing ecclesiological self-understandings of Christian communities in the global church. Thereafter, we will seek briefly to put the differing visions of unity into perspective with regard to the main issues and see what kinds of tasks await us in the future. Finally, having outlined the challenges, we seek to offer a number of potential resources and viewpoints that may further help our churches to grow together in unity and shared mission.

Different Perceptions of the Unity among Church Traditions[11]

For the Orthodox Church, it is not easy to define an official ecumenical standpoint, for the simple reason that official pronouncements are few and far between. What is clear is that the Eastern Church considers schism a grave problem and believes itself to be standing in the unbroken line of the apostolic church. Hence, rediscovering and re-establishing unity is a key concern, as is

---

[8] See Stephen B. Bevans and Roger P. Schroeder, *Constants in Context: A Theology of Mission for Today* (Maryknoll, NY: Orbis, 2004), chap. 7.

[9] Bevans and Schroeder, *Constants in Context*, 227-28.

[10] See further Jaroslav Pelikan, 'Christian Doctrine and Modern Culture (since 1700)', in *The Christian Tradition: A History of the Development of Doctrine 5* (Chicago/London: Chicago University Press, 1989), 282.

[11] This section is drawn from Chapter 7 of my *An Introduction to Ecclesiology: Ecumenical, Historical, and Contextual Perspectives* (Downers Grove, IL: IVP, 2002). For supporting sources, see Harding Meyer, *That All May Be One: Perceptions and Models of Ecumenicity* (Grand Rapids, MI, and Cambridge, UK: Eerdmans, 1999), 15-36. I am also indebted to Risto Saarinen, *Johdatus Ekumeniikkaan* (Helsinki: Kirjaneliö, 1994), 81-110, 113-21.

evident also in the prayers of the divine liturgy. The very minimum for Orthodox Christians to overcome the painful divisions is the recognition of the apostolic succession of the episcopate and sacramental priesthood in addition to the apostolic tradition as formulated in the ancient creeds.[12] The Orthodox Church also argues that 'the unity of the church [is] grounded in its foundation by our Lord Jesus Christ and in the communion of the Holy Trinity and in the sacraments'. Where can this unity be found? According to Orthodox interpretation, this 'unity is expressed through the apostolic succession and the patristic tradition and has been lived up to the present day within the Orthodox Church'.[13]

More thoughtfully and authoritatively than any other Christian family, the Roman Catholic Church has carefully and publicly defined its understanding of Christian unity at Vatican II: 'The restoration of unity among all Christians' which was 'one of the principal concerns' of the council (*Unitatis Redintegratio*, #1). Along with the Orthodox Church, Catholics affirm only one church of Christ on earth. Importantly, *Lumen Gentium*, the defining ecclesiological document, helped correct and balanced features of the Roman understanding of the church that obviously stood in the way of unity. Three points are crucial for our purposes. First of all, rather than considering the Church as the 'perfect society' (after Vatican I), *Lumen Gentium* imagines the church as a Pilgrim People on the way – not yet arrived, still in process (chapter 7). That kind of attitude, of course, facilitates mutual learning, correction, and seeking for unity together with other churches. Second, rather than equating the Church of Christ with the Catholic Church, it teaches rather that Christ's Church 'subsists in the Catholic Church' (#8), leaving open the possibility for the same in other Christian communities.[14] Third, although the Council affirmed that 'the Church, now sojourning on earth as an exile, is necessary for salvation' (#14), it also famously set forth the most comprehensive and inclusive vision of the levels that other Christians and even followers of other faith traditions may be linked to the Catholic Church. Of other Christians with whom the Catholic Church shares so much in common from its Scriptures to the triune God to the sacraments, and so forth, it is said that 'in many ways, she is linked with those who, being baptised, are honoured with the name of Christian' (#15). These and similar ecumenically pregnant statements are not meant to try to 'whitewash' the contemporary Roman Catholic vision of unity in order to make it more appealing.

---

[12] See further C.G. Patelos (ed), *The Orthodox Church in the Ecumenical Movement* (Geneva: WCC, 1978).

[13] The statement of The Third Pan-Orthodox Pre-Conciliar Conference in Chambésy, Switzerland, 1986, in *Episkepsis* 369 (December 1968).

[14] I do not take this statement as necessarily contradictory to that of *Lumen Gentium* #13, which expresses the desire (that could also be said by all church communities which are missionary by nature): 'All men are called to be part of this catholic unity of the people of God which in promoting universal peace presages it. And there belong to or are related to it in various ways, the Catholic faithful, all who believe in Christ, and indeed the whole of mankind, for all men are called by the grace of God to salvation.'

Bishops, among whom the Bishop of Rome, the Pope, has the primacy, are the guardians of the unity of the church in the Catholic understanding of ecumenism.[15] The Roman Catholic Church makes the bold claim that the unity of the church already 'exists' within herself, and therefore they expect that other churches will 'return' to that church. Even though this mentality of the 'return of separated brethren' was qualified by Vatican II, it is still part of the Catholic ecumenical view. 'The unity, we believe, subsists in the Catholic Church as something she can never lose, and we hope that it will continue to increase until the end of time.'[16]

For the Anglican Communion, as explicated in the 'Thirty-nine Articles' (#19 and #34) of 1563 and 1571, the unity of the church is based on the preaching of the Word of God and the sacraments. However, the later 'Chicago-Lambeth Quadrilateral' from 1870 went further in its specifications regarding unity and outlined four aspects which shift the ecclesiological identity definitely towards the Roman Catholic and Orthodox view (and away from the Protestant one): Scripture, the Apostles' Creed, the two sacraments, and the episcopate.[17] Ecclesiologically speaking, it should be noted that, whereas the Reformation churches leave the leadership question open, for Anglicans the unity of the church requires the presence of a bishop. As is well known, within the worldwide Anglican communion is a great deal of plurality and diversity – and recently, the real threat of a split within the Anglican Communion between the predominantly liberal North and conservative South poses an urgent challenge.

The churches of the Reformation have stipulated a very minimum for Christian unity, namely, the preaching of the Word of God and the right administration of the sacraments. This is the position of the Lutheran Church as formulated in the Augsburg Confession #7 (the same principle is to be found also in the Reformed Second Helvetic Confession #17 and is materially followed by most Protestants):

> It is also taught, that one holy Christian church must always be and remain, which is the assembly of all believers, among whom the gospel is purely preached and the holy sacraments are administered according to the gospel. For it is sufficient for the true unity of the Christian church, that the gospel is harmoniously preached and the sacraments administered according to the Word of God. And it is not necessary for the true unity of the church, that everywhere the same ceremonies established by human beings be observed.

As long as there is basic unanimity in the understanding of the gospel, then church structures, liturgies, leadership patterns, and other such matters may differ. Even though the personal faith of individuals is not a matter of indifference, unity can never be based on it (as is the case with Free Churches).

---

[15] See further especially *Lumen Gentium* #23.

[16] *Unitatis Redintegratio* #4.

[17] *The Book of Common Prayer*, Historical Documents of the Church, Lambeth Conference of 1888, Resolution 11. The Lambeth Quadrilateral can be found at http://anglicansonline.org/basics/Chicago_Lambeth.html (accessed 20 April 2009).

The newest Christian churches, the Free Churches, have entertained many kinds of suspicions, even doubts, concerning ecumenism. The guiding principle for them has been the idea of 'spiritual union' according to which God-given unity already exists between either 'true' churches or at least 'true' individual believers. The Free Churches have not located unity either in creeds or even in the Bible, although for most of them these two elements have been very important, but rather in the hearts of believing individuals.[18] The Unions of Baptist Congregations in Austria and Switzerland and the Union of Evangelical Free Churches in Germany defined their understanding in a way that illustrates the wide and diverse movement whose roots go back all the way to the Anabaptists of Reformation times and the sixteenth century, and the Baptists of the early seventeenth century.

> The Christian experiences the communion of the community above all in the local assembly of the faithful. In it, baptism for the confession of faith is performed, and the one bread, bestowed by the one Lord, is broken and shared. That is why the local parish understands itself as the manifestation of the one body of Christ, filled with the one Spirit and fulfilled with the one hope.[19]

Four aspects of this unity are highlighted in the Free Churches: first, the personal faith of every Christian; second, the local church as the focus; third, the priesthood of all believers; and fourth, reservations with regard to the idea of visible unity.[20]

Currently, the largest Free Church constituency and the most rapidly growing segment of Christianity, namely Pentecostals, basically define their ecclesial self-understanding along the same lines. What makes Pentecostalism both theologically and ecclesiastically more complex is that as the usual nomenclature 'Pentecostal/Charismatic movement' suggests, the phenomenon is multi-layered. Whereas 'Pentecostal' refers to diverse and rapidly proliferating movements stemming from the revivals started at the beginning of the twentieth century, 'Charismatic' movements refer to Pentecostal-type movements located within traditional churches. Thus, we can speak of 'Roman Catholic Charismatic Renewal' or 'Lutheran Charismatics'. It is noteworthy that this second layer – let alone the third one, currently named 'Neo-Charismatics' which consists of numerous independent movements around the globe – is larger than the original one. Catholic Charismatics alone number over 100 million, thus making them more numerous than any single Protestant family or Anglican communion. The ecumenical questions

---

[18] For the Baptists, see William L. Pitts, 'The Relation of Baptists to Other Churches', in *The People of God: Essays on the Believers' Church*, Paul Basden and David S. Dockery (eds) (Nashville, TN: Broadman, 1991), 235-50. For the Pentecostals, see Veli-Matti Kärkkäinen, *Spiritus ubi vult spirat: Pneumatology in the Roman Catholic-Pentecostal Dialogue, 1972-1989*, Schriften der Luther-Agricola Gesellschaft 42 (Helsinki: Luther-Agricola Society, 1998), ch. 5.

[19] Bund Evangelisch-Freikirchlicher Gemeinden in Deutschland, ed. *Rechenschaft vom Glauben*, vol 2, no 7 (1977).

[20] Meyer, *That All May Be One*, 24-27.

concerning Pentecostals and subsequent Charismatic movements are understandably different as the latter are part of their own respective church traditions – or, as with neo-Charismatics, they are part of no self-defined tradition!

What Kind of Unity Are We Talking About?

In summary, the various views of unity among Christian churches with all their differences have a common feature: that all churches ground the unity of the church in the unity of the triune God and the apostolic tradition as conveyed to us in the Bible and the ecumenical creeds. It is highly promising that even the currently youngest ecclesial tradition, Pentecostalism, in long-term international dialogue with the Roman Catholic Church, made this highly significant mutual statement. The *Final Report* (1985-89) of the International Dialogue between the Roman Catholic Church and Pentecostal churches opens with an important mutual affirmation (#29):

> Both Pentecostals and Roman Catholics believe that the *koinonia* between Christians is rooted in the life of Father, Son and Holy Spirit. Furthermore, they believe that this trinitarian life is the highest expression of the unity to which we together aspire: 'That which we have seen and heard we proclaim also to you, so that you may have fellowship with us; and our fellowship is with the Father and with his Son Jesus Christ' (1 John 1:3).[21]

That said, there are two wide and deep areas of disagreement and debate that have to be tackled as we hope to grow together towards unity in mission. The first one is the question of 'ecclesiality', namely, what makes the church, the church. Orthodox and Catholics (and to a large extent, Anglicans) regard the episcopate (presence of a bishop) and sacraments (celebrated under the legitimate bishop) as essential to church unity. (Where Orthodox and Anglicans differ from Roman Catholics is that they do not acknowledge the Papacy.) To Protestants and Free Churches, including Pentecostals, ministry patterns are a non-issue in relation to church unity. Furthermore, as already mentioned, Free Churches take the personal appropriation of faith as the requirement for the ecclesiality of the church communion; often this may lead to suspicion about the true churchly nature of other kinds of communities.[22]

The second very difficult question is the topic of visible unity. Let it suffice to mention this much in this context: on the one hand, all traditional churches and the ecumenical movement have set visible unity as the stated goal and ultimate aim of the pursuit of unity. On the other hand, no one can at this point

---

[21] *Perspectives on Koinonia*, #29. Report from the Third Quinquennium of the Dialogue between the Pontifical Council for Promoting Christian Unity and Some Classical Pentecostal Churches and Leaders (1985-1989), #29 (available at the website of Centre Pro Unione: www.prounione.urbe.it/dia-int/pe-rc/doc/e_pe-rc_pent03.html).

[22] See further Miroslav Volf, *After Our Likeness: The Church as the Image of the Trinity* (Grand Rapids, MI: Eerdmans, 1998), 133-35.

tell definitively what the nature of visible unity is! In contrast, it is quite easy to state what visible unity is *not*: it is widely agreed that it does not mean one 'world church', or the deletion of denominational distinctives, or similar solutions. The lack of consensus about what visible unity is means that the nature of unity is a continuing agenda in ecumenical conversations and work.

Moreover, one continuing development in the global church has everything to do with how unity may be realised, namely, the constant and rapid emergence of new congregational models, particularly in the Majority World (Asia, Africa, Latin America), but also in the United States and elsewhere. Many observers of world Christianity hold the opinion that the 'Independent' or Free Church type of congregational model will be the major paradigm in the third millennium. It is significant that the former Pope Benedict XVI (in his capacity as the Prefect of the Congregation for the Doctrine of the Faith), well known for severe reservations about congregational ecclesiologies and their counterparts in the Roman Catholic Church, has admitted that this is the direction into which Christian *oikumene* is heading.[23] The implications for how to seek the unity of the church including these disparate, diverse, and organisationally disconnected movements have not been much reflected on by the ecumenists. What is the vision for unity in that light? What is the ecumenical 'method'?

Having now briefly outlined the current differences in Christian visions of unity, and identified some of the deepest underlying issues, the rest of the essay seeks to tap into potential resources and insights on the way to a fuller unity in Christ's mission and church.

Some Ways and Forms of Seeking Unity in the New Context

In no particular order of importance, let us seek to identify some viewpoints, resources, and insights that may facilitate growth together in unity:

First, I suggest that we discern carefully some of the implications for Christian mission and unity of the radically changing mosaic of the global church. In other words, how would ecumenical work be reshaped as a result of the 'Macro-reformation'[24] taking place before our very eyes as Christianity is moving from the global North (Europe and North America) to the global South? As is well known, by 2050 only about one-fifth of the world's three billion Christians will be non-Hispanic whites.[25] At the same time, the

---

[23] Joseph Cardinal Ratzinger, *The Ratzinger Report: An Exclusive Interview on the State of the Church, Joseph Cardinal Ratzinger with Vittorio Messori* (San Francisco, CA: Ignatius, 1985), 45ff.

[24] Justo L. González, *Mañana: Christian Theology from a Hispanic Perspective* (Nashville, TN: Abingdon, 1990), 49.

[25] See Philip Jenkins, *The Next Christendom: The Coming of Global Christianity* (Oxford: OUP, 2001). Regrettably, Jenkins's book title is most unfortunate: there will never be another Christendom. Yet the basic argument of the book is not compromised by the uninformed choice of title.

composition of the church worldwide is changing dramatically: at present, one half of all Christians are Roman Catholic, another quarter is composed of Pentecostals/Charismatics (in three sub-groups as outlined above), while the rest are Eastern Orthodox Christians, by far the largest segment, and mainline Protestants, including Free Churches.[26] These demographics have several effects: there are going to be two major poles of the Christian church in terms of size and influence, namely, Roman Catholic and Pentecostal/Charismatic. They together comprise three-quarters of all church membership. All this means that conservative and traditional mindsets will be strengthened around the Christian church, even while theological liberalism reigns in western academia and in the worldwide Christian communions led by leaders from the global North. Moreover, the 'Pentecostalisation' of the Christian church in terms of Pentecostal/Charismatic spirituality and worship patterns infiltrating all churches continues to reshape the lives of the churches.

Second, in the light of these dramatic developments, I propose we take another careful look at the issue of ecclesiality, briefly outlined above. We need to rethink the necessary and sufficient conditions for a community to be called the church in the theological sense. The approach of traditional theology has too often been to impose its own, often quite-limited, definition of 'church' on its younger counterparts. Naturally, those churches that define what ecclesiality means usually themselves fulfil the requirements of their own definitions! But ecumenically, this does not further the discussion. For older churches, just to discard the enormous potential and force of non-traditional churches by classifying them as something less than a church is both dangerous and useless. We have to raise this blunt question: is there really any theological justification for denying the true churchliness of hundreds of millions of Christian communities from Pentecostals to other Free Churches to, say, the rapidly growing House Church movement in China or African Instituted Churches, and so on? Isn't such denial just another form of colonialism, a form of exercising power by the 'Old World' (i.e., old Christendom) over the 'New World'?

This leads us to my third suggestion: rather than unilaterally imposing one's own definitions as to what makes for the true church, both the principle of Christian hospitality and the needs of the diverse global church demand that we seek to learn from each other. This mindset was wonderfully present in the drafting of the American Princeton Proposal for Christian Unity. Looking at the younger churches, it says:

> Evangelical and Pentecostal Christians and their institutions also have a unique role. All churches may benefit from their vitality, their zeal for evangelism, and their commitment to Scripture. They demonstrate a spirit of co-operation with each other and sometimes with others that breaks down old barriers, creates fellowship among formally estranged Christians, and anticipates further unity.

---

[26] The basic statistical source is David B. Barrett, George T. Kurian and Todd M. Johnson, *World Christian Encyclopedia,* 2nd edn (New York: OUP, 2001); for global statistics, see especially 12-15, as well as the January 2014 edition of *International Bulletin of Missionary Research.*

> The free-church ecclesiologies of some Evangelicals bring a distinct vision of unity to the ecumenical task.[27]

One hopes that Free Churches and Evangelicals reciprocate in acknowledging the strengths of and lessons from older churches. Moreover, both parties are called to constructive self-criticism and self-scrutiny.

Fourth, we need to work towards finding ways of continuing to affirm the necessity and legitimacy of evangelisation and mission, on the one hand, and the need to involve all Christian communities in the condemnation of proselytism, on the other. Too often, it seems to me; some older Christian traditions fail to make the needed distinction between 'evangelisation' and 'proselytism', as if all forms of evangelistic activities (most often done by the younger Christian communities) were suspicious, if not totally unacceptable. The new WCC document *Together Towards Life: Mission and Evangelism in Changing Landscapes* (2012) represents a historic milestone as a number of Pentecostal and Evangelical communities, known for their missionary enthusiasm, have also been involved in its drafting and endorsement. Working towards finding ways of sharing common witness among Christian churches and collaboration in social work, reconciliation and peace-building are other related challenges and opportunities for Christian unity.

Fifth, let us be humble and modest about the aim of unity. Rather than full communion,[28] which is a hopelessly unachievable goal, at least in the contemporary ecumenical milieu and stage of development, why do we not seek for a partial communion? That is a more modest and realistic standard to begin with. Partial communion 'means mutual recognition despite substantial or significant differences or disagreements'.[29] That kind of goal may better help churches enter into a relationship of communion with another church that may seriously differ from themselves. This notion of communion admits many degrees. Just consider the principle of partial communion in relation to one of the defining aspects of ecclesiality, namely apostolicity, which is also the foundation for the church's missionary nature. The Jesuit ecumenist Roger Haight puts it succinctly: 'The apostolic character of common ecclesial existence provides the grounds for partial communion ... As a common apostolic dimension in all the churches, this ecclesial existence contains the

---

[27] *In One Body through the Cross*, #67, 55-56.

[28] The WCC 1991 Canberra Assembly formulated it this way: 'The goal of the search for full communion is realised when all the churches are able to recognise in one another the one, holy, catholic and apostolic church in its fullness. This full communion will be expressed on the local and the universal levels through conciliar forms of life and action. In such communion, churches are bound in all aspects of their life together at all levels in confessing the one faith, sharing sacramental life, and engaging in common witness, sustained by recognised and reconciled ministry.' O.C. Edwards Jr, 'Meanings of Full Communion: The Essence of Life in the Body', in *Speaking of Unity* 1 (2005): 11 (electronic journal of Faith & Order Commission of the National Council of the Churches of Christ in the USA: www.ncccusa.org/speakingofunity).

[29] Roger Haight, *Ecclesial Existence: Christian Community in History*, Vol 3 (New York and London: Continuum, 2008), 277.

possibility to serve as a basis for partial communion among the churches. Indeed, it urges such communion and even demands it'.[30]

Finally, and related to the goal of partial communion, I believe it is important to imagine flexible, creative, and diverse processes and structures in the service of seeking unity. That kind of imagination, rather than rigid structures, better fits the mosaic of the Christian church at both the local and global levels. Just consider work for unity with the global Pentecostal/ Charismatic movements. There are supreme difficulties even in trying to involve Pentecostals in long-term ecumenical work at the global level – even after the desire has been expressed! There is no global structure or umbrella that unites all Pentecostals, nothing like the global structures uniting traditional church families. Even when granted that there are co-operative organs such as the Pentecostal World Fellowship, one must keep in mind that even this does not represent a majority of Pentecostals, and its organisational capacity or intention is far from that of the corresponding global fellowships among traditional churches. Many more such examples could be given from other younger churches.

In Lieu of Conclusions: A Vision for Unity in Diversity

If we believe that 'Christian unity is given by God through the Holy Spirit',[31] then that is also the key to affirming unity in diversity. More than a convenient ecumenical catchword, the principle of unity in diversity is the way to go about the work of unity in our pluralistic and diverse world. This expression speaks both to the heart of the Christian search for oneness and the late modern appreciation of The Other.

Only the kind of unity that honours the otherness of the other is worth its name. 'The unity of the church does not ... reduce the difference to uniformity. In the New Testament, the church is neither a zone of intimate sympathy among the like-minded nor a space of live-and-let-live.'[32] That principle sets the seeking for Christian unity on a dynamic and challenging path. It is to steer between the Scylla of a 'simplistic celebration of the *different* [that] provides no resources for appropriate attachment', and the Charybdis of an 'anxious fusion to *the same* ... [that] hinders us from appropriate differentiation'.[33] While diversity is a high value both theologically and culturally, we also need to

---

[30] Haight, 285-86.

[31] *In One Body through the Cross*, #5, 13.

[32] *In One Body through the Cross*, #23, 28-29. *The Nature and Mission of the Church*, #62, puts it succinctly: 'Authentic diversity in the life of communion must not be stifled: authentic unity must not be surrendered.' This is also what Schleiermacher emphasised much earlier: see Friedrich Schleiermacher, *The Christian Faith*, H.R. Mackintosh and J.S. Stewart (eds) (New York: Harper Torchbooks, 1963), #150: 'Whensoever separations actually occur in the Christian church, there can never be lacking an endeavor to unite the separated.' See also #151, 152.

[33] Shults, 'Theological Responses to Postmodernities', 3.

beware of diversity that 'is easily conscripted to sinful purposes'; at times, it is not so easy to see the difference between a diversity that is valuable and that which is to be deplored.[34] Yet the difficulty should not hinder our efforts but challenge us to new, creative work together.

[34] *In One Body through the Cross*, #22, 27-28. For a helpful discussion on the 'Limits of Diversity', see #63 in *The Nature and Mission of the Church,* 37-39.

Cooperation and the Promotion of Unity: A Pentecostal Perspective

Cecil M. Robeck, Jr.

Edinburgh and the Pentecostal Movement in 1910

It should come as no surprise to learn that when missionaries from around the world met in Edinburgh, Scotland, for the great World Missionary Conference of 1910, they would overlook the Pentecostal Movement completely. The Pentecostal Movement was no more than a decade old at the time, and most Christian leaders thought it was hardly worth noticing. Pentecostals had only begun to enter full-time missionary service for the first time in 1906.[1] When invitations to the Conference went out, there were very few signs that Pentecostals were here to stay, and there were even fewer signs that they would make any substantive contribution to world missions. If the organisers did notice this tiny movement, they would surely have had little good to say about the Movement. What is more, they would have found it impossible to believe recent reports that spell out the impact that this Movement has had over the past century.

The earliest Pentecostal missionaries were frequently an irritating lot. They were not in the mood to listen to anyone who did not share the experience they called 'baptism in the Holy Spirit'. They publicly criticised all those with whom they disagreed, including veteran missionaries. They did not see any need for advanced theological training, or courses in cross-cultural immersion, or even the need for language study. They ignored most modern missionary wisdom, claiming instead that the Holy Spirit was leading them in a different and powerful way, and that they did not rely upon mere human wisdom. They openly proselytised. Furthermore, they made outlandish claims!

Originally published in David A. Kerr and Kenneth R. Ross (eds.), *Edinburgh 2010 Mission Then and Now,* Regnum Edinburgh Centenary Series 1 (Oxford: Regnum Books, 2009), 290-303.

[1] Cecil M. Robeck, Jr., 'Pentecostalism and Mission: From Azusa Street to the Ends of the Earth', *Missiology: An International Review* 35:1 (January 2007), 75–92, especially 81–83; See also, Allan Anderson, *Spreading Fires: The Missionary Nature of Early Pentecostalism* (London: SCM, 2007).

It should come as no surprise, then, that when they made their appearance on various mission fields, they were criticised and ridiculed. Their unwillingness to cooperate with veteran missionaries except on their own terms, and their swaggering claims that they needed nothing more than the power of the Holy Spirit to spread the Gospel among the 'heathen', left them vulnerable to intense criticism. It is not surprising to realise, then, that they should not even have been invited to participate in such a gathering. It would be safe to say that neither the fledgling Pentecostal Movement nor the Edinburgh Missionary Conference was ready for one another.

Visible Unity for the Sake of Mission

The care and balance with which the authors of the Commission's report approached their subject is obvious. While the Commission acknowledged in an even-handed way the strengths and weaknesses made explicit by differences in perception and thought that arose from regional differences, denominational concerns, and longstanding theological disputes, it did not push its readers into making any specific choice. It made itself quite clear, however, that while no one should be asked to relinquish his or her convictions of truth a way had to be found to reconcile these differences with the 'essential unity' that already existed between Christians of different traditions.[2] It confronted its delegates and readers to take the challenge of visible Christian unity seriously and to act upon it. Moreover, it concluded with the passage of a resolution that put into place a Continuation Committee of the World Missionary Conference that would be multi-national and multi-denominational, with power to follow up on unresolved issues.[3]

Even a cursory examination of the work of Commission Eight reveals that the participants were overwhelmingly representative of historic mainline Protestant and Anglican churches and their missionaries. Furthermore, the delegates were dominantly representative of North American, British and European churches and missionary agencies with missionary input from Asia (primarily China and India) and Africa (primarily from Anglophone countries). Notably absent from the conversation were the ancient Roman Catholic Church and the Orthodox churches. Thus, neither Latin America, which was dominantly Catholic and had been excluded from discussion because it was viewed as a 'Christian' region, nor Russia, which was Orthodox, were represented or formally discussed,[4] although some delegates expressed concern

---

[2] World Missionary Conference, *Cooperation and the Promotion of Unity: Report of Commission VIII* (Edinburgh & London: Oliphant, Anderson & Ferrier; New York, Chicago and Toronto: Fleming H. Revell, 1910), 134.

[3] For a useful summary of the week and the debate surrounding this resolution see, W.H.T. Gairdner, *'Edinburgh 1910': An Account and Interpretation of the World Missionary Conference* (Edinburgh & London: Oliphant, Anderson & Ferrier; New York, Chicago and Toronto: Fleming H. Revell, 1910), 178–214.

[4] It had been agreed beforehand that missions to and among Roman Catholics would be

that the absence of the Roman Catholic and Orthodox churches might be highly significant for the successful implementation of Conference findings.[5] Thus, the Conference was limited by the realities of the East/West split of the eleventh century. It was further limited by the division between Catholic and Protestant/Anglican churches at the time of the sixteenth-century Reformation. In fact, the absence of any substantial voice from either Latin America or Russia was simply reflective of these same realities and not an unwitting omission on the part of Conference planners.

In the same way, there is no reference to the challenges that Pentecostals were already beginning to pose on the mission field. Clearly, the World Missionary Conference of 1910 was also limited either by its lack of knowledge and experience of Pentecostals on the mission field, or by the unwillingness of its organisers to pursue missionaries across the obvious doctrinal differences and class distinctions that separated the churches present at the Conference from Pentecostal missionaries. As a result, the potential contribution of this newest Christian movement was completely ignored or overlooked.[6]

What this meant was that the call to visible Christian unity was limited to those groups that were present at the Conference. It also meant that as important as the World Missionary Conference of 1910 was, and it was very important, it was actually a conference of what would become the representatives of the Christian minority among today's Church. If the Roman Catholic Church, the Orthodox Churches, and Pentecostals, none of whom were present at the World Missionary Conference of 1910, represent the vast majority of Christians around the world today, then by any accounting the churches that were present at the Conference are very much to be reckoned among the minority churches today. To take it one step further, it has been noted repeatedly in recent years that it is the churches that were not present at the Conference where the most substantial growth is taking place, while many of those groups that were present at the Conference now appear to be in rapid decline.[7]

---

excluded because the focus of the conference was to be on missions to 'non-Christians' and 'non-Christian countries'. See, Kenneth Scott Latourette, 'Ecumenical Bearings of he Missionary Movement and the International Missionary Conference', in Ruth Rouse and Stephen Charles Neill (eds), *A History of the Ecumenical Movement*, vol. 1 (Geneva: WCC, 1993 [1954]), 396.

[5] See the comments made in *Cooperation and the Promotion of Unity* by the Right Reverend Bishop Brandt (American Episcopal Church) (198–99), the Right Reverend E. S. Talbot, Bishop of Southwark (Anglican) (201–202; 233–34), and the Reverend R. Wardlaw Thompson (London Missionary Society) (216).

[6] Donald W. Dayton, 'Yet Another Layer of the Onion or Opening the Ecumenical Door to Let the Riffraff in', *The Ecumenical Review* 40 (1988), 87–110.

[7] See, Philip Jenkins, *The Next Christendom: The Coming of Global Christianity* (New York: Oxford University Press, 2002); Konrad Raiser, *To Be the Church: Challenges and Hopes for a New Millennium* (Geneva: Risk Books/WCC Publications, 1997), 101. Here Raiser writes 'We have noted earlier that the ecumenical scope of the WCC is

Pentecostal Responses

Given the fact that the emergence of Pentecostalism was not particularly welcomed by the historic churches it should come as no surprise that Pentecostals did not turn to them for acceptance. Though they held much in common with historic churches, acceptance by these churches was not easily found. Like other Christians in 1910, Pentecostals believed in the inspiration and authority of Scripture, the Trinity, and the person and work of Jesus Christ in classical terms. Like most Protestants, they taught the doctrine of justification by faith, they administered baptism, and they observed the Lord's Supper. Like most Methodists and Wesleyan-Holiness Christians, they were concerned about personal integrity, holiness, and what some called the 'Higher Christian Life'. Like those who convened the World Missionary Conference of 1910 and like most Evangelicals, they were committed to evangelisation and missionary work among non-Christian people. And they did not invent any new polities; they simply adopted those of their forebears, Episcopal, Congregational, and Presbyterian.

What separated them from most Protestants were two things. The first was their approach to the Holy Spirit. They insisted that people could be 'baptised in the Holy Spirit' at a time subsequent to their regeneration, that this baptism equipped them with power for witnessing (Acts 1:8), and that it would be accompanied by some form of evidence such as speaking in tongues (Acts 2:4). They also insisted that the Holy Spirit continues to distribute charisms upon whomever He chooses (1 Corinthians 12:8–10) regardless of age, gender, race, ethnicity, colour, class, or level of education. That many Protestants linked baptism in the Spirit with conversion and baptism, rejected any notion of evidence, and embraced a cessationist theory regarding certain charisms made things challenging at best. These differences led Protestants to reject Pentecostal claims, and because these differences went to the core of Pentecostal identity, they led Pentecostals to distance themselves from many Protestants. This debate ultimately led Aimee Semple McPherson to preach a sermon titled, 'Is Jesus Christ the Great "I Am", or Is He the Great "I Was"?' Sister Aimee appealed to the dominant Pentecostal claim that mainline pastors were preaching a Christ who 'used to be', a distant and powerless Christ who had ceased to deal with the problems of the contemporary world in any meaningful way, while Pentecostals preached a Christ who was 'the same yesterday, today, and forever' (Hebrews 13:8), a Christ who was deeply involved in the everyday lives of ordinary people, just as He had been when he walked the roads of Palestine.[8]

limited because its member churches include only a minority – and probably a shrinking one – of world Christianity. This is the case because the Roman Catholic Church on the one hand and most evangelical and Pentecostal churches on the other have not so far seen the possibility of joining the WCC'.

[8] Aimee Semple McPherson, *Divine Healing Sermons* (privately published, ca. 1923), 11–22.

The second issue that separated Pentecostals from most Protestants, indeed, from most Christians at that time, had to do with the fact that while most Christians viewed the contemporary Church as standing in continuity with the Church of all previous centuries, most Pentecostals viewed themselves as standing in discontinuity with much of that history. Pentecostals embraced a Restorationist reading of church history, and that reading gave a particular spin to their eschatological views. God raised up the Pentecostal Movement at the end of the age when it was incumbent upon the Church to evangelise the world. The time would soon come when a universal religion would emerge, and it would become the tool of the forces of antichrist. As a result, Pentecostals turned their backs on many discussions regarding visible forms of Christian unity. They feared that such discussions would ultimately lead to disaster. And they focused their attention on bringing all non-Christians to salvation and all believers into the fullness of the Holy Spirit.

That being said, Pentecostals were neither consistent nor generally militant in their treatment of all such discussions. This is because the issue of unity had deep roots in the foundations of the Movement. While they tended to emphasise the spiritual reality of their unity in Christ, and thus the invisible character of Christian unity, some early Pentecostals lifted up the challenge of visible unity. Charles F. Parham was troubled by the confusion of denominationalism at the beginning of the century. He came to believe that God had anointed him to be 'an apostle of unity'. Unity did not come through the establishment of denominations, which he described as 'concentration camps', but through the work of God among those who were '...baptised by the Holy Ghost into one Body, the gloriously redeemed Church...'. He viewed himself as the true Elijah who would lead this redeemed Church into fruitful evangelisation in such a way as to result in a single, restored, visible, Pentecostal Church.[9]

The African American pastor of the famous Azusa Street Mission, William J. Seymour, articulated his stand in his publication *The Apostolic Faith.* In every issue of this newspaper, he included these words: 'The Apostolic Faith Movement stands for the restoration of the faith once delivered unto the saints – the old time religion, camp meetings, revivals, missions, street and prison work, and Christian Unity everywhere'.[10]

A decade later, Richard G. Spurling, founder of the Christian Union, the group that ultimately became the Church of God (Cleveland, TN), lamented frequently over the 'strife and confusion' he witnessed in denominational diversity. 'Above all this din of strife and confusion', he wrote, 'I hear Christ praying in John 17:21, that they may all be one.' He knew that some would argue that the answer to Jesus' prayer had already come. It could be found in the spiritual unity of all Christians. It was something that was essentially invisible. But he argued, '... our reason says not so', 'Christ said the world might believe, but there is not a unity that the world can see. No, it is not the

---

[9] Charles F. Parham, *A Voice Crying in the Wilderness* (Baxter Springs, KS: Apostolic Faith Bible College, 1902), 61–65.

[10] William J. Seymour, *The Apostolic Faith* 1:1 (Los Angeles, CA, September 1906), 2.

unity which Christ wanted by any means, but a confusion that He does not want'.[11]

However, in spite of the concern for Christian unity that had been articulated from the early days of the Pentecostal Movement, Pentecostals were slow to reach beyond themselves in any form of a cooperative venture, even when it came to missionary work among non-Christians.

John R. Mott, the man who had so successfully chaired the 1910 Edinburgh Conference also chaired the 1925 Convention of the Foreign Missionary Conference of North America. The 1925 Convention was as close to the 1910 Conference that any Pentecostal would get. His plenary address, titled 'New Forces Released by Cooperation', echoed the theme of Commission Eight.[12] Throughout his message, Mott recalled the lessons learned and the challenges raised by the 1910 Edinburgh Conference, noting that the arguments that had been offered 'in favour of cooperation' then, were 'now accentuated tenfold'.[13] He lamented the divisions that continued to plague the Church, and he pointed out the inconsistency of these divisions with Jesus' prayer in John 17:21 – unity *for the sake of mission.* He also drew from the visions of unity set forth in Ephesians 2 and again in Ephesians 4. Mott tied his vision for unity to the spiritual dimension that was so important to him personally and to the Holiness stream of Methodism of which he was a part.

The 1910 Conference had made it clear that there were times when differences in doctrine and polity needed to be set aside or bracketed in order to make progress in cooperation and the promotion of unity in missionary matters.[14] In 1925, Mott reiterated this point. He repeatedly called for the delegates to lead the way in setting aside their denominational distinctions in order to bring about unity. 'If we can forget that we are Americans, Canadians, British, Chinese, Dutch, French, Germans, Indians, Japanese, Scandinavians', he began,

> … or that we are Baptists, Congregationalists, Disciples, Episcopalians, Friends, Methodists, Presbyterians, Lutherans; in the work of making Christ known to people in Asia, Africa, Latin America, or Europe, or of North America, we have gone a great way toward proving to unbelievers who are moved by facts, that the religion of Jesus Christ is the great solvent of the racial and national alienations of the world, and, therefore, is the mightiest force operating among men. The present is the time of times to present this apologetic.[15]

---

[11] R.G. Spurling, *The Lost Link* (Turtletown, TN: Farner Church of God, 1920; reprint, 1971), 20.

[12] John R. Mott, 'New Forces Released by Cooperation', in Fennell Turner and Frank Knight Sanders (eds), *The Foreign Missions Convention at Washington 1925* (New York: Foreign Missions Conference of North America, 1925; New York: Fleming H. Revell, 1925), 209–22.

[13] Mott, 'New Forces', 209.

[14] *Cooperation and the Promotion of Unity*, 50.

[15] Mott, 'New Forces', 218.

Upon his return from that meeting to the Assemblies of God headquarters in Springfield, Missouri, John W. Welch, the General Superintendent of the Assemblies of God, gave a report that was ultimately published in the denomination's periodical, *The Pentecostal Evangel.* Instead of affirming Mott's message, he made it clear that he did not agree with Mott at all.[16] Welch was clearly opposed to what he termed the 'get together' idea. 'Satan's super-man is on the way', he warned, 'the modern church along with the nations, unconscious of what they are doing, is leading their efforts directly to the establishment of conditions for the antichrist to take supreme control. This "get-together" idea is nothing other than that.'[17] He criticised the Conference for expecting denominations to set aside what he saw as their doctrinal commitments. 'When they lay aside all of the Methodist doctrine, and the Baptist and Presbyterian, etc., so that there will be no friction', he protested, 'there is nothing left much but a name.'[18]

John W. Welch was eight years older than Mott. Originally from Seneca, New York, he had worked with the American Sunday School Union for a number of years and had been a minister with the Christian and Missionary Alliance. After having a Pentecostal experience, he joined the Assemblies of God and pastored several congregations that stood on the margins of the larger Church.[19] Indeed he represented many people who stood on the margins of society. This location on the margins contributed substantially to his feeling that at this missionary conference he was out of place. He described the nearly 5000 delegates who had gathered in Washington D.C. as 'intelligent-looking, well-dressed, and sufficient in themselves'. He judged them as being delighted with their 'reputation of doing a great work in the ends of the world'. He complained that they were '...spending other people's money very lavishly'. 'I saw a lot of missionaries', he murmured, but 'none of them seemed to show any evidence that they were willing to sacrifice.'[20] Rubbing shoulders with so many international players, most of whom were educated far beyond him and supported and clothed beyond his means, must have been a challenging experience. Welch did not fit in, and as a result, he was unable to hear what Mott was actually saying.

---

[16] J.W. Welch, 'The Present Great World Crisis', *The Pentecostal Evangel* 590 (March 28, 1925), 2–3, 8–9; Gary B. McGee, *The Gospel Shall Be Preached: A History and Theology of Assemblies of God Foreign Missions to 1959* (Springfield, MO: Gospel Publishing House, 1986), vol. 1, 120–21.

[17] Welch, 'The Present Great World Crisis', 2.

[18] Welch, 'The Present Great World Crisis', 3.

[19] C.E. Jones, 'Welch, John William', in Stanley M. Burgess and Eduard M. van der Maas (eds), *The New International Dictionary of Pentecostal and Charismatic Movements*, revised and expanded ed. (Grand Rapids, MI: Zondervan, 2002), 1187.

[20] Welch, 'The Present Great World Crisis', 9.

Understanding Pentecostal Approaches to Unity

In the years immediately following 1910, Pentecostals had four concerns. The first of these was its core concern for evangelisation and world mission. From its beginning, it was clearly a missionary movement. As the Movement expanded and divided, it kept this concern at the forefront of its thinking. As new congregations were established, the number of evangelists who crossed the nations and the number of missionaries who went abroad increased. Soon, further organisation would become necessary in order to accomplish with greater efficiency what Pentecostal missionaries were already doing.

Its second concern turned on how Pentecostalism would understand itself. The oldest groups with a Pentecostal self-understanding emerged in the first decade of the twentieth century. They held much in common with the Holiness Movement, though it was clear to both movements that they were different. In point of fact, they shared the identical milieu that had produced John R. Mott, for whom the language of holiness, entire sanctification, and being baptised in the Holy Spirit was quite normal.[21] They would have differed largely on the nature of baptism in the Spirit and the role of speaking in tongues.

In 1911, a different version of Pentecostalism emerged with the teaching of William H. Durham. Instead of viewing sanctification in terms of a crisis experience, Durham viewed it as part of the 'finished work' that Jesus had accomplished on the cross. Thus, sanctification began at conversion and continued as a process throughout the Christian life.[22]

Again, in 1913, a much more radical teaching began to emerge in part of the Pentecostal Movement. In their quest to be truly 'apostolic', some Pentecostals argued that new converts should be baptised 'in the name of Jesus Christ' rather than invoking the traditional Trinitarian Formula. That was the way it had been done by the Apostles throughout the book of Acts (cf. 2:38), they contended. This concern ultimately led to further reflection on the nature of the Godhead, the Name of God, and the place of baptism in the Spirit within the Christian life. Thus, by 1913, three major streams of Pentecostalism had developed.[23]

The third concern that the young Pentecostal Movement addressed revolved around its institutional makeup. As the revival spread, new churches sprang up and new missionary fields were opened. It soon became apparent that some form of organisation was necessary. This led to the clear identification of some denominations as Pentecostal (e.g., Church of God in Christ, Church of God (Cleveland, TN), and the International Pentecostal Holiness Church) that had existed before the Pentecostal revivals in Topeka, Kansas (1900) and in Los

---

[21] Mott was reared within and remained loyal to the Holiness tradition within the Methodist Church. See, C. Howard Hopkins, *John R. Mott: 1865–1955: A Biography* (Grand Rapids, MI: Eerdmans, 1979), 9–46.

[22] William H. Durham, 'The Great Revival at Azusa Street Mission – How It Began and How It Ended', *Pentecostal Testimony* 1:8 (ca. July/August 1911), 3.

[23] On the early years of this movement see James L. Tyson, *The Early Pentecostal Revival: History of Twentieth-Century Pentecostals and the Pentecostal Assemblies of the World 1901–30* (Hazelwood, MO: Word Aflame Press, 1992), 169–76.

Angeles, California (1906). It also led to the formation of new denominations such as the Assemblies of God, the Pentecostal Assemblies of the World, the International Church of the Foursquare Gospel, and the United Pentecostal Church. Within a century Pentecostalism would divide over virtually every issue that had caused division in the rest of the church during its 1900 years of history, producing a multiplicity of denominations worldwide.[24]

This led to the fourth concern, that of unity. As early as 1911, the Norwegian Pentecostal, Thomas Ball Barratt issued 'An Urgent Call for Charity and Unity'. He proposed an international Pentecostal Union. While the form of unity he sought was not accepted immediately, the following year a Consultative International Pentecostal Council was formed in order to provide advice to the growing movement. This council met in Amsterdam in December 1912, and again in Sunderland, England in May 1913 and 1914.[25] World War I put an end to these efforts until 1921, when once again the Council met in Amsterdam. Meanwhile, the question of whether or not Pentecostals stood in unity with one another and what constituted the basis for this unity was being resolved in other ways.

While relationships between the first two streams of Pentecostals, with their different perspectives on the doctrine of sanctification, were strained, they were not completely antagonistic to one another. At times their rhetoric was strong, but in the end, they recognised each other as legitimately sisters and brothers. That was not true for the understanding that developed between these Pentecostals and those who identified themselves as 'Apostolic' or 'Oneness' Pentecostals. Questions simmered for several years while Pentecostal leaders in each of these camps tried to find ways to coexist in fellowship with one another. In 1916, these efforts came to an end. The fact that 'Apostolics' insisted on the invocation of the 'name of Jesus Christ' for a baptism to be legitimate while the others insisted on the Trinitarian Formula might have been managed. But when the Apostolics adopted a modalist position on the Trinity, the older groups, which maintained a classic Trinitarian position, rejected them as legitimate Pentecostal partners.

Once these basic issues had been studied, the majority of Pentecostals sought partnerships with one another even as they opened themselves up to potential partnerships with other Christians. They remained fully committed to the invisible unity that exists between all believers through the Holy Spirit. But they were suspicious about entering into more broadly based partnerships if they suspected that these partnerships might mean that they would be asked to give up any of their own autonomy or authority.

---

[24] Cecil M. Robeck Jr., 'Pentecostals and Ecumenism in a Pluralistic World', in Murray W. Dempster, Byron Klaus, and Douglas Peterson (eds), *The Globalisation of Pentecostalism: A Religion Made to Travel* (Oxford: Regnum Books, 1999), 340–41.

[25] Cornelis van der Laan, 'The Proceedings of the Leaders' Meetings (1908-1911) and of the International Pentecostal Council (1912-1914)', *EPTA Bulletin* 6:3 (1987), 76–96; see also *Pneuma: The Journal of the Society for Pentecostal Studies* 10 (1988), 36–49.

Despite occasional collaboration with Evangelicals, it remains difficult to make a convincing case that the Pentecostal movement participated in efforts for Christian unity. Pentecostals continue to take part in various regional, national, and international associations of Evangelicals, but they have great fear of moving beyond what might be considered the safe space in which they understand many of the factors that are at play. To date, the most significant place where broader ecumenical engagement has taken place is at the bilateral level. An international dialogue between the Catholic Church and certain Pentecostal churches and leaders has existed since 1972, co-founded by David du Plessis and Fr. Kilian McDonnell, OSB. During its thirty-five years of existence, it has made some important findings.

Other dialogues have begun as well. During the 1960s a series of dialogues took place between the Pentecostals and various Reformed denominations in the Netherlands,[26] while during the late 1980s, the Pentecostal Movement in Finland was engaged in discussions with the Finnish Lutheran Church.[27] Since that time, a bilateral dialogue between the World Alliance of Reformed Churches and Pentecostals has nearly completed two rounds of discussions,[28] and a conversation has been initiated between the Institute for Ecumenical Research, in Strasbourg, France, on behalf of the Lutheran World Federation and Pentecostals.[29]

Lessons from Commission Eight

There is no question but that both in the Church's desire to support missionary service and cooperative witness among non-Christians, and in its quest for visible unity during the twentieth century and beyond, the World Missionary Conference that convened in Edinburgh in 1910 was a watershed. It definitively noted the need for some form of visible unity as a compelling force or apology for the reconciling message of the Gospel. Furthermore, it repeatedly called for a clear, compelling, and singular vision and voice to declare Christ to the nations. It contributed substantially to the formation of both the Commission on Faith and Order and the International Missionary Council.

---

[26] See, *De Kerk en de Pinkster Groepen* (S-Gravenhage, Netherlands: Boekencentrum N.V., 1960_.

[27] 'The Official Discussions between the Evangelical Lutheran Church of Finland and the Pentecostal Movement of Finland 1987–1989', in *Dialogues with The Evangelical Free Church of Finland and the Finnish Pentecostal Movement: Documents of the Evangelical Lutheran Church of Finland 2* (Helsinki: Church Council for Foreign Affairs, Ecclesiastical Board, 1990), 33–56.

[28] See 'Word and Spirit, Church and World: The Final Report of the International Dialogue between Representatives of the World Alliance of Reformed Churches and Some Classical Pentecostal Churches and Leaders', *Pneuma: The Journal of the Society for Pentecostal Studies* 23:1 (Spring 2001), 9–43.

[29] Ken Appold, 'Institute Begins Lutheran-Pentecostal Study Group', *Building Bridges: Newsletter of the Institute for Ecumenical Research* 6 (Summer 2005), 2–3.

But Edinburgh proved also to be a moment marked by the finitude of human imagination. Those who convened the Conference did not envision the Church in 2010 as looking anything like it does today. They assumed, perhaps rather naively, that they held all the seeds of the answer to Jesus' prayer in their hands. A few participants in the Commission Eight discussions, especially those from the Anglican community, wanted to engage Catholics and the Orthodox more fully. Coming as it did a decade later, the call of the Ecumenical Patriarch which was developed independently of the Conference, could be interpreted in some way as being fruit borne from his reflection on the subject subsequent to the Edinburgh Conference *and* at it should be viewed as coming at the prodding of the Holy Spirit.[30] Since that time, it has become equally clear that something was also happening among Roman Catholics at the time. It is doubtful that any of those who attended the Conference in 1910 anticipated the changes brought about by the Second Vatican Council, but its ecumenical fruit is now a well-established fact. Still, notably absent from the Edinburgh Conference, and from any deliberation that took place in conjunction with Commission Eight, was even a single representative of the Pentecostal Movement. What seems to be the case is that the Holy Spirit was at work within historic Protestantism, among the Orthodox, within the Catholic Church, and in the latest Christian movement the Pentecostals.[31]

Those on Commission Eight who envisioned the future of world mission were fully aware of the limitations of comity agreements. Even as they encouraged further use of these treaties, they recognised that they were not ultimate solutions to real problems.[32] These limitations would only grow when groups such as the Pentecostals, who had not been part of the implementation process, simply ignored them and crossed lines without regard for those who were already present. They believed that there was no need to respect these agreements when they had not been part of putting them in place, and they sometimes viewed them as standing in the way of the will of the Holy Spirit.

The Commission was also very much aware of the fact that the so-called 'Sleeping Giants' of the world were beginning to stir and at one level they knew that the end of Western Colonialism was at hand. But while recognizing that in light of emerging events the time for action was limited, the commissioners were unable to think beyond the present form of 'Christendom'

---

[30] 'Unto the Churches of Christ Everywhere, Encyclical of the Ecumenical Patriarch, 1920', in Michael Kinnamon and Brian E. Cope (eds), *The Ecumenical Movement: An Anthology of Key Texts and Voices* (Grand Rapids, MI: Eerdmans; Geneva: WCC Publications, 1997), 11–14.

[31] Huibert van Beek, 'Pentecostals-Ecumenicals Dialogue', in André Droogers, Cornelis van der Laan, and Wout van Laar (eds), *Fruitful in This Land: Pluralism, Dialogue and Healing in Migrant Pentecostalism* (Zoetermeer, Netherlands: Boekencentrum Publishing House, 2006), 81–92.

[32] 'The delimitation of territory, as we have seen, can be carried out only under certain limitations, and cannot provide an ultimate solution of the problems of the mission field. But for the present, it has been found to work well, and might be considerably extended in many fields'. *Cooperation and the Promotion of Unity*, 139.

to which they had grown accustomed. Their vision was still highly dependent on the *status quo*. In far too many cases they had failed to educate indigenous clergy to adequate levels to take leadership positions. Indeed, in many cases the neglect was intentional. In some cases, they established schools only to certain levels of attainment to ensure this limitation. They seem to have expected to be in positions of authority even when the financial and political support from colonizing governments and the home offices that frequently oversaw their work began to dry up. As new nations under indigenous leadership began to emerge, many churches seemed to lose their will or ability to proclaim the Gospel through the historic means of evangelisation, preaching, and teaching. They increasingly withdrew, or they turned their funds toward other enterprises, projects associated with health, education, and general welfare. Even so, many churches have withdrawn in the name of cleaning up paternalism.

In a sense, what Edinburgh also demonstrates is that, in the words of the Scottish bard, Robert Burns, 'The best-laid plans of mice and men often go astray'. The Pentecostal and related movements that began to emerge about the time of the Edinburgh Conference were not yet part of the Conference vision. And while their vision of the world and the challenges they would face began to increase, the vision of those who had been so committed to unity for the sake of mission seems to have lost the second part of that vision. For too many, perhaps, unity became an end in itself.[33] As a result, Pentecostals now frequently wonder why they need a relationship with historic churches. They wonder what these churches can bring to the table that they might find of value. Perhaps it can be said that the vision of Edinburgh for the unity of the Church was a large one, just as the missionary vision of contemporary Pentecostals could be said to be large. But in neither case has it been as large as the vision that God has for the Church. God's perspective calls for visionaries who can see beyond themselves. In addition to the many contributions of historic Protestant, Catholic, and Orthodox churches, that vision *must* include a role for the witness of Pentecostal, Charismatic, and related types of groups to the ongoing power of the Holy Spirit through signs, wonders, and witness. In the end, that may even call into question long-held understandings of the marks of the Church.

Commission Eight called the churches to listen to the voices of the churches on the mission field. 'The Churches in the mission field may lead the way to unity', they observed, 'but they cannot move far and move safely without the co-operation of the Church at home'.[34] This possibility was undoubtedly raised in light of the progress that had been made, even by 1910, in the development

---

[33] In his address to the Convention at Washington, D.C. John R. Mott reminded his audience of precisely this concern. 'The unity or oneness among His followers down the generations, for which Christ prayed, was not to be regarded as an end in itself, but rather as a means to ensure the great central end of Christian missions, namely, "that the world may believe".' Mott, 'New Forces', 217. This admonition bears repeating in 2010.

[34] *Cooperation and the Promotion of Unity*, 138.

of what would later be called the united and uniting churches. But more than that, it seems to have been a recognition that the key to the unity of the Church for the sake of mission might rest in the hands of Christians in the South. 'We are only beginning to understand that the beliefs and customs and capacities of the coloured races are in future to be regarded as worthy of attention', they noted.

> These coloured races have their own future, and mean to work out their own political, religious and social history; and they will no longer do so apart from, and with negligible influence on, the community of the civilised nations. We are beginning to see that the Church is again facing a mighty conflict, like that which arose when the living forces of the Gospel contended with the forces of the pagan world in the early centuries.[35]

Over the past half-century or so, we have seen the rise of indigenous Christianity around the world. It looks more like Pentecostalism than it does many of the historic churches. Even many of the historic churches, especially on the African continent, have become part of movements for renewal that are viewed as grounded in the Holy Spirit. The question is whether or not the historic churches have a vision for reaching beyond their time-worn traditions, whether they have the ability to think dramatically new thoughts, and whether they are willing to learn from the newer, younger, vibrant, 'southern' churches. The question must also be raised in the other direction. Do many of these newer Pentecostal, charismatic, third wave, new apostolic, independent, and prosperity driven, 'southern' churches have the patience to learn from the long and valuable experience of the older churches. The option to dismiss one another is not now open. If the conditions that called for the World Missionary Conference were serious in 1910, they are infinitely more serious today. As John R. Mott summarised the issue in 1925,

> The missionary message will be wonderfully enriched through the most intimate cooperation of all true believers. In fact, is not genuine cooperation and unity absolutely essential to ensure the giving of full orbed expression to the message of the Church of Christ? Christ has not revealed himself solely or fully through any one nation, race, or communion. No part of [hu]mankind has a monopoly of His unsearchable riches. Every national and denominational tradition has a contribution to make which can enrich the whole Body of Christ. The help of all who bear His name and who have had experience of Him is necessary adequately to reveal His excellencies and to communicate His power.[36]

The call of Commission Eight for visionary people and the call that John R. Mott reiterated fifteen years later is still a call that is waiting to be answered. The question is, 'When are the churches going to heed the call and rely both on the Lord and on one another instead of on their own strength and wisdom?'

---

[35] *Cooperation and the Promotion of Unity*, 5–6.

[36] Mott, 'New Forces', 21

The Ecumenism of the Spirit: Emerging Contemporary Contexts of Mission in Latin America

Carmelo Alvarez

The theoretical framework of this analysis is based on two biblical, theological and missiological concepts: *missio Dei* and *koinonia. Missio Dei* is analysed in the context of recent ecumenical discussions. The Trinitarian implications of *missio Dei* is studied in relationship to an ecumenical and Pentecostal thinking of the Holy Spirit as it affects its role in mission. The *koinonia* concept is examined as a partnership within the ecumenical movement and its influence on mission theology, particularly that of the Protestant and Pentecostal movements in Latin America.[1]

Sharing in God's Mission: An Ecumenical Partnership

Latin American Protestantism has struggled with the issue of the multifaceted relationship between identity and mission, as manifested in the role of churches as autonomous-autochthonous bodies within the Church universal.[2] This issue has been connected with larger topics such as 'religion and post-modernity', and church leaders are examining their active presence in social life and politics in Latin American society. Jorge Larrain expresses the importance of the 'religious factor' in the modern search for religious identity in Latin America: 'Religion is a crucial dimension of Latin American identity'.[3] He examines the active role of Christianity in the formation of a Latin American cultural identity.[4] Larrain concludes, 'The impact of Catholicism and Pentecostalism upon Latin American culture is very important'.[5]

Originally published in Miguel Alvarez (eds.), *The Reshaping of Mission in Latin America*, Regnum Edinburgh Centenary Series 30 (Oxford: Regnum Books, 2015), 47-64.

[1] In this article, 'Pentecostal' is used as a noun and 'pentecostal' as an adjective.
[2] Valdir Steurnagel, *Obediencia Misionera y Práctica Histórica* (Grand Rapids, MI: Nueva Creación, 1996), 13-29.
[3] Jorge Larrain, *Identity and Modernity in Latin America* (Oxford: Blackwell, 2000), 201.
[4] Larrain, *Identity and Modernity in Latin America,* 201-207.
[5] Larrain, *Identity and Modernity in Latin America,* 206.

In turn, Christian movements in Latin America also reflect the local culture and are shaped by the interaction between the various religious groups. Walter Hollenweger observes several roots of influence within the pentecostal movement in Latin America: a strong oral tradition, an ecumenical frame of reference, a Catholic culture, pacifism, diversity, indigenization, a close relationship between theology and ethics, and a need for autonomy.[6] The resulting search for identity is closely related to *la memoria histórica* [historic memory] – a capacity for examining the roots, development, and destiny of a collective people.[7]

The emphasis on the experience of the Holy Spirit means the recuperation and appropriation of a vital force and presence of Christianity in history. The Holy Spirit has always been calling, challenging, signalling towards a better future and showing the way to transformation. This conviction affirms history as an instrument to discern God's mission in the world to transform the existing realities of sin and injustice.

Doing Mission in a Globalized World

Mission and unity are interconnected. One cannot understand the history of the ecumenical movement in the twentieth century without considering how mission and unity have combined in creative tension to shape present conditions. The significance of this dialectical tension is crucial for any theology of mission and for the emergence of a new 'missionary paradigm' towards the future.[8]

The theology of mission is better understood today as *missio Dei*, which requires a reciprocal relationship of mutuality in an ecumenical understanding of mission. The churches of North and South become mutually accountable. They are real partners in mission and members of a worldwide community.

Koinonia as Sharing in Partnership

Koinonia made a definite impact in the ecumenical movement during the twentieth century. Its influence can be seen in numerous documents of conferences in which the church was the main theme.[9]

Koinonia describes the experiences of the Gospel and life in Christ and the Spirit, incorporating the social dimensions of the concept. It leads to solidarity

---

[6] Walter Hollenweger, 'From Azusa to the Toronto Phenomenon: Historical Roots of the Pentecostal Movement', in Jürgen Moltmann and Karl-Josef Kuschel (eds), *Pentecostal Movements as Ecumenical Challenge, Cocilium* 3 (London: SCM, 1996), 3-7.

[7] See Eduardo Hoornaert, *El Movimiento de Jesús* (Mexico: Editorial Dabar, 1996).

[8] David J. Bosch, *Transforming Mission: Paradigm Shifts in Theology of Mission* (Maryknoll, NY: Orbis Books, 1991), 463-67.

[9] Jean-Marie Tillard, '*Koinonía*', in Nicolas Lossky et al (eds), *Dictionary of the Ecumenical Movement*, 568-74.

with the suffering and the poor, and encourages love to the neighbour without prejudice. This kind of ecclesiology is relevant if the church is going to be successful cross-culturally.

Justo L. González analyses the context and mission of the early church, insisting that *koinonia* means partnership: sharing material goods, and participating in a communal fellowship.[10] In his study of Paul's ecclesiology, Marcelino Legido shows that *koinonia* is a fellowship in obedience that is transformed into a fellowship of service.[11] Sharing in God's mission requires the ecumenical sharing of resources as a concrete manifestation of fellowship in worship and of caring for God's creation.

Sharing in Partnership: Ecumenical and Feminist Perspectives

Partnership is a concept that was introduced in the ecumenical movement in order to apply the biblical word *koinonia.* The concept served as a principle to enhance relationships between churches in the North and the South, particularly with missionary societies. It evolved into terms like 'autonomy', 'reciprocity', and 'respect'. Partnership was essential to establishing better interchurch relations and developing mission and unity among the churches. Finally, partnership was increasingly connected with issues of equality, justice and the integrity of creation.

More recently Andrew Kirk has written a book on the theology of mission containing an entire section on partnership.[12] He is able to combine a progressive evangelical perspective with a sensitive, balanced and sympathetic approach to Liberation Theology. He points to what mission means today and elaborates on some of the challenges that lie ahead. Kirk develops a theology of mission with the foundational principles of *missio Dei* and describes the church's response. 'This means that God's mission is carried out in both the world and the church; to a lesser degree in human history untouched by the Gospel, to a greater degree where the Gospel is believed and obeyed'.[13]

Kirk follows the history of and the contemporary discussion on partnership. His theological conviction is expressed in the following terms:

> It may therefore be even harder to lay hold of the notion that 'partnership in mission' also belongs to the essence of the Church: partnership is not so much what the Church *does* as what it *is.* Churches (theologically) belong to one another, for God has called each 'into the fellowship (*koinonia*) of His Son Jesus Christ our Lord' (1 Cor. 1:9). Partnership is therefore not a nice slogan that some

[10] Justo L. González, *Faith and Wealth: A History of Early Church Ideas on the Origin, Significance and Use of Money* (San Francisco, CA: Harper & Row, 1990), 79-83.

[11] Marcelino Legido, *Fraternidad en el Mundo: Un Estudio de Eclesiología Paulina* (Salamanca, Spain: Ediciones Sígueme, 1986), 210-86, 289-304.

[12] J. Andrew Kirk, *What is Mission? Theological Explorations* (Minneapolis, MN: Fortress Press, 2000), 1-22.

[13] Kirk, *What is Mission?* 37.

clever committee has dreamt up; it is the expression of one, indivisible, common life in Jesus Christ.[14]

Kirk argues that *koinonia* is the closest biblical expression for partnership, and sees four characteristics of discipleship that express this idea: first as a common project, second as a sharing of gifts, third as the sharing of material resources, and fourth as a sharing in suffering. Kirk stresses the fact that this partnership in suffering is based on the incarnation of Jesus Christ.

Kirk expands on the obstacles to partnership, raising very concrete and practical issues like dependency and freedom, mutual learning in trust, shared responsibility in the sharing of finances, and the exercise of power and accountability. He underlines that co-operation in mutual commitment to mission in Christ as the way to improve North-South relations. *Koinonia* as partnership became more identified with solidarity in unity and the sharing of resources.

Identity and Mission: Protestant Interpretations

José Míguez Bonino sees the relationship between history and mission as one of 'heritage-destiny', always searching for the newness of life and a better future.[15] Alberto Rembao interprets Protestantism as 'transcendent democracy' and 'cultural Protestantism'. These phrases exemplify Protestantism as a progressive ideology in Latin America, dealing with aspects of culture as well as with matters of faith.[16] Sante Uberto Barbieri described Protestantism as a creative force for the education of the people, an alternative in the face of nationalism, communism, and rationalism as the full realization of freedom.[17] Julio de Santa Ana underlines the contribution that Protestantism can offer Latin America as the movement seeks to be faithful to a liberating Christ.[18] Samuel Escobar and Orlando Costas see the connection between identity and mission as a clue to understanding the reality, life, and future of Protestantism in Latin America.[19]

---

[14] Kirk, *What is Mission?* 189.

[15] José Míguez Bonino, 'Historia y Misión', in Carmelo E. Álvarez, José Míguez Bonino and Roberto Craig (eds), *Protestantismo y Liberalismo en América Latina* (San Jose, Costa Rica: DEI-Latin American Biblical Seminary, 1983), 15-36.

[16] Alberto Rembao, *Democracia trascendente (*Buenos Aires: La Aurora, 1945).

[17] Sante Uberto Barbieri, *El país de El Dorado* (Buenos Aires: La Aurora, 1962).

[18] Julio de Santa Ana, *Protestantismo, cultura y sociedad* (Buenos Aires: La Aurora, 1970).

[19] Samuel Escobar, 'Identidad, Misión y Futuro del Protestantismo latinoamericano', *Taller del Teología* 3 (1978), 35-60; and Orlando E. Costas, *El protestantismo en América Latina hoy: ensayos del camino 1972-1974* (San Jose, Costa Rica: INDEF, 1975), 41-76.

Mainline Protestant Churches Searching for Identity

The first CCLA Congress on Christian Work in South America was held in Panama in 1916.[20] The delegates representing American missions divided up the southern continent among the different denominations, thus establishing a particular presence in each geographical area as part of a co-ordinated procedure to make better use of resources and to avoid duplicating efforts.[21]

The Panama Congress also improved relations between foreign missions and the national churches. Congress participants agreed to co-operate in several areas, including Christian literature, publishing houses, and literacy programmes. They also agreed to develop a study guide for Christian education. This Congress became the pillar of the initiation of 'Religious Pan-Americanism', a kind of Protestant co-operation similar to the Inter-American co-operation movement between the United States and Latin America, which was promoted in a series of subsequent Pan-American conferences.[22]

Although the participants at the Panama Congress agreed on the importance of co-operation among the churches, many pitfalls had to be overcome before their decisions could be put fully into practice. John Sinclair makes the following observation:

> Six years of planning [after Edinburgh 1910] followed to prepare for the Congress on Christian Work in Latin America held in the Canal Zone in 1916. At the conference, much of the ecumenical agenda was outlined. Yet one of the reasons for the Protestant presence in Latin America was only partially addressed: the witness of Protestantism to Roman Catholic Christianity. The ecumenical pioneers at Panama did not really face the issue culturally and theologically.[23]

Zuinglio M. Dias summarizes from another perspective the promises and failures of the Panama Congress:

> In general, the preoccupation with cooperation and the search for unity dominated the whole spectrum of the Congress. This was the main objective and as a result, in the years [that] followed, much effort was put into establishing local committees for cooperation. However, this desire for unity and cooperation, which so inspired the Panama congress participants, did not prosper. And it could

[20] See Juan Kessler and Wilton M. Nelson, 'Panamá 1916 y su impacto sobre el protestantismo latinoamericano', *Pastoralia* 1:2 (November 1978), 5-21.

[21] Joyce Hill, *CCLA History*, 1. See also John Sinclair, 'The Congress of Christian Work, Panama, 1916' (unpublished manuscript, May 1985), 1-5.

[22] See Samuel Guy Inman, *Problems in Pan Americanism* (New York: George H. Doran, 1921); Harlan Beach, *Renaissant Latin America* (New York: Missionary Education Movement, 1916); and Erasmo Braga, *Panamericanismo, aspecto religioso* (New York: Missionary Education Movement, 1916). These three figures were the leading voices in the Panama Conference of 1916. For the role leadership provided by Samuel Guy Inman, Secretary of the CCLA, see Karla Koll, 'Samuel Guy Inman: Venturer in Inter-American Friendship', *Union Theological Seminary Quarterly Review* 42:3 (1988), 45-66.

[23] John Sinclair, 'The Unfinished Agenda and Unfulfilled Dream of Panama' (unpublished manuscript, October 10, 1992), 3.

not prosper. The lack of a unified theological education, the wide differences in theological approach between the missions belonging to the established churches and the independent missionary Protestant groups in their countries of origin showed what in Panama they refused to accept: the differences which divide the Protestant churches themselves is of the same order as those which divide Catholics and Protestants.[24]

Zuinglio Dias highlights two problems that affected Protestant missionary movements in Latin America from their inception: their strong anti-Catholic sentiment, and Protestant divisions in the United States.

The Panama Congress was a step in the right direction: it encouraged co-operation and unity with the Latin American churches. The next decade was crucial for this process as the subsequent regional conferences[25] tried to promote national councils of churches and co-operation among denominations and local congregations.[26]

The divisions among foreign missions did not originate in Latin America but were imported from the pluralist United States and Europe. José Míguez Bonino stressed the idea that Latin American Protestantism was a 'divisive and divided' movement from its inception.[27] He saw the positive role that Protestant churches could play as a paradigm of human unity based on the calling to reconciliation, unity, and integration offered by Jesus Christ.

Missionary Protestantism within the framework of liberal ideology became the prevailing religious belief in Latin America. This ideology emphasized individualism, freedom for progress, liberal democracy and success.[28] These elements reflect both European Pietism and North American evangelicalism.[29] Samuel Escobar sets forth three major forces that he believes are the Protestant legacy for mission in Latin America and the Caribbean during the 21st century: Pietism, the Wesleyan revival, and the pentecostal movement.[30]

During the Montevideo Congress on Social Responsibility in South America in 1925, an attempt was made to analyse the social conditions in Latin America. During the 1916 Panama Congress, the missionaries presided and controlled the agenda. In Montevideo, however, a more Latin American

---

[24] Zuinglio M. Dias, 'Cooperation and Unity: The Dreams (Unfulfilled) of the Panama Congress in 1916' (unpublished manuscript, n.d.), 6-7.

[25] *CCLA, Regional Conferences in Latin America* (New York: The Missionary Education Movement, 1917).

[26] Arturo Piedra Solano, 'Orígenes e importancia del congreso de Panamá', *Vida y Pensamiento* 16:2 (November, 1996), 8-16.

[27] José Míguez Bonino, *Integración humana y unidad cristiana* (Río Piedras, Puerto Rico: Evangelical Seminary of Puerto Rico, 1969), 57.

[28] See Carmelo E. Álvarez, 'Del Protestantismo Liberal al Protestantismo Liberador', in Carmelo E. Álvarez, Roberto Craig, and José Míguez Bonino (eds), *Protestantismo y Liberalismo en América Latina*, 37-56.

[29] See David Martin, *Tongues of Fire: The Explosion of Protestantism in Latin America* (Oxford: Blackwell, 1990).

[30] Samuel Escobar, *Changing Tides: Latin America and World Mission Today* (Maryknoll, NY: Orbis Books, 2002), 100-10.

perspective was evident within Protestantism. The main topic of conversation was the positive role that Protestant churches could play socially and politically in these nations.[31] According to Samuel Guy Inman, the main architect of Latin Americanization, the emphasis was on 'social responsibility':

> While at Panama there might have been a question in the minds of some as to the advisability of Protestant Missions working in Latin America, at Montevideo, the Evangelical church felt itself as an established part of the life of South America, an institution which is taken for granted. With its firmer establishment as a national institution, therefore, the big question at Montevideo had shifted to the Evangelical church itself, its own pressing problems, those of the community, and what relationships should be between the South American church and the foreign missionaries and Boards which had given it birth and fostered its life up to the present.[32]

An incipient and timid criticism to imperialism was also voiced in Montevideo, as church leaders moved towards a reassertion of their local cultures and strived to stay focused on the authentically evangelical character of the Christian message. Inman was influenced by the Social Gospel movement and was optimistic because of his liberal and conciliatory approach on inter-American relationships.[33] However, he took a more critical stance against United States' intervention in Mexico and other parts of Latin America.

Inman summarized his vision in this way:

> The whole question regarding future ventures in Inter-American friendship may be summed up thus: shall such ventures be made on the basis of economic determinism or on the basis of the principles of Jesus Christ? The one road leads to division, to despair, to chaos; the other leads to unity, to hope, to victory.[34]

Four years later, at the Evangelical Congress in Havana (1929), the liberal influence was even more evident. 'Evangelical solidarity'[35] and the movement towards ecumenical co-operation within the framework of Pan Americanism[36] were the central themes.[37] Issues of education, social action and literature also re-emerged in Havana.[38]

For the first time, at the Havana Congress, Latin American leaders were active participants and affirmed their national and regional identities; the

---

31 Wilton M. Nelson, 'En Busca de un Protestantismo Latinoamericano: De Montevideo 1925 a La Habana 1929', *Pastoralia* 1:2 (November, 1978), 22-33.

32 Samuel Guy Inman, *Ventures in Inter-American Friendship* (New York: Missionary Education Movement, 1925), 18-19.

33 Karla Koll, 'Samuel Guy Inman: Venturer in Inter-American Friendship', 45-51.

34 Samuel Guy Inman, *Intervention in Mexico* (New York: Association Press, 1919); and Samuel Guy Inman, 'Imperialistic America', *Atlantic Monthly* 133:1 (July 1924), 143.

35 See Samuel Guy Inman, *Solidaridad Americana* (Madrid: Editorial Daniel Gorro, 1924).

36 Dafne Sabanes Plou, *Caminos de Unidad* (CLAI, 1994),14-19.

37 Samuel Guy Inman, *Inter-American Conferences 1826-1954: History and Problems* (Washington, DC: University Press of Washington, DC, 1965).

38 Wilton M. Nelson, 'En Busca de un Protestantismo Latinoamericano: De Montevideo 1925 a La Habana 1929', *Pastoralia* 1:2 (November 1978), 29-30.

missionaries were in the minority.[39] Liberal democracy was seen by Latin American Protestant leaders as an answer to the region's social, economic and political problems.

Samuel Guy Inman made the following remarks on the Havana Congress:

> The outstanding result of the Congress was the decision to form a Federation of Spanish American Evangelical churches [including Portugal and Spain]. The proposed Federation will have as one of its major objects the working out of the teachings of Christ to Spanish America. Only then will its religious life take on the fullness, the vigor and the expansive force of which it is capable; only then will its leaders cease to be considered mere echoes of foreign missionaries and appear in their real light, as native of their own soil, redeemers of their own culture.[40]

The Havana Congress of 1929 was the turning point in Latin American Protestantism.[41] In the first stage of Latin American Protestantism, up to 1929, the missionary heritage was strongly felt, but in Havana, the seeds of a more indigenous Latin American and ecumenical faith were sown.[42] After the Havana Congress, Protestant mission and evangelism began to find a place in Latin American history.[43]

Throughout the 1930s the liberal Protestant movement intensified its work, primarily in education for the upper classes to communicate the Gospel to the Latin American people.[44] However, from 1930-1940 ecumenical work decreased, and as the World War II escalated, only the youth groups played a significant role in the ecumenical movement.[45]

The most significant international ecumenical event of that decade was the Madras (India) Conference, 12th-29th December 1938 – also known as Tambaram.[46] This event was organized by the International Missionary Council and included the first Latin American delegation of distinguished ecumenists as participants. The Latin American message was summarized in this way:

---

[39] See Samuel Escobar and Luis D. Salem (eds), *Gonzalo Báez-Camargo: Una Vida al Descubierto* (Mexico: CUPSA, 1985); and Gonzalo Báez Camargo, *Hacia la Renovación Religiosa en Hispanoamérica* (Mexico: CUPSA, 1930).

[40] Samuel Guy Inman, 'Young Churches in Old Lands', *International Review of Mission* 19 (1930), 119.

[41] Dafne Sabanes Plou, *Caminos de unidad*, 16-17.

[42] Luis E. Odell, 'Sesenta y Cinco Años de Ecumenismo en América Latina 1913-1988', *Pasos* 25 (September-October 1989), 6-7.

[43] Pablo Deiros, *Historia del Cristianismo en América Latina*, 720-30.

[44] Agustín Battle, 'El Advenimiento del Protestantismo a América Latina', in Enrique Dussel (ed), *Historia de la iglesia en América Latina* (Barcelona, Spain: Nova Terra, 1972), 330.

[45] Nestor Míguez, 'De Rosario a Oaxtepec: Los Movimientos ecuménicos y la Búsqueda de unidad Cristiana en América Latina', in *CLAI, Oaxtepec 1978* (San José, Costa Rica: CLAI, 1980), 122-31.

[46] Timothy Yates, *Christian Mission in the Twentieth Century* (Cambridge: Cambridge University Press, 1994), 117-24.

> Protestant missions in Latin America rest directly upon the claims of urgent human need and the Christian consciousness of obligation to make disciples of all nations.[47]

The report resulting from this 1938 conference affirmed that Latin America had a role to play in the ecumenical world of the day and showed that Protestantism was a powerful transforming force in Latin America. Protestantism in Latin America continued to be challenged by the intellectual and upper classes to be an enlightened religion. The International Missionary Council was encouraged to implement a series of recommendations enabling these 'younger churches' to play a relevant role in the changing societies of Latin America. The Protestant churches of Latin America were, again, voicing their search for identity and mission in their region as well as asserting a place for themselves in the global ecumenical movement.

Alberto Rembao identifies a transition from the predominant role of foreign missionaries to the leadership of Latin American leaders. He saw the 1929 Congress of Havana as the turning point for Latin Americans.[48]

The first Latin American Evangelical Conference (CELA), held in Buenos Aires, Argentina, in 1949, opened a new era for the Protestant churches in the region. Besides discussing education and theological formation, participants raised an insistent call for an analysis of the social, economic and political situations in the region, examined within the framework of the traditional liberal ideology. CELA raised an awareness of the need for a commitment of the churches to a relevant evangelism that took the social problems of the grassroots and poor sectors seriously.[49]

The 1949 to 1959 decade was a crucial one for Latin America. Among other important international events, the People's Revolution in China closed the doors to western missionaries, and many were relocated to Latin America.[50] Protestant groups like the Pentecostals and evangelicals grew very quickly in this decade. The Cuban Revolution became the most significant political event of the decade, changing the religious and socio-political scenario in the region.[51]

The second Latin American Evangelical Conference (CELA) was held in Lima, Peru, in 1961. While affirming that Christ is the hope for Latin America, the Conference highlighted the need for an effective testimony, an attitude of humility in carrying out mission, and sufficient theological background for proclaiming the Gospel. The participants concluded that the work of carrying

---

[47] *International Missionary Council*, Madras, India, 12th-29th December 1938, Latin American Group (Special Group 2), 2.

[48] Alberto Rembao, *Mensaje, movimiento y masa* (Buenos Aires: La Aurora, 1939), 32-106.

[49] CELA, *El cristianismo evangélico en América Latina* (Buenos Aires: La Aurora, 1949).

[50] Yates, *Christian Mission in the Twentieth Century*, 78-86, 135.

[51] Jean-Pierre Bastián, *Historia del Protestantismo en América Latina* (Mexico: CUPSA, 1986), 198-200.

out God's mission should be done with both personal action and social militancy.[52] They also stated that the churches must increase their presence in national life and in international ecumenical collaboration.[53]

Councils and federations of churches from the different countries in Latin America and the Caribbean initiated a group called Evangelical Unity in Latin America (UNELAM) in Río de Janeiro, Brazil, in 1963. The main purpose of this provisional commission was to promote Christian unity among the churches.[54] UNELAM was an efficient instrument for dialogue, consultation, and planning.[55] When the assembly convened in Oaxtepec, Mexico, in September 1978, UNELAM ceased to exist; it took seriously the provisional character of its mission.

Two new ecumenical movements were founded between 1960 and 1970: Church and Society (ISAL) and the Evangelical Commission on Christian Education in Latin America (CELADEC). Two youth movements had played important roles during the two previous decades: ULAJE (The Evangelical Union of Latin American Youth), and WSCF (World Student Christian Federation).

In 1964 Richard Shaull[56] wrote the most influential article on ecclesiology ever written in Protestant circles in Latin America. Shaull raised questions on the role of churches in crisis and prophetically envisioned a new era for the church in which God created a new people through the active presence of a community based in Christ's incarnation.[57]

This type of renewal was the most promising and crucial element of contemporary theology in Latin America. A church willing to openly discuss its challenges need not fear the consequences and the radical implications of living God's will. Shaull saw the action of the Spirit as a corrective element and constant source of renewal.[58]

The Latin American Council of Churches (CLAI), founded in Oaxtepec, Mexico, in 1978, adopted a yet more prophetic position, pursuing more progressive issues like solidarity with the poor, the defence of human rights, liberation, and the role of women in the churches. This Conference resulted in

---

[52] CELA, *Cristo la Esperanza para América Latina* (Buenos Aires: Confederación Evangélica del Río de la Plata, 1962).

[53] José Míguez Bonino, *Hacia un Protestantismo Ecuménico: Notas para una Evaluación Histórica del Protestantismo entre la I y la II CELA (1949-1960), CLAI, Oaxtepec 1978* (San Jose, Costa Rica: CLAI, 1980), 65-80.

[54] Marcelo Pérez Rivas, 'El ecumenismo en América Latina' in Norman Goodall (ed), *El Movimiento Ecuménico* (Buenos Aires: La Aurora, 1970), 226-28.

[55] Orlando E. Costas, *Theology at the Crossroads* (Amsterdam: RODOPI, 1976), 237-40.

[56] Richard Shaull, 'Las CEBs Y La Ecclesia Reformata Semper Reformanda', *Cristianismo y Sociedad* 115:122 (1993), 52.

[57] Richard Shaull, 'La Forma de la Iglesia en la Nueva Diáspora', *Cuadernos de Marcha* 20 (September 1969), 69-70.

[58] Carmelo E. Álvarez, *Una iglesia en diáspora: Apuntes para una eclesiología solidaria* (San Jose, Costa Rica: DEI, 1991), 87-98.

many programmes and services that are clearly liberationist in content and praxis. CLAI's position is that evangelization and mission have a transforming presence and are committed to abolishing existing structures of injustice. CLAI was the fulfilment of the dream sparked during the Havana Congress in 1929: an ecumenical organization searching for identity and mission, and promoting unity.[59]

The decades between 1960 and 1980 were times of crisis and of hope. The political, economic, social and religious circumstances in the region created a new *kairos* in which the churches had an opportunity to become more contextualized and relevant. The Protestant churches found a way to respond and be faithful.[60] Between 1983 and 1992 these groups organized theological consultations and shared their reflections in books, forums, and seminars.[61]

Pentecostals in Search of Identity: Ecumenism of the Spirit

The Pentecostal movement in Latin America is very diverse. The search for a pentecostal identity and mission can be observed on four levels: first, what do Pentecostals mean by an 'Ecumenism of the Spirit'? The second level points out to leading voices in the search for identity and mission. The third examines how the process of mission and unity evolved. The fourth distinguishes between the diverse pentecostalisms and their various searches for identity and mission.

The 1961 New Delhi Assembly of the World Council of Churches was a turning point for the ecumenical movement[62] because both pentecostal and orthodox churches were received as full members of the World Council. Two pentecostal churches joined this unique ecumenical body: the Pentecostal Church of Chile, and the Pentecostal Mission Church of Chile.[63]

---

[59] Dafne Sabanes Plou, *Caminos de unidad*, 118-32; and Pablo Alberto Deiros, *Historia del cristianismo en América Latina*, 810-12.

[60] Carmelo E. Álvarez, 'Latin American Protestantism (1969-1978)', in Sergio Torres and John Eagleson (eds), *The Challenge of Basic Christian Communities*, 103-106.

[61] This process of organizing consultations was sponsored by the Ecumenical Research Department in San Jose, Costa Rica, through a programme called Protestant Traditions in Latin America, under the co-ordination of José Duque and Carmelo E. Álvarez. The following books were published as part of the programme: José Duque (ed), *La Tradición Protestante en la Teologia Latinoamericana, Primer Intento: Lectura de la Tradición Metodista* (San Jose, Costa Rica: DEI, 1983); Jorge Pixley (ed), *La Mujer en la Construcción de la Iglesia: Una Perspectiva Bautista desde América Latina y el Caribe* (San Jose, Costa Rica: DEI, 1986); Ashton Jacinto Brooks (ed), *Eclesiología: Presencia Anglicana en la Región Central de América* (San Jose, Costa Rica: DEI, 1990); and Carmelo E. Álvarez (ed), *Pentecostalismo y Liberación: Una Experiencia Latinoamericana* (San Jose, Costa Rica: DEI-CEPLA, 1992).

[62] John A. Mackay, *Ecumenics: The Science of the Church Universal* (Old Tappan, NJ: Prentice Hall, 1964), 197-98.

[63] Marta Palma, 'A Pentecostal Church in the Ecumenical Movement', *The Ecumenical Review* 37:2 (April 1985), 223-29.

The context and theological framework for Pentecostals' relationships with other denominations are what many interpreters call an 'Ecumenism of the Spirit'. The phrase caught momentum during the organization of the CEPLA in Chile in 1990, and later at the General Assembly of CLAI in Concepción, Chile, in 1995. Several historic churches have taken seriously the importance and relevance of the pentecostal churches by doing research and promoting dialogues, exchanges and forums.[64]

What is meant by 'Ecumenism of the Spirit'? The late American Methodist theologian and ecumenist Albert C. Outler relates this idea to specific moments in which the Spirit acts in the 'fullness of time' as 'ecumenical epiphanies', moments of unexpected divine revelation, loaded with joy and enthusiasm. These 'ecumenical epiphanies' are always opportunities to live intensely the promise of an ecumenical dialogue in which the Spirit opens new 'frontier spaces of pneumatology'.[65]

José Míguez Bonino introduced the concept during the General Assembly of CLAI in Concepción, 1995:

> An Ecumenism of the Spirit, although it does not determine institutional forms nor structural commitments nor formal decisions, dares its participants to not only pray and sing together (which is more than enough) but also to share experiences and explore new ventures.[66]

Ofelia Ortega reflects on this concept:

> Ecumenism in pentecostalism is permeated with 'ecumenism of the Spirit' in which the concept of unity is a faithful reflection of the unity of the Spirit; this includes all God's creation and its stewardship and integrity, and emerges from the same authentic experience of the Holy Spirit.[67]

All these definitions strive for an ecumenical agenda in which the 'Ecumenism of the Spirit' is a concrete commitment to a praxis and life in the Spirit as witnesses in the world, and an openness to the constant action of the Spirit calling to newness of life in all its fullness.

With regard to the implications of this 'Ecumenism of the Spirit' for Latin America, Guillermo Cook comments:

> Christian unity, for pentecostals, is a theological fact based upon the unity of the Trinity, the present and the future hope that drives them, both a factor in and a

---

[64] See Benjamín Gutiérrez and Dennis A. Smith, *In the Power of the Spirit: The Pentecostal Challenge to Historic Churches in Latin America* (Louisville, KY: Latin American Center for Pastoral Studies [CELEP]-Alliance of Presbyterian and Reformed Churches in Latin America (PC-(USA)/WMD, 1996).

[65] Albert C. Outler, 'Pneumatology as an Ecumenical Frontier', in Emilio Castro (ed), *To the Wind of God's Spirit* (Geneva: WCC, 1990), 19-20.

[66] José Míguez Bonino, 'Ecumenismo y unidad de la iglesia' (General Assembly, CLAI, Concepción Chile, 1995), 4.

[67] Ofelia Ortega, 'Ecumenism of the Spirit', in Benjamín F. Gutiérrez and Dennis Smith (eds), *In the Power of the Spirit* (Louisville, KY: Latin American Center for Pastoral Studies-Latin American Center for Pastoral Studies-PC(USA)/WMD, 1996), 183.

> requirement for the growth of the church and – for an increasing number of perceptive leaders – an imperative in the contemporary era of the divine *kairós*.[68]

This definition provides an inclusive and holistic approach to Christian mission based on the action of the Holy Spirit, manifested in experience and expressed in the commitment to promote unity in the church and the world.

In Search of Pentecostal Mission and Unity

The CEPLA (Latin American Pentecostal Evangelical Commission) process started in 1960. A national crisis in Chile, the 1960 earthquake, provided the ecumenical opportunity for action by both pentecostal and evangelical churches in Chile. The Evangelical *Ayuda Cristiana Evangélica* (ACE) [Evangelical Christian Aid] was established and became an incentive for two pentecostal churches of Chile to join the World Council of Churches in 1961. Several pentecostal churches and mainline denominations started a programme for theological education in Chile known as the Theological Community of Chile.[69]

The first EPLA (Latin American Pentecostal Encounter) was held in Buenos Aires, Argentina, in 1971. This conference, 'Pentecostal Unity in Latin America', was the starting point for an ongoing process of dialogue among pentecostal leaders of Latin America. Fifteen pentecostal leaders from Argentina, Chile, Costa Rica, Colombia, Nicaragua, Peru, and Venezuela established this unique opportunity for future encounters, and a special commission was formed to organize future events.

The second EPLA took place just before the Assembly of Churches in Oaxtepec, Mexico, 1978. Twenty-two pentecostal churches from different countries in Latin America were present. This pre-Assembly event gave an important impulse and visibility to the pentecostal churches, both at the Assembly and in the formation of the Latin American Council of Churches (CLAI).[70] That same year, immediately after the Oaxtepec Assembly, a group of pentecostal leaders from Colombia and Venezuela decided to convene the first Bolivariano Pentecostal Encounter. The *Encuentro Pentecostal Bolivariano* was held in Bogotá, Colombia, in March 1979.[71] The theme 'Unity and Growth of the Pentecostal People in Latin America' shows that the emphasis was on the implications of church growth in Latin America and the

---

[68] Guillermo Cook, 'Interchurch Relations: Exclusion, Ecumenism, and the Poor', in Edward L. Cleary and Hannah W. Stewart-Gambino (eds), *Power, Politics, and Pentecostals in Latin America* (Boulder, CO: Westview Press, 1997), 80.

[69] *CEPLA: Proceso de Unidad y Cooperación Pentecostal en América Latina, 1960-1992* (Maracaibo, Venezuela: CEPLA, 1992), 3.

[70] Roger Cabezas, 'Despertar Ecuménico del Pentecostalismo Latinoamericano', in Gamaliel Lugo and Manuel Quintero (eds), *Jubileo, Fiesta del Espiritu: Identidad y Misión del Pentecostalismo Latinoamericano* (Quito: *CEPLA-CLAI,* 1999), 103.

[71] Comisión de Fraternidad Evangélica Pentecostal Bolivariana, 28 de julio de 1978, 'Carta de San Cristóbal', *Primicia* (January-February 1979), 30.

challenges for pentecostal churches to witness and understand the socio-political reality.

In November 1979, during the second Latin American Congress on Evangelism (II CLADE) in Huampaní, Peru, thirty-one pentecostal leaders, representing churches in Argentina, Chile, Costa Rica, Ecuador, El Salvador, Mexico, Nicaragua, Panama, Peru, and Venezuela, met for dialogue on common issues. The focus of the resulting document was an openness to a 'new era' of fraternal relationships. Participants recognized the divisions within the body of Christ, and the need for a joint testimony to address both personal sins of individuals, and the structural sins and injustices present in Latin America. This document carried an open expression of a pentecostal theology of social concern.[72]

In 1982, during the founding of the Latin American Council of Churches (CLAI), another Pentecostal Encounter took place to examine the role of pentecostal churches in CLAI. Three pentecostal leaders were elected in the new board of CLAI, and many pentecostal churches joined the Council.[73]

In January 1988 another dialogue took place in Salvador, Bahía, Brazil. This included official representatives of CLAI and the WCC. They wanted to know about pentecostal identity and understand the place and role of Pentecostals as a growing movement. They also addressed the issue of social responsibility. The next pentecostal encounter took place during the first General Assembly of CLAI in Indaiatuba, Brazil, 1988. The meeting focused on two issues: 'ecumenical vocation' and 'prejudices against Pentecostals'.[74]

A series of national and regional events took place between 1989 and 1990. The first Cuban Pentecostal encounter was held in February and March 1989, with the topic 'Sharing the Experience of Latin American Pentecostal Encounters and the Challenges of Cuban Pentecostals'. The next EPLA encounter in Buenos Aires, 1989, made a clear appeal to pentecostal and historic churches to 'hope in unity, in fellowship and love, in the communion and solidarity that unites us in Christ'.[75]

In 1990 a group of leaders, sponsored by several ecumenical agencies called by the Ecumenical Research Department of Costa Rica (DEI), convened to discuss 'pentecostal theology' and to analyse the processes that the churches and people of Latin America were confronting in their daily life and work. The result was a volume of articles on Pentecostalism and liberation addressing the following issues: 'Pentecostal identity, pentecostal pastoral ministries, the work of the Spirit and life in the Spirit'.[76] The final article in the volume stresses the

---

72 'Encuentro Pentecostal Latinoamericano, Huampaní, Perú, 26 al 30 de octubre de 1979', *Pastoralia* 2:4-5 (1980), 240-41.

73 Carlos A. Valle, *Semilla de Comunión* (ed) (Buenos Aires: CLAI, 1983), 155-64.

74 Roger Cabezas, 'Despertar Ecuménico del Pentecostalismo Latinoamericano', 105.

75 'A Nuestros Queridos Hermanos y Hermanas Pentecostales de América Latina', in *EPLA, 18 al 23 de abril de 1989*, mimeographed.

76 Carmelo E. Álvarez (ed), *Pentecostalismo y Liberación: Una Experiencia Latinoamericana*, 17-250.

importance of continuing to contribute in an ecumenism of the Spirit, from the perspective of the poor to the ecumenical movement and the mission of the church.

CEPLA was founded and organized during the EPLA 1990 encounter in Chile. The newly constituted CEPLA commission designed a process that culminated in EPLA 1992 in Sao Paulo, Brazil. Two important issues confronted Pentecostals: 'An ecumenism of the Spirit' as a momentum for churches committed to an 'ecology of the Spirit'. These terms were not used during the event, but they were implied in the conference. The future of theological education for Pentecostals was another topic during the event. CEPLA has played an enormous role as a venue for ecumenical dialogue.

In 1994 an important consultation, sponsored by the WCC and supported by CLAI, concluded with this statement: 'In an atmosphere of fellowship and Christian love we have reflected on pentecostal identity, spirituality, evangelism, social responsibility, the participation of women, co-operation and dialogue.'[77]

The process that started in 1960 as a response to a concrete national crisis in Chile evolved to become a more consistent and constant attempt to create an atmosphere of mutuality and respect, to create a process of discernment to affirm a pentecostal identity, and to promote an integral and holistic evangelism that included an openness to dialogue and ecumenical co-operation.

Pentecostal Churches Searching for Identity in Latin America

The pentecostal movement in Latin America is part of the great missionary effort that followed the missionary movement of the nineteenth century. In Latin America, it started as sporadic renewal movements within the so-called mainline churches: Methodists in Chile, and Baptists and Presbyterian in Brazil.[78]

Three models of the pentecostal mission were predominant in Latin America in the twentieth century:

Classic Pentecostalism came from the United States and brought its own mission methods. It is economically and structurally dependent on foreign missions, and although the pastoral bodies were indigenous, ministerial education and training were based on foreign models.

Indigenous Pentecostalism grew out of the local mainline Protestant churches. With strong roots in popular Catholic culture, it is economically and structurally independent of all foreign missions and has an indigenous pastorate.[79]

---

[77] Consulta Pentecostal Latinoamericana, 'Viviendo en la Unidad del Espíritu', Peru, 14th-19th November 1994.

[78] Áureo Bispo dos Santos, *Origens históricas da pentecostalizacao do protestantismo brasileiro* (Salvador: Presbitério do Salvador, 1989), 1-21.

[79] Juan Sepúlveda, 'Pentecostal and Liberation Theology: Two Manifestations of the Work of the Holy Spirit for the Renewal of the Church', in Harold Hunter and Peter D.

The Neo-Pentecostal churches emphasize exorcism and prosperity. They are the offspring of dissident movements within the churches. Modelled on Messianic patterns, they have an entrepreneurial structure with a weak Latin-American pastorate and are dependent on the local charismatic hero-*empresario*-leader. One issue related to Neo-Pentecostals is the prosperity gospel. According to Kate Bowler: 'The prosperity gospel is a wildly popular Christian message of spiritual, physical and financial mastery that dominates not only much of the American religious scene but some of the largest churches around the globe.'[80]

Pentecostal churches in Latin America emphasize the worship service in their liturgy.[81] The life of the community is embodied in worship, a celebration of life in the midst of suffering and pain. Worship is the context for testimony and faith-sharing stories. Pentecostal testimonies express gratitude and tell of a testing of faith. The responsibility to testify begins at the moment of conversion and continues throughout life through witness, first to one's own pre-conversion circumstances, and then proceeding to the miracle of salvation.[82]

Pentecostal churches believe that their most fundamental task is to evangelize. For Pentecostals, the church is mission – the Mission of God.[83] This missiological dimension exists in creative tension with the eschatological dimension – a tension between the old and the new, between present joy and the expectation of the joy to come.[84] The believer lives in the expectation of the miraculous.

Yet pentecostal churches continue to struggle amidst divisions, doctrinal confrontations and misunderstandings by other Christian confessions. During the EPLA Encounter of 1998 in Havana, they expressed their conviction and hope, affirming that in discerning God's calling pentecostal churches find a continent that is suffering but 'impregnated with hope'.[85]

The pentecostal churches initiated a journey in search of identity and mission during the first half of the twentieth century. They embraced the 'Ecumenism of the Spirit', which was promoted through the active

Hocken (eds), *All Together in One Place* (Sheffield, UK: Sheffield Academic Press, 1993), 53.

80 Kate Bowler, *Blessed. A History of the American Prosperity Gospel* (New York: Oxford Press, 2011), 3.

81 Cecilia Castillo, 'Pentecostal Worship: A Healing Community', in Manuel Quintero (ed), *Seeds of Living Hope: Reflections and Challenges in the Churches in the Road to Concepción* (Quito: CLAI, 1994), 83-94.

82 See Manuel Canales, Samuel Palma and Hugo Villela (eds), *En tierra extraña II* (Santiago, Chile: AMERINDIA SEPADE, 1991).

83 Murray A. Dempster, Byron D. Klaus and Douglas Petersen (eds), *Called and Empowered: Global Mission In Pentecostal Perspective* (Peabody, MA: Hendrickson Publishers, 1991), 44-58, 67-97, 203-24, 242-58, 285-98.

84 Samuel Soliván, 'Hispanic Pentecostal Worship', in Justo L. González (ed) *¡Alabadle! Hispanic Christian Worship* (Nashville, TN: Abingdon Press, 1996), 43-56.

85 Manuel Quintero, *Jubileo, fiesta del Espíritu* (ed) (Quito: CEPLA-CLAI, 1999), 194.

participation of key leaders in the ecumenical movement, both regionally and internationally. This action moved them into specific partnerships of ecumenical co-operation with mainline denominations. This 'Ecumenism of the Spirit' affirms that Christian mission and unity requires an openness to the action of the Holy Spirit as an agent of that unity in the struggle for justice, hope, and peace.

Forward in Mission: An Ecumenical Partnership

At the beginning of this article, the author set forth the theoretical framework, and introduced the concepts of *missio Dei* and *koinonia.* It showed the importance of the search for identity and mission, both as a defining factor for denominational identity and as the foundation of relationships between groups. This article described two models of mission strategy (mainline Protestant and Pentecostal), analysed the joint mission strategy of the partnership, and highlighted the Ecumenical Sharing of Resources model of partnership. The theological elements of mission are provided in an examination of different traditions and diverse theological positions, while searching for consensus in the key concept of *missio Dei* as God's missionary action, and emphasizing the integral and inclusive dimensions of mission.

The conciliar process was shown to follow the same path of affirming mission as *missio Dei.* Another predominant motive in ecumenical circles has been *koinonia* as communion in Christian fellowship, worship, and witness in service. The analysis showed that since the church is called to a commitment to solidarity and unity while caring for God's creation, *koinonia* as partnership is seen as ecumenical co-operation in concrete sharing of resources.

The mission strategy of Pentecostal churches in Latin America was delineated, defining their identity and mission as an ecumenism of the Spirit. Pentecostal church leaders were active participants in promoting this style of ecumenism and in establishing partnerships with mainline denominations. Mission and unity were envisioned as a gift of the Spirit that resulted in the promotion of justice, hope, and peace.

As inheritors of 'Ecumenism of the Spirit' blowing in the Azusa Street movement and other revivals and spiritual movements in the United States, Latin America received inspiration and a missionary impulse in what was already a diverse and complex pentecostal movement. The three predominant mission models listed were the 'missionary expansive' model connected primarily with United States-based missions, a 'divine healing Neo-Pentecostalism', and the 'indigenous autonomous' movement. All three mission models responded to the pressing needs of the poor and oppressed that have comprised the majority of members in the pentecostal churches of Latin America today.

Part 2

Spirit Mission Praxis

Deliver Us from Evil: Evangelism, Spiritual Conflict, 'Signs and Wonders'

Tormod Engelsviken

Introduction, Including a Remarkable Norwegian Case

One of the most remarkable public debates in Norway during the winter of 2016 concerned a documentary movie made by the famous Norwegian film-maker Margreth Olin. In this documentary, which was seen by a large number of Norwegians in cinemas all over the country, she portrays Joralf Gjerstad, a well-known psychic and healer with so-called 'warm hands'. The film-maker, who has made several documentaries before, said that this time she wanted to portray goodness rather than evil as she had done in her former films.[1]

Joralf Gjerstad is almost 90 years old, comes from Snåsa, a small community in rural mid-Norway, and has during most of his life received people with problems or diseases into his home where he has counselled them and laid hands upon them for healing. Lots of people from various walks of life have afterwards testified to the fact that they have been healed or become significantly better through Gjerstad's ministry. Remarkably, the film-maker portrays Gjerstad and his ministry positively, and Gjerstad, a confessing Christian layman who has been employed in the local Norwegian Lutheran church, claims that his powers are a gift from God.

In the debate spurred by Gjerstad's ministry, critics have argued that there are no supernatural causes for the 'cures' but that they are a result of the *placebo* effect or the loving and positive attention that Gjerstad shows towards his clients. Many of the clients who have been helped, both Christians and non-Christians, however, reject this simple explanation and attribute their healing to forces yet unknown, or to God. Gjerstad has also been criticized for supporting the 'alternative' movement by offering healing outside the scientific medical tradition, although he himself strongly recommends his clients to seek

---

Originally published in R. Dowsett, I. Phiri, D. Birdsall, D.O. Terfassa, Hwa Yung and K. Jørgensen (eds.), *Evangelism and Diakonia in Context*, Regnum Edinburgh Centenary Series 32 (Oxford: Regnum Books, 2016), 235-250.

[1] Interview with Olin in the Norwegian Christian daily *Vårt Land*, 19th February 2016, 48.

help also from the medical profession. He does not want to be an alternative to medical science, but a supplement.

The reaction of church leaders has been positive. The Lutheran bishop Per Arne Dahl has said publicly during a discussion in Oslo cathedral that he wanted to ask forgiveness for the church's neglect of the healing ministry and to support the practice of anointing for healing and the use of the gift of healing in the church. Jan Olav Henriksen, professor of Systematic theology at MF Norwegian School of Theology, has co-authored a book about paranormal experiences[2] and tells how he himself has 'warm hands' and has laid hands on and prayed for people who have been healed.

One of the most popular television programmes in Scandinavia is called 'The Powers of the Spirits'. It is a reality (!) series, showing people who are bothered by spirits or 'energies' in their homes, and how these disturbances are diagnosed most often as being caused by the spirits of the deceased, who are then removed from the home by psychics or other specialists in dealing with the spirit-world.

These examples may suffice to show that interest in and experience of non-medical healing and dealing with the spirit-world are strong in some of the most modern and secularized countries of the world. This is the context in which I live today but, based on studies and personal experience of quite different cultures in the global South, I would claim that healing and spiritual conflict are *universals* or *constants* that the church has to deal with in all cultures and at all times. Amanda Porterfield argues that '(Christian) healing has persisted over time and across cultural spaces as a defining element of Christianity and a major contributor to Christianity's endurance, expansion, and success'.[3]

When the Lausanne Theology Working Group was planning a new theological consultation in the late 1990s, it consulted evangelical church and mission leaders all over the world to ask what was the most urgent theme for a theological and missiological consultation. The overwhelming majority suggested spiritual warfare or spiritual conflict as the most relevant topic for the consultation. The consultation with the title 'Deliver Us from Evil' was held in Nairobi, Kenya, in 2000. It resulted in a 'Consultation Statement', a short Lausanne Occasional Paper (LOP)[4] and the full volume 'Deliver Us from Evil'.[5] The Statement claims that the church should be engaged in a ministry of

---

[2] Jan Olav Henriksen and Kathrin Pabst, *Uventet og ubedt – paranormale erfaringer i møte med tradisjonell tro* [Unexpected and unasked for – paranormal experiences encountering traditional faith] (Oslo: Universitetsforlaget, 2013).

[3] Amanda Porterfield, *Healing in the History of Christianity* (Oxford: Oxford University Press, 2005), 19.

[4] Tormod Engelsviken, *Spiritual Conflict in Today's Mission* (Monrovia, CA: Lausanne Committee for World Evangelization, Marc Publications, 2001). The Consultation Statement is found on 82-96.

[5] A. Scott Moreau and others (eds), *Deliver Us from Evil: An Uneasy Frontier in Christian Mission* (Monrovia, CA: Lausanne Committee for World Evangelization, Marc Publications, 2002).

spiritual conflict, and it confirms that Satan is a real, personal, spiritual and created being: 'A primary purpose of the life and ministry of Jesus was to expose, confront and defeat Satan and destroy his works.' The Statement further argues that there are striking similarities between what happened in the early church and what is happening in demonic encounters and deliverance today, and that every Christian has access to the authority of Christ. The statement also issues warnings against syncretism, using magical means or taking ideas, methods, and strategies developed in one society and using them uncritically in another.[6]

The question that will be dealt with in this chapter is what is the nature and place of ministries of delivering people from oppression or possession by evil spiritual forces, and prayer for and experience of non-medical healing in relation to the *diakonia* of the church, especially in its missionary outreach.[7]

The Biblical Basis

The mission of the church has its origin and mandate from Jesus Christ. While the mission of the Triune God (*missio Dei*) may be seen in the totality of the biblical narrative, it may nevertheless be appropriate here to focus initially on the mission commissions of the risen Christ.

While the Great Commission in Matthew 28:18-20 does not explicitly mention deliverance or healing ministries as part of the mission of the apostles, this silence cannot be used as an argument for the view that there was a deliberate change in the apostles' task from the one they received from the earthly Jesus when he sent them out to the people of Israel, a task that included expulsion of evil spirits and healing (Matt. 10:1, 6-8).

Luke emphasizes the preaching of repentance and forgiveness to all nations and the witness of the apostles to the ends of the earth without mentioning exorcism and healing (Luke 24:47; Acts 1:8). His narrative of the mission of the early church in Acts, however, includes several accounts of healing and exorcism (e.g., Acts 3:1-10; 8:6-7; 14:8-18; 16:16-18). Sometimes these events are simply summarized as 'signs and wonders' (Greek: *terata kai semeia*, Acts 2:43). The role of these in the mission of the apostles is succinctly expressed in Acts 14:3: 'The apostles stayed there (in Iconium) for a long time, speaking boldly about the Lord who proved that their message about his grace was true

---

[6] *Deliver Us from Evil*, xx-xxv.

[7] We are aware of the fact that the topics we are dealing with here are sensitive, controversial and complex. We should warn against any easy answers to deep existential questions. There is an enormous amount of literature on these and related topics. In a short chapter, we are not able to cover all the important angles – for instance, such questions as the relationship between the natural and the supernatural, what belongs to creation and what to redemption, why some are healed and others not, and what should be the church's view and practice in this regard. Neither are we explicitly addressing the issues raised by the so-called 'prosperity gospel', but we share the views expressed in the *Cape Town Commitment: A Confession of Faith and a Call to Action* (The Lausanne Movement, 2011, 63-65).

by giving them the power to perform miracles and wonders' (Good News Bible). The term that is translated 'proved' is the Greek *martyreo* which means 'to give testimony' or 'to witness'. Here God himself gives corroborating evidence to the apostles' preaching of the Gospel by enabling them to perform signs and wonders. This is a most significant statement on how Luke values the role of signs and wonders for the mission of the church.[8]

The mission commission in John 20:21-22: 'As the Father sent me, so I send you. Then he breathed on them and said, "Receive the Holy Spirit"', has become very important in missiology over the last fifty years or so. There are at least two reasons for this. First, the text lays the basis for an understanding of mission as God's mission: the Father sends the Son, the Father and the Son send the Holy Spirit, and the Son sends the church with the Spirit to the world.[9] The nature and identity of the church as being sent to the world by the Triune God as a witness to the Gospel is central in recent missiology, not least in the 'missional church' movement.

Secondly, and especially relevant for our topic, is the *holistic* understanding of mission that is based on Jesus and his earthly ministry as a model or pattern for mission. The 'as' in John 20:21 is not only understood as a reference to the fact *that* the church is sent by Jesus, but also as a reference to *how* and *for what purpose* the church is being sent. Just as Jesus' ministry included a ministry of the *word* in preaching and teaching the gospel of the kingdom of God, it also included a ministry in *deed*, a demonstration of the character and power of the kingdom, as seen in his healings, expulsion of evil spirits, caring for the needs of the hungry, recognizing and raising up the downtrodden and despised, such as poor people, leprosy sufferers, publicans, prostitutes and Samaritans. The programme of Jesus according to Luke 4:18-19 was preaching the good news of God's salvation in the power of the Spirit, which meant liberty for captives, recovery of sight for the blind, and freedom from oppression. Whether these words are taken mainly metaphorically or literally, they still indicate the comprehensiveness of Jesus' mission in meeting the basic needs of people.

Against this background of Jesus' ministry, one is fully justified in arguing that loving service – or *diakonia* – to people in need is a central task of the church in its mission to the world. Mission is mission in word (evangelism) and deed (*diakonia*).

If we accept this comprehensive nature of the church's missionary task, it is the more surprising that the ministry of Jesus as healer and exorcist is so often

---

[8] The secondary ending of Mark 9:9-20 places great emphasis on the signs that will accompany the believers, including exorcism and healing of the sick through laying on of hands (Mark 16:17-18). Although this was not originally written by the author of Mark's Gospel, it may nevertheless faithfully reflect the view and experience of the early church.

[9] To various understandings of the concept of God's mission or *Missio Dei,* see Tormod Engelsviken, 'Missio Dei: the understanding and misunderstanding of a theological concept in European churches and missiology', *International Review of Mission* 92 (2003), No. 367, 481-97.

ignored or denied as a model for the church's ministry today. Especially in the theology of western post-Enlightenment Protestantism, both in its more conservative and liberal forms, it seems to have caused some embarrassment that Jesus in the gospels is portrayed as a miracle worker, and that this was central to his ministry and even to his proclamation of the coming of God's kingdom.

The kingdom of God is a comprehensive expression of everything that God's redemption includes. The church is the people of the kingdom who believe in, follow, serve and proclaim Jesus Christ as Saviour and Lord. Without entering the discussion of the meaning of the term kingdom of God (Greek: *basileia tou Theou*), I would argue that the concept 'the realm of God's salvation' catches the meaning better than the more common 'the rule of God'. It is generally agreed, however, that the kingdom has *already* arrived with Jesus (Mark 1:14), but that it is *not yet* fulfilled. This 'already' and 'not yet' distinction is important because it raises the question about which of the gifts of salvation have already been given and may be experienced here and now, and which are still future and will not be realized until the return of Christ and the redemption of God's creation. Among the gifts that are given in the present to those who enter the kingdom of God through faith in Jesus are forgiveness of sins, a new and right relationship with God our Father and Jesus the Messiah, freedom from Satan's power, a fellowship of believers (Greek: *koinonia*), eternal life, the gift of the Holy Spirit, righteousness, peace and joy (Rom. 14:17).

In the gospels, healings and exorcisms are signs (Greek: singular *semeion*, plural *semeia*). It is especially in John's Gospel that we find the term 'sign' frequently used about Jesus' miracles (e.g., John 2:11; 20:30). It may also be used in a negative sense when people demand signs in order to believe (Matt. 12:38-39). The signs have various meanings. We may discern at least four dimensions: a Christological, an eschatological, a diaconal, and a missiological.[10]

The *Christological* dimension points to who Jesus is. Jesus did, in fact, refer to the miracles and his preaching of the gospel when asked who he was (Matt. 11:4-6). There is an ongoing debate, prompted by some charismatic teachers, whether Jesus did his miracles as a human being anointed with the Spirit or in his capacity as the Son of God. The Gospels and Acts present Jesus both as endowed with the Spirit and doing his mighty deeds by the power of the Spirit (e.g., Luke 4:14, 18; Matt. 12:28; Acts 10:38). Yet there is something *unique* about Jesus' ministry. His healings and exorcisms were performed through his word and on his own authority without invoking any other power.[11] The

[10] See also Tormod Engelsviken, 'Tegn og under: deres betydning i kirkens og misjonens liv' [Signs and wonders: their significance for the life of the church and its mission], *Norsk tidsskrift for misjon* 41:1 (1987), 32-47.

[11] See the discussion particularly with regard to expulsion of evil spirits in Tormod Engelsviken, *Besettelse og åndsutdrivelse i Bibelen, historien og vår egen tid*

disciples, however, both in the Gospels and Acts healed and expelled evil spirits *in the name of Jesus*, which implies that it was Jesus, not the disciples, who actually healed and expelled the spirits. After Pentecost, it was God or the risen and ascended Christ who performed the signs and wonders through the ministry of the disciples. The earthly Jesus had authority as God both to forgive sins and to heal diseases (Mark 2:6-12). We also notice that Jesus is never said to have faith in God, while the disciples are encouraged to believe in God and Jesus (Matt 17:19-20; John 13:14). There is, therefore, a fundamental difference between the healings and exorcisms done by the earthly Jesus and those done by the disciples in the name of Jesus, although both Jesus and the disciples were empowered by the Holy Spirit for their ministries.

The *eschatological* dimension is primarily expressed by the fact that the mighty deeds were signs of the coming of the kingdom of God. We have mentioned above that the kingdom has *already* arrived with the coming of Jesus, and his message of repentance and faith in the Gospel (Mark 1:14; 4:17). Further evidence of the kingdom is the expulsion of evil spirits from people who are possessed: 'If I cast out evil spirits by the Spirit of God, then the kingdom of God has come to you' (Matt. 12:28; Luke 11:20). The defeat of Satan and the liberation of those who were possessed or oppressed by him or his demons were one of the central features of Jesus' earthly ministry. Together with the healing ministry, they represent a foretaste or anticipation of the kingdom that will come in power at the end of time. Then the devil and his evil powers will finally be defeated, and all disease will be gone forever through the resurrection of the body to eternal life. There is, however, a basic difference between the healings and the exorcisms: in the healings, there are two people involved: Jesus and the sick person; and Jesus speaks words of comfort and encouragement to the sick person who is then healed. In the exorcisms, however, there are three people involved: Jesus, the possessed and the demon. It is the demon(s) that is spoken to and driven out by a strict command from Jesus, while the possessed person is fully restored to life. The expulsions demonstrate that the kingdom of Satan loses its power in the encounter with Jesus and kingdom of God, and that those who have been bound by Satan are set free (Matt. 12:24-29).[12]

Especially significant in the context of the theme of this volume is what we have called the *diaconal* dimension. The wonders and the exorcisms are motivated by Jesus' love and compassion for people who suffer or have deep needs, whether they are sick, marginalized or possessed by evil spirits (e.g., Matt. 20:34). Matthew 9:36 portrays Jesus as being 'moved with compassion' for 'sheep without a shepherd'. This attitude of love and compassion has been correctly used as a foundation for the church's diaconal ministry, yet it should be pointed out that it is Jesus' (and the apostles') preaching of the gospel and

---

[Possession and expulsion of spirits in the Bible, in history and our own time] (Oslo: Lunde forlag, 1978), 40-43.

[12] See Engelsviken, *Besettelse*, 43-54.

miraculous healing ministry which is the context of Matthew 9:36 (Matt. 9:35-10:1).

Finally, the miracles of Jesus presuppose faith or imply a call to faith. This is the *missiological* dimension. This faith may be that of the suffering person, the faith of others or, in the case of the disciples, of those who perform the miracle. Faith, on the part of the suffering person, is not demanded, neither is it seen as a prerequisite for healing. Nevertheless, Jesus encourages people to believe and performs some of his miracles in response to faith. It is not the strength of the person's faith but its direction towards Jesus that is decisive. In the story of the boy with an evil spirit (Mark 9:17-29), Jesus rebuked the lack of faith by the people (v. 19). When the father of the boy asked for Jesus' help, Jesus answered that 'everything is possible for the person who has faith' (v. 23). The father confessed his lack of faith: 'I believe, help my unbelief' (v. 24), yet Jesus threw out the evil spirit and healed the boy. The story ends with Jesus' word about the need for prayer in the ministry of exorcism (v.29).

The wonders of Jesus may also lead to praise of God and faith in Jesus, both among those who are helped and those who witness the healing or the exorcism (Matt. 9:8; 15:30-31; John 2:23; 4:53). This is one of the purposes of Jesus' miracles (John 20:3). There are, however, also texts that warn against demanding signs or making faith dependent upon them (e.g., Matt. 12:38-39; John 4:48; 20:29).

We have looked briefly at some central features of Jesus' earthly ministry that may be carried forward by the church as it emulates the ministry of Jesus, according to Jesus' word in John 20:21. In the early church as described in Acts, the healing and exorcism ministry of Jesus is continued by the apostles and other Christians in Jesus' name and with some of the same dimensions as in Jesus' own ministry – particularly the Christological, diaconal and missiological. There are general references to 'signs and wonders'[13] and specific references to healing[14] and deliverance from evil spirits.[15] The high number of references to these sign and wonders show the importance that Luke attributes to them in the early mission of the church.

A *caveat* is in place here, however, since the healings in themselves are not unambiguous signs. The story of Paul's and Barnabas' healing of a lame man in Lystra (Acts 14:8-18) shows that Christian healing without the accompanying word may be interpreted within and on the basis of the religious worldview of the observers. In this case, Paul and Barnabas were seen as Greek gods rather than representatives of the living God (vv. 11-12, 15). The lesson to be drawn from this incident is that the preaching of the Gospel and the healing ministry should always go together.

The significance of signs and wonders is also corroborated by Paul himself in his epistles. Paul could refer to the experience of the churches in Galatia (Gal. 3:5) and Corinth (1 Cor. 2:4; 12:9-10). When Paul in Rom. 15:15-21

---

[13] E.g., Acts 2:43; 4:30; 5:12; 8:6-7; 14:3.

[14] E.g., Acts 3:6-8, 16; 4:14, 16; 5:15-16; 8:7; 9:34-42; 19:12; 28:8-9.

[15] E.g., Acts 5:16; 8:7:16:16-18; 19:12.

presents his missionary programme and method, he includes 'signs and wonders': 'I will be bold and speak only about what Christ has done through me to lead the Gentiles to obey God. He has done this by means of word and deeds (Greek: *logos* / word, *ergon* / deed), by the power of miracles and wonders (Greek: *semeia kai terata*), and by the power of the Spirit of God' (v. 18-19). It is common in current missiology to speak of mission in word and deed,[16] and rightly so. It should be noted, however, that the deeds that Paul refers to here are not the more common diaconal ministry but the signs and wonders that are a result of the Spirit's power that accompanies Paul's preaching of the Gospel. When this text is used as an argument for holistic ministry, it should not be forgotten that it includes 'signs and wonders' and the 'power of the Spirit'.

In 1 Cor. 12:9 Paul includes gifts of healing by the Spirit among the charisms (from Greek: *charisma* / gift of grace) that are in operation in the church. In the introductory statement in 12:4-5, the gifts are called charisms and services (Greek: *diakonia* / service). We are aware of the fact that the Greek term *diakonia* may be used of any kind of service, yet it is significant that all the gifts that are mentioned in 1 Cor. 12:6-11 are called 'services'. They are supposed to be permanent features of the ministry of the church in the power of the Holy Spirit.[17]

The New Testament text that has most influenced the church's *practice* of healing is James 5:14-16 which describes a simple rite of anointing and prayer. 'Is one of you ill? Let him send for the elders of the church to pray over him and anoint him with oil in the name of the Lord; the prayer offered in faith will heal the sick man, the Lord will restore him to health, and if he has committed sins, they will be forgiven. Therefore confess your sins to one another, and pray for one another, that you may be healed'. This text is the foundation for the Catholic and Orthodox sacrament of the anointing of the sick, and it has also been widely used in Protestant churches in connection with a healing ministry. This is the closest we come to an institutional form of healing ministry in the New Testament. It does not, however, exclude more spontaneous and individual forms of healing with or without anointing or the laying on of hands.

Healing and Exorcism in the Early Church

It is not possible to follow the long history of healing and exorcism in the church down through the ages, but a few observations may be useful. Contrary to the assumptions of some theologians in the past, these ministries did not disappear after the apostolic age. With regard to exorcism, the patristic scholar Oskar Skarsaune has, based on extensive textual evidence from early church

---

[16] See e.g., Michael W. Goheen, *Introducing Christian Mission Today* (Downers Grove, IL: IVP Academic, 2014), 227-63.

[17] Compare also the list of charisms in Romans 12:6-8 which includes a special charism called *diakonia* (v. 6).

fathers such as Tertullian, Justin Martyr, Origen and Athanasius, shown that a particular set of thought was consistent throughout the early church.[18]

First, Christians were convinced that the gods of the Gentiles were demons. Gentiles relate to real powers in their cult, but the powers are demonic idols (cf. Ps. 96:5). Secondly, when people worship these demons in the pagan cult, they risk possession. The early church placed possession in the pagan context and denied that baptized Christians could be possessed, unless they lapsed. Pre-baptismal exorcism has as its purpose getting rid of demonic forces before the seal of baptism. Thirdly, the context of possession and exorcism in the early church was people outside the church. Most of the evidence occurs in apologetic and missionary literature. It happened at the border between church and paganism. Exorcism is seen as a sign that demonstrates that Christ has conquered Satan and his hosts. It was also taken as a proof of the resurrection of Jesus Christ because only a living Lord could exercise authority over demonic powers. The exorcisms made a great impression on people and contributed to the attraction and growth of the church. Fourthly, the church was of the conviction that Christian exorcism could be performed by any Christian. Both Christian and pagan authors confirm that Christians were recognized as effective exorcists without the use of complicated incantation techniques. Exorcisms were so impressive because they functioned as 'miracles of confrontation' where demons had to openly admit who Jesus was, and recognize his superiority and power.

In connection with Christian initiation in the early church, those who were baptized expected to receive the gift of the Holy Spirit and charisms of the Spirit, such as healing and prophecy. The Catholic scholar Kilian McDonnell has shown how widespread the expectation and experience of the charisms were in different parts of the church during the first three hundred years. The charisms that are mentioned by the early church fathers in relation to Christian initiation include prophecy, healing, miracles and, in general, 'all the divine gifts'.[19] Several of the fathers saw the baptism of Jesus as a model. The Spirit came upon Jesus at his baptism, and then he began his public ministry in which healing and miracles were an integral part.[20] McDonnell and Montague conclude with regard to the normativity of the charisms:

> We believe… that the prophetic gifts must continue until the final coming. In some way the charisms, including the prophetic ones, structure the church. If the

---

[18] Oskar Skarsaune and Tormod Engelsviken, 'Possession and exorcism in the history of the church', in *Deliver Us*, 65-90, and Engelsviken, *Spiritual Conflict*, 18-20. To the question of healing and exorcism in the New Testament and the ancient church, see also the study by Andrew Daunton-Fear, *Healing in the Early Church: The Church's Ministry of Healing and Exorcism from the First to the Fifth Century* (Milton Keynes: Paternoster, 2009).

[19] Kilian McDonnell and George T. Montague, *Christian Initiation and Baptism in the Holy Spirit: Evidence from the First Eight Centuries* (Collegeville, MN: Liturgical Press, 1991, 309).

[20] *Christian Initiation*, 319.

> church is built upon the apostles and the prophets (Eph. 2:20), the charisms are in some way essential.[21]

It was the German theologian Adolph von Harnack who first recognized healing as an important factor in the growth of the church during the early period. Others have built on Harnack and argued 'that the new religion provided innovative forms of health care as well as rituals of spiritual healing that contributed to its attractiveness and figured importantly in its expansion'.[22] Although there are not always clear lines of demarcation between ordinary care for the sick and dying and prayer for divine healing, many documents attest that:

> ...early Christians nursed the sick to emulate the healing ministry of Jesus, to express their faith in the healing power of Christ... In their ministrations to the sick, Christians adopted a simple rite, based on the healings Jesus performed, of anointing the sick with oil 'in the name of the Lord'.[23]

The reason why we have put such a strong emphasis on the evidence of the New Testament and the early church, is the need to lay a theological foundation for the practice of healing and deliverance as part of the church's *diakonia* today, and to show the inadequacy of the so-called 'cessationist' position where signs and wonders are seen as having ceased after the period of Jesus and the apostles. Both the New Testament writers and the early church believed in and practised Christian exorcism and healing without in any way assuming that these practices were not supposed to accompany the church at all times.

Exorcism, Healing, 'Signs and Wonders' Today

The biblical and historical perspective does not, however, determine in what way 'signs and wonders' may be part of the diaconal and missionary ministry of the church in today's multicultural and multi-religious world. In the mainline Protestant churches going back to the Reformation in the sixteenth century, the question of 'signs and wonders', including exorcism and healing, has not been very prominent. In the modern Protestant mission movement from about 1800, healing ministry through medical personnel, clinics, and hospitals using the methods of medical science has been an integral part of the work of most missionary societies. It has not, however, in general, included exorcism or what we may call Christian or divine healing through prayer, although many missionaries with an evangelical background have been open to it, at least in principle. In his famous article on 'the excluded middle,' the American Mennonite scholar Paul Hiebert has pointed out how modern mission did not

21 *Christian Initiation*, 333.

22 Porterfield, *Healing*, 44. Porterfield enumerates several studies on healing in the early church in favour of her position.

23 Porterfield, *Healing*, 47.

come to grips with some of the questions raised by the local context with regard to healing and the spirit-world.[24]

It was the healing movement of the last part of the nineteenth century and the classical Pentecostal movement from 1906 onwards that made Christian healing a central part of their understanding of the gospel and of their missionary ministry.[25] The charismatic movement among non-Pentecostal churches from the 1960s spread the ministry of Christian healing and exorcism to most of the mainline churches. It has been especially in the global South that these ministries have flourished, partly due to influence from western evangelists who have held huge healing rallies in many large cities in the South, and partly due to national and local initiatives where reading of the Bible, combined with local cultural and religious experience, have led to healing ministries for the sick and the possessed.[26]

Discussions among evangelicals concerning 'signs and wonders' were strong in the 1980s, not least due to the influence of the Vineyard pastor John Wimber and the development that took place at Fuller Theological Seminary in California, USA. The Lausanne Theology Working Group convened a consultation on the Work of the Holy Spirit and Evangelization in Oslo, Norway, in 1985. In the book based on this consultation, Professor David Wells dealt with the issue of spiritual power encounters and 'signs and wonders'.[27] He takes a cautious stand, arguing that 'miracles' also take place in other religions and that there are false prophets who may produce signs that lead people astray. His conclusion is that '"signs and wonders" in themselves do not advance the gospel; only when they are done in the name of Jesus do they have evangelistic value'. He writes that 'in specific contexts, we may be brought face-to-face with overt demonic activity and its consequences'.[28]

---

[24] Paul G. Hiebert, 'The Flaw of the Excluded Middle', *Missiology: An International Review* 10 (1982), 35-47.

[25] See Vinson Synan, *The Holiness Pentecostal Tradition: Charismatic Movements in the Twentieth Century* (Grand Rapids, MI: Eerdmans, 1997); D.E. Harrell, Jr., *All Things are Possible: The Healing and Charismatic Revivals in Modern America* (Bloomington, IN: Indiana University Press 1975).

[26] The writings of the Ghanaian professor Kwabena Asamoah-Gyadu give very important documentation and evaluation of the characteristics and various healing ministries of the Pentecostal and Charismatic churches in Africa, see e.g., Kwabena Asamoah-Gyadu, 'Pentecostalism in Africa and the Changing Face of Christian Mission: Pentecostal/Charismatic Renewal Movements in Ghana', *Mission Studies* 19:2 (2002), 14-39. See also the description of new models of mission in Africa and in Pentecostalism in Stephen B. Bevans and Roger P. Schroeder, *Constants in Context: A Theology of Mission for Today* (Maryknoll, NY: Orbis Books, 2004), 265-[75]. I have shown that exorcisms and healing ministries were practised with great impact in the evangelical churches in Ethiopia prior to the influence of the Pentecostal movement in that country; see Tormod Engelsviken, 'Exorcism and Healing in the evangelical churches in Ethiopia', *Journal of Mission Theology* 1:1 (1991), 80-92.

[27] David F. Wells, *God the Evangelist: How the Holy Spirit Works to Bring Men and Women to Faith* (Grand Rapids, MI: Eerdmans, 1987), 65-91.

[28] Wells, *God the Evangelist*, 90-91.

In concluding this chapter, I would like to suggest seven characteristics or criteria for a sound practice of the ministries of spiritual conflict, healing and 'signs and wonders'.

First, the ministries should be *caring* (from Latin: *caritas* / love). By this I mean that they should be inspired by God's love and concern for people who are suffering, and come from the love that is poured out into the hearts of Christians by the gift of the Holy Spirit (Rom. 5:5). They should be carried out with an unselfish motivation and full focus on helping others, rather than to achieve anything for those who minister, or use others as a means to an end.

Secondly, the ministries should be *Christ-centred.* This means that they should produce a personal encounter between the suffering or healed person and the risen Christ. The honour and glory should be given to God (as it was in many of the New Testament stories), and the ministries should not be used to glorify any human being, or any effort or method on the part of ministers. The story of Simon in Acts 8 is an example of a man who sought the power of the Spirit and signs and wonders for the wrong reasons and was therefore judged by God (Acts 8:13, 19-24). When the focus is on charismatic personalities, saints, places, special words or material means, healing may draw attention away from Christ who is the real healer by his Holy Spirit.

Thirdly, the ministries should be *charismatic.* By this, I refer to the biblical meaning of charisms (Greek: *charisma*, 'gift of grace') as spiritual gifts of ministry given freely to individual Christians for the building up of the church (1 Cor. 12:4-11). The gifts should be recognized and given place in the church, and they should be allowed to function in an orderly fashion (cf. 1 Cor. 12-14; Rom. 12; Eph. 4). The whole spectrum of gifts that is needed for these ministries should be desired, expected and sought by prayer.

Fourthly, the ministries should be *communal.* The gifts of healing are given to the fellowship of believers, the church, and they should, as a rule, be practiced in a communal setting. This is especially clear in practice recommended in James 5:14-16. Without the prayerful support of the church, those who are healed may not be sustained. Especially with regard to new converts who are the result of an experience of God's healing power, inclusion in the church's fellowship is crucial.

Fifthly, *counselling* of people who seek help or have experienced healing of diseases or liberation from evil powers is important, both in order for them to be incorporated into Christian fellowship, receive attention for their specific needs, and receive instruction on the meaning of what will happen to them or what has happened. This means that, in my opinion, large healing rallies without an opportunity for individual counselling is not an appropriate form of the healing ministry. In private counselling, *confession of sin and reception of forgiveness* may be a part of the healing process. In the teaching and counselling process, it is very important to deal biblically and truthfully with the fact that many or most of those who are prayed for do not experience full healing. Yet, they may receive a blessing from God and strength to endure suffering.

Sixthly, the ministries should be *contextual.* They should take into account the local context as far as religion and culture are concerned. The needs of suffering people may vary depending on their worldview, their relations, their socio-economic situation, etc. The Malaysian bishop Hwa Yung has pointed out how important the spiritual dimension and spiritual conflict are in a contextual Asian ministry.[29] The introduction to this chapter shows how such needs in Scandinavia may be related to fear of spiritual unrest in the home. The method of critical contextualization as outlined by Paul Hiebert may be useful as it aims at confirming and preserving what is good and true in all religions and cultures, and challenging and confronting what is evil in all religions and cultures.[30] This also means that the forms of the ministries may vary, and one form may not necessarily 'work' in another cultural or religious context.

Seventhly, the ministries should be evaluated *critically.* To some, this may seem to go against the need for faith, but the New Testament is very clear that there is a need for the gift of *discernment* (1 Cor. 12:10; 14:29). Spirits should be tested because there are false prophets leading people astray (1 John 4:1-2). Jesus also warned against false Messiahs and prophets who will do great signs and wonders (Matt. 24:24). The criteria mentioned above may be used in the evaluation of the ministries, but first and foremost it is the confession of Christ as the incarnate, crucified and risen Lord that is the final criterion (1 John 4:2-3; 1 Cor. 12:3).

There is a fundamental difference between the preaching of the gospel in evangelism and *diakonia* as ministry to the poor and suffering, on the one hand, and ministries of Christian healing and exorcism, on the other. The former may be carried out by human beings as channels of God's love and grace, while the latter can only be prayed for and hoped for. Even if there is an expectation that Christ will intervene in a seemingly miraculous way, there is no guarantee. The Spirit is sovereign and distributes his gifts as he pleases (1 Cor. 12:11). Healing is in the hands of God. Yet, it is the task of the church in its missionary work to integrate these ministries in such a way that people are given the opportunity to pray for the sick and expel evil powers.[31] One should hope that ministries of healing and spiritual conflict will get a larger place both in the theory and practice of mission.[32]

---

[29] Hwa Yung, *Mangoes or Bananas? The Quest for an Authentic Asian Christian Theology* (Oxford: Regnum Books, 1997), 71-76; Hwa Yung, 'The Integrity of Mission in Light of the Gospel: Bearing the Witness of the Spirit', *Mission Studies* 20:4 (2007).

[30] Paul G. Hiebert, *Anthropological Insights for Missionaries* (Grand Rapids, MI: Baker, 1985), 171-92.

[31] Liturgies for prayer for (and anointing of) the sick are examples of such integration, cf. the Catholic sacrament of anointing the sick, and liturgies in the Anglican Church; see Morris Maddocks, *The Christian Healing Ministry* (London: SPCK, 1995), 243-46. The Church of Norway (Lutheran) has also made a liturgy for a ministry against 'unrest' in homes without offering any explanation of the causes of what is actually happening.

[32] The Commission on World Mission and Evangelism (CWME) of the World Council of Churches (WCC) focused on healing and reconciliation in its conference in Athens 2005. In the official report from the conference there are many useful insights and

discussions on the role of healing in the mission of the church. It is informative about recent developments and does also raise the question of the reality of spiritual powers and exorcism; cf. Jacques Matthey (ed), *Come Holy Spirit, heal and reconcile* (Geneva: WCC, 2008), 98-100. See also the document, 'The Healing Ministry of the Church', in *'You Are the Light of the World': Statements on Mission by the World Council of Churches 1980-2005* (Geneva: WCC, 2005).

Athens 2005: Reconciliation and Healing as an Imperative for Mission

Jacques Matthey

Since the integration between the International Missionary Council (IMC) and the World Council of Churches (WCC) in 1961, a conference on World Mission and Evangelism (CWME) is held every seven to eight years, called and prepared on behalf of the WCC by its Commission on World Mission and Evangelism. The main role of such world mission conferences is to highlight trends in ecumenical mission theory and practice and offer a space for dialogue, debate, often controversial, as well as for fellowship between representatives of the many spiritual, denominational and theological traditions of the ecumenical movement. The particularity of the Athens 2005 conference lies in the decision of the CWME Commission to search for a new style of conference, emphasising spiritual and ecumenical experience over the aim to produce more or less accepted reports and documents. The style of the conference should match the thematic emphasis on reconciling and healing communities.[1]

There is no space for a general presentation of the world context in which the 2005 conference was held. However, a few factors should be mentioned. Athens was the first mission conference clearly influenced by the *Common Understanding and Vision* document[2] in which the WCC revisited its own role as an important, but not the only, instrument of the ecumenical movement, thus opening the perspective to more intentional co-operation with other actors of contemporary world Christianity.[3] The 2005 conference was also the first WCC mission conference held in a majority Orthodox country. This was a consequence of the adoption by the WCC of the report of the 'Special

---

Originally published in Robert Schreiter and Knud Jørgensen (eds), *Mission as Ministry of Reconciliation,* Regnum Edinburgh Centenary Series 16 (Oxford: Regnum Books, 2013), 37-51.

[1] For a full report on the 2005 conference, see Jacques Matthey (ed), *Come Holy Spirit, Heal and Reconcile! Report of the WCC Conference on World Mission and Evangelism, Athens, May 2005* (Geneva: WCC Publications, 2008). The book contains a CD-ROM with all materials from the book, plus the individual listeners' reports. In the following footnotes, it will be referred to as: Matthey (ed), *Conference Report*.

[2] World Council of Churches, *Towards a Common Understanding and Vision of the World Council of Churches – A Policy Statement* (Geneva: WCC Publications, 1997).

[3] The study process for Athens ran parallel to the preparations for a 'Global Christian Forum', which took place two years later in Nairobi, Kenya

Commission for Orthodox participation in the WCC' following several years of thorough and difficult discussions on relations between Orthodox and Protestant/Anglican member-churches. Both the opening up of the WCC to the larger *oikoumene* and the intense dialogues with Orthodox churches can be understood as contributions to reconciliation and healing processes within Christianity, and in that sense very much linked to the theme of the 2005 conference.[4]

Missio Dei and *Missio Ecclesiae*

One of the originalities of the Athens meeting is its double title. It tries to capture the renewed conscient connection between what relates to God's mission and to the church's task within it. In the 1960s, when missiologists developed quite radical understandings of missio Dei after the 1952 Willingen IMC conference, this resulted in a relative or total neglect of the specific role of the church in mission. In the most extreme cases of the debates of the 1960s, missio Dei and missio ecclesiae became catchwords for opposed perspectives on mission. Once the conditions for a renewed dialogue between 'evangelical' and 'ecumenical' missiologists had been developed, it became possible to reconnect a wide perspective emphasising God's mission in the world and the particular role of the church within it.[5] The Athens title connects them as follows:

'Come, Holy Spirit, heal and reconcile' refers to *missio Dei* and reads like a confession of faith to God as the one who wants to heal and reconcile. The prayer reflects confidence that God will act in a way to overcome evil and violence and all that breaks relations. It is also a call to God when humans reach their limits: we cannot 'heal the world', we rely on God – God is our

[4] 'If ever reconciliation is needed, it is needed between PCCs and other Christians. The ecumenical movement must include this large segment of Christianity to be truly ecumenical, and the vast majority of PCC churches must see the importance of being so included. That said, Athens has made significant achievements with regard to PCC participation' (note from editor: PCC stands for Pentecostal and Charismatic Christian). This was written by Allan Anderson, one of the Pentecostal listeners: 'The Holy Spirit, Healing and Reconciliation: Pentecostal/Charismatic Issues at Athens 2005', *International Review of Mission* 94:374 (July 2005), 342. A dozen scholars had been asked to accompany the conference and to comment on it relatively soon after its conclusion. Their individual reports have been published in the above-mentioned issue of the journal, which in subsequent footnotes will be referred to as *IRM: Listeners' Reports*.

[5] This trend is visible in the statement published as a study document by the CWME Commission in the year 2000, cf 'Mission and Evangelism in Unity Today', in Jacques Matthey (ed), *'You Are the Light of the World': Statements on Mission by the WCC 1980-2005* (Geneva: WCC Publications, 2005), 59-89. Cf. also the results of the consultation held in Willingen, Germany, fifty years after the famous IMC meeting. The papers have been published in *IRM* 92:367 (October 2003) issue ('*Missio Dei* Revisited – Willingen 1952').

hope. But out of the depth of suffering, it can also become a prayer in despair, like the psalmist's: 'It's urgent, God – do intervene!'

'Called in Christ to be reconciling and healing communities' describes *missio ecclesiae*. It is a limited, but essential mission – community-building. We cannot be the agents of God's entire mission, but we can at our level contribute to creating communitarian spaces where something of God's healing and reconciling offer can be experienced in daily life and socio-political dynamics.

In my personal view, this connection between *missio Dei* and *missio ecclesiae* is one of the most essential elements of missiology and should be carefully kept also in the future. When we humans are not able to recognise our own limitations and don't accept the necessary distinction between God's and our own agency, we fall into a dangerous messianism, political or evangelistic.[6] When concentration on the church's mission neglects the width of the Spirit's dynamic presence in the whole of the cosmos, mission falls back into ecclesiocentric domestication of a god that has become our denominational idol.

The Holy Spirit and Mission

Seldom had a WCC world mission conference highlighted pneumatology. At the end of the 1980s, issues around the Holy Spirit became prominent in the preparation towards the 1991 Canberra Assembly whose reports contain valuable insights also for mission. Due however to the serious conflict on discernment of the Holy Spirit in cultural and political movements during the Assembly, there was no real immediate follow-up on pneumatology in the WCC. It has been positively noted by several observers of the mission scene that Athens succeeded in revisiting a pneumatological emphasis on mission without leading to similar clashes.[7]

The CWME conference did not aim at offering a unique and uniform understanding of mission and the Holy Spirit. The following observations summarise main trends:

- The spiritual and relational aspects of the gospel receive due attention, overcoming earlier limitations of Christian witness to ethical, verbal and rational approaches. Athens' prayer to the Holy Spirit points to the liturgical dimension of Christian life and community.
- The Spirit, however, must not be considered as a 'tranquilizer', leading to an 'other worldly' spirituality. It is a creational and resurrecting power that reconciles God and humanity and people to one another. It is a force and dynamic of healing, empowering people to raise their voice

---

[6] There is more similarity than is usually admitted between radical militants for justice and extreme evangelistic movements in their understanding of power and their difficulty to enter into dialogue with people defending other positions.

[7] Michael Kinnamon, 'Report on the World Mission Conference Athens 2005', *IRM: Listeners' Reports*, 390.

in witness, to take part in God's overall mission and stand for the values and dynamics of God's kingdom and justice. The Spirit empowers, in particular, the church, by indwelling it, granting charisms for discernment and witness and edifying it into a healing and reconciling community.

- A theology of the Holy Spirit balances between what one could call 'certainty' and 'uncertainty' principles. Present since the Creation and active in it, the Spirit leads not only humanity, but the whole cosmos towards fulness of reconciliation with God at the end of times. One *can* thus discern the Spirit's influence in Creation and humanity. Such 'certainty' is however limited by the Spirit's freedom to blow where she or it wills, often in most unexpected ways and places. This 'uncertainty' principle prevents absolute dogmatics about *missio Dei.*

The Spirit must be received as an 'alien', subversive force, which one cannot and must not try to domesticate. It breaks barriers, challenges forms of exclusion, and enables, in particular, the marginalised to take part in God's mission.[8]

The shift in approaching God, church, and world in terms of the Holy Spirit seemed acceptable to many in Athens.[9] This is a significant shift, since most earlier mission conferences were based on Christocentric universality. One would, however, misread the intentions of the 2005 conference if one thought it moved away from a reference to Jesus Christ. The remarkable freedom and flexibility brought by the new emphasis must not lead to questionable spiritualities.[10] The recognition that the Spirit is constantly at work in hearts, communities, world, and creation does not mean that everything which one likes is good and valuable. In Christian theology, the Spirit cannot be dissociated from the Son; 'in the earthly ministry of Jesus, the economy of the Spirit and the economy of the Word coincide'.[11] When attempting to escape earlier limitations linked to a narrow Christocentric base, one must not fall into post-modern relativism.[12] There is a double credibility test: missiology has to

---

[8] Monica Melanchthon, 'What does a Reconciled and Healed Community Look Like? Questions and Reflections Arising from the CWME, Athens', *IRM: Listeners' Reports*, 398-99.

[9] One can affirm the same for the Edinburgh 2010 conference.

[10] In his plenary address, Wonsuk Ma referred to some segments of the neo-charismatic indigenous movements that 'advocate questionable doctrines with which orthodox Christians are not comfortable. This gives rise to the possibility of having groups that may be 'more Pentecostal, but less Christian': Wonsuk Ma, '"When the poor are fired up": The Role of Pneumatology in Pentecostal-Charismatic Mission', in Matthey (ed), *Conference Report*, 159.

[11] Kirsteen Kim, '"Come, Holy Spirit": Who? Why? How? So What?', in Matthey (ed), *Conference Report*, 153.

[12] Anastasia Vassiliadou, 'Discerning the spirit of Athens: Listeners' Reports', *IRM: Listeners' Reports,* 439, and Athanasios Papathanasiou, 'Reconciliation: The Major Conflict in Post-Modernity: An Orthodox Contribution to a Missiological Dialogue', in Matthey (ed), *Conference Report*, 182.

remain open to the universal and at times surprising or even disturbing utterances of the Spirit, but never lose the major criterion for discernment of spiritual and other forces, which is Christ-centred.

Debate on the Vision of the World

The difficult debate on worldviews between North and South has never featured with any importance at a world mission conference. The preparatory document on healing does so in its attempt to understand suffering, cure, and healing. Kirsteen Kim also asked the participants whether they thought that only one Spirit was blowing in the world, or whether one should take the existence of conflicting spirits as the basis for analysis. The debate, mainly between churches influenced by a rationality rooted in the Enlightenment, and churches whose rationality has roots in cultures in which the invisible world is considered real, has only just started. Due to migration and the multiplication of churches resulting from it, this issue gains particular urgency in many parts of the world, because it predetermines possibilities of common understanding and vision between Christians of different cultures. It touches profound beliefs and theological taboos, but suffers also from political and religious manipulations. In the long perspective, it could be one of the most important contributions of Athens to world Christianity to have broken the silence on the matter in ecumenical circles.[13] Healing and reconciliation between churches of different spiritual and cultural traditions will not be possible short of a dialogue and perhaps an agreement on the significance of worldviews in theology and mission.

Mission as Healing and Reconciliation

Two separate, but related study processes prepared the Athens conference, leading to a main preparatory document on healing, another on reconciliation.[14] At the conference itself, the subjects were presented in different plenaries. The question was rightly raised by participants and listeners whether CWME had

---

[13] Cf. Kirsteen Kim, 'Come Holy Spirit', and the preparatory document on healing, published in 2005: 'The healing mission of the church', in Matthey (ed), *'You Are the Light of the World'*, 127-62. Similar attention started to be given to the matter at the 2004 conference of the International Association for Mission Studies (IAMS) through the creation of a study group on pneumatology.

[14] 'Mission as Ministry of Reconciliation' document approved by the CWME Commission, in Matthey (ed), *'You Are the Light of the World'*, 90-126. The document on healing is mentioned in the previous footnote. Both documents have also been published in the *Conference Report* and are available on the internet at least as Conference Preparatory Papers on the Athens Website (www.mission2005.org). In further footnotes, these documents will only be referred to with their title and the §, not with page numbers, since these differ in each case.

succeeded in sufficiently integrating the two approaches.[15] I wish to submit the following reflections on the interconnection and differences made in Athens between mission as healing and/or as reconciliation.

At first glance, the similarity and difference between reconciliation and healing seem somewhat parallel to the recurrent debate on the meanings of the overlapping terms 'mission' and 'evangelism'.[16] In his plenary address, Samuel Kabue most clearly pointed to the contextual meaning of healing and reconciliation. In societies that have, e.g., just come out of years of conflict and bloodshed, he argued, the terms carry something of the hope of a new future and harmony. Where however bloody killing continues to shake society, speaking of healing or reconciliation can emphasise the present stage of suffering and augment it.[17] It was pointed out repeatedly at the conference how often the language of reconciliation had been misused by Christians to cover injustice and plead for an easy peace, leaving out the responsibilities of perpetrators and demobilising victims struggling for justice.

Missiologists struggle with the overlapping meaning of reconciliation and healing. When examining the 2005 conference documents, it is imperative to make a distinction between what relates to the eschatological nature of God's mission and what relates to the church's or humanity's tasks in history. Indeed, Athens uses healing and reconciliation almost interchangeably when meaning eschatology:

> God Father, Son and Spirit leads creation and humanity towards the full realisation of God's kingdom, which the prophets announce and expect as reconciled and healed relationships between creation and God, humanity and God, humanity and creation, between humans as persons and as groups or societies (healing in the fullest sense as *shalom*, Isaiah 65:17-25). This is what in missiology is referred to as *missio Dei*.... While affirming the dynamic reality of God's mission in world and creation, we also acknowledge its profound mystery which is beyond the grasp of human knowledge (Job 38–41). We rejoice whenever God's presence manifests itself in miraculous and liberating, healing changes in human life and history, enabling life in dignity. We also cry out with the Psalmist and Job to challenge the Creator when evil and unexplainable suffering scandalise us and seem to indicate the absence of a merciful and just God: 'Why, O God? Why me, Lord? How long?' It is in a profoundly ambivalent and paradoxical world that we affirm our belief and hope in a God who heals and cares.

[15] Lalsangkima Pachuau, 'Athens 2005: A Missiological Reflection', *IRM: Listeners' Reports*, 421-22.

[16] David Bosch, *Transforming Mission: Paradigm Shifts in Theology of Mission* (Maryknoll, NY: Orbis, 1991), 409-20. The working definitions of CWME can be found in 'Mission and Evangelism in Unity Today', §7.

[17] Samuel Kabue, 'Addressing Disability in a Healing and Reconciling Community', in Matthey (ed), *Conference Report*, 172. Samuel Kabue from Kenya is general secretary of the Ecumenical Disability Advocates Network (EDAN).

> Jesus' healing and exorcist activity points in particular to the accomplishment of his ministry at the cross: he came to offer salvation, the healing of relationship with God, what Paul later described as 'reconciliation' (2 Cor. 5).[18]

Healing, reconciliation, as well as salvation and fulness of life, seem interchangeable as expressions of the final coming of God's universal reign. The intimate relationship between healing and reconciliation processes is also illustrated by Samuel Kabue. Reflecting on the basis of his experience of living with a disability, he emphasises in Jesus' healing miracles not so much cure from physical disease, but the reintegration of the sick and 'impure' person into the community of the faithful. In that sense, Jesus' healing mission results in restoration of communion, inclusion, unity, and reconciliation.

The essential theological relation between reconciliation and mission was stressed by Orthodox speakers. In his introductory welcome address, HB Christodoulos, the late Archbishop of Athens and all Greece, explained why he rejoiced in the choice of the theme: 'In our ages-long Orthodox theology, the concept of sin was always perceived as breaking and alteration of relationship and estrangement of the human race from God, from one another and with the whole of creation; never, or rather very seldom, as a legalistic guilt. It was on these grounds that salvation is understood as a process of healing and reconciliation with God, with one another and with the whole of creation.'[19]

There are signs of different emphases, however. The earliest document drafted by CWME places reconciliation in relation with 'repairing the broken relationships' and healing with 'health, balance, wholeness of life'.[20] The preparatory paper on reconciliation also affirms that:

> The very notion of reconciliation presupposes the experience of broken communion. This may be in the form of estrangement, separation, enmity, hatred, exclusion, fragmentation, distorted relationships. It usually also encompasses a certain degree of injustice, harm, and suffering. Reconciliation, in biblical as well as secular language, is understood as the effort towards and engagement for mending this broken and distorted relationship and building up community and relationships afresh.[21]

One could thus argue that the term 'reconciliation' refers to situations in which harm has been done by perpetrators to victims, whether individual or collective. There is a need for reconciliation as a result of a conflict. 'Healing' however refers to overcoming or coping with evil and suffering, whatever the cause is. In such a perspective, healing will be the more general term and

---

[18] 'The healing mission of the church', §§37 and 40.

[19] Christodoulos, Archbishop of Athens and of All Greece, '"Come Holy Spirit, Heal and Reconcile": Welcoming Address', in Matthey (ed), *Conference Report*, 144. A powerful and inspiring plenary address including such perspectives was presented in Athens by Papathanasiou, 'Reconciliation: The Major Conflict in Post-Modernity', 178-86.

[20] Commission document 'Called in Christ to be Reconciling and Healing Communities' (2001), in Matthey (ed), *Conference Report*, 13.

[21] 'Mission as Ministry of Reconciliation', §13.

reconciliation a specific case. The complexity of a *theological* reflection on the matter appears when considering with the Orthodox the understanding of sin as a break in relationships. If the break of relations between humans and God is considered the origin of all evil, death, and suffering in creation and the world, then reconciliation brought about by Christ is the overarching reality allowing for healing to take place.

Reconciliation

For Athens' reflection on missio ecclesiae, the shape of the meanings of healing and reconciliation was influenced by the 'ecumenical context', i.e., the former work done on these issues within WCC and in the overall ecumenical movement.

So the study on *reconciliation* was influenced by experiences in recent social and political processes, truth and reconciliation commissions. The particular challenge for CWME was to draw on work done earlier by WCC with human rights and justice/peace movements, so as to formulate the consequences for a contemporary missiology.

What were then the foci of Athens' approach to reconciliation in terms of *missio ecclesiae*?

> Mission as ministry of reconciliation involves the obligation to share the gospel of Jesus Christ in all its fullness, the good news of him who through his incarnation, death, and resurrection has once for all provided the basis for reconciliation with God, forgiveness of sins and new life in the power of the Holy Spirit. This ministry invites people to accept God's offer of reconciliation in Christ, and to become his disciples in the communion of his church. It promises the hope of fullness of life in God, both in this age and in God's future, eternal kingdom.
>
> The ministry of reconciliation also involves the work for reconciliation among persons and societies. In order to understand what this participation in God's mission of reconciliation may mean, we will focus upon the goals and processes of reconciliation and healing. This involves both some general thoughts and reflections upon the dynamics of how reconciliation and healing come about.[22]

It has been critically argued that Athens neglected the *vertical* aspects of reconciliation, at least in its work and deliberations on the church's participation in God's mission. This is to a certain degree correct, but should receive some qualification. The very titles of the Athens event and all preparatory texts refer to the vertical dimension as the ground and essence of Christian mission. Aware of that dimension, the CWME Commission decided to give to the conference a 'liturgical' shape, so that through worship, meditative Bible study (*Lectio Divina*), home group sharing, the reconciliatory initiative of God in Christ through the power of the Spirit could be experienced rather than explained or argued about. The emphasis on spirituality in the

---

[22] 'Mission as Ministry of Reconciliation', §§32 and 33.

programme resulted from the acknowledgment of the essential importance of the vertical dimension.

Critical reports on Athens mention, in particular, its relative neglect of evangelism understood as a specific ministry of *missio ecclesiae* in the vertical dimension.[23] They have a point. However, one must not pretend that evangelism was completely neglected at the conference. Important statements were issued and significant workshops offered on evangelism.[24] The sequence 'reconciliation – evangelism' is trying to make a point: when reflecting on mission as reconciliation, one cannot treat evangelism in the same way as with any other focus in witness. In the context of the thematic emphasis of Athens, evangelism only makes sense if flowing from a healing and reconciling community, as an outpouring of *experienced* restoration of dignity and *shared* forgiveness. The first and most important task is the building and multiplication of welcoming and inclusive communities. Only then can people really be invited to a local church where they can be offered a safe space. There must be such a community whose life and involvement creates a space into which to invite people who suffer, who doubt, who are exploited and victimised, or who live with unhealed memories. The mission strategy pursued for and in Athens sets the building and multiplication of healing and reconciling communities as a core condition for the possibility of an ecumenically responsible evangelism.[25] This priority is reflected in the subtitle of the conference and explains the particular emphasis of the whole process and the priority setting for the conference.

It remains true that CWME could have worked out in much more detail what evangelism then means. Aware of that need, CWME organised soon after Athens a major consultation dedicated to the subject in Bossey, Switzerland and created a specific working group of the Commission, the results of which strongly influenced the draft for a new WCC mission statement.[26]

---

[23] The CWME Commission received letters from Pentecostal participants and from some of its affiliated bodies asking for more intentional treatment of evangelism.

[24] 'Mission as Ministry of Reconciliation', §§20 and 21, and several workshops proposed during the conference. From those published in the conference report, one can refer to the workshop on 'New ways of being church' which opens a discussion on church-planting and new forms of evangelising churches (*Conference report*, 229). The one on mission-shaped church has a specific chapter on proclaiming the gospel (240). Another workshop provides principles for multicultural evangelism (276).

[25] The most careful drafting of the letter to Philemon shows how much Paul was aware of this issue. The credibility of his mission and of the gospel was at stake: either Onesimus would be received as a brother by Philemon and his church and so be able to experience the consequences of resurrection on people's and community's lives, or nothing had changed and Onesimus would have better kept his old pagan religious belief.

[26] See the report from the Bossey consultation in *IRM*, 96:382/383 (July/October 2007) (theme: Evangelism). The result of the study conducted by the evangelism working group of CWME: 'Evangelism: Witnessing to Our Hope in Christ', *IRM* 101:1 (April 2012), 79-104.

It is surely correct to affirm that the *horizontal* aspect of reconciliation received much attention both in the preparations as well as in the conference plenaries and workshops. Athens and CWME owe gratitude to Professor Robert J. Schreiter who was directly involved in the thematic preparations for the Conference since 2001. Much has been written on the particularities, conditions, and difficulties of reconciliation processes, so that there is no need to go into details. Some points deserve to be mentioned, because they have not received overall appreciation in the follow-up to the conference. Considering developments since 2005, I am not convinced that the particular perspectives of the reconciliation model of mission continue to be at the core of the debate in WCC.[27] There could be several reasons for this.

Reconciliation is one of the most difficult tasks. Even in the Bible, there are not many stories leading to full reconciliation. Most are open-ended, such as the famous Parable of the Prodigal Son. Whereas it is easy to speak of reconciliation in theology, in practice it seems almost out of reach – in the context of brutal exploitation, rape, and extreme suffering. In such settings, how can one imagine living together in the future with perpetrators and then act accordingly? A reconciliation process requires truth, memory, repentance, justice, forgiveness, and love, says one of the main preparatory documents for the conference.[28] Truth is almost impossible to establish, because of the contradictory versions of what happened, and it requires long conflicting debates to unveil the distortions of events, mostly by the oppressive powers, but at times also by victims. Healing of memories can take decades, and steps in mutual approaches between humans and societies can be jeopardised by relatively small incidents and provocations.

Repentance, forgiveness, and love are leading features of the Christian theological tradition. However, even the biblical narratives point to them almost as 'miracles', only possible following an initiative or direction by the Holy Spirit. Love in Pauline terminology is the only charism or gift of the Spirit that will have everlasting (eschatological) value, even over faith and hope, but its radicalism cannot easily be equated with good human behaviour or even the sacrifice of one's life (cf. 1 Cor. 13). The particularity of Jesus' use of the term is the widening of its scope to unbearable extremes: love your enemies. Here we point to a difficulty of the move from liberation to reconciliation as a paradigm for mission, a move welcomed by many while criticised by others.[29] In order to have a lasting and real reconciliation, what seemed needed is a militant attitude that safeguards the respect for the humanity of even the most violent – and least respectable – exploiter.

[27] It was not a major mission theme in Edinburgh 2010. Nor does it feature as a priority in the new draft for a WCC mission statement: 'Together toward Life: Mission and Evangelism in Changing Landscapes: Proposal for a new WCC Affirmation on Mission and Evangelism towards WCC's Tenth Assembly in Busan, Korea: Working Draft 11', *IRM* 101:1 (April 2012), 6-42.

[28] 'Mission as Ministry of Reconciliation', §38.

[29] Cf. Kinnamon, 'Report', 391-92.

Mission as reconciliation thus seems less 'militant' than mission as liberation, but this has been considered as a backward step in ecumenical missiology by quite a number of people. They have criticised CWME for being less engaged for justice now than in the past.[30] The study process and the conference surely didn't abandon the centrality of justice, but moved to problematise it by referring to different realms of justice that need different treatments by different actors. In his plenary address, Robert Schreiter carefully distinguishes between *punitive* justice, which is the task of the legally constituted state, *restorative* justice which requires symbolic and socially relevant gestures restoring the dignity of the victims, *distributive* justice and *structural* justice which imply necessary changes in the world of economics, trade laws, land rights and issues of power structures, both national and international.[31] It is a task often overseen by earlier missiologies to carefully distinguish between the specific mandate of churches and that of other actors, such as democratic states and their legal institutions.

Reconciliation efforts also point to the difficulty to draw an absolute line between victims and perpetrators. As happens in interpersonal conflicts, the same persons or groups can at certain times be victims and at other times perpetrators, and this even in a situation where there is a main line of injustice and exploitation. Athens reconnected somewhat with the point made in the early nineties by Raymond Fung who spoke of people as both 'sinners' and 'sinned against',[32] although that terminology was not used at the conference. Missiology that takes this kind of 'uncertainty' principles into consideration may have to distance itself from ideological and globalised visions of historical and political developments and thus appear less radical. In my view, this is, however, a necessary and healthy corrective to the temptation of 'dogmatically messianic' theologies.[33]

There is another point which distances a reconciliation approach from a dogmatically messianic one, and that is the need to reach authentic

[30] See Valdir Raul Steuernagel, 'Reflections on the Athens Conference', *IRM: Listeners' Reports*, 431-32; Namsoon Kang, 'Towards Healing and Reconciliation of "Regardless": Radicalizing Christian Mission for Today', *IRM: Listeners' Reports*, 373-86; Jesudas M. Athyal, 'Come Holy Spirit, Diagnose, Heal and Reconcile: Lingering Questions from Athens', *IRM* 94:375 (October 2005), 535-45, and Kinnamon, 'Report', 391-92.

[31] Robert J. Schreiter, 'Reconciliation as a New Paradigm of Mission', in Matthey (ed), *Conference Report*, 216-17. Many more writings of Schreiter could be referred to, of course. This was his much appreciated keynote address in the last thematic plenary.

[32] Raymond Fung, *Evangelistically Yours – Ecumenical Letters on Contemporary Evangelism* (Geneva: WCC Publications, 1992), 1-5. When he wrote those letters, Fung was Evangelism Secretary of WCC.

[33] By 'dogmatically messianic', I mean a position that affirms without any doubt a direct and immediate relation between the struggles of specific human groups, persons or churches and the advancement of God's kingdom. This has led in the past to crusades, inquisitions and other religiously motivated violence, as well as the dictatorial use of power.

compromises between opposed positions. No reconciliation process will succeed without some kind of search for an understanding of the past and the shape of a future organisation of society that seems at least partly acceptable to all conflicting parties.

A traditional ecumenical mission emphasis that is highlighted by the reconciliation model is 'story-telling', particularly developed in the past by the Urban Rural Mission (URM) networks.[34] A process towards the healing of memories cannot succeed unless victims – all those considering themselves victims – but also perpetrators, find a space where they can tell their story. Reconciliation and truth commissions provide such spaces, but one would consider this to be the task of each Christian church and community as well. Story-telling by one group only may not bear the whole truth, surely? But without the possibility of telling one's story to others who do listen and take it seriously, no solution to conflicts can be found. Mission as reconciliation is based on story-telling. In that sense, one of the best traditions of URM must be kept in future ecumenical missiology.

The link between Athens' work on the Holy Spirit and its reflection on reconciliation seems clear: The excessively difficult task of reconciliation requires persons with exceptional human qualities. Many of them can, however, stand through the difficulties and frustrations only as a result of empowerment by the Holy Spirit to whom they pray, 'Come, Holy Spirit, heal and reconcile'. Theologically speaking, there is no chance for reconciliation in the absence of God the Spirit, a spirit that is of course not limited to Christian or religious circles.

The particular difficulty for the church's involvement in reconciliation is to keep in balance God's priority for the victims – the 'preferential option for the poor' – with the need to follow the path of the Spirit who is a 'go-between',[35] wanting to repair broken parts, at vertical as well as horizontal levels. It also means for Christ's disciples to keep a balance between their faith in God's plan and their confidence in the human agency to contribute to that plan. Losing confidence in the human agency may prevent faithful discipleship in following Christ to the Cross. Over-confidence in one's capacity to do the right thing may lead to *hybris* before God and violence against those humans that do not think the same way. I am not sure that in past and present ecumenical missiology this delicate balance has always been sufficiently respected. In my view, it is an essential ingredient of a faithful contemporary *missio ecclesiae*.

---

[34] URM, a key actor in ecumenical missiology, had for decades a central co-ordinating office in CWME. Due to various developments which cannot be described here, the WCC office of URM has been discontinued. The international network however continues to inspire mission theory and practice. Several workshops were proposed in Athens by URM people, one of them particularly dedicated to story-telling: 'Building the Circle: Community Building Through a Culture of Story-Telling', in Matthey (ed), *Conference Report*, 241-42.

[35] 'Mission as Ministry of Reconciliation', §65, 83. Reference is made to the book of John V. Taylor, *The Go-Between God: The Holy Spirit and Christian Mission* (London: SCM Press, 1972).

Although clearly referred to in the papers, the *cosmic* or circular aspect of reconciliation, reaching to the creation, has not been featured sufficiently in Athens. Aware of the need to deepen the link between mission, spirituality, and creation, CWME has now given it a priority in the process leading to a new mission statement.[36]

Healing Ministry

A last but short word is needed on CWME's treatment of the healing ministry. The study on the healing ministry could build on work done by WCC since the two Tübingen consultations of 1964 and 1967, and the consecutive creation of the Christian Medical Commission. Without repeating what had been well formulated in a key WCC document on health and healing,[37] CWME intended to update the place and significance of a healing community for a contemporary reflection on mission. Several studies prepared Athens: one launched in 2000 involving dialogues with Pentecostals; insights resulting from the experience of the networks of people living with disabilities; and the huge involvement of WCC networks and churches in the HIV-AIDS Initiative in Africa. The conference insisted on the multi-dimensionality of evil, suffering, and healing, and emphasised also the personal, faith-related, even psychological, aspects of cure and healing, the importance of a theology of charisms, and pointed to the 'assets' which religious communities offer, both institutional and ideological, for health politics.[38]

The church's main contribution to humanity's longing for healing is the edification of communities which provide a home to those who suffer, who live with unanswered questions, who need a space to deal with their plight, who need empowering for accompanying sick family members, or who are marginalised in society due to their race, caste, gender, age, cultural or spiritual preferences. The shape and priorities of such communities would depend on the

[36] There was an important intervention in the plenary on reconciliation by Pepine Iosua, pastor, theologian and fisherman from Kiribati, Pacific, strongly advocating global commitment so as to enable the Pacific islands to survive: Iosua Pepine, 'Reconciliation – Rescuing Victims in their Home Islands', in Matthey (ed), *Conference Report*, 204-07. Creation did feature, but not sufficiently, in CWME conferences in the past, cf. Lukas Vischer (ed), *Witnessing in the Midst of a Suffering Creation* (Geneva: John Knox Center, 2007). However, since Athens, the Commission has given due attention to creation and the relation with spirituality, on the basis of the study by a specific working group of CWME who produced a substantial report, now published under the title 'God's Transforming Spirit: Reflections on Mission, Spirituality and Creation', *IRM* 101:1 (2012), 61-78.

[37] World Council of Churches, *Healing and Wholeness: The Churches' Role in Health. The report of a study by the Christian Medical Commission* (Geneva: WCC Publications, 1990).

[38] 'Athens argued explicitly in religious terms, looking particularly at the meaning of faith, the gifts of the Spirit, the sacraments and pastoral care for the individual.' Dieter Becker, 'Listener's Report', *IRM: Listeners' Reports*, 362.

socio-cultural context and the existence or non-existence of sufficiently affordable medical and other care services.[39] As a conference, Athens tried to become something of a healing community itself, by offering healing worship services, home groups, pastoral accompaniment,[40] workshops for debates, time for personal encounters, all within a liturgical flow of the days and the week. In that sense, the conference intended to let the participants experience something that could be repeated locally in their own church, monastery or secular community. The ideal of CWME was to match what the documents on reconciliation and healing affirm on the need for healing communities, with at least part of the experience made during the conference.

Mission and Unity

How far that became a reality for each participant cannot be answered globally. Although many reactions to the conference experience were positive, the very fact that we could not organise large encounters with the local Orthodox church – and that we were severely attacked by conservative Orthodox demonstrations outside the gate of the resort where the conference took place – showed how far Christian churches are themselves from a healing of memories. To emphasise reconciliation and healing as a priority for Christian mission highlights the divisions between denominations as a main obstacle to the credibility of the gospel. Several participants who did experience real community with other Christians felt deeply frustrated by the impossibility of sharing the Eucharist.[41] So although Athens was a success as a kind of reconciliation event in terms of common planning, organisation and meeting between representatives from WCC-related churches and the wider oikoumene, it was only one small step on the decades-long process of the healing of memories and reconciliation between divided Christian churches.

For the future agenda of mission, reconciliation and healing must keep their priority place, but this makes sense only if those involved in such mission do all that is in their power to struggle for the necessary reconciliation processes *within* the Christian family itself.[42] Indeed, if Christian churches are unable to make significant steps to heal their own divisions, what hope, what message,

---

[39] Theoretical summaries and practical case-studies have been published as a follow-up to Athens: World Council of Churches and DIFAEM, *Witnessing to Christ Today: Promoting Health and Wholeness for All*. (Tübingen: DIFAEM, 2010). A contribution towards the Christian healing ministry compiled by a study group on mission and healing from the World Council of Churches (WCC), Geneva, Switzerland, and the German Institute for Medical Mission (DIFAEM), Tübingen, Germany.

[40] A special multicultural pastoral counselling group had been constituted, offering – for the first time in such a worldwide mission conference of WCC – the possibility for personal pastoral counselling at given times in safe spaces. A booklet emphasising the importance of pastoral counselling was prepared and distributed to all participants. It is included in the CD ROM added to the conference report.

[41] Melanchthon, 'What does a Reconciled Community Look Like?', 403-04.

[42] Becker, 'Listener's Report', 363-64.

what credibility do they have for and in the world? The mission agenda is intimately connected with the unity agenda. As the latest conference in the line starting with Edinburgh 1910, Athens once more witnessed to that essential link.[43]

Come, Holy Spirit, heal and reconcile … your churches.

[43] And as seems clear from reconciliation processes requiring structural changes in society, unity between Christians cannot be restricted to some kind of 'spiritual' unity. There is no reconciliation without changes in behaviour, theology, community forms and church orders or structures.

Health and Healing: The Maasai Prophet Isaia Orishi Ole Ndokote and his Evangelistic Mission in Kenya and Tanzania

Christel Kiel

Introduction

When my husband and I were working in Tanzania as UEM missionaries in the North Eastern Diocese of the Evangelical Lutheran Church in Tanzania from 1986-1992, we got to know the evangelist and freelance prophet Isaia Ole Ndokote. He went with us and our fellow Tanzanian pastors on several evangelistic tours and slept in our houses. In reverse we, the white missionaries, visited him several times in Olasiti, his village in Kenya.

His personality seems to be most unusual, at least for Europeans. In his call to conversion, Isaia uses till today an evangelistic method following Maasai tradition and customs, which is highly successful among an ethnic group which withstood social change and the conversion to the Christian religion till the end of the last century. Part of his success was the combination of the call to conversion with an extensive healing and pastoral mission among a people facing the threat of extinction due to the progress of the modern global society. I want to structure my paper along the following five aspects: ethnic background and biography of Isaia, his evangelistic method, his theology, his success, and an evaluation.

The Ethnic Background and Biography of Isaia[1]

Isaia was born as Leiraroi[2] Ole Molonkó around 1940 in Kenya. He belongs to the so-called Plain Nilotes, a group of semi-pastoralists who live both in Kenya

Originally published in Claudia Währisch-Oblau and Fidon Mwombeki (eds), *Mission Continues Global Impulses for the 21st Century,* Regnum Edinburgh Centenary Series 4 (Oxford: Regnum Books, 2010), 211-21.

[1] Until now only two books exist referring to Isaia Ole Ndokote: The dissertations of C. Kiel, *Christians in Maasailand* (Makumira: Makumira Publication Nine, 1997), 260-72; M. Fischer, *Maasai gestalten Christsein* (Erlangen: Erlanger Verlag für Mission und Ökumene, 2001), 302-64.

and Tanzania. They number around a million people all speaking the 'Maa' language. For reasons hitherto unknown, the Maasai have a monotheistic religion. They pray to Enkai and are led in spiritual matters by the so-called IlOibonok, who are found in family clans of prophets and lawyers. On some rare occasions, these clans are controlled and eventually contradicted by single charismatic prophets who are sent and driven by the Spirit of Enkai in times of special need.[3] According to Isaia's own preaching, his grandfather on his mother's side, Ndokote, belonged to an ancient charismatic group, the so-called 'binders': therefore, he calls himself Ole Ndokote. His grandfather could do all kinds of miracles: people stumbled over their own feet, stolen meat got stuck to the mouth of the thief, threatening lions became motionless as if they were frozen, etc.[4] Isaia's charismatic gifts seem to be rooted in the genes and tradition of his family.

When he still was a young elder, the spirit of Enkai called Leiraroi in 1968 into the service of his people. Every time he heard Enkai's loud voice, his ear was extended towards her/him or vice versa: God reached down and extended Isaia's ear. Isaia let his hair grow, wore a black cloth, prayed and offered sacrifices to Enkai.[5] The main scope of his service was to make peace among the rival Maa-speaking groups of the Purko, Loita, Kekonyokie, Kisongo, Parakuyu, Arusha, etc. He soon got the byname 'Orishi' ('mediator', 'peacemaker').[6] He met heavy opposition among the elders of his neighbourhood. They pointed to the fact that Leiraroi was young and not rich. How then could he be called by Enkai, whose blessing was evident if a person owned large numbers of cattle? The young man reacted to the elders' doubts by charging fees in the form of goats and cattle for his counselling sessions. He married two more wives as soon as his herd had been enlarged. Because his prophecies came true most of the time, he had many clients. Since 1973 the government of Kenya has acknowledged his efforts and called him to peace missions as soon as minor or major troubles broke out among the Maasai.[7]

Orishi first opposed Christianity, but when in 1979 the Christian elders of his community prayed for him intensely, he had a vision of Christ himself standing under a rainbow. Christ told him to call his people into the church and to Christian baptism.[8] Orishi left the traditional practice of sheep and cattle offerings behind, no longer took money for his service, shaved off his hair and

---

[2] Personal communication, received during one of our visits to his Kenyan homestead.

[3] For further information about the Maasai, refer to T. Ole Saitoti and C. Beckwith, *Maasai* (New York: Harry N. Abram, 1980). T. Ole Saitoti is a Maasai himself.

[4] Personal communication received during Isaia's visit to the Theological College and Bible School at Mwika-Moshi in 1997.

[5] Fischer, *Maasai gestalten Christsein*, 307ff. The article 'en' points to female entities or to beings larger than human understanding: 'enkop' means 'earth', 'EnKukuu' means 'a monster lurking in the bush', and 'EnKai' refers to 'Goddess', or 'God'.

[6] According to my understanding, differing from M. Fischer, Isaia said the name was given him by the Kenyan Government in acknowledgement of his peace-making work.

[7] Fisher, *Maasai gestalten Christsein*, 348ff.

[8] Fisher, *Maasai gestalten Christsein*, 320ff.

for six months he became a catechumen in the Bible School of the African Inland Church (A.I.C) in Siyapei, Kenya. Because of his extraordinary memory as a member of an oral culture, he memorised large parts of the New Testament and can tell even the book, chapter, and verse of his quotations during his sermons. The church elders of the A.I.C. were sceptical because he continued to refer to his visions and was not willing to separate from his three legal wives. They delayed his baptism. In his vision, Christ had ordered him to become baptised. So in 1980, Orishi turned to a Baptist Church,[9] got baptised and immediately returned to his home church, the A.I.C. He chose the name of the prophet to the nations, Isaia, as his baptismal name because he was convinced that his message was important not only for the Maasai but for all the nations.[10] Unfortunately, Isaia and his fellow evangelists are not fluent in Swahili or English. They speak the Maa language only. Therefore, until now their service has been restricted to the Maa-speaking communities. Isaia explained in 1996, that from the time of his baptism onwards, the voice of Enkai no longer made itself audible by extending his ear as before but that the Holy Spirit told his heart what Isaia needed to know.

At the beginning of 1988, Isaia was evangelizing in the Arusha region with the full support of the Arusha Diocese. We were able to meet with him and with his team and plan an evangelistic journey together with all of them a month later. Several journeys followed. Our missionary colleague in South Tanzania, Rev. Muck, invited Isaia and his team, too. In 1995, when we came back to Tanzania from a three years' home leave in Germany, it was a common practice among all the Maasai missionaries to go with Isaia on evangelistic excursions. Meanwhile, in an official ceremony in December 1993, the Arusha Diocese had made him its special Maasai evangelist.[11] Until today he is evangelizing among the Maa-speaking tribes in Tanzania with great success.

Isaia's Evangelistic Methods

The Team

No Maasai elder of any important social status goes around alone. He is always in the company of some of his friends and age-group mates. During the first years of his evangelisation Isaia's uncle Noah Kandonyo went with him because he had played an important part during Isaia's conversion to Christianity. From 1989 onwards, Noah stayed at home because the extensive travelling put too much stress on the elderly man. Isaia travelled together with his age-group mate Yoshua and his nephew Isaka. Both of them are living in Isaia's home area, in Olasiti, Kenya. Yoshua is a singer, and Isaka leads the

9 Fisher, *Maasai gestalten Christsein*, 341.
10 Personal communication, received in Lushoto, March 1988.
11 Fisher, *Maasai gestalten Christsein*, 343.

prayers.[12] Isaia does the preaching which can go on for more than an hour, depending on the listeners' willingness to agree with Isaia's message. His preaching is never boring since it is interspersed with songs and sketches by the three men. People from the audience are called upon to read from the New Testament, and there is much laughing in between, standing up and sitting down. A listener never knows what will come next. Isaia leaves the organisation of the meetings and the administration of the sacraments to the accompanying pastors.

His Message[13]

Isaia's evangelistic message can easily be summarised:

> Listen regularly to the word of God in the Old and New Testaments – or learn to read it yourselves! Repent and leave your old sins behind so that you will become joyous children of Enkai.
>
> By baptism turn to Jesus Christ, the Child of Enkai = Enkerai Enkai! He will help you to adapt to the new and difficult present times.
>
> Try to till part of the land and send your children to school.

Isaia himself is a good example of his message: he and his team wear European clothes during their evangelistic journeys. By their dress, they signalise two important things: 1) A change is necessary! 2) We are of equal rank to the European missionaries. Our message is by no means less important. Isaia sent his children to school. He has a large field of maize near his home.

The Peace-Maker

From 1993 onwards Isaia put an additional element into the liturgy of his evangelistic preaching:[14] a ritual to reconcile the often bitter feuds between parents and children, elders and their wives, between the several wives of a polygamous household and between rival families and sub-groups of the Maa communities. The public feuds are mostly centred on water and herding grounds for cattle or cattle-thieving. In order to initiate the peace process, Isaia used symbolic actions. He, Yoshua and Isaka called the congregation to stand in a large circle. Then the three of them placed adversaries together, asked them to join hands as soon as they were ready for reconciliation, talked to them and prayed with them individually, giving them God's blessing. After the peace-making sinners and the sick were called into the circle to pray. Then

---

[12] Fisher, *Maasai gestalten Christsein*, 336ff.

[13] Kiel, *Christians in Maasailand*, 261ff.

[14] Fisher, *Maasai gestalten Christsein*, 358ff, following a description of services held in August and September 1997 in the North Eastern and Northern Lutheran Dioceses of Tanzania. Rev. M. Geißner's an e-mail (Jan. 2009) confirms that Isaia continues this peace-making ritual until today.

Isaia drew a large cross in the soil in the middle of the meeting ground. Four accompanying pastors were called to the four ends of this cross. Isaia remained standing in the middle of this cross. The African and white pastors had to say different prayers in their mother tongues: one prayed for the faith and the conversion of the congregation which was a mixture of baptised and non-baptised people, Maasai and Bantu, another at the other end of the cross asked God for peace and reconciliation, a third prayed for the healing of the sick, the fourth for sufficient food for the people. A combined meal of an animal which had been slaughtered ended the gathering. Isaia met with bitter opposition to this last action, the killing and eating an animal according to the Maasai tradition as soon as enemies had been reconciled. The A.I.C excluded him from his work as a church elder, and a Maasai student in 1994 wrote his certificate thesis at the theological college in Makumira attacking Isaia for not having clearly abandoned heathen customs.[15] This ritual, according to him, was too close to the ritual of Holy Communion.

Charismatic Gifts

Rarely mentioned by Isaia himself but clearly recognizable for everyone meeting him are Isaia's charismatic gifts. By the power of the Spirit of Enkai, he can foretell incidents in the near future and divine events in the past history of his clients, and he has the gift of healing. Telepathy is so much part of his inner conviction that he seems to take it for granted in everybody else, too. All these are gifts the Maasai expect in a man or woman who claims to be a person sent by the Deity. For 40 years now, Isaia has proven that he is driven by the Holy Spirit. His fame among the Maa-speaking ethnic groups is enormous. At the beginning of the 1990s we experienced how he was respected as a spiritual authority not only by ordinary people, men, and women, but by the highest IlOibonok, too, the official Maa spiritual leaders. What astonishes us more and more today, as retired pastors ourselves, is the health and vigour with which Isaia continues to live his mission among his people. As soon as he is travelling he has almost no time to himself. As early as seven o'clock clients want to have private counselling with him. The extensive preaching and rites of reconciliation follow. In the afternoon, eventually, follow the transfer to another locality or visits in a nearby village. After that, extensive evening prayers are followed by private counselling till midnight. Even twenty years ago it was my duty to see to it that Isaia got enough food and sleep. Till today, his capacity for self-regeneration seems to be unlimited.

Although Isaia has the gift of healing, he mostly leaves this service to his team worker Isaka. Isaia's peace mission has taken priority in his preaching.

[15] J. Mameo Ole Paulo, 'Historia Fupi ya Isaya Ole Ndokoti na Mchango wake katika Kanisa la Kiinjili la Kilutheri Tanzania Diosisi Mkoani Arusha' [A Short History of Isaya Ole Ndokoti and his Contribution to the Arusha Diosis of The Evangelical Lutheran Church in Tanzania] (KKKT, unpublished, 1994).

The reason for this slowly upcoming development is Isaia's theology. This brings us to our next point.

Isaia's Theology

It has been mentioned already that Isaia's theology sometimes caused nervousness, animosity and even open contradiction. The cause of this trouble is Isaia's conviction that the God who called him into his service and talked to him since 1968 in auditions and visions by his Spirit is also the father of Jesus Christ. Generally speaking, this conviction is shared by all Maasai theologians. The complete Bible, released in Namanga in 1992, calls God Enkai from the first to the last page. Nevertheless, traditional missionary theology is highly sceptical of charismatic gifts, especially auditions and visions. People who claim to be inspired by the Spirit can easily be charlatans, deceiving the faithful. These doubts can be found in the Bible already. But where is the radical conversion to be seen in Isaia's life? Too numerous are the continuing elements like polygamy – an unsolved problem in most of the African churches – his talk of angels and visions and, since the nineties, the slaughter of animals after the peace sessions. The general problem underlying these doubts is the problem of continuity and discontinuity between non-Christian and Christian religion and the relationship between ethnic tradition and the Christian faith in its traditional western habit.

When Isaia himself explains this problem, he is absolutely sure that the God who called him in 1968 is the one who revealed the existence of Jesus Christ to him 11 years later. The same God who first spoke to him in auditions is now putting the truth into his heart by his Holy Spirit, and told him to turn to the churches for further instruction and for baptism. Through incessant prayer and his ongoing visions, the Risen Christ is so real and luminous for him that it is radiating from Isaia's person in constant waves of warmth and laughter and convincing people by the force of Isaia´s personality. Jesus Christ by his life, death and resurrection is the one who removes all the sin and difficulties which stand between Enkai and his people. He is the potent mediator between the Maasai and their present difficulties of adaptation and he alone is able to open up the future for the Maasai. Isaia's theology is fundamentally Christ-centred. The healing of ailments in individual persons and their health are of minor importance compared with the all-embracing message of adaptation to the future. Enkai wants her people to live, not to die. As during the times of the life of God's child, Jesus Christ, healing and personal health are accompanying signs, not the target of Isaia's ministry.

The common meal of a freshly slaughtered animal belongs to the Maasai peace-making tradition. The closeness and eventual rivalry of this 'eating peace' with the sacrament of Holy Communion cannot be felt by Isaia who has no feeling for the exclusivity of the Protestant Lutheran understanding of sacraments. He insisted on his baptism because Christ had ordered him to become baptised. He participates in Holy Communion when it is distributed by the pastors who are present during his evangelisations – but his inspiration, his vitality, his aura of spiritual strength and joy in the presence of God depend on his intense and incessant prayer life.

Like the Old Testament prophets and Jesus Christ, Isaia's clearly stated conviction is that sin stands between God and his blessings for the Maasai. Sin holds up the rain. Without rain there is no grass for the cattle, without grass there is no milk, without milk there is no health among the Maasai. His understanding of health is a holistic one, therefore, from the beginning his preaching admonished his listeners to separate from their sins and make a renewed connection with God.[16] His preaching about sin has nothing to do with scrupulous self-destruction. It is a kind of laughing conviction: 'this burden is unnecessary in your life'. Using his prophetic insight during individual counselling he is ready to put his finger on the dark areas which separate his clients from God. During the peace sessions after his preaching he shows them the way to repent and begin a new life.

Sometimes during his sermons he may mention Satan and his dark powers. During our travelling with him and his team we ourselves experienced the forces which were interested in keeping Isaia away from the people he came to help. Totally unruffled by extreme thunderstorms, broken-down cars, glaring Loibons and similar nuisances he sat and prayed and the difficulties got solved somehow. Even if he had to lie down hungry on the floor of a cold church he remained at peace. Dark forces exist but, unlike in other revivalist theologies, they are no match for Isaia's omnipotent triune God.

His Success

Isaia's team and his charismatic gifts combined with natural eloquence, following traditional Maasai lines, are one side of his great success. The other side is his never-tiring readiness to serve God and the Maasai people under the shelter of God's blessing.

Let me clarify what I mean by the example of one of the most difficult and least successful parts of Isaia's work – his mission to his fellow prophets, the IlOibonok. In their area behind the Usambara Mountains our work stagnated. 70 women together with their children attended our services but men were more than rare. Under these circumstances, evangelisation by Isaia and his team was extremely necessary. But at the end of 1988 the village of the leading area Loibon Kopera, was not accessible by car although his young men tried hard to open up a path with their bush knives. Isaia stepped out of our car and told the youngsters: 'You see we cannot come to you. You must come to us. Tell your father that I expect him and all the members of your family tomorrow morning at eleven here at the roadside'. The following morning my husband and I did not believe that any man would be there. The Usambaras were too far from

[16] One outward sign of this conviction was his insisting on the stripping off of all weapons before unbaptised men entered any church. The baptised knew this custom anyway.

Kenya. How could a completely foreign prophet order a leading Loibon and his entourage to meet him at the roadside! When our Land Rover came to a halt the usual number of women was sitting under the trees of the meeting point – together with forty men! We couldn't believe our eyes. Two years later the leading Loibon Kopera was baptised. Six years later, half of the men in his large family were Christians. The other half had decided to remain members of the traditional religion and had lost a large part of their cattle in a money-making deal with a charlatan.[17] From the length of time between Isaia's evangelisation and the final conversion of half the family to Christianity, one can guess at the resistance of the IlOibonok towards the Christian religion.

Less successful was the mission to the Head Loibon, Loibon Kitok, of all the Parakuyu, Mtare OleMoreto, near Morogoro in 1992.[18] We arrived in the afternoon together with Isaia, Isaka and Yoshua in the Loibon's large village, which to our surprise included a huge school. The Loibon's brother Paulo, a younger son of the former Head Loibon Moreto, had been sent to school, was converted to Christianity and previously had been killed on a peace mission in 1991, when he was trying to pacify a feud between the quarrelling groups of agriculturists and cattle herders of the region.[19] When we arrived, Mtare was in a counselling session from which he returned inebriated. Isaia did not talk to him until the next morning when Mtare was sober. The aging Loibon was obviously a sick person. The alcohol, used as a starter for prophesying by lesser charismatic persons than Isaia, had done its work and made the Loibon half blind. Isaia, in his public preaching, fervently called for repentance and a change of lifestyle. Mtare humbly knelt before Isaia when he called for the prayer with the sick. The Head Loibon died, not baptised, two years later.

The IlOibonok feel responsible for their people, their well-being and their tradition. Therefore, they may build schools on their compounds. They tolerate Christian wives and children in their villages, but they keep themselves and the sons, who might become their successors, away from Christianity. Isaia, on the other hand, feels responsible for his people, too. He is deeply convinced that the old ways of life will not help his people anymore and that salvation lies in conversion to Jesus Christ. He is well aware of the great influence the Loibon have on the Maasai and how they hinder the progress of Christianity because they stick to the continuation of Maasai tradition. He does not give up his evangelistic efforts among his fellow prophets. He is well received in their villages and with astonishing humility attentively listened to, but they seldom follow his call to be baptised.

In summarizing it can be said that the enormous success of Isaia's evangelistic input is lessened by the restraint of the group he originally and foremost felt called to evangelise – the Loibon.

---

[17] Interview with Mattaio Ole Kairanga, Dec. 1995.

[18] 17-18 February 1992, described in C. Kiel, *Maasai Diviners and Christianity* (Köln: Köppe Verlag, 2015).

[19] His son Yacobo Paulo Ole Moreto is the present Bishop of Morogoro Diocese.

Evaluation

The Bible has a holistic concept concerning health and healing: When a person is in harmony with God's creation, with the creator and with him/herself as well as with his or her neighbour, then *shalom* reigns, the heavenly peace which in its realm harbours health and the healing of illness and sins. Fortunately, the indigenous Maasai religion has the same all-embracing worldview. So Isaia, when his visions demanded the incorporation of the idea of the 'Enkerai Enkai', the Child of God, expanded his concept of God, but his worldview remained the same. He had already originally been the peace-maker, Orishi. Through his conversion, he got a holy book and a mighty helper, the power of the risen Jesus Christ, to fulfil his mission. He could become a Christian and fulfil his mission more effectively than before.

Isaia did not lose his identity and, therefore, he has remained credible and convincing to his non-Christian fellow Maasai. Moreover, he became a largely encouraging model of hope for his contemporaries. All of them are aware that change has to come in a changing world. But nobody knew how to put this change into practice. Isaia, by his own convincing personality, has shown them that you can change and through this change still remain economically successful. You can become a Christian and yet remain faithful to the Maasai tradition. You can send your children, even the girls, to school without uprooting your Maasai identity. This man did not preach by mere words, as many missionaries did, he preached with his whole vibrant personality. That this man was highly gifted with charismatic power helped to underline his convincing sermons and peace missions but is not the most essential aspect. What is essential is that by his personal example and by the symbolic actions during his peace missions he brought his audience back into the harmony with Enkai, with their neighbours and with themselves. His peace rituals enable them to make a new start in life which gives them new faith and new hope and yet does not uproot them but empowers them to evaluate their previous life and to make the decisions which are necessary in order to adjust to the challenge of the present time. During this general re-setting of life, many a physical healing process among parents, children, and their neighbours is started and gives courage and energy to make the steps necessary for further adjustments.

Response by Ferdinand Anno

Contextual theology and ministry mean many things. Within the rubrics of both academic and pastoral theology, the phraseology becomes even more interesting. Even the seminaries' / divinity schools' curricula are a little convulsed on the different schools of understanding of contextualisation in relation to the old business of doing theology. Contemporary missiology, however, prompts us into examining the contextuality of faith expressions (from doing theology to doing mission) through the prism of mission work, outside of the ivory towers of academic theology. This paper issues a call to understanding missiology and mission work, literally from the wilderness, in the life and work of a Maasai tribal leader-turned evangelist.

Kiel tried to sum up the message of Isaia as that of calling people to turn toward the good life, to till the land and send children to school, to become joyous children of *Enkai,* who helps believers to adapt to new and difficult times. She also highlighted the peace-making and healing aspects of the Masaai evangelist emphasizing these as central to Isaia's work of evangelisation.

Calling and moving people toward the good life, following the path marked by the ancestors, is truly an amazing feat in missions and/or missionary work. Traditional mission work normally required following the 'different path', necessitating a radical cultural break that, at most times, resulted in the cultural and spiritual colonisation of peoples and communities. The good life according to Isaia, and as presented in the paper, has more to do with the embracing of a culture of peace than the value systems, images, symbols, and rituals of Western culture. Even the case of Isaia's wearing European clothing, as suggested by Kiel, was the evangelist's way of elevating native mission personnel to positions of respectability.

Also, markedly important in the work of Isaia, was his way of demonstrating that peace-making is realizable within indigenous, social, political and cultural processes. The employment of indigenous rites of mediation / peace-making and healing is an innovation that stresses the importance and efficacy of the indigene. More importantly, it also serves to affirm and celebrate in practical ways, the catholicity of the *imago Dei.* Moreover, the paper described the peace-making ritual devised by Isaia as illustrative, in a very concrete way, of how 'laws' are being 'fulfilled', in the tradition of Jesus who affirmed and innovated from tradition to reveal the new in old forms, as well as the old in new forms. The issue of continuity and discontinuity (between non-Christian and Christian religion), an age-old theme in missions that was also partly raised in the paper, should be understood paradoxically within this Christo-praxis of traditioning.

Historically, Protestant missionary enterprise was conversionist, colonial and negative of non-Western culture. It had been more of a Westernisation process that only aggravated the cracks in civilisational faultiness. Kiel correctly addressed Isaia as a prophet since prophecy is basically an exercise in indigeneity. This is one aspect of prophecy that has been neglected in colonial interpretations of biblical religious 'offices'. The fact of the matter is that the prophet-missionary calls people to remember the desert, the covenant – which is the very 'textual' foundation of the Judeo-Christian ways of *shalom / salaam.* The prophet also brings healing to peoples and communities through efficacious ritualisations in and through the ritual-culture that evolved out of narratives of redemption in the desert. That, at the least, is biblical. In the faith tradition of Christianity, the contemporary included, prophecy is about being spatially rooted and radically immersed in societal conditions, whence prophecy, in the full sense, is also about indigeneity, about touching the ground and taking root.

The Edinburgh World Missionary Conference of 1910 was an event populated by perspectives that were yet to fully appreciate indigenizing methods in doing missions and the theology of mission. What Kiel achieved in this short essay is a re-surfacing of one of those methodologies in mission that should serve as a corrective to our hitherto colonial-neocolonial paradigms.

Power Encounters: Evangelisation and Local Religious Spirits in Latin America

Raimundo C. Barreto, Jr.

> And I saw Salvador: Salvador da Bahia de Todos os Santos, the 'black Rome', with three hundred and sixty-five churches, which stand out against the line of hills or nestle along the bay, churches where the gods of the African pantheon are honored.[1]

I grew up in Salvador, Bahia, one of the most religiously effervescent cities of Brazil. One can sense the African influence everywhere one looks at in Salvador. Most Brazilians identify themselves as Roman Catholic, and that by no means mean a uniform religious confession. Catholicism takes traditionalist, charismatic, popular, and liberationist forms in Brazil. In Salvador, popular Catholicism also means black Catholicism. Every week, the Igreja Nossa Senhora do Rosário dos Pretos, an eighteenth-century Catholic church in the heart of the city, draws crowds of natives and tourists to an 'inculturated mass',[2] which combines elements of Afro-Brazilian traditional religions and popular Catholicism. *Candomble*,[3] an Afro-Brazilian religion based on the

---

This is an extended and revised version of the chapter originally published in Atola Longkumer, Jorgen Skov Sorenson, and Michael Biehl (eds), *Mission and Power: History, Relevance and Perils*, Regnum Edinburgh Centenary Series 33 (Oxford: Regnum Books, 2017), 159-176.

[1] Umberto Eco, *Foucault's Pendulum* (Orlando, FL: Harvest Book, 1988), 169.
[2] For more on inculturated Catholic mass, see John Burdick's study of the field of popular Christianity in Rio de Janeiro, chapter two in John Burdick, *Blessed Anastacia: Women, Race, and Popular Christianity in Brazil* (New York: Routledge, 1998), 51ff. As for the black devotion to Our Lady of the Rosary in Brazil, see Elizabeth W. Kiddy, *Blacks of the Rosary: Memory and History in Minas Gerais, Brazil* (University Park, PA: Pennsylvania University Press, 2005) and Carlos Ott, 'A Irmandade de Nossa Senhora do Rosario dos Pretos do Pelourinho', *Afro-Ásia* 6/7(1968), 83-90.
[3] Candomble is 'essentially a religion which teaches people a way to live in harmony with the energies of nature, which are manifested in the *Orixás*, the spirit emanations of the supreme divinity'. It emerged as 'a religion of slaves and freed slaves', which created 'an Afro-Brazilian synthesis of the African religious heritage brought by the slaves to Brazil'. For more on this topic, see Raimundo C. Barreto, Jr. & Devaka Premawardhana, 'Protestantism and Candomblé in Bahia: From Intolerance to Dialogue (and Beyond)', in Arvind Sharma (ed), *The World's Religions after September 11* (Westport, Conn: Praeger, 2009), vol. 3, 139, 141.

worship of the Orishas, was formed in Salvador, in 1830, and remains strongly active in the city today. *Umbanda,*[4] Spiritism,[5] and different sorts of Protestantism, particularly Pentecostalism, are also important players in this religious mosaic. Each of these Brazilian religions and spiritualities can only be fully understood when considered in relationship with each other in this vast pluralistic context.

Such a lively spirituality was part of my spiritual formation growing up in Salvador da Bahia. At a very young age, I learned about spirit possession as something that was just another part of day-to-day life. However, in the context of an Evangelical Christian church, I was taught to perceive that phenomenon as being associated with demonic activities. Such association of the Afro-Brazilian and African religions with evil spirits is not mere coincidence. Instead, it is an outcome of a Eurocentric worldview that can be traced back to the first encounters between modern European missionaries and African religions. According to John Mbiti, European missionaries, both Catholics and Protestants, understood their mission in Africa in terms of bringing God to a dark continent, which did not have a religion.[6]

> Part of the problem on their part was pure arrogance, racial prejudice, insufficient knowledge, misunderstanding and a narrow concept of anthropology and unwillingness to be challenged and enriched by other peoples and cultures.[7]

In Latin America, the prevailing attitude among Catholic and Protestant missionaries towards indigenous and Africa-derived religions was not different. The formation of Christianity in that region took place in the context of a violent conquest, which brought together military power and cultural/religious

---

[4] Umbanda is 'a deliberate synthesis of various aspects of traditional Brazilian religious beliefs and practices'. It is considered a Brazilian religion *par excellence* because it integrates elements of all traditions that make up Brazilian culture. Many *umbandistas* identify themselves also as Catholics. Whereas Umbanda has sometimes been identified with whitening initiatives in Brazil, others have noticed, instead, its important role in spreading the cultural values of the lower classes and minority ethnic groups to mainstream life in Brazilian society. See Harmon A. Johnson, 'Umbanda: A Modern Brazilian Religion', in David J. Hesselgrave (ed), *Dynamic Religious Movements: Case Studies of Rapidly Growing Religious Movements Around the World* (Grand Rapids: Baker, 1978), 250.

[5] The Spiritism of Allan Kardec, or Kardecism, was imported from France to Brazil in the mid-nineteenth century. Mixing philosophy, science, and religion, and emphasizing the immortality of the soul and communication with spirits, it attracted primarily the white Brazilian bourgeoisie. Over the years it has incorporated elements from other Brazilian religions, in particular from Catholicism. See, Tina Gundrun Jensen, 'Discourses on Afro-Brazilian Religions: From De-Africanization to Re-Africanization', in Christian Smith and Joshua Prokopy (eds), *Latin American Religion in Motion* (New York: Routledge, 1999), 277-78.

[6] John Mbiti, 'Challenges Facing Religious Education and Research in Africa: The Case of Dialogue Between Christianity and African Religion', *Religion and Theology* 3/2 (1996), 171.

[7] Mbiti, 'Challenges Facing Religious Education', 171.

domination. As Justo Gonzalez has rightly stated, 'God's work was done with the sword as well as with the cross'.[8]

Whereas a dominant Christianity willingly advanced the colonial project, Gonzalez identifies some 'voices of compassion' among the European missionaries,[9] highlighting that not all Christians were guided by greed in the evangelisation of Latin America. Those voices, however, did not oppose colonisation as such. Instead, they stood in solidarity with the indigenous people opposing cruelty and advocating for a more peaceful or 'evangelical conquest'.[10]

This chapter considers the power relations involved in the intercultural encounter that informs both Christian evangelisation and the relationship between Christianity and local spirits in Latin America. Although I address the systemic and enduring nature of the oppression perpetrated by colonial powers, I do not portray indigenous peoples and enslaved Africans simply as victims of violence and abuse. On the contrary, I pay serious attention to the agency of Afro-Latino/as and Amerindians.

Furthermore, I do not see Latin America as encompassing a cultural unity. There are multiple cultures in the region, and such cultural diversity must not be overlooked. The only kind of unity I assume when referring to Latin America is the shared history that began with the violent experience of conquest and colonisation and impacted in different ways all peoples who have ever since lived in the region. I use the plural 'Latin American Christianities'[11] to refer to the plurality of Christian expressions that emanate from varied encounters between Latin American cultures and the Gospel. In contrast with dominant missionary-oriented narratives, my approach in this chapter pays greater attention to indigenous interpretations of the Christian faith in the region. As a consequence of that choice to name the different Christian faces in Latin America, I use the term colonial Christianity to refer to the religion originally brought to the region by the colonial empires and later by Protestant missionaries, in contrast with the indigenous recreations that are the focus of this essay. Colonial Christianity was the first kind of Christianity the indigenous peoples of Latin America ever met. As an essential element of the colonial matrix of power, colonial Christianity did not disappear with the demise of the Iberian empires. It has taken new forms in the era of neo-colonialism and continue to exist. Nevertheless, as I will show below, indigenous peoples and Afro-descendants began to embrace the Christian faith

---

[8] Justo L. González & Ondina E. González. *Christianity in Latin America: A History* (New York: Cambridge University Press, 2008), 23.

[9] Justo Gonzalez, 'Voices of Compassion Yesterday and Today', in Guillermo Cook (ed), *New Face of the Church in Latin America* (Maryknoll, NY: Orbis, 1994), 3-12.

[10] Gonzalez, 'Voices of Compassion', 8.

[11] As I stated above, I use the plural 'Christianities' simply to highlight the diversity of Christian expressions in the region. But this is not a dogmatic choice. In different parts of this this chapter, I will also refer to Latin American Christianity in the singular, particularly when referring to the Christian faith in non-specific ways.

as their own. By doing so, they contributed to creating other Christian expressions, which have not merely mimicked the European Christianity originally disseminated by the missionaries, but have instead developed its own characteristics, creatively incorporating elements of the diverse Latin American cultures.

Changing the Focus

It is unnecessary to say these days that Christianity is not a European religion. Christianity was born in the Middle East, and has ever since been a traveling religion, making itself at home in many different cultures. By the end of the first millennium of the Common Era, a larger number of Christians were located in Europe. Such a trend reached its peak in the sixteenth century, when 92 percent of all Christians were Europeans.[12]

Due to, at least in part, the amalgamation between the Christian faith and the Roman Empire, the Christianisation of Europe also resulted, over the centuries, in the Europeanisation of Christianity. This phenomenon became more evident towards the middle of the second millennium of the Common Era, when more than 90 percent of all Christians were found in Europe. Thus, the Christianity that most Africans, Asians, and Latin Americans first encountered during the missionary era that started in the 16th century was a Christianity culturally dressed in European clothes.

Given the prominence of the European aggression, and the apparent subjugation of non-European peoples, historical narratives of those encounters have privileged the European perspective. However, despite that power asymmetry, there was human agency on both sides of that encounter. Whether merely trying to survive or making a more conscious effort to resist cultural annihilation, Latin American indigenous peoples and enslaved Africans never completely lost their agency as historical subjects. The simple fact that they have managed to survive the worst genocide in history or centuries of slavery is a proof of their colossal resilience.

Latin American Christianity emerges in the context of that violent encounter, and as a result of multiple agencies, including the agency of Amerindians and enslaved Africans. Without their participation as cultural actors, Latin American Christianity would be merely an extension of European Christianity. Today it is clear that the history of Christianity in Latin America is not merely the history of the expansion of European Christianity. Instead, the history of Latin American Christianity is shaped by an intense interaction between the Gospel and local religious spirits. In such a context, evangelisation in Latin

---

[12] As Todd Johnson and Sun Young Chung have shown, in the first Christian centuries, the demographic epicentre of Christianity was in the Eastern Mediterranean. Christianity had quickly been translated into different languages and cultures from Egypt and Syria to India and Central Asia. Todd M. Johnson and Sun Young Chung, 'Tracking Global Christianity's Statistical Centre of Gravity, AD 33-AD 2100', *International Review of Mission* 93/369 (2004), 166-181.

America must be interpreted in terms of the outward movement of the Gospel in its interaction with specific Latin American cultures. The Gospel, meaning the salvific gift of God as seen through the life, words, and deeds of Jesus, is embraced and interpreted in the particularity of different local cultures. Nevertheless, Gospel and culture are never the same. The Gospel incarnates in distinctive ways in every culture without ever being fully contained by any culture. Furthermore, neither the gospel nor culture are ready-made commodities. Both are dynamic forces, which can never be fully captured in purist or abstract definitions.

If the Christian faith is always experienced in the concrete context of a particular culture, it is important to pay attention to the way cultured Christian identities are formed. John Mbiti is right when he states that Christianity is always indigenous.[13] It is always the result of an encounter between the Gospel and a given culture. Therefore, as I will show in the course of this paper, Latin American Christianity is more than simply an indigenised expression of a universal religion. Thus, again, the choice to refer to the plurality of Christianities and to name them distinctively in the course of Latin American history. Because Christianity is always culturally shaped,[14] instead of referring to the European Christianity Latin Americans encountered when Columbus arrived in the Caribbean merely as 'Christianity' in the abstract, I opt for using the embodied expression 'European colonial Christianity' to name it. Indeed, such Christianity had universal aspirations as a central piece of an incipient world system that began to take shape at the time of the European invasion of the Americas.[15] And yet it never ceased being culturally, socially, and historically located.

---

[13] I follow John Mbiti's view on the indigeneity of Christianity, which is well captured in the following statement: '...I do not think that we need to or can 'indigenise Christianity'. Christianity results from the encounter of the Gospel with any given local or regional community/society. To speak of 'indigenizing Christianity' is to give the impression that Christianity is a ready-made commodity, which has to be transplanted to a local area. Of course, this has been the assumption followed by many missionaries and local theologians. I do not accept it anymore. The Gospel is God-given'. This quote comes from John Mbiti's response to John W. Kinney's paper 'The Contribution of John Mbiti to the Development of Christian Theology in Africa: An Overview and a Critique' (a study presented at the American Society of Church History at the Dallas, TX meeting in December 1977), quoted in John W. Kinney, 'The Theology of John Mbiti: His Sources, Norms, and Methods', *Occasional Bulletin of Missionary Research* 3:2 (1979), 66.

[14] John Mbiti, 'On the Article of John W. Kinney: A Comment', *Occasional Bulletin of Missionary Research* 3:2 (1979), 68.

[15] European modernity created the modern world system, turning itself into the center of that system and all other peoples and societies into its margins. Christianity was the European religion at the time of the conquest. As Dussel says, interpreting Hegel, Christian Europe was the eschatological fulfillment of Christianity. As such it had nothing to learn from other cultures. It had achieved its full realisation. Enrique Dussel, *The Invention of the Americas: The Eclipse of 'The Other' and the Myth of Modernity* (New York: Continuum, 1995), 9, 24.

It is particularly important to name that Christianity when one thinks about it in relation to Latin America. For those who have experienced modernity from 'the underside of history',[16] it is difficult to talk about an abstract, ahistorical, and universal Christianity, which is simply indigenised in Latin America. Such a perspective would force someone speaking from the same locus of enunciation as I to either overlook that Christianity's ties to the colonial project, or completely reject it on moral grounds. Those choices have been made in Latin American history. But there is a third possible response, which I am advancing in this essay, which requires, though, a radical historicisation of Christianity, which treat it always in its historical and concrete manifestations. The following anecdote about the encounter of Peruvian indigenous leaders and Pope John Paul II, during his visit to the Andes, illustrates this point.

> When John-Paul II visited Peru he received an open letter from various indigenous movements which contained the following passage: John-Paul II, we, Andean and American Indians, have decided to take advantage of your visit to return to you your Bible, since in five centuries it has not given us love, peace or justice. Please take back your Bible and give it back to our oppressors, because they need its moral teachings more than we do. Ever since the arrival of Christopher Columbus a culture, a language, religion, and values, which belong to Europe, have been imposed on Latin America by force. The Bible came to us a part of the imposed colonial transformation. It was the ideological weapon of this colonialist assault. The Spanish sword, which attacked and murdered the bodies of Indians by day at night, became the cross, which attacked the Indian soul.[17]

After telling this story, though, Chilean theologian Pablo Richard argues for a more radical move. Instead of giving the Bible back to the colonisers, why don't we 'make it our own'?[18] This anecdote speaks about the moral rejection of the religion of the Coloniser. If Christianity is equalled to that religion, those indigenous leaders are pointing the way: it must be rejected. If, however, Christianity can only be shaped historically, in the encounter between the Gospel and particular cultures, and if the Bible can be read from different loci of enunciation, then, on top of a Christianity that is colonial (associated with both colonisation and the coloniality of power),[19] there can be alternative Christianities, formed through different cultural and social embodiments, as a result of initiatives like the abovementioned, when people like the indigenous leaders who met Pope John II in Peru have opted for making the Bible their own, reading it in their own terms. In short, if there have been multiple

---

[16] See Linda Martin Alcoff and Eduardo Mendieta (eds), *Thinking from the Underside of History: Enrique Dussel's Philosophy of Liberation* (Lanham, MD: Rowman & Littlefield, 2000).

[17] Pablo Richard, '1942: The Violence of God and the Future of Christianity', in Leonardo Boff and Virgil Elizondo (eds), *The Voice of the Victims, Concilium* (London: SCM, 1990), 66.

[18] Richard, '1942', 66.

[19] For the distinction between colonialism and coloniality of power, see Anibal Quijano, 'Coloniality of Power, Eurocentrism, and Latin America', *Neplanta: Views from South* 1:3 (2000), 533-580.

encounters between gospel and culture in Latin America, multiple Christian narratives must be heard and engaged.

For a long time, the story of Latin American Christianity, told in the singular, as the only available narrative, predominantly paid attention to missionaries as its main protagonists, while other actors appeared mostly as they reproduced or expanded that master narrative. The capacity of Latin American peoples to shape their own faith has been often neglected. In such a context, popular forms of Latin American Christianity were dismissed as deviations or as signs of a failed evangelisation. Even some of the most recent historical accounts of Latin American Christianity, like Todd Hartch's excellent book *The Rebirth of Latin American Christianity* (2014),[20] have failed to fully capture the agency of indigenous peoples.

Hartch has the merit of moving beyond the antagonistic narratives that dominated the study of Latin American Christianity in the 1990s and 2000s, which saw the Pentecostal boom in the region over against the backdrop of a declining Catholicism. In those narratives, the success of the former represented the fading of the latter.[21] Hartch, instead, takes a more nuanced approach, emphasizing the mutual reinforcement of Pentecostal growth and Catholic revitalisation, and highlighting the importance of stronger ecumenical relations for the future of Latin American Christianity. He fails, however, to pay adequate attention to the agency of Amerindian and African peoples in Latin America, often depicting popular religion in not very friendly ways. Interfaith relations, especially the intricacies of Christian relations with Indigenous and Afro-Latin American religions, do not seem to be a priority in his work.[22]

---

[20] Todd Hartch, *The Rebirth of Latin American Christianity* (Oxford: Oxford University Press, 2014).

[21] One example is the analysis made by British sociologist David Martin in the early 1990s. See David Martin, *Tongues of Fire: The Explosion of Protestantism in Latin America* (Oxford: Blackwell, 1990). Martin argued that Latin American Pentecostalism is the third wave of religious change movements, seen through the lenses of a cultural pattern that characterises the Anglo-Saxon Protestant cultures. That cultural pattern contains the seeds of voluntarism and religious democracy and is in clash with the Hispanic monolithic empire that has dominated Latin American culture for over four hundred years. One of the problems with Martin's analysis is his imposition of a foreign model, which emphasises the clash of two European-born imperialistic projects. He does not take Latin American native culture seriously, as having any significant element of its own, which can subvert and transform both projects as it interacts with them.

[22] Although Hartch emphasises the rise of laity as a characteristic of the revitalisation of Latin American Christianity (see chapters 7 and 8), and often refers to the success of Protestant witness exactly due to its Latin American leadership, making it 'truly indigenised' (See Hartch, *The Rebirth*, 36), he lacks a more nuanced analysis of Latin American colonial history, and of Christianity's participation in the colonizing project. His modernist impetus leads him to portray traditional indigenous values and lifestyle basically in negative ways (see, for instance, 172). The survival of traditional religious beliefs and practices, and their presence in popular forms of Christianity come across as a failure, mostly on the part of Catholics to evangelise, or as an expression of

Likewise, liberation theology, which emerged as a key prophetic face of Latin American Christianity in the 1960s, was slow to recognise the protagonist role of Indigenous and Afro-Latin American cultures in the process of liberation. In its initial years, Latin American liberation theology limited itself to the use of socioeconomic categories to interpret the context of injustice and oppression in the continent. Since the late 1980s, though, it has experimented a cultural turn. Categories such as 'the poor' and 'the oppressed' have been expanded to incorporate non-socioeconomic aspects of oppression, such as race, gender, and sexuality. Furthermore, for a long time, Latin American liberation theology was predominantly the work of middle-class white males who saw their role as that of organic intellectuals standing in solidarity with the poor and oppressed. It is true that there was an expectation on the part of some founders of the movement like Gustavo Gutierrez that liberation theology would evolve to the point in which the economically, racially, socially, gendered, and sexually oppressed would raise and speak in their own voices.[23] However, for most of its history, liberation theology's place of enunciation has predominantly been one of solidarity of those who in spite of their privilege decide to live and stand in solidarity with the subaltern.[24] Thanks to the significant changes in the demographics of Latin American Christianity in the past few decades the number of women, Afro-Latin Americans, Amerindians, and Pentecostals articulating their own theological discourses is increasing.

Brazilian educator Paulo Freire was one of the first intellectuals in Latin America to pay attention to the cultural agency of the oppressed peoples. His critical pedagogical theory affirmed that only the oppressed can liberate themselves, and their oppressors, on the basis of the contradictory power of their weakness.[25] Such agency, however, depends on *conscientização*, the process of awareness raising, which depends on the work of organic

---

syncretism. More problematic yet is how Hartch does not mention slavery or the contribution made by millions (4.9 million only in Brazil) of enslaved Africans to religious life in general, and to Latin American Christianity.

[23] That expectation of a 'new presence' can be noticed in Gutierrez's use of the expression 'the irruption of the poor': Gustavo Gutierrez, *A Theology of Liberation*, 15th anniversary edition (Maryknoll, NY: Orbis Books, 1988), xx.

[24] The Boff brothers distinguish between the socio-economically poor and the evangelically poor. The latter, even if not socio-economically poor, make themselves poor 'out of love for and in solidarity with the poor', joining them in their struggle against unjust poverty, and for liberation and justice. See, Leonardo Boff and Clodovis Boff, *Introducing Liberation* Theology (Maryknoll, NY: Orbis Books, 1987), 48. In spite of how important taking such a stand is, it is not yet the poor who are becoming the 'subjects of their own history'.

[25] Paulo Freire, *The Pedagogy of the Oppressed*, 30th anniversary edition (New York: Bloomsbury, 2000), Kindle locations 538-541. 'This, then, is the great humanistic and historical task of the oppressed: to liberate themselves and their oppressors as well. The oppressors, who oppress, exploit, and rape by virtue of their power, cannot find in this power the strength to liberate either the oppressed or themselves. Only power that springs from the weakness of the oppressed will be sufficiently strong to free both'.

intellectuals or cultural agents among the poor.[26] In spite of its phenomenal impact on movements like the Christian Base Communities, Freire's analysis is still too dependable on Western rationality. Indeed, *conscientização* can be instrumental and empowering for those who are oppressed or marginalised as they advance the process of their own liberation. However, even prior to such *conscientização*, moral agency, resistance, and even liberationist aspirations already exist. That aspect of agency is often missed.

There are many ways through which people's agency in a situation of oppression may be displayed.[27] Although I support liberation theology's preoccupation with the structures of oppression that perpetuate injustice, and its commitment to dismantle them whenever and wherever possible, scholars studying Latin America must pay greater attention to the agency of the indigenous peoples, their more subtle strategies of survival and resistance, and the extent to which they have contributed to shape Latin American Christianity.

Beyond Indigenised Christianity

Because Christianity always happens as a result of a concrete encounter between Gospel and culture, sooner or later it will be claimed as indigenous.[28] In this sense, Lamin Sanneh, one of the pioneers in the field of World Christianity, is right when he makes a preferential option for indigenous voices.

> I have decided to give priority to indigenous response and local appropriation over against-missionary transmission and direction, and accordingly, have reversed the argument by speaking of the indigenous discovery of Christianity rather than the Christian Discovery of indigenous societies.[29]

Mine is a similar perspective. Although paying attention to the varied intercultural dynamics in the formation of different expressions of Latin American Christianity, I am especially interested in understanding how the Gospel has been appropriated, interpreted and understood by Latin Americans, particularly the poor, ethnically and racially minoritised groups, and women.[30] The continuous and dynamic encounters between Latin American cultures and

[26] According to Freire, '*conscientização* is the deepening of the attitude of awareness characteristic of all emergence'. *Pedagogy of the Oppressed* (Kindle Location 1577).

[27] See, for instance, James C. Scott, *Weapons of the Weak: Everyday Forms of Peasant Resistance* (New Haven: Yale University Press, 1985).

[28] Mbiti, 'On the Article of John W. Kinney', 68.

[29] Lamin Sanneh, *Whose Religion is Christianity?* (Grand Rapids, MI: Eerdmans, 2003), 10. As he puts it, 'It is difficult to overestimate the implications of this indigenous change for the future shape of the religion' (11).

[30] Once again, 'The Gospel' is a category 'always understood and enunciated from the particular cultural location of whoever reads the Scripture. But it is also always related to the proclamation of God's salvation in Jesus, in accord with the Christian Holy Scriptures'. The interpretations of 'The Gospel' may vary from a cultural context to another. What keeps it 'Christian', though, is the centrality of the Biblical narrative as its 'primary and essential source for theological development'. See Kinney, 'The Contribution of John Mbiti', 65.

the Gospel have produced a number of Latin American Christianities. Therefore, scholars of Latin American Christianity are justified as they turn their attention more specifically to the Christians voices that have been overlooked in dominant narratives, and who are increasingly becoming protagonists of their own history.

Latin American Christianity, in its multiple forms, is, like other Christianities around the world, a faith whose vocation is outwardly and intercultural. It moves beyond itself, towards the other, concerned with 'the world beyond the boundaries of the Church'.[31] However, this outwardly vocation must not be accepted without caution. Latin American Christians are pretty aware, for instance, of the close association between the European/U.S. missions that reached the region and Western colonialism. They understand that in light of that past, Christian mission must be de-colonised.

In his work on the conversion of the Maya people, William Hanks states:

> The Spanish conquest of Yucatan rested on two major columns, military subjugation and the so-called *conquista pacifica* 'peaceful conquest'. The military conquest was carried out by a relatively small number of soldiers, armed with swords, armour, muskets, horses, and dogs, and assisted by their indigenous allies. After decades of advançes, setbacks, and regroupings, it came to an end, at least officially, in 1547. The peaceful conquest, by contrast, was carried out by an even smaller number of missionaries and their recruits, armed with monumental built spaces, the cross, religious vestments, the Bible and doctrine, the Host, wine and oil, and speech.[32]

As history shows, Latin American Christianity has always faced the temptation of a religious-political monism that results from the close association between the Iberian colonial project and the Christendom ideal that European colonisers and missionaries brought to these lands.[33] This is not a privilege only of Catholicism. In fact, a similar mindset can be found in the North American Protestant missions that came to Latin America in the nineteenth century. Whereas helping to break the monopoly of European colonial Catholicism, those missions functioned as the religious legitimisation of neo-colonialism, announcing U.S. 'free-tradism' as the new age of modernisation. As Bonino says,

---

[31] Paulus Y. Pham, *Towards an Ecumenical Paradigm for Christian Mission: David Bosch's Missionary Vision* (Roma, Italy: Gregorian & Biblical Press, 2010), 315.

[32] William F. Hanks, *Converting Words: Maya in the Age of the Cross* (Berkley, CA: University of California Press, 2010), Kindle locations 217-221.

[33] Jose Miguez Bonino quotes Lucio Gera as saying, 'To annex a territory to the crown of Spain and to bring it to the altar of the Lord were one and the same thing; the cause of Jesus Christ and the cause of Spain were identical for that country which had just completed "under the banner of the Catholic faith" the expulsion of the Moslems from its territory and the unification of the kingdom': Lucio Gera, 'Apuntes Para Una Interpretation de la Iglesia Argentina', *Vispera* 15 (1970), 59ff, quoted in Jose Miguez Bonino, *Doing Theology in a Revolutionary Situation* (Minneapolis, MN: Fortress, 2007), Kindle Locations 143-145.

> Protestantism, in terms of its historical origin, of its introduction to Latin America, and of its ethos, came into our world as the religious accompaniment of free enterprise, liberal, capitalist democracy.[34]

Christendom, as a colonial force, benefited from genocide and slavery, and, in its neo-colonial forms, continues to contribute to the economic and cultural oppression of millions in Latin America. The colonial nature of European Christendom has particularly impacted 'the darker nations'[35] of the world. The colonial/modern project in the sixteenth century set in motion a new understanding of race, and a subsequent process of racialisation, which deeply informed the relations between the colonial powers and their subjects in the colonised nations. European Christian missions were not only the ambassadors of a 'superior religion', but also of an idea of cultural and racial superiority which they spread in Africa, Asia, and Latin America.

Duncan Forrester refers to the painting by Thomas Barker in the London National Portrait Gallery as an example of that imperialist sentiment and of its religious and theological justifications. In that painting, a young queen Victoria delivers a Bible to an African chief who humbly kneels at her feet. 'The message' that painting communicates is:

> Christian mission is an element of the imperial project; colonialism and evangelism belong together; and the expansion of empire is providential, part of God's plan, the fulfilment of which has been delegated to the imperial power. The chieftain who kneels and cowers before the queen apparently receives the Bible from her hand in awe, reverence and gratitude. That striking picture captures something of the complex and important interweaving of imperialism and Christianity, which, for long, was considered by many as essential to both.[36]

Implicit in this portray is the idea of subservience on the part of the African leader who kneels before the white queen to receive from her the book of life, which contains the directions for the salvation and subsequent progress of dark-skinned Africa; the adoption of the core elements of the 'superior' British civilisation.

The evangelisation promoted by both European Catholic and Protestant Christianities in Latin America similarly demanded a break with the indigenous past and the adoption of the superior way of life exemplified by the European missionaries. Speaking of the conversion of the Mayas, Hanks says:

---

[34] Bonino, *Doing Theology*, Kindle Locations 231-232.

[35] 'Darker nations' is the provocative epithet Vijay Prashad uses in his thoughtful analysis of the 'third world project'. an attempt on the part of predominantly dark-skinned nations to fight the imperial forces on both sides of the Cold War. This epithet refers to the way Eurocentric projects have often associated predominantly dark-skinned peoples with barbarism, attributing to them a childish behaviour, which legitimises paternalistic and imperialistic attitudes toward them. Vijay Prashad, *The Darker Nations: A People's History of the World* (New York and London: The New Press, 2007).

[36] Duncan B. Forrester, 'Preface', in David Joy and Joseph Duggan (eds), *Decolonizing the Body of Christ: Theology and Theory After Empire?* (New York: Palgrave MacMillan, 2012), xi.

> For the missionaries in colonial Yucatan, the focal object of conversion clearly was Indian behavior and beliefs, as is evident from their actions and from the standard definition of *convertir(se)* as 'convince, be convinced or repentant' (Covarrubias 1995 [1611], 350)...By combining conviction with repentance, conversion designates a voluntary turning away from past and current rent ways, to take on different, better ways. It must be kept in mind that while force was in fact liberally used in the *conquista pacifica*, its defining features were persuasion, habituation, and discipline.[37]

The social space in which conversion initially took place in colonial Latin America was the *reduccion*, a controlled environment where

> [t]he *Indios* [sic] would continue to speak their own language, but it had to be a new version of that language, purged of the 'vomit of idolatry' and the insubordinate genres of hieroglyphic reading and history telling: reduced by erasure, yet incremented with the means to speak to and of God and his designs.[38]

Embedded in this idea of evangelisation was the racist ideology of a new world order that had Europe as its self-proclaimed centre.[39] Colonial Christianity not only justified such power matrix in the name of evangelisation, but also provided a religious language that implied the inferiority of indigenous worldviews.

The good news, though, is that, in spite of all this, a darker-skinned, indigenously Latin American Christianity was formed in that process due mainly to the cultural and spiritual agency of indigenous and Afro-Latin American peoples. The year 1992 marked the 500th anniversary of the arrival of Christianity in Latin America. It provided an occasion for that darker-skinned Christianity to speak up, forcing Latin American Christians to face the ambiguity of evangelisation in the continent, and for alternative narratives of that story to be told. For the first time, many in Latin America heard the memories of its original peoples, the descendants of the millions killed and silenced in the conquest. Amerindian theologians who had been so far ignored began to be heard.

Amerindians began to tell the five hundred years of common history since the European invasion on their own terms.[40] Those indigenous narratives were a big reminder that, contrary to what some dominant narratives suggested, indigenous cultures remained alive. It is still common in some parts of Latin America to refer to indigenous peoples as having been wiped out. Aiban

---

[37] Hanks, *Converting Words*, Kindle locations, 285-89.

[38] Hanks, *Converting Words*, Kindle locations, 308-310.

[39] Walter Mignolo, 'Delinking: The Rhetoric of Modernity, the Logic of Coloniality, and the Grammar of De-coloniality', *Cultural Studies* 21:2-3 (March/May 2007), 449, 514.

[40] Aiban Wagua, 'Present Consequences of the European Invasion of America', in Leonardo Boff and Virgil Elizondo (eds), *The Voice of the Victims* (London: SCM,1991), 47.

Wagua, a Kuna Catholic priest, and others have strongly rejected that false premising by saying, 'no, we are still here'.[41]

The resilience and persistence of indigenous cultures and religions in Latin America is in itself an act of resistance. For Latin American indigenous peoples the struggle against colonialism remains 'a present history, history that is not over but still going on, a living history of oppression and resistance'.[42] As Wagua affirms, the retelling of 'the marginalisation, the violence, the genocide or ethnocide perpetrated against our indigenous communities of Abia Yala',[43] as painful as it is, is also a remembrance of 'our indomitable will'.[44] The genocide continues, but so does resistance.

As a Christian, Wagua addresses the crucial role played by Colonial Christianity in the desecrating of indigenous religions, condemned as superstition.[45] In the same way Vitalino Similox Salazar, a K'aqchiquel Maya Protestant minister from Guatemala, highlights the cultural and religious dimension of the invasion by referring to the encounter of his Maya people with European Christianity as 'the invasion of Christianity into the world of the Mayas'.[46] Because of its underlying racism, European Christianity was unable to learn from the indigenous communities. Instead, considering indigenous ways of life superstitious and idolatrous, it set in motion a process of cultural genocide.[47]

As these indigenous Christians began to speak up, it became evident that they had never been merely passive objects of evangelisation. For the most part, they never made a clear-cut break with their indigenous cultures, values, and spirituality. In spite of missionary misguiding perceptions, they continued to be important cultural actors, making important contributions to the development of indigenous Latin American Christianities. The same happened with Afro-Latin Americans who preserved their spirituality and worldview. In spite of the continuous efforts on the part of white colonisers to separate enslaved Africans from their cultural and religious roots, those efforts did not succeed. Peter Paris' insight that 'Africans brought their worldviews with them into the diaspora' remains important. In the midst of 'their interaction with their

---

[41] See that the kind of argument and the indigenous response, 'still here, have always been', in Tony Castanha, *The Myth of Indigenous Caribbean Extinction: Continuity and Reclamation in Borike (Puerto Rico)* (New York: Palgrave McMillan, 2011), xiff.

[42] Wagua, 'Present Consequences', 49.

[43] Wagua, 'Present Consequences', 49.

[44] Wagua, 'Present Consequences', 49.

[45] Wagua, 'Present Consequences', 48.

[46] Vitalino Similox Salazar, 'The Invasion of Christianity into the World of the Mayas', in Guillermo Cook (ed), *Crosscurrents in Indigenous Spirituality, Interface of Maya, Catholic and Protestant Worldviews* (Leiden: E. J. Brill, 1997), 35.

[47] Guillermo Cook, 'Introduction: Brief History of the Maya Peoples', in *Crosscurrents in Indigenous Spirituality*, 15. Cook connects the cultural genocide with the missionary aim of eradicating all non-Christian religion and beliefs.

new environments, their African worldviews were gradually altered into a new-African consciousness'.[48]

What I am calling Latin American Christianity is the embracing of the Gospel by the Latin American peoples on their own terms. It is true that many native peoples and enslaved Africans transported to the region were coerced into the Christian faith. However, even under those coercive circumstances, a number of them managed to embrace Christianity as their own. Instead of being simply Christianised, they found ways to make Christianity indigenous. Whereas forced to relinquish outward signs of their indigenous and African spiritualities, they interpreted Christianity through their own cultural lenses, transforming it in the process. Those who viewed the indigenous peoples as *tabula rasa* were dead wrong. Missionary efforts to Christianise the individual indigenous souls and their surrounding culture met indigenous and Afro-Latin American communities that were extremely resilient, and whose ways of life continued to exist, even if in adjusted forms.

The lesson here is that the common assumption that Latin American Christianity was basically monolithic until the late 19th century must be re-examined. From the beginning there have been many facets to Latin American Christianity; in other words, different Latin American Christianities. There has always been, for instance, at least a Catholicism of the church and a Catholicism of the people, even though sometimes they were not clearly distinguished from one another. Popular religion has shaped Latin American Christianity from its inception.[49] Thus, when observed from the perspective of the colonised and marginalised people, popular religion is the most visible example of the active agency of indigenous and Afro-Latin American cultures as they create meaning in the face of new and changing realities. The persistence of indigenous spiritualities in the context of popular religion has often been met with suspicion and evaluated negatively.[50] From the perspective of the indigenous peoples, however, the endurance of their ways of life has a profound meaning in their struggle for survival, varying from creative adaptation to various forms of resistance.

Popular Catholicism remains an important expression of popular religion in Latin America. It has in many ways subverted the European dominant interpretation of Christian devotions with the infusion of a spirituality that keeps the traditional indigenous worldview alive. One major example is the

---

[48] Peter J. Paris, *The Spiritualities of the African Peoples: The Search for Common Moral Discourse* (Minneapolis, MN: Fortress, 1995), 24. For Paris, integral to that worldview was African spirituality, which he defines as 'synonymous with the soul of a people: the interpreting centre of their power and meaning' (22).

[49] Popular religion includes popular Christianity but is also present outside of it. As Miguel de la Torre and Edwin David Aponte state, 'through popular religion Latina/o peoples voice and act out their own theological and spiritual understandings of the Divine, themselves, and the world'. It urges that the faith of the people be given proper attention. Miguel de la Torre and Edwin David Aponte, *Introducing Latino/a Theologies* (Maryknoll, NY: Orbis, 2001), 118.

[50] Salazar, 'The Invasion of Christianity', 40.

devotion of Our Lady of Guadalupe, *La Morenita*, in Mexico. Our Lady of Guadalupe appears to Juan Diego, a Nahua peasant in 1531, on the hill of Tepeyac, present-day Mexico City. There was a shrine for the female Azteca deity Tonantzin in that location. In that event, Mary, a Christian symbol, is turned into a dark-skinned woman dressed in indigenous clothes. Indigenous spirituality appropriates a Christian symbol. As Judith Gleanson puts it,

> The Virgin of Guadalupe came to life in response to the putting down of her Nahuatl predecessor, Tonantzin, whom she continues in mysterious ways to embody.[51]

On the hill where the Azteca mother goddess had been worshipped, a brown Catholic Saint emerges to remind a Nahuatl convert that she remains the mother-goddess of her people.[52] The Virgin, as an indigenous mother, chooses to address her indigenous son, not the Spaniard.[53] Commonly dismissed by early scholarship, such expressions of popular religion are now being taken more seriously as '"the faith of the people" on their own terms'.[54]

There is an enormous body of literature discussing categories such as *mestizage*[55] and syncretism to discuss the combination of indigenous, African, and European elements in Latin American popular culture and religion.[56] However, more recently, dissatisfied with approaches that emphasise mixture but not as much difference, some scholars have looked for a new language to talk about the hybridity of Latin American and Latina/o religion. One of those approaches is the perspective of liminality.[57] According to this approach, religious experience happens in transitional, interstitial spaces. Such spaces become an avenue for creativity.[58] Thus, for instance, the disguising of Afro-Brazilian religions within Catholic symbols during the colonial era does not simply mean a melting of African traditional values and European Catholicism. Such understanding does not capture the singularity and significance of each religious worldview in that relationship. In fact, instead of blending different traditions indiscriminately, Latin American popular religion

---

[51] Judith Gleanson, 'Oya in the Company of the Saints', *Journal of the American Academy of Religion* 68:2 (2000), 265.

[52] See Robert Orsi, 'She Came, She Saw, She Conquered', *Commonwealth* 124:5 (1997), 24. This is a book review of *Goddess of the Americas: Writings on the Virgin of Guadalupe*, edited by Ana Castillo (New York: Riverhead Books, 1996).

[53] Enrique Dussel, *The Invention of the Americas: Eclipse of 'The Other' and the Myth of Modernity* (New York: Continuum, 1995), 126.

[54] De La Torre and Aponte, *Introducing Latino/a Theologies*,119.

[55] Virgilio Elizondo, *The Future is Mestizo: Life Where Cultures Meet* (Boulder, CO: University Press of Colorado, 2000).

[56] Tânia Lima (ed), *Sincretismo Religioso: O Ritual Afro-Brasileiro* (Recife: Editora Massangano, 1996). Also, Gustavo Benavides, 'Syncretism and Legitimacy in Latin American Religion', in Anita Maria Leopold and Jeppe Sinding Jensen (eds), *Syncretism and Religion: A Reader* (London: Equinox, 2004), 194-216.

[57] Luis C. Nascimento, 'Religion and Immigration: Towards a Transformative Prophetic Spirit' (Ph.D. Dissertation, Princeton Theological Seminary, 2012), 17ff.

[58] Nascimento, 'Religion and Immigration', 18.

bring together different symbolic worlds in a way that allows them to occupy common physical space and still hold on to their distinctive meanings. For example, in situations where coloniser outsiders would see African slaves in Brazil bowing before Catholic Saints, Afro-Brazilian insiders knew that they were indeed bowing to the Orixás. In other words, they crafted a way to keep their distinct worldview alive in a different and oppressive context where they were not free to worship as they pleased. According to Omari-Tunkara, in the midst of such processes Afro-Brazilian religions continued to create new sacred symbolic spaces where the 'cumulative cultural cognizance and worldviews of enslaved Africans transported to the New World during the trans-Atlantic slave trade (1538–1888) remain[ed] operative'.[59]

Discussing the hybridity of Latin American and Latina/o Christianity, Mara Medina has offered another interpretation to indigenous responses to the conquest through a creative analysis of the Nahuatl word *nepantla*—which means middle or in-between space.[60] According to her, with the advent of the conquest, the world as the pre-Columbian peoples had known was mortally wounded. A Christian order, imposed by the Iberian conquistadores, was in the process of full implementation. Indigenous peoples were caught in between two worlds, being challenged to keep their heritage alive whereas making sense of an overwhelming new reality. Medina's contribution is particularly important for our discussion of indigenous agency, as she points out that the indigenous responses to the events which overwhelmingly changed their world went beyond resistance.

> Indigenous peoples did not merely resist the imposition of Christianity but they responded to the foreign tradition by crafting their religiosity, developing unsanctioned traditions, reinforcing their community networks, and ultimately asserting their religious autonomy. They became Christian on their own terms and in the process Christianity was changed.[61]

The story of the initial documentation of the word *nepantla* is enlightening. According to Medina, this word was first recorded by a Dominican Friar in the sixteenth century to describe an indigenous new convert who was still *nepantla*, i.e., in the middle, not yet firmly rooted in the Christian faith. *Nepantla* described the trauma of living between ancient institutions and new, incomprehensible, ones brought by the colonisers. However, it did not represent a state of confusion, but one of creative survival.

The in-between space that the indigenous worldview inhabits encompasses multiple manifestations of the divine, which co-exist without losing their

---

[59] Mikelle Smith Omari-Tunkara, 'Candomblé', F. Abiola Irele and Biodun Jeyifo (eds), *The Oxford Encyclopedia of African Thought*, 2 vols. (Oxford: Oxford University Press, 2010), found at Oxford African American Studies Centre (http://www.oxfordaasc.com/article/opr/t301/e085), accessed on April 10, 2018.

[60] Lara Medina, 'Nepantla Spirituality: Negotiating Multiple Religious Identities among U.S. Latinas', in Miguel A. de La Torre and Gaston Espinosa (eds), *Rethinking Latino(a) Religion and Identity* (Cleveland, OH: Pilgrim Press, 2006), 248-66.

[61] Medina, 'Nepantla Spirituality', 251.

distinctiveness.[62] *Nepantla* is a complex area, a space of discomfort. It does not allow for easy reconciliation of multiple worldviews without consideration of difference. An emphasis on *mestizaje* and syncretism that simply focuses on the idea of a shared culture risks overlooking the significance of the Indigenous worldview. In light of the history alluded above, true Reconciliation between Indigenous and Christian traditions in Latin America demands the privileging of the former's mother culture, the Indigenous, to the extent that it can be fully respected on its own merits. Thus, the reclaiming and reinterpretation of Indigenous epistemology are vital tasks for Latin American theology.[63]

These and other constructive interpretations of Latin American popular religion and Christianity have emerged as alternatives to perspectives that reinforce the colonial spirit and ignore the local peoples and cultures. These emerging theological insights represent a viable way for Latin American Christians to rethink their journey in a continent that experienced genocide and slavery in conjunction with the idea of Christian evangelisation.

Pentecostalism as Popular Religion

As I suggested earlier, the survival, resilience, resistance, and creative agency of indigenous and Afro-descendent cultures in Latin American and the Caribbean do not depend on an external Western rationality to take place. It has been operative from the moment the first *conquistadores* began to occupy their land and, in the process, set to Christianise them. Orlando Espin that it is almost impossible to study any U.S. Latina/o community in the U.S. without encountering popular religion. And this religious experience profoundly marked by Amerindian and African elements is still considered an embarrassment by some churches.[64] Popular religion was, for a long time, despised as a degeneration of orthodoxy, or a failure in the process of evangelisation. However, it has been recently rediscovered as a prominent sign of how indigenous and Afro-descendent communities in the region have creatively kept their cultural values and symbols alive, in the midst of a violent evangelisation. Popular religion takes on multiple forms in Latin America and the Caribbean. Cubans, Haitians, Brazilians, and Colombians, among others, have combined elements of African, indigenous, and Christian traditions (among others) to create new African-derived syntheses that would later receive particular names, thus taking the form of specific African-derived traditions.

---

[62] Medina, 'Nepantla Spirituality, 253-54.

[63] Medina, 'Nepantla Spirituality', 249, 250. Medina speaks from a Chicana perspective, as Chicana liberation theologian. I believe, though, that her insights similarly speak to the different liberating theologies that have emerged in Latin America and in the U.S. Latino/a communities.

[64] Orlando Espin, *The Faith of the People: Theological Reflections on Popular Catholicism* (Maryknoll, NY: Orbis, 1997), 95, 101.

Likewise, the indigenous agency has been key to the formation of popular Catholicism. This popular face of Catholic religiosity has largely shaped Latin American countries and societies, to the point that many have identified it as a key component of what one would call a Latin American culture. But, another form of popular religion, which needs to receive more attention as such, is Pentecostalism. Pentecostalism is the fastest-growing religious expression in Latin America today. Consequently, it has received considerable scholarly attention in the past half a century. In spite of that, though, there is still some deficit in the study of Pentecostalism as a Latin American popular religion, one that exists in relationship with other popular religious expressions, being strongly informed by indigenous and African-derived traditions. As Bernardo L. Campos has highlighted, Latin American Pentecostalism has not spread in a cultural vacuum. Latin American Pentecostalism is a form of popular religion.[65]

Many people converting to Pentecostalism in Latin America today come either from popular Catholicism or from other religions strongly influenced by indigenous and/or African-derived spirituality. In fact, the explosive growth of Pentecostalism in Latin America, in contrast with the experience of almost every other form of Protestantism, results from its unique capacity to engage the language and symbols of popular culture in a way that those who come from other popular religions into Pentecostal churches do not feel they have been stripped of their worldview.

Brazilian Pentecostal scholar Alexandre Souza rightly states that Pentecostalism is a religious practice born in the soul of the poor. It has a unique capacity to express 'the pain, the anxieties, the dreams, and the challenges of the poor'.[66] There is a power in Latin American popular religiosity to the dominant culture, which can clearly be found in many forms of Pentecostalism. The way and intensity as Pentecostals interact with surrounding expressions of popular religion and culture vary from one church to another. But even in situations when they adopt antagonistic discourses against popular Catholicism or against African-derived religions, they still operate within a worldview that is familiar to the people in those religious traditions they purportedly oppose.

As part of their spiritual warfare strategies, for instance, Neo-Pentecostal churches such as *Igreja Universal do Reino de Deus* (IURD), in Brazil, adopt a number of popular symbols that are part of the universe of Brazilian popular culture. Therefore, rather than actually effecting a radical rupture with popular religion, Neo-Pentecostal spirituality in Brazil, and elsewhere in the continent, is shaped in continuity with other popular religions. French sociologist Jean-Pierre Bastian states that Latin American Pentecostalism exists in

---

[65] Bernardo L. Campos, 'In the Power of the Spirit: Pentecostalism, Theology and Social Ethics', in Benjamin F. Gutierrez and Dennis A. Smith (eds), *In the Power of the Spirit: The Pentecostal Challenge to Historic Churches in Latin America* (Drexel Hill, PA: Skipjack, 1996), 41-50.

[66] Alexandre C. Souza, *Pentecostalismo: Um Desafio às Leituras Contemporâneas da Religiosidade Brasileira* (Viçosa, MG: Ultimato, 2004), 24.

continuity with the traditional values of Latin American society.[67] The kind of Pentecostalism represented by the IURD, and many other Latin American Pentecostal churches, reflects the fluidity of the Latin American religious landscape, and the persistence of indigenous and African-derived heritages. In spite of its antagonistic discourses, those churches exist within the realm of indigenous and African-derived traditions. As Brazilian scholar Wagner G. da Silva affirms, churches like the IURD owe their success to the Exús.[68]

Some Latin American Pentecostals are, indeed, moving towards greater acknowledgement of their indigenous and African-derived roots. The revitalisation of indigenous and African-derived identities in the region has led some Latin American Christians to see themselves as part of a larger indigenous and/or African-derived heritage. Such experience has led some of them to re-examine a learned negative attitude toward their own culture. Indigenous Protestants in Guatemala, Peru, Ecuador, and Brazil are intentionally incorporating some ancestral traditions into their Christian practices, starting to relate more deeply to ceremonies and symbols they were taught to reject. Others have come to the conclusion that as Christians they must stand in solidarity with people of traditional religions in the struggle for racial justice. Luiz de Jesus, an Afro-Brazilian charismatic Baptist pastor in Sao Paulo, Brazil, is an example of Evangelicals and Pentecostals who are reclaiming their African roots after having become more aware of the dominant racism in the Christian structures within which they have been raised. Using poetry to turn his pain into a protest, pastor Luiz has started to read the Bible as an Afro-Brazilian, rejecting the distortions of a Eurocentric reading of the Bible that erases its African elements. At the same time, he has embraced afresh his African roots. In contrast with the paradoxical acknowledgement of African deities seen above in the case of the IURD—which acknowledges their existence but still demonises them—Pastor Luiz de Jesus can praise *Yalorixás* such as Menininha do Gantois and Estela de *Oxóssi, or make a positive reference to the African deity Oxalá* in one of his poems.[69]

The Evangelical Black Movement (*Movimento Evangélico Negro* – MNE), organised in 2003, is another example of this recent development. MNE is a

---

67 Jean-Pierre Bastian, *La Mutación Religiosa de América Latina: Para una Sociología del Cambio Social en la Modernidad Periférica* (Ciudad del Mexico: Fondo de Cultura Económica, 1997), 125. Bastian affirms that the rupture brought by Pentecostalism has been a rupture with the hierarchical manipulation of the Catholic clergy rather than a rupture with its religious imaginary. He says, 'This abandonment of the images, the saints and the rhythms of the Catholic feasts does not imply a rupture with the ancestral religious universe. This universe is, on the contrary, revivified by the elective affinity between Pentecostalism and the shamanic beliefs and practices, which found, then, a renewed legitimisation' [translation is mine]. It is exactly by means of this flexibility that Pentecostalism goes beyond other forms of Protestantism in its engagement of Latin American culture.

68 Wagner Goncalves da Silva, 'Religião e Identidade Cultural Negra: Católicos, Afrobrasileiros e Neopentecostais', *Cadernos de Campo* 20 (2011), 298.

69 Reference to unpublished poems which Pastor Luiz shared with the author.

network of Afro-Brazilian Evangelicals and Pentecostals who, like Pastor Luiz de Jesus, are becoming increasingly aware of their African heritage. As a consequence, they are also turning into more prominent participants in the fight against racial discrimination and injustice. They find in the MNE a platform where black evangelicals and Pentecostals can make sense of their faith in the larger context of the struggle of black Brazilians for racial justice. Such a process has led a number of them to critically reflect on the nature of their Christian faith and its relation to the Afro-Brazilian community, culture, traditions, and struggle. The Forum of Black Christian Women, formed in both Sao Paulo and Rio de Janeiro, in 2001, with the participation of representatives from both historical and Pentecostal churches, is another example of this increasing trend, which is slowly challenging hegemonic understandings of Latin American Pentecostals and of how they relate to indigenous and African-derived cultural identity.[70]

On top of being a public forum for self-conscious black Evangelicals and Pentecostals, the MNE provides an opportunity for the reconsideration of the relationship between black Pentecostals/Evangelicals and the Unified Black Movement. Although not a religious movement, many of the leaders in the MNU (Black Unified Movement) have close ties with Afro-Brazilian religions. Up to the mid-1990s, Evangelicals and Pentecostals were basically absent in the MNU and its struggle for racial justice in the country. Black Pentecostals in the Black Evangelical Movement, different from other Pentecostals, have been able to develop a more open attitude towards members of other religions, looking for common ground at least on the level of political alliances in the struggle for civil and human rights. Black Pentecostals/Evangelicals such as Hernani da Silva (one of the founders of the MNE), Marco Davi de Oliveira (a black Baptist pastor known for his prophetic denunciation of racial discrimination in Brazilian Protestant circles),[71] and Luiz de Jesus are pioneering the development of an Evangelical/Pentecostal 'theology of African roots' with the view towards articulating 'an anti-racist message in clear, theologically sophisticated biblical terms'.[72] Along with that, they are also revisiting the history of Brazilian Protestantism by looking into it from the perspective of the Afro-Brazilian experience. As they reread unquestioned historical narratives, these Black Evangelicals and Pentecostals are contributing to resituate and re-subject Brazilian Protestant identity, retelling its history from a different point of view.

---

[70] See John Burdick, 'Why is the Black Evangelical Movement Growing in Brazil?' *Journal of Latin American Studies* 37:2 (2005), 311-32.

[71] Marco Davi de Oliveira is also the author of the well-known book, *A Religião Mais Negra do Brasil: Por que os negros Fazem Opção Pelo Pentecostalismo?* 2nd ed. (Viçosa, MG: Ultimato, 2015). He argues that Pentecostalism is the largest black religion in Brazil, given the number of Black Brazilians who weekly worship in Pentecostal churches.

[72] Burdick, 'Why is the Black Evangelical Movement Growing in Brazil?', 325.

Hernani da Silva, one of the MNE founding leaders, for instance, has relocated forgotten black preacher Agostinho Jose Pereira to the centre of Brazilian Protestant history, claiming him as the founder of the first Portuguese speaking Protestant church in Recife, in 1841. That is a perspective previously unheard of, the history of Brazilian Protestantism, told from the missionary's perspective, started with Scottish missionary Robert Reid Kalley at the centre as the founder of the first Portuguese speaking Protestant congregation in Brazil (1855). Hernani da Silva, nevertheless, has relocated the perspective of a Brazilian black evangelist and of a black church that did not survive to the centre stage of that narrative.[73] Black Evangelicals and Pentecostals such as Hernani Da Silva enrich the Brazilian Protestantism tradition, by expanding its horizons and recovering forgotten memories. Furthermore, they denounce the racist legacy of a persisting Eurocentric Christianity. Although many in the MNE still resist deeper association with members of Afro-Brazilian religions, the movement creates opportunities for continuous reflection on how deeply racial discrimination has impacted Brazilian culture and society.[74]

Concluding Thoughts

With the rise of liberation theology in the late 1960s, the theological voices emerging out of Latin American Christianity began to be more widely noticed. As a consequence of that awakening, in the following decades, new theological voices emerged in the Latin American scenario. Indigenous peoples, Afro-Latin Americans and women have found their own theological voices and 'locus of enunciation'.[75] By doing that, they are reclaiming their places as subjects of their own history. This is the context in which the relation between Christianity and culture must be discussed today in Latin America.[76]

The question about evangelisation in Latin America has to be asked again. Amerindians and people of African descent in Latin America can no longer be understood as passive objects of European and North American evangelism. Furthermore, new questions must be raised as to the extent to which they have, in fact, transformed Latin American Christianity.

The time has come for a full irruption of the poor in Latin America. Since the late 1980s, new actors, women, indigenous peoples, black-Latin Americans, and Pentecostals have emerged as key actors in the Latin American religious landscape, giving birth to Pentecostal theologies, indigenous theologies, and

---

[73] Hernani da Silva, *O Movimento Negro Evangelico: Um Mover do Espirito Santo?* (São Paulo: Selo Negritude Cristã, 2011), 9.

[74] Although the examples I chose to use come from the context I know best in Brazil, similar experiences and responses can be found among Amerindian Christian communities in Guatemala, Mexico, Ecuador, Bolivia, and Peru, just to mention a few, or among Hatian, Cuban, or Colombian black communities.

[75] Walter Mignolo, 'Introduction', *Cultural Studies* 21:2-3 (2007), 158.

[76] Emilio Castro, 'On Evangelism and Culture: Some Reflections', *International Review of Mission* 84:335 (2001), 365.

black theologies in Latin America which have not yet received proper treatment. They are contributing sophisticated insights on socioeconomic justice, whereas integrating relevant contributions from critical cultural and race theories into the conversation.[77]

Latin America is experiencing a renewed understanding of its religious pluralism. Catholicism remains the religious majority, and one of the largest cultural influences in the region. However, it is not a monolithic religious power. Pentecostalism has unquestionably become an important player, serving on many levels as the venue for popular Protestant religiosity in the region. Just like in the case of Catholicism, Latin American Pentecostalism is plural in its makeup. More than ever before, Latin American Catholicism and Protestantism are challenged to find creative ways of engaging traditional indigenous and Afro-Latin American religions.

At the end of the day, what is really potentially revolutionary in Latin American Christianity is its increasing self-awareness. Latin American Christianity is increasingly realizing the distinctiveness of its cultural location identity. It has realised that it is a 'Cristianismo Moreno',[78] a dark-skinned Christianity. There is a new evangelisation taking place in the region. That evangelisation, however, cannot be described simply in terms of Christian revitalisation. It also implies a revitalisation of Indigenous and Afro-Latin American identities. Whereas some indigenous and Afro-Latin Americans choose to reaffirm their ethnic and cultural traditional heritages by joining their traditional religions, for many others who remain Christian, such revitalisation means a renewal of Christianity and of its attempts to reconcile with indigenous and Afro-Latin American spiritualities. Each of the new theological voices mentioned above turns out to be 'a voice in search of freedom, independence, and autonomy...a voice that wishes to lay claim to its own reality and experience, give expression to its own view of God and the world, and charts its own future.'[79] Whereas they do not represent the whole of Latin American Christianity, these voices are expressions of the most obstinate, creative and liberating movements one can see in Latin American Christianity these days.

---

[77] See for instance Thia Cooper (ed), *The Reemergence of Liberation Theologies: Models for the Twenty-First Century* (New York: Palgrave Macmillan, 2013).

[78] Eduardo Hoornaert, *O Cristianismo Moreno do Brasil* (Petropolis, RJ: Vozes, 1991).

[79] Fernando F. Segovia, 'Two Places and No Place in Which to Stand', in A. Banuelos (ed), *Mestizo Christianity: Theology from the Latino Perspective* (Maryknoll, NY: Orbis, 1995), 35, cited in Maria Pilar Aquino, 'Theological Method in U.S. Latino/a Theology', in Orlando Espin and Miguel H. Diaz (eds), *From the Heart of Our People: Latino/a Explorations in Catholic Systematic Theology* (Maryknoll, NY: Orbis, 1999), 9.

The Transculturalization and the Transnationalization of the Government of 12: From Seoul to Bogota to Charlotte, North Carolina

Philip Wingeier-Rayo

Traditionally missionary movements have spread from the north to the south, or from the west to the east, following the European colonial power structure. This was the model in 1910 at the time of the World Missionary Conference in Edinburgh where the overwhelming majority of the delegates were from the mission-sending nations of Europe and North America. Today, however, there are new post-colonial and omnidirectional missionary movements. This article will research a relatively new mission model that began in South Korea and moved to Bogota, Colombia, and is now going north to the United States. It is moving against the traditional missionary flow using new creative models for evangelism and discipleship that are transnational and transcultural. This article has three main objectives: 1) to trace this particular style of small group methodology and theology from Yoido Full Gospel Church in Seoul, Korea through Bogota, Colombia to Charlotte, North Carolina, 2) to understand the social and cultural adaptations of the small group methodology, and lastly 3) to analyse the theological implications of Cho and Castellanos' theology.

David Yonggi Cho

Our story begins in southern Korea where Paul Yonggi Cho (later he changed his name to David) was born on February 14, 1936, under Japanese occupation. Cho came from a working-class Buddhist family, and his father was a very active lay Buddhist. When Cho was 18 years old, he was diagnosed with tuberculosis and was given three or four months to live. He prayed daily to the Buddha for healing, but nothing happened. One day he decided to pray to the Christian God: 'Oh God! If you really exist, come and help me. If you help me to recover my health, I promise to live my life for you and for the well-being of others.'[1] Shortly after this prayer a young woman came to visit him and offered

Originally published in Afe Adogame, Janice McLean, and Anderson Jeremiah (eds), *Engaging the World Christian Communities in Contemporary Glabal Societies,* Regnum Edinburgh Centenary Series 21 (Oxford: Regnum Books, 2014), 153-168

to speak to him about Jesus Christ. That young missionary returned every day saying the same things, and Cho was tired of her and finally shouted: 'That's enough! Don't say another word! I am tired of your stories. Let me die in peace!'[2] She left him a Bible, and Cho began to read until he finally accepted Christ. Within six months he was completely healed of tuberculosis and began attending a Full Gospel Assembly of God Church.

In 1956 he began seminary at Full Gospel Bible College in Seoul. After graduating in 1958, he held a worship service in the home of his friend and future mother-in-law Choi Ja-Sil. Three years later the congregation bought a plot of land at Seodaemun-gu and built a 1,500 auditorium. He worked hard visiting people to fill up the new building and in 1965 suffered a collapse. At this time he realized that he could not do the pastoral work alone and divided the city of Seoul into 20 zones or 'cells' and trained a team of lay leaders to offer Bible studies in homes. Then in 1969 he felt called to buy land on Yeouido Island where the government was building its central offices. There Cho built a church auditorium that now has a capacity for 25,000 people.[3] Today the congregation has a membership of 763,000 and offers seven services on Sundays and three on Wednesdays.[4] In addition to the church itself, Cho has established two organizations: Church Growth International and the David Cho Evangelistic Mission to help spread his message beyond South Korea.

From South Korea to Bogota

Given the geographical distance, the language and cultural differences between Korea and South America, Colombia is an unlikely place for his methodology to spread. Yet on the opposite side of the world, a young pastor was struggling with the same issues as Cho did early in his ministry. Cesar Castellanos began his pastoral work in 1973 in Bogota, Colombia. By 1982 his congregation had grown a little, but he realized that although people came to church on Sunday, he was tired of having to beg parishioners to come to church. Castellanos recalls having to:

> chase after the people begging them, 'Don't leave, you are needed and you are important to us.'...I said, 'Lord is this what you called me for, to beg people to come back to You? I don't want this! If this is what shepherding is then this is not what I want.' He resolved not to return to the pastorate until God 'confirmed the more specific purpose of my call.[5]

While taking a break from the ministry, Castellanos went on a vacation at the beach and had a vision. In the dream Castellanos heard God speaking to

---

[1] David Yonggi Cho, *The Fourth Dimesion*,2nd ed. (Editiorial Peniel, 2002), 11.

[2] Cho, *The Fourth Dimension*, 12.

[3] Cho, *The Fourth Dimension*, 16.

[4] Website of the Yoido Full Gospel Church, http://english.fgtv.com/yfgc.pdf (Accessed on 30 September 2008).

[5] Cesar Castellanos, *Dream and You Will Win the World* (Hollywood, FL: G12 Editors, 2004), 24, 25.

him about dreaming big: 'Dream of a very big church because dreams are the language of My spirit!'[6] Castellanos heard God promising him that: 'The church that you will shepherd will be as numerous as the stars in the sky and the sand on the seashore. It will be so big that it will be countless.'[7] Castellanos founded a new church in 1983 under the name *Mision Carismatica Internacional* (MCI). Yet he still had not discovered the methodology that would put the legs under his new vision.

Hearing about the success of David Yonggi Cho in South Korea, Castellanos, and his wife visited the Yoido Full Gospel Church in 1983 to learn about Cho's methodology and theology first-hand. He saw how the city of Seoul was divided up into cells, and how lay leaders lead home Bible studies across the city. Castellanos brought this idea back to Bogota and implemented it. However, after seven years, he was still dissatisfied with growth. 'We tried it [Cho's system] but just didn't experience the growth we longed for,' Castellanos said. 'From 1983 to 1990, we only had 70 cells,' Castellanos reported.[8] For most churches, 70 small groups would be a success, but Castellanos was not satisfied that only 30% of church members were involved.[9] He wanted more cell groups, a higher percentage of participation, and a larger congregation.

While praying in 1991, Castellanos received what he had been waiting for: '[the] extraordinary revelation of the Principle of Twelve.'[10] Castellano reported that 'God removed the veil from my mind and I received the model that is now revolutionizing church growth. God validated the model by reminding me [of] the way Jesus had worked with His twelve disciples.'[11] Based on this vision Cesar Castellanos together with his wife, Claudia Rodríguez de Castellanos, adapted and refined Cho's methodology to the Colombian context. Castellano heard God saying to him: 'If you train twelve people and you manage to reproduce in them the character of Christ which is in you and if every one of them does the same with another twelve people and if these, in their turn, do the same with another twelve, transmitting the same vision to each other, you and your church will experience unprecedented growth.'[12] Castellanos called his new hybrid methodology 'the Government of 12'. Basically the G12 builds on the methodology of David Yonggi Cho of cell group ministries, but limits attendance to twelve and instead of organizing the groups by neighbourhood, they allow each cell group leader to seek out his or her twelve disciples of the same gender wherever they may live. By not

[6] Castellanos, *Dream and You Will Win*, 25.

[7] Castellanos, *Dream and You Will Win*, 25.

[8] Found in http://www.charismamag.com/display.php?id=7978 Sept. 26, 2008

[9] Castellanos, *The Ladder of Success: A Practical Guide* (Bogota: Editorial Vilit and Co., 2001), 25.

[10] Castellanos, *The Ladder of Success*, 81. Also see website for Mision Carismatica Internacional.

[11] Castellanos, *The Ladder of Success.*

[12] Castellanos, *The Ladder of Success,* 25.

dividing up cell groups geographically, the G12 model allows families to stay together – which is fundamental in the Latino context.

Castellanos also builds on Cho's fourth-dimension concept and the importance of success. Castellanos advocates 'dreaming' or envisioning one's goal in order for it to come true. He writes: 'First of all, it is necessary to point out that an attitude of success is something that must be inside you. It is not possible to attain any measure of growth and success in the life of the believer unless his attitude and lifestyle reflect that of a winner.'[13] Castellano uses the Old Testament figure of Joshua as the epitome of a successful man who was happy, healthy, prosperous, had peace of mind and good friends.[14] Castellanos applies his method of 'dreaming' to parish ministry, where pastors and leaders should envision multiplying cell groups and mega-churches.

This ecclesiology comes from Castellanos' model in the MCI that starts with Cesar Castellanos and his wife Claudia who have a core group of twelve couples. Pastor Castellanos shepherds the men and Pastor Claudia the women. In turn, each of these twelve men and women also shepherds twelve men and women. The G12 movement envisions each new Christian to be a leader and create his or her own cell group, so that theoretically the movement would multiply by twelve with the Castellanos being at the top of the pyramid. The cell groups are divided into categories of men, women, youth, and children, and like the Yoido Full Gospel Church, are hosted in private homes. Today the *Misión Charismatic Internacional* (MCI) has 15,000 cell groups with a total of 120,000 members in the capital city of Bogota. Nationwide the MCI has 25,000 cell groups and a total of 170,000 members.[15] The MCI also has spread outside of Colombia through missionaries and immigration and has 120,000 members in Brazil, Chile, Bolivia, Ecuador, and the United States. Pastors are also implementing the vision in Peru, Argentina, Mexico, and Canada.[16]

Castellanos, like Cho, formed an international organization to spread his movement to other countries. Individual churches not associated with the MCI can join the G12 organization for $120 monthly membership fee. In exchange, they will receive publications, a monthly communication and a discount on registration to the annual convention, which are held in Puerto Rico, Venezuela, Miami, Atlanta, as well as the large annual G12 convention in Colombia.

From Bogota to Charlotte, NC

In 1995 Luis and Marta Montoya emigrated as a lay people from Colombia to North Carolina and began attending *Vida Nueva Iglesia de Dios* in Charlotte

[13] Castellanos, *Dream and You Will Win*, 87.
[14] Castellanos, *Dream and You Will Win*, 89-91.
[15] http://www.mci12.com.co/index.php?option=com_contentandtask=viewandid=62and Itemid=81
[16] Andrea Tunarosa, 'Spreading the Word – Fast: A New System Makes Church Membership Grow Exponentially', *Wall Street Journal*, 28 July, 2006.

where José Chacon was the pastor of a congregation of about 175 people. Shortly afterwards Chacon experienced some conflict in the church and departed for Puerto Rico leaving another pastor in charge. The church split, and Chacon returned to pastor the larger group of about 135 people, and he asked Montoya to be the associate pastor in the fall of 1996. Chacon travelled a lot giving Montoya pastoral experience until finally, Chacon convinced the congregation to financially support his missionary efforts and left to become a missionary in Africa in 2000.

Montoya became the senior pastor for the first time, but the congregation maintained strong personal and financial ties to support Chacon's mission. Gradually people began to buckle under the imposed financial obligation and leave the church in 2001. Amidst this crisis, Montoya saw church attendance decrease causing him to question his calling. In his own words, Montoya said: 'I came face-to-face with God…and I asked God to reveal to me what to do. God told me to go to Colombia.'[17] So he and another leader from the church went to Bogota to attend the introductory training of the G12 and brought back curriculum to read. Montoya studied the materials and compared it to the doctrine of the *Iglesia de Dios* (Cleveland, Tennessee). Montoya recalled: "I felt that in my church we had a good doctrine, but we were not developing leaders." After joining the G12 leadership in Bogota assigned John Espinosa as an advisor to us, and he said that our first step was to come to an 'Encounter'. So Montoya went back to Colombia with six women and one man from our congregation in March of 2002. Montoya describes the Encounter:

> It was a great experience because all the participants were new believers. They separated us between men and women and sent us on buses [to the retreat center]. There were many drug addicts, thieves, homosexuals, as well as former military and paramilitary. In our church we had had retreats of 15 people, but this was a much much bigger. It was amazing to see the transformation of people.[18]

Montoya returned to Charlotte with his lay leaders and hosted their own 'Encounter' in May of 2002. Then Montoya went back to Colombia again for 'Re-Encounter' with nine or ten people from his church. But from then on they have hosted their own 'Post-Encounter' and began the School of Leaders.

Montoya asked the whole congregation to go through this process, but some long-standing members did not agree and left the church. According to Montoya, once they started this new G12 vision they have not lost members. They only lost former members in the transition. Since adopting the vision, they have grown to have an average weekly attendance of 500, and have built a new multipurpose facility and expanded their sanctuary to have a seating capacity for 600 – the largest Hispanic congregation in Charlotte.

Montoya has adapted the G12 vision and not only offers these 'Encounters' for new believers in his congregation, but also for surrounding congregations. They have churches who have come with their pastor and key leaders in the congregation from Winston-Salem, Concord, Myrtle Beach and as far away as

[17] Interview with Pastor Luis Montoya, 15 October, 2008 in Charlotte, NC.
[18] Interview with Pastor Luis Montoya.

Virginia. Montoya's church provides financial support to his brother-in-law, Alvaro, who works with the G12 back in Bogota leading a cell group for drug addicts.

Methodology of *Vida Nueva Iglesia de Dios*

As each new Christian converts, he or she starts the G12 process beginning with the 'Ladder of Success', which is a combination of discipleship classes and spiritual retreats to transform new believers into leaders. The Ladder of Success consists of four objectives: winning, consolidating, discipleship and sending. In order to achieve these objectives, the Ladder of Success takes the new convert through the process of consolidation, Pre-Encounter, Encounter, Post-Encounter, School of Leaders, Re-Encounter with accompaniment through the process by consolidators and a cell group.

A new convert in the G12 process is assigned a 'consolidator' to answer basic questions about the Bible and generally encourage beginners in the faith. A consolidator may call or visit new Christians and offer one-on-one Bible studies to strengthen a new believer during his or her first steps in the faith. The reason the consolidator position was created was to prevent new converts from dropping out. Many churches have hundreds if not thousands of visitors every year. Although a few might convert to Christ and start off on fire, just as many often become disenamoured and stop attending. The consolidator position in the G12 was created to precisely 'close the backdoor' of the movement. In traditional Protestant ecclesiology, a 'consolidator' might assume the responsibilities of discipleship often performed by the pastor, evangelism team or usher.

After one's first steps in the movement, one would continue the 'Ladder of Success' by taking the 'Pre-Encounter' classes. These twelve classes can be taught by the pastor, but it is more likely taught by one of the pastor's 'twelve', or the inner circle of leaders immediately shepherded by the pastor. The men take classes separate from women. Over the course of twelve weeks, the new believer prepares for a weekend spiritual retreat called an 'Encounter'. These classes play the educational role of discipleship, but in addition, they create high expectations for the 'Encounter'.

Participants are told very little about the actual content of the 'Encounter' creating a sense of mystery. A lot of weight and expectation is placed on this weekend retreat as a 'make or break' moment in the life of a new Christian. New believers who have not yet attended an 'Encounter' are not authorized to hold any leadership positions in the church. This also goes for people who have served in leadership positions, or even pastors, in other denominations. When the long-awaited weekend of 'Encounter' arrives new Christians are asked to prepare for a serious encounter with Jesus Christ. Participants are told that this will not be like any other retreat they have been on and not to expect to have fun.

The 'Encounter' is a weekend retreat of 17 talks, similar to the Roman Catholic model of 'Crysalis'. Cesar Castellanos recommends that the 'Encounter' be held at a camp ground or retreat center away from the town where one lives. The 'Encounters' that I attended were held at a YMCA camp in the Smokey Mountains and the experience is often referred to metaphorically as 'going up to the mountain'. The pastor and his or her twelve inner leaders give the talks and pray for the participants. These leaders are called 'guides' for the weekend, and no other visiting pastor or lay leader is allowed to give counselling. Participants are encouraged to seek out a guide for any additional prayer or counselling that arises during the 'Encounter.' The goal of the retreat is to confront each individual with traumatic or sinful experiences from the individual's his or her past and seek spiritual liberation. The talks have titles such as 'Hero of Heroes', 'Identifying the Media that Contaminate your Mind', Recognizing and Removing Bondage in your Life', 'Christ: Characteristics of a New Man', 'The Other and I', 'Health and Body', 'The Best Friend, The Holy Spirit', and 'Restoring Family Unity'. Their content is quite introspective asking the participants to recall painful childhood experiences that have marked one's life. Any past sins such as adultery, fornication, idolatry, and lust are considered demons possessing the individual and must be rebuked.

The G12 theology believes that sins committed in the past, even by an ancestor, cast a curse upon the present and future generations. Even if one was a victim of rape or abuse, for example, the G12 believes that these traumatic experiences leave demonic possession which requires liberation. Thus it is necessary to repent of these sins and break the curse from continuing in one's life and transmitting it to future generations. The prayers following the talks at the 'Encounter' could be described as exorcisms to cast out demons and seek spiritual liberation. The 'Encounter' is supposed to be an honest encounter with Christ and with one's past. The retreat becomes a watershed event in the life of a new Christian and has an almost sacramental place in the G12 movement. Before attending an 'Encounter' new comers are considered neophytes in the faith, yet once attending believers are considered 'Christians' and can begin to assume leadership roles.

After coming 'down from the mountain', the G12 movement attempts to continue the momentum of the 'Encounter' with 'Post-Encounter' classes. These nine classes are taught by the same leaders of the 'Encounter.' These are follow-up classes to prevent the new convert from 'cooling off' after the mountain-top experience. These classes have titles such as: 'Be a Person Firm in Your Decisions', 'The Bible: the Book That Will Transform Your Life', 'Knowing the Will of God', 'Think Like a Winner', and 'God Created Man to be Prosperous'. I found that the 'Post-Encounter' classes offer a slight contradiction from the teachings of the 'Encounter.' The 'Encounter' taught that one must repent from past sins and cleanse oneself in order to be liberated. The assumption is that once the encounter is finished, one will be free of these sins. However, the Post-Encounter classes continue to emphasize these past sins as though they were still present.

The 'Ladder of Success' continues after the Post-Encounter with more classes to prepare for 'Re-Encounter'. This is another retreat experience similar to the 'Encounter', but supposedly deeper. I found this second retreat experience to be more of the same of the first encounter. Again there were 17 talks given by the pastor and his inner circle of male leaders, as well as more exorcism of demons. Of course, it is less of a mystery because all the participants have necessarily attended the first encounter. The 'Re-Encounter' does focus more on applying the G12 theology to one's lifestyle. The title of some of the talks is: 'Health and our Body', 'Marriage and Sexuality', 'Devotional Life', and 'A Christian Vocation'.

Although the G12 produces and publishes its own curriculum for the 'Ladder of Success' in Colombia, Pastor Luis Montoya in Charlotte is beginning to adapt the vision to his context. For example, transporting over a hundred people two hours to the mountains and renting a YMCA camp has become cost-prohibitive for several potential participants, so he is adapting the talks to be more accessible. Given the reality of most Hispanic immigrants in the United States, it is very difficult to find disposable income to spend $110 for registration in addition to the rising cost of transportation. Moreover, it is challenging for laborers without such benefits as paid vacation time to get two days off. Therefore Pastor Montoya has started to shorten the 'Encounter' to only one day and consolidate two similar talks into one. Now he can have the 'Encounter' all-day on a Saturday for only $40 and provide the meal in his local church. In addition, the 'Encounter' only has eight talks, and fewer leaders are needed to facilitate the 'Encounter.'

Following 'Re-Encounter' the participant is now prepared for a leadership role within the G12 – usually becoming a consolidator or cell group leader. The individuals will continue to prepare themselves once a week in the School of Leaders. The leadership classes are also taught by one of the pastor's inner circle of twelve. This process of training continues for about two years in several different levels. The School of Leaders has three levels of three months each. Then the individuals will go through three months of teacher's school where the curriculum focuses more on pedagogy. Finally, the leadership school reaches its pinnacle with two levels of seminary entitled simply: Seminary I and II. When one reaches this level, then it is expected that he or she has a cell group and is prepared to be a guide in the encounters and a teacher in the School of Leaders.

At *Iglesia de Dios Vida Nueva* in Charlotte, the G12 vision has been implemented into the life of the congregation, and they offer 'Encounters' and leadership classes to promote the vision for other churches. They offer two or three 'Encounters' and 'Re-Encounters' every year for men, women, and youth. They also offer the leadership school once a week for members of their congregation and other nearby missions who would like to enter into the vision.

Theological Analysis of David Cho

I will now transition from the ethnographic description of the methodology to a theological analysis. David Yonggi Cho attended the Full Gospel Bible College related to the Assembly of God denomination and claimed to be Christian. However, his theology has some tendencies toward shamanism, spiritualism and the self-help philosophy of 'the power of positive thinking'. In his book, *The Fourth Dimension*, Cho argues for a law of faith called 'Incubation'. He states 'the Bible says that faith is the substance of things hoped for, a substance which first has a stage of development – of incubation – before its usage can be full and effective'. Based on the 17th-century physicist Isaac Newton who said that the material world is comprised of three dimensions, Cho argues that the spiritual realm is the fourth dimension. Founded in the creation story where God creates the world *ex nihilio* (out of nothing), Cho argues that the spiritual realm has the ability to incubate or envision a new reality for the material world.[19]

> So men, by exploring their spiritual sphere of the fourth dimension through the development of concentrated visions and dreams in their imaginations, can brood over and incubate the third dimension, influencing and changing it.[20]

As the word Incubation suggests, Cho likens envisioning to a 'hen sitting on her eggs.'[21] In his book, Cho offers the example of a single woman who had prayed to God for a husband without success. When Cho asked her what traits she preferred in a husband she responded: 'Well, I don't know…may he be whatever God wills.'[22] Cho scolded her for being so vague in her prayer and instructed her to pray for specific physical, social and emotional traits. A year later Cho visited that zone of the city and learned that the woman had married to the man of her dreams.

It is well documented that Cho grew up studying Buddhism and his father was a Buddhist lay leader in his community. One of the Buddhist beliefs is that enlightenment is an individual matter and one cannot receive much help from other persons, institutions or even the gods.[23] The individual must envision his goals through meditation and eliminate all outside distractions. Cho's 'fourth dimension' metaphysics places a great deal of emphasis on the human ability to visualize the change in the physical world and influence it through prayer. His beliefs diminish the role and interaction between God's will, human responsibility and the natural sciences for understanding the physical universe.

Another influence on Cho's theology of incubation is modern psychology. In 1952 Norman Vincent Peele published *The Power of Positive Thinking*, which became a best seller and ushered in the pop psychology books known as

---

[19] Cho, *The Fourth Dimension*, 39.
[20] Cho, *The Fourth Dimension*, 39-40.
[21] Cho, *The Fourth Dimension*, 43.
[22] Cho, *The Fourth Dimension*, 39.
[23] Lewis M. Hopfe, *Religions of the World* (Upper Saddle River, NJ, Prentice Hall, 2001), 140.

'self-help'. Peele's psychology was extremely popular during Cho's formative years. Peele argues that too many people become consumed by the problems of everyday existence and do not find peace of mind and happiness. He writes that one can caste these problems from the mind and channel positive energy toward success. According to Peele, one can even overcome physical ailments and achieve physical and emotional health.[24] Cho adds onto Peele's theory of the power of positive thinking, positive speaking and positive visualization of what you want.

Theologically speaking, Cho's belief challenges the orthodox position of the sovereignty of God. When God created the world, there were no human beings present envisioning the creation. The Bible states in Genesis 1:1 'In the beginning God created heaven and earth.' God simply willed it. To assume that human beings can influence or imagine a future material change is to lift theological anthropology to the level of divine. Also, God's will is defined in the Bible as 'good, pleasant and perfect', which may not be the same thing for all people.

Cho's answer to this challenge is that God's will is too broad and emphasizes the difference between the New Testament use of '*logos*' and '*rhema*'. While *logos* is the Word of God, Cho defines *rhema* as 'a specific word to a specific person in a specific situation.'[25] Like the woman praying for a husband, her general petition to God was not answered. However, when she wrote a list of the specific traits that she desired, God rewarded her with a husband. Cho believes that it is not enough to have a general knowledge of God through the *logos*, rather we must pray for specific petitions and incubate our design into the physical realm. Cho's doctrine of the spiritual realm have power over and influencing the physical realm becomes dangerous when it deals with prosperity.

Theology of Cesar Castellanos

Cesar Castellanos has also implemented incubation theology and incorporated the *rhema* word into the theology of the G12. Meanwhile, Cho says incubate, Castellanos says: 'Dream, and you will win the world.' While a positive word can become reality in the physical realm, so then can a negative word. The tremendous influence placed on the 'Encounters' within the G12 structure is based on the undue emphasis on curses. All past sins, whether they be one's own or those of one's ancestors, are believed to have placed a curse on one's life. Before attending an 'Encounter', a new believer is not allowed any leadership in the G12 structure. Even if they have been previously baptized or have been leaders (even pastors) of other denominations, unless they have attended a G12 'Encounter' to receive spiritual liberation, then they remain under the curses of past sins. Castellanos states that 'it is absolutely vital to

---

24 Norman Vincent Peele, *The Power of Positive Thinking* (Philadelphia, Running Press), 2002.

25 Peele, *The Power of Positive Thinking*, 91.

break the chains and the power of curses.'[26] Demonology is a central tenant of Castellano's theology.

Another aspect of Castellano's theology is the tremendous emphasis and expectations for the weekend 'Encounter' experience. Orthodox theology refers to justification by faith as the moment following repentance when God's grace forgives a new believer for his or her sins. This moment has generally been referred to as conversion. Jesus emphasizes the importance of 'being born of the water and the Spirit' in his conversation with Nicodemos (Jn 3:3). The timing of justification is different in the life of each believer, and it occurs in God's time depending upon the readiness of the seeker and life circumstances. It seemed to me that the 'Encounters,' however, attempt to force the issue. Participants felt peer pressure to confess and repent for events in their past for which they may or may not have been responsible. The closed environment seemed to have the effect of 'programming' the Holy Spirit to work on a time-table whether or not the individual was prepared. The role of an 'Encounter' is so paramount in the G12 theology that it creates a dualistic 'before and after' effect. Before an 'Encounter' a new believer is under a curse and possessed, and after the 17 talks and prayers then one can begin the 'School of Leaders' and participate in leadership roles. I agree that in the life of a Christian there should be a moment of justification by faith. However, I have difficulty with the forced feel of programming when and where the Holy Spirit will work in the life of a believer.

The reason that this 'Encounter' is so necessary in the G12 theology and order of salvation is the belief in 'ancestral curses' or 'family curses'. G12 theology interprets cancer, poverty, obesity, adultery, poor self-image could be the result of a generational curse.[27] According to Cesar Castellanos, these conditions can be the result of the sins of one's ancestors, but this curse can be broken by the power of the blood of Jesus Christ during the '*Encuentro*'. Therefore if a person wants to attend a G12 church and assume leadership responsibilities, it is necessary for he or she to attend an 'Encounter' first – even if one has been baptized and been a Christian for some time.

The structure of the G12 is in the shape of a pyramid, which can lead to the monopolization of power. The pastor has a group of twelve male followers who he disciples, and in turn, each of them has twelve disciples, and so on, and so. Likewise, the pastor's wife has twelve female followers, and each of them has twelve disciples. This tiered ecclesiology creates a hierarchical structure that makes it difficult for individual followers to have access to the senior pastor or to ascend in decision-making ability or power. The whole church is organized into cell groups, and there are no other committees. So the husband and wife pastoral team at the top wield a tremendous amount of power. They may consult with their team of twelve leaders who have a great deal of influence down to the bottom rungs of the pyramid. The other followers down the chain

---

[26] Castellanos, *The Ladder of Success*, 30.

[27] Marilyn Hickey, *Break the Generation Curse: Overcoming the Legacy of Sin in Your Family* (Denver, CO: Marilyn Hickey Ministries), 1988.

do not have access to the pastors and have little influence over the decision-making process. If there is a lack of opportunity in the structure, then frustration and resentment can build up causing schisms. The lifestyles of those at the top of the structure can exacerbate these differences. A cell group leader with a following of twelve can have personal aspirations and feel that his leadership ability is underappreciated and can split from the G12 and create his own independent church.

Gender Roles in the G12

The cell structure separates the small groups according to men, women, youth, and children. According to Castellanos, co-ed cell groups did not grow as fast as the homogeneous model.[28] The G12 model believes that men should disciple men, and women should disciple women. Separation allows for gender-specific curriculum in the cell groups and limits intergenerational and cross-gender interaction. While this might be a good source of support for men and women, the content of the lessons has a tendency to encourage stereotypes and reinforce traditional gender roles. For example, men are encouraged in the G12 theology to be the spiritual guide and head of the household, while women, on the other hand, are encouraged to submit to their husbands. In a book entitled *Post-Encounter for Women*, Claudia Castellanos writes: 'The attraction God designed is specific – men towards women and women towards men, nothing else. God gave Adam a helper, the woman. She would become his support, and together they would represent a team.'[29] The G12 interprets the Bible in such a way as to reinforce the traditional gender roles in Latin America.

Although Latin American culture is changing, traditionally men and women have very gender-specific roles. In her book, *The Reformation of Machismo: Evangelical Conversion and Gender in Colombia*, Elizabeth Brusco describes the traditional roles assigned with each gender as women being homemakers and men being the breadwinners.[30] However, she acknowledges that men often spend their earnings on alcohol, gambling, and other women. Feminists have historically criticized evangelicalism as reinforcing the traditional gender roles citing Scripture (i.e., Ephesians 5:22) to justify patriarchy. Yet Brusco's study indicates that conversion can be liberating when the husband upholds his domestic responsibilities. In other words, conversion of the male partner to evangelicalism is tantamount to domestication. While Brusco's study was in Colombia, it was not specifically related to Castellanos' movement, yet it does apply to the G12's effect on gender relations, namely, that the conversion and subsequent domestication of men can actually be 'liberating' for the wives.

The flip side of the gender separation in the G12 is Claudia Castellano's emphasis on a pastoral team resulting in a higher profile for women. Mrs

[28] Castellanos, *The Ladder of Success*, 30.

[29] Claudia Castellanos, *Post-Encounter for Women* (Bogota: G12 Editors, 2004), 51.

[30] Elizabeth Brusco, *The Reformation of Machismo: Evangelical Conversion and Gender in Colombia* (Austin: University of Texas Press, 1995).

Castellano, in her own right, is not a traditional stay-at-home mother. She forms a pastoral team with her husband as preacher and workshop leader and is a senator to Colombia's National Assembly. Yet she advocates the G12 method where women are ministered to separately from men, and a pastoral team of a man and woman are needed for counselling couples. Rather than the traditional role of a male pastor playing a leadership role, and the female spouse working behind the scenes, the G12 raises the profile of the wife to '*pastora*' and partner.

Iglesia de Dios Vida Nueva in Charlotte has a pastoral husband and wife team of Luis and Marta Montoya. Following the model of Cesar and Claudia Castellanos, Luis pastors the men and Marta, the women. At times I have called, and Marta answers the phone, and she will promptly refer any questions to pastor Luis. During worship services, both will speak, lead Bible studies and prayers. Luis preaches regularly on Sunday, but Marta is always there in a prominent leadership role. They both are working and available in the church office throughout the week. Together they supervise a group of twelve couples with Luis overseeing the husbands and Marta the wives.

The G12 vision creates a unique relationship between clergy and the laity. On the one hand it embraces the Protestant slogan of 'the priesthood of all believers' and empowers lay leaders to preach, teach and counsel new believers in the cell groups. The ladder of success provides ongoing training where students learn Old Testament, New Testament, hermeneutics, homiletics, pedagogy, pastoral care, and counselling techniques – although the hermeneutical emphasis is fundamentalist and does not admit any findings from social sciences that would in anyway contradict Biblical teaching as understood by Castellanos. The teaching in these fields, especially Bible, is text-proofing as bits and pieces of theories are appropriated to support the G12 vision. So, on the one hand, the lay people are encouraged to prepare themselves to be a quasi-pastor as the leader of a cell group. Yet, on the other hand, the pyramid structure creates an accountability structure where there is always someone looking over one's shoulder who can arbitrarily contradict, correct or reprimand a cell group leader. This hierarchical structure opens the door for abuses of power – especially by the person on top. On one occasion Pastor Luis Montoya announced that their G12 advisor, John Espinosa, was coming to Charlotte and would lead a three-day workshop on cell groups. At midnight the night before departing from Bogota Castellanos called him and said that he could not go. So Espinosa called Montoya and Charlotte and told him to cancel the workshop. After Castellanos learned that the leader had cancelled the event with no protest, he called Espinosa back and said that now he could go as he was only testing his loyalty. When Espinosa arrived in Charlotte, he told this story as an example of loyalty and submitting to authority.

On another occasion, one key couple in Montoya's inner circle of twelve grew to have their own group of twelve couples, and all of them had their own group of twelve. So basically this one couple had direct supervisory influence over 144 men and 144 women. This allotted them a tremendous amount of power in a congregation of 500 members, and they started questioning

Montoya's decisions and challenging him. Last year Montoya decided to remove them from his inner circle of twelve, and they left the church taking many of their followers with them. Obviously, this was a painful departure for Montoya, and it underlines one of the weaknesses of the G12 structure, namely the hierarchical pyramid structure. Loyalty, submitting to authority and respect for one's overseer are important values in the G12 vision.

Transculturation of the G12

As anyone who has crossed borders and cultures knows, what is successful in one context is not necessarily successful in another. Very few models or structures, whether they be religious or secular, have been transplanted successfully across cultures. The cell group model of David Yonggi Cho works in the Korean context because of a natural sense of loyalty and respect for one's elders within the Korean culture. The society holds together out of veneration for one's elders and this lends itself to a cell group structure without the fear of schisms and divisions. While Cesar Castellanos went to Seoul and studied Cho's model, it did not work in Colombia because of the different cultural context. Castellanos eliminated the geographical assignment to allow for close family connections in the Latino culture that want to gather together in homes regardless of geographical location. To prevent schism Castellanos capped the group size to twelve and then divided groups before they became large enough and powerful enough to consider starting a new church. The pyramid structure and 'Ladder of Success' also keep leaders closely supervised to avoid aberrations in doctrine.

In Charlotte, Luis Montoya has also needed to make adaptations to the model to allow for the immigrant lifestyle. For example, the weekend 'Encounters' were too expensive and too long for most day laborers to afford to miss one or two days of work. Also, Montoya consolidated the number of talks from 17 into eight and adapted their content to fit the Hispanic immigrant context. Moreover, the talks encouraging believers only to buy new cars and new furniture have been adapted to the reality of immigrants who earn minimum wage. The talks calling upon believers to own their own business have been modified to fit the reality where many Hispanic immigrants are undocumented do not have the legal status to obtain a license to own their own business. Therefore, there are real material barriers that exist that cannot be overcome purely in one's individual mind, or in the spiritual sphere.

Conclusion

It is fascinating to trace the small group movement as a transnational and transcultural mission model from Seoul, Korea to Bogota, Colombia to Charlotte, NC. It defies the traditional missionary movements that moved from north to south and west to east. Yet Cho's incubation theology and Castellanos' 'dream and you will win the world' theology become problematic when understood in the hard reality of the poor and immigrant populations in the world. There are real concrete economic, racial and legal barriers for certain populations to obtain their dreams. As much as one may dream or envision a successful future, certainly obstacles are insurmountable until there are changes in the legal rights of immigrants. In the case of undocumented workers in *Iglesia de Dios Nueva Vida*, the threat of deportation is real, and the dream of owning one's home or starting a business cannot be achieved by dreaming or envisioning only in one's head until real legislative change occurs in US immigration law. Montoya wisely adapted Castellanos' dream theology not to offend or frustrate the aspirations of undocumented workers. There comes a moment where one cannot change reality only in one's mind. One must see reality as it is and work in the real world for a systemic change.

The spiritual realm is not so separate or distinct from the physical world – the two are more entwined and inter-related than Cho and Castellanos' theology acknowledge. It is unfair to new believers to give them the illusion that these harsh realities can be overcome simply by envisioning a more successful future. To narrow down the '*logos*' (collective) to '*rhema*' (individual) is to create an individualized prosperity theology and lose the collective will of God. Globalization has made previous barriers more porous, distances more accessible through technology, identities more hybrid, and created opportunities for missionary movements to move from anywhere to everywhere, but it has also exacerbated the split between the 'haves' and the 'have-nots.' It is unrealistic and unjust to offer new believers the illusion that everyone can become prosperous when there are real legal and economic barriers. It is exciting to observe new transcultural and transnational missionary movements challenging the traditional north-south colonial paradigm. However I would hope that their message would not confuse God's blessing with material prosperity.

Christian Spirituality and the Diakonic Mission of the Yoido Full Gospel Church

Younghoon Lee

The History and Growth of the Korean Church

After Catholicism was first introduced in Korea in 1784, many Catholic believers suffered persecution and martyrdom partly because of the problems that had arisen from the cultural differences between the Korean society and the Western world. Protestant Christianity was introduced in 1885, and Protestant Christians experienced no less persecution. Robert J. Thomas, a Presbyterian missionary from Wales, arrived in Korea on board the General Sherman ship in 1866 with high hopes for evangelising the country. As soon as he approached Pyongyang, however, he was arrested and beheaded in Yanggak-do's Ssuk Island in Pyongyang. He was only twenty-seven years old, and he was not able to proclaim a word of the gospel before his death.[1] He was reported as saying to his slayer, '*Yaso, Yaso*' (Jesus, Jesus) and offered him a package. It contained many copies of the Bible. However, his martyrdom was not fruitless at all. In fact, the blood of the martyrs – either the Western missionaries, or early national believers – is the very secret of how the Korean churches have been able to grow so fast in such a short time, with 12 million believers today.

In the history of the evangelisation of Korea, there is a unique feature: Korea had voluntarily sought for the gospel, even before any missionary was able to set foot on Korean soil. By the time the first Protestant missionaries reached Korea, most parts of the Bible had already been translated into Korean – either by Western missionaries, or by Korean believers who lived or studied abroad, such as in China, Japan or in the U.S. or who were international traders – so

Originally delivered at the Plenary 2, Case Study 1: Mission Worldwide on Friday, 4 June 2010 at the Edinburgh 2010 Conference and subsequently published in Kirsteen Kim and Andrew Anderson (eds), *Edinburgh 2010 Mission Today and Tomorrow*, Regnum Edinburgh Centenary Series 3 (Oxford: Regnum Books, 2011), 85-97.

[1] More detail on the martyrdom of Robert J. Thomas is available in many sources, such as Manyeul Lee, *A Study on the History of Acceptance of the Korean Christianity* [in Korean] (Seoul: Dooraesidae, 1998), 38; Kyungbae Min, *The History of the Korean Church* [in Korean] (Seoul: Yonsei University Press, 1993), 101-102, 136-139.

that the earliest missionaries to Korea were able to preach with Korean Bibles.[2] Evidence abounds to attest to the enthusiasm of the earliest Korean believers over the Christian faith with the attitude and fervour of inquirers.[3]

There is another important feature of the growth of the Korean church: the attitude of humility found both among the missionaries and national believers. For example, Rev. Henry G. Appenzeller lived a simple life based on John Wesley's famous teaching, 'sanctification, justification, and one penny a week', and dedicated himself to be a missionary to Korea at the early age of 26.[4] He came to Korea as one of the first Western official Protestant missionaries in 1885.[5] Another remarkable characteristic of Appenzeller's missionary work was his respect for local culture and the situation of Korea as much as possible. For instance, he made every effort not to violate any rule that the Korean government had set for the foreign missionaries. Consequently, he devoted himself primarily to educational activities for a considerable period of time.[6] He sat with his legs folded on the floor of the small sanctuary in Korean fashion at the first worship service at Chung-dong First Methodist Church in 1887. He powerfully demonstrated his adaptability to local Korean culture.[7] In summary, in the birth and development of the Korean churches, humility, devotion, and obedience were evident both among the missionaries and national leaders. Their resolute commitment to the scriptural teaching resulted in persecution and martyrdom.

Brief History of the Pentecostal Movement in Korea

At the beginning of the twentieth century, God poured out the Holy Spirit simultaneously throughout the whole world. In 1904, God used a young man named Evan J. Roberts to spread the fire of the Holy Spirit in the United Kingdom centred on Wales.[8] In the United States, William Seymour, a son of an African American slave, was used by God to ignite the United States and

---

[2] The Library of the British and Foreign Bible Society, *Historical Catalogues of Printed Editions of the Holy Scriptures* (London: The Bible House, 1903); M. Lee, *A Study on the History*, 38-44; K. Min, *The History of the Korean Church*, 165-167.

[3] M. Lee, *A Study on the History*, 458-68.

[4] William E. Griffis, *A Modern Pioneer in Korea: The Life Story of Henry G. Appenzeller* (New York: Fleming H. Revell Co., 1912), 70; M. Lee, *A Study on the History*, 202-49.

[5] Appenzeller, a formally appointed Methodist missionary to Korea, arrived in Korea on the Easter day (April, 5), 1885, with Horace Underwood, an appointed Presbyterian missionary. *Annual Report of the Missionary Society of the Methodist Episcopal Church*, 1885, 237; Tongshik Ryu, *A History of Chung Dong First Methodist Church, 1885-1990* (Seoul: Editorial Committee of Chung Dong First Methodist Church, 1992), 38.

[6] Jonghae Noh, *New View on the History of Korea Methodist Church* [in Korean] (Seoul: Poongman, 1988), 198-99; Tongshik Ryu, *A History of Chung Dong First Methodist Church*, 40-46.

[7] Henry G. Appenzeller, *Diary*, on October 11, 1887.

[8] Young-hoon Lee, *The Holy Spirit Movement in Korea: Its Historical and Doctrinal Development* (Oxford, UK: Regnum Books International, 2009), 27.

Europe with the Holy Spirit from his humble Azusa Street Mission from 1906 to 1909.[9] Also in South America, countries like Brazil, Chile, and Argentina experienced great Pentecostal outbreaks. India, influenced by the Wales revival movement, also experienced the flames of the Holy Spirit in the Khasa region and many other parts of India. The news of the Indian revival eventually reached the Korean Peninsula.

In 1903, Methodist missionaries invited Rev. M.C. White, who was ministering in China, for a revival meeting. White's spirituality had been shaped by the Keswick higher life movement, which emphasised the convention for the promotion of scriptural holiness.[10] In his Wonsan meeting, a strong manifestation of the Holy Spirit was felt by the participants. The revival in Wonsan had a direct influence on the Great Pyongyang Revival of 1907.[11] The Holy Spirit movement in the Korean churches started with repentance. On January 4, 1907, Pyongyang's Jangdaehyun Church, greatly inspired by the revival throughout the world, including Wales and India, held a revival meeting for two weeks.[12] People were not being changed until the end of the event. Sun-joo Gil, an elder who participated in the revival as a church leader, just led a prayer meeting. During the time of repentance, he publicly confessed his sins in front of the congregation as follows:

> I am like Achan, and because of me, you could not experience the grace of God. Once my friend pleaded with me at his dying hour and said, 'I'm dying now, and I want you to dispose of all my fortune. My wife cannot do anything because she is uneducated, so I plead with you', and with these words, he passed away. While I was disposing of his fortune, I took 100 *Won* for myself and deceived God. Early tomorrow morning I will give that money back to the widow.[13]

Gil's public repentance challenged and inspired many others to follow his example in open confession of their sins. Missionaries also joined in their own public confessions.[14] The Holy Spirit's conviction of sins was the hallmark of

---

[9] Y. Lee, *The Holy Spirit Movement in Korea*, 66-67.

[10] 'Keswick Higher Movement', in Stanley M. Burgess & Eduard M. Van Der Maas (eds), *The New Dictionary of Pentecostal and Charismatic Movements* (Grand Rapids, MI: Zondervan Publishing House, 2002), 820-21.

[11] Y. Lee, *The Holy Spirit Movement in Korea*, 25.

[12] 1910 Edinburgh World Missionary Conference described the great revival in 1907 in Korea as a 'pure Pentecostal experience': World Missionary Conference 1910, *Report of Commission I: Carrying the Gospel to All the Non-Christian World* (Edinburgh and London: Oliphant, Anderson, & Ferrier; New York, Chicago, and Toronto: Fleming H Revell, 1910), 77-80.

[13] William Newton Blair & Bruce Hunt, *The Korean Pentecost and the Suffering Which Followed* (Edinburgh: The Banner of Trust, 1977); Kwangsoo Kim, *The History of the People in Korean Christianity* [in Korean] (Seoul: Kidokgeomunsa, 1981), 140-41; for more detail on the ministry and the theology of Rev. Sun-joo Gil, see Y. Lee, *The Holy Spirit Movement in Korea*, 34-39.

[14] For instance, Rev. Hardie confessed his errors and arrogance in public and asked fellow missionaries and national Christians for forgiveness. All the participants then began to weep and repent altogether: Blair and Hunt, *The Korean Pentecost*, 71.

the Pyongyang Revival. Other manifestations of the Holy Spirit also appeared: speaking in tongues, and being slain in the Spirit until the next morning by the power of the Holy Spirit. One child was under the conviction of the Holy Spirit and repented for stealing a Chinese pancake. Soon he went back to the store and paid for it. The revival of Pyongyang's Jangdaehyun Church spread throughout the country with the characteristic repentance.[15]

Korea had to go through an extremely difficult time until its independence in 1945, and so did the church. The revival brought an explosion of the church, and its flame was continued by several revival leaders in the next four decades, although the revival itself ran its own course. Christianity, once considered a vanguard of nationalism and independence spirit, became a formidable force for the transformation of individual life. The revival has brought a unique prayer life to the Korean church, beginning with the daily early morning prayer and unison prayer traditions. They were later followed by the prayer mountain movement, weekly (usually Friday) all night prayer, and mass prayer rallies. The revival tradition laid a firm foundation for the surge of the Pentecostal movement. Korean Christianity in general, but the revival tradition in particular, also contributed to social transformation. For example, numerous campaigns promote a biblical lifestyle, including the prohibition of alcohol and smoking,[16] and taking concubines, as well as promoting a prudent life, diligence, love for farming, the purchase of national products to support industries, and many other initiatives.

David Yonggi Cho and the Yoido Full Gospel Church

God had a plan for the Holy Spirit revival not only to impact Korea, but also to spread to many parts of the world. He took a nation which went through harsh colonial rule and the pains of the Korean War (1950-1953). God also raised up an unlikely individual and his tiny congregation on the outskirts of Seoul among the poor and marginalised. This young man was David Yonggi Cho, and his Yoido Full Gospel Church has now grown to be the largest congregation in the world.[17]

The basis of the growth of Yoido Full Gospel Church is the Pentecostal Holy Spirit movement.[18] Cho started his first church at Daejo-dong, a suburban area

[15] Y. Lee, *The Holy Spirit Movement in Korea*, 29-33; K. Min, *The History of the Korean Church*, 276-81.

[16] International Theological Institute, *A Minister in Yoido: A Biography of Rev. Yonggi Cho* [in Korean] (Seoul: Seoul Logos, 2008), 232; K. Min, *The History of the Korean Church*, 266-267.

[17] Yonggi Cho launched a tent church with his five family members as church members on May 18, 1958 (Y. Lee, *The Holy Spirit Movement in Korea*, 95).

[18] Vinson Synan, *The Holiness-Pentecostal Tradition: Charismatic Movements in the Twentieth Century* (Grand Rapids, MI: Eerdmans, 1997), 287; Myung Soo Park, 'David Yonggi Cho and the international Pentecostal/ Charismatic movement', *Journal of Pentecostal Theology* 12:1 (2003), 107.

of Seoul in 1958.[19] This congregation was quickly known for claims of healing and miracles. First, an alcoholic was healed, and then two women who were deaf and blind. Even a shaman came to repent. Soon the congregation was known for speaking in tongues as the Holy Spirit gave utterance. The message was clear: sin and suffering comes from human separation from God's lordship, and thus the proper solution to any human problem is God's lordship in life. According to this belief, the gospel impacts not only the spiritual aspect of human life, but also the physical and material dimension of daily life. The Daejo-dong tent church grew to six hundred members in three years.[20]

In 1961, when the church moved from the impoverished Daejo-dong to Sudaemun, Seoul's central business district, and the work of the Holy Spirit intensified.[21] Initially, people suspected a preference of the wealthy over the marginalised. However, soon the church proved to be a sanctuary for the poor, the sick, and the socially marginal. Once a woman missionary asked Cho, 'Reverend, why are there only sick people in this church? I can't stand the smell. How can our holy Lord come to this smelly place? Try not to gather these people anymore. And go out and preach the Gospel. Teach your congregation how to take a bath'. Cho's answer to the missionary reveals his view of the church's role to the poor and suffering:[22]

> Rightly said, missionary. These people are from heaven's first complex. Why is it the first complex? Because when Jesus comes, they will be the first ones to go to heaven. It is not that these people are not cleaning themselves because they do not know how to take a bath. During the winter they have to go to a public bath for washing, but they cannot afford to as they are poor. They can only clean themselves in the summer in the Han River. As a missionary, you must know this. Do you think that Jesus ever took a bath? Foxes have holes and birds have nests, but Jesus had to sleep on the mountains and fields because He did not have a place to rest His head. Jesus could only take a bath in the Galilee beach when it rained. Jesus likes poor and smelly people because he belongs to them. Is there any greater news than healing the sick and helping the poor? Isn't this the gospel? Isn't God our healer, and healing the gospel?

Like the Daejo-dong Church, the Full Gospel Central Church was also a church for the poor and the sick. When the Holy Spirit started to work among them, their lives began to be transformed. First, there is regeneration, realising that what is visible in this world is not the full reality. People began to live with hopes of heaven, and naturally began to dedicate themselves to the Lord. They also began to live a sanctified life. Violent husbands became faithful to their wives and families, and those who always borrowed money from others started to lend and share their possessions with others. Church revival was the natural result of such dedication and service to the Lord.

---

[19] Y. Lee, *The Holy Spirit Movement in Korea*, 95-96.

[20] Y. Lee, *The Holy Spirit Movement in Korea*, 95; Frank J. Lechner and John Boli, *World Culture: Origins and Consequences* (Oxford: Blackwell Publishing, 2005), 173.

[21] Y. Lee, *The Holy Spirit Movement in Korea*, 96-97.

[22] Yonggi Cho, *A Commentary on the Gospel of Matthew* (Vol. 2) [in Korean] (Seoul: Seoul Logos, 2008), 240-42.

In 1973, Cho made another move for his church to Yoido. In this new location, the church continued its growth, but this time, increased its influence on the wider Christian world. For example, from 1977 until today, the annual Church Growth International (or CGI) conference has been held with thousands of ministers from around the world.

To provide its members with a clear identity of faith, vitality in faith and hope in life, Cho developed a theological framework later known as 'The Fivefold Gospel and Threefold Blessing'.[23] The 'Fivefold Gospel' is five principal themes of the Bible: (i) salvation (by faith); (ii) fullness of the Holy Spirit; (iii) (divine) healing; (iv) (divine) blessing; and (v) the second coming of Jesus Christ. His holistic theology of salvation found its expression in 3John 2: 'enjoy good health and that all may go well with you, even as your soul is getting along well'.[24] He tried to emphasise the fact that Jesus came to this world not only to save souls, but also to heal the sick and resolve human suffering.[25] Cho even argued that in the Gospels Jesus often treated salvation and healing as synonymous.[26]

The significance of this theological thinking is not only the new interpretation of salvation, but also its close attention to the social context where the gospel is proclaimed. The message of the fivefold gospel and threefold blessing was a message of hope to the nation, which was suffering poverty, devastation, and destruction after the Korean War. To Cho, Christian salvation is holistic, encompassing spiritual, emotional, relational, physical and material levels of human existence.[27] The work and intervention of the Holy Spirit are embodied in the message of hope, healing, miracle, and blessing based on the fivefold gospel and the threefold blessing, and this has attracted the poor and marginalised to Yoido Full Gospel Church, which has eventually grown to be the largest congregation in the world.[28] The emphasis on holistic salvation was also expressed at a corporate level when Cho revolutionised church leadership by recruiting, training, empowering and appointing women lay leaders of the church's vast network of cell groups. Considering the male-dominant social culture of Korea, this was a radical decision, but theologically it is well traced to the Pentecostal theology of empowerment.

---

[23] Prof. Jürgen Moltmann succinctly summarises and analyses Cho's 'Fivefold Gospel and Threefold Blessing' in his article 'The Blessing of Hope: The Theology of Hope and the Full Gospel of Life', *Journal of Pentecostal Theology* 13:2 (2005), 149-150; Y. Lee, *The Holy Spirit Movement in Korea*, 100-102.

[24] Y. Lee, *The Holy Spirit Movement in Korea*, 97-99.

[25] Some references to the healing ministry of Jesus are Matt 4:23; 8:2-4, 14-17, 28-34; 9:1-8, 18-26, 27-31, 32-35, and so on; for Jesus' feeding ministry, see Matt 14:13-21; 15:29-39; Mark 6:34-44; 8:1-9; Luke 9:12-17; John 6:1-13.

[26] For example, Matt 9:21,22; Mark 5:23,28,34; 10:52; Luke 8:36,48,50; 17:19; 18:42; Acts 4:9; 14:9.

[27] Cf. David Yonggi Cho, *Salvation, Health and Prosperity: Our Threefold Blessings in Christ* (Altamonte Springs, FL: Creation House, 1987).

[28] As our church moved to the Yoido area in 1973, it was renamed from Full Gospel Central Church to Yoido Full Gospel Church.

Nonetheless, it is important to note that Cho's notion of salvation until the early 1980s was focused on the personal level.

Yoido Full Gospel Church's Missionary Engagement

Yoido Full Gospel Church's missionary engagement includes salvation, engagement with society and beyond. First, the church has been strong in missionary engagement in the sense of saving souls. As a congregation committed to Pentecostal beliefs, in 1976 the church sent its first missionaries to minister to overseas Koreans. From 1993, the church has had a strong emphasis on cross-cultural mission.[29] Cho's highly publicised overseas crusades have also changed their focus from North American and European countries to Asia, Africa, Latin America and East Europe. YFGC missionaries have been establishing Bible schools throughout the world to train national workers and leaders. Today's annual World Missions Conference of the church celebrates its missionary work in many countries of the world.[30]

The cross-cultural missionary work of the church has a strong emphasis on the empowerment of national leadership. This approach is based on its reading of the Great Commission: 'Go and make disciples of all nations, baptising them in the name of the Father and of the Son and the Holy Spirit, and teaching them to obey everything I have commanded you. And surely I am with you always, to the very end of the age' (Matt 28:19-20). The core of this commandment is 'making disciples'. This is understood as Jesus' disciples going to 'all the ethnic groups' and *making* their leaders *disciples* so that they may, in turn, take this mandate to their own country and people, and beyond.[31]

Second, the church's mission vision includes the poor and suffering. As Korean society became politically stabilised and economically developed in the 1980s, the church's ministries and the focus of its mission gradually started to change. Up to this point, much of the pastoral attention was focused on spiritual regeneration and empowerment to live a victorious Christian life. As theological maturity demanded that Christians reach for a higher purpose, there was a deep process of reflection. The faith of Threefold Blessing was clarified as not self-centred teaching, but a missional commitment to bring transformation to personal and corporate life by practising Christ's ethical teachings. This theological change has given rise to several distinct ministries as a concrete expression of the theological awareness.

The church began to serve the needy in society. The initial inspiration was drawn from Acts 2:44-47 which defines the church's impact on society. The church responded to disasters, both at home and overseas, with relief programmes. In 1982, the church established a non-profit social programme

[29] Yoido Full Gospel Church, *The Fiftieth Anniversary of Yoido Full Gospel Church*, 197. To date, our church has sent 727 missionaries in 65 countries; among them are 152 native missionaries in fifty countries.

[30] Yoido Full Gospel Church, *The Fiftieth Anniversary*, 197-99.

[31] Yoido Full Gospel Church, *The Fiftieth Anniversary*, 197.

called the 'Movement of Sharing', and it supported orphanages, nursing homes, the rural poor, impoverished slums and village churches. Support was offered in various forms: voluntary workers, finance, logistics, supplies, and books. Free medical aid was given to orphans, seniors living alone, and social welfare recipients. A feeding centre was established to offer hearty meals to unattended seniors. This is a significant shift in the church's mission thinking and practice by bringing the social diakonic element into the existing mission emphasis on evangelism.

This ministry of serving is intensifying as Cho has created another instrument. Around Cho's retirement from his fifty-year pastoral ministry at the church, the 'Sharing of Love and Happiness Foundation' was created in 2008. He is now devoting himself to a worldwide social relief and development ministry. This full-thrust ministry requires not only many resources but a more fundamental theological realignment from self-centred faith to self-giving lifestyle. For this reason, the message of 'Threefold blessings' is now adapted to a godly purpose of blessing others. It is encouraging to see the wholehearted and enthusiastic support of, and participation of, the church in this ministry. As the new senior pastor, I publicly pledged my own commitment to fully support Cho's social ministry by equipping and empowering the church to be an instrument of God's transforming power of individuals and society.

Third, the church has been nurturing the future of society. Among the various ministries of social service, the church's attention to children and youth is noteworthy. In December 1982, the church constructed and donated a building complex including a dormitory and a chapel to the Holt Children Services, Inc., a major institution caring for abandoned children and arranging foster families.[32] In 1987, the church also constructed the Elim Welfare Town to provide youth with skills training while caring for homeless seniors.[33] Since 1984, the church has committed approximately 11 million dollars to underwrite the heart operations for 4,268 children. The church's role to serve society was formally recognised in 1996 by the Korean government which awarded Cho the 'Order of *Mugungwha*', the highest recognition offered to a civilian by the Korean government. This honour recognised the church's contribution to children's welfare particularly through the heart operations programme for underprivileged children and ministry to orphans.

Fourth, the church has taken an important decision to play a substantial role in the formation of public culture. This was an important theological shift on the Christian understanding of the world. Christianity is not called to stay isolated from the world, but to transform the world with the gospel teaching. In December 1988, the church began a massive media project by launching the *Kukmin Daily News*, a daily newspaper with a distinct perspective drawn from the gospel teaching.[34] It requires enormous financial, personnel and logistical

---

[32] Yoido Full Gospel Church, *The Fiftieth Anniversary*, 181. The English website of Holt Children's Services Inc. is www.holt.or.kr/holten/main/main.jsp.

[33] Yoido Full Gospel Church, *The Fiftieth Anniversary*, 185.

[34] Yoido Full Gospel Church, *The Fiftieth Anniversary*, 189.

resources. Through the prayer and financial support of the members of the church, the newspaper today has a half million daily subscribers as one of the country's top five newspapers.

The YFGC's heavy investment in education ministries is also another platform for Christianity to contribute to the public platform of national life. To cultivate committed leaders to the Christian faith, the church recognised the role of higher education. Conscientious Christian professionals can permeate the Christian principle in their workplaces, thus, contributing to national life and global world. The church transformed the former Full Gospel Theological School into Hansei University, a reputable Christian liberal arts university.[35]

Fifth, Yoido Full Gospel Church works toward bringing churches together. Just as it is taught in the book of Ephesians to make every effort to keep the unity of the Spirit (Eph. 4:3), the church has exerted every effort to create unity and agreement among the Korean churches. As Pentecostals are often blamed for creating divisions among Christians, this role is significant. Cho emphasises the personal experience of the Holy Spirit, but he seldom uses the Pentecostal term, 'the baptism of the Holy Spirit'. He prefers to use the term, 'the fullness of the Holy Spirit'. This is to prevent any theological disputes which may cause discord among denominations.[36]

I experienced the Holy Spirit of Pentecost when I was a child, and I am now here in this place to celebrate the centennial of the ecumenical movement because I share with the Holy Spirit the hope to achieve unity. Every year Yoido Church holds an international academic seminar and engages in various joint projects with churches from different denominations. I was a former director of the Theological Committee of The National Council of Churches in Korea (or NCCK), and am now serving as a co-chairperson of the Christian Council of Korea (or CCK), the national body for evangelicals. Furthermore, as the senior pastor of Yoido Full Gospel Church and as the moderator of the NCCK, I am actively involved in various kinds of ecumenical events throughout the country. The pulpit of the Full Gospel Church accommodates a wide breadth of church traditions, while I am frequently invited to speak among

---

[35] Yoido Full Gospel Church, *The Fiftieth Anniversary*, 191-93. Dr. Sunghae Kim, who is Rev. Yonggi Cho's wife, is currently the president of Hansei University (www.hansei.ac.kr/global/en/index.html).

[36] Dr. William Menzies, who is a theologian of the U.S. Assemblies of God, has often asked Rev. Yonggi Cho, who likes to use the term, 'the fullness of the Holy Spirit', to use the term, 'the baptism in the Holy Spirit' instead in public because the former is not the terminology of the Assemblies of God. However, Rev. Cho has thus far refused his request for the sake of the unity of the churches. Jack Hayford, who is a pastor of the U.S. Four Square Church suggested at the Lausanne Conference in Manila in 1989 to use the 'group of the Fullness in the Holy Spirit' instead of 'charismatic' or 'Pentecostal' churches: Russell Spittler, 'Perspectives on the Pentecostalism' in Harold Smith, *Pentecostals from the Inside Out* (Wheaton, IL: Victor Books, 1990). As long as the theological debate on the baptism in the Holy Spirit is still going on, we had better use the term 'the fullness in the Holy Spirit' for the pastoral intention to narrow the distance between denominations, and to be united as one in Christ.

a wide variety of church bodies. For example, in 2009 I delivered the opening message at the general assembly of one of the largest Presbyterian denominations as it commemorated the centennial of its mission to Jeju Island, the southern providence of the nation.

Additionally, the YFGC has participated in, and provided leadership for, many interdenominational joint projects. Every year the church records the highest number of worshippers at the Joint Easter Service. I was invited as the main preacher at the 2010 Joint Easter Service, at which more than twenty thousand believers from all different churches and denominations gathered at the City Plaza in downtown Seoul early Easter morning.

As I look back on the past century, I find it regrettable that the Holy Spirit movement and ecumenism have been regarded as mutually incompatible. In the Pentecostal movement, there have been ecumenical heroes. Seeking to achieve unity and agreement in church, David du Plessis, who is called Mr Pentecost, preached a Pentecostal message to the Pope in Rome, even though he was threatened with losing his denominational affiliation if he did so.[37] The Holy Spirit, however, is the Spirit of unity. On the instruction of the Holy Spirit, Peter risked exposing himself to criticism by entering the house of Cornelius, the Gentile, and sharing the Gospel with him (Acts 10:1-11:18). The Yoido Full Gospel Church will continue to exercise its ecumenical leadership in the coming years not only within Korea but also at the global levels.

Sixth, love and peace-building is a unique gift that Christians can offer to divided society and broken relationships. One strong motivation for the care for the poor and marginalised is to bring reconciliation in society. Often the marginalised are the victims of unequal distribution of wealth or an unjust social structure. The victims are socially wounded, or people of *han* ('grudge'), according to Korean minjung theology. Therefore, without the practice of love and peace-building, restoration of harmony and justice is simply impossible. True people of God's blessing are those who embrace their neighbours and society with Christian love to foster peace and harmony.[38] This is the goal of Yoido Full Gospel Church's Sharing of Love and Happiness Foundation.

In spite of continuing social and economic development, the Korean society is currently facing numerous social challenges. The biggest is the current tension between North and South Korea, with the steady flow of North Korean refugees to South. Other social problems are labour-management disputes, ideological divisions, an increase in marital breakdown, unwanted and abandoned children, abortions, babies born out of wedlock, low birth rates, and so on. Some of these are symptoms of the steady slide of moral values, family life, and increasing egoism, and they call for a strong role for the church. For example, the churches have a unique role in providing humanitarian support to

---

[37] Because of this, David du Plessis was deprived of his certificate of affiliation by the Assemblies of God in the USA.

[38] Yonggi Cho, 'Sharing of Love and Happiness' (Sermon at the thanksgiving worship service for the Fifty Anniversary of the Foundation of Yoido Full Gospel Church on 18 May 2008).

lessen the food shortages of North Korea. Yoido Full Gospel Church's great investment in North Korea in building a large-scale cardiac hospital is a visible expression of the church's commitment to this national agenda. Another area which demands the church's immediate missional attention is the increasing number of immigrant workers in Korea and the many problems which arise from this new social situation. Like many churches, the Yoido Full Gospel Church has developed not only an English-speaking congregation, but also services for various language groups. Often such spaces provide social networking among immigrant workers from the same country. Such a social change also provides unprecedented missionary opportunities. Many of the immigrant labourers return home now as Christians, and some with completed seminary education in Korea. Many Chinese Koreans and Taiwanese have experienced the transforming work of the Holy Spirit at Yoido Full Gospel Church. As they return, they often go home with a deep sense of the missionary mandates. Naturally, the church makes efforts to support their ministries by providing training, prayer, and financial support.

Finally, Yoido Full Gospel Church is experiencing another important mission paradigm shift. In 2005, during the church's opening service for the New Year, Cho confessed the shortcoming of his concept of holistic salvation. In his assessment, he said the message of personal salvation and social engagement is not sufficient to fulfil God's missional call. Interpreting John 3:16, he pointed out that 'God so loved the world', and the world is more than human beings.

> Just recently I found out many insufficiencies of my forty-seven years of ministry. The Bible says, 'For God so loved the world that he gave his only Son, so that everyone who believes in him may not perish but have eternal life' (NRSV). All these years, I had misinterpreted it. I understood that God so loved 'human beings', not 'the world', that he gave his only Son. What is the world? In the world, there are all things, including people, society, sky, land, ocean, plants, insects, and animals. The Bible says that God so loved the 'world' that he gave his only Son; it does not limit the scope of the world to human beings, and say that God so loved them all. 1 John 5:19 also reads that the world is under the control of the evil one. I thought that the evil one only controlled human beings, not the world, which is why my message and salvation ministry, up to now, have been restricted to human beings.[39]

He contended that his limited understanding of the scope of God's plan for salvation had kept him from participating in God's integral salvation ministry in personal, social and environmental dimensions. He believed, 'The fall of Adam is a universal event that became the origin of social evil and the decay of the environment. As a result of Adam's sin, the devil took control not only of humankind, but also of the society as well as the environment. Therefore, salvation without including our commitment to care for the ecosystem cannot be considered holistic salvation'. Cho declared, 'From this New Year [that is, the year 2005], we will bring about the salvation of our souls, get rid of social

[39] Yonggi Cho, 'Sermon at the Opening Service for the New Year 2005'.

evils, and actively work toward environmental protection'. This shift toward stewardship of God's creation has since had a strong impact on each member of the church, and its mission policies and practices. This message was welcomed by many scholars from within and without. Prof. Jürgen Moltmann, for instance, learned of Cho's message and completely supported his 'shift in policy' by sending Cho an e-mail message. Moltmann said, 'If the Yoido Full Gospel Church can save souls, save society and restore the environment, then I can assure you that this church can be a church that will embrace the world'.[40]

The Best Way…

Having surveyed the formation of the Holy Spirit movement in Korea and the missionary engagement of the Yoido Full Gospel Church, several points deserve our attention. The shift in mission and pastoral ministry of the YFGC does not imply any change in the traditional Pentecostal understanding of the person and work of the Holy Spirit. Experience of the fullness of the Holy Spirit is all the more required to fulfil the church's mission to bring good news to the poor and the sick (Luke 4:18-19). The book of Acts teaches us that supplying one another's needs in the early church was a natural expression of hearts filled with the Holy Spirit. In fact, without the transforming work and power of the Holy Spirit, no true change can be possible, ranging from spiritual regeneration to behavioural change and social transformation. Without the Holy Spirit touching our hearts, we cannot even practise love. This is the true expression of the Spirit's empowering presence. The missionary work of the church will continue to anchor itself on belief in the Holy Spirit.

When I look back on modern Pentecostal history, I cannot but acknowledge the criticism of Pentecostals' spirit of triumphalism. The glowing success in missionary work and the exponential spread of the Pentecostal movement may have contributed to this perception. However, the truth is that all missionary work is the work of the Holy Spirit and it has been done only through the grace of God. Thus, one should humble oneself and approach ministries with the spirit of *humility*. We must glorify God alone, and our confession should be 'We are unworthy servants. We have only done our duty' (Luke 17:10b). We are only messengers of the gospel of the cross and God's love. God empowered us to achieve his goal faithfully. We at Yoido Full Gospel Church will recognise this point and will do our best to bring God's message of salvation and love in the power of the Spirit with the heart of humility. So may God help us all to be faithful to our missionary call.

[40] The entire content of Prof. Moltmann's email is in the 13 February 13 2005 issue of the *Full Gospel Family Newspaper* (www.fgnews.co.kr/).

Holistic Ministry of the Pentecostal Church

Julie C. Ma

Introduction

Pentecostals have traditionally maintained their unique belief that the empowerment of the Holy Spirit is for the preaching of the gospel. However, in recent decades, they have broadened the concept and scope of mission to include social issues.[1] One immediate challenge, then, is how Pentecostals can continue to maintain their evangelistic commitment and passion, while existing as contributing members of society. This will require a rather substantial shift in their mission thinking and practice. This can be seen in two larger contexts. First, since the Lausanne Congress in 1974, Evangelicals have struggled to maintain the two 'pillars' of Christian mission in healthy tension, between proclamation and social service.[2] Secondly, Pentecostal believers and churches have been trying to respond to challenges brought about by rapid social changes. They are trying hard to minister particularly to the socially marginalised and vulnerable.

One of the immediate goals of today's Pentecostal mission engagement, especially in the social context of the global South, is achieving a peaceful living environment as God's missional people to the world. Today, Pentecostal churches and missionaries are involved in a broad spectrum of social work such as HIV/AIDS intervention and care, serving the hungry and destitute, media, education, relief work, and others. The rise of such 'progressive Pentecostals'[3]

Originally published in R. Dowsett, I. Phiri, D. Birdsall, D.O. Terfassa, Hwa Y., and K. Jorgensen (eds), *Evangelism and Diakonia in Context*, Regnum Edinburgh Centenary Series 32 (Oxford: Regnum Books, 2016), 107-119.

[1] Wonsuk Ma, '"When the Poor are Fired Up": The Role of Pneumatology in Pentecostal Charismatic Mission', *Transformation* 24 (January 2007), 29.
[2] See the *Manila Manifesto* of the Lausanne Movement on affirmations of the *Lausanne Covenant*: www.lausanne.org/manila-1989/manila-manifesto.html and Rose Dowsett's article in this volume.
[3] A term adopted by Donald E. Miller and Tetsunao Yamamori, *Global Pentecostalism: The New Face of Christian Social Engagement* (Los Angeles, CA: University of California Press, 2007).

may have contributed in part to the rise of Pentecostal Christianity in the global South where the church is compelled to engage in the daily struggles of people. This does not diminish, however, the Pentecostals priority in proclaiming the gospel. They somehow find ways to embrace the new, not at the cost of the old. In fact, such social works are a significant means of bringing people to Christ, thus serving both goals.

This study will introduce and discuss a number of selected social works which Pentecostal churches and missionaries have undertaken in different locations, especially in engaging with the marginalised. Three out of five are, or were, led by nationals, and two by missionaries. Two are led by women, and three by men. The challenges which each ministry takes up as a mission task are different from one another, but they all aimed at, and resulted in, the transformation of lives and communities.

The Orphanage Work in Egypt

Lillian Trasher (1887-1961) was an early Pentecostal believer from the United States. She once met Mattie Perry who ran the Faith Orphanage in Marion, North Carolina. Having shared how the orphanage was managed, Perry surprisingly invited her to work in his orphanage, which, according to him, was a faith operation.

As Lillian gained experience working in the orphanage, her trust in God was tested in the supply of daily needs. She entered a Bible school in Cincinnati, Ohio, to prepare herself for ministry.

Lillian had a strong desire for mission, and spent much time in prayer to discern God's guidance. At that time, she was engaged to a young Christian, Tom Jordan. Ten days before their wedding in June 1910, she attended a worship service to hear a missionary from India. In the meeting, the Holy Spirit clearly spoke to her to go into mission. As her fiancée did not share her missionary call, she had to make the excruciating choice to break off her engagement with him.[4] And yet, she did not find any country open to her. Shortly after having a concerted time of prayer, God opened the door to Egypt. Lillian arrived in Egypt on 10th November 1910. After settling in Asyut, she had a desire to start an orphanage, though there was no funding, nor anyone who promised to support her project.

Lillian approached several people for help, and the first funds she received was thirty-five cents. It was just enough for one day's food supply for herself. She survived entirely on faith, and she journeyed on a donkey to different areas to visit churches to ask them to help the children. Government officers were astounded that no one tried to hurt her or threaten her life.[5] The miraculous

[4] Kelly Boxer Sagert, *Inspirational Christians: Lillian Trasher Biography*: www.inspirationalchristians.org/biography/lillian-trasher – 2015.

[5] Since she was a white woman, ill-intended men could easily have attacked her. *Assemblies of God World Missions-Eurasia: Orphanage Celebrates 100 Years:* http://worldmissions.ag.org/regions/eurasia/__.cfm?targetBay=4bab7a5e-cb12-48a0-878

provision was made by a local businessman for her to purchase property for an orphanage.[6] In 1915, an orphanage was started with a few children, and by 1916 the number of fifty children outgrew the facility. An adequate place to house them became an urgent priority, but she had no funds available. She hatched a plan to make bricks by using the labour of the children.[7]

By 1941, the orphanage had grown in number so that every day 2,700 meals were served and in the 1960s the number of children had increased to 1,500, and she served 4,500 meals each day, on a site that consisted of more than eleven buildings.[8] Lillian provided accommodation even for widows who had lost their husbands and had nowhere to live.

Lillian's essential desire was for a spiritual awakening. She prayed for a long period for this to take place among the orphans and widows. In 1927, there was an unusual spiritual occurrence that took place at an evening devotional meeting, when children and widows experienced a moving of the Holy Spirit. She was reading a passage from the Bible and explained its meaning to them when suddenly a number of them began to weep and, kneeling down, they openly repented of their sins to God and asked him for forgiveness. The gathering went on at length into the night.[9]

Lillian devoted most of her adult life, fifty years to be precise, to take care of children and women in Egypt. This missionary, affectionately identified as 'Mama Lillian', or 'Mother of the Nile', went home to be with the Lord on 17th December 1961.[10] The orphanage has provided a comfortable home, hope, Bible teaching, and training to more than 25,000 children throughout its one hundred years of operation. Currently, it is one of the biggest and best orphanages in the world.

HIV/AIDS Intervention and Care and the 'Lazarus Project Care for Street Children' in Zambia

Since 1992, Joshua Banda, the senior pastor of Northmead Assembly of God Church in Lusaka, has experienced events that led to a paradigm shift in his mission thinking and practice. As a typical Pentecostal minister, he was awakened to the social responsibility of the church only recently. In his study entitled 'The role of the church in crime prevention',[11] he presented a

8-486b7cfbbfb7&Process=DisplayArticle&RSS_RSSContentID=18467&RSS_OriginatingChannelID=1164&RSS_OriginatingRSSFeedID=3689&RSS_Source

[6] *Assemblies of God World Missions – Eurasia: Orphanage Celebrates 100 Years.*

[7] Janet and Geoff Benge, *Lillian Trasher: The Greatest Wonder in Egypt* (Seattle, WA: YWAM, 2004), 93-94.

[8] Christie Florence, *Called to Egypt* (Wichita Falls, TX: Western Christian Foundation, 1997), 44.

[9] Benge, *Lillian Trasher,* 138-39.

[10] *Assemblies of God World Missions – Eurasia: Orphanage Celebrates 100 Years.*

[11] Joshua Banda, 'Engaging with the Community: The Fight against AIDS', in Brian Woolnough (ed), *Good News from Africa: Community Transformation through the Church* (Oxford: Regnum, 2013), 41.

soul-searching question: 'Is the church actually involved in a crime prevention ministry?' It was evident that this was an unexplored area of mission. With a disturbed heart, he offered prayer to God, asking for his help and new ideas.

From 1992, he has been involved in a holistic ministry providing care for HIV/AIDS patients and their families. He was well aware that the church's response to this pandemic had to be holistic, encompassing spiritual, medical, educational, social and community care. In 1999, he began to care for street children, most of whom were AIDS orphans, and gradually other work followed. As a nation, Zambia's future was threatened by a growing rate of AIDS infections. According to a 2011 UNICEF report, AIDS patients in Zambia consisted of 337,316 adults and 43,625 children.[12] It became an urgent concern for the government and social sectors.

The Circle of Hope was established in September 2005 to provide Christian-based prevention and holistic care for HIV/AIDS patients, including free anti-retroviral treatment (ART), and their families.[13] Openness to the test is the most difficult and yet most crucial part of HIV/AIDS prevention and care. They also expressed their sincere desire to contact people who were in similar situations. With their consent, the church began a specialised ministry among those who were infected with HIV/AIDS.[14] It was reported:

> To date, COH has counselled and tested over 7,429 people, of whom 5,326 are HIV-positive and have been enrolled in care. Of the number that are positive, 2,310 are currently on full ART, of which 516 are children. A group in excess of 200 community adherence personnel, care givers and counsellors have sensitised, educated and monitored clients on treatment in their homes. Approximately 80 people visit the COH Centre per day, while 120 patients are enrolled monthly.[15]

The Health Care Association of Zambia, to which Banda's Northmead Assembly's programme belongs, accounts for over 50% of healthcare provision in the nation.[16] Christian intervention in AIDS by local congregations has made a substantial impact on society. As a result, Banda was invited to lead the National AIDS Council in 2007.[17]

The Lazarus Project is another social care programme of the church. It provides holistic care to orphans and vulnerable children.[18] As the years went by, the Lazarus Project developed into a community of seventy former street children, providing its own housing with a 40-acre farm. Using a vigorous family search programme, relatives of most of the rehabilitated children were

---

[12] UNICEF, 'HIV & AIDS: Key Statistics': www.unicef.org/zambia/5109_ 8459.html
[13] Banda, 'Engaging with the Community', 48.
[14] Banda, 'Engaging with the Community', 49.
[15] Banda, 'Engaging with the Community', 49.
[16] Banda, 'Engaging with the Community', 42.
[17] Wonsuk Ma, 'A Pentecostal Reflection on Christian Unity in the New Christian Millennium'. Paper presented at Global Forum for the Future of World Christianity, Jeju, Korea, May 2015), 2. See also 'A Changing Africa', Joshua Banda 1/1: https://www.youtube.com/watch?v=p3cB63qmoew – 2012.
[18] Banda, 'Engaging with the Community,'44.

traced. While the farm community helps the children to readjust to the social system, approximately fifty children were reunited with their relatives towards the end of 2005. To date, almost 1,000 orphans and vulnerable children have gone through its training, with amazing stories of transformation.[19]

Both programmes have been providing a wide range of care and help to the most vulnerable in society. Through all these programmes, the power of the gospel is central. Banda, his church, and various ministries are all inspired and motivated by the gospel mandate. They also regularly share the good news of Jesus with HIV/AIDS patients, their families and the children under their care. In fact, the proclamation of the gospel and responding to the immediate needs of the vulnerable have been going hand-in-hand from the very beginning.[20]

Female Education in Burkina Faso

The rate of female education is among the lowest in Burkina Faso, as in other Sahel area countries. 'Reports tend to support the view that this situation is also true, especially of some Francophone West African countries.'[21] In many countries and throughout many societies, there is an essential cultural prejudice in favour of boys. Girls have only a tiny chance to receive an education, and it consequently limits female involvement in areas of child care, nutrition, physical work, freedom of movement and marriage.[22]

The earliest Assemblies of God missionaries, Harold Jones, and his wife came to Burkina Faso in January 1921. They were warmly welcomed by the Mossi king Naaba Koom II, who offered them a property to begin their mission at Gounghin, currently Sector 8 of the capital Ouagadougou. They established educational programmes for literacy, evangelistic work, and 'economic development.'[23] Their educational programme was mainly informal to help girls and women to read and write.[24] Later, churches were significantly involved in education.

> Sixty years later that church influences 50% of the private Evangelical schools. The 2006 results paper shows that 33 Assemblies of God schools represented 77.91% of the national primary schools. The national records in 2006 had 99 private Protestant schools of which 50% are related to the church, individuals or NGOs who opened schools with the Christian ethos. This indicates what an important role the church is playing in formal primary education. The remaining

---

[19] Banda, 'Engaging with the Community,'45. Numerous similar accounts are found in Miller and Yamamori, *Global Pentecostalism*.

[20] Joshua Banda, 'A Request' (email message to the author, 9th September 2015).

[21] Philippe Ouedraogo, *Female Education and Mission: A Burkina Faso Experience* (Oxford: Regnum, 2004), 2.

[22] C. Brock and N.K. Cammish, *Factor Affecting Female Participation in Education in Seven Developing Countries*, 2nd ed (London: DFID, 1997), 21.

[23] Ouedraogo, *Female Education and Mission,* 44.

[24] Ouedraogo, *Female Education and Mission,* 44.

> 50% of schools comes from other denominations and church leaders, families and associations.[25]

Philippe Ouedraogo, an Assemblies of God leader, began to be involved in girls' education in 1991 through his congregation. In the same year, the Association Evangélique d'Appui au Développement (AEAD), under his leadership, signed an agreement with the National Institute of Literacy. This initiative was a response to the low literacy rate of the nation, as AEAD was seeking to bring its contribution to the national need for female education.[26] In 1992, different churches, mission organisations and Christian non-governmental organisations (NGOs) came together under AEAD to strategise the Christian response to national education needs.[27] This provided an important platform for various Christian entities to bring their experiences and resources together for co-operative work. Their educational work was its focus:

> Since 2006, an intense and accelerated nine-month educational programme [called 'Speed School'] has been set up in the northern region of the nation, where about 80% of its population is Islamic. By 2012, a total of 2,255 boys and girls between 9 and 12 years of age, who had missed their opportunity for elementary education, had completed this programme. After the nine-month fast track programme, 90% of them achieved the three-year equivalent of a formal elementary education, when they are placed in public schools.[28] In addition, local churches run formal schools under AEAD, and an overwhelming majority of the 5,035 students in 2008-2009 were girls (or 62.5%).[29]

Churches soon realised that education was a great means of bringing children to Christ. Between 2012 and 2015, there were about 342 conversions to Jesus Christ, consisting of 153 girls and 189 boys from the Speed School.[30] In other schools like the Protestant College in Ouagadougou, over 700 students came to Christ within the academic year 2014-15. AEAD currently operates eleven schools where more than 5,000 children and adults receive their education, while hearing the good news of Jesus Christ.[31]

The co-operative work of this interdenominational network has proved to have real potential for changing the future of the country. Tertius Zongo, the former Prime Minister, endorsed this education programme as an 'innovative way to improve female education', swaying the government's strategies, making an input to a 'gender balance', and encouraging the use of the 'national

---

[25] Ouedraogo, *Female Education and Mission*, 47.

[26] P. Ouedraogo, 'A request'. Email sent to the author, 1st September 2015.

[27] Ma, 'A Pentecostal Reflection on Christian Unity', 1.

[28] Ma, 'A Pentecostal Reflection on Christian Unity', 1.

[29] Ma, 'A Pentecostal Reflection on Christian Unity', 1.

[30] Philippe Ouedraogo, 'Transforming Community through Education', in *Good News from Africa*, 87. It explains that Speed School is 'aimed at those youngsters, aged 9-12, who have missed out on primary education and are thus not able to enter the national formal education schooling'.

[31] Ouedraogo, 'A request', states that this information on the Protestant College of Ouagadougou was reported on 26th August 2015 in the Assemblies of God Executive meeting by the Principal, Emmanuel Kalkoundo.

language in education'. The quality of its education was highly praised: '... the schools continually dominate in the national examination league tables.'[32] The influence of change provided by the churches working hand-in-hand has inspired wider cooperation together with Catholics and Muslims. The effectiveness of Ouedraogo's passion for girls' education and his leadership in bringing various Christian bodies together have affected national education policies. AEAD's education programme has now been handed over to the government and has become a nationwide programme.[33]

Integral Mission in India

Pandita Ramabai (1858-1922) was described as an Indian female Christian[34] 'reformer, Bible translator and social activist, particularly involved in the revival movement in her mission'. Ramabai turned to God from the Brahmin caste by vetoing the Hindu 'propriety' and marriage system. She had been widowed with her daughter less than two years after her marriage. She began to attend a church during her three-year stay in England where she studied education at Cheltenham Ladies' College. During this time, in 1883 she was baptised in the Church of England. Later she obtained her degree in education in America.[35]

She came back to India in 1889 after her studies, and pioneered a ministry for widows close to Bombay (now Mumbai), which after a year was moved to Pune. In 1895, she started a mission on a farm she had purchased at Kedgaon, close to Pune. By this time, she had changed her work from a 'religiously neutral' offering to an explicitly 'evangelical Christian organisation'.[36] This change had a devastating effect: her support from Hindu parents vanished, followed by the resignation of her committee. Ramabai and her working team named this mission 'Mukti', which means 'salvation'. Its primary aim was to offer shelter for deprived girls and young women. Many of them had suffered from child marriages, and had become widows. Others were rescued from starvation due to a shortage of food. There were 48 young women and girls in 1896, but throughout that year, 300 girls were liberated from starvation in Madhya Pradesh. By 1900, nearly 2,000 people were cared for.[37] This mission

---

[32] Tertius Zongo, 'Foreword' to Philippe Ouedraogo, *Female Education and Mission: A Burkina Faso Experience* (Oxford: Regnum, 2014), xiii.

[33] Ma, 'A Pentecostal Reflection on Christian Unity', 2.

[34] See Allan Anderson, *Spreading Fires: The Missionary Nature of Early Pentecostalism* (London: SCM, 2007), 77: 'Ramabai is both significant in the origins of Pentecostalism and in the acceptance of its phenomena among some in the wider Christian community. The importance of her revival movement is born out by the prominence given to it in reports in the emerging Pentecostal press, both in India and especially in Britain and North America.'

[35] Anderson, *Spreading Fires*, 77.

[36] Anderson, *Spreading Fires*, 77.

[37] Jessie H. Mair, *Bungalows in Heaven: The Story of Pandita Ramabai* (Kedgaon, India: Pandita Ramabai Mukti Mission, 2003), 87-88.

had become famous overseas by 1905 before revival took place.[38] Ramabai was convinced that Hindu women could experience complete liberty by coming to Christ. At the same time, her mission provided training in income-generating skills.[39] Ramabai's solid mission vision progressed, regardless:

> But by 1907 the Mission had expanded to include a rescue mission, a hospital, an oil-press, a blacksmith forge, a printing press, a complete school that provided college entrance training, a school for the blind, and training departments in teaching, nursing, weaving, tailoring, bread and butter making, tinning, laundering, masonry, carpentry and farming. [40]

Ramabai had a strong belief in and experience of the work of the Holy Spirit. She once expressed, 'I found it a great blessing to realise the personal presence of the Holy Spirit in me, and to be guided and taught by Him.'[41] Later she developed a strong desire to be 'filled with the Spirit' to 'enter into a new experience of God's power to save, bless and use'.[42] After learning of the Welsh Revival and the Australian revival led by R.A. Torrey, in 1904 she communicated with Manoramabai and Minnie Abrams to learn the necessary elements of a revival. Through this interaction, she became convinced that prayer and 'pouring out your life' were the key components for revival.[43] In January 1905 Ramabai started a 'special early-morning daily prayer meeting, where 70 women would meet and pray'. She expressed her commitment 'for the true conversion of all the Indian Christians including ourselves, and for a special outpouring of the Holy Spirit on all Christians of every land'. The number of people who attended this daily prayer meeting steadily went up to 500. The revival continued for a year and a half, and resulted in '1,100 baptisms at the school, confessions of sins and repentance, prolonged prayer

---

[38] Rajas K. Dongre and Josephine F. Patterson, *Pandita Ramabai: A Life of Faith and Prayer* (Chennai, India: Christian Literature Society, 1963), 13-18.

[39] See Anderson, *Spreading Fires,* 77; and S.M. Adhav, *Pandita Ramabai* (Chennai, India: Christian Literature Society, 1979), 114-15: 'Ramabai became nationalistic because of the repression of "British rulers" and their arrogance towards Indian social structures…' 'She was a dedicated ecumenist before the word was coined in the twentieth century, deploring the divisions within Christianity and pleading for a united Indian church.' See also R.E. Hedlund, *Quest for Identity: India's churches of Indigenous origins – the 'Little Tradition' in Indian Christianity* (Chennai and Delhi, India: Mylapore Institute for Indigenous Studies and Indian Society for Promoting Christian Knowledge, 2000), 160: 'Gauri interprets Ramabai's conversion as a quest for intellectual and spiritual freedom… Ramabai set about "refashioning Christianity to her own requirements," says Gauri. If so, it is not surprising that in Ramabai one finds an incipient Indian Christian nationalism expressed in a critique of missionary paternalism and rejection of colonial control.'

[40] *Mukti Prayer-Bell* (Kedgaon, India: Pandita Ramabai Mukti Mission, 1907), 21-22.

[41] Dongre and Patterson, *Pandita Ramabai: A Life of Faith and Prayer,* 18, 24.

[42] Anderson, *Spreading Fires,* 79.

[43] Gary McGee, 'Minnie F. Abrams: Another Context, Another Founder', in James R. Goff, Jr. and Grant Wacker (eds), *Portraits of a Generation* (Fayetteville, AR: University of Arkansas Press, 2002), 87-104.

meetings and the witnessing of 700 of these young women going out in teams into the surrounding areas'. She also began a 'Bible school' of 200 young women to form 'Praying Bands' to pray and 'to be trained in witnessing to their faith'.[44] According to Ramabai's knowledge, no revival such as this took place before 1905.

Latin America Childcare

Latin America Childcare (LACC) was started in 1963 by John Bueno, an American who spent much of his time in Chile, pastoring the Centro Evangelistico, San Salvador. He had a strong desire to help children move away from their chronic cycle of deficiencies. The children made up 50% of Latin America's population, half of them underprivileged, frequently malnourished and without fundamental health provision. One-third of them had no access to education. LACC was intended to offer an 'institutional alternative' to these children. The first school, named Liceo Cristiano, was started in February 1963 with 152 children in Sunday school classrooms in several churches. This venture was effective from the beginning. Initially offering primary-level education, it soon added schools of a higher level with a considerable number of students enrolled.[45]

Liceo Cristiano and several other schools throughout Central America operated totally on their own funds, only occasionally receiving fairly small help from outside, normally for classroom goods and supplies. Years later, a three-storey school building was erected. In its inaugural ceremony, members of the large church were recognised for providing funds for the building project.[46]

Liceo Cristiano expanded by launching a satellite campus in 1973 in El Granjero. It was a slum area populated by refugees of civil war in the countryside. This extension started with 300 students, and in 1976 another campus was established in Candelaria. In 1977, an additional school was started in *Soyapango*, a suburb of San Salvador.[47] In 1983, Liceo Christiano acquired a university charter to offer professional programmes in education. Eventually, over 50% of the institution's over 500 teachers received their professional degrees from Universidad Christiana de El Salvador.[48]

The dream of helping the children in the slum area led to the opening of Liceo Cristiano of El Salvador. In turn, this led to the founding of LACC or Programa integral de educacion de las Asambleas de Dios (PIEDAD) in

[44] Anderson, *Spreading Fires,* 79.
[45] D. Petersen, *Not by Might nor by Power: A Pentecostal Theology of Social Concern in Latin America* (Oxford: Regnum, 1996), 152-55.
[46] Petersen, *Not by Might nor by Power,* 155-56.
[47] José Alfredo Guerrero, 'Origin, Desarrollo Y Filosofia de los Liceos Christianos', SIEELA (San Salvador, El Salvador: Documents of PIEDAD, 1984), 1-3.
[48] Petersen, *Not by Might nor by Power,* 157.

November of 1977.[49] Between 1978 and 1985, the educational programmes of LACC stretched from Belize, Costa Rica, Guatemala and Honduras, to Panama and Nicaragua, and are now in eighteen countries in Latin America.[50]

Pentecostal Theological Reflection on Wholeness

As a general perception would suggest, Pentecostals have given much attention to the salvation of souls as its mission priority. However, this does not necessarily reflect a narrow view of mission. In their relatively short history, Pentecostals have intuitively demonstrated their holistic view of life, the gospel, and mission. It is true that Pentecostal mission theology starts with the significant work of the Holy Spirit and encompasses not only soul-saving but also (physical) healing. An equally significant practice is the miraculous intervention of the Holy Spirit in human needs, which includes physical and material, as much as spiritual, relational and circumstantial needs. Although not fully developed in an articulated mission theology, this points to the life-giving work of the Holy Spirit, evidenced from the very beginning of history (or from Genesis). This includes life-sustaining and life-restoring.

Several Pentecostal missionary practices, such as Teen Challenge, reveal a theological logic in dealing with the destitute (or, in Teen Challenge, for example, drug addicts in urban centres). As the current state of human sinfulness began from rebellion against God, its undoing will have to begin with the spiritual realm of human existence.[51] That is one reason why Pentecostal mission takes conversion seriously. Once the relationship with God is restored, the logic contends, the effect of God's redemption expands to behaviour, physical wholeness, work habits, family life, and morality. This partly explains the upward social mobility that is observed among Latin American Pentecostals.[52]

The vision of individual and communal restoration through the Holy Spirit is at the heart of Pentecostal mission. It encompasses a full spectrum of life – from spiritual and physical restoration to emotional, mental and communal *shalom*. Isaiah 32 explicitly presents this vision as the work of God's Spirit:

> ... until a spirit from on high is poured out on us, and the wilderness becomes a fruitful field, and the fruitful field is deemed a forest. Then justice will dwell in the wilderness, and righteousness abide in the fruitful field. The effect of righteousness will be peace, and the result of righteousness, quietness, and trust forever. My people will abide in a peaceful habitation, in secure dwellings, and in quiet resting places (Is. 32:15-18).

[49] Petersen, *Not by Might nor by Power,* 158.

[50] Petersen, *Not by Might nor by Power,* 160.

[51] Wonsuk Ma, '"When the Poor Are Fired Up": The Role of Pneumatology in Pentecostal-Charismatic Mission', *Transformation*, 24:1 (Jan 2007), 28-34.

[52] David Martin, *Tongues of Fire: The Explosion of Protestantism in Latin America* (Oxford: Blackwell, 1990), 90-92.

Jeremiah 33:6 similarly envisions the restoration of the city of Jerusalem in the language of healing: 'I will bring health and healing to it [the city, Jerusalem]; I will heal my people and will let them enjoy abundant peace and security…' Here lies a theological challenge for Pentecostal mission:

> If Pentecostals develop the theological capability to apply their prized heritage of healing to broken families, relationships, divided churches and societies, racial conflicts and moral decay, the impact of Pentecostal mission will be unimaginable.[53]

Pentecostals have brought into the world of mission a radical set of gifts, and we need to celebrate this. One of them is definitely the holistic vision of God's mission. At the same time, especially in theological exploration and articulation, its practice has not been matched by a corresponding reflection. For example, in reconciliation or church unity as God's mission, Pentecostals have been either indifferent and uninterested in such important aspects of God's mission, or even responsible for many divisions (of the church). It is the Holy Spirit who plays a crucial role in reconciling humans with God through the death of Christ, and this should cause the people of the Spirit (as Pentecostals claim) to want to take reconciliation as an integral part of its missionary thinking and practice. The implications, such as creation care, can go on and on. The Pentecostal idea of mission is integral and holistic, but its practice appears otherwise, with a strong emphasis on evangelism, perhaps fuelled by its eschatological expectation in the early years. Pentecostal mission now faces an immediate challenge for theological reflection to articulate its holistic vision.

Conclusion

This study gives five examples of holistic Pentecostal ministries in different countries, combining the proclamation of the gospel and social works. There is a common perception among Evangelicals that Pentecostal churches or missions tend to focus on only one side, declaring the gospel, ignoring the social aspect. But these case studies strongly suggest that, even from the initial period of its existence, Pentecostals have been consistently conscious of both proclamation and social work, even if their concern and awareness for social involvement have increased during recent decades.

Lillian Trasher, a single lady, wholeheartedly committed herself to mission in Asyut, Egypt. Her loving passion for the destitute caused her to embrace hungry and abandoned children, and to provide food and shelter. Joshua Banda's ministries for HIV/AIDS patients in society made a significant impact, not only on the community but also on the nation. He, a Spirit-filled pastor of a Pentecostal church, developed a mission strategy that extending a helping hand to those struggling with deadly disease and daily survival is at the very heart of mission. Philippe Ouedraogo's involvement in female education has affected

[53] Julie C. Ma and Wonsuk Ma, *Mission in the Spirit: Towards a Pentecostal/Charismatic Missiology* (Oxford: Regnum Books, 2010), 25.

the national education programmes of Burkina Faso, where girls have much less chance for education than boys. His education programme set a benchmark for the national education policies.[54] Pandita Ramabai in India strongly felt an urgent need to provide women suffering deprivation with a means of escaping the cycle of poverty. Her work for underprivileged women was noteworthy in empowering them to regain their self-respect. Ramabai's early morning prayer meetings for revival with seventy women were remarkable, and countless believers experienced the outpouring of the Holy Spirit. Latin American Child Care, established by John Bueno for the education of underprivileged children, made a huge impact in Latin America.

Having discussed these examples, it would be appropriate to offer an analysis of the features they have in common. First, the main players were Spirit-filled leaders. All of them considered prayer as a crucial part of their ministry planning and execution. They were deeply interested in the root causes of suffering, including the spiritual aspects. Their ministries were marked by strong spiritual activities. Secondly, all these examples have been taken from the global South. Poverty and oppression call Pentecostal believers to immediate action. Thirdly, their level of commitment to ministering to the suffering stands out. This can be attributed to the empowering role of the Holy Spirit for witness. Each one of them made a strong commitment to fulfilling their God-given tasks. Such committed dedication bears marvellous fruit, not only in the success of such ministries, but also in the holistic transformation observed in all these examples. Fourthly, social works prove to be an effective means of evangelism. In fact, as the *Lausanne Covenant* states, proclamation and social service are 'partners' in mission. Actions sometimes speak louder than words. Many non-believers have seen and experienced the loving care of the church. Fifthly, although not evident in all these examples, social works with a strong spiritual emphasis have the potential for triggering spiritual and social renewal. Ramabai's ministry became the epicentre of a significant revival which predates the Azusa Street Revival in 1906. In a similar way, Trasher's daily evening devotions led to the experience of the Holy Spirit among the children. Some, after their spiritual revival, reached out to other children with the gospel. As a result, many people came to Christ. Lastly, social works have the power to provide opportunities for ecumenical relationships and inter-religious dialogue for work among different churches and with other religions. Female education in Burkina Faso witnessed co-operation with Muslim authorities in providing education for girls. After all, the Holy Spirit is the Giver of life, and so Pentecostals, the people of the Holy Spirit, should be in the forefront of the flourishing of such life.

[54] Zongo, 'Foreword'.

The Emerging Church in Africa and Holistic Mission: Challenges and Opportunities

Nicta Lubaale

Introduction

Holistic mission is given many understandings, from linking the gospel with social services to linking the gospel with social justice and to being a prophetic voice in various realities that require change. This chapter explores the nature of holistic mission in a group of churches in Africa I refer to as 'emerging church', but which are also called African Independent, African Instituted, and African indigenous churches. I will be looking at three categories of emerging church: the 'nationalist' churches and the Spiritual churches (which by and large emerged in the colonial period), and the newer Pentecostal churches. The Pentecostal churches I will be referring to are those who fall in the category of community-based churches, and I will be using this term to refer to all the other churches because the given definition fits all of them. All these churches have their own distinct ways of doing mission, but they have two common traits. They are engaged in community building in sectors of society that are largely excluded from the benefits of the formal economy, and they are in most cases led by people who are as vulnerable to poverty as their followers.

Initiatives in Holistic Mission by the Founding Generation of AICs

The emergence of the African Independent or African Instituted Churches (AICs) in the early twentieth century was a response to what the founders of these churches saw as the political, cultural, spiritual, and to a certain extent, economic challenges the colonial era. To understand the holistic mission of the AICs during this era, one has to look at the different values and actions of the various categories of AICs.

Key to the founding of these churches was the availability of the scriptures in local languages. This has enabled Africans to understand the place of the Holy Spirit in their lives both as individuals and as a community. The consequent integration of the work of the Holy Spirit in the mission of the AICs has helped local communities to contextualise Christianity in the local realities and to bring security in the lives of those who have abandoned their traditional beliefs for a new faith.

In colonial Kenya, the working of the Holy Spirit in the emerging churches brought about the integration of a discourse of liberation in their mission in two distinct ways. The Nationalist churches like the African Independent Pentecostal Church of Africa (AIPCA) and the National Independent Church of Africa (NICA)[1] understood their mission during the colonial era as one of liberation from colonial domination in politics and culture, and getting back their land which had been taken by the foreign commercial farmers. The struggle for liberation became part of their liturgy and hymnology. They also went ahead to establish their own educational system – which reflected their emphasis on African cultural values. It is this understanding of mission that led the AIPCA to participate in the Mau Mau struggle for the independence of Kenya from 1952 onwards.

The Roho or Spiritual churches,[2] on the other hand, expressed their understanding of liberation principally through the ministries of the Holy Spirit. They brought drums into the church. They introduced Christian prophets into the community of faith, reflecting the reality that the Spirit of God can speak to local communities in their own languages. Even women were empowered by the Spirit to prophesy, and their voice gained space in the worship and in the life of local communities. Peasants, plantation workers, and factory workers were empowered after being filled with the Holy Spirit to start creating new communities of Christians who developed a spirituality that engaged with the emerging reality of colonialism. The Roho churches distrusted the use of money in church, expressing in this way their desire to separate themselves from the overarching power of the emerging capitalist economy which was so different from the economy of reciprocity that they had known. They may not have had all it takes to understand the newly emerging economy based on market values, but they made a clear moral statement: you cannot use money to commodify life and then use it in church.

To the Roho churches, holistic mission also meant the integration of the Christian faith in the African worldview. It was the Holy Spirit's presence in the lives of the people and the community that enabled them to overcome the evil that had always kept them in fear. They started facing issues like witchcraft, the fear of spirits and other areas of African traditional belief systems which had not been adequately handled by the Mission Founded Churches (MFCs). These churches also participated in the political struggles,

---

Originally published in Brian Woolnough and Wonsuk Ma (eds), *Holistic Mission God's Plan for God's People*, Regnum Edinburgh Centenary Series 5 (Oxford: Regnum Books, 2010), 76-86.

[1] These are the post-colonial names given to two denominations that emerged from the church that was known as the African Independent Pentecostal Church in the colonial period.

[2] *Roho Mtakatifu* is Swahili for 'Holy Spirit', often shortened to *Roho*, or 'Spirit'.

but in a way a little different from that of the nationalist churches. They acted through prayer, prophecy against the colonial domination, and the development of radically different liturgies to the liturgies of the MFCs. Two of the innovations of the Spirit churches were the re-definition of priesthood, making it accessible to the common people, and the transformation of the worship space into a place where the day-to-day struggles, hope uncertainties and success of ordinary people are shared. On the political front, the churches drew on the empowerment of the Holy Spirit to reject what they understood to be structures of economic and political domination. The refusal to use money in the church, the refusal to wear ties and suits by some churches, and the use of their own flags (Padwick) reflects the attempts by the Roho churches to develop a spirituality on which their mission to create moral communities – acting as counter communities to the colonial society – was based. Part of the mission of the church was to assert local citizenship – the power and right of ordinary people to act at the local level to control the spiritual and moral and hence the material development of their communities – rejecting in the process the model of development that was being imposed on them from the north, which had few moral foundations in African life.

The challenge Roho and Nationalist churches are faced with is that they challenged a number of practices in the local cultures but did not go far enough to understand the gospel of Jesus Christ in certain areas. The place of women in society is one of those areas. Their closeness to African culture is resourceful but has also been a barrier because these churches easily relate to the Old Testament when it comes to relations between men and women.

For the Roho churches – especially in the rural areas – their understanding of wholeness goes beyond individual wellbeing. So there is a constant search for what has gone wrong in the community whenever there are unwanted situations like sickness, deaths whose cause cannot be explained, drought and any other calamities. This search will always end up identifying spiritual causes which require repentance, forgiveness, correction of those who have gone wrong, casting out evil spirits and some other processes which can heal in individuals and communities. This understanding of wholeness and wellbeing, however, ignores the structural causes to the suffering of individuals and communities. The contradiction is that these churches had a clearer understanding of structural issues during the colonial era – and that is why they came up with initiative mentioned earlier in this chapter. They also retain an understanding of just systems in relation to the moral economy at the micro level, where all are expected to use part of their resources for the well-being of the community, but all this is not linked to the process of building just systems at the national and international levels.

The Case of Community-Based Pentecostal Churches

The more recent emergence of newer forms of Pentecostalism on the continent brings another dimension into the mission of the church. This movement is attracting people who are demographically diverse – young and old, male and female, rich and poor.[3] Consequently, the movement is producing a rich and ever-expanding variety of different models of church. The focus of this chapter will be on the Pentecostal churches that have been called community-based.[4]

In many ways, these community-based Pentecostal churches are close to the Roho churches in their understanding and practice of mission. Mission is based on the empowerment that comes with the baptism of the Holy Spirit and the gifts that believers receive after this experience. Like the Roho churches, these Pentecostal churches depend on the gifts of the Holy Spirit for ministries such as healing and deliverance from demonic oppression. Many of the missioners in these churches have not had any formal theological education. The new Pentecostal churches are largely independent – in that, they are not linked by denominational ties – but they have local, national, and regional networks. The Pentecostal churches have been clearer in the demands of the gospel of Jesus Christ on some areas where many of the older AICs did not pay adequate attention. The place of women and young people in the mission of the church is an area of great strength. They are also clearer in dealing with the cultural values and attitudes that prevent women from being in senior leadership in the church. So bringing the demands of Jesus Christ, the Bible, together with the understanding of the place of the Holy Spirit, is bringing a new dimension of mission at the grassroots.

In contrast to the nationalist and Roho churches, however, the lack of a clear history of political and social struggles among the new Pentecostals limits their participation in the public space. It leaves them without an adequate tradition to engage with contemporary issues from the position of social justice. The resources which they use to empower themselves in the form of sermons on TV and FM radio stations, and books and magazines, focus rather on individual effort through faith, prayer, and giving. All these are strengthened by sermons that stress the role of personal achievement. It is these resources which enable the missioners to participate in the contemporary environment with skill but at the same time uproots them from the concrete realities of their mission environment. Because their discourse is wanting in the area of social justice, in their engagement with these realities they can use only spiritual tools.

The other challenge for the Pentecostal churches is their understanding of prosperity and how it relates to coming out of poverty. Naturally, prosperity is desired by many. Even in the African traditional religion, people go to mediums to get guidance on how to prosper or thrive in their businesses, careers, marriages and other areas of life. However preaching of prosperity in

---

[3] Adelaide Maame Akwa Boadi, 'Engaging Partriachy: Pentecostal Gender Ideology and Practice in Nigeria', in Chima J. Korieh and Ugo G. Nwokeji (eds), *Religion, History and Politics in Nigeria: Essays in Honour of Ogbu U. Kalu* (Lanham, MD: University Press of America, 2005), 173.

[4] Centre for Development and Enterprise, *Dormant Capital: Pentecostalism and its Potential and Social Economic Role* (Johannesburg: Centre for Development and Enterprise, 2008), 15.

the community-based Pentecostal churches becomes unbalanced when giving, tithing, faith and overcoming spiritual barriers like curses in the lives of individuals, families, and communities, are understood as the only keys to prosperity. The failure to include socio-political causes of poverty in this understanding of well-being holds back the leadership and members of these churches from engaging with the broader issues that keep masses of people in poverty.

Challenges Faced by Emerging Churches from Outside

The Struggle to Affirm Their Own Methodology of Doing Mission

Below is an interaction between students from mainline churches, a lecturer from St. Paul's University, Limuru, and pastors from Roho and Pentecostal churches at Tafakari centre in the large informal settlement of Kibera, in which I participated.

> *Student*: You Pentecostals are always looking for money because of the way you propagate the prosperity gospel.
> *A Pentecostal pastor from Kibera*: If you want money, you go to the city centre and plant a church in a place where you can attract people who have money.
> *A pastor from a mainline church in Kibera*: We have also started singing in our worship services the choruses you sing.
> *A pastor from a small Pentecostal church in Kibera*: That is fine, but for us, these choruses are sung on a daily basis. They are part of us throughout the week. So make sure that you are not limiting them to the confines the church walls.
> *Student*: Our churches do ministry in these places [meaning the informal urban settlements] by reaching out with services and food donations.
> *A pastor from a Roho church*: You do ministry by reaching out. For us, we live here and work with the people through their difficulties on a daily basis.
> *A lecturer*: You've said that Roho churches can raise their voices in public through raising the flag. You've said that it is at the foot of the flag that the evils that hurt the community are named and thrown out. What if they name people living with HIV as part of the evil?
> *Author's response*: It's at the foot of the flag that the church should name stigma, discrimination against people living with HIV, and the marginalisation of women as issues that harm the community.

This brief discussion brings to the surface a number of issues in the way we understand mission. The participants from the mainline churches seem to come from a position of power, the pastors from the independent churches have to counteract the stereotypes developed by others, and finally the need for constructive engagement between different church traditions on mission for us all to benefit.

The Lack of Appropriate Processes to Mobilise and Engage the Emerging Churches

The emerging church is lagging behind because of the lack of scholarship about the place of Spirit-led churches in the public space and the lack of appropriate resources for education. As a result, these churches either try to copy what the mainline churches are doing – hence failing because they do not have similar structures and opportunities of access to financial resources – or they copy what the evangelical churches do in North America – hence ending up with a strong voice that only emerges in seasons when there are moral issues in the public discourse.

In the case of Roho churches and the nationalist churches, their invisibility in the public space is also partly due to:

- their failure to build on the resources in their histories of struggle during the colonial era and a subsequent shift from reading the scriptures in the context of both political and social realities to that of social realities only;
- their weak institutional frameworks especially at national levels;
- their historical and continuing exclusion from the public media;
- the trust that the Independent churches had in the pre-independence nationalist movements, and which was carried forward into the post-colonial governments, has consequently blunted their ability to speak prophetically into the contemporary issues that face Africa.

Engaging with the Values of the Global Development Industry

A faith-based response to any issue should be the action that comes out of the interaction of people's faith with their realities. It is people's faith that gives them the ideological framework for understanding and explaining their realities. Kurt Alan Ver Beek who defines spirituality 'as a relationship with the supernatural or spiritual which provides meaning and a basis for personal and communal reflection' affirms this fact. [5] The international development discourse, however, does not fully recognise faith and spirituality as a basic and fundamental resource in development. Indeed, the development industry is often driven and managed in a way that makes Africa a participant in the jargon and themes that are continuously generated elsewhere – as a result of the analysis of situations but also as a way of establishing control. The values behind this discourse are suspicious of faith and look at it as a barrier to achieving development objectives. The end result has been their appreciation of the physical infrastructure and the human resources of the church only, and not their belief systems. As a result, churches tend to apportion their mission resources to provide a framework for the non-faith-based development agencies

---

[5] Kurt Allan Beek, 'Spirituality: a development taboo', *Development in Practice* 10:1 (2000), 31-43 http://www.informaworld.com/smpp/content~db=all?content=10.1080/09614520052484.

to work with, and they hold back from using their faith resources and in consequence deny themselves the opportunity of developing and building on their belief systems. The tragedy is that many Christian agencies in Europe and the rest of the north had also been caught up in the secularisation going on in their midst and had started designing programs for the developing countries in a way that focused only on the structures of the churches, leaving out the real resources of faith. It is only recently that many of these agencies are beginning to recognise the value of faith in the lives of people in developing countries. Initiatives by Christian Aid and ICCO are an example.

Limiting the Search and Understanding of Justice and Human Dignity to the Context of Small Communities

In most parts of Africa people have learned to build social support systems on which they rely to face the difficulties of poverty and exclusion from the formal economy and their lack of access to basic social services. These support systems are in the form of women's groups, farmers' groups, youth groups, and various church ministry groups, and operate on the values of reciprocity and a moral economy. The mission of the congregations of community-based churches is built on similar values. These communities of support have with time become an alternative to a contracted state that is not well established in the lives of the people because of its failure to provide basic social services to many. In these circumstances, the Christian faith and mission of the churches is to bring harmony and to continuously rebuild lives that are broken by their exclusion from the formal economy and their lack of access to basic social services. The songs, the testimonies, the prophecies, the sermons in the churches, and the day to day conversations of their members reflect this reality. People can share their problems in relation to poverty, but they rarely refer to themselves as the poor when they are on their own. Rather, they are apostles, prophets, pastors, and evangelists. In the fellowships and other groups where the people at the margins meet, all the issues that affect them are shared. The fellowship or church service becomes a space of collective lamentation or collective celebration. This is the space where those who are battered by poverty and other forms of hardship look for support. It is a space where those who live in indignity find dignity. It is a space where those who do not have a voice in the public space – which is controlled by politicians and the visible civil society organisations – find space for their voice. Here people share their hardships, dreams, visions, songs, success, and information on any economic opportunities. Unfortunately, this also results in ordinary citizens withdrawing from laying a claim on the public and governmental structures and institutions that are responsible for providing essential social services and the defence of their rights. Instead, they seek mutual support and comfort in spiritual fellowship, in 'a place to feel at home' in the midst of a harsh world.

What it Will Take for the Emerging Church to Play a Greater Role in the Public Arena?

Transform Claims Making

The prophetic voice of the community-based churches should be linked to claims-making. Spector and Kitsuse define 'claims-making' as a form of interaction, a demand made by one party to another that something is done about some putative condition.[6] A claim implies that a claimant has a right at least to be heard. In the context of the emerging churches, claims-making is practiced on a daily basis; only that the claims made are directed to God in prayer – on the basis of the scriptures where promises have been made for a good and prosperous life, to members of the congregation where there is a right to be cared, and to community groups. In these churches, claims are rarely directed to the political and economic structures of this world. This could mean that claims-making in this context is directed to where people actually expect they can get some measure of justice. People at this level participate in shaping the structures-fellowships, ministry groups, etc. – in a way that makes them responsive to their needs. So there is a heavy engagement in building just communities in the mission of the community-based churches. What the missioners need to do is to study the scriptures in a fresh way and understand that God stands with the weak and has made a claim on the larger political and socio-economic structures that are responsible for keeping people in indignity. The day this will be internalised in the understanding of God who demands for righteousness as well as justice will be the time to see a fresh wave of revival deeply rooted in the voice of the Spirit for a just world.

Recovery of the Prophetic Voice for the Older AICs

For some of the Spirit churches like the Roho churches in Kenya, one way ahead is through the recovery and updating of the vision of the founders. The founders spoke truth to the colonial structures and developed liturgical and hymnal resources that supported their mission. There are enormous resources in the theology of these AICs. What is required here is the updating of these visions to make them relevant to the contemporary environment where Africa has to deal with poor governance at the local, national, and international levels

Illuminating Reality and Transforming Existing Theologies

What affects the churches at the margins is a partial understanding of reality. For the OAIC the development of appropriate mobilisation and training processes has been critical in mobilizing the member churches to expand their

[6] Malcolm Spector and John I. Kitsuse, *Constructing Social Problems* (New Brunswick, NJ: Transaction Publishers, 1987).

understanding of mission to include critical issues like HIV and AIDS in their mission.

'Now I know the reason why cotton farming has disappeared'. This is a statement by Eliazaro Onyando – a peasant farmer who is also a bishop from an African Independent Church in rural Kenya in conversation with the author. He made this remark after a two-day interdenominational workshop on the on-going Economic Partnerships Agreements (EPAs) between the European Union and African states. Cotton farming which was one of the major economic activities in his community collapsed over 25 years ago. It was in that workshop that the impact of agricultural subsidies in developed countries was explained in very simple terms. Bishop Onyando had lived with and felt the reality of the loss of income due to the collapse of the cotton industry, yet he didn't understand the cause. Onyando has since then developed an interest in trade policies.

Another clear example where churches in Africa faced a challenge in their response is the HIV and AIDS pandemic. Since the mode of transmission is mainly through sex, initially most churches held the view that AIDS was a result of sin – hence looking at it as a judgment from God. The churches' reading of scriptures in this context was selective and geared towards affirming the negative understanding of the reality of HIV and AIDS in the community. As a result, the churches – especially those at the margins of society which act as safety nets for the poor – held back their resourcefulness from supporting the people living with HIV. To respond to this challenge, the OAIC transformed its mobilisation program from simply giving scientific facts about HIV to the analysis of the theological, cultural, political and economic issues. This process helped the church leaders to root their reading of the Bible in the social realities of the communities they serve. One of the major revelations was the vulnerability of women because of the power relations at the family level, in the church, and in the wider society. As a result, women and young people started making a claim on the governance structures of the churches, and the church leaders started listening to the voices of women and young people who wanted them to allocate more of their resources to HIV and AIDS programs. The OAIC terms these processes as laboratories for developing the capacity for civic engagement among the churches and community groups.

This process requires opening up the scriptures, reflecting on the language used in church and outside the church and enabling people to acquire the knowledge and skills they need to participate effectively in the public space to address injustices that are keeping people in indignity. Corwin Smidt says that, whereas citizens do not need become policy experts to fulfil their civic responsibilities, lacking knowledge on the specific issues they want to address impairs their participation.[7]

[7] Corwin E. Smidt et al, *Pews, Prayers: Participation and Civic Responsibility in America* (Washington, DC: George Town University Press, 2008).

Expand the Understanding of the Role of the Holy Spirit in Society

Healing, seeing into the future, identifying and overcoming what harms the community (especially evil spirits) – these practices clearly manifest belief in a God who heals and builds the community, a God who is known to be present in their midst. Wilhelmina Kalu[8] refers to this role as the calling of a Christian 'to discern the spirits that are at work in communities, families and individual lives and confront them with the power of the spirit, the water of the word and the blood of Jesus'. It is this calling that should be expanded to include discernment in the area of social justice, to the causes of social inequalities, unjust international policies, and the plunder of national resources by the political and business elite from both Africa and beyond. It is this that will liberate the mission of the Spirit-led churches.

For such transformation to take place, the Spirit-led churches have to overcome the fear of losing the Spirit. In an Urban Missions conference held in Nairobi in 2009, one Pentecostal pastor from an informal settlement asked his colleague – who was involved in multiple community projects – how he gets involved in studying for a degree in a theological college, leads a church, initiates and gives oversight to an expanding income generating project without losing the Holy Spirit. Such an understanding of the work of the Holy Spirit is limiting and calls for engagement through theological reflection. It is time for the Spirit-led churches to re-read the Apostle Paul in I Thessalonians 5:19, 'do not quench the Spirit'. This scripture is used in relation to allowing the Holy Spirit to speak, rebuke, correct, guide, and exhort the church. But the Spirit's voice must also not be quenched from speaking into the social, political and economic issues that affect Africa.

This Spirit of God must also be allowed to speak to issues that have not been handled at family and local community levels. It is at this level of society that the impact of poverty is reflected in the gender and generational inequalities. The empowerment and liberation of the Spirit has to be felt and experienced by the women of Africa who are the majority in the church

Conclusion

In social contexts where many people are living in deprivation, holistic mission is not an option. There is no line between what is termed as the gospel – the proclaimed word – and the social gospel. Such demarcations are created by Christians writing or speaking from a middle or upper-class context. Missioners in contexts of deprivation and exclusion from the benefits of the formal economy and basic social services develop mission approaches that are born out of their faith's interaction with the realities the communities they are part of. They may not understand fully each and every issue, but they have the

[8] Wilhemina Kalu, 'Soul Care in Nigeria: Constructing Pentecostal Models in Pastoral and Counseling', in *Religion, History and Politics in Nigeria: Essays in Honour of Ogbu U. Kalu.*

ability to learn from and engage with their belief systems and to transform their methods of doing mission. This process leads to a continuous review of the beliefs, and a consequent expansion of the frameworks of action which in turn transforms mission. This doesn't mean that the missioners at the margins of society are adequate in themselves. The fact that they are immersed in the realities of the excluded and to a great extent are themselves the excluded, means that they need accompaniment for them to be able to reflect objectively on their calling and the actions that come out of it.

Holistic Mission in Post-Communist Romania: A Case Study on the Growth of the 'Elim' Pentecostal Church of Timişoara (1990-1997)

Marcel V. Măcelaru

A Missiological Turning Point

However else it may have been interpreted, I regard the anti-communist uprising that took place in Timişoara, Romania, in the last weeks of December 1989, to be a turning point, with deep missiological implications, in the history of the region.[1] On the one hand, the events in Timişoara marked the 'beginning of the end' for Nicolae Ceauşescu's 24-year rule of Romania, which is considered to be one of the most repressive totalitarian regimes communist Eastern Europe has known. Thus, it made space for much-needed and long-awaited political, economic and societal reforms. On the other hand, it also revealed, quite dramatically, the failure of decades of communist propaganda. The cry for freedom that somehow united the thousands of demonstrators filling the streets of Timişoara during those days had strangely turned out to be a defying 'God exists!' This challenged foundational communist notions of materialistic atheism.

To me, that was a cry of vindication. As a believer, I had been mocked and despised for my 'naïveté' by those who had had the 'benefit' of communist atheistic education. But now, the people who were once taught to deny God's existence were proclaiming something I had believed all along. Here was a testimony to the fact that longing for God is part of who we are, and that humanly devised ideologies could neither fulfil nor suppress this inherent need for transcendence. And even more than vindication, the cry of the demonstrators was reason for hope – hope that the oppressive context in which

Originally published in C. Constantineanu, M.V. Măcelaru, A. Kool, and M. Himcinschi (eds), *Mission in Central and Eastern Europe: Realities, Perspectives, Trends*, Regnum Edinburgh Centenary Series 34 (Oxford: Regnum Books, 2016), 327-44.

[1] On 'turning points' and their significance, see Romeo V. Turcan, 'The Philosophy of Turning Points: A Case of De-Internationalization', *Advances in International Management* 26 (2013), 219-35.

I had lived would, at last, end; hope that my country would become a society in which freedom and truth would prevail; and hope that the newly discovered religious liberty would trigger a resurgence of true Christian commitment, perhaps even a fully-fledged, revival.

Needless to say, as I am writing these thoughts now, more than 25 years after the fall of communism, the better Romania I had hoped for continues to be a 'dream' in the making. As we have had to discover, the change of political regimes did not bring about changed mentalities; therefore, much more remains to be done and many wrongs have yet to be corrected. However, one also has to recognise that vital steps towards a truly democratic, prosperous society have been taken. And more importantly, a shift in the way Romanians perceive and relate to Christianity has definitely taken place. As the 2011 census showed, a staggering 93% of the citizens of Romania nowadays consider themselves Christian.

Admittedly, since the census could not measure Christian commitment, the numbers being circulated do not prove that a Christian revival is underway. They point however to the fact that the anti-communist 'revolution' (as the 1989 uprising is otherwise referred to) did create unprecedented opportunities for mission which, over the past 25 years, have been fruitful, in some places more than in others, as various missionary enterprises were undertaken in the region.

The case study below presents one such 'enterprise': the mission strategy and praxis of the 'Elim' Pentecostal Church in Timişoara, Romania (henceforth EPC)[2] during the period 1990-1997. This is, I propose, an outstanding example of holistic mission undertaken during the confusing time of 'transition' that succeeded the fall of communism in Eastern Europe, the transition for which most churches in the region were by no means prepared. The intelligence of the vision driving the praxis of this church during those years and its successful outcome justify, I propose, the inclusion of EPC's story in the present volume.[3]

---

[2] Although named 'Elim', EPC is neither a part of, nor connected with, the 'Elim' Pentecostal Movement in UK and Ireland. EPC is one of the many churches that form Cultul Creştin Penticostal – Biserica lui Dumnezeu Apostolică din România (The Pentecostal Christian Denomination – The Apostolic Church of God of Romania). The congregation adopted the name 'Elim' on 20th November 1988, at the inauguration of the worship facilities it has used ever since. See 'Inaugurarea unui lăcaş de închinăciune la Timişoara', *Buletinul Cultului Penticostal* 37:1 (January-February 1989), 4-5. For the sake of simplification, the abbreviation EPC is used in this paper to identify the congregation throughout its entire history.

[3] Most of the information regarding EPC provided below is available in Elim, a magazine EPC has published beginning with 1992; on EPC's website: www.elim.ro; and in *Cuvântul Adevărului*, the official bulletin of the Romanian Pentecostal Denomination: <http://digitallibrary.usc.edu/cdm/search/collection/p15799coll14/searchterm/Pentecostal%20Theological%20Institute,%20Bucharest,%20Romania/field/parta/mode/exact/conn/and/order/nosort>. Data was also obtained through personal observation (during the period under scrutiny, I have been an active member of EPC), interviews with various

EPC – The Story up to 1990

EPC represents a unique case of church growth within the Romanian, and indeed, Eastern European context. After the fall of communism, in a relatively short period of time (seven years), membership of the congregation more than doubled. Over thirty new satellite churches were planted in the region. The impact of the church within the country grew significantly due to various ministries addressing social needs that sprung out of it, and news of the 'revival' that was taking place in Timişoara began spreading in Romania[4] and beyond.[5]

No success, however, happens in a vacuum. In fact, I suggest that the seeds of EPC's missiological ethos were sown earlier in the history of the church and its 1990-1997 mission praxis was rooted in strategies that were tested and proven effective during the long years before the fall of communism. Therefore, I will preface the discussion on the 1990-1997 period with an overview of EPC's story before 1990, aiming to identify such 'seeds' and to show the development of such strategies.

---

members of the church, and from EPC's official records, to which I had access during December 1999-January 2000.

[4] Information about EPC appears in different publications (primarily Christian) in Romania. For example, see the listings in footnotes throughout this paper. For specific references to EPC's growth, see Teodor Codreanu, 'Biserica Penticostală Elim – Timişoara', *Cuvântul Adevărului* 3:8 (2nd series, August 1992), 19; 'Semicentenarul Bisericii Penticostale Filadelfia din Timişoara', *Cuvântul Adevărului* 7:1-2 (2nd series, January-February 1996), 24; 'Botez nou-testamental la Biserica Penticostală "Elim", Timişoara', *Cuvântul Adevărului* 8:4 (2nd series, April 1997), 2; Ioan Bochian, 'În vizită la pastorul Teodor Codreanu – Timişoara', *Cuvântul Adevărului* 13:9-10 (2nd series, September-October 2002), 18; Cornelius Merca, 'Elim-ul… la 15 ani', *Cuvântul Adevărului* 15:1 (2nd series, January 2004), 2; 'Teodor Codreanu, 1928-2004', *Cuvântul Adevărului* 15:11 (2nd series, November 2004), 23; and Pavel Riviş Tipei, 'Aniversare – 85 de ani', *Cuvântul Adevărului* 19:2 (2nd series, February 2008), 6.

[5] Although references to EPC in non-Romanian literature are more recent, their very existence proves that information about EPC's unique case has spread beyond Romania's borders long enough and to the extent that it became worth mentioning even within academic contexts. See, for instance, Rodica Pandrea, 'A Historical and Theological Analysis of the Pentecostal Church in Romania', *The Journal of the European Pentecostal Theological Association* 21 (2001), 117; Peter Kuzmič, 'Pentecostal Theology and Communist Europe: Pentecostal Power under Political Pressure', in William K. Kay and Anne E. Dyer (eds), *European Pentecostalism*, Global Pentecostal and Charismatic Studies 7 (Leiden: E.J. Brill, 2011), 350; Bill George, '"To All Who Are Afar Off": The Incredible International Growth of Pentecostalism', *Evangel* 103:5 (May 2013), 15; and Bill Prevette, 'Evangelical Faith Based Agencies and Churches involved with Children and Youth at Risk in Romania since 1989' (OCMS Seminar Paper, 26 Jan. 2015), 6: http://prevetteresearch.net/wp-content/uploads/image/all/January%2026th%20OCMS%20Seminar%20paper.pdf (accessed 13th July 2016).

EPC – The Early Years (1928-1946)

The story of EPC,[6] up until the years in view here, covers two distinct periods of time; each of these has had its specific challenges, but also each one is a testimony to the congregation's unique focus on mission. The first period starts sometime in the year 1928, with a few Pentecostal believers who began gathering for prayer and Bible study in various private homes within the city of Timişoara, and concludes with the official inauguration of the church as a religious entity, within the legal framework of the time, on 3rd November 1946, under the name *Biserica Apostolică Penticostală* (The Pentecostal Apostolic Church).

Information about this period is scarce, as much of the life of the church took place 'underground'; Pentecostalism – which in its early years was regarded a dangerous 'sect' – did not become a legally recognised 'religion' within the legal framework of Romania until 1946. We know, however, that about 1928 prayer and Bible study meetings became regular events and that they continued, in various locations throughout the city of Timişoara, until 1935. These, I suggest, are the years in which the core identity of the group as a 'church' began to take shape, for in their aftermath, from 1935 onwards, the believers organised themselves into a congregation, initially of about thirty members, under the leadership of Pastor Alexandru Izbaşa, and met regularly in the house of Ioachim Ţunea.

Not much is known about the mission praxis of the group either. Unquestionably, the data available shows progress, as eleven years later, when the 'legalisation' of the church took place, the congregation had allegedly grown to about 100 members. This would translate as an average growth rate of 7% per annum. However, since no membership records are available, it is unclear how many of these were adult members and how many were children, and also how many members were new converts and how many were believers coming from other congregations who had simply joined the newly-founded church.

[6] For EPC's story presented here, see Codreanu, 'Biserica Penticostală Elim – Timişoara', 19; Cornelius Merca, 'Din istoricul Bisericii Apostolice Penticostale "Elim" Timişoara', in *Elim* 36-37 (1998), 14-15; Ibid. 'Elim-ul… la 15 ani', 2; and the historical overview provided on EPC's website 'Biserica "Elim" de-a lungul timpului': www.elim.ro/despre-biserica-penticostala-elim-timisoara/biserica-elim-de-a-lungul-timpului (accessed 14th April 2016). See also Mărioara Măcelaru, *Însemnări pe uşiorii casei* (Timişoara, Romania: Casa Literaturii Creştine, 2007), an autobiography that makes various references to EPC's post-1960 history. The historical data available in these publications has also been used to corroborate information about EPC obtained from several interviews with members of the congregation (see footnotes below).

EPC – The Communist Era (1946-1989)

The second period in EPC's history covers the years under the communist totalitarian regime (1946-1989).[7] On the one hand, these are years marked by persecution and restrictions – methods of control exercised by communist authorities who endeavoured to curb the progress of the congregation. Thus, in 1960 communist authorities withdrew EPC's 'approval' to exist as a congregation on its own and 'decreed' that believers who wanted to continue meeting should share the worship hall with Hungarian and German believers in a facility that was both small and inadequate. Also, during the 1960s, strict interdictions in terms of worship practices were applied. No music, preaching, prayer or other kinds of manifestations were allowed during church meetings, nothing other than what was sanctioned beforehand by the Departamentul Cultelor (the Department of Religious Affairs – the branch of government through which communists controlled religious groups and implemented repressive anti-religious policies).[8]

This situation continued until 1973, when, in the context of Ceauşescu's bid for better trade relations with the West, some relaxation in communist policies regarding the status of religious communities in the country became necessary.[9] This created an opportunity for re-launching EPC as a congregation on its own. On 11th March 1973, a group of Romanian believers, which by now was numbering about 300 members under the leadership of Pastor Teodor Codreanu, began gathering in a new location; admittedly, in a property in need of much renovation, but one used solely by EPC. The limitations imposed by communist authorities, however, did not come to an end there, for it took another fifteen years of 'negotiation' with the Department for Religious Affairs and finally the demolition of the building EPC was using before the church

---

[7] Besides the sources listed in footnote 6 above, information for this part of EPC's story comes from Maria Măcelaru, interview by the author (Timişoara, Romania, 17th December 1999), and Dorel M. Măcelaru, interview by the author (Timişoara, Romania, 20th January 2000), both interviews using written notes.

[8] On these, see Măcelaru, *Însemnări pe uşiorii casei*, 74-75.

[9] As early as 1962, communist Romania had refused to integrate fully with the Council for Mutual Economic Assistance (COMECOM) of the Soviet bloc. Beginning in 1965, after Ceauşescu became the General Secretary of the Romanian Communist Party (and therefore the *de facto* ruler of Romania), a western-oriented foreign policy was pursued, aiming to diminish Soviet influence in the country and to increase trade and other opportunities with western nations. This indeed resulted in Romania being granted the MFN (Most Favoured Nation) trade status by the USA in 1975. Among the (cosmetic) changes Ceauşescu had to make in pursuing his goals was the granting of more freedom to religious groups in the country. Of course, this 'relaxation' of communist policies did not bring the end of the communist oppression of religious communities in Romania; changes implemented were superficial, and communist persecution continued, albeit admittedly in subtler ways. On these, see further, Juliana Geran, 'Why Romania No Longer Deserves to be a Most Favoured Nation': www.heritage.org/research/reports/1985/06/why-romania-no-longer-deserves-to-be-a-most-favored-nation (accessed 15th July 2016).

received permission to build the adequate facilities currently in use (see an image[10] of the current facilities below).

The period 1946-1989, on the other hand, is also testimony to God's faithful protection and provision, and to the believers' steadfast commitment to God and his mission in the world. Thus, after moving into its own facilities in 1973, in spite of further restrictions and harassment, the church continued to register steady growth, records showing that by December 1989, when the communist period ended, EPC's size had surpassed the 2,000-member threshold. This translates as an average 5.83% annual growth rate over the entire period (1946-1989).

It should be noted, however, that in fact, during this period, the development of the congregation took place in three distinct stages. During 1946-1973, harsh communist restrictions were imposed. For instance, EPC's leadership during these years was changed seven times. They were not necessarily because of the wishes of the congregation. It was a typical practice of communist authorities to impose on congregations the leaders they could control. As a consequence, growth was slower: an average annual rate of 4.15%.

The situation changes significantly from 1973 onwards, for by April 1987, when construction of the current worship facilities was approved, the congregation had already reached approximately 1,200 members – that is, an average annual growth rate of 10.41%. This increase in growth was undoubtedly helped by the re-launching of EPC as a congregation, in its own facilities, in 1973, and the stabilisation of EPC's leadership.[11] More

[10] For this, and other images of EPC's current facilities, see: www.elim.ro/gallery-list/arhiva-aur-biserica-penticostala-elim

[11] Teodor Codreanu continued as pastor of EPC until his death in September 2004. It should be noted though that during the last six years of his life he suffered a series of severe vascular accidents which gradually impaired him, thus making 1997 his last year of full-time service as EPC's pastor. As a result, from 1998, EPC entered a six-year period of transition during which a new leadership emerged and new priorities were defined. Consequently, although EPC's focus on mission has remained a constant

importantly, however, the missiologically significant turning point seems to be the appointment of Teodor Codreanu as EPC's pastor. Being mission-oriented, Pastor Codreanu developed a mission strategy tailored to work in spite of the constraints of the communist context. He taught the congregation to adopt four fundamental practices which, with hindsight, very effectively nullified the impact that the restrictions imposed by the communist authorities would have had on religious communities. As described by Pastor Codreanu, these practices were:[12]

1. *The participation of each EPC member into an unbroken 'chain' of fasting and prayer.* This 'chain' began in 1973, when each EPC member voluntarily choose one day a week in which (s)he would fast and pray for the well-being and progress of the congregation; this continued over the years, as each new convert that became part of the congregation was invited to join in and commit to fasting and prayer as well. Specifically, explains Pastor Codreanu, people prayed that God's power would become manifest within the congregation in ways which would challenge the absurd claims of the communist atheists that no spiritual reality was really available and the Marxist charge: 'Die Religion… ist das Opium des Volkes'.[13] Such propaganda was intended to extirpate the idea of divine transcendence from society; however, manifestations of divine power attracted non-believers to turn to God, especially when they needed to see God working in similar ways in their own lives. Needless to say, the numerous stories of conversion in the aftermath of divine miraculous interventions in the life of believers and non-believers alike are proof of the effectiveness of this practice.[14]
2. *Pastor Codreanu's emphasis in his sermons of the importance of living a moral, exemplary life as a mission strategy.* Such morality helped to counteract the communist claim that Christians – 'repenters', as we were labelled – were a danger to society, a 'contagion' that had to be eradicated. Evidently, the purpose of such lies was to alienate believers from society, to isolate them and eventually eliminate any public influence they might have had. The moral quality of the believers' lives, however, contrasted powerfully with the corruption, demagogy, and

priority, methods and emphases have shifted sufficiently to justify the marking of 1997 as the end of a distinct mission period in the life of the church. Thus, the 1997 time limit chosen for the present study. On Teodor Codreanu as EPC's pastor, see 'Noi ordinări de păstori', *Buletinul Cultului Penticostal* 5-8 (1976), 38; 'Absolvenţii cursului Biblic, Seria IV, 1975-1976', *Buletinul Cultului Penticostal* 5-8 (1976), 38; Bochian, 'În vizită la pastorul Teodor Codreanu – Timişoara'; 'Teodor Codreanu, 1928-2004'.

[12] Teodor Codreanu, taped interview by author (Timişoara, Romania, 18th December 1999).

[13] Karl Marx, 'Zur Kritik der Hegel'schen Rechtsphilosophie', in Arnold Ruge and Karl Marx (eds), *Deutsch-Französische Jahrbücher* (Paris: Bureau der Jahrbücher, 1844), 71 – republished as 'Zur Kritik der Hegelschen Rechtsphilosophie', in *Marx-Engels-Werke, Bd. 1* (Berlin: Dietz Verlag, 1976), 378.

[14] E.g., Măcelaru, *Însemnări pe uşiorii casei.*

falsehood that characterised the communists and their propaganda, thus attracting non-believers to the church. In Codreanu's words: 'People were seeking the church because that was the only place within Romanian society where they could hear the truth.'[15]

3. EPC members were encouraged to talk one-on-one to family members, friends and neighbours about God's existence, in spite of the fact that any attempt to 'pass the faith on' was regarded by the communists as a grave political error. Also, they would extend invitations to non-believers they came in contact with to attend church meetings. Thus, although public, open proclamation of the gospel was restricted by the communists, preaching in the church itself, which was usually evangelistically oriented, provided non-believers with the opportunity to hear the good news. In addition to these sermons, evangelistic messages were also delivered on most occasions when meetings outside the church building were permitted: at wedding parties, during funerals, and even during the Christmas season when the traditional carol-singing on Christmas Eve would turn into night-long Christian musical strolls of church youth on the streets of Timişoara. Pastor Codreanu also explained that children from non-believing families who befriended children from EPC's families and began attending Sunday school classes, were encouraged to tell their parents everything they had heard in EPC. All these ensured that the message of the gospel would reach beyond the 'walls' which the communists attempted to raise around believing communities.
4. The fourth practice adopted by EPC as mission strategy during the communist years was grassroots social assistance and charity work. Since the communists denied the right of religious organisations to participate in education, charity, and other community-directed activities, mission outreach and social work at the institutional level was not possible. EPC's function as a social agent was therefore severely limited, for such separation of faith from the reality of everyday practice would make any religious community socially irrelevant. However, as Pastor Codreanu explained, a large mission board was formed within EPC which was charged with the task of visiting every EPC family, with the purpose of intervening and helping in situations of illness, poverty, loneliness, disability, etc. Such visits became a testimony of true sacrificial love to non-believers in the city of Timişoara, and when faced with similar liminal situations, many of these specifically asked to be visited and helped. Needless to say, it was often the very gesture of love one would receive that would prompt him/her to inquire about God and eventually to convert.

[15] Teodor Codreanu, taped interview by author (Timişoara, Romania, 18th December 1999).

Needless to say, these practices were crucial in shaping EPC's missiological ethos from 1973 onwards. Furthermore, as will be seen below, these provided a foundation for the mission praxis of EPC after the fall of communism as well.

Finally, the third stage of growth during the communist era refers to the period between April 1987 and January 1990. I have identified this as a distinct stage because documents show that, within only three years, the number of adult believers in EPC increased from 1,200 to 2,130.[16] This would translate as a record 21.08% annual growth rate, which effectively marks EPC as the fastest-growing Pentecostal congregation during that period in Romania, and probably in Eastern Europe. I suggest that the 'secret' of such increase in growth is to be found in two specific events which enhanced and added to, the mission practices described above.

The first of these was the September 1985 Billy Graham evangelistic campaign in Romania, which concluded in Timişoara with a meeting that gathered some 150,000 people in the central square of the city.[17] Although no altar call or other such 'follow-up' was permitted by the communist authorities, I submit that this event contributed to bringing the Christian message (and therefore EPC and other similar communities) to the fore in both talk and general awareness. Admittedly, Billy Graham's sermon itself could not have had much impact, for the Securitate (the communist Secret Police) confined the evangelistic meeting to the Timişoara Metropolitan Cathedral and did not allow the service to be broadcast to the people gathered outside, so only approximately 5,000 people actually heard the message. However, the believers who had gathered in the square hours before the meeting actually used this opportunity to speak to others about their faith and made their 'presence' widely known as they sung Christian choruses together throughout the entire time the meeting was taking place in the cathedral.[18] All in all, I suggest that this event helped non-believers realise that Christianity was neither extinct nor a phenomenon on the margins of the society – both claims made by communist ideologues. Rather, the high international profile of Billy Graham and the turn-out of tens of thousands of people in the square provided sure proof that 'there was something there worth exploring'.

The 'awakening' provided by this evangelistic campaign was followed in Timişoara, and more specifically in EPC's case, by another significant event which, I suggest, created the unique context of growth being documented. I refer to the 1987-1988 demolition of EPC's old church building and the

---

[16] On these statistics, see A. Trip, 'Biserica Elim 1992 – Retrospectivă', *Elim* 1 (1992), 11.

[17] See Billy Graham, *Just As I Am: The Autobiography of Billy Graham* (HarperCollins, 1999), 942-43; John Pollock, *The Billy Graham Story* (Grand Rapids, MI: Zondervan, 2003), 223-31. For a Romanian perspective, see 'Reflections on Billy Graham's Trip to Romania', *Religion in Communist Lands* 14 (Summer 1986), 224-27.

[18] Information about the event also comes from personal observation as I was one of the thousands who did not gain access to the cathedral and ended up spending the time singing Christian hymns in the square of Timişoara.

construction of the current facilities. To be sure, the demolition programme was not an act of repression directed against EPC alone. Rather, it was part of a master 'urbanisation' plan Ceauşescu began implementing in the early 1980s.[19] Paradoxically, though, the very tool of oppression – Ceauşescu's 'urbanisation' plan – became, in EPC's case, an opportunity for mission. First, it provided for the creation of an emotional bond, as private citizens who had suffered similar treatment by the communist authorities began to identify and sympathise with the church.

Secondly, the subsequent construction of new facilities became a testimony in and of itself, for not only was it completed in seventeen months of intensive labour round the clock, but also it was done entirely by members of EPC and other Christian brethren who joined in as volunteers in order to help the project. Moreover, the expenses of the construction were supported by EPC from donations given by its members, who each committed to contribute the equivalent of twenty monthly incomes (salaries, pensions, and other forms of revenue), payable in installments over a period of ten years. Even those who could not commit to financially support the project, or to work at the construction site, found ways to contribute by waiting long hours in queues to purchase the food and fuel needed by the workers (which at that time in Romania were scarce and available only in the form of strict rations). These sacrifices were not ignored, for news about what was happening started spreading throughout the city, and non-believers who had been wavering with indecision began joining in both the work and the congregation.[20] As records show, within the three short years taken by the construction project and its aftermath, over 900 new converts joined EPC,[21] bringing the number of adult

---

[19] Ceauşescu's 'urbanisation' plan consisted of the demolition of tens of thousands of private properties and the construction of 'efficiency' apartment buildings instead – apartments within which families that were left without a home in the demolition process were forced to live but now, of course, paying rent to the communist government. This was, evidently, a strategy through which the communist government gained more control over people's lives. The information comes from personal observation, as the present author has experienced Ceauşescu's forced urbanisation first-hand.

[20] As a volunteer worker myself, I have personally witnessed the events described. See also Codreanu, 'Biserica Penticostală Elim – Timişoara', 19.

[21] The impact the construction project had on the growth of the church is a recurring motif in several interviews. E.g., Teodor Codreanu, taped interview by author (Timişoara, Romania, 18th December 1999; D. Tecar, interview by author (Timişoara, Romania, 19th December 1999), using written notes; V. Goagără, interview by author (Timişoara, Romania, 19th December 1999), also using written notes. According to Tecar, this impact is undeniable, for after the inauguration of the new building in 1989, an upsurge of new converts was recorded: during 1989, EPC held five water-baptism services, with the service held on 23rd April 1989 adding a record 158 new members to the community, thus making this the second highest number of candidates baptised in one baptism service in the history of EPC – the highest number being recorded at the service on 10th May 1992, with 189 candidates. This was a clear departure from a pattern of three water-baptism services per year, of an average of 100 candidates each.

believers in EPC at the beginning of the period under scrutiny (1990-1997) to 2,130.

EPC – Mission in Post-1989 Romania (1990-1997)

The decade after the fall of communism in Romania represents a time of transition in two levels. At the macro-level, these are the years during which the ideals of freedom that had animated anti-communist demonstrators in December 1989 were challenged at every turn by neo-communist agendas. They were promoted by elected officials, such as Ion Iliescu (president of Romania 1990-1996 and 2000-2004) and other such figures that were clinging to the past. At the micro-level, these are also the years during which the stabilisation of new leadership structures and a search for a genuine Pentecostal identity, untainted by the compromises of the past,[22] began taking place within the Romanian Pentecostal denomination. For EPC, however, these are years during which the mission work of the congregation resulted in unprecedented growth. These are also the years in which the mission strategy of the church, tested and sharpened during the communist era, became the foundation upon which new endeavours, that would not have been possible prior 1989, were undertaken. The result: according to available membership records, coupled with oral reports obtained via interviews, was an average annual growth rate of approximately 20%, reaching in 1997 some 7,000 adult believers and over 2,500 children and adolescents.

It should be clarified, however, that while the figures above include a fairly precise estimate of new converts that joined EPC from 1990 until 1997, they only approximate the number of converts in the over thirty satellite churches established by EPC during the same period.[23] Also, it takes into account (again, an estimate) the number of people that converted in EPC and subsequently left Romania as work-migrants, and the converts that left EPC and joined other

Published figures confirm this estimate: Codreanu, 'Biserica Penticostală Elim – Timişoara', 19 (10th May 1989 – 189 candidates); 'Botez nou-testamental cu 136 de suflete la Timişoara', *Cuvântul Adevărului* 5:4 (2nd series, April 1994), 20 (9th January 1994 – 136 candidates); 'Pe scurt', *Cuvântul Adevărului* 5:12 (2nd series, December 1994), 19 (25th September 1994 – 70 candidates); 'Botez nou-testamental la Biserica Penticostală "Elim", Timişoara', 2 (19th January 1997 – 106 candidates); A.M. Anescu, 'Legământ', *Cuvântul Adevărului* 9:3 (2nd series, March 1998), 20 (11th January 1998 – 82 candidates); Ghiţă Bodrojan, 'Primul rod în anul 2000', *Cuvântul Adevărului* 11:2-3 (2nd series, February-March 2000), 5 (16th January 2000 – 93 candidates); Corneliu Merca, 'Botez la Elim, Timişoara', *Cuvântul Adevărului* 15:5 (2nd series, May 2004), 2, 20 (2nd April 2004 – 58 candidates).

[22] On the duplicitous attitude shown by some of the Pentecostal leaders during the communist period, including collaboration with communist oppressors and compromise for personal benefits, see Vasilică Croitor, *Răscumpărarea memoriei: Cultul Penticostal în perioada communistă* [Redeeming the Memory: The Pentecostal Denomination during the Communist Period] (Medgidia, Romania: Succeed Publishing, 2010).

[23] E.g., 'Pe scurt', *Cuvântul Adevărului* 9:11 (2nd series, November 1995), 15.

newly established congregations in Timişoara. Since precise information on all these categories is not available in EPC's records, such estimates are the best that can be provided.[24]

There is, of course, a clearer record with regard to the growth of EPC itself. This shows that, even when considered alone, EPC's average growth rate remained impressive: 10.66% per annum, with 1992 and 1994 being the years with the highest yield (with growth rates of 14.37% and 14.87% respectively), by contrast with 1996, when there was only a 6.95% increase.[25] The highest number of converts that joined EPC over a one-year period was recorded in 1994, with 440 new members, while the total number of new converts over the seven-year period under scrutiny was 2,198 – that is, a total growth of 103.19%. The four charts provided below help 'paint' a clearer picture.

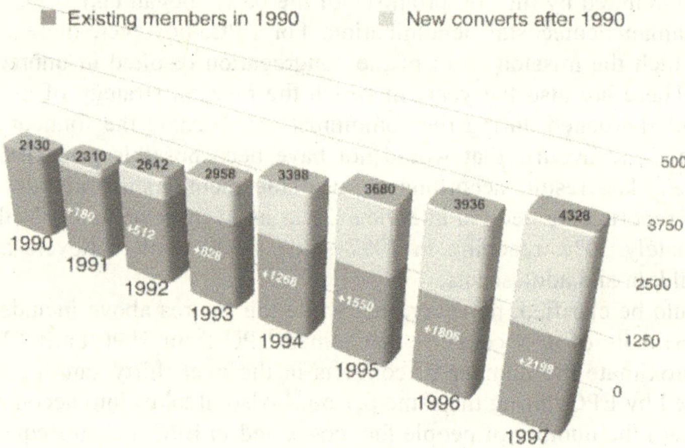

Total growth during 1990-1997 (number of new converts)

[24] On these, see further Merca, 'Elim-ul… la 15 ani', 2.

[25] Discrepancies appear at some points between the records of EPC that I had access to and figures given in various publications or stated in interviews. Where such was the case, I generally sided with the more conservative numbers. For published figures, see Trip, 'Biserica Elim 1992 – Retrospectivă', 11; Codreanu, 'Biserica Penticostală Elim – Timişoara', 19; Merca, 'Din istoricul Bisericii Apostolice Penticostale "Elim" Timişoara', 14-15; Ibid. 'Elim-ul… la 15 ani', 2; 'Teodor Codreanu, 1928-2004', 23; and 'Biserica "Elim" de-a lungul timpului': www.elim.ro/despre-biserica-penticostala-elim-timisoara/biserica-elim-de-a-lungul-timpului (accessed 14th April 2016).

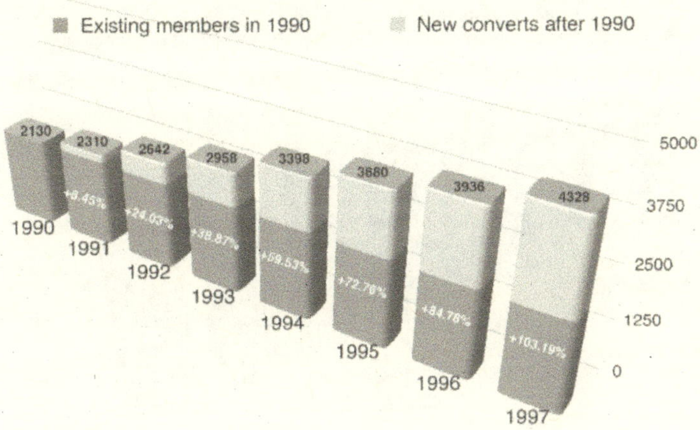

Total growth during 1990-1997 (percentages)

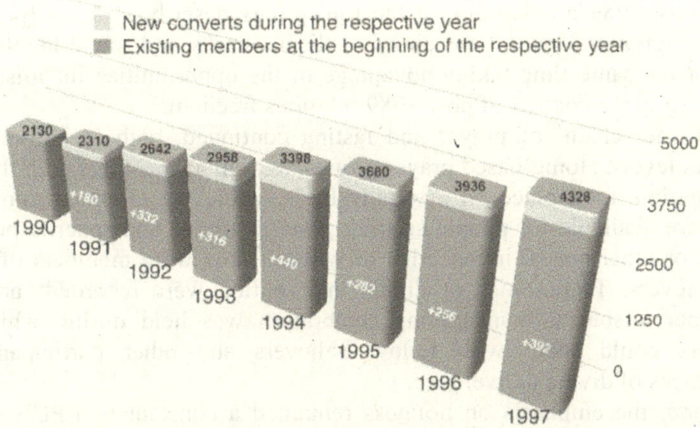

Annual growth (number of new converts)

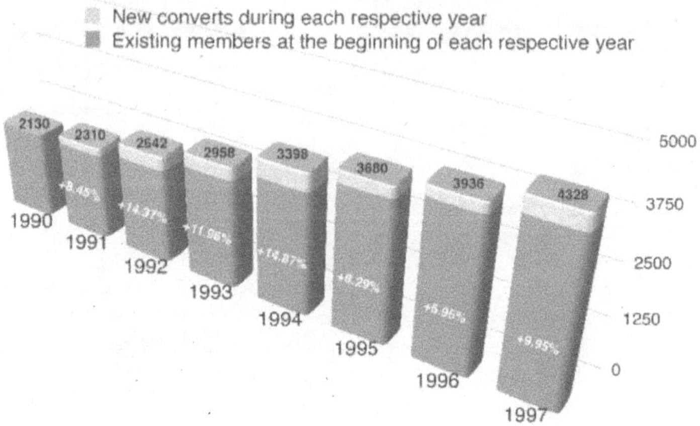

Annual growth (percentages)

In terms of mission strategies, the research undertaken has revealed that EPC's post-1989 praxis built on the four pillars described earlier (prayer and fasting; high morality; a focus on evangelism; charity and social involvement), while at the same time taking advantage of the opportunities for mission that opened up in the context of post-1989 religious freedom.

First, the 'chain' of prayer and fasting continued, both at individual and ecclesial levels. Home-based prayer groups, as well as meetings with the whole congregation, took place on a weekly basis, while the ordained ministers of EPC were available for people seeking pastoral advice and specific prayer for healing or other needs, irrespective of whether they were members of EPC or non-believers. Testimonies of divine intervention were recorded[26] and every December a special thanksgiving celebration was held during which EPC members could share with fellow believers and other participants their experiences of divine deliverance.

Second, the emphasis on holiness remained a constant of EPC's ethos as well, although, according to Pastor Codreanu, the 'enemy' to be unmasked was no longer communist propaganda, but the 'shocking' customs and unprecedented accessibility to western cultural features that had the potential to become a threat to the integrity of Romanian believers. Also, during this period, due to the cross-cultural exchanges that took place between Romanians and visitors from abroad, new concepts of worship and service to God became available. In EPC's answer to all this, one could observe a tendency to preserve the traditions of the past, although there was also much openness from EPC's leadership to enter fruitful partnerships with foreign mission agencies and

[26] E.g., Codreanu, 'Biserica Penticostală Elim – Timişoara', 19; Viorica Coman, 'Lanţul vindecărilor', *Cuvântul Adevărului* 7:8-9 (2nd series, August-September 1996), 16.

missionaries for as long as these paid due attention in their approach to mission to the specifics of the Romanian Christian ethos.

Third, the new-found freedom of expression was seen by EPC as an opportunity to increase its evangelistic efforts. Thus, during the period in view, EPC was involved (as a partner or as sole organiser) in several evangelistic rallies in the city of Timişoara:[27]

- June 1990, with evangelist Luis Palau (Argentina / USA) as speaker – CFR Stadium, Timişoara (EPC as a partner, together with other evangelical churches from the city).
- 10-12 April 1992, with evangelist Len Linstrom (Canada) as speaker – CFR Stadium, Timişoara (EPC as organiser).
- 13-14 April 1992, with the Rev. Al Smith (USA) and Pastor Teodor Codreanu as speakers – 'Olimpia' Sports Hall, Timişoara (EPC in partnership with the Romanian Mission of Chicago).
- 20-22 July 1992, with the Rev. Al Smith (USA) and Pastor Teodor Codreanu as speakers – 'Olimpia' Sports Hall, Timişoara (EPC in partnership with the Romanian Mission of Chicago).
- 24-26 July 1992, with evangelists Lennart Charlsson and Leif Svenson (Sweden) as speakers – 'Olimpia' Sports Hall, Timişoara (EPC in partnership with the Romanian-Swedish Humanitarian Christian Centre).
- 6-8 November 1992, with evangelists Lennart Charlsson and Leif Svenson (Sweden) as speakers – 'Olimpia' Sports Hall, Timişoara (EPC in partnership with the Romanian-Swedish Humanitarian Christian Centre).
- 4-6 June 1993, with evangelists Lennart Charlsson and Leif Svenson (Sweden) as speakers – 'Olimpia' Sports Hall, Timişoara (EPC in partnership with the Romanian-Swedish Humanitarian Christian Centre).
- 7-8 May 1994, with evangelist Iohan Maasbaah (Holland) as speaker – 'Olimpia' Sports Hall, Timişoara (EPC as organiser).

In addition to these, EPC has participated every year in the so-called 'Marşul Învierii' (Resurrection March), an ecumenical event involving all Christian denominations (including the historic churches) in Timişoara. The event has taken place every Easter Monday since 1990, and it consists of a procession through the city, which is concluded with an evangelistic service in an open arena in one of the parks of Timişoara.

It should be noted in this context that 1992, the year in which EPC was involved in five evangelistic rallies, has also been identified in the charts above as one of its best years in terms of growth.

Besides the evangelistic rallies listed above, in 1991 EPC, in partnership with the Evangelical Theological Seminary of Osijek, Croatia, launched a

[27] On these, see 'Info Elim: 20 Noiembrie 1988-20 Noiembrie 1998', *Elim* 36-37 (1998), 20.

theological educational programme (which later developed into the 'Elim' Evangelical Theological Seminary) with the purpose of training mission workers and church planters.[28] As a result, in 1992 EPC organised twelve missionary teams which were charged with planting a new church in every city and village in the Banat area (the western part of Romania) that did not have at least one Pentecostal church in it. The impact and scope of this ministry increased over time to the point that church-planting teams were sent to reach other areas of the country (Oltenia – southern Romania)[29] and Romanian ethnics living in Serbia.[30] The fruits of this ministry are evident in the over thirty satellite churches that were started during the period in view.

Finally, regarding EPC's fourth mission strategy, the charity work and social involvement of the congregation during the seven years under scrutiny was remarkably broad in its scope and diversified in its impact. Although not all the activities that could be listed under this category were recorded, research shows clearly that it is in this area that EPC's mission agenda was most obvious. Thus, records show that over 30% of EPC's budget during this period was directed at funding charitable and other social care activities.[31] Below, I describe the most representative occurrences, many of which also represent starting-points for long-term (sometimes still ongoing) ministries:

- 1992 onwards – in the aftermath of a disastrous earthquake which took place in the city of Voiteni and the surrounding area, EPC, in partnership with the Romanian-Swedish Humanitarian Christian Centre, provided humanitarian aid to affected families, especially families that had many children. This was the beginning of a longer-term partnership between the two institutions and the Romanian regional authorities, which later on focused on providing humanitarian aid to orphanages in

---

[28] 'Elim' Evangelical Theological Seminary is recognised as one of the denominational educational institutions: Pavel Riviş Tipei, 'Raportul Consiliului Bisericesc la Congresul al VI-lea al Bisericilor Apostolice Penticostale din România: Mandatul noiembrie 1994-noiembrie 1998', *Cuvântul Adevărului* 10:1 (2nd series, January 1999), 8.

[29] See 'Biserica "Elim" de-a lungul timpului'; see: www.elim.ro/despre-biserica-penticostala-elim-timisoara/biserica-elim-de-a-lungul-timpului.

[30] See G. Mozor, 'Binecuvântări pe Meleagurile Banatului Iugoslav', *Elim* 1 (1992), 5.

[31] In most cases, charitable and social activities are not mentioned beyond expense entries in the budget of EPC. As such, the information provided in this section was obtained primarily from announcements of, and reports about, such activities recorded in EPC's periodical *Elim*. The periodical, published since 1992, has become one of the most respected Pentecostal publications in Romania, widely distributed in the country, and abroad among Romanian diaspora churches. For references confirming the impact of *Elim*, which appear in the official periodical of the Romanian Pentecostal Denomination, see 'Biblioteca redacţiei', *Cuvântul Adevărului* 7:5 (2nd series, May 1996), 12; 'Pe scurt', *Cuvântul Adevărului* 8:4 (2nd series, April 1997), 16; 'Lumina vechilor cărări', *Cuvântul Adevărului* 9:5 (2nd series, May 1998), 2; and Pavel R. Tipei, 'Raportul Consiliului Bisericesc la Congresul al VII-lea al Bisericilor Apostolice Penticostale din România pentru mandatul 1998-2002', *Cuvântul Adevărului* 13:11 (2nd series, November 2002), 7.

the cities of Timişoara, Lugoj, and Periam.[32] The ministry developed further as members of EPC began individual involvement in the lives of orphan children from these institutions, through donations as well as by welcoming them into their homes and, in some cases, by adoption.[33]

- 1992-1995 – EPC sent aid to war orphans in Osijek, Croatia.[34]
- 1992-1995 – EPC provided aid for Serbian refugees in the camps in Călacea and Buziaş.[35]
- 1993 onwards – EPC organised special church events, coupled with material aid for children with disabilities[36] and orphan children infected with HIV.[37]
- 1993 onwards – EPC organised and funded summer camps for orphan children and children coming from families without material means.[38]
- 1993 onwards – EPC began providing regular aid to elderly people in asylums or hospitals, especially those without relatives. Also, volunteers from among EPC members started providing transport for elderly people to and from the church.[39]
- Late 1993 – the EPC's Women's Association was launched. Its primary function was involvement in various types of charitable activities for the benefit of both believers and non-believers. The organisation was self-funded.
- December 1993 – EPC launched a hospital ministry: teams of believers were organised and funded to visit patients in the Timiş County Hospital every Sunday. The purpose of the ministry was to identify and help people who had no family support.[40]
- December 1993 – EPC launched a prison ministry: teams of believers were organised and funded to visit and, when permitted, give aid to inmates in the 'Popa Şapcă' Prison in Timişoara. Also, when permitted, inmates were invited to visit EPC and worship together with the congregation.[41]

---

[32] See Ion Pitic, 'Avem o colaborare bună în toate domeniile: interview by G. David', *Elim* 1 (1992), 5.

[33] See 'Ştiaţi că…?', *Elim* 2 (1993), 9.

[34] See E. Codreanu, 'De la inimă la inimă', *Elim* 8 (1994), 21; J. Paulus, 'interview by C. Constantineanu', *Elim,* 10 (1994), 14; E. Codreanu, 'Un zâmbet fericit pe feţe nevinovate', *Elim* 17 (1995), 18.

[35] I. Moroşan, interview by author (Timişoara, Romania, 19th December 1999), using written notes.

[36] L. Măcelaru, 'Mâinile care vindecă', *Elim* 42-43 (1999), 8.

[37] E. Codreanu, 'Stropi de binecuvântare', *Elim* 4 (1993), 14.

[38] C. Constantineanu and T. Stoia, 'Tabăra de vacanţă Petroşani – 1993', *Elim* 6 (1993), 14.

[39] G. Gui, 'Sărbătoare la Azilul din Ciacova', *Elim* 5 (1993), 15.

[40] M. Măcelaru, 'Alege să slujeşti', *Elim* 7 (1993), 10.

[41] C.G. Câmpan, 'Două ore deosebite petrecute de Biserica Elim împreună cu tineri din Penitenciarul Timişoara', *Elim* 42-43 (1999), 27.

- June 1995 – EPC began sending aid to the leprosy colony in Tichileşti, Brăila, the last place of its kind in Europe.[42]

From the record of EPC's ministries provided above, it is evident that the most significant year from a social assistance perspective was 1993. Most ministries of this type in EPC had their beginning at some point during that period. I suggest that the effects of this emphasis were evident in the upsurge of new converts that led to the peak of EPC's growth registered in 1994.

Conclusion

EPC's unique record of growth presented above provides a telling example of how the praxis of a congregation animated by a proper vision and informed by the right strategy can have effective outcomes even if operating within unfavourable contexts. Although EPC's success story is most visible in the period after 1989, the information provided above shows that the seeds of that success were sown in the years preceding the fall of communism. This, I suggested, was due to the mission intelligence of Pastor Teodor Codreanu, whose fourfold mission strategy made EPC an efficient 'engine' of mission in both the pre- and the post-1989 Romania. Thus, in the midst of a regime that aimed to silence religious communities and to smother any desire for social engagement, the mission strategy adopted kept the outward orientation of the congregation alive and the rate of its growth high. After the fall of communism, the same mission strategy provided a foundation for notable evangelistic efforts and broad social involvement, which together contributed to unprecedented upsurges in both EPC's membership and influence.

In the light of these, I conclude that the practices of prayer and fasting, the leading of a moral life, the focus on speaking out the message of the gospel, and charitable social involvement, all provide a model for ministry that reflects a holistic understanding of our God-given charge to be his witnesses in the world (Acts 1:8). They should not be taken as separate mission objectives but as an integrated mission plan – an 'edifice' that will stand tall for as long as its four pillars are equally developed.

[42] V. Păscălin, 'Tichileşti – tabăra de leproşi din România', *Elim* 16 (1995), 20; Ibid., 'Noi veşti din tabăra de leproşi de la Tichileşti', *Elim* 23 (1996), 15.

A Guatemalan Perspective on Pentecostal and Neo-Pentecostal Theology in the Twenty-First Century

Rigoberto M. Gálvez Alvarado

Introduction

When writing a document like this, it is important to guard against generalisations or simplification, especially when we refer to the vast pentecostal [1] diversity in the world. However, there are some unique considerations that raise questions in any analysis of Pentecostalism. Furthermore, the term 'Pentecostal' is not just an adjective of a specific religious denomination, but of a movement with doctrinal and spiritual structure, which embraces a large number of denominations and churches, mostly originating in the pentecostal experience in the early years of the twentieth century. Since the movement continued to grow worldwide, even to this day, it is appropriate to analyse it as a religious phenomenon that also made it to the 21st century with numerous forms and practices.

In this article I will write about Pentecostalism and Neo-Pentecostalism in Guatemala. Based on my observations of the past and present of these two Christian streams, I will make some remarks about the future of Pentecostalism and Neo-Pentecostalism in Guatemala and in Latin America. Even though it is impossible to exhaust the subject in a presentation like this, I would at least like to touch on some of the most visible characteristics observed in contemporary Pentecostalism and Neo-Pentecostalism. In the particular case of Guatemala, I will focus on some characteristics, strengths, and challenges of the two movements. Moreover, I will look into some definitions that seem to be typical of each movement. Then, as I said, I will elaborate on future perspectives that might be predicted, based on historical and current developments. All my

Originally published in Miguel Alvarez (eds), *The Reshaping of Mission in Latin America,* Regnum Edinburgh Centenary Series 30 (Oxford: Regnum Books, 2015), 144-160.

[1] For the purpose of this presentation I am using the words: 'Pentecostalism' as a noun, and 'pentecostal' as an adjective.

observations are related to ecclesiological and theological practices by both movements.

Definitions

Pentecostal: According to Robert Menzies, a Pentecostal is a Christian who believes that the book of Acts provides a model for the contemporary church and encourages all believers to experience the baptism in the Holy Spirit. This baptism is understood as a spiritual experience that follows the model of the book of Acts. According to Menzies, through the baptism of the Spirit, Christians are also empowered for mission and enabled to use the charismatic gifts as the Spirit makes them available to them.[2] For classic Pentecostalism, tongue-speaking is evidence of the baptism with the Holy Spirit, which is different from the experience of regeneration. Menzies also states: 'Signs and wonders including all the gifts mentioned in 1 Corinthians 12:8-10 should characterise the life of the church today'.[3]

Neo-Pentecostal: A Christian who agrees and acts in accordance with all the principles mentioned above, except that he or she does not believe that speaking in tongues is the initial evidence of this baptism or that the same serves as a regulatory signal for the baptism in the Holy Spirit.[4]

Charismatic: A Christian who believes that all the gifts described in 1 Corinthians 12 are available for today, but rejects the claim that the baptism with the Holy Spirit endues the believer with power for mission other than regeneration.[5]

Non-Pentecostal: A Christian who rejects the claim that the baptism of the Holy Spirit endues Christians with power for mission, distinct from regeneration, and rejects at least one or all of the gifts of the Spirit described in 1 Corinthians 12:8-10.

Pentecostalism

Characteristics

The Bible: Pentecostals have the highest regard for the Bible. They believe it is the inspired and infallible Word of God and the final authority in matters of faith and conduct. The Bible is the spiritual model of life, faith, worship and

[2] Robert Menzies, *Pentecostés, Esta Historia en Nuestra Historia* (Springfield, MO: Gospel Publishing House, 2013), 13.

[3] Menzies, *Pentecostés, Esta Historia en Nuestra Historia*, 13.

[4] See Paul Barnett and Peter Jensen, *The Quest for Power: Neo-Pentecostals and the New Testament* (Sydney: Anzea Publishers, 1973), 3-6.

[5] For more information on this subject, see Norberto Saracco, 'Charismatic Renewal and Social Change: An Historical Analysis from a Third World Perspective', *Transformation* 5:4 (1998), 14-18.

evangelistic witness for the church. They believe in the baptism of the Holy Spirit and that the Lord has empowered them to witness to the world. The Bible, first by faith and experience, shapes Pentecostal faith and practice, as may be observed in their theological and practical commitments.[6]

Holiness: The doctrinal and practical commitments of Pentecostals teach them to live a 'separate' life from the 'world'. As a system, the world is morally contaminated by sin. Christians are called to seek holiness in the Word and the Spirit. They are taught that through faith in the cleansing blood of Jesus Christ they can live in purity and testify of their faith to the world. Living in holiness is understood as 'being different', which includes external appearance, vocabulary, behaviour, and attitude. Pentecostals are in accordance with the whole concept of holiness, which not only means separation, but distinction too.

Service: In Pentecostalism, all believers are commissioned to serve and all seek to serve. Ecclesiologically, they call it the priesthood of all believers, although most of them do it without explicit awareness. In Pentecostalism, everyone can and should speak in tongues, which is the initial evidence of the baptism with the Holy Spirit who empowers them to exercise the priesthood effectively. Everyone can and must evangelise, and the strength for evangelisation lies in the fact that all Pentecostals 'should be' potential preachers and evangelists. Everyone can testify, and everyone can have ministerial privileges. Spiritually, everyone has access to the power of the Holy Spirit, and biblically, all have access to the free examination and interpretation of Scripture.

Liturgy: After one hundred years there have been no significant changes in pentecostal liturgy. Lay people participate in worship services through testimonies, while Christian songs and Bible readings occur without much preparation or pre-planning. Historically, Pentecostalism did not have significant development. Most praise, songs, and other specials are presented *impromptu*, in spontaneous and repetitive forms without much preparation. They are not driven by excellence in praise and worship, because they are focused on 'experiencing the freedom of the Spirit' and convinced that 'the Lord looks at the heart, not at the preparation'.

Leadership: Pentecostals focus on securing full recognition of local leadership, which grants them the authority to send and to be sent as workers to open new places for preaching. This practice is considered part of the ministerial training for new believers, and has no limitations for the completion of their evangelistic effort.

Evangelisation: Pentecostal evangelism is aggressive, constant and is seen as part of a Christian lifestyle. Most evangelistic efforts remain focused on the poor, both urban and rural. Pentecostals are spontaneous in providing immediate aid to the needy. They lead people to repentance of sin, do the prayer for salvation, and pray for the healing of the sick. They submit to civil

[6] See Miguel Alvarez, *La Palabra, El Espíritu y la Comunidad de Fe: Entendiendo la Hermenéutica Pentecostal* (Cleveland, TN: Editorial Evangélica, 2007), 41-46.

authority without prejudice. They do not depend at all on higher levels of church government for social assistance.

Social Needs: Pentecostals never consider the social aspects of their communities as most social activist typically do. They have a different approach to social concern. They care for the poor and are eager to assist them regardless of the cost, but they see it as part of God's redemptive plan for them. Pentecostals are focused on guiding the poor to salvation in preparation for the imminent return of Christ. That urgency of saving 'souls' is part of the millennial dispensationalist teachings that they incorporate in their faith and practice. For them, it is very important to separate the sacred and the profane. That may be the reason Pentecostals do not have theological teaching that focuses on social action alone. They are taught to win souls for Christ, and that is the source of their social impact. For them, any social action is the result of evangelism, and they are not involved in any political participation in civil life.

Preaching: Miguel Alvarez sees pentecostal preaching with a Christological emphasis: he associates pentecostal preaching with the fivefold ministries of Christ: he saves, heals, sanctifies, baptises with the Holy Spirit, and is coming back as King.[7] Although the bulk of the congregation may not appear to notice these teachings, they are very much part of what they believe and depend on when they preach.

A second pneumatological emphasis is also seen in the baptism of the Spirit. This baptism is the source of spiritual power that operates in the preacher, which enables him or her to serve effectively. Another emphasis of their preaching lies in the manifestations of the gift of tongues, interpretation of tongues, prophecy and physical healing.

Another distinctive aspect of preaching is that, in most cases, it is thematic. Their preaching does not feature expository sermons on passages, chapters, books or complete epistles. There are exceptions, as always, because there are pentecostal preachers with solid biblical and theological training who present well designed and well-delivered sermons.

Pentecostal preaching is spontaneous, passionate and compelling, with an urgent call to conversion. It invites sinners to repent and to raise their hands as a signal of acceptance of the message and to move forward to the altar to be prayed for. They are taught to wait on the Lord for what they have asked for, to believe and expect signs and wonders, and to be ready for miracles in the same way as they took place when Jesus preached: the blind saw, the deaf heard, the lame walked, the sick were healed, and demons were cast out. Along the same lines, Peter Wagner makes an interesting observation: 'I see that each of the five times the Great Commission is mentioned in the New Testament, it has a powerful promise':[8] a) Believers received the Spirit (John 20:22), b) These signs followed those who believe (Mark 16:17); c) The disciples waited in Jerusalem until they were endued with power (Luke 24:49), d) They received the Holy Spirit' (Luke 24:49), e) They received power (Acts 1.8).

---

[7] Alvarez, *La Palabra, el Espíritu y la Comunidad de Fe*, 28.

[8] C. Peter Wagner, *Señales y Prodigios Hoy* (Miami, FL: Editorial Vida, 1985), 12.

Theological education: Historically, theological education has not been a priority among Pentecostals, but in recent years they are showing genuine interest in it. Daniel Chiquete admits that they have neglected theological education owing to the typical conditions of their beginnings. Early in the twentieth century, Pentecostals lacked government and structural policies, and they had to cope with the problem of illiteracy. Most Pentecostals did not have access to secular or theological education; however, that was not intentional; they just happened to be part of a limited society composed mostly of peasants who were among the poor. The situation started to change at the end of the century and continued to improve in recent years.

Soteriology: The Pentecostal doctrine of salvation has Wesleyan and Arminian roots and, as Pearlman noted, 'The experience confirms the possibility of a temporary fall from grace known as relapse or recurrence.'[9] Classic Pentecostals emphasise the ministry of the Holy Spirit in the life of the believer. It is the work of the Holy Spirit that makes it practically impossible for a genuine believer to fall from grace. When a Christian lives in the Spirit, he or she is guided through holiness to experience the fullness of God's grace. For Pentecostals, the ministry of the Holy Spirit is indispensable in their lives and service. Such ministry of the Spirit is taken holistically. It is very much a part of the total being, thinking and doing of Christians committed to Christ.

Positive Aspects of Pentecostalism

Significant Growth. The historical expansion and strength of the Pentecostal movement are unquestionable. From the smallest congregation to the largest, their liturgy is oriented towards the participation of all believers. Their praise and worship reflect the reality of the human context where the church is located. The ordinances of the church are made simple and available to all members of the community of faith.

Pentecostals have permeated most Christian churches with their passion for evangelism and their emphasis on the spiritual gifts. Christians from different denominations are now speaking in tongues and practising ministry which reflects the pentecostal distinctive. The Pentecostal movement has dozens of names, millions of followers, and the fastest growth among all Christian movements.[10]

Church Planting: Pentecostal workers have not stopped in the face of difficulties and limitations that stand in opposition against the church. They are enabled to withstand adversity even with very basic education and training. Hence, through prayer and fasting, they hold on and plant new churches in the most remote areas of the nation. While some theologians and historic churches

---

[9] Myer Pearlman, *Teología Bíblica y Sistemática* (Miami, FL: Editorial Vida, 1989), 299.

[10] C. Peter Wagner, *Avance del Pentecostalismo en América Latina* (Miami, FL: Editorial Vida, 1987), 16.

criticise their theology and methods, they continue to preach and plant churches everywhere.

Spontaneity: Pentecostals are spontaneous in the practice of their faith and the fulfilment of their ministry. This major and decisive characteristic has contributed to spontaneous evangelism. They approach praise and worship with the same spontaneity, which strengthens their witness and prayer, without having to fit into liturgical and rigid methods.

Passionate Testimony: Generally Pentecostals do not show any fear or shame in testifying about their conversion to Christ. They love to tell others about their personal experience with Christ. So they testify with passion and conviction, believing that the hearers will respond positively to their preaching. That has gained them much, for people overlook some inaccuracies when they hear them speak with vehemence. But generally, people dislike boring speeches that fail to communicate the gospel effectively.

A Lifestyle of Evangelism: Pentecostals are taught from the moment of conversion that they have to be committed to Christ. They are instructed to show good testimony to the people with whom they interact. They are compelled to be baptised in water, to seek the baptism with the Holy Spirit, and to evangelise wherever they go. These practices are seen as virtues or fruits of their new life as believers in Christ.

Open Participation: The entire congregation is constantly encouraged to participate in all activities of the church. All Christians have opportunities to serve in the ministerial departments of the church. If they do not become involved, they will be considered as inactive members.

Commitment: Christian commitment is taught to believers at the moment of conversion. Committed believers will seek water baptism quickly. They will also be guided to receive the baptism with the Holy Spirit. Once the two baptisms are received as new members of the church, and they are considered to be loyal witnesses, they can partake of all the privileges reserved for them such as faithful stewardship and tithing. The latter are considered privileges that show healthy growth as active members of the church. In turn, the church considers them regular members for they fulfil all the spiritual and church commitments expected of faithful Christians.

Loyalty: For Pentecostals, loyalty to their leaders is crucial, especially to the pastor. They also show loyalty to deacons and leaders generally, as those to whom the church has entrusted authority in ministry.

Membership: For Pentecostals, being a church member is crucial. Membership makes them feel welcome, accepted and taken seriously into consideration. As part of the congregation, they develop a sense of belonging, which is seen in two ways: they are considered members of the church for their loyalty, commitment and service, and they, in turn, feel fully identified with the church by giving great importance to membership. To have a good testimony means a member is in full communion with other members. This practice is hardly seen in other churches or Christian traditions.

Affectionate Co-existence: There is an affectionate fellowship and mutual acceptance among members that make Pentecostals appealing to non-believers.

People are attracted to them by their simplicity of life and testimony. The poor welcome them as part of their own culture. This is one reason that makes pentecostal congregations attractive. People get prayed for, their human needs are met, and they are welcomed into a fellowship of believers who care for them holistically.

Lukan Focus: Pentecostals believe in the Pauline approach of Spirit baptism as a source of regeneration and sanctification, but they also believe, practise and teach the Lukan approach to the power of the Holy Spirit for effective service. They are aware of the need for spiritual empowerment when they witness, preach or evangelise. They insist that the infilling of the Holy Spirit is necessary for ministerial success.

Challenges

Suspicious of Theology: According to Carlos Ramos, Pentecostals have shown an attitude of rejection or indifference to formal theological education, which seems to be universal.[11] Such a negative attitude may be rooted in the very origin of the movement. Pentecostalism was initiated among the poor, and at some point, the movement represented the poor before the rest of evangelical bodies. Nonetheless, the new generation is moving towards theological training and general education, which may incorporate new sources of education for the advancement of the movement. One positive attitude is that they have been able to incorporate theological education into their prayer, fasting and Bible study. Pentecostal theologians have departed from their historical roots.

Legalism: Historically, Pentecostals have associated the doctrine of holiness to external appearance rather than developing strong spiritual disciplines for the practice of the faith. They are inclined to construct a gospel of prohibitions. For them, spirituality contains many of these, and at times they associate it with poverty, which include stereotyped forms of external appearance, speech, and conduct, thus causing 'true isolation' from the world.

Technologically Challenged: Pentecostals have not responded properly to the contemporary challenge of the mass media. They are not making proper use of TV, the Internet, social media or the press. There is scope for them to use local radio, but they lack adequate training for this, so opportunities are missed.

Isolation. Pentecostals do not show interest in the biblical response to 'mundane' issues that interest the rest of society. They do not pay attention to culture, politics, social issues, globalisation, religious pluralism or such other matters. This may result from their cultural and social condition.

Denominationalism. Pentecostals also show a lack of flexibility for new projects, developments, and changes. This may be due to internal rules of denominationalism, bureaucracy, red tape or negative 'denominational yokes'.[12]

---

[11] Carlos Ramos Ampudia, 'Un Siglo del Movimiento Pentecostal', in *P. Arieu Theologies Web*: https://lasteologias.wordpress.com/2010/07/23/un-siglo-del-movimiento-pentecostal (accessed 16th January 2015).

[12] Wagner, *Avance del Pentecostalismo en América Latina*, 16.

Sometimes they are compelled to observe denominational standards that stand over the Bible itself.

Refocus

In the context of Guatemala, the Pentecostal movement has not paid much attention to mission theology. As a matter of fact, this seems to be the case with most of Latin America. It was only recently that two Pentecostal scholars, Darío López of Peru and Miguel Alvarez of Honduras, published their works on mission theology from a Pentecostal and Latin American point of view.[13] They have developed mission theology following the teachings of renowned evangelical missiologists such as Samuel Escobar[14] and René Padilla.[15] These scholars have approached the biblical model of mission as found in some of their books on mission theology.

The disciples in the early church had a clear understanding of the fulfilment of the prophecy of Joel at Pentecost. On that day they were filled with the Spirit, who provided them with power, passion, commitment, and definition. They did not do theology before taking action. Instead, they went everywhere proclaiming that Jesus was the Messiah, who was raised from the dead and who would return. They made a call to repentance, conversion, and baptism in water. Pentecostals have followed this pattern until now. They are focused on worship and seek the baptism of the Holy Spirit. They also look for the gifts of the Spirit and believe that signs and wonders follow the work of evangelisation. Their challenge today is to move from theology to mission without losing its essence.

Another challenge is to move freely and quickly into the fields of education and, more importantly, into formal theological training. Although things have begun to change in the pentecostal world, that is not enough. There have been pentecostal scholars and academicians, mostly European and American, who laid the foundations for pentecostal hermeneutics, theology, and apologetics. Hence, there are some Latin American pentecostal scholars who are developing

---

[13] See the books of Darío López, *La Misión Liberadora de Jesús: Una Lectura Misionológica del Evangelio de Lucas* (Lima: Ediciones Puma, 1997); López, *Los Evangélicos y los Derechos Humanos* (Lima: Centro Evangélico de Misiología Andino-Amazónica, 1998); and López, *Pentecostalismo y Transformación Social* (Buenos Aires: Ediciones Kairós 2000). See also the works of Miguel Alvarez: 'Integral Mission in Contemporary Perspective: Exploring an Appropriate Model of Mission for the Pentecostal Churches with Special Reference to Honduras' (Ph.D. dissertation, Oxford Centre for Mission Studies, 2012); and 'Pentecostals, Society and Christian Mission in Latin America', in Wonsuk Ma, Veli-Matti Kärkkäinen and J. Kwabena Asamoah-Gyadu (eds), *Pentecostal Mission and Global Christianity* (Oxford: Regnum, 2013), 302-24.

[14] Samuel Escobar, *De la Misión a la Teología* (Buenos Aires: Kairós, 1998), 13.

[15] See for instance, C. René Padilla, 'An ecclesiology for integral mission', in Tetsunao Yamamori and C. René Padilla (eds), *The Local Church, Agent of Transformation: An Ecclesiology for Integral Mission* (Buenos Aires: Kairos Ediciones, 2014).

solid academic works. But they are small in proportion to the number of Pentecostals in the region. Along these lines, it is pertinent to mention that pentecostal preachers and theologians move forward to balance spirituality with scholarship.

Pentecostal theology should strive to become more skilled in the use of biblical tools, such as systematic theology and scientific methods that develop a broader understanding of Christian issues. They need to pour all their abilities into biblical interpretation, pentecostal spirituality, and social concern. Pentecostal theology needs to move from words and experience to written theology. They need to deliver a rational and systematic discourse, without abandoning the spontaneity and spirituality that has characterised them historically.

Pentecostal believers, teachers, preachers, and pastors have a basic knowledge of Christian doctrines and various branches of theology. They have stayed close enough to evangelicals to receive basic formation for ministry. But that is not enough. Their teaching and academic training are limited. By the same token, their theology is also called systematic theology, but in reality, it is more a biblical theology that expounds the doctrine of God, Christ, Holy Spirit Church, man, salvation, and eschatology. And that is where academic theologians need to contribute to pentecostal theology.

Another challenge for Pentecostals is the need to develop and disseminate a well-structured Lukan theology. Robert Menzies has suggested that Pentecostals will have to work on building a strong biblical exegesis and solid systematic theology. They need to establish foundations for a Pentecostal Theology. They cannot continue borrowing doctrine and theology from the evangelicals.[16] Their theology has to demonstrate the work of the Holy Spirit in the church. They also need to prove that Luke did write as a theologian, for most evangelical theologians take the book of Acts as a narrative, not as a theological record.

Pentecostals also need to incorporate a new perspective of women in Pentecostal theology, mission and ministry. The number of women in ecclesiastical authority seems to be limited. This is contrary to the traditional understanding that women are the majority in the pentecostal churches. To accomplish this, Pentecostals will have to educate women and make room for them in leadership positions and every area of ministry in the church.

Pentecostal theology must be more self-critical and not only apologetic. Pentecostal theology has received enough reviews from other Christian theologians who always end with the same conclusions about Pentecostals.[17] On the other hand, Pentecostals need to accept with humility that they have made mistakes. A humble attitude will revitalise their achievements, and they

---

[16] Menzies, *Pentecostés, Esta Historia en Nuestra Historia*, 15.

[17] One of those scholars is Bernice Martin, 'Interpretations of Latin American Pentecostalism: 1960s to the Present', in Calvin L. Smith (ed), *Pentecostal Power: Expressions, Impact and Faith of Latin American Pentecostalism* (Leiden: Brill, 2011), 112.

will be able to withstand the challenges of a globalised, multicultural and technological world. They will also succeed in social, economic and political contexts amid rampant religious pluralism.

New Perspectives for the Twenty-First Century

If current trends continue, the future may not look so bright for Pentecostalism. Even though they may continue to pursue formal theological education, their growth, in general, has entered a certain stagnation. Classic Pentecostal denominations are losing members to Neo-Pentecostals, and their finances have entered a severe recession. Their institutionalised government is obsolete, and they do not seem to find viable solutions to this problem.

Classic Pentecostalism will remain a) pre-millennial, b) mostly Arminian in their approach of salvation, c) dispensationalist in eschatology, d) their final authority will remain in their assembly, and e) the liturgy will remain the same. Pentecostals will seek to maintain and guard the teachings of the previous century. Those who are interested in new theological fields and education will be marginalised from mainstream leadership.

There will be some Pentecostals in Latin America that will be open to dialogue with other Christian streams and with emerging ministries in the area. In Latin America, Pentecostals will continue to grow among the poor and those living on the margins of society. Daniel Chiquete states that there are at least three initiatives that are relevant in Latin America: a) local denominational seminaries, b) solid educational projects arising under local church efforts, and c) strong interdenominational associations recognised by other Christian organisations.

Another initiative comes out of the Latin American Network of Pentecostal Studies (RELEP) that seeks to promote and coordinate the work of Pentecostal theological reflection in the region.[18] These efforts are connected with the Society for Pentecostal Studies (SPS), the European Pentecostal Theological Association (EPTA) and similar networks in Asia and Africa. Clearly, there is much to be done and many tasks to accomplish, but it is also true that these initiatives may help classic Pentecostals to renew their spirituality and ministry.[19]

In Latin America, the Pentecostal movement has leaders, pastors and theologians increasingly educated with access to seminars, universities and research centres with high academic levels. Such would include ISEDET in Buenos Aires, the Comunidad Teológica Evangélica de Chile (Evangelical

[18] Daniel Chiquete y Angelica Barrios, 'Mirada Común al Pentecostalismo: Entre Cronos y Kairós', in *Consejo Evangélico de Madrid. La Casa Común Protestante*. http://protestantedigital.com/magacin/12970/Mirada_comun_al_pentecostalismo_entre_cronos_y_kairos (accessed 10th Feb 2015).

[19] Luis Orellana, 'El Futuro del Pentecostalismo en América Latina', in Daniel Chiquete and Luis Orellana (eds), *Voces del Pentecostalismo Latinoamericano* (Haulpén, Chile: RELEP, 2011), 141-56.

Theological Community of Chile), the Universidad Bíblica Latinoamericana (Latin American Biblical University) in Costa Rica, the Seminario Teológico Matanzas (Matanzas Theological Seminary) in Cuba, the Universidade Metodista de São Paulo (Methodist University of Sao Paulo) in Brazil, and the Seminario Bíblico Pentecostal de Centro América (SEBIPCA) (Pentecostal Bible Seminary of Central America) in Quetzaltenango, Guatemala. Also, a number of pentecostal scholars have enrolled in doctoral studies at prestigious theological schools and universities in the United States and Europe, but they are still a minority.

However, the future of Pentecostalism is moving towards institutionalisation. Historically, this pattern seems to be unavoidable. This phenomenon can be observed in historical Protestantism, which ensured institutional continuity, but the challenge is to ensure the institution while keeping the spiritual movement alive and healthy.[20] Unfortunately, history shows that once a movement becomes institutionalised, it is very difficult to be revived spiritually.

Neo-Pentecostalism

Some scholars like Buhene Wolfgang suggest that Neo-Pentecostalism was the result of a new wave of revival among the classic Pentecostal movements,[21] but I argue that Neo-Pentecostalism is a new movement that has convergences with Pentecostalism, while both differ from each other. I also argue that Neo-Pentecostalism was an activity of the Spirit moving believers to a revival in response to the coldness and indifference of traditional denominations that claimed ownership over charismatic manifestations of the Spirit. Besides the classic Pentecostal denominations, the Neo-Pentecostal movement also reached Lutherans, Presbyterians, Episcopalians, Baptists, and Methodists altogether. The movement began in the 1980s, at a time of profound social change and transformation in Latin America. Since then it has influenced the liturgy and ministry of most classic Pentecostal denominations.[22]

Characteristics

Not all Neo-Pentecostal churches and pastors are exactly alike. Each congregation has its personality and particularities in theology and ministry. Neo-Pentecostals show a strong influence from the Reformed tradition in the doctrine of salvation. In its preaching, Neo-Pentecostalism emphasises the

[20] Jean-Pierre Bastian, *Protestantismo y Sociedad en México* (Mexico: Casa Unida de Publicaciones, 1983), 58.

[21] For a broader understanding of this subject as related to the Pentecostal, Charismatic and Neo-Pentecostal movements, see Buhene Wolfgang, *Explosión Carismática. Un Análisis Crítico de las Doctrinas y Prácticas de las Llamadas Tres Olas del Espíritu Santo* (Barcelona, Spain: Clie, 1996), 16-17.

[22] See Wolfgang. *Explosión Carismática*, 17.

supernatural power of God, experienced through signs and wonders here and now.

For Neo-Pentecostals, a high level of preparation and quality for praise and worship is called for. Its musicians, singers, and their songs have transcended all Christian denominations.

Biblically, they believe and seek all the gifts of the Holy Spirit as found in 1 Corinthians 12.[23] Doctrinally, they believe in the baptism with the Holy Spirit, but do not consider speaking in tongues as evidence of this baptism. Neither do they consider this necessary in order to acquire power for evangelisation.

Neo-Pentecostals highlight the importance of small groups for fellowship and teaching in homes. Their ministry permeates the upper strata of society and politics of the country. They make good use of television, radio, written press, Internet and social networks. They are very creative, so they have developed innovative methods of church growth.

Neo-Pentecostal liturgy is practical, simple, pragmatic, spontaneous and live. They have used these tools to build more mega-churches. They also use their influence to collect significant amounts of money by implementing certain fund-raising techniques that at times could be questionable.

Neo-Pentecostals' governance and management revolve around a recognised charismatic leader known for his gifts of leadership, influence, power, communication, persuasion, and preaching. Capable and professional personnel surround this leader whose role is to protect the leader's reputation and safety.

The management of the church is mostly run from a business-like perspective, but the leader claims that his or her priority is to seek the guidance of the Holy Spirit.

In Guatemala, these were the first churches that were able to remove the financial obstacles imposed by the banking industry on Christian organisations. Their success took off when they consolidated churches as companies, creating good accounting systems, and set up structures of qualified managerial operations.

Neo-Pentecostals know and teach the great doctrines of the Christian faith, like the doctrines of God, Christ, Holy Spirit, the church, etc. but they do not have a fully articulated systematic theology. This is one of their great challenges for the future.

Positive Aspects of Neo-Pentecostalism

Some of the positive aspects of Neo-Pentecostals were noted by the Synod of the Christian Reformed Church.[24] By way of example, Neo-Pentecostals show a warm and vital relationship with God. They have practical leadership; they

---

[23] Gálvez, *Prácticas Dudosas en el Ejercicio de Nuestra Fe*, 153. Here I studied the characteristics of Neo-Pentecostalism in general.

[24] Serafín Rose, *Renovación Carismática Como una Señal de los Tiempos* (Grand Rapids, MI: Subcomisión de Literatura Cristiana, 1977), 15.

experience brotherly love and do not repress their emotions. They acknowledge the role, presence and guidance of the Holy Spirit in every work. They are aggressive in evangelism, manifest freedom in worship, and maintain a positive attitude in their commitment to Christ.

Neo-Pentecostals put an emphasis on the individual's religious experience. They show great interest in the presence of the Holy Spirit combined with a devotion centred on Christ. They also take great enthusiasm in testifying of what happens in their lives.

Neo-Pentecostals seem to be inclined to certain Calvinist teachings, and consequently, some believe the doctrine of eternal security. They practise freedom in worship with songs, gestures, and dance; yet sometimes these end in disorder. Other Neo-Pentecostal ministers wear their robes at worship, which reveals the influence of Presbyterian churches.

Challenges

As we have seen, Neo-Pentecostals show a lack of structured systematic theology. Sometimes the Scriptures do not sustain their doctrinal teachings. As a result, they hold onto poor or fanciful hermeneutics, and their preaching is more thematic than expository.

From a theological point of view, Neo-Pentecostals are prone to implement popular religious practices, which are not even sociologically backed up. In 1995 I started researching these doubtful practices, which I documented in my thesis before obtaining a bachelor's degree in theology.[25] In 2003 the first edition of my book, *Dubious Practices in the Exercise of our Faith*, I explained in detail these practices, and in recent years we completed the second edition that described the following dubious practices by some Neo-Pentecostals:

- The anointing of objects
- Laying hands on objects
- Idolizing the Bible
- The anointing of today's saints
- Evangelical superstitions
- Formulas and learning of new methods for healing
- The deliverance ministry applied to Christians
- The ministry of inner healing
- The gospel of faith and prosperity
- Hyper-faith and positive confession
- Spiritual warfare
- The popular Messianic movement
- The revival of laughter and being slain in the Spirit
- Signs of 'Gold Dust' in worship and revivals
- The world apostolic movement[26]

[25] Gálvez, *Prácticas Dudosas en el Ejercicio de Nuestra Fe*, 154.
[26] For more information on the Apostolic movement in Latin America, see Emilio A.

- The modern prophetic movement
- Humanism. Some churches study more humanistic books than the Word of God.[27] Undoubtedly, the Neo-Pentecostal movement needs a profound reorientation in many aspects, without losing the positive ones.

New Perspectives for the Twenty-First Century

The future of Neo-Pentecostalism in Latin America is still uncertain, but the movement will continue to grow; however, it is wise to observe its development over the coming years.[28]

I believe that the construction of mega-churches has come to an end, for several reasons – such as the global economic crisis, the high costs of construction and maintenance, demographic mobilisation and the saturation of parking lots. Churchgoers will migrate to satellite churches. These satellite congregations will become the venues for preaching by pastors, live via communication media. This is already happening in some countries and in some cities of North America.

More preachers are now using social networks for their preaching and worship online. In this regard, Harvey Cox argues that Neo-Pentecostalism (and following only slightly behind Pentecostalism) is the religion of the 21st century.[29]

Eventually, Neo-Pentecostalism will start its own process of institutionalisation and the shaping of its theology will occur, although it will be at a slow pace.

Three will be at least three well-identified Neo-Pentecostal trends: Conservatives, moderates and those who show excesses.

Neo-Pentecostals will continue to advance and grow while moving around entrepreneurial leaders with great vision. These leaders operate without excessive bureaucracy or denominational tie to make the transitions and succession of command at the right time.

They will continue to respond to the challenge of the media and making the best use of them.

Their interest in formal theological education remains low, although there will be some exceptions.

Self-Criticism of Neo-Pentecostalism

Neo-Pentecostal churches have tried to respond to multiple economic, cultural, social and spiritual challenges. They have sought solutions to these needs

---

Núñez, *El Movimiento Apostólico Contemporáneo* (Guatemala: Marlor, 2001), 62-71.

[27] Some of these Neo-Pentecostals teachings can be found in Cash Luna, *En Honor al Espíritu Santo: ¡No es un Algo, es un Alguien!* (Grand Rapids, MI: Zondervan, 2010).

[28] Orellana, 'El futuro del Pentecostalismo en América Latina', 152.

[29] Harvey Cox, *Fire from heaven: The Rise of Pentecostal Spirituality and the Reshaping of Religion in the XXI Century* (Cambridge, MA: Da Capo Press, 2001), 153.

consciously or unconsciously, employing preaching or evangelical popular religious practices to connect with the power structures, and in some cases, under the support of US financial ties and theological coverage. The purpose has been to solve spiritual problems and social issues.

The Neo-Pentecostal churches have grown in number and have influenced other Christian denominations despite some intolerance shown by non-Pentecostal denominations, as we have already indicated. Some of the growth strategies are questionable, but not all, since many of these are well planned, structured, and require a lot of discipline and hard work. Other Pentecostal churches do not seem to be willing to assume these responsibilities.

The Neo-Pentecostal churches have challenged the theological thinking and traditional practices of non-Pentecostal theology and so have forced conservative theologies to review their pneumatological teaching. Neo-Pentecostals have recovered the pneumatological dimension of the action and power of the Holy Spirit, though disproportionately, and very often they abandon the historic churches completely.

The Neo-Pentecostal churches have recovered the hermeneutics of the Spirit, experience, and the theology of subjectivity that fit within the gospel. I contend that the gospel is objective and subjective. It is objective because of the work of Jesus, and subjective because by faith we appropriate his work to be saved. Those who believe know, somehow, that they are saved.

The gospel contains doctrine and experience, word and power. It is knowledge but also a guide or intuition of the Spirit. It is the Spirit but also the word that appeals to the intellect, but does not eliminate the feelings or emotions. Hermeneutics of the Spirit and experience is legitimate if it subordinates to the biblical text, correctly interpreted without dogmatic or denominational prejudice. The hermeneutic of experience not only checks the doctrine, but makes it crisp and clean. The historical churches reject this hermeneutics of the Spirit and experience because they do not lead to an intellectual faith.

However, we are aware that experience and subjectivity are dangerous extremes and have led to a gospel of private interpretation. At the same time, the established churches need the spontaneity of Neo-Pentecostalism. At the end of the day, we have to love one another as brothers and sisters, tolerate and respect one another, because one does not choose who will be one's brothers or sisters. This decision is made by God the Father.

Conclusion

In broad terms, according to the development of historical Protestantism, with its ups and downs, the Spirit guides actions and reactions and all churches or renewal movements that are led to plant new churches or denominations. They are responding to the need of the hour and serving a life cycle that ends with the next generation. Another cycle of stagnation follows the first cycle of revival, and the third cycle leads to a waning due to new social and economic conditions. This was the case of the 'father' of the evangelical movement: Methodism. The Methodist movement was the Father of modern movements such as Holiness, Pentecostalism, and evangelical families like Baptists, etc. The movements that survived are those who managed to pass the 'sect' phase, to use the sociological meaning of Max Weber, into the phase of 'church' with its new institutions, doctrinal body and 'hierarchy'.[30] Those are the ecclesiological devices that support and channel the enthusiasm and first emotions without getting lost in personalities and charismatic leaderships that vanish when the person who holds leadership disappears. The challenge is to make the variants converge by seeking unity in the gospel and service to the community (love for God and neighbour). Unity strengthens those beliefs, which are the spine that supports the entire building and encourages spirituality that covers the nerves, tendons, and muscles of the body.

---

[30] For instance, Max Weber makes a distinction between 'sects' and 'churches' on the basis of numerical growth. Sects are small and dynamic communities whereby an individual, by choice, and only after a careful examination by the sect, is admitted as a member. By contrast, a church, according to Weber, is an entity that offers a religious and cultural acceptance to its parishioners. See Max Weber, *The Protestant Ethic and the Spirit of Capitalism* (London and New York: Routledge, 2001), 52; and Colin Loader and Jeffrey C. Alexander, 'Max Weber on Churches and Sects in North America: An Alternative Path toward Rationalization', in *Sociological Theory*, 3:1 (Spring, 1985), 1-6.

Challenges Facing the Ethiopian Evangelical Church Mekane Yesus (EECMY): A Growing Charismatic Churches in the Global South

Dawit Olika Terfassa

1. Introduction

Like many other churches in the global south, the Ethiopian Evangelical Church Mekane Yesus (EECMY) is among the rapidly growing Lutheran churches in the global south. The fact that the membership of EECMY grew from around 20.000 in 1959 to 8.4 million in 2017[1] places this church among the largest Lutheran churches in the world. The different waves of charismatic movements experienced by the church in the 1970s and 80s are among the important reasons for such rapid growth.[2] But the charismatic movement in EECMY is not without problems and challenges. Diverse problems and crises connected to the wrong view and practices of charismatic gifts have been and are still challenging the mission and theology of EECMY. This is a common challenge which even other Evangelical, Charismatic and Pentecostal churches in Ethiopia are encountering daily. In this study, the focus is given to EECMY which is one of the several charismatic churches from the global south that are struggling with a similar challenge. And the main challenges relate to the understanding and practice of charismatic gifts, particularly the gift of prophecy. The view and practice of charismatic prophecy are what I have paid much attention to.

A revised version of the chapter originally published in Beate Fagerli, Knud Jorgensen, Rolv Olsen, Kari Storstein Haug and Knut Treiteried (eds), *A Learning Missional Churches: Reflections from Young Missiologists*, Regnum Edinburgh Centenary Series 11 (Oxford: Regnum Books, 2012).

[1] World Council of Churches, https://www.oikoumene.org/en/member-churches/ethiopian-evangelical-church-mekane-yesus, Accessed 20180427.

[2] Dawit Olika Terfassa, *Prophecy, a Blessing or a Problem?: A Critical Study of the Practise [Sic] and Understanding of Prophecy in Ethiopian Evangelical Church Mekane Yesus* (Oslo: D.O. Terfassa, 2007), 18-19. Magnus Hagström, 'Reasons for the growth of the Ethiopian Evangelical Mekane Yesus', *Swedish Missiological Themes* 98:2 (2010).

An increasing amount of studies have been devoted to the multifaceted challenges and problems connected to the experience, view, and practice of charismatic gifts and revival in EECMY without necessarily excluding the positive impact of the experience. The investigations have been conducted by nationals from different parts of Ethiopia and synods of EECMY with a focus on the different periods of the history of the church. Few expatriates who have closely followed the development and the challenges have also chosen this area as a focus of their study.[3] Therefore, the challenges EECMY faces regarding charismatic gifts are large and complex. This study is intended to provide useful tools and guidelines derived from teachings of the scripture and the tradition of the early church.

2. General Background and Overview of the Challenges

The charismatic experience has played a significant role in the remarkable growth of EECMY.[4] But contrary to the positive effect or impact of charismatic revivals different types of problems are increasingly observed in the church. Due to problems related to the experience of charismatic gifts in general and specifically the understanding and practice of prophecy, many Christians have withdrawn from their Evangelical faith to return to their old religion or have become atheists. Their bad experience with the practice and understanding of prophecy has made them hostile to Christian belief, church and even to God.[5] They have lost their interest in evangelical faith as a result of all the lies, deceptions, false promises and empty hopes they have seen and heard within the practice and understanding of prophecy.[6] Also, this controversy has become a hindrance for non-believers from coming to evangelical faith.[7] Many believers likewise experience disappointments and frustrations caused by false prophecies. The reason for deciding to remain in the church is that they don't feel comfortable about leaving the Christian community. But they maintain a

---

[3] For example, A.A Gingmo, 'The Challenges of Lutheranism in Ethiopian Evangelical Church Mekane Yesus Tabor Congregation' (MTh these, Ethiopian Graduate School of Theology, 2015); Tesso Jaleta, *The Work and Use of the Spiritual Gifts* (Addis Abeba, Ethiopia: EECMY-Gospel Ministry Department, and Christians Education Section, 2000); Johnny Bakke, *Christian Ministry: Patterns and Functions within the Ethiopian Evangelical Church Mekane Yesus*, Studia Missionalia Upsaliensia (Oslo: Solum Forlag, 1987); Magnus Hagström, 'Reasons for the Growth of the Ethiopian Evangelical Church Mekane Yesus (Eecmy) in Western Wollega, Central Synod, 2004-2009: A Quantitative Study', *Swedish Missiological Themes* 98:2 (2010); A. Øyvind, 'The Problematic of Church Growth in Southern Ethiopia', in Egil Grandhagen, Kjell Olav Sannes, and Tormod Engelsviken (eds.), *Med Kristus Til Jordens Ender: Festskrift Til Tormod Engelsviken* (Trondheim: Tapir akademisk forl., 2008).

[4] Hagström, 'Reasons for the Growth', 157-68.

[5] Interview with Mr. Temesgen Alemu and Mrs. Elisabeth Terfa, Nov 17, 2006, Nekemte.

[6] Interview with Mr. Motuma Bedhassa, Nov 13, 2006, Nekemte.

[7] Interview with Rev. Gilo Si'a, Nov 20, 2006, Arjo.

sceptical attitude toward prophecy,[8] resulting in mistrust in all charismatic gifts and ministry of the church.[9]

3. History of Charismatic Revivals/Experiences in EECMY

During the half-century of explosive growth, the church faced the challenge of the shortage of trained workers. The charismatic movement started in the Central Synod, and Illubabor Bethel Synod, which spread to all 29 Synods.[10] The Central Synod was one of the four Synods that constituted the national church EECMY. Rev Belina Sarka is a well-known figure in the country regarding charismatic revival; It is confirmed that the beginning of charismatic renewal in the central synod 'was the first charismatic renewal in the history of Mekane Yesus Church'.[11] The two great waves of revivals that came to the EECMY in the 1970s and 80s highly contributed to the growth of the church in many ways.

Some of them were: the spread of news about charismatic healings, exorcisms, and fulfilled prophecies; passionate sharing of the gospel with others; the rise of many highly devoted lay minsters.[12] The experience of transformed Christian life ushered in a new spiritual dimension which attracted many non-believers to Christian faith.[13]

Charismatic revivals, expressions, and experience in EECMY had a variety of inputs. The main inputs were from traditional religious life and practice,[14] Pentecostal teaching, practice, and experience.[15] In some cases, the movement occurred as an indigenous movement in remote Mekane Yesus congregations where and when it was not expected. However, soon problem rose due to the lack of sufficient teaching on the right use and practice of spiritual gifts. The use and practice of prophecy were particularly controversial within the EECMY.

4. Seven Common Problematic Areas Related to Prophecy In EECMY

Before discussing the problem of prophecy, it is important to affirm the important and wonderful role of this particular gift in the growth of the church. The exercise of the gift of prophecy has also kept alive the biblical

---

[8] E.g., interview with Rev. Miressa Berhanu, Dec 5, 2006, Addis Ababa.

[9] Interview with Mr. Asefa Woyessa, Nov 13, 2006, Nekemte.

[10] Debela, 'The Effect of Charismatic Renewal', 12-14., Interview with Mr. Fekadu Bengna, Nov 14, 2006, Nekemte.

[11] Debela, 'The Effect of Charismatic Renewal', 14.

[12] Fogi, 10., Debela, 'The Effect of Charismatic Renewal', 22.,

[13] Godebo, 18., Interview with Rev Kano Galan, Nov 30, 2006, Addis Ababa.

[14] The parallelisms are seen in many aspects. See Dawit Olika Terfassa, 'Parallelisms between Charismatic Prophecy in Eecmy and Qallu Institution in Oromo Traditional Religion' (Mekane Yesus Theological Seminary 2003), 25ff.

[15] Tesema, 56-57. Interview with Mrs. Tadelech Mekonen, Nov 17, 2006, Nekemte.

understanding and practice of the various gifts of Spirit. It also had a positive effect in transforming lives, introducing Christians into a new dimension of spirituality by strengthening and refreshing the personal faith of the members. This was the cause of many new converts, producing committed voluntary ministers and bringing inspiration to the global church.

On the other hand, prophecy and the so-called prophets have affected the church in a negative way, hindering and threatening the growth and the charismatic life of the EECMY. There has been a growing trend to uncritically copy charismatic experiences and their expressions from surrounding Pentecostal Churches. Often lacking sufficient biblical instruction, people are influenced by traditional religions regarding attitudes, beliefs, and practices. They are the main factors for the many problems about the understanding and practice of charismatic gifts in EECMY.[16] Some of the main problems observed can be summarized as follows:

1. Unfulfilled Prophecies

The number of people who call themselves prophets has been and is incredibly growing within EECMY and almost all Protestant churches in Ethiopia. They provide uncountable false prophecies in the form of empty promises. Unfulfilled prophecies include promises of pregnancies for a barren woman. Sometimes promises are made to a woman whose womb has been removed because of cancer and other reasons. Promise and hope are also made for healing to those who are diagnosed as HIV – positive, and the promise of raising of the dead who have been buried for some days.[17] The most grotesque example was shown on Ethiopian TV, involving a woman who had been buried for two days. A group of prophets ordered the grave to be dug open and that the body be brought into the church, promising that she would wake up. They prayed and prophesized over the dead body for several hours in vain after which the police intervened and arrested the prophets and reburied the woman.[18] The challenge is that the types of prophecies and promises of healing intensify and grow extensively.

2. Interest in Gaining Power and Popularity

Instead of becoming humble servants of God, most of the alleged prophets, the healers, or apostles are often characterised by a strong desire to obtain power and popularity. These types of prophets claim to be the most authoritative persons in the church because of their close and personal communication with God. Majority of prophets in EECMY and within other denominations in the

[16] Terfassa, 10-24.

[17] Badassa, 29-30. Interview with Rev Gilo Sia, Nov 20, 2006, Arjo. Interview with Mr. Amensissa Ulfata, Nov 28, 2006, Addis Ababa. Interview with Evangelist Abdi Megersa, Dec 5, 2006. Addis Ababa

[18] Benti, 27-28. Interview with Rev. Diriba Atomsa, Nov 20, 2006, Arjo.

country want to take over the church leadership. Often a church is established by enticing some supporters from an existing church. In general, they desire for all the church members and leaders to become subject to their prophetic authority. They are neither willing to submit to the leadership of the church, nor let their prophecies be subjected to testing, questioning, and evaluation by the word of God. Rather they often use a tactic of drama, by loud and threatening, judgemental voice/message to scare people, nor to prevent them from challenging their authority. They avoid cooperation with one another but level harsh criticism at their competitors. Sometimes they do this in the form of character assassination just to be the lone ruler. According to the understanding of the and experiences of both the leaders and members of the church, these people that claim to have the gift of prophecy or had the gift earlier '...abuse their gifts for the sake of getting popularity and due to intoxication by the thirst of power'.[19]

3. The Use of Prophetic Office as a Means to Material and Financial Benefits

The claim of a gift of prophecy or healing is regarded as a good source of income by many of the so-called prophets. They use the gift they claim to have to gain all kinds of personal gains whether in kind or in cash.[20] Most of them can tell any prophecy if that will give them some benefit, no matter whether it is true or false. They promise good fortunes when their hosts pay well, but pronounce curses and misfortunes on those that refuse to pay well or may be attempting to resist/question their authority/prophecy. Most of these prophets who are benefit-driven, regularly visit the rich and well-to-do families but not the poor and the sick. They act as advisers and intercessors of the rich and influential, thus becoming powerful characters.[21] This is what most of the informants expressed their disappointments on the exploitations by such prophets. Estifanos Tesema who conducted a similar study confirms that 'People who claim to have been manipulated financially as well as in-kind by those who claim to have the gift are not few. The underlying reason for such economic manipulation is that most people with the gift do not want to think that their prophetic message is subject to the scrutinising and validating authority of the Bible'.[22]

---

[19] Tesema, 'Charismatic Experience on Trial', 62. Interview with Eva, Abdi Megersa Dec 5, 2006, Addis Ababa.

[20] Interview with Rev. Wakseyoum Idossa, Dec 15, 2006, Addis Ababa.

[21] Interview with Mr. Bizuayehu Kebede, Nov 20, 2006, Nekemte. The society is used to bring gifts of money, material and cattle etc. whenever they were going to Qallu, the traditional prophet to know their future of receive healing from sickness or internal problems. No matter if what Qallu told them is true or false, fulfilled or not fulfilled, they were expected to bring gifts and this mentality is in some ways retained and reflected in the prophetic experience in EECMY today. Terfassa, 12.

[22] Tesema, 'Charismatic Experience on Trial', 62-65. Interview with Rev. Belayneh Gashare, Dec 8, 2006, Addis Ababa.

4. The Wrong Use and Attitude toward the Bible

During the early charismatic history of EECMY in the 1970s and 80s, Bible studies and correct teaching of scripture played an important role in forming the charismatic expressions and promoting proper growth of a church. But this is no longer the case because many of recent prophets including their sympathizers do not only lack biblical knowledge but show no interest at all in learning it and ground their understanding and practice of charismatic gifts on it. They avoid Bible courses and teachings; instead, they constantly refer to the guidance of the spirit (illumination of the spirit).[23] They regard themselves as superior as they claim extra-biblical revelations. In many aspects, the believer's life, understanding, and future are dominated by and bound to the words of the prophets rather than the word of God.[24] They do not accept anyone who questions or tests their prophecies. They are especially sensitive to those with theological training whom they usually refer to as 'dry theologians'. Observation of where they place their prophecies, revelations or words of healing makes their ambition to 'compete with the scripture or even replaces scripture, in giving guidance concerning God's will'.[25]

5. Attitude Related Problems towards the Prophets and the Gift of Prophecy

Many of the EECMY and other Protestant church members in Ethiopia originate from the traditional religious background. They are used to visit the traditional healers or prophets (*qallus*, diviners or spirit mediums) to resolve their problems. They try to get security from fear of evil spirits and hear how their future is going to be.[26] Because of this and their key role, these traditional healers and prophets are highly respected almost like superhuman beings. Critical analyses of believer's attitude toward the charismatic prophets were made based on the view and experiences of the informants and leaders of the church. Many Christians seem to have retained their attitude towards the traditional prophets, and transferred to the charismatic prophets. These prophets are given and demanding very high respect and are feared by church members. People treat the prophets as if they are more than ordinary human beings, and commit so much of their time on listening to their prophecies and promises of healing than to the word of God in preaching and teaching. They prefer a prophet predicting good future in their home to attending church services. Many Christians are totally dependent on the prophets with high regard for their words.[27] The prophets themselves are doing all they can to reinforce their control over the members' life through their words, teaching, and actions.

---

23 Interview with Evangelist Kidanu Mosissa, Dec 8, 2006, Addis Ababa.

24 Interviewwith Rev Wakseyom Idossa, Dec 15, 2006, Addis Ababa.

25 Wayne Grudem, *The Gift of Prophecy in the New Testament and Today* (Wheaton, IL: Crossway Books, 1988), 245.

26 It is many people in the church today that looks up on prophets in the church in the same way as they were looking up on their traditional prophets. Benti, 9-10.

27 Interview with Rev. Wakseyoum Idossa, Dec 15, 2006, Addis Ababa.

6. Prophecy as a Cause for Spiritual, Economical, and Social Crises

The experience of unfulfilled prophecies has led many Christians and churches to various forms of spiritual crises. They include frustrations and disappointment with God and the church; withdrawing from faith and becoming atheists. Many Christians feel that they have been misled and their faith damaged.[28] Economically, a large number of Christians have put themselves in debt to meet the prophet's demands, to the extent of relinquishing their houses and cars. As pointed out by Estifanos Tesemas, '... they [prophets] request (or command) people to give them money or any help in kind, underlining that the command comes directly from God'[29] Youths give up their jobs and studies to follow these prophets to idly wait for the things God will do through them. They are losing all sense of responsibility for themselves, parents, the community and a work moral.[30]

There is also a social crisis which results from the prophet's regular engagement in marriage relationships through prophecy. They often pressure a certain man to marry a particular woman, command a married couple to divorce or break engagement ties. In many cases, the prophet himself marries a divorced wife or a lady who has been loosened from an engagement bond. The prophet claims that such commands come from God, and failure to obey it will result in punishment and curses. Further, prophets are also behind the splits and divisions among different groups and leaders in the congregations.[31] The existence of these problems in EECMY is a serious challenge to the mission and theology of the church, which has claims to have committed to 'wholistic ministry', encompassing physical, social, economic and spiritual restoration.

7. The problem of Uncontrollable Emotionalism

The practice of prophecy in EECMY as well other Protestant and charismatic churches has one common feature: uncontrollable emotionalism. Often, the prophet aims to address the believers or followers emotional state through the immature expression of emotions of ecstasy. The practice includes the repetition of few words and shouting, shaking and falling to the ground as proof of the presence of the Spirit. Such gatherings can last hours with heightened ecstasy. A common perception is that the louder and wider are these ecstatic expressions, the more intense is to believe the presence of the Holy Spirit:[32] '...although prophets often performed symbolic acts which they then

[28] Interview with Rev. Gilo Si'a, Nov 20, 2006, Arjo.

[29] Tesema, 'Charismatic Experience on Trial', 65ff.

[30] In EECMY more than 60% of the church members are youngsters between 16-30. They are the ones that have highly welcomed the charismatic movements. They are also the victims of all problems that result from the misuse of the spiritual gifts/prophecy. Interview with Berhane Temesgen, Dec 2, 2006, Addis Ababa.

[31] Interview with Rev. Bekeuma Sura. Nov, Dec 1, 2006, Addis Ababa.

[32] Debela, 'The Effect of Charismatic Renewal', 28. Interview with Rev. Wakseyom Idossa, Dec 15, 2006, Addis Ababa.

interpreted, the mainstream of prophetic activity, at least as it came to be canonized, had very little to do with 'ecstasy'.[33]

Factors Contributing to an Increasing Demand for and Dependence on Prophetic Activity in EECMY

Despite the problems some of which are discussed above, both in EECMY and Ethiopia as a whole, there is a growing trend of spirituality and revival with an emphasis on prophecy and healing. The number of prophets and prophetic activities has increased beyond control. Many new churches emerge again both in EECMY and other denominations under the name of prophets. Here are several factors which contribute to the increase in prophetic activity.

1. Increasing Poverty and Unemployment

'Ethiopia is one of the bottom line countries in its economy, most of whose people live below the poverty line (44% according to World Bank assessment and the Official poverty line is US1.50)'.[34] Evangelicals in Ethiopia are no exception. The lack of all the basic needs like food, house and cloth, etc is something people experience daily. People come to the church with questions such as their daunting economic situations, their financial depravity, and their joblessness, They seek relief from these challenges; they look for answers and ways out.[35] So the ears of people are always open to any message that would bring good news. Many are in desperate need of economic, social and medical assistance. Thus, anyone who promises a way for improved living conditions and health has a ready audience. Most of the prophecies uttered in EECMY are concerning material issues: promises of a good source of income in the future, an open door and opportunity for jobs, a chance to go abroad, etc. They invoke a psychological feeling of satisfaction and relief, however short-lived. 'The false prophet is empty, the people who come to him are empty, and the answers are empty too'.[36]

---

[33] Gordon D. Fee, *The First Epistle to the Corinthians* (Grand Rapids: Eerdmans, 1987), 595.

[34] Lorenzo Guarcello and Furio Rosati, 'Child labor and youth employment: Ethiopia country study' (http://siteresources.worldbank.org/SOCIALPROTECTION/Resources/SP-Discussion-papers/Labor-Market-DP/0704.pdf, March 2007), 3.

[35] Tesema, 'Charismatic Experience on Trial', 65. Interview with Rev. Waksyoum Idossa, Dec 15, 2006, Addis Ababa.

[36] J. Reiling, *Hermas and Christian Prophecy: A Study of the Eleventh Mandate* (Leiden: Brill, 1973), 38-39.

2. Traditional Religious Background

Many of believers came from traditional religions, bringing their experience with them to their Christian life. What is common for almost all the religious backgrounds are the dependency on mediators, fortune-tellers, diviners, witchcraft, and *qallus* to know the future. People bring their inquiries to them in times of problems, to get security and protection from fear of evil spirits.[37] This mentality is retained by many Christians. They often find a strong similarity between the functions of *qallus* or mediums and the activity of many charismatic prophets within the EECMY.[38]

The danger of syncretism is evident because of retained attitudes and beliefs from traditional religion and the traditional prophets. The issue of syncretism in EECMY was pointed out by many researchers. Amsalu Tadesse observes:

> The ties to old tribal religions are not totally broken. Some Christians believe in suppressions. For example, belief in the power of 'evil eye' is still strong. 'Fortune' is one of the common suppression practiced also among some Christians.[39]

His observation confirms the necessity of theological reflection and research on this challenge. Öyvind Aadland made visits the rural areas of Sidama over the last three decades after observing strong 'charismatic' elements. He called for thorough attention to this problem. He 'recognized and identified elements that have created a sense that the mission and/or church has left this area 'too early' without having paid enough attention to Christian education and to contextualizing Christianity into the Sidama culture in a real sense'.[40]

3. Being Born (Spiritually) in a Charismatic Church

Many of the present members and prophets in EECMY were spiritually born in the charismatic context or history of the church especially in the 1970s and 80s. They saw a church that was experiencing charismatic gifts with healings, prophecies and speaking in tongue. For most of them, it seemed that this is the normal and natural characteristics of the church to have as many healing announcements and prophecies as the church had at that time. A church life without such healings and prophecies, followed by people's applause, the shouting of hallelujah's and amen's, was not accepted as a normal and good Christian life. It was rather seen as a sign of weakness in prayer in one's (church's) Christian life, lack of holiness caused by sin against God, as a result of which God withdrew his gifts from the church. Out of great interest and

---

[37] In Africa it is very common to think that someone is under the influence and control of spirit whether that spirit is good or bad. John S. Mbiti, *Introduction to African Religion (African Writers)* (Heinemann Educational Books 1991), 43, 68ff.

[38] Interview with Rev Wakseyoum Idossa, Dec 15, 2006, Addis Ababa.

[39] Amsalu Tadesse, 'A case study: Demonization and the practice of exorcism in Ethiopian Churches' (study presented at the Lausanne movements issue-based gatherings, Nairobi, 2000).

[40] Øyvind, 'The Problematic of Church Growth', 203-13.

pressure to keep as close as possible to the standard of charismatic church life as prophets continued to feel they had to prophesy and the people continued to expect it regularly.[41]

Insights from the Teachings of the New Testament and Early Church Traditions

Prophecy is defined as the reception of divine revelation of God's will, which originates from God and is communicated through inspired intermediaries with intelligible words, actions or signs (1Cor 14: 29-30). Prophecy in a broad sense is the prediction of future events or the speaking of divine words (divine revelation) through the chosen human messengers (prophets). Prophecy is a general term for assertions presented as the revelation of divine will.[42]

Prophecy is one of the spiritual gifts for the NT church. This points to the fact that the understanding of charismata, gifts of grace, should not be limited to the supernatural gifts like gifts of healing and speaking in tongues, but be understood broadly including all other gifts like encouraging, generous giving, the gift of celibacy or gift of marriage, with the gift of salvation itself as the core of all gifts. Paul makes an interesting shift in 1 Cor 12:1 from spiritual gifts (*penumatikon*), a term the Corinthians preferred, to gifts of grace (charisma), a term he preferred to emphasize grace.

The diversity of all the different gifts of the Spirit, as shown by the body metaphor used in 1 Corinthians, should be understood based on the unity of adhering to one common confession and inspired by the same Spirit. This helps to see the gift of prophecy as one gift among the many and shows the importance and interdependence of all the different gifts.

The motivation for manifesting and having the gifts of the Spirit should not be for personal status or benefit,[43] but the common good. On this, Carson admonishes,

> ...some charismatic leaders and their followers treat prophecies of their leaders as if they possess the unqualified authority of God himself... God has given the leader a prophecy that commands him to build something and to tell the people to send in some money. No community of believers carefully checks out this claim, nor does the leader submit himself to the evaluation of a spiritually-minded community. The resulting exploitation is manipulative, arrogant, sometimes dishonest, and corrosive of the leader's humility and destruction of the follower's spiritual maturity.[44]

Prophecy and other spiritual gifts should be exercised in the congregation in an orderly manner so that they may edify the believers and convict the non-

---

[41] Interview with Rev. Jira Dhufera, Nov 29, 2006, Addis Ababa.

[42] Grudem, *The Gift of Prophecy*, 69, 116-19.

[43] Herman's mandate XI 7, 16, The Didache: Text, Translation, Analysis, and Commentary, by Aaron Milavec, *The Didache: Text, Translation, Analysis, and Commentary* (Collegeville, Minnesota: Liturgical Press,, 2003), 73.

[44] Carson, *Showing the Spirit*, 121.

believers. This demands the provision of intelligible content during the exercising of the gifts.[45] Prophecy should always be subject to the testing and judging role of the congregation in line with the teaching of Scripture (1 John 4:1-6, 1 Thess 5: 19-21 and Didache 11: 7-12).

Finally, it is important to underline that church leaders can play an important role in the process of correcting the practice and understanding of prophecy by the teaching of the New Testament and the early church. But '...sometimes it [prophecy] competes with the scripture or even replaces scripture, in giving guidance concerning God's will'.[46] Therefore, churches leaders and educated theologians need to set a good example in testing all kinds of prophecy based on the Scripture and by equipping Christians with enough Biblical instruction concerning spiritual gifts. These insights and guidelines which are derived from the general teaching in NT and the preserved tradition in the Early Church concerning the view and practice of prophecy. They are thought to help EECMY and other churches that have similar challenges, to come to terms with the misuse of the gift of prophecy and other spiritual gifts in general.

---

[45] Different analogies (instruments and different languages) used by Paul to argue for intelligibility Fee, *The First Epistle to the Corinthians*, 661-65.
[46] Grudem. *The Gift of Prophecy*, 245.

Mission and Three South African Metropolitan Megachurches: Middle-Class Masses in Search of Mammon?[1]

Genevieve Lerina James

Megachurches have incurred strong disapproval from segments within the global Christian community. These churches are often at the receiving end of jokes pertaining to their size. Mocked with names like 'soul garage', 'McChurch' and 'faith-factories' megachurches have certainly unintentionally and in some cases intentionally encouraged a lively discussion and debate about the new face of Christian presence in our cities today. According to Shelley and Shelley,[2] megachurches are the 'newest feature on the ecclesial landscape of large metropolitan areas'. The strong presence of these churches in the major cities of South Africa warrants exploration.

This article will describe the ethos, practise, and presence of three Pentecostal/Charismatic megachurches in three South African cities. The research on which this article is based is located in the cities of Johannesburg, Durban, and the administrative capital, Pretoria. These cities were selected on account of their dominance in shaping the political, economic, cultural and religious landscape of the country. The descriptions and explorations in this article are based on participant observation over the first decade of the twenty-first century. Participant observation as the fieldwork strategy of this research has provided extensive opportunities to experience and view the phenomena discussed here.

In this article, I will discuss the significance of size as the most obvious characteristic of the megachurches. I will move on to explore forms of megachurch mission engagement strategies, thereafter tackling what I call mega-hazards, which include potentially risky mission practice.

Originally published in B. Fagerli, K. Jørgensen, R. Olsen, K.S. Haug and K. Tveitereid (eds), *A Learning Missional Church Reflections from Young Missiologists,* Regnum Edinburgh Centenary Series 11 (Oxford: Regnum Books, 2012), 171-184.

[1] The study contains content from my doctoral dissertation titled, 'And God Said "Let There Be Charismatics in the City": A Study into the Practice and Presence of a Charismatic Megachurch in the City of Durban' (PhD dissertation, University of South Africa, 2000).

[2] B. Shelly and M. Shelly, *The Consumer Church: Can Evangelicals Win the World Without Losing Their Souls?* (Grand Rapids, MI: Kregel, 1992), 204.

Size Counts

The megachurches' most obvious characteristic is their size. Rothauge (in Shelley and Shelley)[3] suggests that there are four basic sizes of churches. A small church is called a 'family church', and can have up to 50 active members, while a medium size church with 50 to 150 members is a 'pastoral church'. Here the pastor's role is to provide the common purpose and identity of the church. A large church with 150 to 350 people is a 'programme church'. The extra-large church has 350 or more people and can be called a 'corporation church'. Thumma[4] describes a megachurch as constituting a minimum weekly attendance of 2000 people. All three South African congregations in question have memberships of well over 15 000 people. National membership of these congregations could in some cases surpass 50 000 people. One news reporter[5] described one of the congregations as an '... empire called the fast-food of spirituality, [that] has been growing steadily and in the last four years attracted 10 000 new members... National membership exceeds 70 000'.

To experience the megachurch multitudes, a Sunday morning church visit is necessary. A traveller on the roads leading to these churches may not recall that it is actually a Sunday morning, since the traffic that leads to these churches resembles the Monday morning peak hour. It is not uncommon to witness people queuing in long lines just to get into the service. Ushers skilfully filter the crowd in and out of the massive halls. As the auditoriums fill to capacity, rows of chairs are often set up for the overflowing crowd at the back of the church or outside. In some instances when popular guest preachers are invited, people occupy aisle space, hallways, and entrance areas to accommodate the influx. Crowds bring delight to the leadership of these churches. The presence of crowds indicates the success of the churches' evangelistic and marketing efforts. Further to this, statistics play a huge role in megachurches self-value and appraisal. It is common to hear about the number of people who were saved or baptised in the last church meeting.

The other major observation is that the three megachurches have an overwhelmingly middle-class membership. The churches have become brand names that have massive brand loyalty from the middle class. One of the reasons that these South African megachurches grow can be ascribed to the simple theory that big crowds attract big crowds; however, there is more to the growth of these churches. Given the phenomenal rate of urbanisation in post-apartheid South Africa, the megachurches also attract people who are first-generation urban dwellers.

The pastors and congregants often suggest that the growth of their churches should be attributed to the prompting and guiding of the Holy Spirit who leads people to these churches. Several members of the three congregations believe

---

3 Shelley and Shelley, *Consumer Church*, 203.

4 S. Thumma, 'Megachurches Today' (hirr.hartsem.edu/org/faith_megachurches_FACTsummary.html, 2000).

5 A. Eliseev, 'Stressed out Pastor McCauley Heads for Durban', *The Mercury* 20 (April 2006), 1.

that people are attracted to their church, since it is a 'spirit-filled church'. The term 'spirit-filled church' is commonly used in Pentecostal and Charismatic circles. It refers to a church that allows the move of the Holy Spirit as opposed to churches that abide by a strict liturgical structures and time limits. Exuberant worship styles, lively musical instruments, testimonies, healing, and prophetic services are often elements of Spirit-filled churches.

Megachurch Mission Engagement Strategies

The South African urban megachurches reflected in this article have a wide array of mission strategies. I will briefly focus on four main strategies, which are as follows: Evangelism, Mobilised masses – the agency of the flock, Social interventions, 'Send us the power Lord!'

Evangelism

Megachurches in South Africa are deeply evangelistic in their practice. Evangelism is often considered to be the core function of the church and the primary priority. Congregants are conscientised about their role as messengers of the gospel and 'proof producers' that Christianity works. 'Give us souls Lord' is the recurrent prayer at these churches. The churches spend generously on hosting evangelistic campaigns and crusades. The senior pastors travel around the country and the world preaching and teaching and 'leading the lost to Christ'. As mentioned earlier, the statistical gain is crucial, as the senior pastors often return home sharing the news of the number of people who 'came to the Lord'.

The megachurches teach that every Christian is responsible for the communication of the good news of Jesus Christ. Things start to get murky when we explore the megachurches' interpretation of the good news. The good news of the fullness of life through Jesus is often mixed with references to emotional well-being, secure and happy families, riches, living luxuriously, better jobs and houses. The message of Jesus is communicated as a message of a better life. Now, this is a very South African message, in fact, a slogan of the ruling political party is 'a better life for all'. Given the massive discrimination and inequality that plagued South Africa during the apartheid era, this is a pertinent and powerful message, rich with promise. Unlike the transitory nature of political parties, the good news of the better life courtesy of Jesus, who through the Holy Spirit will always be with us, is a compelling and comforting message for South African urban masses.

Mobilised Masses – the Agency of the Flock

Another significant form of mission engagement is the special prayer and bible studies that take place in the homes of the megachurch members. The congregants are mobilised to reach their communities through 'home cells' or 'life groups', which are gatherings of small groups of people. Members are encouraged to bring along 'unsaved' families and friends to house meetings. These meetings form an indispensable feature of the growing megachurches. The house becomes a neutral space for people who do not attend church services and who would feel uncomfortable and intimidated in an actual church building. The guest is nurtured and encouraged through other members of the home group who share their personal narratives of strength in situations of crisis. Stories of healing, salvation and answered prayer are part of the appeal of the house meeting. The megachurches grow as a direct result of the social networks established at the home level.

Social Interventions

Realising their capacity to contribute to change in their cities, the megachurches have engaged in a wide range of social interventions ranging from HIV and AIDS awareness and treatment, youth and children mentorship programmes, counselling services, places of safety, children's homes, employment clinics, and migrant integration support services. These churches offer valuable support to the already-strained city social development and relief programmes. It could be said that the overriding mission themes behind these interventions is that of evangelism through compassion and acts of social good as acts of blessing, this since the megachurches often explain that they are 'blessed to be a blessing'.

'Send Us the Power Lord!'

One of the major reasons why people are attracted to the megachurches is their need for power. The old Pentecostal song 'Send us the power Lord' aptly describes the congregations of the three churches. According to Schreiter,[6] the primary answer to the question, what does an individual seek from participation in popular religion, is 'access to power in times of crisis'. The three congregations confirm Schreiter's analysis, as weekly Sunday church services reveal an emphasis on the acquisition of personal power. The worship leader or preacher often refers to crisis situations reflected in the news and general family or individual situations such as divorce, financial, health and employment predicaments. Congregants are told that they can tap into the 'same power that raised Jesus from the dead' to transform their situations. Access to power in times of crisis is one of the dominant mission themes at these churches and amongst the dominant reasons that people attend these churches. The communication of the availability of power to the overwhelmed, beleaguered and stressed urban populace is a key mission strategy in these

[6] R. Schreiter, *Constructing Local Theologies* (Maryknoll, NY: Orbis, 1985), 139.

megachurches. At this point, it necessary to ponder the purpose of the power of God as John Hamby[7] so aptly states:

> The power of God turned despairing doubters into dynamic disciples. They had received the promise of the Holy Spirit and were clothed with power from on high. But power for what? Did they receive the power of God simply so they could feel good about themselves? Did they receive the power of God to keep it to themselves? No! They received the power of God to energize them to be witnesses to Jesus Christ in a secular society. The power of the Holy Spirit was for people; to enable the disciples to reach out and touch human need and share the liberating truth of the Gospel of Christ.

Mega-Hazards

While the megachurches in question boast an array of mission activities too many to account for in this article, there are mega-hazards in their current mission praxis. I outline them in the following section.

Middle-Class Masses in Search of Mammon?

A popular Pentecostal song I remember singing at church as a child was Ira Stanphil's 'Mansion over the hilltop'. This song dealt with the eschatological hope of prosperity and longevity. This hope was eschatological, since Pentecostals at that time were mainly poor working-class people, who did not have many 'worldly possessions'. Now many Pentecostals and Charismatics have become upwardly mobile and are comfortably located in the middle-class bracket. So, 'Mansion over the hilltop' is no longer sung at these Pentecostal/ Charismatic megachurches. Songs like Stanphil's are placed in archives and called 'old school' or 'classics', for the simple reason that they are considered irrelevant today. This is because many megachurch members who, when referring to a mansion over a hilltop, would probably be referring to their own houses here on earth, and not some hope in the afterlife. The megachurch congregants have moved from the romanticism of poverty and the hope of a better life in heaven to a global, public embracing of prosperity and abundance here and now. The 'prosperity gospel' has influenced the masses attending the three churches. Owing to the globalization of Charismatic Christianity, prosperity teachings of Western proponents have permeated the three megachurches. American prosperity preachers are household names in South Africa, since their television programmes are broadcast almost daily on Christian TV channels.

I would hope that the churches consider the reflections of Ronald Sider and Walter Hollenweger. Sider's 1977 thought-provoking book 'Rich Christians in an Age of Hunger'[8] discusses the folly and injustice of the gratuitous

---

[7] J. Hamby, 'Ministering in the Holy Spirit's Power' (www.antiochchurchofchrist.com/Sermons/2010-01-10%20Ministering%20in%20the%20Spirits%20Power.pdf).

[8] R. Sider, *Rich Christians in an Age of Hunger* (London: Hodder and Stoughton, 1977).

acquisition of the material amongst the Christian community while people continue to hunger and starve in the world. This still holds true today. Hollenweger [9] offers a spirited disapproval of affluent Pentecostals. He describes the 'insulation of elite Pentecostals from a meaningful dialogue' with poor Pentecostals. He laments the disinterest and disrespect shown to the poor primarily by those who have become rich. He then reminds us that Pentecostalism began as a religion of the poor. Now the upward mobility of Pentecostals has brought with it a sense of elitism, 'money-based power structures and world conformism'.[10] Though poor Pentecostals became rich through the 'work and life discipline that Pentecostal conversion entails'[11] and their ability to 'actively create, work in the informal sector of the economy',[12] they lose sight of their humble beginnings and join the race for 'more', more power, money and recognition. Hollenweger [13] further asserts that Pentecostalism has to be 'delivered from its Babylonian bourgeois captivity'.

Since the churches in this article have mastered the art of ministry to the middle class, they continue to attract a steady stream of upwardly mobile individuals. These churches often use the concept of 'excellence' to explain why they insist on only the best in life. The quest to attain the living standard of the bourgeois is being marketed as the quest for God-ordained wholeness. The megachurches in question have indeed reached outside the walls of the church and are involved in several social interventions in their respective cities. Despite this, I believe, the megachurch leadership of the three churches are far removed from the day-to-day struggles of the poorest people in the cities in which they operate. This lack of proximity to the poor has created a deficit in understanding the total plight of the disadvantaged and the urgency needed to authentically advocate for the poor. One megachurch pastor put up his five-bedroom house for 10 million Rands. The reporter[14] described the house as a 'palace' of '800m^2 of luxury'. The pastors live in unapologetic luxury compared with the South African urban poor. Their theology that it is God's will for people to prosper and enjoy the finer things in life (also known as 'abundant life' in these circles) justify their lifestyle choices. The megachurch pastors will further vindicate their lavish lifestyles by using the sow–reap principle. They often talk about what they personally sowed into the work of God, how they sacrificed, and how God has subsequently blessed them. These pastors believe that they are in control of riches and that riches are not in control of them.

---

[9] W. Hollenweger, 'The Pentecostal Elites and the Pentecostal Poor – A Missed Dialogue?' in K. Poewe (ed), *Charismatic Christianity as a Global Culture* (Columbia, SC: University of South Carolina Press,1994).
[10] Hollenweger, 'Pentecostal Elites', 205.
[11] Hollenweger, 'Pentecostal Elites', 203.
[12] Hollenweger, 'Pentecostal Elites', 204.
[13] Hollenweger, 'Pentecostal Elites', 208.
[14] Eliseev, 'Stressed out Pastor McCauley', 1.

The flaw in the logic above is that there is a failure to consider the full reality of the context in which the pastors live. The blessing of God is not the issue that I personally dispute; my dilemma is with the justification of extreme wealth and affluence in the presence of gross poverty and lack. The cities of Johannesburg, Durban, and Pretoria are by no means without visible signs of poverty, inequality and injustice. Thousands of people in South Africa live in a labyrinth of tin and plastic makeshift structures, which we have clinically named 'informal settlements'. Megachurch ministers should ask the popular question, 'What would Jesus do?' Would Jesus have opted for ostentatious crusades, luxury cars, business-class air travel, and palatial mansions, or would Jesus have identified with the poor and marginalised? If the pastors considered a simpler lifestyle for the sake of authentic identification with the poor, the impact of such a lifestyle choice may have a great influence on the thousands of middle-class congregants who hold in high esteem the very words of these leaders.

In South Africa, the number of people living on less than a dollar a day has 'more than doubled since the first democratic election in 1994'.[15] What is more disturbing is that 'black economic empowerment[16] and the surge in the black middle-class have worsened inequality amongst black South Africans by boosting wealth and incomes at the middle and top end'.[17] It could be said that the megachurches in question contribute to the widening gap between the poor and the rich by unconsciously encouraging the black middle class who throng to these churches to maintain the status quo of middle-class individualism and consumerism. This is achieved through constant references to personal prosperity and blessings.

Megachurches, Capitalism and Consumerism

The next mega-hazard to consider is what Luisa Kroll[18] wrote about in *Christian capitalism: megachurches, megabusiness*. Kroll notes the similarities between corporations and churches. After presenting these similarities, she offers a welcome to the world of megachurches, 'Where pastors often act as chief executives and use business tactics to grow their congregation'. This entrepreneurial approach, Kroll believes, has contributed to the explosive growth of megachurches. Kroll ventures to mention that churches have 'learned valuable lessons' from business corporations, and 'maybe they can teach businesses a thing or two'. Kroll is certain that companies would appreciate 'having the armies of non-paid, loyal volunteers'.

---

[15] G. Steyn, 'Different Conclusions', *Finweek* 2006, 47.

[16] In an African special report, Robinson discusses how the spoils of black economic empowerment are benefiting a few. S. Robinson, 'The New Rand Lords', *Time* (6 June 2005), 30-33.

[17] Steyn, 'Different Conclusions', 47.

[18] L. Kroll, 'Christian Capitalism: Megachurches, Megabusinesses' (www.forbes.com/2003/09/17/cz_lk_0917megachurch.html), accessed on 17 Sept 2003.

The Learning Annex Real Estate Wealth Expo, where consumers learn about wealth creation and real estate opportunities, was held in several American cities in 2007. Keynote speakers include the likes of real estate mogul Donald Trump, founder of the multinational 'Virgin' enterprise Richard Branson, former boxer and entrepreneur George Forman, and life strategist Anthony Robbins. What is fascinating about this conference is that amidst the lineup of keynote speakers, there was a megachurch pastor, Paula White, who 'taught on why God wants you to be wealthy'.[19] The presence of a megachurch pastor at a wealth-creation conference is a conspicuous example of how megachurch leaders have become proponents for capitalism and consumerism. The American influence of size and wealth fixation has become deeply embedded in the consciousness of the South African megachurches in this study. There is little critical consciousness to counter the relentless sway of American megachurch values.

The South African megachurches' enthusiastic adoption of corporate-style growth strategies is giving them an advantage in the business of church growth. The churches display the savvy use of corporate strategies. They are major shareholders in the religious economies of the cities of Johannesburg, Durban, and Pretoria. The contemporary business strategy of these churches is not without theological backing. They prescribe to a theology that suggests that it is God's wish for his peoples' expansion, excellence, success, and prosperity.

Individualism

The mega-hazard of individualism is a serious threat to the Mission of God. I have observed that the worship service content of the megachurches is intentionally directed towards the upliftment and encouragement of the individual. Although the Sunday services are described as the equipping of the saints for the harvest field, the services' striking resemblance to psychotherapy sessions and motivational workshops cannot be ignored. Sermon content is largely confined to themes that deal with positive confessions, self-esteem, self-actualization, and self-empowerment. Vanhoozen[20] describes individualism as a:

> Distinctly modern ideology that promotes the sacred value of the self: individual freedom, private prosperity and personal wealth, personal fulfilment, self-improvement and the self-made man [sic] and the right to pursue one's own happiness

The megachurches appeal to the desires, needs and senses of the individual is crucial. Individualism is what drives many members of the megachurches.

---

[19] Donald Trump at The Learning Annex Real Estate & Wealth Expo (www.thefreelibrary.com/Donald+Trump+at+The+Learning+Annex+Real+Estate+%26 +Wealth+Expo.-a0159654740).

[20] K. Vanhoozer, 'Evangelism and the Church: The Company of the Gospel', in C. Bartholomew, R. Parry and A. West (eds), *The Futures of Evangelicalism* (Leicester: Inter-Varsity Press, 2003), 58.

People can dispense with a church that is not meeting their needs or fancies. Bellan (in Vanhoozen)[21] describes this as: 'a group of persons united by their shared interest in a project that they believe will contribute to their individual good'. Vanhoozen[22] states that individualism is followed by consumerism. 'To elevate the individual is to focus on my needs, my want, and my fulfilment',[23] this is the ethos of individualism. The prosperity gospel adds to the notion of individualism, despite the fact that this gospel is marketed as 'blessed to be a blessing'. Individualism also contributes to the ease of which Pentecostal/ Charismatic theology ushers its followers on to the road to capitalism and neo-liberalism.

Go Tell It on the Mountain, over the Hills and Everywhere: Mega-Marketing

The next mega-hazard is the thin line between marketing and evangelism. In general, marketing activities are all those associated with identifying the particular wants and needs of a target market of customers, and then going about satisfying those customers better than the competitors.[24] Though the megachurches' theology can be considered conservative, the marketing is certainly progressive. The purpose of marketing is to draw people to the church. The churches use the usual marketing means from expensive glossy brochures, welcome booklets and weekly bulletins to electronic advertising boards located at the entrance to the church premises. What used to be weekly announcements is now transformed into *Coming Attractions,* which is presented in a high-tech, action-packed video format during the Sunday morning services.

The churches target people at every stage of their lives. There is specific targeting of children and youth with weekly contemporized versions of Sunday school with trendy name brands. I once witnessed costumed mascots walk through the crowds, gathering the children in order to take them to the children's church. Here the children are not only educated about the Bible, but also come to enjoy high-quality entertainment.

The intentional use of captivating contemporary names for the programmes, sensational language and the call to be part of something greater is a common thread in the three churches' advertising campaign targeting younger people. The focused targeting of children and youth in these megachurches is not without reason, since it is thought that if children become attached to the church, their parents will certainly follow.

One of the churches once marketed itself as 'More than just a Church'; this was presented on large billboards outside the church facing the street. This captures the essence of what these churches want to be known and experienced

---

[21] Vanhoozer, 'Evangelism and the Church', 58.
[22] Vanhoozer, 'Evangelism and the Church', 58.
[23] Vanhoozer, 'Evangelism and the Church', 58.
[24] Boone and Kurtz, *Contemporary Marketing Wired* (Dryden Press: 1998), leasingtoolkit.org/lease_production.

as. It is important at this point to reflect on the Theology of Church. What does it mean to be Church? Why do churches have the desire to be more than just a Church? Will this lead to the diminishing prioritising of the true purpose of Church? I will not go into a long systematic theology discussion on the doctrine of the Church in this article, I will merely state that the megachurches would do well to revisit the Church as the Bride of Christ and the Body of Christ. The Church is also viewed as the alternative community of mercy and justice, the sign of the Kingdom of God that is not yet but already here. This understanding seems far from the savvy sales pitch and bumper-sticker reductionism that emanates from the megachurches.

If the instructions of Jesus had to be marketed, I believe few people would be interested in signing on. Consider Jesus' answer to the rich man who asked how he could enter the Kingdom of God: 'Sell all you have and give it to the poor'. I am certain that this kind of radical instruction is not the kind of catch phrase that will be used in the megachurches' marketing. Imagine passing a church with a billboard saying 'take up your cross and follow Jesus' or 'die to self' or 'wash one another's feet' or 'If the world hates you know that it hated me before it hated you', or 'why do you call me Lord, Lord and don't do the things I say?' These statements will not attract people to megachurches, since these churches market a softer more 'user-friendly' version of Jesus, the Jesus who is Healer, Provider, Saviour, the Prince of Peace and the Jesus through whom we are now heirs of the Father who owns the whole earth. The Jesus who passionately opposed the oppression and negligence of the poor is not marketable amongst middle-class circles who, while climbing the socio-economic ladder, need a Jesus who keeps them at peace in times of stress, provides them with luxury goods and assets, and facilitates their upward mobility through promotions and salary increases.

Crucial Missional Considerations for the Metropolitan Megachurches

In order to conclude the reflections of the three megachurches in the three South African cities, I propose three crucial mission considerations in this section.

Convert the Middle Class

Pixley and Boff[25] assert that 'the main objective of the pastoral care of the non-poor has to be to associate them with the cause of the poor'. Further to this, they advise the non-poor to 'take on the cause of justice, adopt the viewpoint of the poor, to show solidarity with their struggle, and be their companion'. The gospel speaks of the conversion of the middle class and rich. This conversion is

[25] G. Pixley and C. Boff, *The Bible, the Church and the Poor* (Maryknoll, NY: Orbis, 1990), 230.

the need for a decision to choose between the 'plan of mammon (accumulation), or that of God (freedom and sharing)'.[26] The megachurches' interpretation of excellence should be interrogated and revised. Excellence cannot be the aligning to the mission and vision of corporatism and the super rich. The quest for excellence should be in the churches' sustained, prophetic and vigorous engagement with the injustice of our time.

Although the economic well-being of the middle class is crucial to the economy of the country, this well-being cannot come at the cheap satisfaction that supporting a children's home or an AIDS clinic through the church is sufficient. Vincent[27] succinctly states that pastoral action must move past the comforting of the middle class. He argues that the church in the city must 'submit to becoming vile'. The church must have a legitimate presence amongst the poor of the city in order to truly be a church of the city. The black middle class and all the members of the megachurches should be personally involved in advocacy and justice for the poor. Members should be discerning and ask critical questions about the way money is spent: is it just to spend millions on sound and light technology? Is it fair to use the money set aside for 'the extension of God's kingdom'[28] for flashy conventions and hosting budgets for superstar evangelists? Are the megachurches really aware of what the extension of Kingdom of God entails? I believe that extending the Kingdom of God is extending and increasing the environment or conditions of justice, mercy and shalom. While I am attracted to the Jesus of the middle class, I am also aware that part of God's dissatisfaction over the twin cities of Sodom and Gomorrah was over the economic injustice that they perpetuated. I fear that South African cities are also guilty of this serious indictment.

Understand the Power of the Small

Being part of the Pentecostal/Charismatic movement myself, over the years, I have observed the transvaluation of the value of weakness to strength and material simplicity to extravagance. Many proponents in Pentecostal/Charismatic churches have become bloated with pride and intoxicated with triumphalism. Humility is a crucial characteristic in the mission of the church. While strength in the megachurches discussed in this study is manifested through size, power rhetoric and wealth, it is necessary for me to concur with Hall,[29] who points out that all the metaphors Jesus used 'to depict the community of witness... are metaphors of smallness':

> Little things that perform some essential service for bigger things-salt, yeast, a candle, a litte town on a hill in a dark night, a pearl, a mustard seed. He speaks of

---

[26] Pixley and Boff, *The Bible*, 231.

[27] J. Vincent, "The Public Presence of the Church in the City" (a public lecture delieverd at the Universidade Metodista de Sao Paulo, September 2005).

[28] It is common to hear the words 'bless this money for the extension of your kingdom' when an offering is taken.

[29] D.J. Hall, *The Cross in our Context* (Minneapolis: Fortress, 2003), 189.

> his 'little flock', which he sends out 'as sheep into the midst of wolves' (Matt.10:16). He assumes that the missionary vocation of this koinonia will involve excruciating isolation, rejection, and suffering – should not the disciple follow the master?[30]

The imagery contained in these metaphors of smallness point to the power and possibility contained in the small, less obvious, or seemingly insignificant. The small groups that meet across the city in the homes of megachurch members are the actual sites of mission. These are the communities of witness. Megachurch leaders would do well to invert their power hierarchies and support the local area networks and house meetings.

We Must Decrease

I am profoundly moved by the writing of Koyama[31] who advocated for the 'crucified mind' and not the 'crusading mind' in the missionary. He asserts that the crusading mind is not the mind of biblical communicators. Koyama's reflection rings true for the churches in this study. The megachurches' statistic-driven, increase-hungry empire lusts need to be carefully critiqued. Unfortunately, the expansionist objectives of church growth could become a serious hindrance to the Missio Dei.

Koyama[32] laments the crusading mind in mission, imploring for the Johannine principle that 'he must increase, but I must decrease' (John 3:30). He states:

> What does this decrease mean? Decrease in number? Decrease in influence? Decrease in prestige? I understand it in the framework of the history of 'reviled' (decrease) – bless (increase) – persecuted (decrease) – endure (increase) – slandered (decrease) – conciliate (increase)… It is a mind that does not seek profit for itself. It is a mind which is happy in becoming refuse (decrease) of humanity since it brings increase to others.

Can the megachurches apply the Johannine principle to their mission discourse, consciousness, and engagement? Are they willing to become insignificant, small, vulnerable and powerless? Are they willing to allow the names of their leaders to fade away so that the name of Jesus can be lifted up? Are they willing to disparage their brands so that people will only know the crucified Christ, the suffering servant? Are they ready to be persecuted and not praised? Is the megachurch ready to decrease so that He can increase in the pain and poverty and torment of many in the cities of Johannesburg, Durban, and Pretoria?

---

30 Hall, *The Cross in our Context*, 189.

31 Kosuke Koyama, 'What Makes a Missionary? Toward Crucified Mind Not Crusading Mind', in Gerald H. Anderson and Thomas F. Stransky (eds), *Mission Trends No. 1: Crucial Issues in Mission Today* (New York: Paulist Press, 1974), 132.

32 Koyama, 'A Moratorium', 131.

Conclusion

This article has embarked on the journey of discovery of three South African megachurches and their mission engagement strategies. A critical evaluation of the practice and presence of the megachurches in the three South African cities was conducted in order to attain an account of the churches' missional presence.

The similarities between South African megachurches and their American counterparts was discussed in order to provide evidence of the influence of American models of Christianity on segments of South African Christianity. The megachurches' attraction of large crowds can be attributed to the agency of the congregants, their advertising prowess and the diverse programmes that target young people and children and the middle class in general. Realising that the congregants are religious consumers, the churches ensure that the peoples' senses are appeased.

In this article, I have made several references to the megachurches' individualism, brand consciousness, consumerist middle-class lifestyles and their appetite for mammon. At this point, I have to admit that although some Christian traditions and theologians may not share the Charismatic theologies of prosperity and blessing, this does not preclude their quest for riches. The Pentecostal/Charismatic megachurch middle class is not the only segment in society that has a penchant for the material. The government, multinational corporations, and even *some* liberation theologians are in the 'get all you can' mode. This is the prevailing spirit of our time.

According to Davey,[33] Jesus taught about 'the economy of God', which is concerned with the 'reordering of relationships and resources through a just and gracious liberality'. Davey[34] adds that the apostle Paul believed that economy was the 'Christ-centred activity of God'. The following view of an alternative economy is necessary for us all to consider.

> As God encourages generosity, the economy is about the possibility of new communities: a new pattern of relationship, internally and with other communities; it is an involving system that seeks to include and empower those who are not 'economically active', which should not lack the gifts necessary to its life and mission. It is an economy with a critique that offers radical criteria for the valorisation of people, places, and activities, concerned with bringing the experience of the future into the present in its exploration and embodiment of the possibilities that its experience of the Spirit makes possible.[35]

Finally, megachurches are not to be discounted in the mission endeavour. While I have covered elements of megachurch mission praxis that are hazardous, I would end this article by emphatically stating that in spite of some faulty perceptions, flawed theologies and imperfect mission engagements people are discovering the liberating presence of Jesus Christ in these churches.

---

[33] A. Davey, *Urban Christianity and Global Order* (Peabody, MA: Hendrickson, 2002), 111.

[34] Davey, *Urban Christianity*, 111.

[35] Davey, *Urban Christianity*, 111.

Countless personal stories of renewal, healing, and restoration are heard across the three cities. I seem to be making an about-turn in my final analysis of the three megachurches. What I want to convey is that all churches are flawed by virtue of their susceptibility to the spirit of the age. This is what churches all over the world need to be aware of. The half-truths and ideal visions we have of our own churches need constant interrogation. I am from the Pentecostal/ Charismatic background, so this article is an exploration of my own tradition. I believe that there are mission merits to the presence of these megachurches, and that would have to be considered in another paper. My only cry is that the three megachurches who claim to be intimately connected with the Holy Spirit and the will of God should be at the forefront of advocacy and action for the poor and the marginalised. Super-sized urban congregations may be the bother of mainline churches, but for many Pentecostals/Charismatics across the globe, megachurches are viewed as signs of the next move of God, a revival of faith, and the churches' ability to blend into an increasingly urban, market-driven society.

Selected Bibliography

Alvarez, Miguel. 'Pentecostals, Society and Christian Mission in Latin America'. In Wonsuk Ma, Veli-Matti Karkainan and J. Kwabena Asamoah-Gyady (eds.). *Pentecostal Mission and Global Christianity.* Oxford: Regnum Books, 2014: 301-319.

Anderson, Allan. 'Towards a Pentecostal Missiology for the Majority World'. In Grant McClung (ed.). *Azusa street & beyond.* Gainesville, Florida: Bridge-Logos, 2006: 169-89.

Anderson, Allan. *An Introduction to Pentecostalism.* Cambridge: Cambridge University Press, 2004.

Aune, David E. *Prophecy in Early Christianity and the Ancient Mediterranean World.* Grand Rapids, MI: Eerdmans, 1983.

Aygei, Ahmad. *Sharing the Love of Christ with Your Muslim Neighbour.* Kumasi: UGC, 2002.

Balia, Daryl and Kirsteen Kim (eds.). *Edinburgh 2010: Witnessing to Christ Today.* Oxford: Regnum Books, 2010.

Banda, Joshua. 'Engaging with the Community, the Fight against AIDs'. In Brian Woolnough (ed.). *Good News from Africa: Community Transformation through the Church.* Oxford: Regnum Books, 2013.

Bastian, Jean-Pierre. *La Mutación Religiosa de América Latina: Para una Sociología del Cambio Social en la Modernidad Periférica.* Ciudad del Mexico: Fondo de Cultura Económica, 1997.

Bauman, Chad M. *Pentecostals, Proselytization, and Anti-Christian Violence in Contemporary India.* Oxford; Oxford University Press, 2015.

Beltrán, William Mauricio. *Del Monopolio Católico a la Explosión Pentecostal: Pluralización Religiosa, Secularización y Cambio Social en Colombia.* Bogotá, Colombia: Centro de Estudios Sociales de la Universidad Nacional de Colombia, 2013.

Braaten, Carl E. and Robert W. Jenson (eds.). *In One Body through the Cross: The Princeton Proposal for Christian Unity.* Grand Rapids: Eerdmans, 2003.

Brunner, Daniel L., Jennifer L. Butler, and A.J. Swoboda. *Introducing Evangelical Ecotheology: Foundations in Scripture, Theology, History, and Praxis.* Grand Rapids, MI: Baker Academic, 2014.

Brusco, Elizabeth. *The Reformation of Machismo: Evangelical Conversion and Gender in Colombia.* Austin: University of Texas Press, 1995.

Burdick, John. *Blessed Anastacia: Women, Race, and Popular Christianity in Brazil.* New York: Routledge, 1998.

Castellanos, Claudia. *Post-Encounter for Women.* Bogota: G12 Editors, 2004.

Cho, David Yonggi. *The Fourth Dimension.* Editorial Peniel, 2002.

Cook, Guillermo (ed.). *Crosscurrents in Indigenous Spirituality, Interface of Maya, Catholic and Protestant Worldviews.* Leiden, The Netherlands: E.J. Brill, 1997.

Cuvântul Adevărului [The Word of Truth], formerly Buletinul Cultului Penticostal (1931-2010), online at: <http://digitallibrary.usc.edu/cdm/search/collection/p15799coll14/searchterm/Pentecostal%20Theological%20Institute,%20Bucharest,%20Romania/field/parta/mode/exact/conn/and/order/nosort>.

Croitor, Vasilică. *Răscumpărarea memoriei: Cultul Penticostal în perioada communistă [Redeeming Memory: The Pentecostal Denomination during the Communist Period]*. Medgidia, Romania: Succeed Publishing, 2010.

Davey, Andrew. *Urban Christianity and Global Order: Theological Resources for an Urban Future*. Peabody, MA: Hendrickson Publishers, 2002.

Donovan, Vincent J. *Christianity Rediscovered: An Epistle from the Maasai.* London: SCM Press, 1978.

Dovlo, Elom, and Alfred Ofosu Asante. 'Reinterpreting the Straight Path: Ghanaian Muslim Converts in Mission to Muslims'. *Exchange* 32:3 (2003): 214-38.

Engelsviken, Tormod. 'Missio Dei: The Understanding and Misunderstanding of a Theological Concept in European Churches and Missiology'. *International Review of Mission* 92:4 (2003): 481-97.

Engelsviken, Tormod. *Besettelse og åndsutdrivelse i Bibelen, historien og vår egen tid.* Oslo: Lunde Forlag, 1978.

Engelsviken, Tormod. *Spiritual Conflict in Today's Mission.* Monrovia, CA: Lausanne Committee for World Evangelization, Marc Publications, 2001.

Escobar, Samuel. *A Time for Mission: The Challenge for Global Christianity*. Leicester: IVP & Langham Partnerships, 2003.

Escobar, Samuel. *Changing Tides: Latin America and World Mission Today*. Maryknoll, NY: Orbis Books 2002.

Fischer, Moritz. *Maasai Gestalten Christsein.* Erlangen: Verlag für Mission und Ökumene, 2001.

Gairdner, W.H.T. *'Edinburgh 1910': An Account and Interpretation of the World Missionary Conference.* Edinburgh & London: Oliphant, Anderson & Ferrier, New York: Chicago and Toronto: Fleming H. Revell, 1910.

Gifford, Paul. *Ghana's New Christianity: Pentecostalism in a Globalizing African Economy*. Indianapolis, IN: Indiana University Press, 2004.

González, Ondina E., and Justo L. González. *Christianity in Latin America: a history*. Cambridge: Cambridge University Press, 2008.

Grudem, Wayne. *The Gift of Prophecy in the New Testament and Today*. Wheaton, IL: Crossway Books, 1988.

Gutiérrez, Benjamín and Dennis Smith (eds.). *In the Power of the Spirit. The Pentecostal Challenge to Historic Churches in Latin America*. Louisville, KY: CELEP-AIPRAL 1996.

Gutiérrez, Benjamin F. and Leonildo Silveira Campos. *Na Força do Espírito: Os Pentecostair na A,érica Latina: um desafio às igrejas históricas. [In the Power of the Spirit: The Pentecostals in Latin America: A Challenge to the Historical Churches)*. São Paulo: Associação Evangélica Literária Pendão Real, 1996.

Hanciles, Jehu J. *Beyond Christendom: Globalization, African Migration and the Transformation of the West.* Maryknoll, NY: Orbis Books, 2008.

Hiebert, Paul G. 'The Flaw of the Excluded Middle', *Missiology: An International Review* 10 (1982), 35-47.

Hodges, Melvin L. *The Indigenous Church.* Springfield, MO: Gospel Publishing House, 1953.

Hollenweger, W. 'The Pentecostal Elites and the Pentecostal Poor – A Missed Dialogue?' In K. Poewe (ed.), *Charismatic Christianity as a Global Culture.* Columbia, SC: University of South Carolina Press, 1994.

Hopfe, Lewis M. *Religions of the World.* 8th ed., Upper Saddle River, NJ: Prentice Hall, 2001

Hopkins, Howard C. *John R. Mott: 1865–1955: A Biography.* Grand Rapids, MI: William B. Eerdmans Publishing Company, 1979.

Hwa Yung. *Mangoes or Bananas? The quest for an Authentic Asian Christian Theology*. Oxford: Regnum Books, 1997

Hwa Yung. 'Missiological Implications of Dr. David Yonggi Cho's Theology'. *CyberJournal for Charismatic-Pentecostal Research*, April 2004.

Ingalls, Monique M. and Amos Yong (eds.). *The Spirit of Praise*. University Park, PA: Penn State University Press, 2015.

International Review of Mission 93 (July /October 2004) featuring 'Divine Healing, Pentecostalism and Mission'.

International Review of Mission 94 (July 2005) featuring 'Athens 2005 – Listeners' Reports'.

James, G. *And God said 'Let there be Charismatics in the City', A Study into the Practice and Presence of a Charismatic Megachurch in the City of Durban.* Pietermaritzburg, South Africa: University of Kwa Zulu Natal Pmb. 2007.

Johnson, Alan R. *Apostolic Function in 21st Century Missions.* J. Philip Hogan World Missions Series. Pasadena, CA: William Carey Library, 2009.

Kalu, Ogbu, Chima J. Korieh, G. Ugo Nwokeji, and Obioma Nnaemeka. *Religion, History, and Politics in Nigeria: Essays in Honor of Ogbu U. Kalu.* Lanham, MD: University Press of America, 2005.

Kärkkäinen, Veli-Matti. 'Ecclesiology'. In Kapic, Kelly and Bruce McCormack (eds.). *Mapping Modern Theology.* Grand Rapids: Baker Academic, 2012: 345–46.

Kärkkäinen, Veli-Matti. *Hope and Community: A Constructive Christian Theology for the Pluralistic World.* Grand Rapids: Eerdmans, 2017.

Kiel, Christel. *Maasai Diviners and Christianity*. Köln: Rüdiger Köppe Verlag, 2016.

Kim, Kirsteen & Andrew Anderson (eds.). *Edinburgh 2010: Mission Today and Tomorrow.* Oxford: Regnum Books, 2011.

Kirk, J. Andrew. *What is Mission? Theological Explorations*. Minneapolis, MN: Fortress Press, 2000.

Kuzmič, Peter. "Pentecostal Theology and Communist Europe: Pentecostal Power under Political Pressure". In William K. Kay and Anne E. Dyer (eds.). *European Pentecostalism.* Global Pentecostal and Charismatic Studies 7. Leiden: E.J. Brill, 2011: 333-354.

Lamp, Jeffrey S. *The Greening of Hebrews: Ecological Readings in the Letter to the Hebrews.* Eugene, OR: Pickwick Publications, 2012.

Larbi, Emmanuel Kingsley. *Pentecostalism: The Eddies of Ghanaian Christianity.* Accra: Blessed Publications, 2001.

Lim, Timothy T.N. "Towards a Protestant Pneumatological-Ecclesiology: Outside the 'Two Lungs of the Church'", *De Gruyter's Review of Ecumenical Studies* 7:2 (2015): 211-229.

López, Darío. *Pentecostalismo y Misión Integral: Teología del Espíritu, Teología de la Vida.* Lima, Perú: Ediciones Puma, 2008.

Ma, Wonsuk. '"When the Poor are Fired Up": The Role of Pneumatology in Pentecostal Charismatic Mission'. *Transformation* 24 (2007): 28-34.

Ma, Wonsuk, Veli-Matti Kärkkäinen, and J. Kwabena Asamoah-Gyadu (eds). *Pentecostal Mission and Global Christianity.* Oxford: Regnum Books, 2014.

Macchia, Frank D. *Justified in the Spirit: Creation, Redemption, and the Triune God.* Grand Rapids, MI: Eerdmans, 2010.

Măcelaru, Mărioara. *Însemnări pe uşiorii casei [Writing on the Doorposts].* Timişoara, Romania: Casa Literaturii Creştine, 2007.

Martin, David. *The Explosion of Protestantism in Latin America.* Oxford: Blackwell, 1990.

Matthey, Jacques (ed.). *'You are the Light of the World': Statements on Mission by the WCC 1980-2005.* Geneva: WCC Publications, 2005.

Matthey, Jacques (ed.). *Come Holy Spirit, Heal and Reconcile! Report of the WCC Conference on World Mission and Evangelism, Athens, May 2005.* Geneva: WCC Publications, 2008.

McDonnell, Kilian and George T. Montague. *Christian Initiation and Baptism in the Holy Spirit: Evidence from the First Eight Centuries.* Collegeville, MN: Liturgical Press, 1991.

McGee, Gary B. *This Gospel Shall Be Preached: A History and Theology of Assemblies of God Foreign Missions to 1959.* Springfield, MO: Gospel Publishing House, 1986.

Meyer, Harding. *That All May Be One: Perceptions and Models of Ecumenicity.* Grand Rapids: Eerdmans, 1999.

Miller, Donald E. and Tetsunao Yamamori. *Global Pentecostalism: The New Face of Christian Social Engagement.* Berkeley, CA: University of California Press, 2007.

Mol, Frans. *Maa, A Dictionary of the Maasai Language and Folklore, English-Maasai, Marketing & Publishing* Ltd. Nairobi, 1978.

Moreau, A. Scott and others (eds.). *Deliver Us from Evil: An Uneasy Frontier in Christian Mission.* Monrovia, Ca.; Lausanne Commission for World Evangelization, Marc Publications, 2002.

Olika, Dawit T. *Prophecy: a blessing or a problem (a critical study of the understanding and practice of prophecy in EECMY.* Oslo: MF, 2007.

Ouedraogo, Philippe. *Female Education and Mission: A Burkina Faso Experience.* Oxford: Regnum Books, 2004.

Padilla, C. René. *¿Qué es Misión Integral?* Buenos Aires: Ediciones Kairos, 2006.

Padilla, C. René. *Bases Bíblicas de La Misión: Perspectivas Latinoamericanas [Biblicas Bases for Mission; Latin American Perspectives]*. Buenos Aires: Fundación Kairós, 1998.

Padilla, René. 'Evangelism and Social Responsibility: From Wheaton '66 to Wheaton '83', *Transformation* 2:3 (July-September 1985): 27–34.

Pandrea, Rodica. 'A Historical and Theological Analysis of the Pentecostal Church in Romània'. *Journal of the European Pentecostal Theological Association* 21 (2001): 109-135.

Petersen, D. *Not by Might nor by Power: A Pentecostal Theology of Social Concern in Latin America.* Oxford: Regnum Books, 1996.

Pixley, G. and Boff, C. *The Bible, the Church and the Poor.* Maryknoll, NY: Orbis, 1990.

Porterfield, Amanda. *Healing in the History of Christianity.* Oxford: Oxford University Press, 2005.

Reiling, J. *Hermas and Christian Prophecy: Study of the Eleventh Mandate.* Leiden: E.J. Brill, 1973.

Rouse, Ruth and Stephen Charles Neill (eds.). *A History of the Ecumenical Movement.* Vol. 1. Geneva: WCC, 1993 [1954].

Samwini, Nathan I. *The Muslim Resurgence in Ghana since 1950: Its Effects Upon Muslims and Muslim-Christian Relations.* Berlin: LIT, 20006.

Saracco, Norberto. 'Las Opiniones Liberadoras de Jesú'. *Misión* 3:10 (1989): 3-9.

Snodderly, Beth & A. Scott Moreau (eds.). *Evangelical and Frontier Mission. Perspectives on the Global Progress of the Gospel*. Oxford: Regnum Books, 2011.

Stott, John. 'The Bible in World Evangelization'. In *Perspectives on the World Christian Movement.* 3rd ed. Pasadena: William Carey Library, 1999.

Swoboda, A.J. and Steven Bouma-Prediger (eds.). *Blood Cries Out: Pentecostals, Ecology, and the Groans of Creation*. Eugene, OR: Pickwick Publications, 2014.

Swoboda, A.J. *Tongues and Trees: Toward a Pentecostal Ecological Theology.* Blandford Forum, UK: Deo Publications, 2014.

Synan, Vinson and Amos Yong (eds.). *Global Renewal Christianity*, 4 vols. Lake Mary, FL: Charisma House, 2015.

Tesema, Estifanos. *Charismatic Experience on Trial: Towards a Theology of Charismatic Experience*. Addis Ababa: Ethiopia: EGST, 2005.

Vanhoozer, K. 'Evangelism and the Church: The Company of the Gospel'. In C. Bartholomew, R. Parry and A. West (eds.). *The Futures of Evangelicalism.* Leicester: Inter-Varsity Press, 2003.

Volf, Miroslav. *After Our Likeness: The Church as the Image of the Trinity.* Grand Rapids: Eerdmans, 1998.

Wilson, Everett A. *Strategy of the Spirit: J. Philip Hogan and the Growth of the Assemblies of God Worldwide 1960-1990.* Carlisle, Cumbria: Regnum Books, 1997.

World Council of Churches and DIFAEM (German Institute for Medical Mission). *Witnessing to Christ Today. Promoting Health and Wholeness for All.* Tübingen: DIFAEM, 2010.

World Missionary Conference, 1910. *Cooperation and the Promotion of Unity, Report of Commission VIII.* Edinburgh & London: Oliphant, Anderson & Ferrier; New York, Chicago and Toronto: Fleming H. Revell, 1910.

Wright, Christopher J.H. *The Mission of God's People: A Biblical Theology of the Church's Mission.* Grand Rapids, MI: Zondervan, 2010.

Wynarczyk, Hilario. *Ciudadanos de dos mundos. El Movimiento Evangélico en la Vida Pública Argentina 1980-2001.* San Martín, Argentina: UMSAM EDITA, 2009.

Yates, Timothy. *Christian Mission in the Twentieth Century.* Cambridge: Cambridge University Press, 1994.

Yong, Amos. *Missional Spirit: Christian Mission Theology in the Third Millennium Global Context.* Eugene, OR: Cascade, 2014.

Yong, Amos. *The Spirit Poured Out on all Flesh: Pentecostalism and the Possibility of Global Theology.* Grand Rapids, MI: Baker Academic, 2005.

Contributors

Rigoberto M. Galvez Alvarado is Rector of the Seminario Bíblico Teológico de Guatemala (SETEGUA) and professor of the Consorcio de Seminarios de Latinoamérica (CONSELA).

Carmelo Alvarez is a long-term volunteer missionary of the Board of Global Ministries, United Church of Christ and Christian Church (Disciples of Christ) in the US and Canada, also serving as Visiting Professor of Pentecostal Studies at Evangelical Theological Seminary, Matanzas, Cuba.

Mireya Alvarez is Vice-President of Academic Affairs at the Asian Seminary of Christian Ministries, Manila, Philippines. She is an ordained minister and has been involved in pastoral and missionary work in Ecuador and among Latino churches in the Northeast Region of the United States.

Raimundo César Barreto Jr., an ordained Brazilian Baptist minister, is assistant professor of world Christianity at Princeton Theological Seminary, Princeton, New Jersey, USA. He is also the general editor of the 6-volume series World Christianity and Public Religion (Fortress Press).

Bernardo Campos, a Peruvian Pentecostal, is Professor of Theology at Protestant seminaries, while serving as Coordinator of the Pentecostal Forum for Latin America and the Caribbean, a regional expression of the World Christian Forum, and director of the Systematic Theology Hispanic Perspective Series of the Kerygma Publishing House in Oregon, USA.

Tormod Engelsviken, a Norwegian Lutheran, is Professor Emeritus of Missiology at MF Norwegian School of Theology in Oslo, Norway. He has served as a missionary in Ethiopia, been member of the Lausanne Theology Working Group, moderator of the Church of Norway Council for Ecumenical and International Relations, member of the WCC Commission on World Mission and Evangelism and visiting professor at Minzu University, Beijing, China.

Andreas Heuser, a theologian and political scientist, is Professor for Extra-European Christianity (with a focus on Africa) at the Faculty of Theology at the University of Basel, Switzerland. His multi-sited research on African Instituted Churches (AIC) and the Pentecostal movement covers sub-Saharan Africa as well as on migrant Christianity in Germany and Switzerland.

Genevieve Lerina James is the Deputy Director of Community Engagement at the University of South Africa. She previously served as a senior lecturer in the missiology at the same university.

Alan R. Johnson serves as a missionary in Thailand with Assemblies of God World Missions (1986-present). He is an adjunct professor with the Intercultural Doctoral Studies program at Evangel University, Springfield, Missouri, USA.

Veli-Matti Kärkkäinen is Professor of Systematic Theology at Fuller Theological Seminary, Pasadena, California, USA, and Docent of Ecumenics at the University of Helsinki. Native of Finland, he has also lived and taught theology in Thailand. An ordained Lutheran minister (ELCA) and an expert in Pentecostal-Charismatic theologies, he has participated widely in ecumenical, theological, and interreligious work.

Abednego Keshomshahara is a bishop of the North-Western Diocese of the Evangelical Lutheran Church in Tanzania. He has served as a lecturer at different institutions of education.

Christel H. Kiel is an ordained minister of the Lutheran Church in Braunschweig, Germany. Together with her husband she served in Tanzania, East Africa, and now lives in retirement in Wolfenbüttel, Germany.

Young-Hoon Lee serves as Senior Pastor of Yoido Full Gospel Church, Seoul, Korea.

Timothy T.N. Lim, a Singaporean and an ordained Presbyterian minister (U.S.A.), is Director of Chinese Research and Training at Carey Baptist College, Auckland, New Zealand.

Nicta Lubaale is General Secretary of the Organization of African Instituted Churches (OAIC), Nairobi, Kenya, involved in mobilizing and training church leadership from OAIC member churches to participate in holistic mission.

Julie C. Ma is Associate Professor of Intercultural Studies at Oral Roberts University, Tulsa, Oklahoma, USA.

Wonsuk Ma is Dean and Distinguished Professor of Global Christianity at Oral Roberts University, Tulsa, Oklahoma, USA.

Marcel V. Măcelaru, a Romanian Pentecostal, is Professor of Theology at the Pentecostal Theological Institute in Bucharest, Romania and Founding President of the Centre for Faith and Human Flourishing in Timişoara, Romania.

Jacques Matthey, Swiss Reformed missiologist, before retirement served as Secretary of the Commission on World Mission and Evangelism of the World Council of Churches.

Antonia Leonora van der Meer has served with the International Fellowship of Evangelical Students, including a pioneer service in Angola and Mozambique. She also served Professor and Dean of the Evangelical Missions Center in Viçosa, Brazil.

Opoku Onyinah is the chancellor of Pentecost University College, Accra, Ghana. He is Chairman Emeritus of the Church of Pentecost, Ghana.

Cecil M. Robeck, Jr. serves as Senior Professor of Church History and Ecumenics and Special Assistant to the President for Ecumenical Relations at Fuller Theological Seminary in Pasadena, CA, USA.

Dawit Olika Terfassa is a member of the Ethiopian Evangelical Church Mekane Yesus and Swedish Evangelical Mission. He pastors an immigrant church in Sweden.

Amos Yong, an Asian American Pentecostal, is Professor of Theology and Mission at Fuller Theological Seminary, Pasadena, California.

Philip Wingeier-Rayo is Dean and Professor of Missiology and Methodist Studies at Wesley Theological Seminary, Washington, DC, USA.

Olga Zaprometova serves in the faculty of St. Philaret Christian Orthodox Institute, Moscow, Russia. Previously she served as Academic Dean of the Evangelical Theological Seminary, Moscow, Russia.

Index

Ad Gentes, 149
African, 5, 26, 28, 56, 73, 96, 97, 99, 100, 101, 102, 103, 107, 117, 126, 128, 130, 131, 132, 133, 134, 135, 136, 141, 157, 165, 173, 224, 226, 227, 233, 234, 239, 243, 246, 247, 248, 249, 251, 252, 253, 271, 286, 294, 295, 296, 297, 302, 347, 350, 351, 352, 355, 356, 357, 359, 360, 362, 366, 367, 371, 372
African Instituted Churches, 294
African-derived religions, 250
AIDS, 302
Althouse, Peter, 123
American Sunday School Union, 167
Anderson, Allan, 99
Anderson, Wilhelm, 99
Anglican, 114, 153, 154
Anglican Church, 208
Anglican Communion, 153
Arminian, 115
Asia, 43, 112, 117, 121
Assemblies of God, 112, 116, 167, 169
Athens, CWME Consultation in Athens, 207, 208, 209, 210, 211, 212, 213, 214, 215, 216, 217, 218, 219, 220, 221
Aygei, Ahmad, 95, 96
Azusa Street Mission, 165, 168
Baptism, 136, 201
Baptist, 112, 115, 224
Bauman, Zygmunt, 120
bishop, episcopacy, 153, 155
Bitrus, Ibrahim, 132, 133, 134
Brazil, 120
Buddhist, 54
Bultmann, Rudolf, 134
Cape Town Commitment, 149, 195
Capitalism, 356
Carey, William, 40, 45, 46
Castelgandolfo, 114
Charismatic expressions, 114
Charismatic Renewal, 154
Chicago, 117
Childcare, 290
children, 20, 24
China, 117, 157
Christ, Christological, 209, 210, 213, 214, 215, 218, 220
Christendom, 163, 171
Christian and Missionary Alliance, 167
Christian Union, 165
Christianity, 352, 354, 355, 362
Christological, 197, 199
Church at home, 172
Church of God (Cleveland, TN), 165, 168
church planting, 46
Cleveland, 116, 121, 122
Colonialism, 171
Commission on World Mission and Evangelism (CWME), 117, 118, 205, 207, 208, 209, 210, 211, 212, 213, 214, 215, 216, 217, 218, 219, 220, 371, 373
conflict, conflict resolution, 209, 212, 213
Consejo Latinoamericano de Iglesias (CLAI), 180, 181, 183, 185, 186, 187, 188, 189
Consultative International Pentecostal Council, 169
Continuation Committee, 162
Convention of the Foreign Missionary Conference of North America, 166
co-operation, partnership, 157
cosmic, 15, 17, 21, 22, 23
creation, 13, 15, 16, 17, 18, 19, 21, 22, 23, 24
creation care, 24
Cross, 129, 134
database, 43, 51
David Yonggi Cho, 7, 36, 38, 107, 255, 256, 257, 263, 268, 273, 274, 275, 278, 279, 280, 365, 367
Day of Pentecost, 14, 20
Deification/theosis, 141
development, 16, 131, 135, 297, 299
Diakonia, 193, 282
Dialogue, 24, 113, 114, 115, 133, 138, 154, 155, 170, 171, 207, 208, 209, 210, 211, 233, 234, 355, 367

diaspora, 54
disciples, 53
discipleship, making disciples, 218
Doctrine of creation, 5, 6, 13, 14, 15, 16, 17, 18, 19, 21, 22, 23, 24, 57, 70, 71, 72, 73, 74, 75, 76, 77, 78, 79, 93, 118, 121, 123, 124, 132, 176, 185, 190, 195, 197, 210, 211, 212, 213, 214, 219, 230, 263, 264, 281, 292, 314, 357
Doctrine of redemption, 17, 19, 20, 22, 23, 55, 62, 74, 75, 77, 195, 197, 231, 291
earth, 13, 15, 17, 18, 19, 20, 23
Eastern Orthodox, 151, 157
Ecclesiology, 114, 119, 123, 124, 149, 150, 151, 330, 367
ecological crisis, 15
Ecology, 369
Ecumenical, 113, 114, 116, 117, 119
Ecumenical dialogue, 113
ecumenical movement, ecumenism, 150, 153, 154, 155
Ecumenism, 114, 150, 169, 174, 184, 185, 186, 189, 190
Ecumenism of the Spirit, viii, 174, 184, 185, 189, 190
Edinburgh 2010, 1, 3, 4, 5, 6, 8, 9, 13, 25, 26, 40, 54, 55, 71, 83, 95, 105, 108, 112, 114, 126, 128, 137, 149, 161, 162, 166, 170, 171, 172, 174, 178, 193, 207, 210, 216, 221, 222, 232, 233, 255, 270, 272, 282, 295, 305, 323, 339, 350, 365, 366, 367, 370
Education, 286, 287, 288
Edwards, Denis, 15, 16
Elim Pentecostal Church, viii, 277, 305, 306, 307, 308, 313, 314, 315, 316, 318, 319, 320, 321, 322
embodiment, 15
Emotionalism, 345
Emotions, 139
empowerment, 218
environment, 17, 23, 24
Ephesians, 166
eschatological, 212, 216
ethics, 15
Ethnolinguistic, 41, 42, 43, 44, 46, 49, 50, 53
evangelical(s), 43, 44, 116, 121, 123, 282, 292
Evangelist, 203
evangelization, 44, 50, 164, 165, 168, 172
Exorcism, 99, 107, 200, 201, 202, 203
Faith and Order, 113, 170
Female education, 293
Foreign Mission, 166, 167
forgiveness, 214, 215, 216, 296
Fraternidad Teológica Latinoamerica (FTL), 85
Free Churches, 153, 154, 155, 157, 158
frontier mission(s), 40, 41, 42, 47, 49, 53, 54
Gender, 297
Genesis, 18
Ghana, 5, 95, 97, 101, 107, 110, 203, 366, 369, 373
Global South, 3, 29, 65, 71, 81, 339
Global/globalization, 169, 355, 362
gospel, 40, 41, 42, 43, 44, 45, 46, 48, 49, 50, 51, 52, 130, 131, 354, 357
Government of 12, viii, 255, 257
Great Commission, 195
Green, Michael, 135
Guatemala, 91, 117, 245, 251, 253, 291, 323, 330, 333, 334, 336, 371
Healing, viii, 92, 136, 164, 171, 189, 194, 200, 201, 202, 203, 205, 206, 207, 208, 209, 211, 212, 213, 214, 215, 216, 217, 218, 219, 220, 222, 303, 367, 369
Hindu, 54
Holiness, 14, 29, 33, 42, 43, 62, 116, 118, 166, 168, 203, 325, 338
Holiness Movement, 168
Holistic Mission, viii, 294
Hollenweger, Walter, 114
Holy Communion, 226, 227
human rights, 214
Humility, 360
Hungary, 115
Identity and Mission, 177
incarnation, 15, 19
Incarnational, 128
Independent Church, 5, 26, 28, 295, 302
India, 43, 120, 283, 288, 289, 293
Indigeneity, 45

indigenous, 44, 45, 46, 49, 50, 210
Individualism, 357
Institute for Ecumenical Research, 170
Integral mission, 85
International Church of the Foursquare Gospel, 169
International Missionary Council, 170
International Review of Mission(s), 112, 120
Inter-religious, 97
Islam, 95, 96, 97, 98, 101, 102, 103
Italy, 114
Jenkins, Phillip, 40
Joshua Project, 43
justice, 209, 210, 212, 214, 216, 217
Keane, Marie-Henri, 128
Keswick, 118
Kim, Sebastian, 210, 211
Kingdom of God, 56, 58, 65, 72, 78, 83, 86, 89, 90, 92, 93, 94, 142, 146, 359, 360
Koinonia, 155
Korea(n), 216
Kreider, Alan, 116
Kreider, Eleanor, 116
Lausanne, 42
Lausanne Covenant, 282, 293
Lausanne Movement, 149, 195, 282
liberation, 16, 295, 303
liturgy, 152
Lumen Gentium, 152, 153
Luther, Martin, 128
Lutheran, 114, 115, 126, 128, 130, 131, 132, 133, 134, 136, 150, 153, 154, 222, 225, 227
Lutheran World Federation, 114, 115
Ma, Wonsuk, 113
Maasai Prophet, viii, 222
majority world, 42, 50, 52, 53
Mammon, ix, 350
Matthew, Craig, 116, 117, 123
Matthey, Jacques, 207, 208, 210, 211, 212, 213, 217, 218, 219
Mau Mau, 295
Mbiti, John, 130, 133, 135
McFague, Sally, 15, 16
Megachurch, 350, 352, 356, 361, 367
Melanchthon, Monica, 210, 220
Mennonite, 114, 116
Methodology, 116, 135, 260, 298
Middle East, 43
Miller, William, 112, 117
Missio Dei, 174, 196, 208, 361, 366
missiological, 44, 45, 46, 47, 48, 49
Missiology, vii, 17, 23, 24, 40, 41, 42, 44, 47, 49, 52, 161, 203
mission agency(ies), 41, 44, 46
Mission Frontiers, 52
mission of God, 14
Moltmann, Jürgern, 129
Mott, John R., 166, 167, 168, 172, 173, 367
Mukti, 288, 289
Muslim, 54, 95, 96, 97, 99, 100, 101, 102, 103
Nationalist churches, 295, 296
Neo-Pentecostalism, 83, 85, 88, 90, 91, 93, 132, 133, 134, 146, 190, 323, 333, 334, 336, 337
New York, 117, 120, 122
Newbigin, Lesslie, 128, 129
Nigeria, 117
North America, 113, 117
Orphanage, 283, 284
Orthodox Church, 163, 207, 210, 213, 214, 220
Oxford, 112, 113, 114, 120, 121
Pannenberg, Wolfhart, 150
Partnership, 45, 46, 49, 50, 51, 77, 174, 175, 176, 190
Pasadena, 115
Pentecostal Assemblies of the World, 168, 169
Pentecostal mission under communism, 177, 306, 307, 313, 315, 322
Pentecostal movement, 3, 4, 6, 7, 8, 25, 30, 33, 35, 37, 42, 53, 54, 56, 62, 67, 70, 108, 119, 134, 146, 170, 174, 184, 203, 273, 279, 281, 327, 330, 332, 333, 371
Pentecostal World Fellowship, 159
Pentecostalism in Romania, viii, 305, 306, 307, 308, 309, 311, 312, 313, 314, 315, 320, 321, 322, 366, 368, 369, 372
people group(s), 40, 41, 42, 45, 46, 50, 52
Pinnock, Clark, 124
Pluralism, 171
Politics, 297, 303

poor/poverty, 20, 282, 291, 293, 355, 359
Popular religion, 246, 249
Poverty, 134, 135, 136
power, 157, 209, 214, 217, 220, 354
prayer, 51, 52, 289
Promotion of Unity, viii, 161, 162, 163, 166, 171, 172, 173
Prophecy, 14, 42, 339, 341, 344, 345, 346, 348, 349, 365, 366, 368, 369
proselytism, 158
Protestant, 15, 150, 151, 153, 154, 227, 231
Reconciliation, viii, 158, 207, 208, 210, 211, 213, 214, 215, 216, 217, 218, 219, 249
redemption, 17, 19, 20, 22, 23
Reformed, 114
religion, 48
Renewal, 203
repentance, 216
resurrection, 20, 21, 22
Revelation, 135
Revival, 134
Robeck, Cecil (Mel), 112, 114
Roho, 295, 296, 297, 298, 299, 301
Roman Catholic, 15, 114, 126, 129, 149, 152, 153, 154, 155, 156, 157
Roman Catholic Church, 162, 163, 164
Romania, viii, 305, 306, 307, 308, 309, 311, 312, 313, 314, 315, 320, 321, 322, 366, 368, 369, 372
Ross, Kenneth, 114, 120
sacraments, eucharist, 152, 153, 155
salvation, 213
Sanneh, Lamin, 120
schism, 151
Schreiter, Robert, 216, 217
Seymour, William, 112
Signs and wonders, 197
South/southern, ix, 350, 351, 352, 354, 355, 356, 357, 359, 360, 362
Spiritual churches, 294
Spiritual life/spirituality, 14, 15, 16, 26, 27, 28, 31, 32, 34, 80, 89, 121, 123, 130, 140, 145, 146, 147, 148, 157, 188, 209, 214, 219, 234, 245, 246, 250, 272, 295, 296, 299, 329, 331, 332, 338, 342, 346, 351
Spirituality, viii, 31, 115, 134, 137, 142, 145, 146, 209, 214, 219, 245, 248, 249, 270, 299, 336, 365
story-telling, 218
Straightway Chapel, vii, 95, 99, 103
Strategy, 48, 49
Syncretism, 247
Tafakari, 298
Tampere, 115
Teen Challenge, 37, 291
Teodor, Codreanu, 307, 308, 309, 310, 311, 312, 314, 316, 318, 319, 321, 322
theology, 13, 14, 15, 16, 17, 18, 19, 22, 24
theology of mission, 13
Theology/-ical, 359
Tillich, Paul, 134
Transformation/transformational development, 282, 284, 291
Trinity, 129
Trinity, triune God, 152, 155
uniformity, 159
union, 154
Unitatis Redintegratio, 152, 153
United Pentecostal Church, 169
United States, 283
Unity, viii, 113, 114, 146, 149, 150, 151, 155, 156, 157, 158, 159, 161, 162, 163, 165, 166, 168, 169, 171, 172, 173, 179, 183, 186, 208, 212, 220, 261, 285, 287, 288, 338, 365, 370
Unity, Disunity, 213, 221
unity, spiritual unity, visible unity, models of unity, 149, 150, 151, 152, 153, 154, 155, 156, 157, 158, 159
unreached, 41, 42, 43, 44, 45, 46, 47, 48, 49, 50, 51, 52, 53, 54
Vatican, 114
Vatican II, 151, 152, 153
Visible unity, 162
Vocation, 262
Wariboko, Nimi, 116
Wealth/wealthy, 357
Wesleyan, 118
Western, 354
Wilfred, Felix, 122
William Carey Library, 40, 45, 46
Winter, 46, 51, 52

Winter, Ralph D., 46, 51, 52
World Alliance of Reformed Churches, 170
World Christianity, 285
World Council of Churches, 7, 106, 113, 117, 119, 120, 149, 152, 158, 163, 171, 184, 185, 186, 187, 188, 205, 207, 208, 209, 214, 215, 216, 217, 218, 219, 220, 339, 368, 369, 370, 371, 373
World Council of Churches (WCC), WCC Conference(s), 207, 208, 209, 214, 215, 216, 217, 218, 219, 220
Worship, 133
Yoido Full Gospel Church, iv, viii, xi, 6, 28, 255, 256, 257, 258, 270, 273, 275, 276, 277, 278, 279, 280, 281, 372
Yong, Amos, 113, 117, 118, 119, 122, 123, 124
Yung, Hwa, 112
Zurich, 115